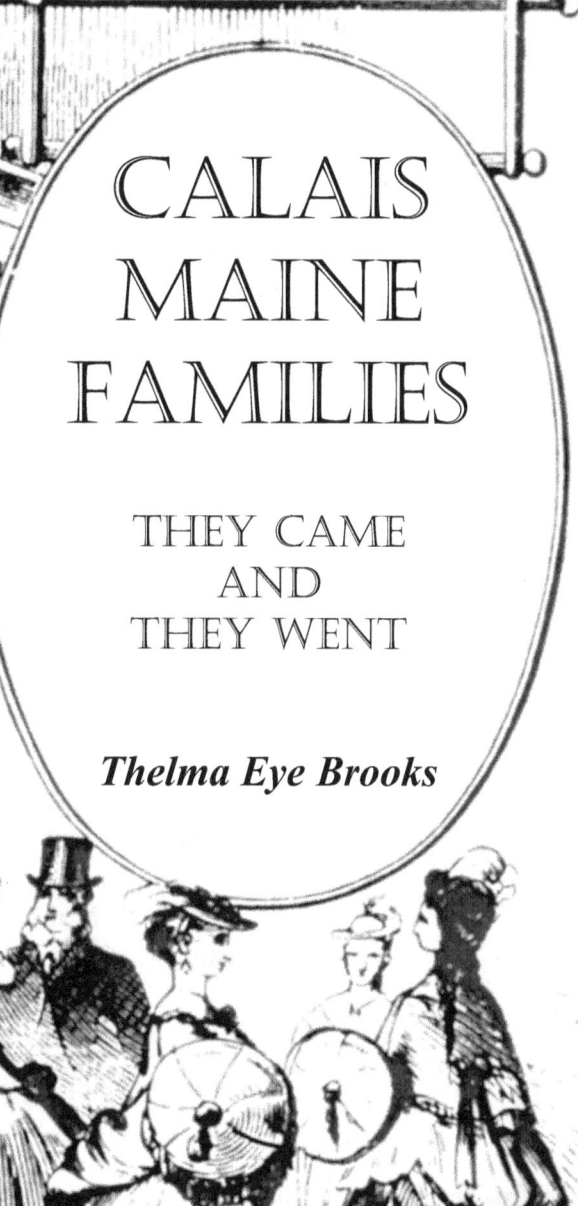

CALAIS MAINE FAMILIES

THEY CAME AND THEY WENT

Thelma Eye Brooks

HERITAGE BOOKS
2006

HERITAGE BOOKS
AN IMPRINT OF HERITAGE BOOKS, INC.

Books, CDs, and more—Worldwide

For our listing of thousands of titles see our website
at
www.HeritageBooks.com

Published 2006 by
HERITAGE BOOKS, INC.
Publishing Division
65 East Main Street
Westminster, Maryland 21157-5026

Copyright © 2002 Thelma Eye Brooks

All rights reserved. No part of this book may be reproduced or transmitted in any form or by any means, electronic or mechanical, including photocopying, recording or by any information storage and retrieval system without written permission from the author, except for the inclusion of brief quotations in a review.

International Standard Book Number: 978-0-7884-2135-2

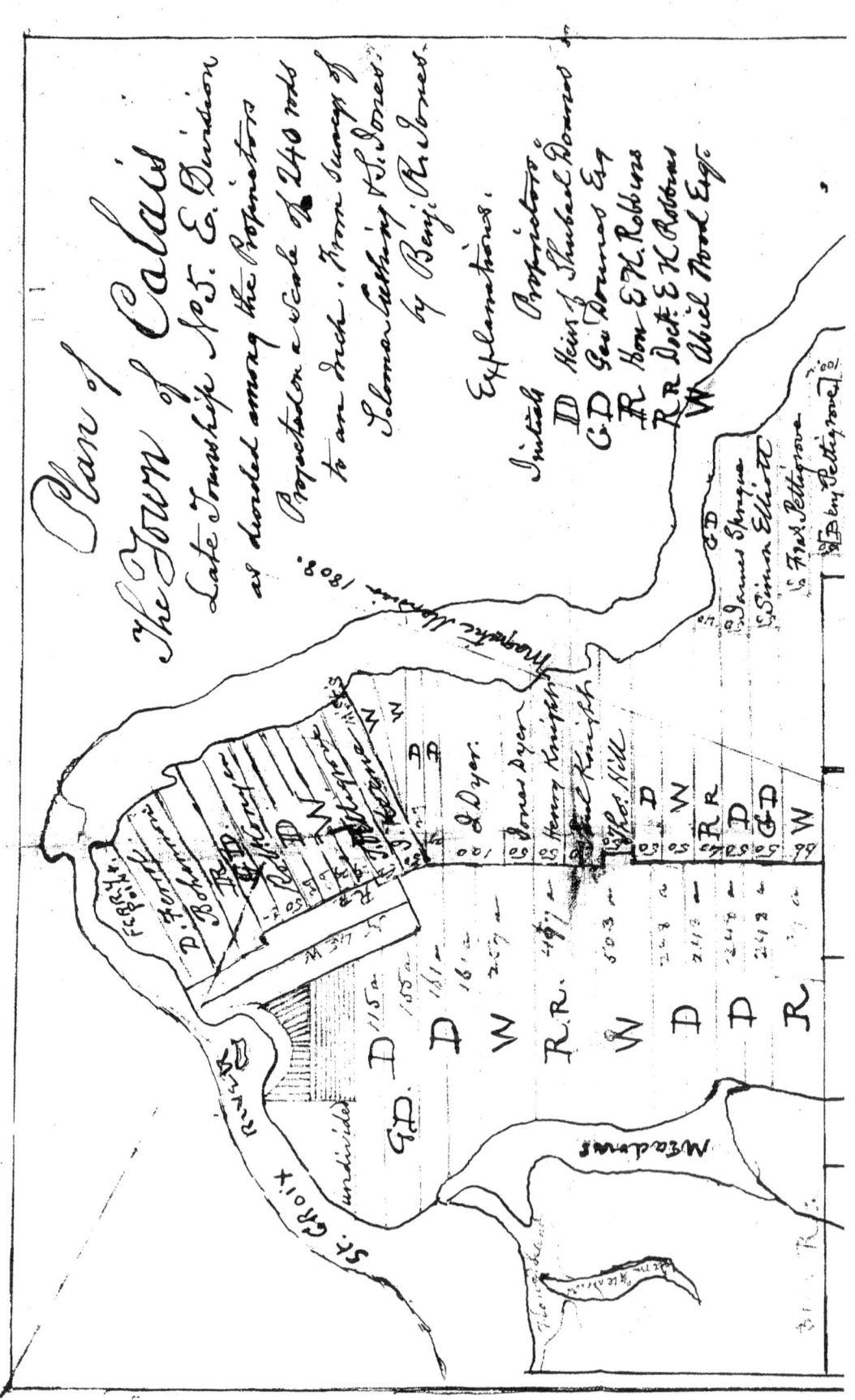

"Recorded with the Deeds of Washington County
Book No. 14 p. 550-551."
Original map in the James S. Pike Papers, Folger Library, University of Maine.

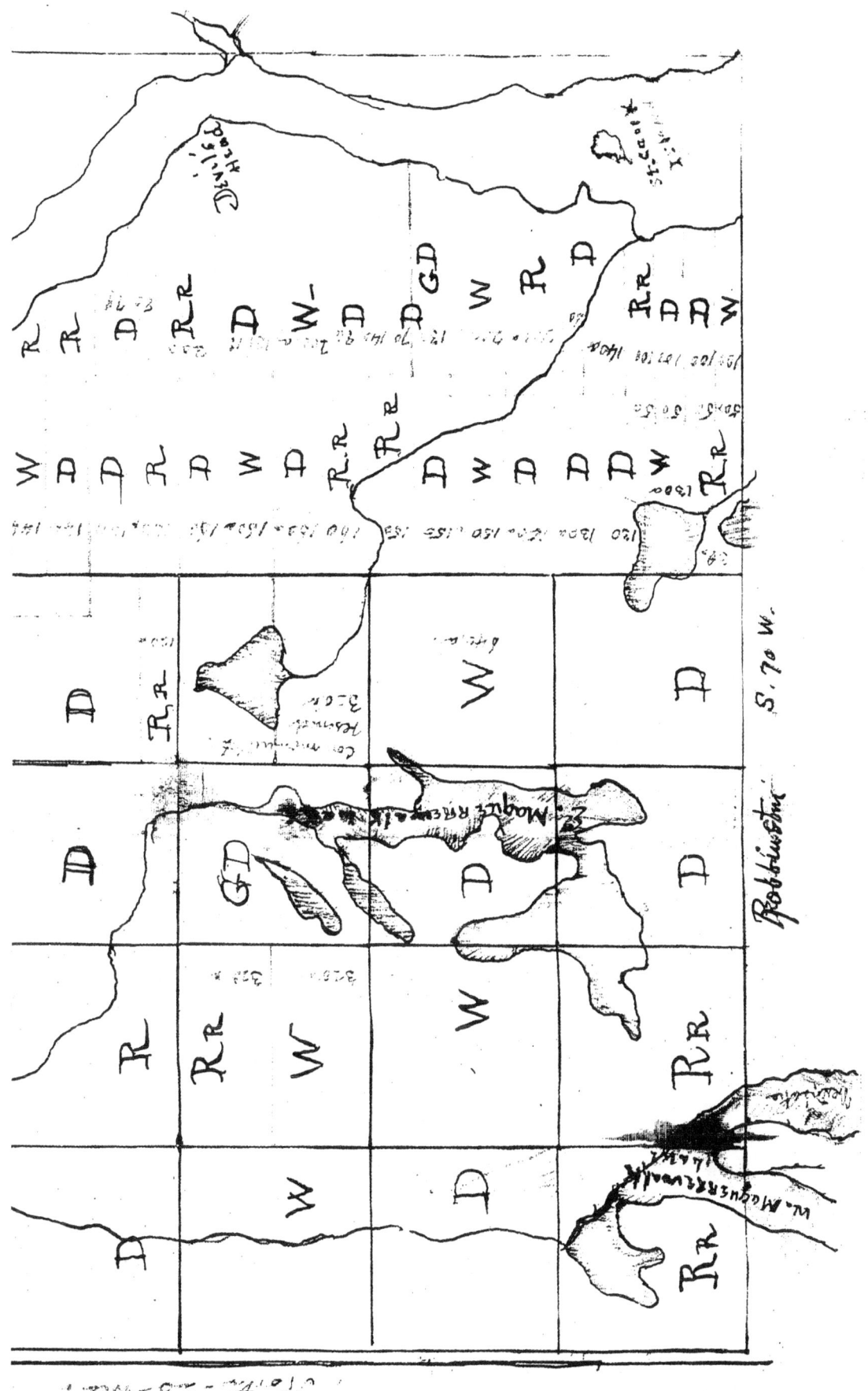

CALAIS, MAINE FAMILIES
THEY CAME AND THEY WENT

The families included in this book are the families listed in Book I of Calais Vital Records. I have placed the names in alphabetical order with the page number of the original record following the name of the head of family. The goal of this project was to find three generations of each family - one back from the head of the family and his wife, and the children and their spouses.

INTRODUCTION

In 1820 in the Calais census there were 61 males between 16 – 26 years living in 64 households. By 1830 there were 399 males between 21 & 30 years living in 225 households. Ten years later, in 1840, there were 204 males between 31 & 40 years living in 439 households. Young men came to Calais in large numbers in the late 1820's, some stayed but many left by 1840 and many others left by 1850, thus the name of this book - *CALAIS, MAINE FAMILIES: THEY CAME AND THEY WENT.*

The 346 families represented in this book are the families who had children's births registered in the Calais City Hall's earliest [as of 1993] book of Vital Records. An earlier book of records has recently been found and published. This recently located book is not the basis of this book, although some of the information found in the older book was used to clarify some dates and names. A few additional families have been included to show relationships of other families living in Calais during this period, in some cases the grandparents or siblings of the 346 families. An effort has been made to find where each of these families came from and where they resided if they left Calais. Where possible the census was used to follow these families from 1820 through 1920. Whenever known the place where they lived during the time of the census is indicated in the text.

There are several families that had births recorded in Book One and also in Book Three [as known in 1993] with a difference in dates. Also some records found in both Perry and Calais have a difference in birth dates. Where more than one record was found and there were differences, both are noted in the text. When date of birth could not be determined from the facts as found, the individual's age as indicated in census, the individual's age at death, or the individual's age found on any other source, is given as listed. I will leave it to the reader to decide on the factual age.

This book is the result of eight years of research. Every effort has been made to find where these families came from and where they went; however, there may be some misinterpretations of records, some unanswered questions and a few yet untraced families that left the area. There is an index of the 1850 census available at the Maine State Archives, this was searched to try to locate all the families in other localities within the state after they left Calais. It may be presumed that the missing families left the state before 1850. Perhaps these missing families went west to the Gold Mines of California or other places along the way. In trying to match similar names, without collaborating evidence, with the families, some presumptions that were made, may be incorrect.

The main purpose of this book is to help descendants of Calais Families and other genealogists to find some clues to lead them to further their research. The following family is an example of the distribution of the extra male population of Calais in the 1830 census.

CHENEY FAMILY

One of the families that fits into the title of my book is the family of Amasa Cheney.
Amasa was born in NH in 1787 and died in Calais in 1827. He moved to Eastern Maine as a young adult. He married Nancy C. Todd in Eastport, Me and had four children born there in 1812, 1814, 1817, and 1819. Another child born ca 1821 place unknown at this time and the last child was born in Milltown, NB in 1825.

Amasa died in Calais in 1827 and his wife, Nancy, appears in Calais in the 1830 census of Calais with her children: a male under 5; a male born bet. 10-15; a female bet. 5-10; a female bet. 10-15; 2 females bet. 15-20. Also in this household are 8 males and 1 female between 20-30. In the 1840 census Nancy has only one male 10-15 and one male 20-30 with her.

Who are the nine persons living with Nancy in 1830? Being a young widow with six children she probably took in boarders. Many Calais families had additional persons in their households in 1830 mostly male. Where did they come from is a mystery at this time. Where they went before 1840 is another mystery.

The Cheney family is found listed in the Eastport Records on page 20 (printed edition).
Eliza Jane born 10 Feb 1812; Nancy Maria born 1 June 1814; Mary Ann born 2 Apr 1817; William born 8 Aug 1819.

Comparison of the 1830 census: Eliza would be one of the females bet. 15-20, she does not appear in 1840 with her mother because she married Mark Ellsworth of Calais before 1832 when their 1st child was born in Calais.
Nancy Maria would be the other female bet. 15-20, she does not appear in 1840.
Mary Ann would be the female bet. 10-15 in 1830 and she does not appear in 1840 with her mother because she married 7 Sept 1834 Amos Clark of Calais.
William would be the male bet. 10-15 in 1830 and the male bet. 20-30 in 1840 with his mother.
Abigail Peris b. ca 1821 (Cheney Genealogy) would be the female bet. 5-10 in 1830 and does not appear in 1840 census. She married 16 Oct 1845 Samuel B. Jackson in Calais.
Amasa William b. 14 Mar 1825 in Milltown, NB (Cheney Genealogy), would be the male under 5 in 1830 and the male bet. 10-15 in 1840.
This leaves the 8 males and 1 female in 1830 unaccounted for.

WILLIAM & MARAGRET ABERNATHY p.190.

William ABERNATHY, born circa 1815, in St. Stephen, NB (1850 census). A William Abernathy filled for citizenship 4 Sept 1852, born Danathadic, Co of Down, Ireland 1814, left Ireland 1 Oct 1818, arrived St. Andrews, NB 1 Dec 1818, arrived Eastport, Me June 1832 and to Calais May 1833 where he since resides (SJC:9:47). He was a painter. Died 1 Apr 1857 in Calais. Buried in Calais Cemetery. Census: 1850 (age 35 living with James Belmore) in Calais. He married (int.) 1 Nov 1843, ca 1843-1844 by Rev. S. H. Keeler in Calais (VR:1:130, mrwc:39) MARGARET SAVAGE, born circa 1821, died 1848 in Calais (g.s.), buried 9 Nov 1848 in Calais Cemetery (sext).

- Marriage intentions were filed on 4 Dec 1855 between WILLIAM ABERNATHY & EMELINE BARTON of Columbia, Me in Calais (VR:1:71).

Children of William & Margaret:

i. SARAH JANE ABERNATHY, born 4 Jan 1845 in Calais (VR). Died 20 Nov 1846 age 1y 10m in Calais (VR:1:233, g.s.). Buried: 22 Nov 1846 in Calais Cemetery (sext).

ii. MARGARET HELEN ABERNATHY, born 28 Jan 1847 in Calais (VR). Died 4 Apr 1848 in Calais (g.s. =age 10m). Buried: Apr 1848 in Calais Cemetery (sext).

JAMES & MARGARET ALLEN p. 200

JAMES ALLEN, born _____.

He married 23 Apr 1840 in Calais (FJ) MARGARET HAMILTON. Children:

i. JAMES ALLEN, Jr., born 28 Jan 1841 in Calais (VR).
ii. JANE ALLEN, born 12 Aug 1846 in Calais (VR).

JOHN JUDSON & EMILY AMES p. 204

JOHN JUDSON AMES, son of Capt. JOHN AMES, born circa 1820. He presented the first bible to the St. Croix Lodge #46 in 1845 (lodge:20). In 1850 he was the editor of the Pacific News (times). Died circa 1861, in San Diego, CA (balch: 290).

He married 6 Jun 1844 in Lubec Me (lubec:164, gaz) EMILY BALCH, born 8 Aug 1820 in Lubec (balch: 290), daughter of Dr. HORATIO GATES BALCH and RHODA DUTTON. She died 13 Dec 1892 in Weaverville, CA (balch). Emily received a divorce on 6 June 1854, on 2nd of July 1848 he had deserted her in Boston, MA. The court awarded her $5000.00 in alimony (SJC 12:52). In 1849 her father in his will left her a home for herself and daughter, Patia as long as no husband is with her (prbt). Children:

i. GEORGE GORDON BYRON AMES, born 3 Jun 1845 in Calais (VR). Died 1 Jun 1847 in Calais (VR, FJ). Buried in Calais Cemetery.
ii. PATIA MCLEAN AMES, born 2 Sep 1847 in Calais (VR). Died 29 May 1865, in Peabody, MA (balch:290, name Helen P., name Patia McLellan on divorce rec.).

BENJAMIN & MARY ARNOLD p. 194

BENJAMIN ARNOLD, born circa 1780. Died 14 Apr 1838, in Boston Ma (gaz, g.s.). Buried in Calais Cemetery. Probate of Estate: 23 Jun 1840, in Machias Me (petition to remove, son, Lloyd as co-exec.). Census: 1830 (7 males & 6 females) in Calais.

He married ca 1813 MARY (_____), born circa 1789. Died 23 Sep 1868 age 80y 10d in Calais (VSNB:27:355, union, g.s.). Buried in Calais Cemetery. Census: 1840 widow (1 male & 5 females), 1850 & 60 in Calais. Children:

i. THOMAS S. ARNOLD, born circa 1808. Died 17 Sep 1822 age 19 in Calais (g.s.). Buried in Calais Cemetery.

ii. JULIA ARNOLD, born ca 1810. Died 17 Nov 1877 age 62y 2m in Calais (g.s.). Buried in Calais Cemetery. Census: 1850, 60 & 70 in Calais. She married before 1829 JACOB KIMBALL born ca 1804 in NH. He was in the 1st Brigade, 7th Div Maine Militia as a Pvt. in 1828 (mil). Died 25 Jan 1869 age 65 in Calais (union). Census: 1840 (2 males, 6 females), 1850 & 60 in Calais. 1850 Jacob & Julia Kimball, had Mary, Benjamin K., Bertha V.S. & Lloyd Arnold and his family, living with them. In 1830 census a female born between 1811 & 1820 could be Julia and male born between 1801-1810 could be Jacob. No other evidence that she is the child of Benjamin & Mary.

iii. GEORGE ARNOLD, born between 1811-1815 (1830 census), died 2 Aug 1816 age 18 mos. (g.s.). Buried in Calais Cemetery

iv. MALE CHILD ARNOLD, born between 1811-1815 (1830 census).

v. LLOYD ARNOLD, born ca 1814 (see BELOW).

vi. SAMUEL ARNOLD, poss. he is the male in the family of Benjamin, born between 1816-20 (1830 census). He was a ship carpenter. Census: 1830, 50 & 60 in Calais. He married before June 1852 when son was born in Calais (VR:3:252), MARGARET (_____) born ca 1828 in Ireland. Census: 1850 & 60 in Calais.

vii. LUCINDA B. ARNOLD, born circa 1819. Died 4 Jan 1881 age 63y in St. Stephen, NB, the same day her son, David H. died in St. John, NB age 26 (adv). Buried in Rural Cemetery in St. Stephen. Census: 1861(widow with 4 children) in St. Stephen. She married 28 Dec 1837 by Rev. Thomson in St Stephen, NB (CCMR, gaz) ABRAHAM H. MARKS, born ca 1797, died 28 Mar 1859 age 62 (g.s.), buried in Rural Cemetery in St. Stephen, NB (rural:83). He may be the son of NEHEMIAH & HANNAH H. MARKS who are buried in same cemetery lot.

viii. SARAH ELIZABETH ARNOLD, born circa 1820 in Waldoboro, ME (1850 census). Died 6 May 1884 in Calais (g.s., congo, times obit). Buried in Calais Cemetery. Census: 1850, 60 & 70 in Calais. She married 29 Jul 1843 CALVIN RICE GOODNOW, son of CALVIN GOODNOW & SALOME PHILLIPS (see GOODNOW).

ix. JAMES W. ARNOLD, born circa 1824. Died 2 Mar 1833 age 9y in Calais (g.s.). Buried in Calais Cemetery.

x. BERTHA V. S. ARNOLD, born circa 1825. Census: 1850 in Calais.

xi. ENOCH D. ARNOLD, born 23 Jun 1826 in Calais, died 25 Sep 1846 in Calais (VR:3:234, g.s.). Buried in Calais Cemetery.

xii. MARY/Mercy J. ARNOLD, born 8 Oct 1828 in Calais (VR). She was a teacher. Died 14 Jul 1883 age 54y 9m in Calais (times, g.s.). Buried in Calais Cemetery. Census: 1850 (with b-in-l Calvin Goodnow), 1860 & 70 (age 39 living with Calvin Goodnow) in Calais.

xiii. BENJAMIN K. ARNOLD, born 28 Jan 1834 in Calais (VR). Died 25 Apr 1855 in Calais (g.s.). [union, he died 15 Apr 1855 by drowning]. Buried: 27 Apr 1855 in Calais Cemetery. Census: 1850 (with Jacob & Julia Kimball) in Calais.

LLOYD & MARY ARNOLD p. 194

LLOYD ARNOLD, born circa 1814. In 1840 he resided Galveston, TX, when he was named administrator of his father's will (Probate of Benjamin's Estate: 1838, in Machias Me). Died 28 Apr 1888 in Galveston, TX in his 75th year (obit adv). Census: 1850 (living with Jacob & Julia Kimball also Mary Arnold age 61) in Calais.

He married 5 Dec 1844 in Calais by Rev. S. H. Keeler (gaz) MARY SMITH, born circa 1822 in NB. Probably died in Texas. Census: 1850 in Calais. Children:

i. ALICE EMMA ARNOLD, born 22 Oct 1845 in Calais (VR). Died circa 1848 (sext). Buried: 16 Dec 1848 in Calais Cemetery (sext).

ii. ABBOTT L. ARNOLD, born circa 1849. Census: 1850 (with uncle, Jacob Kimball) in Calais.

iii. UNNAMED CHILD ARNOLD, born circa 1852, died Sep 1852 in Calais (sext). Buried: 11 Sep 1852 in Calais Cemetery.

WILLIAM B. & MARY ANN ATWOOD p. 222

WILLIAM BOYDEN ATWOOD, born circa Feb 1793 poss. in Mass. before the move to Livermore with his parents, son of Capt. SAMUEL ATWOOD (died age 47 at Livermore 1816) & HANNAH BOYDEN (died age 84 in 1854) who was born in

Berkley, MA moved to Livermore 1795 (VR, liver:57, buck:523). He was in Calais by Sept 1825 when he appeared in Court, he was a farmer, trader & carpenter in the firm of Wait & Atwood (CCP). Died 29 Mar 1853 (g.s.). Buried: 2 Apr 1853 in Calais Cemetery. Census: 1830 (2 males, 2 females), 40 (2 males, 6 females), 50 (George Campbell age 27 living with him) in Calais.

He married (int) 3 Dec 1825 in Calais (cal2:24) MARY ANN REGAN (liver:57). She doesn't show up in 1850 census (however his grave stone says erected by wife, Mary). [Mrs. Mary Atwood removed from rolls 20 Jan 1879 reason died in Calais age 88y 3m (congo)]. Children: from early census there were possible 2 or 3 other children who died young.

i. WILLIAM HARRIS ATWOOD, born 25 Dec 1826 in Calais (buck:185, cal2:9). Attended Calais High School, went to Buckfield, ME to work for his uncle, Ephraim Atwood, became a partner in E. Atwood & Co in 1848, went into business for himself in North Turner, ME, returning to Buckfield in 1856, later established the first Department Store in Oxford County (buck:186). Died 12 Dec 1900 age 73y 11m 12d in Buckfield. Census: 1860 and 1900 in Buckfield. He married 1st 10 Sept 1849 HELEN M. ATWOOD, daughter of NATHAN ATWOOD AND RUTH ROGERS, she died 8 June 1865 (buck:186). Census: 1860 in Buckfield. He married 2nd JANETTE LORING, daughter of Major LUCIUS LORING, she died 6 Jan 1903 (buck:186). She died 6 Jan 1903 in Buckfield, d/o LUCIUS SPRING b. Turner & SALLY LONG b. Buckfield (MSA). Census: 1900 in Buckfield.

ii. MARY HANNAH ATWOOD, born 3 Dec 1828 in Calais (cal2:9).

iii. SARAH JANE ATWOOD, born 22 Sept 1830 in Calais (cal2:10)

iv. ANN LOUISA ATWOOD, born 29 Aug 1833 in Calais (VR).

v. CAROLINE PRISCILLA ATWOOD, born 10 Feb 1836 in Calais (VR).

vi. MINERVA LOWELL ATWOOD, born 10 Apr 1838 in Calais, died 18 Aug 1838 in Calais (VR). Buried in Calais Cemetery.

PETER & NANCY AVERY p. 217

PETER AVERY, born circa 1810 in Jackson, ME (1850 census). Census: 1840 (3 males, 2 females), 50 & 60 in Calais.

He married circa 1839 by Rev. E. D. Very (mrwc:29, brack:324) NANCY BRACKETT, born circa 1822, in Robbinston Me (1850 census), daughter of JOHN BRACKETT & NANCY JOHNSON. Census: 1850 & 60 in Calais (see BRACKETT). Children:

i. GEORGE JOHNSON AVERY, born 8 Oct 1839 in Calais (VR). He was a RR Conductor. Census: 1850 & 60 in Calais.

DANIEL & HANNAH BAILEY p. 217

DANIEL BAILEY, born _____ .
He married HANNAH (_____), born _____ . Children:

i. EDWARD BYRON BAILEY, born 16 Aug 1846 in Calais (VR).

SAMUEL & MARY ANN BAILEY, p. 219

SAMUEL BAILEY, Sr. born in Bakerstown Plantation, ME 17 Aug 1775 (bail:70). Died 22 Mar 1830 in Baileyville ME (Alexander, ME VR). He married JANE FROST born 23 Sept 1790 in St. Stephen, NB, daughter of JEREMIAH FROST, Sr. died 12 Nov 1859 in Baileyville ME (bail:70). Their 2nd son named Samuel Bailey, Jr. settled in Calais, the 1st son named Samuel died in 1814 age 2 years.

SAMUEL BAILEY, Jr., born, 22 May 1818 in Baileyville ME (bail:70, Alexander VR:18). He was a millman. Census: 1850 & 60 in Calais.

He married 20 Dec 1840 in Alexander, ME (VR) MARY ANN RUMERY /RUMNEY, born 15 Oct 1823 in Lubec Me (lubec:17, Perry VR), born (2): 5 Oct 1824 in Lubec (Alexander VR), daughter of JOHN RUMERY / RUMNEY & MEHITABLE PHINNEY. Census: 1850 & 60 in Calais. Children:

i. ESTHER ANN BAILEY, born 9 Aug 1842 in Alexander ME (VR:115, bail:73). She was a teacher. Census:

1850 & 60 in Calais.
- ii. LORING LORENZO BAILEY, born 26 Mar 1844 in Calais (bail:73, Alexander VR). He worked in a mill. Census: 1850 & 60 in Calais.
- iii. MOSES EMERY BAILEY, born (1) 5 Dec 1847 in Calais (VR), born (2) 5 Sept 1847 (Alexander VR). He was named for an uncle who died in 1846 (bail:73). He worked in a mill. Census: 1850 & 60 in Calais.
- iv. MARY E. BAILEY, born circa 1851. Died Sep 1869 in Calais (deaths in 1870 census). Census: 1860 in Calais.
- v. ANSON RUMERY BAILEY, born 3 Apr 1852 (bail:73, Alexander VR).
- vi. SAMUEL BAILEY, (III), born circa 1854. Census: 1860 in Calais.
- vii. FRANKLIN BAILEY, born circa 1856. Census: 1860 in Calais.
- viii. THEODORA E. BAILEY, born circa 1859, died 18 Jan 1860 age 3 m. 15 d. in Calais (g.s.). Buried: 19 Jan 1860 in Calais Cemetery.
- ix. THEODORE BAILEY, ca 1860 (age 3/12) in 1860 census in Calais.

JAMES E. & SARAH BALKAM p. 224

JAMES E. BALKAM, born circa 1809 in Anapolis, NS (1850 census). He was a farmer, carpenter & sheriff. Died Jan 1882 in Calais (obit adv). Census: 1840 (2 males, 1 female), thru 1880 in Calais.

He married 7 Dec 1837 in Calais (mrwc:23) SARAH ANN BEEDY, born circa 1810 in Berlin, ME (now Phillips 1850 census). Died 9 Jun 1881 in Milltown ME (obit adv). Census: 1850 thru 1880 in Calais. Children:

- i. HENRY ALLEN BALKAM, born 14 Apr 1839 in Calais (VR). Served in both Co. D and Co. E. of 6th Maine in Civil War and was wounded (NRMS:238). He was 5'9" with blue eyes and sandy hair (cwcard). He never regained the use of one hand (trib). He was a Customs Officer. Died 4 Aug 1911 in Calais (obit adv). Census: 1850 thru 1910 in Calais He married 1st 21 Jan 1864 in Calais (VR) CORDELIA DENSMORE, born 1849 in St. George, NB, daughter of SAMUEL DINSMORE (b. NS) & AMY MILLBURY (b. NB). She died 14 July 1894 in Calais (MSA). Census: 1880 in Calais. Henry was listed in 1896 Calais Directory as a sheriff and had only a daughter living with him. Census: 1870 & 80 in Calais. He married 2nd 11 Jan 1899 by Rev. W. Morgan in Oak Bay NB (MSA) AGNES V. TOAL, born ca Dec 1846 in Oak Bay, NB, daughter of HORATIO N. & MARTHA TOAL of Oak Bay. Census: 1900 & 1910 in Calais, not listed in 1920 census.
- ii. ANN ELIZA BALKAM, born 30 Jan 1843 in Calais (VR). Died 4 Oct 1864 age 21y 7m in Calais (VR:3:310). Census: 1850 & 60 in Calais. She married 18 Nov 1863 in Calais (VR:3:194) WILLIAM SHERMAN.
- iii. SARAH ADALINE BALKAM, born 23 Jun 1844 in Calais (VR). Died 15 Aug 1895 age 49 in Ashland, WI (obit adv). Census: 1850, 60 (age 15) in Calais. She married 3 June 1867 in Calais (VR:3:302) by Rev. H. V. Dexter in Calais JOSEPH W. COCHRAN.
- iv. JAMES EDWIN BALKAM, born 12 Jul 1846 in Calais, died 1 Jul 1859 in Calais (VR). Buried: 19 Jul 1859 in Calais Cemetery. Census: 1850 in Calais.
- v. GEORGE F. BALKAM, born circa 1849. Census: 1850 & 60 in Calais. He was a machinist. Died 10 Mar 1918 in Tacoma, WA (obit adv). Census: 1860 in Calais. He married (int.) 3 Apr 1870 in Calais (VR:3) LUCY HARMOND MCDONALD. (poss. the daughter of William & Deborah McDonald see McDonald)

DAVID B. & ISABELLA BARCLAY p. 211

SAMUEL BARCLAY, born circa 1794 in Ireland. Died 15 Dec 1861 in Calais. Census: 1850 in Calais. He married MARY LINDSAY, born circa 1796 in Ireland. He was a wheelwright. Died circa 1886 (g.s.). Buried in Calais Cemetery. Census: 1850 & 60 in Calais. One of their sons, David B. Barclay has a family listed in the early VR of Calais.

DAVID B. BARCLAY, born 15 Sep 1822 in St. Andrews, NB (MSA). He was a wheelwright. He served in Civil War as Private in Co G Coast Guard, described as 5' 11" with blue eyes and light hair (cwcard). Died 15 Sep 1903 age 82 in Calais (MSA). Census: 1850 thru 1880 in Calais.

He married (int.) Nov 1844 in Calais, married (1844-1845) by Rev. S.H. Keeler (mrwc:44) ISABELLA MILLIGAN, born circa 1827 in Ireland, daughter of SAMUEL MILLIGAN & ISABELLA (_____) [she was born ca 1797, died after 1870 census in Calais, when she was living with David & children]. David's wife died 21 Feb 1864 age 38 in Calais (g.s.). Buried in Calais Cemetery. Census: 1850 & 60 in Calais. Children:

i. ISABELLA {1} BARCLAY, born circa Aug 1847 in Calais, died 15 Aug 1847 age 15d in Calais (g.s.). Buried: 17 Aug 1847 in Calais Cemetery.
ii. ISABELLA {2} BARCLAY, born 17 Nov 1847 in Calais (VR). Died 4 Apr 1853 age 5y 4m in Calais (g.s.). Buried: 5 Apr 1853 in Calais Cemetery. Census: 1850 in Calais.
iii. DAVID FILMORE BARCLAY, born Jun 1850 in Calais (1850 census). Died after 1870. Census: 1850, 60 & 70 in Calais.
iv. MARY EVA BARCLAY, born 23 May 1853 in Milltown ME (VR). Died 16 Apr 1929 in Calais (sfh:7:182). Buried in Calais Cemetery. Census: 1860, 70, 1900 & 1920 in Calais. She married 14 Sept 1873 in Calais by Rev. A. S. Townsend (VR:3:327) JOSEPH E. COLLINS, born 25 Nov 1850 in Baring, Me (MSA), son of HIRAM P. COLLINS (born St. John, NB) & HARRIET BRIGGS (born South China, Me). Joseph, died 18 July 1933 in Calais, buried in Calais Cemetery (MSA). Census: 1870 (with mother), 1900 &1920 in Calais.
v. ANNABELLA BARCLAY, born circa 1853. Died after 1870. Census: 1860 & 70 in Calais.
vi. SARAH J. BARCLAY, born circa 1856. Died after 1880. Census: 1860, 70 & 80 in Calais.
vii. JAMES M. BARCLAY, born circa 1859, died 3 Apr 1907 in Calais, unmarried (MSA). He was a lumberman. Census: 1860 & 70 in Calais.
viii. SAMUEL R. BARCLAY, born circa 1861. Died Jan 1882, his obit reads: The body of Samuel R. Barclay s/o David Barclay of Milltown, Me recently killed at Lowell, MA, while in the act of shackling cars, was brought home on Monday last for burial. He was at one time member of City Council (VSNB:58:1840 SCC of 2 Feb 1882). Census: 1870 & 80 in Calais.

SAMUEL F. & ANNIE D. BARKER p. 178

TIMOTHY BARKER, born 4 Jan 1774 in Buxton/Wells ?, Maine (biorev:428).
He married SUSAN BOWEN, born 15 Feb 1774 (biorev: 428). Died ? One of his children, Samuel F. Barker, had a family listed in the early Calais VR.

SAMUEL FOSS BARKER, born 20 Feb 1803 in Buxton, ME (biorev:428). Served in War of 1812 from Nov 1812 to Oct 1813 in Capt. A. Gregory's Co., Col. Ulster's Regt {9yrs old?} and received a land grant from the U.S. Government (biorev:428, copy of muster roll record, dated from Nov 1812 to Oct 1913, from National Archives). He was a Merchant. He was a Deacon in Congo Church. Died 10 Oct 1849 in Calais (congo, probate at Machias). Buried in Calais Cemetery. Census: 1830 (4 males, 1 female), 40 (5 males, 4 females) in Calais.

He married 1st 2 Apr 1826 (biorev:429) LURENA KILBURN, born circa 1805 (g.s.). Died 9 Jan 1829 age 23 in Calais (cal2:15, biorev:428). Buried in Calais Cemetery. Children:

i. SAMUEL FOWLER BARKER, born 23 Jul 1827 (biorev:429, cal2:9). Bapt. 4 Dec 1831 in Calais (congo). He left Calais about 1845, returned once when his {step}mother died and again with his wife [probably a second wife] to visit in Sept 1890 (adv). He married 27 Aug 1853 in San Francisco, CA (east:130) ANN AMELIA LABORTIER of Boston. She died 19 May 1881 in Winter Hill, Somerville (adv).

He married 2nd 31 Jan 1830 (dem: 92) ANNE D. DEMING, daughter of CHARLES DEMING & MEHITABLE FULLER, born 17 Feb 1798 in Needham, MA (VR, biorev). She was a teacher. She was a sister of William Deming (see DEMING). Died 21 Nov 1876 in Calais (obit adv, congo). Buried in Calais Cemetery. Census: 1850 & 60 in Calais.

ii. EMILY LOUISA BARKER, born 18 Oct 1830 in Calais (biorev, g.s.). Bapt. [Louisa Emily] 4 Dec 1831 (congo). Died circa 1902 (g.s.). Buried in Calais Cemetery. Census: 1850 in Calais. She married (_____) JOHNSON.
iii. ELIZABETH ADALINE DEMING BARKER, born circa 1832, bapt. 4 Aug 1833 in Calais (congo). She died 24 Apr 1835 in Calais (VR, g.s.). Buried Calais Cemetery.
iv. JOHN BARKER, born 19 Apr 1834 in Calais (VR, biorev:428). Bapt. 8 June 1834 in Calais (congo). He was a merchant and in 1863 he was a partner in the firm of Chase, Barker & Co. and became one of the leading businessmen of Calais (biorev:430). Died 16 Jan 1909 age 74y 9m in Calais, dropped dead on

street (sfh:1:142, MSA, obit). Census: 1850 thru 1880, & 1900 (age 64, born Apr 1836) in Calais. He was a merchant. He married 31 Aug 1868 by Rev. Edgar L. Foster in St. Stephen, NB (CCMR, biorev:428) ANNA M. ANDREWS, born ca May 1838 in Milltown, NB (congo), daughter of JOHN D. ANDREWS & ALMIRA ALBEE. She died 24 Jan 1915 age 76y 8m in Calais (MSA, sfh:2:161). Census: 1870, 80 & 1900 in Calais.

- v. STEPHEN BARKER, born 19 Apr 1836 in Calais (VR). Census: 1850 in Calais.
- vi. ANNA DEMING BARKER, born 12 Mar 1838 in Calais. Bapt. 1 July 1838 in Calais (congo). She was a teacher of painting. Died after 1860. Census: 1850 & 60 in Calais.
- vii. WILLIAM SEWELL BARKER, born 9 Feb 1841 in Calais (VR). Bapt. 4 July 1841 in Calais (congo). Died Aug 1842 in Calais (obit gaz, g.s.). Buried: 23 Aug 1842 in Calais Cemetery.

BARNARD FAMILIES

JOHN[4] BARNARD b. 19 May 1743; son of Robert[3], Stephen[2], Robert[1]. Died 19 May 1825. He married ELIZABETH FAIRBANK 21 July 1768. They had eleven children. Their 1st child was John b. 26 May 1769 who married Annie Kendall. The 2nd child was Timothy Barnard b. 3 Nov 1770, who married Esther Newhall. The 10th child, Abel Barnard, and three of their grandchildren were among the families listed in the Book I of the VR. Information on this Barnard Family can be found in "Robert Barnard of Andover, Mass, and His Descendants" by Robert M. Barnard of Everett, Mass., 1899, found at MSL Augusta.

ABEL & MARY W. BARNARD p. 202

ABEL BARNARD, born 1 Nov 1792 in Sterling, MA (RBD:12,20). He was a merchant. Died 12 Oct 1859 in Calais (obit adv). Buried in Calais Cemetery. Census: 1830 (1male, 3 females) & 1850 in Calais.

He married 24 Aug 1826 (RBD:20), MARY W. PIKE, born circa 1801 in Westbrook, ME (1850 census), daughter of SAMUEL DEAN PIKE & MARY WEBB [daughter of Jonathan Webb and Mary Carver (mar. July 1802) of Westbrook] (biorev: 615). Bapt. 8 Aug 1830 in Calais (congo). She is a sister of Abby Barnard (see below). Died 13 Aug 1889 age 82 in Calais (g.s., congo., east:427). Buried in Calais Cemetery [her mother, Mary born 26 Sept 1784, died 28 Oct 1868 is also buried in their lot in Calais Cemetery]. Census: 1850, 60 & 70 in Calais. Children:

- i. CHARLES WILLIAM BARNARD, born 11 Jun 1827 in Calais (VR). Died 2 Sep 1828 in Calais (VR, RBD:20).
- ii. MARY CAROLINE BARNARD, born 14 Jul 1829 in Calais (VR). Died 30 Jul 1871 (RBD:20). Census: 1850 & 60 in Calais. She married 23 Sep 1864 in Calais (RBD:20) WILLIAM H. MCGREGOR.
- iii. ANN ELIZABETH BARNARD, born 7 Oct 1830 in Calais (VR, RBD). Died 19 Feb 1903 age 72y 4m in Calais (MSA, congo, obit adv). Buried: 21 Feb 1903 in Calais Cemetery. Census: 1850, 60, 70 & 1900 in Calais. Never married.
- iv. CHARLES HENRY BARNARD, born 6 Jan 1832 in Calais (VR). Died 6 Apr 1838 in Calais (VR,RBD:20, obit gaz). Buried in Calais Cemetery.
- v. EDGAR PIKE BARNARD, born 9 Oct 1833 in Calais (VR, RBD:20). He was a clerk & accountant. Died 24 Jan 1897 age 60 in Calais (MSA). Living with his sisters, Ann and Ellen, in the homestead at time of death. Unmarried. Census: 1850, 60 & 70 in Calais.
- vi. MARTHA BURNHAM BARNARD, born 30 Aug 1836 in Calais (VR), died Jul 1887 (RBD:20). Census: 1850, 60 & 70 in Calais. She married 1st 8 Jan 1863 in Calais (VR, RBD) JAMES B. HORNE of Brooklyn, NY. She married 2nd 4 Oct 1878 (RBD) S. W. ADAMS.
- vii. GEORGE FREDERICK BARNARD, born 15 Sep 1838 in Calais (VR, RBD:20). Died after 1860, prob. killed by Indians in Oregon (RBD: 20). Census: 1850 & 60 in Calais.
- viii. ELLEN 'NELLIE' PIKE BARNARD, born 11 Oct 1844 in Calais (VR, RBD). After her husbands death she returned to Calais and lived in the house where she was born, called the Barnard Place, where she died 28 Apr 1907 age 62 in Calais (obit adv, MSA). Buried in Calais Cemetery. Census: 1850, 60, 70 & 1900 (a widow) in Calais. She married 1 Sep 1871 by Rev. William Carruthers in Calais (VR, adv) CHARLES E. LIBBY, who was a photographer, after their marriage they moved to Salina, KS where he died ca 1883.

ALBERT W. & ABBIE BARNARD p. 196

ALBERT WEBSTER[6] BARNARD, born 14 May 1812 in Pembroke NB (RBD:18), the son of TIMOTHY[5]

BARNARD & ESTHER NEWHALL, [JOHN⁴, ROBERT³, STEPHEN², ROBERT¹]. Died 6 Sep 1870 in Calais (RBD, congo, obit SCC). Census: 1840 (4 males, 2 females) thru 1870 in Calais.

He married 24 Jan 1837 in Calais by Rev. William A. Whitwell (mrwc:21) ABBY/ABBA C. PIKE, born circa 1818 in Westbrook, ME (1850 census), daughter of SAMUEL DEAN PIKE & MARY WEBB, sister of Mary, wife of Abel Barnard (see above). In October 1882 she and daughter, Abby Woods & her children moved to Des Moines, IA to join Mr. Woods who is employed there (adv). Died 28 Feb 1893 in Des Moines, IA, moved there 1882 (congo, RBD). Census: 1850 thru 1880 in Calais. Children:

i. HERBERT WEBSTER BARNARD, born 27 Feb 1838 in Calais (VR, RBD:29 = 1839). Died 1 Feb 1929 in Portland age 90y 11m 27d (MSA). Census: 1840 thru 1880 in Calais, 1900 in Portland, ME. He married 1 Jun 1863 in Calais (VR:3:195, RBD:29, east:195) ELLEN 'NELLIE' AUGUSTA YOUNG, born 1 Mar 1842, daughter of CYRUS YOUNG & ELECTRA EMERSON. Died 9 Dec 1914 in South Portland, ME (MSA). In 1899 they resided in Portland, ME (congo, RBD). Census: 1870 & 80 in Calais.

ii. LYMAN PAGE BARNARD, born 20 Apr 1839 in Calais (VR, RBD has 16 Aug 1840). Died 16 Jul 1873 age 32y 10m in Augusta, ME (adv). Census: 1850 & 60 in Calais.

iii. CHARLES WILLIAM BARNARD, born 16 Aug 1841 in Calais (VR, RBD has 20 Aug 1842). He was a merchant. Died after 1870. Census: 1850, 60 & 70 in Calais.

iv. ALFRED GORDON BARNARD, born 19 Jun 1845 in Calais (VR, RBD has 10 June1846). He was a merchant. Died Jan 1888 (RBD). Census: 1850, 60 & 70 in Calais. He married 1st 28 Apr 1870 by Rev. William Carruthers in Calais (VR:3:233, adv) HATTIE N. CAREY, born ca 1850 in NB. Census 1870 in Calais. He married 2nd 30 Aug 1882 by C. B. Rounds, JP in Calais (VR:2:18, 19) SARAH A. BURNS.

v. ABBIE/ABBA E. BARNARD, born, 6 Mar 1851 (RBD:29). Died after 1880. Census: 1860, 70 & 80 in Calais. She married 17 Sep 1873 by Rev. William Carruthers in Calais (RBD, adv) JOSEPH G. WOODS of Calais at marriage, they resided in Des Moines, IA after 1882.

vi. LAURA E. BARNARD, born 13 Aug 1855, died 21 Feb 1881 (RBD:29, adv). Census: 1860 & 70 in Calais.

EDWARD A. & MARY ANN BARNARD p. 207

EDWARD AUGUSTUS⁶ BARNARD, born 12 Jan 1814 in Boston MA (RBD:18, 27), son of JOHN⁵ BARNARD (JR.) & ANNIE KENDALL, [JOHN⁴, ROBERT³, STEPHEN², ROBERT¹]. He came to Calais in 1836 (beg:122). He was a merchant and Councilman in the city of Calais, and a State Representative (biosk: 7). He was in business as E. A. Barnard & son in 1887 Calais directory. Died 5 Apr 1899 in Quincy, MA (obit gaz, times). Buried in Calais Cemetery. Census: 1840 (1 male, 3 females) thru 1880 in Calais.

He married 12 Dec 1837 in Calais by Rev. William Whitehall (RBD, news clip gaz) MARY ANN SHEPPARD, born 10 Jul 1814 in Jefferson, ME (g.s., congo, RBD) daughter of DAVID SHEPPARD & MARY HILL. Bapt. 3 May 1840 in Calais (congo). Died 2 Nov 1897 age 83 in Calais (MSA, adv, congo, g.s.). Buried in Calais Cemetery. Census: 1850 thru 80 in Calais. Children:

i. ANNA KENDALL BARNARD, born 4 Feb 1839 in Calais (VR). Resided in Milwaukee, WI in 1875 (beg:122). Died 11 May 1904 in Milwaukee, WI Buried in Forest Home Cemetery in Milwaukee (DEA 12:2:71). Census: 1850 & 60 in Calais. She married 23 Jul 1863 in Calais (RBD:27) JULIUS M. KUMMELL of New York.

ii. HARRIET LARKIN BARNARD, born 11 Apr 1841 in Calais (VR, g.s.). Graduated from Calais Academy. Died 13 Jan 1904 in Calais (g.s., RBD). Buried in Calais Cemetery. Census: 1850, 60 & 70 in Calais. She married 25 Jun 1863 in Calais GEORGE THATCHER PORTER, son of CHARLES CURTIS PORTER & SOPHIA B. DYER (see PORTER).

iii. FRANK AUGUSTUS BARNARD, born 16 Sep 1843 in Calais (VR). Graduated from Calais Academy. Enlisted in Civil War, 5 Aug. 1862, Co D of 6th Maine, at age 18 years 10 months, father signed consent (enlist). He was 5'5" with gray eyes and brown hair (cwcard). Died of wounds 1 Dec 1863 in Armory Sq. Hospital, in Washington, DC (NRMS:242, east:201, RBD). Census: 1850 & 60 in Calais.

iv. HENRY HARRIS BARNARD, born 13 Aug 1846 in Calais (VR). He was a merchant at time of his death he was a member of the firm of Church E. Gates & Co. extensive lumber dealers (obit). Died 8 Feb 1921 age 62 in NY (obit adv, g.s.). Buried in Calais Cemetery. Census: 1850 in Calais (congo says he moved to NYC

23 Feb 1890). Census: 1860, 70 & 80 in Calais. He married 24 Aug 1871 in Calais by Rev. William Carruthers (adv, east:255) LUCY GATES, born 27 June 1845 (RBD, g.s.), daughter of EPHRAIM GATES AND VASHTI. R. PICKENS (see GATES). She died 28 Feb 1921 in New York City age 75y 7m 27d (g.s., sfh:3:222). Buried Calais Cemetery. Census: 1880 in Calais.

v. CLARA EVERETT BARNARD, born 21 Oct 1850 in Calais (g.s., RBD = Sept 1849). Died 28 May 1926 age 78y 8m 7d in New Rochelle, NY (g.s., sfh:5:95, obit adv, single). Body brought by train and buried in the family lot where 3 generations are buried in Calais Cemetery (obit). Census: 1850, thru 80 in Calais (congo has she moved to Cambridge, MA 20 June 1900).

GEORGE S. & FRANCES L. BARNARD p. 180

GEORGE SULLIVAN BARNARD, born 3 Jun 1808 in Lunenburg, VT (RBD:18,28) son of TIMOTHY BARNARD & ESTHER NEWHALL, brother of Albert (above). He was in the 1st Brigade, 7th Div Maine Militia as a Pvt. in 1832 (mil). Died 27 Oct 1861 in Calais (g.s., RBD). Buried: 29 Oct 1861 in Calais Cemetery. Census: 1850 & 60 in Calais.

He married 11 Oct 1832 in Calais (RBD:18) FRANCES L. STARBOARD, born 1 Apr 1815 in Eastport ME (RBD, dem, VR Eastport has 1816), daughter of EBENEZER STARBOARD AND SARAH BELL. Died 27 May 1887 age 79 in Calais (RBD, g.s., adv). Buried in Calais Cemetery. Census: 1850 thru 1880 in Calais. Children:

i. SARAH ELIZABETH BARNARD, born 20 Jan 1834 in Calais (VR). Died after 1860 and before 1880. Census: 1850 & 60 in Calais. She married 30 May 1859 in Calais (RBD:28, VR) CHARLES LEONARD DEMING, son of WILLIAM DEMING AND SARAH M. WILCOX (see DEMING).

ii. LUCY JANE BARNARD, born 3 Nov 1841 in Calais (VR). Died 11 Aug 1845 age 3y 9m in Calais (RBD:28, g.s.). Buried: 18 Aug 1845 in Calais Cemetery.

iii. FREDERICK S. BARNARD, born 22 Mar 1843 in Calais (VR, RBD). He served in Civil War (1861-1865) as Serg't in Co K 15th Inf. and Capt. in Co G 14th Inf., 5' 5" with blue eyes and brown hair (cwcard). Died 1 Dec 1874 in St Louis, MO (RBD:29). Census: 1850 & 60 in Calais. He married 1st 3 Jan 1869 LAURA F. MERRILL she died 17 Dec 1871 (RBD:29). He married 2nd MATTIE F. HINDMAN (RBD:29). Resided in St. Louis, MO (RBD).

iv. FANNIE PAINE BARNARD, born 23 Oct 1858 (RBD). Died 27 Jan 1882 in Calais (g.s., east: 348, - RBD has date Jan 1884). Buried in Calais Cemetery. Census: 1860, 70 & 80 in Calais. She married 21 May 1878 in Calais (adv, congo, times, RBD:29 gives date 1880) EDWIN B. TODD, born 16 Jan 1852, died 12 Mar 1902 and buried in Rural Cemetery in St. Stephen, NB (rural:200). He was employed in firm of F. H. Todd & Sons. Census 1880 with a 1 year old child in Calais.

MICHAEL & ANN BARRETT p. 222

MICHAEL BARRETT was born 20 September 1814 in Dromorenorth, County Sligo, Ireland arrived Calais 11 June 1831. Witnesses to establish his residence were William L. McAllister of Alexander and Joseph Granger of Calais. He was naturalized 3 Sept 1840. [Naturalization Papers in the Sept. 1840 Term of the Washington County Court Records, at MSA]. He was a grocer and trader. Died after 1871. Census: 1840 (6 males, 1 female) & 50 in Calais, 1851 (p.20), 61 & 71 in St. Stephen, NB.

He married ANN (_____), born in Tipperary, Ireland (1850 census). Died between 1861 & 1871. Census: 1850 in Calais, 1851 & 61 in St. Stephen, NB. Children:

i. JAMES BARRETT, born 2 May 1838 in Calais (VR). Census: 1850 in Calais, 1851 in St. Stephen, NB.

ii. JOHN BARRETT, born 9 May 1841 in Calais (VR). [A John Barrett served in Civil War 6 Jan to 6 July 1865 as Pvt. in Co G Coast Guard born in Calais age 18 at enlistment, 5' 5 ¾" blue eyes and dark hair, occupation, printer (cwcard) parents consent not filled in on enlistment paper]. Census: 1850 in Calais, 1851 & 61 in St. Stephen, NB.

iii. MARY ANN BARRETT, born 23 Jul 1843 in Calais (VR). Census: 1850 in Calais, 1851 & 61 in St. Stephen, NB.

iv. BRIDGETT BARRETT, born circa 1848. Census: 1850 in Calais, 1851, 61 & 71 in St. Stephen, NB.

v. MICHAEL BARRETT, Jr., born circa 1851 in NB. Census: 1861 & 71 in St. Stephen, NB.

vi. WILLIAM H. BARRETT, born circa 1853 in NB. Census: 1861 & 71 in St. Stephen, NB.

JAMES & CATHARINE BARRY p. 201

JAMES BARRY, born _____ .
He married, Catherine (_____), born _____ . Children:

i. JOSEPH BARRY, born 29 Dec 1842 in Calais (VR).
ii. BRIDGET BARRY, born 24 Jan 1846 in Calais (VR).

James may be the son of JACOB BARRY, whose will was dated 7 May 1822 and his wife Brigit. Sons mention in will; James, Thomas and Nicholas. (Early New Brunswick Probate Records, by R. Wallace Hale, 1989. p. 30).

JOHN & MARGARET BARRY p. 201

JOHN BARRY, born _____ .
He married Margaret (_____), born _____ . Children:

i. CHARLES BARRY, born 24 April 1842 in Calais (VR).

THOMAS & ALICE BARRY p. 201

THOMAS BARRY, born ca 1812 in Ireland (daughter Mary's obit). Died before 1880 wife was a widow in 1880 census. Census: 1860 (age 48), 70 (age 55) in Biddeford.

He married ALICE MAHER, born ca 1828 in Ireland. Died 27 Jan 1911 age 83 in Biddeford (mart, MSA). Census: 1860 (age 34), 70, 80 & 1900 in Biddeford. Children:

i. ELLEN BARRY, born 8 Feb 1847 in Calais (VR). Died 14 Dec 1921 age 73 in Lowell, MA (Lowell Sun of 15 Dec 1921, mart). Married 6 Feb 1871 (mart) JOHN J. LEARY, born June 1851 in Milford, NH, died June 1926 (Lowell Sun of 28 June 1926, mart).
ii. ELEANORA 'NORA' BARRY, born ca 1950 in Biddeford. Census: 1860 (age 10) & 70 in Biddeford. Married before 1880 _____ TREFETHER. Resided in Portsmouth NH 1932 (sister's obit).
iii. MARGARET BARRY, born ca 1853 possibly in Biddeford, ME. Unmarried. Died after 1932. Census: 1860 (age 7), 70, 80, 1900 & 1920 (age 63) in Biddeford.
iv. WILLIAM BARRY, born ca 1855 in Maine. Resided in Salem, MA in 1921 (Ellen's obit). Not mentioned in Mary's obit. Census: 1860 (age 5) & 70 in Biddeford.
v. MARY ANN BARRY, born ca 1857, in Biddeford. Died 28 May 1932 age 75 in Biddeford (MSA, obit pph). Unmarried. Census: 1860 (age 3), 70, 80, 1900 & 1920 (age 58) in Biddeford.
vi. JAMES BARRY, born ca 1860 in Biddeford. Listed as a survivor living in Norwich, CT in Ellen's obit. Not mentioned in Mary's obit. Therefore probably died between 1921 & 1932. Census: 1860 (age 6/12), 70 & 80 in Biddeford.
vii. KATHERINE BARRY, born ca 1861 (age 36 at marriage) in Biddeford. Probably died before 1911 not mentioned in mother's obit, may have died in child birth as her 6months old son living with her mother and sisters in 1900 cenus. Census: 1870 & 80 in Biddeford. Married 4 May 1897 (MSA, her 1ST his 2ND) in Biddeford EDWARD RICKER, born ca 1851 in Saco (MSA), son of HUMPHREY RICKER & MARTHA HOOKER.

Thomas may be the brother of James above.

DAVID & MARIA BASSET p. 195

DAVID BASSET, born circa 1805 in Livermore ME (1850 census). He was in the 1st Brigade, 7th Div Maine Militia a Pvt. in 1828, as a Cpl. 1829-1832 (mil). Died after 1880. Census: 1820 (5 males, 7 females, see below), 40 (3 males, 1 female), 1850 in Calais, 60 (living with Warren Sawyer), 1870 & 80 {pauper age 78 in Poor Farm since Nov 1867} in Calais. {In 1820 census of Calais there is a David Basset with 5 males & 7 females, this David may be his father}. There was a David Basset who was an original land grantee in Magaguavavic, NB 5 Feb 1812 (PANB film #F1252). There is a marriage rec. in VR of Livermore for David Basset and Miss Hannah Stockman on 29 Mar 1802 by Cyrus Hamlin, JP, poss. his parents.

He married 13 Sep 1829 by Rev. Samuel Thomson in St George NB (angch) MARIA SWIM, born circa 1815 in St George NB (1850 census). They were both of St. George at marriage. She was a nurse. She may be the sister of Sarah (Swim) Sawyer of Calais. Maria got a divorce from her abusive husband in Oct 1856 and got custody of the children (SJC:14:274). Died after 1870. Census: 1850, 60 & 70 in Calais. She married 2nd before 1860 GEORGE KELLEY born ca 1834 a harness maker. Census: 1860 in Calais. Children of David & Maria:

i. JOHN BASSET, born circa 1832 in St George NB (1850 census). He was a sailor. Died after 1860. Census: 1850 & 60 in Calais.
ii. GEORGE FREDERICK {1} BASSET, born 11 Oct 1837 in Calais, died in Jan 1840 in Calais (VR:1:234).
iii. ANN MARIA BASSET, born Jan 1839 in Calais, died Mar 1841 in Calais (VR:1:234).
iv. GEORGE FREDERICK {2} BASSET, born 11 Oct 1840 in Calais (VR). Census: 1850 & 60 in Calais.
v. WILLIAM HENRY BASSET, born 4 Jul 1842 in Calais (VR). Died after 1860. Census: 1850 & 60 in Calais.
vi. WYMAN/HYMAN BASSET, born 11 Dec 1845 in Calais, died in Mar 1847 in Calais (VR:1:234).
vii. CHARLES EDWARD BASSET, born circa 1848 in Calais (1850 census). Served in Civil War Co G 1st Cavalry, described as 5' 4" with gray eyes and brown hair, died 5 May 1913 near Landers Station, CA (cwcard). Census: 1850 & 60 in Calais.
viii. ELLA JOSEPHINE BASSET, born circa 1852. Died after 1868. Census: 1860 in Calais. She married 19 Oct 1868 (VR:3) FRANK DURGAN.

THOMAS R. & ANN BASSET p. 206

THOMAS R. BASSET, born circa 1806 in Spencer, NY (1850 census). He was a ship carpenter.. He was still in Calais in 1854 when he was a party in a court action (SJC:3:475). Died after 1854 Census: 1850 in Calais

He married circa 1844 by Rev. S. H. Keeler in Calais (mrwc:44), int. 5 Oct 1844 (VR) ANN BROWN, born circa 1826 in St Andrews, NB (1850 census). Census: 1850 in Calais. Children:

i. JOHN BASSET, born 28 Jan 1845 in Calais (VR). Census: 1850 in Calais.
ii. MARY BASSET, born 17 Aug 1847 in Calais (VR). Census: 1850 in Calais.
iii. CHARLES BASSET, born Jan 1850 in Calais. Census: 1850 in Calais.

ASHER B. & MEHITABLE BASSFORD p. 210

ASHER BENJAMIN BASSFORD, born Aug 1805 in Mt. Vernon, Me, came to Calais in 1826 (obit). His father was a foreman when the Boston State House was built (pkjdt:52). He was in the 1st Brigade, 7th Div Maine Militia as a musician in 1828 and Sgt. 1829-1832 (mil). He was an architect and master-builder also the Chief Engineer on the Fire Dept. He was a member of the Calais Band, played the clarinet. Died 4 Aug 1887 age 82 in Calais (congo, obit SCC, adv). Buried in Calais Cemetery. Census: 1830 (1 male, 1 female), 40 (5 males, 3 females) thru 1880 in Calais.

He married 1st Oct 1829 in Calais (east:104), MEHITABLE M. GETCHELL born circa 1809. Died 2 Oct 1831 age 22 in Calais (VR:1:237, east:117). Buried in Calais Cemetery, stone buried. Child:

i. FRANCES CAROLINE BASSFORD, born 25 Jul 1830 (VR). Died after 1887. Resided in Watertown, Col. when her father died in 1887. Census: 1850 in Calais (living with James Sargent family). She married 15 Jun 1851by Rev. Mr. Barrett in St. Stephen, NB (CCMR, FJ) GEORGE W. WASHBURN,

He married 2nd 13 Oct 1833 in Calais (cal2:36) LUCY JANE STUART/STEWART, born 29 Jul 1815 in Oak Bay, NB (1850 census = St David, NB). They celebrated their 50th wedding anniversary on Nov 7, 1883 (adv). Died 9 May 1898 in St. Stephen, NB (g.s., prbt, adv). Buried: in Calais Cemetery. Census: 1850 thru 1880 in Calais. Children:

ii. LEVI LINCOLN LOWELL BASSFORD, born 30 Nov 1834 in Calais (VR). Bapt. 1 Nov 1835 in Calais (congo). Served as Sgt. in Co. D 6th Me Infantry, and transferred and promoted to Capt., Co. B 6th Maine. Died 1898 in LaGrange, Ill. (NRMS:238). He 5'7 ½" with blue eyes and black hair (cwcard). He was a Civil Engineer. Census: 1850 & 60 in Calais. He married 23 May 1863 in Eastport ME (east:195) MAGGIE J. CARY, daughter of Capt. THEODORE CARY of Eastport.

iii. EDWARD PAYSON BASSFORD, born 7 Jun 1837 in Calais (VR). Bapt. 7 Jan 1838 in Calais (congo). He was an Architect. In 1898 he resided in St. Paul, MN (mother's probate). Died 12 Jul 1912 age 32 in St. Paul, MN (adv) Census: 1850 & 60 in Calais. He married 1st 15 Aug 1866 by Rev. J. Caldwood in Calais (VR:3:224) HANNAH W. TODD, born ca 1843, daughter of JOHN WORTHY TODD (1815-1898) & MARIA BIXBY. She died 8 or 10 Sept 1875 in St. Paul, MN (g. s., obit) buried Rural Cemetery, St. Stephen, NB (rural:204). He married 2nd CATHERINE 'Kate' MURPHY. She died 5 Nov 1874 age 39 in St. Paul, MN (adv).

iv. LAURA MEHITABLE BASSFORD, born 17 Mar 1840 in Calais. Bapt 23 Oct 1842 in Calais (congo). She graduated from Calais Academy and was a teacher. Died after 1898, resided in St. Louis (mother's obit). Census: 1850 & 60 in Calais. She married C. M. HOLBERT 15 June 1873 in Chicago by Rev. C. D. Helmer (adv). Her name was Mrs. Holbrook of St. Louis in 1887 when her father died, also when mother died 1898, her signature reads Holbert on probate document.

v. MARY DOWNES BASSFORD, born 13 Jul 1843 in Calais, died 25 Feb 1846 in Calais (VR:1:237). Buried: 26 Feb 1846 in Calais Cemetery.

vi. LUCY J. BASSFORD, born 30 Mar 1845 in Calais (VR). Died 11 Mar 1919 age 78y 11m 11d in St Stephen, NB (sfh:3:60). Buried: 11 Mar 1919 in Calais Cemetery. Census: 1850, 60 & 70 in Calais. She married 5 Jun 1874 in Calais (adv) as his second wife (mop:249 has Jan 1872) MARSHALL NOAH MCKUSICK, born 7 Mar 1841 in Baring, ME, son of LEVI E. MCKUSICK & ADELAIDE A. MARSHALL (biorev:345, mop:248). He attended academies in Milltown, NB and Fryeburg, Me (biorev:347). In Civil War he was in the 6th Battery, Lt. Artillery, commissioned Lieutenant in 1862, and commanded his unit in battles of Antietam, Gettysburg, and the Wilderness, where he received a wound in his right shoulder from which he never fully recovered (mop:248, obit). In the City of Calais he served as; Postmaster, Overseer of the Poor, Alderman, and was Mayor of Calais in 1889-91 among other public offices (biorev:347, obit served 5 terms ending 1907). Died 28 May 1908 age 67 in Calais (obit adv, mck:118, MSA has mother's name Fannie A. Marshall, she died 1901 her death rec. name Frances A. d/o Robert & Jessina Marshall, MSA). Census: 1850 (age 9) in Baring, ME.

vii. ASHER BENJAMIN BASSFORD, Jr. born 13 Sep 1847 in Calais (VR). Graduated from Calais Academy. Resided in St. Paul, MN in 1888 when they visited Calais (adv), resided Landownes, PA in 1898 (mother's will). He was a building contractor, some of the building constructed by him were: Post Offices in Altanta and Tampa, and a 15-story building in Savannah (article in Calais Adv. of 30 Dec 1914). Died 24 Aug 1932 in Tampa, Fl (obit adv). Buried in Savannah, GA. Census: 1850 & 60 in Calais. He married 12 Feb 1874 in Calais (adv) ANNA ELIZA MARSHALL, daughter of BRADFORD MARSHALL & ELLEN SHEEHAN (see MARSHALL).

CHARLES & BETSEY M. BATES p. 187

CHARLES BATES, born circa 1809, in NB (g.s.), son of AMBROSE BATES & MERCY GREENLAW (geng). Died 1861 in Princeton Me (g.s.). Buried in Princeton Me. Census: 1840 (5 males, 1 female) in Calais, 50 & 60 in Princeton.

He married 9 Aug 1835 by Joseph Granger, JP in Calais (VR) ELIZABETH 'BETSEY' M. EATON, born circa 1817 (g.s.) in Blue Hill, ME (MSA). Died circa 1880 in Princeton Me. Buried in Princeton. Census: 1850 thru 1880 in Princeton. Children:

i. JAMES AMBROSE BATES, born 29 Sep 1836 in Calais (VR, g.s. = 1837). Before leaving for service he was a mill man. Served in Civil War as Corp'l in Co. H 9th Maine (g.s.) described as 5' 4" with hazel eyes and dark hair (cwcard). Died 29 Sept 1864 killed in action (cwcard, g.s.). Buried in Princeton Me. Census: 1850 & 60, in Princeton.

ii. MELISSA BATES, born 20 Jul 1838 in Calais, died 21 Aug 1838 in Calais (VR). Buried: 23 Aug 1838

in Calais Cemetery.
- iii. CHARLES EDWIN BATES, born 2 Jul 1839 in Calais (VR, MSA=1840). He was a farmer. Died 19 May 1918 age 78y 10m 17d in Princeton, Me (MSA, g.s.). Buried in Princeton. Census: 1850, 60 & 80 in Princeton.
- iv. GORHAM AUGUSTUS BATES, born 1 Jul 1841 in Calais (VR). Died circa 1862 in Princeton (g.s.). Buried in Princeton. Census: 1850 & 60 in Princeton.
- v. JOHN ALONZO BATES, born 14 Apr 1844 in Calais, died 20 Dec 1845 in Calais (VR).
- vi. VIOLA ALBINA BATES, born 14 Aug 1846 in Calais (VR). Census: 1850 & 60 in Calais. She married, 18 Aug 1866, in Princeton (VR). WILLIAM H. SMITH, [poss. the William H. Smith, born in Canada, who died 31 May 1905 in Eastport, son of GIDEON & ANN SMITH (MSA)].
- vii. LEORA A. BATES, born circa 1848 in Princeton. Census: 1850, 60 & 70 in Princeton.
- viii. HIRAM A. BATES, born 7 Mar 1851 in Princeton (MSA). He was a farmer & potato dealer. Died 9 Aug 1921 age 70y 5m 2d in Princeton Me (MSA, prinvr:46,47, g.s.). Census: 1860, 70 & 80 in Princeton.. He married 2 Nov 1884 by Rev. George E. Chapin in Princeton (VR) BESSIE M. FIELD, born 13 Aug 1864 in Princeton, died 27 (Dec?) 1940 (MSA, g. s.). She was the daughter of JOHN FIELD born in Waite. Both are buried in Princeton.
- ix. WILLARD ALBERTUS BATES, born circa 1854 in Princeton Me. He was a harness maker. Died 10 Aug 1905, in Princeton (MSA). Buried in Princeton. Census: 1860, 70 & 80 in Princeton.
- x. IVAETTA BATES, born circa 1856 in Princeton. Died after 1880. Census: 1860, 70 & 80 in Princeton.

EDWIN & LYDIA M. BATES, p. 188

EDWIN BATES (death rec. has father as A. BATES no mother given), born circa 1815 in St Andrews, NB. He was a Customs Toll Collector. Died 16 Jan 1893 age 76 11m 7d in Calais (MSA, obit adv, g.s.). Buried: 18 Jan 1893 in Calais Cemetery. Census: 1850 thru 1880 in Calais.

He married 30 Apr 1846 by Rev. Eaton in Calais (gaz, mrwc:47) LYDIA M. LANE, born circa 1820 in Calais. Died 5 Jan 1891 age 70y 8m 16d in Calais (times, adv, g.s.). Buried: 7 Jan 1891 in Calais Cemetery. Census: 1850 thru 1880 in Calais. Children:

- i. EDWIN CASSIUS BATES, born (1) 7 Feb 1847 in Calais (VR), born (2) 7 Feb 1846 (VR 3:256). He enlisted in Civil War Co C 9th ME Inf., he was a clerk 5'6 ½" with blue eyes and brown hair (cwcard). Died at age 17y 6m at Point Lookout, MD where his body lies 12 Apr 1864 from wounds received near Petersburg, VA (g.s. in Calais Cemetery). Census: 1850 & 60 in Calais.
- ii. ADA M. BATES, born 10 Jun 1852 in Calais (VR:3:256). She was a housekeeper. Died 10 May 1906 age 54y in Calais unmarried (MSA). Buried: 12 May 1906 in Calais. Census: 1860, 70 (listed as Adam, male) & 80 in Calais.
- iii. DAVID HUME BATES, born 18 Oct 1854 in Calais (VR:3:256). Died 19 Mar 1913 in St. Stephen, NB (SCC, adv). Buried: 22 Mar 1913 in Calais Cemetery. Census: 1860, 70 & 80 in Calais. He married FANNIE GRANT, born 1857, died 1938 (g.s. in Calais Cemetery).
- iv. HERBERT MONROE BATES, born 31 Mar 1857 in Calais (VR 3:256). Died 4 May 1927 age 70 in Calais (MSA, sfh:7:40, g.s.). Buried: 6 May 1927 in Calais Cemetery. Census: 1860, 70 & 80 in Calais.

JOSEPH & JANE BEEDY, p. 221

JOSEPH EVELETH BEEDY, born in Industry, Me, son of DANIEL[4,3,2,1] BEEDY & POLLY EVELETH [d/o JAMES EVELETH & BETSEY WILLIAMS] (indr:510, 'he married an Irish lady at Calais and removed to Iowa'). Census: 1840 in Calais.
He married JANE (_____). Child:

- i. EMMA FEDELIA BEEDY, born 4 Jul 1847 in Calais (VR).

WILLIAM B. & MARY ANN BELLOWS, p. 204

WILLIAM B. BELLOWS, born circa 1813, in Mass. Census: 1850 in Calais (living with Henry & Mary Bates family).

He married 2 May 1846 in St Stephen, NB (CCMR) MARY ANN BATES, born circa 1823 in Cooper ME (1850 census), daughter of HENRY BATES & MARY BECKFORD. She died 24 Aug 1898 age 78y 11m in Boston Ma (east:583). Census: 1850 (living with her parents) in Calais. Children:

i. DANIEL B. BELLOWS, born 13 Feb 1847 in Calais (VR). Census: 1850 (living with Henry & Mary Bates family) in Calais.
ii. MARY BELLOWS, born circa 1849 in Calais (1850 census). Census: 1850 (living with Henry & Mary Bates family) in Calais.

JAMES & ANNE BELMORE, p. 190

JAMES M. BELMORE, born 19 Dec 1817 in St Andrews, NB immigrated 10 Apr 1830 from NB, Naturalized 5 Sept 1840 (naturalization papers at MSA). He was a lumberman. Died 6 Nov 1883 age 65 in Calais (times, probate rec.). Census: 1840 (3 males, 1 female) thru 1880 in Calais.

He married 28 Jul 1838, by John Knowlton in St Stephen, NB (CCMR: A: 915) ANNIE COLSON, born circa 1822 in St George NB (1850 census). Died 7 Sep 1898 in Calais (times). Census: 1850 (Josiah Colson age 53 living with them thru 1880 in Calais. (In 1860 & 70 Josiah Colson age 76, poss. her father). Children:

i. MARY HELEN BELMORE, born 21 Dec 1845 in Calais (VR). Died 9 Aug 1908 age 61y 8m 11d at her home on North St. in Calais (MSA, obit adv). Census: 1850 thru 1880 in Calais. She married 15 Nov 1865 by Rev. W.S. McKellar in Calais (VR) GEORGE WASHINGTON HUTCHINS, son of JOSEPH HUTCHINS & MARY ANN MANSFIELD (see HUTCHINS, see also Frank Hall).
ii. JAMES BELMORE, born circa 1848 in Calais, died 6 Aug 1849 age 17m in Calais (g.s.). Buried in Calais Cemetery.
iii. CATHERINE `CASSIE' E. BELMORE, born Jun 1850 in Calais. Died after 1880. Census: 1850 thru 80 in Calais. She married 4 Nov 1875 by Rev. William Carruthers in Calais (VR, adv) ALEXANDER F. ANDERSON, of Boston, MA, not living with her in 1800 census, she and children with her parents.
iv. JULIA BELMORE, born circa 1852, died Nov 1859 (1860 census deaths). Buried: 30 Nov 1859 in Calais Cemetery.
v. OSSIAN W. BELMORE, born, circa 1854 in Calais, died 1 Oct 1855 age 1y 6m in Calais (g.s.). Buried: 3 Oct 1855 in Calais Cemetery.
vi. JAMES OSCAR BELMORE, born circa 1857. Died 29 July 1880, his father brought his remains home for burial in Calais Cemetery (adv no age or place of death given). Census: 1860 & 70 in Calais.
vii. ANNE BELMORE, born Jan 1859, died Dec 1859 in Calais (sext, 1860 census deaths). Buried: 8 Dec 1859 in Calais Cemetery.
viii. JULIA A. BELMORE, born circa 1861 in Calais. She died after 1890. Census: 1870 in Calais. She married 1st 13 Jan 1880 by Rev. Mr. Lovejoy in Calais (VR:1:332, times) MERTON DAVID GARDNER, born circa 1858, son of DANIEL MORGAN GARDNER AND DEBORAH BRADFORD (see BRADFORD). He was a hotel prop. Census: 1880 in Calais. She divorced Merton Jan 1890 (SJC:28:478). She married 2nd 14 Apr 1890 in Summerville, MA by Rev. F.O. Cunningham FRED D. NORTON of Cambridge, MA (east: 440). [He married 2nd before 1892 NELLIE TOWNSEND]

RICHARD W. & REBECCA BISHOP, p. 198

JOSHUA BISHOP born 15 Apr 1772 in Greenwich, Horton Township, NS, son of WILLIAM[3], JOHN[2], ELEAZER[1], died 11 Dec 1848. He married JANE WILLIAMSON. Their oldest son, Richard W. Bishop, went to Calais, where he married and had a family. At this point there is no data available on them. It is said that he died from the kick of a horse [bish:2:4].

RICHARD W. BISHOP, born, circa 1810, in Horton, NS (1850 census). Immigrated Mar 1832 to Eastport ME, later to Calais, when he was naturalized 26 Feb 1846 (irmch). In 1844 he was doing business as Bishop & Berry with Stephen O. Berry (SJC July term 1849). It is said that he died from a kick of a horse (bish:2:4). Died circa 1854. Buried: 26 Mar 1854 in Calais Cemetery. Census: 1850 in Calais.

He married before 1842 REBECCA (_____), born circa 1822 in Brownfield, Oxford Co., ME (1850 census). Census: 1850 in Calais. Children:

i. WILLIAM HENRY BISHOP, born 1 Oct 1842 in Calais (VR). Died circa 1848 (g.s.). Buried: 24 Apr 1848 in Calais Cemetery.
ii. FRANCES AUGUSTA BISHOP, born 23 Feb 1845 in Calais (VR). Census: 1850 in Calais.
iii. EDWARD JOSHUA BISHOP, born 29 Mar 1847 in Calais (VR). Census: 1850 in Calais.

THEOPHILUS & SOPHIA BISHOP, p. 217

THEOPHILUS BISHOP, born circa 1805 in Quebec, Canada (1850 census). Immigrated in 1849, no port of entry on record, naturalized 2 Oct 1855, while living in Calais (irmch). Died after 1882 (mentioned in wife's will). Census: 1850, 70 & 80 in Calais.

He married SOPHIA (_____), born circa 1805 in Quebec, Canada. Died circa 1883. Probate of Estate: 12 Jun 1883 in Machias Me (will dated 8 Mar 1882, no children mentioned). Census: 1850, 70 & 80 in Calais. Children:

i. ELIZABETH BISHOP, born circa 1831 in Canada. Census: 1850 in Calais.
ii. ALMEIDA BISHOP, born circa 1833 in Canada. Census: 1850 in Calais. She married 5 Apr 1855 by M. D. Mathews, DANIEL CARMICHEL of Calais (VR:1:160).
iii. THOMAS BISHOP, born 4 Nov 1835 in Madawaska, ME (Calais VR).
iv. CHARLES F. BISHOP, born circa 1836 in Madawaska, ME (1850 census). Census: 1850 in Calais.
v. THEOPHILUS BISHOP (jr.), born circa 1838 in Fredericton, NB (1850 census). He worked in saw mill. Census: 1850 & 60 (age 21 with Thomas & Mary Sprague & family) in Calais.
vi. RACHEL BISHOP, born circa 1840 in Oramoncto, NB (1850 census). Census: 1850 in Calais. She married (int.) 14 Oct 1856 in Calais (VR:1:76) WILLIAM H. CAMPBELL of Calais.
vii. JOHN BISHOP, born 4 May 1843 in Calais (VR). Died 15 Mar 1873 age 29, of consumption in Calais (adv). Census: 1850 in Calais. He married (int.) 13 May 1865 by Rev. S. H. Keeler in Calais (VR:1:115) Mrs. MARY C. BROWN of Minot, ME.
viii. MARY ANN BISHOP, born 11 Jun 1847 in Calais (VR). Census: 1850 in Calais.
ix. DANIEL C. BISHOP, born circa 1848. Census: 1850 in Calais.
x. SOPHIA BISHOP, born Jul 1850. Census: 1850 in Calais.

SILAS & MARY BLANCHARD, p. 216

SOLOMON^6 BLANCHARD baptized 28 Nov 1762, Weymouth MA, removed to Yarmouth, Me (wey:105) married ca 1789 ARDRA ROBINSON of Dresden. [Solomon was born in Weymouth, MA ca 1762, died 25 Jan 1853 in Dresden, Me, he served in the Rev. War (DAR # 161489)]. Solomon was son & grandson of SAMUEL$^{4-5}$, JOHN^3, NATHANIEL^2, THOMAS^1 BLANCHARD](wey:91-105).

SILAS BLANCHARD, born 24 Oct 1797, in Dresden, ME (VR, 1850 census), son of SOLOMON & ARDRA. He was a Teamster and lumberman. Died July 1879 (1880 census mortality schedule, age 81 years). Census: 1830 (5 males, 3 females), 40 (4 males, 3 females) thru 1870 in Calais. * Note: they lost three sons in the Civil War.

He married ca 1826 (DAR:161489) (int) 17 Sept 1826 in Calais (cal2:26) MARY BRIGGS LAMB, born circa 1805 in Philipsburg, ME (1850 = Hollis), daughter of JAMES LAMB AND BETSEY DUNN (poss. sister of Nathaniel, Robert & Eleanor, SEE LAMB & HARMON). Died 4 Jul 1896 age 91 in Calais (MSA, SCC). Buried in Calais Cemetery. Census: 1850, 60, 70 & 1900 (with son, Charles) in Calais. Children:

i. CHARLES ROBINSON BLANCHARD, born 17 Dec 1827 in Calais (VR). He worked in a mill then was a druggist. Died 11 May 1903 age 74y 5m in Calais (MSA, adv, SCC, DAR). Buried in Calais Cemetery. Census: 1850 thru 1880 in Calais. He married 6 June 1858 in Calais (VR:3:171) MARGARET E. MILLIGAN, born April 1830 in Calais (1900 census) (1830-1911 DAR No. 161489). Daughter of SAMUEL MILLIGAN & ISABELLA KIRK (both born in Ireland), she died 15 Oct 1911 in Calais age 76 (MSA). Census: 1880 & 1900 in Calais.
ii. ORVILLE STANWOOD BLANCHARD, born 18 Mar 1830 in Calais (VR). Died 1 Oct 1831 in Calais (VR).
iii. ELIZA TURNER BLANCHARD, born 6 Dec 1833 in Calais (VR). Census: 1850 & 60 in Calais. She married 30 May 1853 (VR:3:153) CHARLES C. WEST, born ca 1832 in NY. He was a painter. Census: 1860 in Calais.

iv. MARGARET M. BLANCHARD, born circa 1835. Census: 1860 (age 25) in Calais.
v. GEORGE PARKS BLANCHARD, born 30 Dec 1835 in Calais (VR). He was a RR fireman. Served in Civil War, Co. D 6th Maine as a Sgt., was promoted to 2nd Lt. in 1863. Died of wounds 15 Aug 1864 (NRMS:238) described as 5' 10" with blue eyes and black hair (cwcard). Buried National Cemetery, Arlington, VA (cwcard). Census: 1850 & 60 in Calais.
vi. SILAS ALBION BLANCHARD, born 3 Mar 1838 in Calais (VR). Died 2 Mar 1843 in Calais (VR).
vii. MARY EMMA BLANCHARD, born 21 Jun 1840 in Calais (VR). At age 19 she was a teacher. Census: 1850 & 60 in Calais. She married 10 Mar 1864 by Rev. B. M. Mitchell in Calais (VR:3:195) ROBERT J. GRAY of Houlton .
viii. SOLOMON BLANCHARD, born 21 Mar 1843 in Calais (VR). He was a house painter. He served in Civil War a Private in Co G 22nd Inf., described as 5' 9" with blue eyes and dark hair (cwcard). Died 14 Mar 1863 of fever in Baton Rouge, LA (cwcard). Census: 1850 & 60 in Calais.
ix. ALBION BLANCHARD, born 14 Feb 1845 in Calais (VR). Served in Civil War a Private in Co F D.C. Cav and Co C 1st Me Cav described as 5' 9" with blue eyes and sandy hair, died 7 Nov 1864 in prison (cwcard). Census: 1850 & 60 in Calais.
x. EMILY ARDRA BLANCHARD, born 4 Nov 1847 in Calais (VR). Census: 1850, 60 in Calais & 70 in Houlton, ME. She married 4 Apr 1867 by Rev. B. M. Mitchell in Calais (VR:3:220) THEODORE A. HEYWOOD, born ca 1840 of Houlton, ME. He was a store clerk. Census: 1870 (age 30) in Houlton.

WILLIAM & ESTHER W. BOARDMAN, p. 217

TAPPAN/TOPPAN FAMILY

STEPHEN^4 TAPPAN b. 6 Dec 1756, son of EDWARD^3 TOPPAN & SARAH BAILEY, ABRAHAM^2, JACOB^1. He married 1 Jan 1786 EDNA LITTLE of Newburyport, MA. He died 7 Oct 1839. They had eight children. The 4th child, ESTHER W. TAPPAN married WILLIAM BOARDMAN and moved from Newburyport, MA to Calais between 1824 and 1829 (tapp:81, topp:14). Descendants of this family live in Calais and vicinity today (2002).

WILLIAM BOARDMAN Jr., son of Capt. WILLIAM BOARDMAN AND MARY SHORT, born 20 May 1789 in Newburyport, MA (VR, beg:122). He was a bookkeeper. Died 2 July 1866 age 72 (g.s., union). Buried in Rural Cemetery, St. Stephen, NB (rural: 210). Census: 1830 (5 males, 4 females), 40 (4 males, 4 females), 50 & 60 in Calais.

He married 12 Mar 1815 in Newburyport, MA (tapp:85, board) ESTHER WIGGLESWORTH TAPPAN, born 28 Jun 1793 in Newburyport, MA (VR, tapp:85), daughter of STEPHEN TAPPAN/TOPPAN & EDNA LITTLE. She came to Calais with her husband about 1827 (obit). She died 31 May 1877 age 83y 11m in Milltown (g.s., adv). Buried in Rural Cemetery, St. Stephen, NB (rural:210). Census: 1860 & 70 with Elwell Lowell in Calais. Children:

i. ADALINE BOARDMAN, born 5 Dec 1815 in Newburyport, MA (VR). Died 17 Jun 1882 in St Stephen, NB (obit adv, g. s.). Census: 1861 & 71 in St Stephen, NB. She married 20 Dec 1838 by Rev. William Whitwell in Calais (mrwc:27, topp:17), FREEMAN HALE TODD, born 7 Aug 1809 born in Yarmouth (g.s.), son of, WILLIAM TODD & ANNA WORTHLY, he died 9 Sept 1885 in St. Stephen, NB. (probate of a foreign will, Washington Co. # T-1-196). Both are buried Rural Cemetery, St. Stephen, NB (rural:199). Census: 1861 & 71 in St. Stephen.
ii. WILLIAM HENRY BOARDMAN, born 3 Jan 1817, in Newburyport, MA (VR). He was a master mariner and was Mayor of Calais 1878-82. Died 12 May 1893 age 76y 4m 9d in Calais (adv, MSA). Buried in Rural Cemetery in St. Stephen, NB Census: 1840 thru 1880 in Calais. He married 5 Aug 1840 in St. Stephen, NB (topp:17, board) MARY QUINCY, born 16 Dec 1819 in Portland, ME (g.s.), daughter of HORATIO G. & MARY (PETTIS) QUINCY. Mary died 22 Aug 1905 (MSA, g.s.). Buried Rural Cemetery in St. Stephen, NB (rural:210). Census: 1880 in Calais.
iii. GEORGE A. BOARDMAN, born 5 Feb 1818 in Newburyport, MA (topp:17). Graduated from Calais Academy. He was a merchant and lumber manufacturer. In his spare time the studied natural History of Maine & New Brunswick. Died 10 Jan 1901 in Calais (adv, MSA). Buried in Rural Cemetery in St. Stephen, NB. Census: 1851, 61 & 71, in St Stephen, NB. He married 19 Dec 1843 in St. Stephen, NB (topp:17, board) MARY JANE HILL, born in Milltown, NB, daughter of JOEL HILL & MARY JAMISON TODD. She died 4 Mar 1894 in Calais (MSA). Buried in Rural Cemetery in St. Stephen (rural:223). Census: 1861

in St. Stephen.

iv. CAROLINE MOODY BOARDMAN, born 23 Mar 1820 in Newburyport, MA (VR). Resided: 1875 in Eastport ME. She married 18 Jun 1839 by Rev. E. D. Very in Calais (topp:17, MRWC:29) CHARLES HENRY HAYDEN, born 4 May 1804 in Eastport (VR), son of AARON HAYDEN & RUTH RICHARDS JONES (BHM:7:134), brother of Hannah Hayden who married Elijah Green (Eastport VR). He was town treasurer 1841 – 1847 (bhm:7:135). He died 19 Oct 1851 at age 41 in Eastport (Me Farmer of 31 Oct 1851, adv has he died at home of E. D. Green).

v. ANNA LOUISA BOARDMAN, born 12 Dec 1822 in Newburyport, MA (VR, topp:17). Died 14 Mar 1895 age 73y 3m 2d in Calais (biorev:307., MSA). She married 17 Oct 1842 in Calais (VR:1:130, mrwc:39) HENRY FRANKLIN EATON, born 22 Nov 1812 Groton, MA, died 21 Mar 1895 age 82 (MSA, adv, g.s.), son of JONAS EATON & MARY COREY (biorev:306). He was a lumber merchant in Milltown, NB, doing business as H. F. Eaton & Sons (MOP:187). Both buried Rural Cemetery, St. Stephen, NB (rural:36). Census: 1871 in St. Stephen.

vi. GORHAM B. BOARDMAN, born, 23 Oct 1824, in Newburyport, MA (VR, topp:17). Died 13 Feb 1908 age 84y in Brooklyn, N Y (obit adv). Resided: 1875 in New York, NY (beg:122). He married 23 Oct 1851 in Boston Ma (topp:17, board) MARY L. LORD.

vii. CHARLES EDWIN BOARDMAN, born 15 Mar 1829 in Calais (VR, topp:17). Died 10 Apr 1899 (g.s.). Buried Rural Cemetery in St. Stephen, NB. Census: 1850 in Calais, 1861 & 71 in St. Stephen. He married 15 Sep 1859 in St. Stephen, N B (topp:17) ELIZABETH ANNA GRANT, born ca 1832, died at age 39 on 21 Apr 1871 (g.s.). Buried in Rural Cemetery in St. Stephen, NB (rural:208). Census: 1861 in St. Stephen.

viii. MARY EDNAH BOARDMAN, born 28 Apr 1831 in Calais (VR, topp:17). Died 30 Oct 1908 age 77 in Kennebunkport, Me (obit). Census: 1850 in Calais. She married 20 Jan 1851 in Calais (VR:1:149, adv, topp:17) HENRY VAUGHAN DEXTER, born 3 Apr 1815 in Wayne, Me. Graduated from Colby College in class of 1842, Newton Theol. Inst., 1845; Pastor in Calais 1860-1871; also in Augusta, Kennebunkport and Baldwinville, MA. He died in Baldwinville, MA 23 July 1884 age 69y (colby, adv).

ix. EMILY FRANCES BOARDMAN, born 4 Mar 1833 in Calais (VR, topp:17). Died 30 Jun 1918 in Calais (VR, sext). Buried: 2 Jul 1918 in Calais Cemetery. Census: 1850, 60, 70, & 1900 in Calais. She married 9 Jan 1859 by Rev. I.J. Burgess in Calais (VR:1:182, topp:17, adv) (low:569 = 1860 in Middletown, MN) ELWELL LOWELL, born ca 1830 in Wiscasset, Me, son of JOHN LOWELL & MELINDA HATCH (low:569). He was a trader & clerk. Census: 1860 (with her parents), 70, & 1900 in Calais.

JAMES & MARY ANN BOIES, p. 182

JAMES BOIES /BOYCE, born circa 1796 in Bedford, NH (1850 census). In June 1832 he was in court for non payment of rent of $500.00 for the Franklin Mill in 1828 (SJC). He appeared in court records with his business partner David Pineo, Jr. on 11 Nov 1837 (DC:2:207). He was a truckman. Census: 1830 (16 males & 5 females), 1850 & 60 in Calais.

He married 9 Aug 1820 in Machias Me (VR, east:25) MARY ANN PINEO, born circa 1802 in Machias (1850 census), daughter of DAVID PINEO AND PRISCILLA HILL, and sister of Hannah Tinker (see David Pineo). Bapt. 17 Aug 1825 in Calais (congo). Died 8 Jan 1872 in Chelsea, MA (congo, union). Census: 1850 & 60 in Calais. Children:

i. JAMES S. BOIES, born circa 1822 in Calais (see below).
ii. JOHN H. BOIES, born circa 1823, died 27 Feb 1844 age 21 years 2 months in Calais (VR, gaz). Buried in Calais.
iii. MARY ANN PRECILLA BOIES, born 5 Sept, 1826 in Calais (cal2:13).
iv. LUCY HILL BOIES, born 25 Sept 1830 in Calais (cal2:13).
v. ADELINE BOARDMAN BOIES, born 5 June 1832 in Calais (cal2:13). Census: 1850 in Calais. Married in 1856 or 57, by Rev. S. H. Keeler, in Calais (VR) JAMES W. BROCKWAY.
vi. ANDREW JACKSON BOIES, twin, born 16 May 1834 in Calais (cal2:13). Census: 1850 in Calais.
vii. HENRIETTA H. BOIES, twin, born 16 May 1834 in Calais (cal2:13). Census: 1850 & 60 in Calais.
viii. STEPHEN E. BOIES, born 24 Aug 1840 in Salmon River, NB (Calais VR). Died 25 Feb 1844 in Calais (VR, obit gaz). Buried: 26 Feb 1844 in Calais Cemetery.

JAMES S. & F. L. BOIES, p 182

JAMES STILLMAN BOIES, born circa 1822 in Calais (1850 census), son of JAMES & MARY BOIES (see above). He appeared in court records several times with his business partner, Stephen S. Pineo in Dec 1843 & Feb 1845, doing business as J. S. Boies & Co. (DC:63: 193, 460). He died 10 Apr 1853 age 31 in Calais (obit FJ). Census: 1850 in Calais.

He married 11 Nov 1843 by Nathaniel Whitman, in Calais (VR:1:132, gaz), FRANCES LOUISE WHITMAN, born 18 Apr 1823 in Billerica, MA (1850 census, bill:161), daughter of Rev. NATHANIEL WHITMAN & SARAH HOLMAN (bill:161). Died 11 Aug 1873 in Newberry, S.C. age 50 (union, adv). [On 30 May 1853 Louisa F. Boies widow of James S. Boies states she prefers to have Edward S. Dyer be executor of James' estate (prbt:18:215)]. Census: 1850 in Calais. Children:

i. JAMES N. BOIES, born 18 Nov 1844 in Calais (VR). Died Oct 1846 (sext). Buried: 8 Oct 1846 in Calais Cemetery.
ii. ELEANOR ELIZABETH BOIES, born 17 Oct 1846 in Calais (VR). Census: 1850 in Calais.
iii. HARRISON C. BOIES, born, circa 1849 in Calais (1850 census). Died Oct 1851. Buried: 15 Oct 1851 in Calais Cemetery. Census: 1850 in Calais.
iv. EDWIN H. BOIES, born circa 1850 in Calais (1850 census). Died 10 Sep 1850 in Calais (FJ). Buried 11 Sep 1850 in Calais Cemetery. Census: 1850 in Calais.

JOHN & CAROLINE BOOLE, p. 216

JOHN BOOLE, born circa 1808 in Shelburne, NS (1850 census). Called to court in Jan 1855 but did not appear (SJC:12:421). He was a millman). Died after 1855. Census: 1840 (John Bolle, 2 males, 3 females), 50 in Calais.

He married CAROLINE [DICKEY?], born circa 1819 in Anson ME (1850 census). Census: 1850 in Calais. Children:

i. AMELIA BOOLE, born ca Apr 1841. Died 7 Sep 1841 (g.s.). Buried: 8 Sep 1841 in Calais Cemetery.
ii. CAROLINE BOOLE, born 7 Jul 1842 in Calais (VR). Census: 1850 in Calais.
iii. JOHN ORLANDO BOOLE, born 7 May 1845 in Calais (VR). Died 25 Sept 1848 (g.s.). Buried in Calais Cemetery.
iv. GEORGE FRANCIS BOOLE, born 31 May 1847 in Calais (VR). Census: 1850 in Calais.
v. CHARLES Y. BOOLE, born ca 1849 in Calais. Census: 1850 in Calais.
vi. OLIVE A. BOOLE, born ca 1854, died 26 Apr 1854 age 3m 14d (g.s.). Buried in Calais Cemetery.

JAMES & JANE BOYCE, p. 203

JAMES BOYCE, born circa 1815 in Londonderry, NH (1850 census). He was a lumberman. Census: 1850 in Calais.

He married JANE (_____), born circa 1822 in St Patrick, NB (1850 census). Died 7 Oct 1850 in Calais (adv). Census: 1850 in Calais. Children:

i. SARAH E. BOYCE, born, circa 1840 in St John, N B (1850 census). Census: 1850 in Calais.
ii. MARY E. BOYCE, born, circa 1843 in St Patrick, NB (1850 census). Census: 1850 in Calais.
iii. JOHN W. BOYCE, born, 9 Jan 1846 in Calais (VR). Census: 1850 in Calais.
iv JAMES H. BOYCE, born, circa 1848 in Calais. Served in Civil War as Private in Co I 32nd Inf., described as 5' 5" with gray eyes and light hair, died 21 June 1864, died of wounds, in Petersburg, VA (cwcard). Census: 1850 in Calais.
v. ELLEN BOYCE, born, circa June 1849. Died ca Nov 1849 age 5 mos. in Calais (deaths in 1850 census).

JAMES & MARY (sic) ANN BOYD, p. 209

JAMES BOYD, born circa 1822 in St Andrews, NB (1850 census). He was a ship carpenter. Died 22 Jul 1850 (congo). Buried in Calais Cemetery. Census: 1850 in Calais.

He married 4 Oct 1846 in St Stephen, NB (CCMR) SARAH ANN DILLON, born 12 May 1825 in Calais

(VR), daughter of EDWARD & MARGARET DILLON (see DILLON). Census: 1850 & 60 in Calais. Children:
- VR has her name written as Mary Ann all other records have Sarah Ann.

 i. EDWARD BOYD, born 25 Sep 1847 in Calais (VR). Census: 1850 & 60 in Calais.

JOHN BRACKETT FAMILY
These next two families inserted to show relationships to other Calais families.

JOHN[7] BRACKETT, son of JOSEPH[6] BRACKETT & JEMIMA ROBERTS; (JAMES[5], SAMUEL[4-3], THOMAS[2], ANTHONY[1]), born 9 Feb 1786, in Berwick, ME soon after birth moved to Osipee, NH by 1830 lived in Robbinston (brack:324). Died 25 Nov 1853 in Robbinston Me (g.s.). Buried in Robbinston Me (Brackett Pvt. Cemetery). He was a Farmer. He married NANCY JOHNSON. Three of their daughters married and resided in Calais.

1. MARY ANN BRACKETT, born 25 Jan 1818 in Robbinston Me (brack:324). Died 19 Sept 1904 age 87 in Calais (MSA, dow:725). Census: 1850 thru 80 in Calais. She married 1st 26 Oct 1837 in Calais THOMAS McNEAR (see McNEAR). She married 2nd after 1858 OLIVER DOW (see DOW).
2. NANCY BRACKETT, born, circa 1822 in Robbinston Me (1850 census). Census: 1850 & 60 in Calais. She married PETER AVERY (see AVERY).
3. HARRIET BRACKETT, born 9 Oct 1832, in Robbinston Me (MSA, brack:324). Died 25 Mar 1921 in Robbinston (MSA.). Buried Brewer Cemetery in Robbinston. Census: 1880 & 1900 in Robbinston. She married SETH TURNER LAMB, son of NATHANIEL LAMB & ELMIRA/ALMIRA CARLE (see LAMB).

JAMES BRACKETT FAMILY

JAMES[7] BRACKETT, born 30 March 1784 in Berwick, brother of above John[7] Brackett, resided in Ossipee, NH, Fairfax, Kennebec County, Maine, China, Maine and Weston in Aroostook County, Maine, where he Died 7 Apr 1845. He married 9 Dec 1855 (Brack p. 322-323) ABIGAIL FAIRFIELD, born 30 Mar 1787, in Vassalboro, Me. She also died in Weston (brack:322). Their 1st child of 14, Luther born 25 Apr 1806 married Abigail Todd born 30 Dec1812, daughter of John C. Todd and Abigail Nichols in Eastport (VR) died 24 Apr 1891 in Farmington, MN (brack:331). Abigail was the sister of John N., Alexander, & William Todd (see TODD). Their 2nd child, CAROLINE BRACKETT, born 29 Feb 1808, died 27 May 1886 in Grand Rapids, MI, married LEVI PEARL of Calais (see PEARL).

DANIEL & JANE BRADFORD, p. 185

DANIEL[6] BRADFORD, born circa 1775 in St Andrews, NB (1850 census), son of BENJAMIN[5] BRADFORD & MARTHA STUDLEY (JOSHUA[4], ISRAEL[3], MAJOR WILLIAM[2], GOV. WILLIAM[1]). He was in Calais at least by 1820 when he appeared in Court (CCP). He was a peddler. A pauper living at Poor Farm in 1856 when overseers went to court to get payment of his board from three sons, Benjamin, James & Josephus (SJC 14:516 October Term 1857). Died 14 Apr 1859 (g.s.). Buried in Calais Cemetery. Census: 1850 (age 75) living with Esther Reding (possibly his daughter) in Calais.

He married before 1804 (court rec. & son's death rec.) JANE LUNT, born 24 July 1780 (bouch) in Brooksville, ME (VR, 1850 census has Portland), daughter of BENJAMIN LUNT and ESTHER PERKINS (bouch). Died 5 Sep 1855 age 74 in Calais (g.s.,). Buried: 9 Sep 1855 in Calais Cemetery (saint). Census: 1850 (age 66, daughter & gr. daughter with her) in Calais. Children:

 i. JOHN BRADFORD, born 9 Dec 1804 in St. Andrews, NB (see below).
 ii. SARAH BRADFORD, born 30 Jan 1806 in Brooksville, ME to Daniel Bradford & Jane his wife (VR of Brooksville).
 iii. ESTHER BRADFORD, born ca 1806 (possible daughter), married EBENEZER REDDING. Census: 1850 in Calais (Daniel Bradford age 75 living with them).
 iv. JOSEPH BRADFORD, born 24 Aug 1811 (see below).
 v. BENJAMIN W. BRADFORD, born ca 1814 (probably in St. Andrews, NB). He was a resident of Topsfield in 1839 when he appeared in court records to dissolve partnership with M[anley]. B. Townsend (DC:29:571) also in 1856 when he was named son of Daniel in court action to recover board & room for his father (SJC). He died after 1870 before Feb 1878. [Administrators Notice in Calais adv – Estate of Benjamin Bradford, anyone with claim on his estate contact O. B. Rideout, Admin. Calais 1 Feb. 1878]. In the census of 1860 in Topsfield living with Mary A. Johnson and his four children, 1870 census also in Topsfield. He married 1st before 1849 in Topsfield MARY E. JOHNSON, born ca 1823 in Topsfield, the daughter of THOMAS & JUDITH JOHNSON. She died 2 July 1856 age 33 in Topsfield (VR, g.s.). Buried in Town Cemetery, Topsfield. He married 2nd 21 Oct 1862 in Topsfield Mrs. MARY ANN (RUGGLES) JOHNSON, born ca 1812 (VR Topsfield at MSA), poss. daughter of Gilbert & Mary Ruggles. She married 1st Nov 1843 in Topsfield Moses S. Johnson, brother of Mary E., Benjamin's first wife (Topsfield VR:1:129). Census: 1860 & 70 in

Topsfield.

vi. JAMES BRADFORD, immigration record states: born 31 Jan 1815 in St Andrews, NB, arrived in U.S. at Calais May 1821, naturalized 25 June 1838, witnesses were: John Bradford and M. B. Townsend of Calais (NAW:4-49). Living in Calais by 1839 when he appeared in court records (DC:42:303) also in 1857 & 1865 at which time he was in Court, when overseers of Poor Farm tried to collect for his fathers room & board (SJC). He was a peddler & grocer. [Calais adv of 17 Sept 1873- James Bradford was robbed on his way home from his shop between 9-10 p.m. on 11th Sept. He had a small box under his arm containing about $240.00]. Census: 1850 thru 1880 in Calais. Died 30 Apr 1894 age 79 in Calais (VR, adv, MSA, obit says he was a descendant of Gov. Bradford of Mass., prbt). Buried in Calais Cemetery. He married (int.) 11 Apr 1847 in Calais (VR:1: 31) MARY CONDELL, born ca 1814 in Sullivan, ME (1850 census), daughter of JOHN CONDELL. She died 23 July 1895 age 81 in Calais, buried in Calais Cemetery (MSA). Census: 1850 thru 1880 both in Calais.

vii. JOSEPHUS BRADFORD. He applied for citizenship and stated that he was born 12 June 1819 in St. Andrews, NB, he left from St. Andrews to Calais at about 2 years of age (DC:761). Arrived in US at Calais 1821, naturalized 19 Sept 1840 (NAW:2-486). Living in Auburn, ME in 1857 & 1865 at which time he was in Court when overseers of Poor Farm tried to collect for his fathers room & board (SJC). Census: 1850 (living with Thomas Bassett) in Calais. Died 31 Jan 1896 in S. Berwick, ME (MSA, g.s. has birth date 17 June 1819). Buried in Portland Street Cemetery in S. Berwick. He married 1st 20 May 1848 in Calais (VR:1:141, adv) by Rev. H. V. Dexter, ELIZABETH W. BRUNELL born ca 1815 in Dorchester, NB (1850 census). Died before 1858 (when son was born to 2nd wife). Census: 1850 (age 35 living with Thomas Bassett) in Calais. He married 2nd ca 1857 HELEN M. SMITH born 11 May 1834 in Auburn, ME, died 20 Sept 1913 (MSA, g.s.), buried with her husband in Portland Street Cemetery in So. Berwick (MOCA). Census: 1900 in S. Berwick (alone).

viii. MARY JANE BRADFORD, born 1 Sep 1823 in Calais (VR). Census: 1850 [had a daughter, Amanda Melvina b. 3 Jul 1844 father unknown in Calais (VR:1:185, MSA) (name Amanda Wright age 6 in 1850 census)].

JOHN & MARY BRADFORD, p. 192

JOHN BRADFORD, immigration record states: born 9 Dec 1804 in St Andrews, NB, arrived in U.S. at Calais May 1821, naturalized 25 June 1838, witnesses were: Joseph and James Bradford of Calais (NAW:B-631) He and his father signed a promissory note in 1827 (DC:26:148) [he was alive in 1856 why wasn't he taken to court with brothers?] He was a butcher. Died 9 Jan 1884 in Calais (times). Census: 1850 thru 1880 in Calais.

He married (int) 6 Mar 1836 in Calais (cal2:40) MARY DAVIS, born circa 1810 in Calais (from dau death rec., 1850 census = Portland). Died 8 Jul 1886 in Calais (times). Buried in Calais Cemetery. Census: 1850 thru 1880 in Calais. Children:

i. PEREZ GEORGE BRADFORD, born circa 1836 in Calais, died Mar 1854. Buried: 16 Mar 1854 in Calais Cemetery (sext, saint). Census: 1850 (age 14) in Calais.

ii. MARY JANE BRADFORD, born 11 Dec 1839 (bouch) in Calais, died 28 Jul 1908 age 68y 7m 17d at her home on North St. in Calais (obit adv, sfh:1:94, MSA). Buried in Calais Cemetery. Census: 1850 & 60 in Calais. Married JAMES TOOLE, born in St. Andrews, NB (sfh). Died 12 Dec 1884 (bouch) in Calais.

iii. PHEBE SAWYER BRADFORD, born 13 Jul 1842 in Calais (VR). Bapt. 11 Aug 1851 in Calais (saint). Census: 1850 & 60 in Calais. She married 28 Sep 1862 by D. F. Smith, in Calais (VR) JOHN DEMICK.

iv. HENRY BRADFORD, born circa 1844 in Calais. Died before 1860 (not in census). Census: 1850 (age 6) in Calais.

v. DEBORAH ELIZABETH BRADFORD, born 3 Feb 1846 in Calais (VR). Bapt. 11 Aug 1851 in Calais (saint). Census: 1850 & 60 in Calais. Married 14 June 1866 by Rev. E. W. Murray in Calais (VR:3:214) WILLIAM H. HAYMAN.

vi. WILLIAM HENRY BRADFORD, born circa 1848 in Calais. Bapt. 11 Aug 1851 in Calais (saint). He was a hostler. Census: 1850 & 60 in Calais. He married 1 June 1869 in Calais (VR:3, bouch) MARY ELLEN NEW, born ca 1845, in Pleasant Ridge, NB (son's birth rec. MSA), daughter of JOSEPH & JANE NEW. Census: 1850 (age 5 with parents) in Calais.

vii. GEORGE THOMAS BRADFORD, born circa 1851 in Calais. Bapt. 11 Aug 1851 in Calais (saint). Died after 1880. Census: 1860, 70 & 80 in Calais.

viii. UNNAMED CHILD BRADFORD, born 28 Aug 1852, died 28 Aug 1852 in Calais. Buried: Aug 1852

in Calais Cemetery.
  ix. CHARLES AUGUSTUS BRADFORD, born Sep/Oct 1853. Bapt. 26 Nov 1853 in Calais (saint). Died Feb 1854. Buried: 25 Feb 1954 in Calais Cemetery.
- Two of his children named Perez & Deborah may indicate a relationship to Perez Bradford (see below).

JOSEPH & LUCRETIA BRADFORD, p. 194

JOSEPH BRADFORD, immigration record states: born 24 Aug 1811 in St Andrews, NB, arrived in U.S. at Calais May 1821, naturalized 25 June 1838, witnesses were: John and James Bradford of Calais (NAW:4-403). Died after 1870. Census: 1840 (Joseph 2 males, 1 female), 1850, 60 & 70 in Calais. *His name Joseph in VR and in 1850 census he is Josephus (age 39); in 1860 census he is Josephus (age 46); in 1870 he is Joseph (age 68) and a keeper of beer shops, each year with wife Lucretia.

He married circa 1835 LUCRETIA (_____), born circa 1820 in Calais. Died 24 Jan 1886 in Calais (times). Census: 1850, 60 & 70 in Calais. Children:

  i. ESTHER BRADFORD, born 24 Oct 1836 in Calais (VR, 1850 census has St. Stephen). Died: May 1855, buried 20 May 1855 in Calais Cemetery (sext). Census: 1850 in Calais.
  ii. UNNAMED CHILD BRADFORD, born circa 1849. died May 1850 in Calais, buried 7 May 1850 in Calais Cemetery (sext).

PEREZ & DEBORAH BRADFORD, p. 196

PEREZ[7] BRADFORD (Jr.), born 9 Sep 1791 in Plympton, MA (VR), son of PEREZ[6] BRADFORD {Rev. War} (Capt. JOHN[5], SAMUEL[4], JOHN[3], Major WILLIAM[2], Gov. WILLIAM[1]) & SARAH KIMBALL PRINCE. Died 9 Aug 1853 age 62 (FJ, g.s.). Buried: 26 Aug 1853 in Calais Cemetery. Census: 1840 (5 males, 6 females) & 50 in Calais.

He married 22 Aug 1819 in St Andrews, NB (CCMR:31 # 132) DEBORAH DAVIS, born circa 1802 in Bangor Me (1850 census). Bapt. 9 Feb 1851 in Calais (saint). She was the owner of a boarding home. Died 17 Apr 1882 Calais (adv). Census: 1850, 60, 70 & 80 in Calais. Children:

  i. LOUISA BRADFORD, born 6 Apr 1822 (bouch) in St Andrews, NB (1850 census). Died 10 Apr 1887 in Erie, PA (obit, times). Census: 1850 in Calais. She married 18 Nov 1850 by Rev. Mr. Wells in Boston MA (FJ, adv) ROBERT LANGLANDS who died 6 Mar 1876 age 65 in Pittsburgh, PA (adv).
  ii. HEZEKIAH BRADFORD, born 26 Mar 1824 (bouch) in St. Andrews, NB (1850 census). Died 1 May 1870 age 46 in Calais (adv). Census: 1850 in Calais.
  iii. GEORGE J. BRADFORD, born circa 1827 in St. Andrews, NB (1850 census). Died Mar 1854. Buried: 7 Mar 1854 in Calais Cemetery. Census: 1850 in Calais.
  iv. MARY SOPHIA BRADFORD, born 16 Feb 1829 (bouch) in St Andrews, NB. Census: 1850 in Calais (with her parents). She married 24 Feb 1848 in St Stephen, NB (adv) THOMAS OLIVER PAINE, poss. he is Oliver Paine, son of Thomas and Nancy Paine (see PAINE).
  v. DEBORAH BRADFORD, born 1 July 1832 (bouch) in St Andrews, NB. She was hostess of American House and later Border City Hotel operated by her husband (obit). Died 13 Sep 1898 in Calais (MSA, obit adv has date 6 Sept). Buried in Calais Cemetery. Census: 1850, 60, 70 & 80 in Calais. She married 8 Jun 1853 in Calais (VR:1:160, saint has 1854) DANIEL MORGAN GARDNER, born 6 Jan 1834, in Charlotte ME (VR), or Pembroke (biorev:696), son of JACOB D. GARDNER AND SARAH MORGAN. Served in Civil War, Sgt. Co. F, 22nd Regt., Vol. Inf., enlisted 10 Sept 1862. He was a harness maker, had a livery stable, and later owned the American House in 1878 and the Border City Hotel in 1885, he was an alderman and Mayor in Calais (biorev: 696). Died 6 Oct 1897 age 63y 10m in Calais (MSA, prbt = 4 Oct). Census: 1860, 70 & 80 in Calais.
  vi. SALOME BRADFORD, born circa 1834 in St. Andrews, NB (1850 census). Bapt. 9 Feb 1851 in Calais (saint). Died in California in a drowning accident many years before 1887 when her husband wrote a letter to the Calais Advertiser. Census: 1850 in Calais. She married 28 Apr 1859 in Calais (VR) WILLIAM BREWER HEYWARD, son of ZIMRI BREWER HEYWARD AND HANNAH COOPER (see HEYWARD).

vii. PEREZ BRADFORD, III, born 23 Feb 1838 in Calais, died 6 Sep 1840 in Calais (VR:1:235, MSA). Buried: 8 Sep 1840 in Calais Cemetery.
viii. SARAH ELIZABETH BRADFORD, born 16 Mar 1840 in Calais (VR). Bapt. 23 Feb 1851 in Calais (saint). Census: 1850 in Calais.
ix. LUCY ELLEN BRADFORD, born 16 Feb 1842 in Calais, died 20 Nov 1842 in Calais (VR:1:235, MSA).
x. ELIZA BRADFORD, born 21 Jul 1844 in Calais, died 13 Aug 1844 in Calais (VR:1:235, obit, adv). Buried in Calais Cemetery. [*note on birth records for Lucy & Eliza mother's name is Deborah on both death records her name is Ellen. Could she be Deborah Ellen Davis?]

JAMES & MARY BRANNAN, p. 225

JAMES BRANNAN, born _____ .
He married MARY (_____), born _____ . Children:

i. CHARLES BRANNAN, born 16 April 1851 in Calais (VR).

CHARLES & AGNES BROCKWAY, p. 214

CHARLES BROCKWAY, born circa 1803 in NB. Census: 1840 (3 males, 7 females), 1850 in Calais (of St. George, NB at time of marriage).
He married 25 Oct 1826 in NB (CCMR) AGNES McCURDY, a widow, born in Whitefield ME (1850 census, lived St. Patrick, NB at time of marriage). Census: 1850 in Calais. Children:

i. KESIAH BROCKWAY, born circa 1824, in St Patrick, NB (1850 census). Census: 1850 in Calais. [age 26 in 1850 census with Charles & Agnes, she is much older than other children she might possibly be a child from a previous marriage or a relative of Charles. There was also living with them in 1850, James McKenzie age 26 and Charlotte Ricker age 6].
ii. CHILD BROCKWAY, born circa 1829. Died Jul 1845 age 16. Buried: 23 Jul 1845 in Calais Cemetery.
iii. ROXANNA BROCKWAY, born circa 1833, in St George NB (1850 census). Census: 1850 in Calais.
iv. HENRY AUGUSTUS {1} BROCKWAY, born 3 Oct 1839 in Calais, died 12 Sep 1840 in Calais (VR). Buried: 13 Sep 1840 in Calais Cemetery.
v. MARY ELLEN BROCKWAY, born 3 Oct 1839 in Calais (VR). Census: 1850 in Calais.
vi. ISABELLA PRATT BROCKWAY, born 5 Jun 1842 in Calais, died 24 Aug 1843 in Calais (VR). Buried: 27 Aug 1843 in Calais Cemetery.
vii. HENRY AUGUSTUS {2} BROCKWAY, born 25 Sep 1845 in Calais (VR). Census: 1850 in Calais.

ALFRED & MARY BROOKS, p. 221

ALFRED BROOKS, born circa 1811 in Jonesboro, Me (1850 census). He was a partner in Brooks & Waldron with Sumner T. Waldron (SJC:3:446). In Aug 1839 he was a defendant in court with Warren Brooks who might be his brother (SJC). Died before 1880 (wife widow in 1890 directory). Census: 1840 (7 males, 5 females), 50, 60 & 70 in Calais.
He married 11 Dec 1836 by Rev. James Huckins in Calais (mrwc:20) MARY CARPENTER born circa 1821 in Robbinston ME, daughter of Doctor ALFRED[6] CARPENTER & JOANNA JONES (bhm:7:131), and grand daughter of BENJAMIN[5-4-3-2], JOSEPH[1] CARPENTER. Died 6 Jan 1898 in Calais (MSA). Buried in Calais Cemetery. Census: 1850 thru 1880 in Calais. Children:

i. SARAH JONES BROOKS, born 24 Oct 1837 in Calais (VR). Died 14 Oct 1855 in Calais (sext). Buried in Calais Cemetery. Census: 1850 in Calais.
ii. MARY CAROLINE BROOKS, born 20 Apr 1839 in Calais (VR). Died: 16 June 1898 age 59 in Calais (MSA). Census: 1850 & 60 in Calais. She married JAMES CRANGLE. He died before his wife.
iii. GEORGE ALFRED BROOKS, born 18 Aug 1840 in Calais (VR). Died Feb 1861. Buried: 15 Feb 1861 in Calais Cemetery. Census: 1850 & 60 in Calais.
iv. EDWARD VERY BROOKS, born 30 Aug 1842 in Calais (VR). He was a dealer of stoves. Died 20 Jul 1896 age 53y 10m in Calais (MSA). Buried: 21 Jul 1896 in Calais Cemetery. Census: 1850, 60 & 70 in Calais. He married 28 Apr 1876 in Calais (VR:3:239) AMANDA R. ESTABROOKS, born Dec 1851 (1900

census) in NB. Died Mar 1914 in Malden, MA (adv), buried in Calais Cemetery. Census: 1880 & 1900 in Calais. [in 1880 census Lilly Estabrooks age 11, step daughter living with them]

v. HOWARD ALBERTUS BROOKS, born 12 Nov 1844 in Calais (VR). He was a tinsmith. Died 23 Oct 1932 age 87y 11m 11d in Milltown ME (MSA, sfh:6:187). Buried in Calais Cemetery. Census: 1850 thru 80, 1900 & 1920 in Calais. He married HARRIET McNEAR, daughter of THOMAS McNEAR AND MARY ANN BRACKETT (see McNEAR).

vi. NETTIE BROOKS, born circa 1855 in Calais. Census: 1860, 70 & 80 in Calais. She may be the child of A. Brooks who died 18 Mar 1862 age 7 years in Calais (VR:1: 243). There is also a Brooks child age 2 buried in Calais Cemetery on 19 Sept 1854 (sext).

vii. HATTIE E. BROOKS, born ca 1862, census of 1870 (age 8).

WILLIAM D. & ELIZA BROWN, p. 200

WILLIAM D. BROWN, born circa 1811 in Horton, NS (1850 census). Census: 1850 in Calais. He was a painter.

He married ELIZA (_____), born circa 1810 in Horton, NS (1850 census). Census: 1850 in Calais. Children:

i. EDWARD BROWN, born circa 1833 in Bridgetown, NS (1850 census). Census: 1850 in Calais.
ii. STEPHEN BROWN, born circa 1835 in Bridgetown, NS (1850 census). Census: 1850 in Calais.
iii. CHARLOTTE BROWN, born circa 1839 in St Stephen, NB (1850 census). Census: 1850 in Calais.
iv. CHARLES W. BROWN, born circa 1841 in St Stephen, NB (1850 census). Census: 1850 in Calais.
v. FRANCES BROWN, born circa 1844 in St Stephen, NB (1850 census). Census: 1850 in Calais.
vi. HENRY/HARRY BROWN, born 5 Jun 1846 in Calais (VR). Census: 1850 in Calais.
vii. FREDERICK BROWN, born circa 1849 in Calais. Census: 1850 in Calais.

PATRICK & ELLEN BUCK, p. 201

PATRICK BUCK, born _____ .
He married ELLEN (_____), born _____ . Children:

i. MARTIN BUCK, born 29 Jan 1848 in Calais (VR).

RICHARD & SARAH J. BURPEE, p. 220

RICHARD BURPEE, born circa 1822 in St John, N B (1850 census). Census: 1850 in Calais.
He married SARAH J. (_____) , born circa 1824 in St John, NB (1850 census). Census: 1850 in Calais. Children:

i. GEORGE UMPHREY BURPEE, born 22 Sep 1844, in NB. Census: 1850 in Calais.
ii. UNNAMED CHILD BURPEE, born Sep 1846, died 22 Sep 1846 in Calais (sext). Buried: 22 Sep 1846 in Calais Cemetery.
iii. CHARLES EVERETT BURPEE, born 17 Nov 1847 in Calais. Census: 1850 in Calais.
iv. MARJORIE L. BURPEE, born circa 1849 in Calais. Census: 1850 in Calais.

- Note – child of Richard Burpee buried 13 Mar 1853 no age given in Calais Cemetery (sext).

JOHN & REBECCA BUTLER, p. 213
JOHN & FRANCES BUTLER, p, 213

JOHN BUTLER, born 23 Oct 1795, in Kingston, NB (Alexander, Me VR, 1850 census has St. John, NB). Died before 1864 when wife signed son's consent for Civil War. He was in Calais by 1826 when he appeared in Court (CCP:4:419). He was a house carpenter. Census: 1830 (5 males, 1 female), 40 (5 males, 3 females), 50 in Calais.

He married 1st 6 Sep 1819 (Alexander VR) REBECCA FANJOY born 7 Feb 1798 in St John, NB (Alexander

VR). Died 22 Sep 1835 in Calais (VR). Children:

i. SAMUEL BUTLER, born 9 Jun 1820 in St John, NB (Alexander VR).
ii. WILLIAM HENRY BUTLER, born 8 Dec 1822 in St John, NB (Alexander VR).
iii. EPHRAIM HARVEY BUTLER, born 17 Aug 1825 in Calais (Alexander VR). Died 13 Sept 1826 in Calais (Alexander VR).
iv. JOSEPH EPHRIAM BUTLER, born 5 Jul 1827 in Calais (VR). Possibly married Margaret Fanjoy.
v. JOHN MANLY BUTLER, born 19 Jul 1829 in Calais (VR).
vi. DANIEL GRAY BUTLER, born 9 Sep 1831 in Calais (VR).
vii. ELIZA BUTLER, born 25 Jan 1835 in Calais (VR).

He married 2nd (int) 18 Oct 1835 in Calais (cal2:40) FRANCES JONES (poss. widow of CALVIN JONES, see JONES), born circa 1800, in Pettijack, NS (1850 census). Died after 1870. Census: 1850 & 1870 (alone age 70) in Calais. Children:

viii. EDWARD I. JONES (poss. s/o Calvin & Frances Jones, not listed in VR of Butler family but is in 1850 census age difference of three years may be son of John Butler named for her son by Calvin Jones), born circa 1836 in Calais. Census: 1850 in Calais.
ix. REBECCA BUTLER, born Aug 1836, died 10 Sep 1838 in Calais (g.s.).
x. DAVID BUTLER, born 15 Nov 1838 in Calais (VR). Died 13 Sep 1864 age 25y 9m 22d (g.s.). Buried in Calais Cemetery. Census: 1850 in Calais.
xi. ISAIAH BRIDGES BUTLER, born 22 Sep 1840 in Calais (VR). Died 15 Nov 1858 age 18y 19d in Calais (g.s.). Buried in Calais Cemetery. Census: 1850 in Calais.
xii. CAROLINE MATILDA SARAH BUTLER, born 22 Dec 1842 in Calais (VR). Died 20 Apr 1861 age 18y 4m in Calais (g.s.). Buried: 27 Apr 1861 in Calais Cemetery. Census: 1850 in Calais.
xiii. GEORGE HENRY BUTLER, born 15 Jun 1845 in Calais (VR), in St Stephen, NB (enlist). Served in Civil War, Co M 2nd Me Calvary, enlisted in Pembroke age 18 (mother signed consent 17 Mar 1864). Died 22 Sep 1864 age 19y 3m 7d in Barrancas, FL (service rec. = left service. 22 Sept 1864 died in Hospital). Buried in National Cemetery, Barrancas, FL (also g.s. in Calais Cemetery). Census: 1850 in Calais.
xiv. ALMIRA BUTLER, born circa 1850 in Calais. Died 28 Mar 1853 in Calais (g.s.). Buried: 29 Mar 1853 in Calais Cemetery. Census: 1850 in Calais.

SAMUEL & HANNAH CALLAGHAN, p. 189

SAMUEL CALLAGHAN (poss. s/o William Callaghan of Columbia, ME), born circa 1788 in Jonesport, Maine (1850 census = Columbia). He was a ship carpenter. Died before 1860 in Princeton Me (1860 census deaths). Census: 1830 (6 males, 2 females), 40 (7 males, 3 females), 50 in Calais.

He married circa 1814 (census rec.) HANNAH EASTMAN born circa 1792 (?) in St Andrews, NB (1850 census). Died after 1870. Census: 1850 in Calais, 1860 & 70 in Princeton Me (with son William). Children:

i. WILLIAM CALLIGHAN, born 4 Jul 1815 in Eastport ME (mason). He was a farmer. Moved to Princeton in 1846 and after 1886 to Chippewa Falls, WI to live with their youngest child. Died 1 Dec 1895 in Chippewa Falls, WI (mason). Census: 1850, 60, 70 & 80 in Princeton Me. He married Aug 1836 (mason), (int) 26 July 1835 in Calais (cal2:39), SARAH JANE CAMPBELL, born 10 Sept 1819 in St. John, NB, daughter of JAMES CAMPBELL of St. John, NB. Died 18 Mar 1911 in Chippewa Falls (mason – from death cert.). Census: 1850, 60, 70 & 80 in Princeton.
ii. THOMAS CALLAGHAN (possible son), born circa 1818 in St. George, NB (1850 census). Census: 1850 in Calais.
iii. SAMUEL CALLAGHAN, Jr., born circa 1826 in Calais (1850 census). Died before 1860. Census: 1850 in Calais. He married circa 1845 (mrwc:44). PHEBE ABIGAIL ELLSMORE, born ca 1826 in Machias (1850 census) (poss. d/o MOSES ELSEMORE & LUCY FOSTER). Census: 1850 in Calais.
iv. MARY HANNAH CALLAGHAN, born 31 July 1827 in NB, bapt 12 Mar 1828 in St. Stephen, NB (kmc, mason). Died: probably before 1870. Census: 1860 in Calais. She married ca Mar 1845 in Calais (mrwc:46), by Rev. Seth H. Keeler (int.) 22 Mar 1845 in Calais (VR:1:136). WILLIAM COCHRAN, born ca 1821 in NB, a lumberman (age 39 1860 census). Census: 1860 & 70 (wife's name Angia H.) in Calais.

v. TIMOTHY CALLAGAN, born 16 Aug (year not given), bapt. same day as sister, Mary, 12 Mar 1828 (kmc).
vi. PHINEAS H. G. CALLAGHAN, born 24 Mar 1830 in Calais (VR). Died Jul 1839 age 10 in Calais (g.s.). Buried: 20 Jul 1839 in Calais Cemetery.
vii. LYDIA ELTHEA CALLAGHAN, born 25 Dec 1833 in Calais (VR). Census: 1850 in Calais. She married (int.) 21 Apr 1854 RANDAL MCDONALD of Calais (VR:1:58), son of WILLIAM McDONALD & DEBORAH WADSWORTH (father's obit, see McDonald).
viii. WARREN CALLAGHAN, born 16 Mar 1835 in Calais (VR). He was a lumberman. Died 12 Aug 1904 in Oconto, WI (mason from death cert.). Census: 1850 in Calais. He married 13 Aug 1864 (mason, union) MARY M. CALLIGAN, born 13 Nov 1841, daughter of HOLLIS CALLIGAN & RACHEL ROBINSON (mason from death cert.). Died 16 Dec 1923 (mason). After 1860 they resided in Oconto, WI (mason).
ix. UNNAMED CHILD CALLAGHAN, born Jul 1838 in Calais, died 26 Sep 1839 in Calais (mason).

ALEXANDER & LYDIA CAMERON, p. 205

ALEXANDER I. K. CAMERON, born ca 1898 in NB, died 21 Jan 1890 age 91y 6m in Bangor, buried in Mt. Hope Cemetery, Lot # 1181CG, buried 23 Jan 1890 (hope).
He married before 1841 LYDIA (_____), born ca 1810, died 3 Feb 1903 age 93y 3m 10d in NY, buried in Mt. Hope Cemetery, Bangor (Lot #1181CG hope). Children:

i. ISABEL CAMERON, born 24 Mar 1842 in Calais (VR).
ii. GEORGE FREDERICK CAMERON, born 1 Feb 1844 in Calais (VR). He was a merchant in the Company of Whitney & Cameron in Bangor and also a member of the city council (obit BDN). Died 9 Sept 1918, age 75y 7m 8d in Bangor, buried in Mt. Hope Cemetery, Bangor, ME (MSA, hope lot # 1181). Census: 1880 & 1900 in Bangor. He married before 1877, PATHENIA F. WHITNEY, born 20 Mar 1843 in Pittsfield, ME, daughter of JOHN WHITNEY & SARAH J. PUSHOR (obit). She died 30 Mar 1945 age 102 in Bangor, ME (obit BDN). Buried in Mt. Hope Cemetery, Bangor (lot # 1181 hope). Census: 1880 & 1900 in Bangor.
iii. MARY FOSTER CAMERON, born 1 May 1846 in Calais (VR).

MICHAEL & JANE CARRY, 211
(Name spelled Carey in other records)

MICHAEL CAREY /CARRY/CARY, born circa 1822 in Ireland (1850 census), {Michael Carey, born 13 Sept 1821 in St. John, entered U. S. June 1831 at Calais, naturalized 5 Oct 1852 (irmch, SJC:11:39)}, son of MICHAEL CAREY, SR. & EMMA BAKER, both born in Ireland (Topsfield VR)- (son's marriage record and family tradition says he was born on the ocean) He was a farmer & lumberman. He was in the Civil War Co E of 6th Maine Vols. (NRMS:247). He was 5'9 1/2" with blue eyes and brown hair (cwcard). Died 18 Nov 1886 of blood poisoning in wound received in war, in Topsfield, Me (VR:93). Buried Town Cemetery, Topsfield (cemetery rec. has 19 Nov 1887 age 67). Census: 1850 in Calais, 1870 & 80 in Topsfield.
He married 27 Nov 1845 in Calais (mrwc:47 & Calais VR:1:137) [5 June 1848 in Calais, by Rev. Allen Barrows (Topsfield VR)] ANN JANE LARNER of Calais, born July 1824 in Eastport ME (1850 & 1900 census), daughter of ISAAC LARNER & JANE WILSON (both born in Ireland). Died: 10 June 1908 age 85 in Topsfield (MSA). Census: 1850 in Calais, 1870, 80 & 1900 in Topsfield. Children:

i. GEORGE F. CAREY, born 26 Aug 1846 in Calais (VR), (Topsfield VR has 1850 as b. date). Died 1937 (g.s.). Buried Town Cemetery, Topsfield. Census: 1850 in Calais. He married 17 Oct 1869 in Topsfield (VR:58) Miss ADELIA RIPLEY of Waite.
ii. CHARLES EDGAR CAREY, born 1 May 1851 in Calais (Topsfield VR). He was a farmer, moved to Danforth ca 1926. Died 12 Dec 1937 age 87y 4m 11d in Danforth ME (MSA, g.s.). Buried in Town Cemetery, Topsfield. Census: 1870, 80, & 1920 in Topsfield. Married 15 Nov 1894 by O. H. Taylor, JP in Topsfield, AMANDA JUDITH KNEELAND, born Jan 1852, daughter of EPHRAIM KNEELAND & CARRIE JOHNSON (MSA). Died 18 Apr 1928 age 76y 1m. in Danforth, ME (MSA). Census: 1920 in Topsfield.
iii. EMMA JANE CAREY, born 27 Dec 1854 in Calais (Topsfield VR, death rec. has 1852). Died 5 May 1940 in

Topsfield (MSA, g.s.), buried Town Cemetery, Topsfield. Census: 1870, 80 &1900 in Topsfield. She married 8 June 1873 by William F. Johnson, Esq. in Topsfield (VR, adv) GEORGE WILLIAM BEAN, born 9 Apr 1852 in Topsfield (VR:9), son of STEPHEN BEAN, b. Bethel, ME & ANNIE Y. NOYES, b. Topsfield (MSA). Died 13 May 1929 in Topsfield (MSA, g.s.), buried Town Cemetery, Topsfield. Census: 1880 & 1900 in Topsfield.

iv. MARY ANN CAREY, born 2 June 1856 in Topsfield (VR).

v. JAMES SHEPARD CAREY, born 10 Jan 1858 in Topsfield (VR). Died 1940 (g.s.), buried Town Cemetery, Topsfield. Census: 1870, 80,1900 & 20 in Topsfield. At age 48 he married 7 Oct 1907 by O. H. Taylor, JP in Topsfield FLORENCE DAVIS, born ca 1882 (g.s.). in Milltown, ME, daughter of WILLIAM DAVIS & AGNES McLAUGHLIN (MSA). Died ca 1967 (g.s.). Buried in Town Cemetery, Topsfield. Census: 1920 in Topsfield.

vi. ISAAC MONROE CAREY, born 19 Apr 1859 in Topsfield (VR). Census: 1870 & 80 in Topsfield

vii. CLARA CAREY, born 1861 in Topsfield (VR). Census: 1870 in Topsfield.

ANSON G. & ANNIE E. CHANDLER, p. 225

General JOHN [6] CHANDLER, son of JOSEPH [5-4-3], THOMAS[2], WILLIAM[1], served in the Revolutionary War and afterwards settled in Monmouth, Maine. General John Chandler was Selectman of Monmouth 1792-1803, Town Clerk 1892-1804, was in the State Legislature and Senate, President of Senate in 1820 and member of U.S. Congress in 1820-29. He was a Brigadier General 11 Aug 1801, in the Mass. Senate 1803, and also a Kennebec County Sheriff (jojc). He died 25 Sept 1841 in Augusta. He married MARY WHITTIER/WHITCHER, born 16 Feb 1764 (chand:401). Their son Anson Chandler resided in Calais.

ANSON GONZALO[7] CHANDLER, born 14 Oct 1793 in Monmouth, ME (chand:404, g.s.) graduated from Brown University in 1814. He was a Judge Advocate and Division Advocate of the Militia in Calais from 1823 to 1827 (milit). He ran for Governor of Maine in 1852 in opposition to Gov. Hubbard and received 21,774 votes. He was a Justice of the District Court for the Eastern District from 1840 to 1845, he was indeed an upright Judge. In 1856 or '57 he was appointed U.S. Consul at Lahaina, Sandwich Islands to succeed Hon. George M. Chase who died while holding the office. Mr. Chandler always took an active interest in railroad and other public enterprises in our State, although delicate health for a long series of years prevented arduous labor. By 1820 he was in Calais, in 1834 he was a Justice of Peace in Calais, he also was a Div. Advocate in the State Militia, an Attorney and Judge. He was admitted to the Bar July 1823 (SJC). Died 16 May 1863 age 69, in Bethlehem, PA (argus obit, g.s., Calais VR:3:303, adv, chand:754). Buried in Calais Cemetery. Census: 1860 in Calais. Note: he does not appear in other census, he must have been out of town when census were taken.

He married 1st 25 Dec 1825 (chand:404, east:72) ELIZABETH ANN PIKE, born 21Feb 1803, daughter of WILLIAM C. PIKE SR. AND ELIZABETH CHRISTOPHER (pkjdt:4). She died 21 Nov 1847 age 44 in Calais (adv., g.s.) (see PIKE) Buried in Calais Cemetery. No children.

He married 2nd 9 Jun 1852 (chand:404) ANNIE ELIZA BRADBURY (sister of BION BRADBURY), born 28 May 1819 in York, ME (obit, g.s.), daughter of JEREMIAH BRADBURY & MARY LANGDON STORER (chand:754). Died 26 Mar 1865 in Providence RI (obit adv, g.s.). Buried: 3 Apr 1865 in Calais Cemetery. Probate of Estate in Machias Me (will dated 6 Oct 1863). Census: 1860 in Calais. They had only one child who died when only a few months old:

i. ANSON BRADBURY CHANDLER, born 11 Jan 1856 in Calais (VR). Died 30 Mar 1857 age 14m 20d in Eastport ME (east:153).

AMASA L. & SUSAN B. CLAPP, p. 182

AMASA LYMAN CLAPP born 30 Oct 1813 in Boston, Ma, son of SALMA CLAPP AND ABIGAIL MONROE. He was a jeweler and watchmaker, business first established in 1836 and was later sold to Ross Brothers Jewelry. He was a deacon in the Congo church in Calais from 1854 to 1900. He died 13 Oct 1900 in Calais (MSA, adv). Buried in Calais Cemetery. Census: 1850 thru 1880 in Calais.

He married 1st Nov 1839 in Calais (Bangor VR) SUSAN B. YOUNG, born 1 May 1818 in Meddybemps ME (g.s.). Died 27 Dec 1866 age 48y 8m in Calais (union, g.s.). Buried: 31 Dec 1866 in Calais Cemetery. Census: 1860 in Calais. Children:

i. ANNE YOUNG CLAPP, born 29 Dec 1841 in Calais (VR). Bapt 1 May 1842 in Calais (congo). Graduated from Calais Academy. Died 7 Aug 1914 age 72 in Calais (MSA, adv, g.s.). Buried in Calais Cemetery. Census: 1860 & 1900 in Calais. She married 28 Jul 1864 in Calais (VR:3:308) CHARLES B. COLLINS, born Sept 1840 in Calais, son of BRADBURY COLLINS, (born Harrington), ME & CHARITY G. PATTEN, (born Cherryfield). Died 16 Apr 1903 in Calais (MSA). Buried in Calais Cemetery. Census: 1860 & 1900 in Calais.

ii. MARY LYMAN CLAPP, born 27 Mar 1845 in Calais (VR). Died 19 Apr 1845 in Calais (VR:1:229, obit). Buried on 21 Apr 1845 in Calais Cemetery.

iii. MARIA LOWELL CLAPP, born 22 Nov 1846 in Calais (VR). Died after 1900 (father's obit) Census: 1860 & 70 in Calais. She married 9 Nov 1887 in New York, NY (times) CHARLES BEAUCHAMP ANDERSON. They were in Kansas City in 1893 (adv).

iv. MONROE F. CLAPP, born 4 Sep 1853 in Calais, died 9 Dec 1927 in Kennebunk Me (MSA). Buried: Dec 1927 in Calais Cemetery. He was a jeweler. Census: 1860 & 70 in Calais. He married 12 Sep 1886 in Aurora, IL (times) LINA DYCKMAN. Resided in Columbus, OH in Apr 1891 when parents visited him (adv).

v. HORACE CLAPP, born circa 1857 in Calais. Died Sep 1859 age 21m in Calais (sext, 1860 mort. schedule). Buried 26 Sep 1859 in Calais Cemetery.

He married 2nd 9 Jan 1868 in Calais (VR:3:227, union) ALMEDA M. (JONES) MITCHELL, born 12 Oct 1829 in Calais (MSA), daughter of JOHN Y. JONES & MYRA VOSE and sister of Sarah Tinker. Died 15 Oct 1922 age 93y 3d in Calais (MSA, adv, sfh:4:64). Buried: 17 Oct 1922 in Calais Cemetery. Census: 1870 & 80 in Calais.

AMOS & MARY ANN CLARK, p. 213

AMOS[7] CLARK, born 8 Jan 1802 in China, ME (VR, 1850 census = Lebanon, ME), son of EPHRAIM[6] CLARK & OLIVE BRALEY they married 23 Sept 1795 in Vassalboro, Me (VR) [grandson of JONATHAN[5], THOMAS[4], JOHN[3], THOMAS[2], JOHN[1](folley)]. He was a shoemaker. He was an old time abolitionist, great anti-slavery fighter, did more perhaps to create abolition and republican sentiment in Washington county than any other private individual (biosk on son, Judson). Died 29 Jun 1879 age 71y (probate rec., g.s., adv). Will dated 14 June 1879, probate of estate: 16 Sept 1879 in Machias Me. Buried in Calais Cemetery. Census: 1840 (1 male, 2 females), 50, 60 & 70 in Calais.

Family tradition says 'Amos was a farmer in China until his disappearance around 1838. Amos left China & fled east to Calais, where he married a second time (without benefit of divorce). Esther & family had Amos officially declared dead, around 1845, after waiting the allotted seven years, and she had a grave stone erected in the China Cemetery'.

He married 1st 5 Feb 1822 in China, ME (VR) ESTHER ROBINSON BURRELL, born 12 Mar 1804 in China (VR), daughter of SAMUEL BURRELL & ESTHER DEXTER. She died 20 Nov 1884 in Jackson, ME (VR:48) at home of her daughter, Lydia Edwards, and is buried in the Snow Cemetery there. Census: 1860 in China, 1880 in Jackson. Children:

i. ESTHER CLARK, born in China.

ii. THOMAS F. CLARK, born ca 1829 in China. He enlisted in Civil War 30 July 1862 in Co G 19th Me Inf. a farmer 5'9" with dark eyes and dark hair, born and res. in China (cwcard). Census: 1860 in China (his mother, Ester, with him). He married int. 7 Dec 1851 in China ROXANNA BRAGG (China VR at MSA). Census: 1860 in China.

iii. LYDIA A. CLARK, born 10 Nov 1831 (Jackson, Me VR). She died in 1911 (g.s.). She married (int) 1 Nov 1851 in Jackson (VR). ELISHA EDWARDS, born 16 July 1825 in Jackson (VR, MSA) son of AARON EDWARDS & SUSANNA DAVIS. Died: 27 Oct 1900 in Jackson (MSA, g.s.). They are both buried in Snow Cemetery in Jackson. Census: 1860, 70 & 80 in Jackson (both).

He married 2nd 7 Sep 1834 in Calais by Rev. Edward N. Harris (mrwc:13) MARY ANN NICHOLS[8] CHENEY, born 2 Apr 1817 in Eastport (VR), daughter of AMASA[7] CHENEY & NANCY CAMPBELL TODD (both born in Cherryfield) [granddaughter of WILLIAM[6], TRISTRAM[5], JOHN[3-4], PETER[2], JOHN[1] (folley)]. Bapt. 26 Apr 1840 in Milltown, ME (lord:8). She was the administrator of husband's will. Died 3 Aug 1902 age 85y 4m 1d in Calais (MSA, g.s.). Buried in Calais Cemetery. Census: 1850, 60 & 70 in Calais (see TODD). Children:

iv   SARAH MARIA CLARK, born 23 Oct 1835 in Calais (VR). Her father left her $1.00. She ran a Dry, Staple and Fancy Goods store in Milltown established in 1872 (MBM:38). In her will dated 12 Apr 1913 she gave to Izetta Clark the income of my estate ------ in her lifetime if she doesn't use all --- devise remains to Ethel H. Gerrish in trust for her father Judson S. Clark. Izetta to use as she deems best for the said Judson's support. Hiram Gerrish to be sole exec. of will (probate #H-4-287). Died 13 Oct 1914 age 79 in Calais (MSA, adv, sfh:bk2). Census: 1850 & 70 in Calais. She married 21 Nov 1855 in Calais (VR) ASA HAMILTON, born ca 1814. He was a machinist. He died before his wife. Census: 1870 in Calais.

v.   ALICE DODGE CLARK, born 13 Aug 1838 in Calais (VR). Her father left her $25 a year for 5 years. Died 23 Nov 1910 in Milltown, NB (folley). Buried in Calais Cemetery. Census: 1850 & 60 in Calais, 1870, 80 & 1900 in Princeton. She married 20 Mar 1864 SANDERS GILL SPOONER (see SPOONER).

vi.   GEORGE HALLET CLARK, born 5 Feb 1841 in Calais, died 12 Mar 1841 in Calais (VR). Buried: 14 Mar 1841 in Calais Cemetery.

vii. EUGENE BRACKETT CLARK, born 8 Dec 1842 in Calais (VR). Graduated from Calais Academy. His father left him $25 cash and shoes & boots from Judson when needed. He served in the Civil War in Co C of 32nd Maine, 5' 6 ½" tall, hazel eyes and dark hair (enlist, cwcard), he was a member of G.A.R. Post #34 in Calais. He was a teacher. Died 17 Aug 1896 age 53y 8m in Calais (MSA, g.s.). Buried in Calais Cemetery. Census: 1850 & 60 in Calais.

viii. HENRY HOWARD CLARK, born 6 Mar 1845 in Calais. His father left him $1.00. He resided in Anapolis, MD in 1914 (sister, Sarah's will, was a Chaplain in US Navy in her obit). Name is on grave stone in Calais no dates. Census: 1850 & 60 in Calais.

ix.   ABIGAIL 'ABBY' JACKSON CLARK, born 29 Dec 1847 in Calais (VR). Her father left her $25. A year for 5 years. Died 22 Jan 1913 in Calais (MSA). Census: 1850 thru 1900 in Calais. She married 9 Oct 1873 by Rev. Porter in Milltown ME (adv) GEORGE PRATT, born Apr 1827 in St. George, NB (1900 census). He was a surveyor. Died 1 Feb 1906 in Calais (MSA).

x.   CARRIE ELSEWORTH. CLARK, born circa 1850 in Calais. Her father left a store on Main St. to her. In her will dated 1 May 1907, she left her sister, Sarah Hamilton, her home known as the "Old Amos Clark Homestead", and her brother, Judson a life estate in the house he resides. Died 11 May 1907 age 56y 9m in Calais (MSA). Census: 1860 & 70 in Calais. Never married.

xi.   HARRIET 'Hattie' EMMA CLARK, born circa 1852 in Calais, died age 15 y 5m on 17 June 1867 (union, g.s.). Buried in Calais Cemetery. Census: 1860 in Calais.

xii. JUDSON STORER CLARK, born 31 Jul 1857 in Calais (MSA = 1856). His father left him a store on Main Street. In 1890 he owned three stores; boots, shoes & skins and groceries in Milltown, shoes etc. in Calais. Also was a farmer; and a member of the state legislature in 1886 and 1887; he was also an alderman and member of the school committee (MBM:37). He died 9 May 1928 age 71y 9m 22d in Brownville, Me at home of his daughter, Ethel Gerrish (obit adv, MSA, g.s.). Buried in Calais Cemetery. Census: 1860, 70 & 80 in Calais. He married 21 July 1879 by Rev. W.L. Brown (adv) IZETTA ROGERS, born ca 1861, daughter of STEPHEN EDWARD ROGERS & SARAH JANE CARR (conn). Died 25 Sept 1920 (g.s.) (no will found in Machias for either Izetta or Judson). Buried in Calais Cemetery. Census: 1880 in Calais.

SAMUEL B. & EVELINA C. CLARK, p. 182

SAMUEL or Lemuel B. Clark.
    He married EVELINA C. (_____).Children:

i.   WILLIAM DWIGHT CLARK, born 15 Nov 1845 in Calais.
ii.   UNNAMED CHILD CLARK, born Sep 1847, died Oct 1847, buried 5 Oct 1847 in Calais Cemetery (sext).
iii. ANNIE JANE CLARK, born 18 Sep 1848 in Calais (VR).

RICHARD & LIBERTY CLAYBORN, p. 212

RICHARD CLAYBORN, born circa 1804 in Hull, England (1850 census). He enlisted in Civil War at age 44, in Co K 15th Me Inf. on 24 Dec 1861, discharged for disability in Barrancus, FL (no date), a butcher with gray eyes and brown hair, born in England, res. Calais (cwcard). He was a millman. Died after 1870. Census: 1850 & 70 in Calais.

He married 29 Sep 1836 in St Patrick, NB (CCMR) ELIZABETH/ LIBERTY BURNS born circa 1815 in Down, Ireland (1850 census), daughter of HUGH & BRIDGET BURNS (MSA). Died 24 Dec 1892 age 90 in Milltown, ME (MSA, adv). Buried in Calais Cemetery. Census: 1850 & 70 in Calais. Children:

i. RICHARD CLAYBORN (Jr.), born circa 1840 in Maguadanic, NS (enlist, 1850 census = St Patrick). Service in Civil War, enlisted 23 Dec. 1863, Co. D 6th Maine, 5' 6" with brown hair and blue eyes, MIA 10 May 1864 (enlist, NRMS:239). He probably never returned from war, his son had a guardian appointed after Jane's death. Census: 1850 in Calais. He married 3 Sep 1859 by Rev I. J. Burgess in Calais (VR:3:182, adv, union) JANE FITZSIMMONS, born ca 1835. Died 23 Sep 1867 age 32 in Calais (VR:3:313). Probate of Estate, in Machias, in her last illness she gave her son, William, to Patrick Levi as guardian, dated 1 Oct 1867.

ii. FRANCES CLAYBORN, born 27 Mar 1843 in Calais (VR, death rec. = b. St. George, NB). Died 9 Jun 1918 in Calais (MSA, g.s.). Buried in Red Beach Cemetery in Calais. Census: 1850 thru 1910 in Calais. She married 9 Jun 1863 in Calais (VR:3:196) DANIEL MINGO, born ca Mar 1840 in Red Beach, son of MICHAEL MINGO & SARAH DOBSON (both born NS). He was a fireman. Died 4 Aug 1905 age 65y 4m 4d in Calais (MSA, g.s.), buried Red Beach Cemetery. Census 1870, 80 & 1900 in Calais.

iii. WILLIAM JAMES CLAYBORN, born circa 1848 in Milltown ME. He was a plaster mill employee. Died 27 Jun 1910 age 60 in Red Beach Me (MSA, sfh:1:284). Buried in Catholic Cemetery in Calais. Census: 1850, 60 (age 11 with Bernard McGraw) & 70, 1910 age 59 living with sister, Frances in Calais. Unmarried.

JOHN & ELIZA ANN COFREN, p. 192

JOHN COFREN/COFFREN.
He married ELIZA ANN (_____).Children:

i. JOHN STILLMAN COFREN, born 18 Nov 1840 in Calais, died 15 Sep 1842 in Calais (VR).
ii. MARY ANN COFREN, born 10 Apr 1843 in Calais (VR).
iii. MARIA GERTRUDE COFREN, born 16 May 1845 in Calais (VR).

GEORGE N. & OLIVIA COLE, p. 192

GEORGE NATHAN COLE, born circa 1821 in Boston Ma. (1850 census). Bapt. 1 May 1836 age ca 15 (congo). He was a merchant. Died 24 Sep 1860 in Boston MA, while in Boston purchasing stock for his store (obit). Buried: 27 Sep 1860 in Calais Cemetery. Census: 1850 & 60 in Calais.

He married ca 1846 OLIVIA P. PATTEN, born circa 1824 in Granville, NS (1850 census), daughter of WILLIAM PATTEN AND RUTH FOSTER, died 7 Apr 1897 age 74 in Calais (MSA, adv, prbt will dated 13 Apr 1870). Buried in Calais Cemetery. She left her estate to son, William H. (prbt). Census: 1850, 60 & 70 (she & children living with Charles Deming), 80 (with son William H.) in Calais. Children:

i. WILLIAM HOWARD COLE, born 21 Oct 1846 in Calais (VR). He enlisted in the Civil War in Co C of Coast Guard, a clerk 5'8" with gray eyes and dark hair (cwcard). His mother signed his enlistment paper. He was a bookkeeper. Died 30 Nov 1909 age 63y 1m 3d in Calais (VR, obit). Buried: 2 Dec 1909 in Calais Cemetery (sext). Census: 1850 thru 80 & 1900 in Calais. He married before 1875 ELIZABETH WING, born ca July 1851, daughter of DAVID WING & LYDIA PITTS, died 22 June 1902 in Calais (MSA). Buried in Calais Cemetery. Census: 1880 &1900 in Calais.

ii. GEORGE E. COLE, born circa 1851 in Calais. Resided in Everett, MA when mother died in 1897. Died after 1897. Census: 1860, 70 & 80 in Calais. He married 30 Dec 1881 LAURA S. WHIDDEN, daughter of CHARLES & MILA WHIDDEN (see WHIDDEN).

BENJAMIN & ANN CONDELL, p. 197

BENJAMIN W. CONDELL born circa 1810 in Sullivan, ME (from daughter's death rec), (Calais Cemetery records have a Benjamin Condell who d. 26 Jan 1854 may be his father) (VR of Sullivan has Benjamin Condle & Mariam Johnson married 8 Aug 1808 may be his parents). He was a stevedore. [Benjamin Condle & Samuel G. Thompson, who went from Calais in the brig "B. M. Prescott" for San Francisco, arrived in town last Friday (FJ of 2 Apr 1851)]. Died 26 Apr 1883 in Calais (times). Buried in Calais Cemetery. Probate of Estate: 7 Aug 1883 in Machias Me. Census: 1850 thru 1880 in Calais.

He married 13 Jun 1841 by L.L. Lowell in Calais (gaz, adv) ANN W. WAKEFIELD born circa 1815 in Deer Isle, NB (daughter's death rec., 1850 census = Steuben). Died 5 Sep 1888 age 62y 6m in Calais (times). Census: 1850, 60 & 80 in Calais. She was not listed with husband & children in 1870 census, insane in 1880 special census. Children:

i. UNNAMED CHILD CONDELL, born circa 1841 in Calais, died Sep 1842 in Calais (g.s.). Buried: 13 Sep 1842 in Calais Cemetery.

ii. GEORGE H. CONDELL, born 2 Feb 1843 in Calais (VR). Served in Civil War in Co. D 6th Maine. (NRMS:242). He was 5'7" with gray eyes and brown hair (cwcard). He was a mariner & stevedore. Died 9 Mar 1925 in Calais (MSA). Buried in Calais Cemetery. Census: 1850, 70, 80 & 1910 in Calais. He married on 6 Dec 1866 by Rev. John Turnbull in St. Stephen, NB (Dir. 1901, SCC, CCMR) BARBARA M. MORRISON, born 26 Oct 1843 in Scotch Ridge, NB, daughter of GEORGE MORRISON (b. Scotland) & MARGARET SINCLAIR (b. NB)(MSA, her death rec.). Died 6 Mar 1919 age 76y 4m 8d in Calais, buried in Calais Cemetery (MSA, sfh:3:57). Census: 1851 in St. James, NB, 1870, 80 & 1910 in Calais.

iii. MARY E. CONDELL, born 9 Feb 1845 in Calais (VR). Died 1 Jan 1910 age 64y 10m in Calais (sfh:1:234). Buried in Calais Cemetery. Census: 1850, 70 & 80 in Calais. She married on 16 Sep 1863 in NB (CCMR). ALEXANDER A. MORRISON, born 23 Apr 1838 in St. James, NB, son of GEORGE MORRISON & MARGARET SINCLAIR (MSA). He was a millwright. He died 29 Oct 1900 in Calais (MSA). Census: 1851 in St. James, NB, 1870 & 80 in Calais.

iv. DAVID CONDELL, born 4 May 1847 in Calais (VR). Died circa 1849 in Calais (g.s., 1850 census deaths). Buried: 1849 in Calais Cemetery.

v. UNNAMED CHILD CONDELL, born Apr 1852 in Calais, died Aug 1852 in Calais (g.s.). Buried: 29 Aug 1852 in Calais Cemetery.

COLUMBUS & LOUIS COOPER, p. 194
COLUMBUS & SARAH COOPER, p. 194

COLUMBUS COOPER, born 21 Oct 1811 in Livermore, ME (VR), son of WILLIAM & REBECCA COOPER. History of Livermore has Deliverance Lovell as his mother. Died 21 Feb 1871 age 59 in Oak Ranch, CA (obit adv). Census: 1840 (10 males, 5 females), 50 in Calais (Left by ship for Calif. early 1850 from Calais, (FJ) article didn't mention if any of his family was with him).

He married 1st 1 Oct 1835 by Moses Stone in Jay, ME (VR:I:25), LOUIS/LOIS STARR LEACH, born 3 June 1814 in Jay, ME, daughter of LUKE LEACH & POLLY STARR (jay:483). Died 9 Jun 1843 in Calais (g.s.). Buried: 11 Jun 1843 in Calais Cemetery. Children:

* Note: VR in Calais & Jay have her name Louis, grave stone and marriage have Lois.

i. AUGUSTUS AMORY COOPER, born 28 Jul 1837 in Calais (VR). He attended Westbrook Seminary in Maine, went to California in 1850, became a lawyer, died 20 July 1870 in Chico, CA, survived by his wife (no name mentioned) and aged father (obit, adv). Census: 1850 in Calais.

ii. FREDERICK COLUMBUS COOPER, born 7 Nov 1839 in Calais (VR). Died 24 Nov 1871 age 32, killed by Indians in Arizona, he was of Downeyville, CA (obit adv). Census: 1850 in Calais.

iii. WILLIAM F. COOPER, born May 1843 in Calais. Died 29 Jun 1843, in Robbinston Me (FJ, g.s.). Buried 1 Jul 1843 in Calais Cemetery.

Columbus married 2nd circa 1845 SARAH (_____), born circa 1822 in Limerick ME (1850 census).

Census: 1850 in Calais. Children:

iv. STILLBORN COOPER, born circa 1846 in Calais. Died circa 1846 in Calais (sext). Buried: 9 Jul 1846 in Calais Cemetery.
v. FRANKLIN COOPER, born circa 1848 in Calais. Census: 1850 (age 2) in Calais.
vi. UNNAMED GIRL COOPER, born Apr 1850 in Calais, in 1850 census (age 3/12) in Calais.

JAMES & SUSANNA COOPER, p. 221

JAMES COOPER, born in Robbinston Me. He married MARY HAYWARD, born in England. Their son, James S. settled in Calais.

JAMES S. COOPER, born Jan 1816 in Robbinston Me(1900 census). He was a mill laborer and a tailor. Died 29 Jul 1906 in Calais (MSA). Census: 1850 thru 1900 in Calais.
* Note: there were two James S. Coopers living in Calais at same time, other one was a lawyer.

He married 22 Jul 1843 by Elias Kelsey, Esq. in Calais (mrwc:40, gaz) SUSANNA CAVERT or Covert or Colbert, born Apr 1819 in Belfast, Antrium, Ireland (1850 & 1900 census), daughter of JAMES & MARY COLBERT/CAVERT. Died 7 Apr 1904 age 84 in Calais (MSA, SSC, probate of estate). Census: 1850 thru 1900 in Calais. Children:

i. JOHN COOPER, born 1844, died 18 Oct 1845 age 1y 18d in Calais (g.s.). Buried in Calais Cemetery.
ii. SAMUEL JAMES COOPER, born 10 Jan 1847 in Calais (VR). He worked in a sawmill. Died after 1904 (mothers estate address unknown). Census: 1850, 60 & 70 in Calais.
iii. DAVID COOPER, born Jan 1850 in Calais. Died after 1904 (mothers estate) Census: 1850, 60 & 70 in Calais.
iv. ALBERTUS COOPER, born circa 1852 in Calais, died 3 Nov 1865 age 13y 6d in Calais (g.s.). Census: 1860 in Calais.
v. ROBERT C. COOPER, born circa 1855 in Calais, died 7 Mar 1864 age 9y 21d in Calais (g.s.). Buried: 9 Mar 1864 in Calais Cemetery (sext). Census: 1860 in Calais.
vi. ANNA/ANNIE JANE COOPER, born 25 Sep 1857 in Calais (MSA). She was a boarding home operator at time of marriage in Baileyville, ME. Died 12 Nov 1933 age 76y 1m 16d in Calais (sfh:6:263, MSA). Buried in Calais Cemetery. Census: 1860 & 70 in Calais. She married 5 Feb 1908 in Calais (MSA) JAMES EDGAR BLANEY, born ca 1882 in Boston, NS, age 26 at marriage, son of WILLIAM H. BLANEY & JOSEPHINE JONES both born in Boston, NS (MSA, Baileyville VR:10). He was a cook in her boarding home.
• Records of her age are interesting, especially since her husband was much younger, in 1860 age 3; 1870 age 11; 1900 age 31; 1908 age 32; at death in 1933 age 76.
vii. JOHN CAVET COOPER, born 13 Apr 1863, in Milltown ME (sfh:6:256, MSA). His mother in her will left the homestead to him and he was to care for his father during his lifetime. Died 7 Oct 1933 age 70y 5m 24d in Milltown ME (MSA, sfh). Buried in Calais Cemetery. Census: 1900 age 36 with parents in Calais. He married 10 Aug 1904 in Calais by Rev. W.H. Robinson BESSIE LOUISE OLIVER or Elliot, born 13 Apr 1873 in Greenfield, NB (MSA), daughter of [FRANK OLIVER & CATHERINE SMITH both were born in NB (on marriage record)] [FRANK ELLIOT & KATHERINE FROST (on death record)] [Katherine Frost age 72 living in Calais with John & Bessie in 1920 census]. [Son, Vernon F. Cooper b. 22 Aug 1905 mother's name Bessie L. Oliver b. Centerville, NB (MSA)]. Bessie died 1 Jan 1948 in Calais (MSA).
viii. MARY COOPER, born ca Apr 1864 (1900 census). She does not appear in 1870 census, her existence discovered through marriage records of her daughter, Anna C. Colson, who was living with grandparents in 1900 census. Her name Mary Colson in mother's will of 1904. Census: 1900 & 1920 in Calais. She married 6 Sept 1883 in Calais (VR:2:31) JOSIAH COLSON, born ca Mar 1865. Census: 1900 & 1920 in Calais.

JOHN & CAROLINE COOPER, p. 202

JOHN COOPER, born circa 1823. Census: 1850 in Calais.
He married CAROLINE M. (_____), born circa 1830 in Wiscasset, ME (1850 census). Census: 1850 in Calais. Children:

i. ALBERT COLBY COOPER, born 15 Feb 1848 in Calais (VR). Died 7 Sep 1848 (sext). Buried in Calais Cemetery.
ii. CHARLES C. COOPER, born Sep 1850 in Calais. [A Charles C. Cooper graduated from Calais Academy, might not be this Carles]. Census: 1850 in Calais.

MOSES & CLARINDA CORSON, p. 217

MOSES CORSON. Died before 1860.
    He married before 1831 CLARINDA [COGGINS ?], born circa 1811. Died 15 Jan 1884, probate of estate in Machias Me (Wash. Co. Probate rec. - will dated 7 Sept 1883). Census: 1860 (living with Samuel, age 73 born in Blue Hill, ME) & Rebecca, age 70 born Orland, ME, Coggins) in Calais. Children:

i. GEORGE DEXTER CORSON, born 15 Sep 1832 in Calais (VR). Died Oct 1832 in Calais (VR:1:239).
ii. HARRIET MELINDA CORSON, born 25 May 1833 in Calais (VR). Died after 1884. She married (_____) CORMIER (her name in mother's probate).
iii. LUCINDA BARRET CORSON, born 26 Apr 1835 in Calais (VR). Died after 1884. She married (_____) SMITH (her name in mother's probate).
iv. GEORGE HARRISON CORSON, born 15 Mar 1837 in Calais. He was a machinist. Died after 1896. Census: 1860, 70 & 80 in Calais. He married 18 Oct 1863 in Eastport ME (east:200) LUCY A. BROWN of Eastport. Probably died before 1880. Census: 1860 & 70 in Calais. He divorced her in Apr 1876 for neglecting family, marriage date on divorce 8 Sept 1863 by Rev. Charles Tibbetts at Eastport (SJC docket # 279).
v. JOSEPHINE L. C. CORSON, born 20 Oct 1843 in Calais. Died after 1900. Census: 1860, 70 & 1900 (age 54) in Calais. She married 30 Sep 1863 in Calais (VR). EDWARD OWENS b. ca 1838 in Maine (age 32 1870). He died before his wife. Census: 1870 in Calais.

CHARLES & PHOEBE COTTEL, p.200

CHARLES COTTEL, born 21 May 1809 (alex:VR:7), in Portsmouth NH (1850 census), son of SAMUEL COTTELL & ELIZABETH HATCH, first white woman to settle in Crawford {adv 8Mar 1870}. He was a trader, in a court case Jan 1854 he was in business with his brother, Hampden C. Cottell (SJC:12:146). In a letter to the editor of Calais Advertiser 21 May 1888, he wrote from Elwood, Will County, Illinois, "This is my birthday and I enter upon the last year of my fourth score today." Died after May 1888. Census: 1840 (3 males, 2 females) in Crawford, 50 in Calais. Charles was the Assistant Marshall who recorded the Census for Crawford in 1840. Family moved to Illinois after 1850.
    He married 23 Jul 1835 in Calais (mrwc:16) PHOEBE HANSCOM, born 21 Nov 1813 in E. Machias, Me (VR:51, cenmem:164), daughter of NATHANIEL & RUTH HANSCOM. Died 8 Apr 1879 age 65 in Florenceville, ILL (times, adv). Census: 1850 in Calais. Children:

i. PHOEBE A. COTTEL, born circa 1836 in Crawford ME (1850 census). Census: 1850 in Calais.
ii. HAMPDEN S. COTTEL, born circa 1838 in Crawford ME (1850 census). Census: 1850 in Calais.
iii. EMMA E. COTTEL, born circa 1840 in Crawford ME (1850 census). Census: 1850 in Calais.
iv. CHARLES W. COTTEL, born circa 1843 in Crawford ME (1850 census). Census: 1850 in Calais.
v. URSULA COTTEL, born circa 1845 in Calais (1850 census = Alexander). Census: 1850 in Calais.
vi. ADA W. COTTEL, born circa 1846 in Calais. Died 19 Jan 1873 in Florenceville, ILL (adv, d/o Charles Cottelle ? formerly of Calais, age 27y 11m). She married THOMAS PENINGTON.
vii. ALBERT HENRY COTTEL, born 7 Jan 1847 in Calais. Census: 1850 in Calais.

SOLOMON & JANE COY, p. 191

SOLOMON COY, born circa 1804, in Lewiston, ME (1850 census) (poss. son of Solomon Coy b. 1786 & Deborah Holmes of Poland, Me). He was a lumber surveyor and Justice of the Peace. Died ca 1871 in Oshkosh, WI (g.s.). Buried in Riverside Cemetery Oshkosh. Census: 1840 (3 males & 2 females) 1850 & 60 in Calais, 1870 in Algoma, WI.
    He married 16 Sept 1834 in Calais by Rev. E. N. Harris (cal2:48) JANE MORRISON, born circa 1810 in

Boston Ma (1850 census). In May 1881 she received $8.00 per month federal pension, she had two sons of her son, John Homer Coy, who was killed in the Civil War, in her care [list of pensioners on the roll 1883, vol. 4 Oshkosh Public Library]. She died 24 Sep 1881 in Oshkosh (times, obit north). Census: 1850 & 60 in Calais, 1870 in Oshkosh. Children:

i. JOHN HOMER COY, born 16 Jul 1835 in Calais (VR). Enlisted in Civil War 5 Aug 1862 in Co. K 6th Maine (enlist). He was a surveyor 5'8" with blue eyes and brown hair (cwcard). Died 23 Dec 1863 28y 5m 7d of wounds received Nov 7th (cwcard, NRMS:268, g.s.) in Washington, DC, at Armory Sq. Hospital. Buried: 6 Jan 1864 in Calais Cemetery (sext). Census: 1850 & 60 in Calais. He married 10 June 1855 in Calais by Justice Solomon Coy, MARY ELLEN CRAIG, born ca 1835 of St. Stephen, NB. Probably died before 1881 when her children in care of Jane in Oshkosh. Census: 1860 in Calais.
ii. BARBARA OLIVE COY, born 29 Apr 1839 in Calais, died 12 Aug 1840 age 1y 3m 15d in Calais (VR, adv, g.s.). Buried: 14 Aug 1840 in Calais Cemetery.
iii. SARAH JANE COY, born 6 Dec 1840 in Calais (VR). Died after 1870. Census: 1850 in Calais, 1870 in Oshkosh, WI. She married 2 Sep 1858 by Justice Solomon Coy in Calais (VR & adv of 9/9/1858) GUSTAVUS A. LAWRENCE, son of WILLIAM LAWRENCE AND LYDIA BRACKETT. By 1870 they resided in Oshkosh, WI. (see LAWRENCE).
iv. WILLIAM WALLACE COY, born 31 Jan 1843 in Calais (VR). Served in Civil War Co. D 6th Maine, 5'6 ½" with hazel eyes and brown hair (cwcard). Died 7 Nov 1863 age 20y 9m killed at Battle of Rappahannock Station, VA (cwcard, NRMS:239). Buried: 29 Jan 1864 (?) in Calais Cemetery. Census: 1850 & 60 in Calais.
v. JAMES K. COY, born 31 Aug 1846 in Calais, died 18 Mar 1847 age 7m in Calais (VR, g.s.). Buried in Calais Cemetery.
vi. BARBARA E. COY, born circa 1847 in Calais. Census: 1860 in Calais (not in 1850), 1870 in Oshkosh (age 23 married living with parents, married name not clear M___field).
vii. ROBERT BRUCE COY, born circa 1848 in Calais. He was a lumberman and drove a raft. Census: 1850 & 60 in Calais, 1870 in Oshkosh, 1880 in Algoma, WI. He married 1st 11 Sept 1873 in Oshkosh LAURA A. LULL, born ca 1846, daughter of LEVI & FANNY LULL, she died 16 Feb 1889 age 43, buried in Riverside Cemetery, Oshkosh (north, wmr & wdr at Oshkosh Library). Census: 1880 in Algoma, WI. He married 2nd 29 Nov 1890 in Oshkosh, BARBARA JANE MORRISON daughter of JOHN MORRISON & N. SOPHIA McROY of Wisconsin (wmr at Oshkosh Library).
viii. MARY E. COY, born circa 1853 in Calais, died 22 Aug 1853 age 6m in Calais (g.s.). Buried: 24 Aug 1853 in Calais Cemetery.
ix. UNNAMED DAUGHTER COY, born circa 1857 in Calais, died 20 Oct 1858 age 1y 6m in Calais (g.s.). Buried in Calais Cemetery.
x. CATHERINE COY, born circa Feb 1868 in Calais, died 2 Mar 1868 age 13d in Calais (g.s.). Buried in Calais Cemetery.

DONALD & CHARLOTTE CREARAN?, p. 185

DONALD CREARAN (? Spelling - record not clear), born _____ .
He married before 1847 CHARLOTTE (_____), born _____ . Children:

i. HENRY CREARAN?, born 27 Nov 1847 in Calais (VR).

JOHN & CATHERINE CURRAN, p. 185

JOHN CURRAN, born circa 1811 in Down, Ireland (1850 census). He was a house carpenter. Died before 1860. Census: 1850 in Calais.

He married 7 Oct 1843 in Calais by Elias Kelsey, JP (mrwc:40) CATHERINE MCFARLAND, born circa 1814 in Down, Ireland (1850 census). She was a tailoress. Died June 1879/80 (Mortality Schedule 1880 census). Census: 1850, 60 & 70 in Calais. Children:
- Note – first two children born before marriage date, was there another wife?

i. MARGARET CURRAN, born circa 1836 in St Stephen, NB (1850 census). She was a tailoress. Census: 1850 & 60 in Calais.

* Note – Marriage intentions 30 Apr 1866 VR:1:120 John Leahan and Margaret Curran.

ii. JAMES CURRAN, born 12 Nov 1842 in St Stephen, NB (MSA). He was a truckman. Died 7 Aug 1920 in Calais (MSA). Census: 1850, 60, 70, 80 & 1910 in Calais. He married ca 1879 MARY E. McCONNELL, born ca 1842 in St. Stephen, NB, daughter of PATRICK McCONNELL & MARGARET CANAVAN b/b Ireland. Census: 1880 (age 38), 1910 in Calais.

iii. JOHN CURRAN, born circa 1844 in St Stephen, NB (1850 census). He was a rope maker. He died 14 Mar 1872 age 28 in Calais (adv, sext). Buried in Calais Cemetery. Census: 1850, 60 & 70 in Calais. He married before 1866 ELIZABETH (_____), born ca 1842 in Canada. Census 1870 in Calais.

iv. GEORGE A. CURRAN, born 31 Aug 1846 in Calais (VR). He was a rope maker. Census: 1850, 60 & 70 in Calais.

v. THOMAS CURRAN, born 18 Feb 1847 in Calais (VR). Died 10 Jun 1918 age 72y 3m 5d in Calais (MSA). Census: 1850 thru 1900 (b. Apr 1847) in Calais. He filed marriage int. 3 Nov 1874 in Calais (VR), KATHERINE AHEARN born 21 Aug 1855 in Calais, daughter of THOMAS AHEARN & AUST(?IS) POWERS. She died 11 Apr 1936 in Calais (MSA).

vi. FRANK CURRAN, born circa 1848 in Calais. He was an iron molder. Census: 1860 & 70 in Calais.

vii. ESTHER CURRAN, born circa 1848/50 in Calais (1850 census, age 2). She was a dressmaker. Died 28 Apr 1920 age 70 in Calais (MSA, sfh:3:144). Census: 1850 thru 80, 1900 & 20 in Calais. She married 22 Sept 1873 in Calais by Rev. Father Conton (adv) JOSEPH STEELE, born 16 June 1848 in P.E.I. son of DONALD STEELE & MARY CAMERON. He was of Calais at time of marriage and was a carpenter. Died 14 May 1922 age 74y 11m in Calais (MSA). Census: 1880, 1900 & 20 in Calais.

ANSEL & MARY ANN DAILEY, p. 202

ANSEL DAILEY, born ca 1804 (1850 census has birth in Jay ca 1804, ages in census and death indicate 1804 as birth date) [there is an Ansel born 6 May 1799 in Livermore, ME (VR poor copy on film MSA) son of (Nezar?) Dailey & Elizabeth (_____)]. He was a merchant. Died 6 Feb 1878 age 74 in Calais (obit adv, congo, g.s.). Census: 1850 (age 46), 60 (age 56) & 70 (age 66) in Calais. Buried in Calais Cemetery.

He married MARY ANN (_____), born circa 1810-15 in St Stephen, NB (1850 census). Died 10 Nov 1895 age 81y 15d in Tonawanda, NY (g.s.). Buried in Calais Cemetery. Census: 1850 thru 1880 in Calais. Children:

i. CAROLINE DAILEY, born circa 1835 in St Stephen, NB (1850 census). Died 25 Mar 1897 in Hawaii, where she had lived for about 40 years and she had been a successful teacher (obit adv). Census: 1850 in Calais. She married (_____) KINNEY (her name at time of death).

ii. LAURA H. DAILEY, born circa Oct 1837 in St Stephen, NB (1850 census). She was a teacher. She died age 38y 10m 14 Dec 1875, Machias (obit, g.s.). Buried in Calais Cemetery. Census: 1850 & 60 in Calais. She married 16 Sept 1868 by Rev. E.L. Foster in Calais (VSNB:27:338, int. VR) JAMES H. ROBBINS son of JAMES & MARY ROBBINS (see ROBBINS).

iii. GEORGE S. DAILEY, born 23 Feb 1842 in St Stephen, NB (1850 census, g.s.). Graduated from Calais Academy. Died 14 Jan 1910 in New York (sfh:1:243, g.s.). Buried in Calais Cemetery. Census: 1850 & 60 in Calais. He married 9 Apr 1880 in Albany, NY (times) MINNIE/EMMA A. BIRCHALL, born 18 Aug 1853, died (probably in NY) 12 Oct 1927 (g.s.). Buried in Calais Cemetery.

iv. MARY H. DAILEY, born circa 1844 in St Stephen, NB (1850 census). Died 31 Mar 1881 in Calais (times, g.s.). Census: 1850 thru 1880 (partial paralysis of lower limbs) in Calais.

v. ANSEL DAILEY, Jr., born 24 Apr 1847 in Calais (VR). Died after July 1885 when he was visiting his mother in Calais (adv). Census: 1850, 60 & 70 in Calais. He married 10 Dec 1876 in Foxboro, Ma by Rev. Dyke, GEORGIA PROCTOR of San Jose, CA (adv).

REUBEN & KEZIAH DAMOTH, p. 200

REUBEN DAMOTH, born circa 1802 in Waldoboro, ME (1850 census). Died 16 Feb 1869 age 70 in Calais

(SCC). Census: 1850 & 60 in Calais.

He married 29 Dec 1824 in St Stephen, NB, (CCMR, Jones & Elizabeth Jackson, witnesses at her wedding) KEZIAH JACKSON born circa 1807 in St Stephen, NB (1850 census) d/o WILLIAM JACKSON & MARY DYER, {grand daughter of Jones Dyer, Sr. & Hannah Harrington} (dyerf). Census: 1850 & 60 in Calais. Children:

   i. HARRIET N. DAMOTH, born 15 Jan 1828 in Calais (VR). Probably died in Bennington, NH. Census: 1850 & 60 in Calais. She married ca 1863 FRANK G. SMITH, born in Francestown, NH ca 1827. In 1872 they resided in Antrim, NH and in 1876 Bennington, NH where they remained (antr:685).
   ii. MARY ANN DAMOTH, born circa 1830 in St Patrick, NB (1850 census). Died Nov 1856 in Calais (g.s.). Buried: 4 Nov 1856 in Calais Cemetery. Census: 1850 in Calais.
   iii. MEHITABLE W. DAMOTH, born circa 1833 in St Patrick, NB (1850 census). Census: 1850, 60 & 70 in Calais. She married 29 Sep 1869 by Rev. Howard Sprague in Calais (VSNB:28:2007, union) JOHN MITCHELL.
   iv. UNNAMED CHILD DAMOTH, born circa 1835 in NB. Died age 10 Sep 1845 in Calais (g.s.). Buried: 10 Sep 1845 in Calais Cemetery.
   v. UNNAMED CHILD DAMOTH, born circa 1837 in NB. Died age 8 Sep 1845 in Calais (g.s.). Buried: 7 Sep 1845 in Calais Cemetery.
   vi. SARAH N. DAMOTH, born circa 1840 in St Patrick, NB (1850 census). Bapt. 11 May 1854 in Calais (saint). Census: 1850 & 60 in Calais.
   vii. LOUISA DAMOTH, born circa 1842 in St Patrick, NB (1850 census). Census: 1850 & 60 in Calais.
   viii. GEORGE WILLIAM DAMOTH, born 5 Aug 1846 in Calais (VR). Bapt. 11 May 1854 in Calais (saint). Census: 1850 & 60 in Calais.

DANIEL & MARY ANN DAVIDSON, p. 206

DANIEL DAVIDSON, born circa 1784 in Nova Scotia. He was a ship carpenter. Died Oct 1847 age 85 in Calais (Adv, g.s.). Buried: 22 Oct 1847 in Calais Cemetery. Census: 1830 (3 males, 4 females).

He married MARY ANN CAMPHOR, born circa 1795 in Fredericton, NB (1850 census). Died 16 Mar 1864 age 73y 4m in Calais (VR:3:308, congo). Buried in Calais Cemetery. Census: 1850 & 60 in Calais. Children:

   i. PARKER DAVIDSON, born circa 1816 in St. David, NB (1850 census). He was a ship carpenter. Died 27 May 1895 in Calais (VR, times, MSA). Census: 1850, 60 (age 44 with mother), & 80 (age 70 a pauper, resident in Poor Farm since June 1876) in Calais. He married 1st (int.) 31 May 1846 in Calais (VR:1: 41), married June 1846 (Maine Farmer of 2 July 1846) EDITH TUCKER of Robbinston. He married 2nd 19 Dec 1850 by Thomas D. Williams, JP in Calais (VR:3:146, FJ) ELIZABETH SITE of Calais (VR). Died before 1895 (husband was widower).
   ii. GEORGE DAVIDSON (see BELOW)
   iii. MARIA/MARIE DAVIDSON, born 19 May 1828 in Calais (wnact, MSA). Died 16 Apr 1903 age 75y 18d in Calais (wnact). Census: 1850, 60 & 70 in Calais. She married (int.) 23 Apr 1843 in Calais WILLIAM F. WHITEKNACT, son of JOHN WHITEKNACT & ESTHER CULVER (see WHITEKNACT).
   iv. MARY ANN DAVIDSON, born 16 Dec 1831 in Calais (VR).
   v. ORREN DAVIDSON, born 26 Aug 1834 in Calais (VR). Census: 1850 in Calais.
   vi. ABRAHAM DAVIDSON, born circa 1838 in St. Andrews, NB (1850 census). On a list of men drafted for Civil War but no record of service found. Died after 1875. Census: 1850 & 60 in Calais. He married by Rev. William Carruthers 24 Aug 1871 (adv, VR:3:233) in Calais SARAH C. HATT, she divorced him for non support and intoxication in Apr 1875 (SJC docket # 273).

GEORGE & SARAH DAVIDSON, p. 199

GEORGE H. DAVIDSON, Sr., born 11 Apr 1823 in Calais (VR). son of DANIEL DAVIDSON AND MARY ANN CAMPHOR.. He was a butcher. Died 26 Dec 1890 age 68y 10m in Calais (east:453, adv). Buried in Calais Cemetery. Census: 1850 thru 1880 in Calais.

He married (int.) 18 July 1846 in Calais (VR:1:29) to SARAH `SALLY' SMITH, born May 1822 in St.

David, NB (1850 census). Died Apr 1907 age 85 in Calais (obit, adv). Census: 1850 thru 1900 in Calais. Children:

i. JAMES DAVIDSON, born 24 Mar 1843 in Calais (VR). Died 30 Jan 1927 age 82y 10m in Calais (MSA, sfh:6:145). Census: 1850 thru 1900 in Calais.

ii. GEORGE H. DAVIDSON, Jr., born 29 Dec 1846 in Calais (VR). Enlisted 7 Jan 1865 at age 18 in Co G Me Coast Guard, disc. 6 July 1865, 5'5" with black eyes & dark hair and was a butcher (enlist, cwcard). Died 17 Oct 1887 age 41 (east:396, g.s.). Guardianship for Edward M. & Julie was granted to Henry A. Davidson. Census: 1850 thru 1880 in Calais. He married 8 Apr 1868 by Rev. Dexter in Calais (VR:3:229) REGINA 'JENNIE' CREAMER. Died 21 Feb 1881 in Calais (VR:3:267, g.s.). Buried in Calais Cemetery. Census: 1880 in Calais.

iii. CHARLES F. DAVIDSON, born circa 1849 in Calais. He was a Grocer. Died after 1870. Census: 1850 thru 80 in Calais. Married 2 Nov 1870 by Rev. William Carruthers in Calais (adv) LOVINIA A. DINSMORE, born ca 1848 in NB. Census: 1880 in Calais. [adv of 26 Sept 1900 – News received in Calais of death of Charles Davidson formerly of Calais, which occurred on a steamer, on the passage from Cape Nome to Seattle].

iv. ANNIE DORCAS DAVIDSON, born 7 Oct 1851 in Calais (MSA). She was a dressmaker. She died 7 July 1935 age 83y 9m in Calais (MSA). Census: 1860, 70, 80 & 1900 in Calais. She married 15 Sept 1882 in Calais (VR:2:19) NOAH SMITH McGERRY (see McGERRY).

v. AMOS HENRY DAVIDSON, born circa 1853 in Calais. He was a designer & builder of yachts and boats and senior member of Davidson Bros. Boat Builders. Died 2 Nov 1901 age 48y 2m 21d in Calais (adv, MSA). Buried in Calais Cemetery. Census: 1860 thru 1900 in Calais. He married ELLA F. (_____), born ca June 1860. She died after her husband (his obit). Census: 1880 & 1900 in Calais. She married 2nd 10 Jan 1926 in Ballouville, CT to George L. Cook (adv).

vi. JOSEPH T. DAVIDSON, born 1 Mar 1857 in Calais, died 29 Oct 1933 in South Portland, ME (MSA). He was a boat builder. Census: 1860 thru 1880 in Calais, 1900 in So Portland. He married 8 Apr 1883 in Calais (VR:2:25) CARRIE M. LEEMAN. She was born 24 May 1862 in Deer Isle, NB, daughter of HENRY LEEMAN & MALETIA ABBOTT, died 5 Sept 1920 in South Portland, ME (MSA). Census: 1900 in So. Portland.

vii. ORRIN DAVIDSON, born Apr 1860 in Calais. In 1887 Dir. he was a brick mason. Died Jan 1951 (g.s.). Buried in Calais Cemetery. Census: 1860 thru 1900 in Calais. He married 1 Aug 1882 by Rev. Padelford in Calais (VR:2:19) AMY ELLEN WOODBURY, daughter of WILLIAM T. WOODBURY AND FRANCES D. WINCHELL (see WOODBURY).

viii. WILLIAM DAVIDSON, born circa 1863 in Calais. Died in Mar 1863 age 9weeks in Calais (sext). Buried: 8 Mar 1863 in Calais Cemetery.

WILLIAM & SARAH DEMING, p. 179

CHARLES DEMING born 6 March 1774 in Needham, MA the son of JONATHAN DEMING & ESTHER EDES. He also resided in Brighton, MA where he kept "The Bull's Head Tavern"; also in Marlboro, NH and Fitzwilliam, NH, where he became active in the Masons. He married 24 July 1793 in Needham, MA MEHITABLE FULLER born 9 January 1777 the dau. of MOSES FULLER & ELIZABETH NEWELL, she died 5 Sept 1867. They had thirteen children the 8th being William of Calais. Their 4th child, Anne, married Samuel F. Baker who also resided in Calais (see BARKER). [dem: 92, 307, biorev:431].

WILLIAM DEMING, Sr., born 21 Feb 1804 in Marlboro, NH (biorev:431, obit dem). In 1818 he was working with his uncle, Moses Fuller of Lubec, as a clerk (pkjdt:12). He was a bank cashier, ran a Variety store, was treasurer of the International Steamship Co. and treasurer of City of Calais (obit). Resided in Calais after 1824 when he moved from Brighton, MA, he was a Lt. Col. in State Militia 1834 (dem:170). Died 3 Mar 1882 age 78 in Calais (dem:170, times, adv). Probate of Estate in Machias Me (owned land in Superior, WI, mentioned in will of 3 Aug 1880). Census: 1830 (2 males, 2 females), 40 (3 males, 4 females), 50, 60 & 80 in Calais.

He married Oct 1826 (dem:170) SARAH M. WILCOX, born 24 Feb 1806 in Dartmouth, MA (dem:170, 1850 census), daughter of BENJAMIN WILCOX & JANE ATWOOD. She died 21 Oct 1878 age 72 in Calais (obit, adv). Buried in Calais Cemetery. Census: 1850 & 60 Calais. Children:

i. WILLIAM DEMING, Jr., born 22 Oct 1828 in Calais (VR, demo:307, cal2:9= b. 1827). Bapt. 4 Oct 1835 in Calais (congo). He was a clerk. Resided in Nova Scotia and St. Stephen, NB. Died 26 Jan 1872 age 43 in Calais (demo:307, obit, prbt of will 10 May 1872, adv). Buried in Calais Cemetery. Census: 1850, 60 & 70 in

Calais. He married 3 Nov 1852 in Calais (VR) MARY ELIZABETH WAITE, daughter of BENJAMIN FRANKLIN WAITE & HANNAH TOWNSLEY TODD (see WAITE).

ii. SARAH JANE ATWOOD DEMING, born 18 Feb 1831 in Calais (VR, dem:170). Bapt. 4 Oct 1835 in Calais (congo). Died 21 Mar 1901, just a few days before her sister, in the house where she was born in Calais (adv, dem, mentioned in father's will 1882, MSA, g.s.). Buried in Calais Cemetery. Census: 1850, 60, & 80 in Calais. She married at home of her parents 8 Jun 1851 in Calais (VR, dem:170) ISAAC PURINGTON Jr. born 30 Jan 1822 son of ISAAC & MARY R. PURINGTON, Sr. He was a master mariner, captain of ship *Golconda* & *Congress of Boston*. His wife traveled around the world aboard ship with him, for several years. He died 30 Jan 1881 on his 59th birthday (adv, prbt, g.s.). Census: 1880 in Calais.

iii. CHARLES LEONARD DEMING, born 24 Jan 1834 in Calais (VR, dem:307). Bapt. 4 Oct 1835 in Calais (congo). He was a merchant & grocer, he succeeded his father in the family business, Deming & Sons (CEV:17). Died 3 Jan 1905 age 70 in Calais (obit adv, MSA). Buried in Calais Cemetery. Census: 1850, 60 & 80 in Calais. Served in Civil War in 1863 (Home Guards). He married 30 May 1859 in Calais (VR, dem:307) SARAH ELIZABETH BARNARD, daughter of GEORGE SULLIVAN BARNARD & FRANCES L. STARBOARD. (see BARNARD).

iv. EMMA MARCELIA DEMING, born 23 Apr 1836 in Calais (VR, dem:171). Bapt. 10 Dec 1837 in Calais (congo). She was mentioned in father's will in 1882. Died 6 May 1883 age 47 in St. Stephen, NB (obit, bay, times, at home of brother-in-law, Clement Eaton). Census: 1850, 60 & 80 in Calais. She married 25 Sep 1865 in Calais (saint, dem, east:216) Gen. GEORGE FREDERICK GRANGER, born (1) 10 July 1837 in Calais (cal2:12) born (2) 13 June 1838 (obit), son of JOSEPH & HARRIET (GRANGER) GRANGER. He was in the Civil War in Co A of the 9th Maine, attended Bowdoin College, worked in his fathers law office, and was a member of City Council (obit). He was a surveyor & lawyer. Census: 1850, 60 & 80 in Calais. Died 10 Feb 1883 age 45y in Calais (east:357, adv). Census 1850 & 60 in Calais.

v. REBECCA LEONARD DEMING, born 13 Jul 1839 in Calais (VR, dem:171). Bapt. 14 June 1840 in Calais (congo). Died 2 Apr 1901 just a few days after her husband, and her sister in Calais (adv, mentioned in father's will in 1882). Census: 1850 in Calais, 1861 & 71 in St. Stephen, NB. She married 11 Oct 1859 in Calais (VR, eaton: 70, dem:171) CLEMENT BELCHER EATON, born 26 Apr 1824 in Cornwallis, NS, son of WILLIAM EATON & NANCY DeWOLF (eaton:101). He was in the wholesale grocery business, a member of the town council and held office of Mayor of St. Stephen in 1877 (obit adv). Died 29 Mar 1901 in Calais (MSA). Both are buried in Rural Cemetery in St. Stephen, NB (rural: 34). Census 1861 & 71 in St. Stephen, NB.

vi. ALBERT EDWIN DEMING, born 21 Mar 1842 in Calais (VR). Died 14 Sep 1842 in Calais (obit, gaz). Buried: 18 Sep 1842 in Calais Cemetery.

vii. MARIETTA HUNT DEMING, born 21 Jan 1850 in Calais (VR, dem:171). Died 19 Feb 1856 in Calais (VR:3302, dem:171). Buried: 21 Feb 1856 in Calais Cemetery. Census: 1850 in Calais.

JOHN P. & SARAH B. DESHON, p. 192

JOHN P. DESHON, born 28 May 1801 in Mass (1850 census, g.s.). He was a painter. Bapt. 6 Mar 1836 in Calais (congo). Died 25 Sep 1854 in Calais (g.s.). Buried: 26 Sep 1854 in Calais Cemetery. Census: 1830 (3 males, 1 female), 40 (4 males, 2 females), 50 in Calais.

He married circa 1822 SARAH BRINLEY JONES, born 8 Jun 1803 in Ellsworth Me (VR, g.s.), daughter of THEODORE JONES & KATHERINE WINTHROP SARGENT. Died 28 Jan 1849 in Calais (VR, FJ). Buried: 30 Jan 1849 in Calais Cemetery. Children:

i. ELIZABETH DESHON, born 22 Sep 1823 in Calais, died 22 Oct 1826 in Calais (VR:1:233, g.s.). Buried in Calais Cemetery.

ii. MARY ELIZABETH DESHON, born 15 May 1826 in Calais (VR, g.s.). Died 22 Feb 1827 in Calais (VR:1:233). Buried in Calais Cemetery.

iii. HENRY SARGENT DESHON, born 19 Feb 1828 in Calais (VR). Bapt. 13 Mar 1836 in Calais (congo). Died Jul 1909 in New York, NY (obit, adv).

iv. CHARLES DESHON, born 2 Jan 1830 in Calais. Bapt. 13 Mar 1836 in Calais (congo). Visited Calais from Pittsfield, PA in Sept 1888 for the first time since he left in 1841 (adv). Census: 1850 in Calais.

v. LEONARD ABOTT DESHON, born 16 Jan 1835 in Calais, died 30 Aug 1839 in Calais (VR:1:233, g.s.). Bapt. 13 Mar 1836 in Calais (congo). Buried in Calais Cemetery.

vi. FRANCIS DESHON, born 9 Nov 1837 in Calais. Census: 1850 in Calais.
vii. CATHERINE DESHON, born 26 Mar 1839 in Calais, died 5 Nov 1840 in Calais (VR:1:233, g.s.). Buried in Calais Cemetery.
viii. CHARLOTTE TWEED DESHON, born 19 Apr 1840 in Calais, died 19 Nov 1848 in Calais (VR, g.s.). Buried in Calais Cemetery.

JOHN P. DESHON married 2nd in 1850/51 by Rev. S. H. Keeler JOSEPHINE CLARK of Calais (VR:1:147), born ca 1831 in Machias. Census 1850 (age 19 born in Machias, in household of John P. Deshon with her daughter, Caroline N. Clark age 2).

EDWARD & MARGARET DILLON, p. 209

EDWARD DILLON, on his application for citizenship 9 Aug 1838 he states he was born in 1788 at Belleymanoh, Ireland, he left Ireland 5 May 1819, arrived at St. Andrews, NB 17 June 1819, arrived at Calais 5 May 1821 where he now resides (SJC:16:178 doc # 805). Died 14 Jan 1840 in Calais (VR). Probate of estate, George Downes appointed executor, Margaret appointed guardian of daughter, Sarah Ann. Census: 1830 [Dilling] (1 male, 2 females).

He married MARGARET (_____), born circa 1781 in Antrim, Ireland (1850 census). Died ca 1862 (union dated 17 June 1862 death of Margaret Dillon age 80). Census: 1840 (widow, 2 females), 1850 with dau & husband, James Boyd, 1860 in Calais. Children:

i. SARAH ANN DILLON, born 12 May 1825 in Calais (VR). Died after 1891 when she was dropped from rolls at Congo. church. Census: 1850 & 60 in Calais. She married 1st 4 Oct 1846 in St Stephen, NB JAMES BOYD (CCMR), born circa 1822 in St. Andrews, N B (see BOYD). She married 2nd 21 Jun 1864 by Rev. S. H. Keeler in Calais (VR:3:207) JAMES ROBERTSON.

JOSEPH & ELIZA DIXON, p. 190

JOSEPH DIXON, born circa 1816, in St. John's River, NB (1850 census). Census: 1850 in Calais.

He married (int.) 4 Dec 1842 in Calais (VR) ELIZA COFFRIN born Sep 1814 in St. Andrews, NB (1850 census). Census: 1850 in Calais. Children:

i. CHARLES DIXON, born 13 Jan 1844 in Calais (VR). Census: 1850 in Calais.
ii. SAMUEL DIXON, born 24 Jun 1846 in Calais (VR). Census: 1850 (name Jane age 4) in Calais.
iii. MARGARET DIXON, born circa 1848. Census: 1850 in Calais.

EVERARD H. & ANNA DOE, p. 193

Dr. THEOPHILUS[6] DOE born Parsonsfield, ME 10 Nov 1795 son of Levi[5], John[4], Daniel[3], John[2] and Nicholas[1]. Name of his 1st wife is unknown. He married 2nd CORDELIA BLAKE born Brewer, ME. He studied medicine with Dr. Colby of Ossipee, NH and practiced at Lubec, ME and Deer Island. Records of Washington County show his first purchase 10 April 1827, and many more up to 1865. He was very successful both as a physician and in real estate speculations. He died in Bangor, ME 10 Feb 1879 (doe:.62). The only child by his 1st wife was EVERARD H. DOE of Calais. [? That there was a 1st marriage – In VR of Lubec there were children born to Theophilus and Cordelia in 1825 and 1828 but no birth recorded for Everard].

EVERARD H. DOE born circa 1830 in Lubec Me, resided in Castine, ME moved to Calais in 1847 (doe:62-94). Died 9 Nov 1848 age 27y 7m in Calais (g.s.). Buried: 12 Nov 1848 in Calais Cemetery.

He married 15 May 1845 ANNA[8] EATON born 11 Oct 1819 in Cornwallis, NS daughter of WILLIAM[7] EATON and NANCY DeWOLF, granddaughter of Elisha[6], David[5], James[4], Jonathan[3], Thomas[2], John[1], sister of Clement Eaton who married Rebecca Deming (eaton:42,56, see Deming). Anna died 2 Sept 1862 age 42 (VR, g.s.). Census: 1860 (name Caroline) in Calais, 1861 (with sister Rebecca Eaton) in St. Stephen, NB. Children:

i. FLORA ETTA DOE, born 26 Mar 1846 in Calais (VR). Died after 1916 (doe:94). Census: 1860 in Calais. She married 1 Oct 1867 (VR) FRANCIS A. EVERETT. Resided in San Jose, CA in 1918 (doe:94).
ii. FRANCES M. DOE, born circa 1848 (eaton:42). Died 26 Apr 1864 age 15y 8m in Calais (g.s.). Buried: Apr 1864 in Calais Cemetery. Census: 1860 in Calais, 1861 with uncle Clement Eaton, in St. Stephen, NB.

JONATHAN & MARGARET DOW, p. 223

JONATHAN DOW, born 12 May 1805 in Whitefield ME (VR, 1850 census has Jefferson), son of JERIMAH DOW & REBEKAH GLIDDEN (dow:627). He became a in Lt. in 1st Brig 7th Div. on 20 Mar 1831 in the Militia in Calais (milit). He was a millwright, then a bridge builder & engineer. He moved with is family to St. Anthony, Minneapolis, MN about 1855 (dlund). Died 30 July 1859 in St. Anthony, MN (bible). Census: 1830 (6 males, 1 female), 40 (6 males, 2 females), 50 in Calais.

He married 14 Aug 1828 in Calais by Rev. Josiah Eaton (cal2:46) MARGARET DYER, born 7 Aug 1809 in Calais (1850 census, bible). Died Sept 1895 (bible). Census: 1850 in Calais. Children:

i. WILLIAM LEWIS/Louis DOW, born 29 Aug 1829 in Calais (VR). He was a millwright. Died 9 Mar 1903 in Minneapolis, MN (dlund). Census: 1850 in Calais. He married, with parents consent, on 8 Jun 1851 in St Stephen, NB (CCMR) MARY E. SAVAGE, born 24 Mar 1834, daughter of ANDREW SAVAGE, died 20 July 1918, poss. in MN (dlund).

ii. HENRY AUGUSTUS DOW, born 18 Feb 1831 in Calais (VR). Died 9 Feb 1889 in St. Anthony Falls, MN (bible) Census: 1850 in Calais. He married 22 Sept 1860 in Minneapolis, MN LEONIECE B. McKENZIE, born 15 Sept 1831, Columbia Falls, Me, died 31 Oct 1907 St. Anthony Falls, MN (bible).

iii. MARGARET MELISSA DOW, born 6 Feb 1833 in Baring ME (Calais VR). Died 9 Feb 1838 in Calais (VR:1:240). Buried in Calais Cemetery.

iv. LLOYD ULMER DOW/ LEWIS DOWD, born 28 Jul 1835 in Calais (VR). He enlisted 29 Apr 1861 at Fort Snelling, MN in Co. E of the 1st Minnesota Infantry and was wounded, partially incapacitated, (military records under Lloyd W. Dow), he worked as a mailman (dlund). Died 7 Oct 1906 Mawrer, McLean Co. ND, buried in Forest Hill Cemetery, Owatonna, MN (dlund). Census: 1850 in Calais. He married 13 Oct 1863 in St. Anthony, MN, ANNA MARIA SCOTT, born 30 Dec 1837 (poss. in Calais), died 21 Sept 1911 at age 73 in Little Falls, MN, buried in North Star Cemetery, St. Cloud, MN (obit, dlund). Lloyd walked out of his Sauk Rapids home on 28 March 1878 never to return. He set up a house at Clinton Falls with EVA JOHNSON, born ca 1856 in NY, died 12 May 1907 and two of his sons by Anna, changed his name to Lewis Dowd and also his sons last name and lived there as a happy family until his death, Lewis Dowd & Eva Dowd are buried together in Forest Hill Cemetery, Owatonna, MN, according to cemetery records (dlund).

v. ABIGAIL AZUBY/AZUBA DOW, born 7 Oct 1837 in Calais (VR). Census: 1850 in Calais.

vi. JOHN FAIRFIELD DOW, born 27 Dec 1837 in Topsfield, ME (Calais VR). Died 6 Oct 1844 in Calais (VR:1:240). Buried: 8 Oct 1844 in Calais Cemetery.

vii. PAULINA JOSEPHINE DOW, born 27 Dec 1841 in Calais, died 5 Sep 1845 in Calais (VR:1:240). Buried: 7 Sep 1845 in Calais Cemetery.

viii. THIRZA SOPHIA DOW, born 17 Feb 1844 in Calais, died 10 Feb 1848 in Calais (VR:1:240). Buried: 17 Feb 1848 in Calais Cemetery.

ix. ADELBERT FAIRFIELD DOW, born 17 Apr 1846 in Calais (VR). Died 10 Sept 1863 (bible), poss. in MN. Census: 1850 in Calais.

x. JOHN DOW, born circa 1848 in Calais. Died circa 1850 in Calais (Mortality schedule age 2 1850 census). Buried in Calais Cemetery.

- NOTE. Family bible of Jonathan Dow of Calais dated March 1850 copied by Katherine Stone Moore in 1969 (sent by Ruth E. Dow of Nobleboro, Me).

OLIVER & ELIZABETH DOW, p. 214

OLIVER DOW, born 27 Dec 1802 (g.s.), in Vassalboro, ME, son of JOHN DOW AND ZELPHAH LINCOLN (china:28). He was a millwright. Died 13 Jun 1874 in Milltown ME (g.s., dow:207). Buried in Calais Cemetery. Census: 1840 (4 males, 2 females), 50, 60 & 70 in Calais.

He married 1st 6 Oct 1831 in Westmoreland Co., NB (milb), ELIZABETH 'Betty' MILLBURN, born circa 1810 in Winsyke, Eng. (g.s. has 2 l's in Millburn), bapt. 30 Oct 1813, in Black Cleugh, Stanhope Parish, Durham, England (milb), Wardell Parish, Durham, England (dow:207), daughter of JEREMIAH MILBURN & SARAH SMITH, they were married 24 Dec 1808 (milb). She died 8 Aug 1857 in Calais (obit, adv). Buried on 9 Aug 1857 in Calais Cemetery. Census: 1850 in Calais. Children:

i. JOHN W. DOW, born in NB. Died 1 Sep 1834 in Calais (?).
ii. ISAAC WASHINGTON DOW, born 7 May 1833 in Hopewell, NB (1850 census). He was a millwright in Calais, he moved to Kansas about 1852, where he was Treasurer of Woodson, Co. KS in 1869 (VSNB:28:2002:2042). He served as Cap't in Civil War (dow:208). Died 27 Sept 1913 in Neosho Falls, Kansas (dow:208). Census: 1850 & 60 in Calais. He married 1st SARAH MILLER, who died 8 Apr 1866 (dowr). He married 2nd 18 Dec 1872 MARY J. CONNOR, born 31 Dec 1833, died 14 Apr 1895 (dow:208).
iii. SARAH JANE DOW, born 8 Feb 1835, in Grand Manan, N B. In 1887 she visited Calais from Eldorado, Kansas (adv). Died 20 June 1907 in New Hampton, Iowa (dow:208). Census: 1850 & 60 in Calais. She married 1856/57 by S. H. Keeler in Calais (VR, lisa = 8 June 1856) HARRISON HENRY INNESS, born 1 Apr 1833 in St. Stephen, NB, son of GEORGE INNESS & MARCIA HALL (lisa, 1851 census). Harrison Inness who has long resided in Milltown, recently [Dec 1869] removed to Neosho Falls, Kansas. We learn from Kansas 'Patriot' he has leased the Falls House and is keeping a good hotel (VSNB:28:2068). In Jan 1883 he was running the Dexter House under the firm name of H.H. Inness & Co. (adv). Later had a hotel in Pierce City, MO (milb:2:14-16). He died 23 Dec 1893 in Neosho Falls (dow:208). Census: 1851 in St. Stephen, NB, 1860 in Calais.
iv. JOHN OLIVER DOW, born 15 Nov 1836 in Calais (VR). Served in Civil War, a Cpl. in Co. D 6th Maine (NRMS:238). He was a machinist. Died 12 Feb 1905 in Neosho Falls (dow:208). Census: 1850 & 60 in Calais. He married 28 Mar 1865 MARY CATHERINE MANN, born 27 June 1843 in Hillhall, PA, she was living in Neosho Falls in 1918 (dow:208).
v. ISAIAH LINCOLN DOW, born 3 Jun 1839 in Calais (VR, death rec. = Millinocket). He was a millwright then a carpenter and master builder, he built many of the houses in Danforth. Died 7 Apr 1918 age 78y in Danforth Me (weston:212, MSA, dow:208). Buried: Maple Cemetery Danforth (moca). Census: 1850 & 60 in Calais. He married 1st 29 Nov 1865 in Amity, ME (VR) SARAH H. MAXELL /MAXWELL, born Mar 1841 in Orient, ME, daughter of THOMAS JEFFERSON MAXELL & JOANNA LIBBY. Died 27 July 1871 30y 4m (weston:212). Buried Peter's Cove Cemetery in Orient, ME. He married 2nd 1 Jan 1872 in Amity (VR) EMILY JUDSON MAXELL /MAXWELL, born May 1853 in Orient, sister of his first wife (weston:213). She died 11 Sept 1916 (dow:208, g.s.). Buried: Maple Cemetery Danforth (moca).
vi. MARY ELIZABETH 'Lizzie' DOW, born 6 Apr 1842 in Calais (VR). She was a teacher. Died 30 May 1914 (dow:208). Census: 1850 & 60 in Calais. She married 4 Jan 1862 by Rev. H. A. Philbrook in St. Stephen, NB (CCMR) JOHN ALEXANDER INNESS, born 28 Feb 1831, son of GEORGE INNESS & MARCIA HALL (lisa, brother of Harrison, above). He was a carpenter and millman. He died 11 Oct 1903 (lisa). Census: 1851 & 61 in St. Stephen, NB.
vii. JEREMIAH EDWIN DOW, born 6 Apr 1842 in Calais, died 11 Apr 1842 age 6 days in Calais (g.s., VR). Buried: 12 Apr 1842 in Calais Cemetery.
viii. GEORGE WILLARD DOW, born 1 Jul 1849 in Calais (VR). He served in Indian Wars in 19th Kansas Vol. in 1868 a farmer (dowr). He was a carpenter of Guthrie, OK (dow:209). Died 26 Aug 1940 in San Gabriel, CA and is buried in Sawtelle National Military Home Cemetery (dowr). Census: 1850 & 60 in Calais, 1880 in Neosho Falls, KS. He married 1 Nov 1874 SARAH LUELLA 'ELLA' McCLANAHAN at her home in Neosho Falls, KS (dowr), born 7 Apr 1844 (dow:209, dowr: Beverly Murphy's chart).

He married 2nd 6 Nov 1868 in Calais (VR:3, SCC) MARY ANN BRACKETT born ca 1818, daughter of JOHN BRACKETT AND NANCY JOHNSON, and widow of Thomas McNear (see BRACKETT & McNEAR). Died 19 Sept 1904 in Calais (MSA). Census: 1880 (living with daughter Harriet Brooks family).

GEORGE & BETSEY DOWNES, p. 210

Capt. SHUBAEL DOWNES, born 31 Oct 1741, son of SAMUEL DOWNES & TEMPERANCE TYLER, was one of the original proprietors of Calais (beg:22, 44). He married 7 May 1775 LYDIA BANGS, born 14 Sept 1754, daughter of JOSHUA BANGS & MARY HATCH. (bangs: 66). Their 6th child, George Downes settled in Calais. Their 2nd child, Shubael, Jr., born in Walpole, MA (VR), also lived in Calais, but does not have children listed in book 1 of the Calais Vital Records.

GEORGE DOWNES, born 29 Aug 1793 in Walpole, MA (bowcat:8). Bapt. May 1830 in Calais (congo). Attended Bowdoin College (bowcat:8). Came to Calais in 1816 and was the first regularly established lawyer. He was admitted to practice law June 1822 (SJC). He became a Capt. on 22 Apr 1824, a Maj. On 22 June 1826, a Lt. Col. on 17 Sept 1827 and a Col. on 31 May 1829 in the 1st Brig. 7th Div. of the Militia in Calais (milit). He was Master of St. Croix Lodge, No. 46 in 1829 (lodge:43). He was a deacon in Congo Church 1838-1869. He served in both the State Legislature 1822 and State Senate 1855. When Calais was incorporated as a city in 1850 he was elected its first Mayor. He was the first president of the Calais Bank, serving from 1832 until compelled by old age, he relinquished the duties of the office to his son, Lemuel G. Downes (biorev:336). Died 4 Oct 1869 in Calais (congo., g.s., east:241). Buried in Calais Cemetery. Probate of his estate in Machias, he left no will. Census: 1830 (4 males, 6 females), 40 (5 males, 5 females) thru 1860 in Calais.

He married circa 1821 in Calais (biorev:336, east:241) BETSEY L. DANFORD, born circa 1802 in Wiscasset, ME, daughter of PAUL DANFORD & MARY COTHRAN. Bapt. 25 May 1828 in Calais (congo). Died 13 Nov 1881 age 79y 9m in Calais (congo, g.s., east:346). Buried in Calais Cemetery. Census: 1850 thru 1880 in Calais. Children:

i. CAROLINE DOWNES, born 8 Dec 1822 in Calais, died 27 Jan 1824 in Calais (VR:1:237). Buried in Calais Cemetery.

ii. MARY DANFORD DOWNES, born 14 Aug 1824 in Calais (VR, g.s.). Bapt. May 1830 in Calais (congo). Died 9 Jul 1851 age 25 in Calais (congo, adv, g.s.). Buried in Calais Cemetery. She married Sept 1849 in Calais CHARLES EDWARD SWAN, born 5 Sept 1822 in Winslow, ME, son of FRANCIS SWAN AND HANNAH CHILD (mop:255). He was a physician and graduated from Bowdoin Medical School in Brunswick, ME (bowhis:603). He began his practice in 1847 in Calais working with Dr. Job Holmes, at that time they made their own medicines, until 1864 when Dr. Holmes died. He was the director of the choir of the Congregational Church in Calais. After Mary died leaving twin daughters, who both died young, He married 8 Sept 1890 Mrs. Minerva (King) Horton, widow of Thomas and daughter of Gilman King who survived him. He was Mayor of Calais 1897-98. He died 13 July 1908 (obit, g.s.) in Calais. Buried in Calais Cemetery (see also SWAN).

iii. GEORGE DOWNES, born 29 Aug 1826 in Calais, died 23 Aug 1827 in Calais (VR:1:237). Buried in Calais Cemetery.

iv. GEORGE EDWARD DOWNES, born 29 Apr 1828 in Calais (VR). Bapt. May 1830 in Calais (congo). Graduated in class of 1851 from Bowdoin College, in Brunswick ME. He was in Civil War 1861-1862, a Pvt. in Co A 5th Regt. Maine Inf. (cwcard). He was an attorney and municipal judge. Died 17 Sep 1882 in Calais (g.s., will probated 1883, bowd:alumni files). Buried in Calais Cemetery. Census: 1850, 60 & 70 in Calais. He married 24 Aug 1858 by Rev. Mr. Jackson in Calais (adv). MARTHA PRESCOTT PIKE, daughter of WILLIAM CORNELIUS PIKE JR. AND FRANCES CAMPBELL TODD. Divorced Oct 1879 in Machias Me (east:329). Census: 1880 with daughter and sister in Calais (see PIKE).

v. CAROLINE PIKE DOWNES, born 12 Feb 1830 in Calais (VR). Bapt. May 1830 in Calais (congo). Died 25 Jun 1901 in Calais (MSA, obit). Census: 1850, 60 & 80 in Calais. She married 11 Nov 1863 by Rev. S. H. Keeler in Calais (VR, congo) LYMAN C. BAILEY, born ca 1835, died 1890 (g.s.). Census: 1880 in Calais.

vi. HENRY RICHARD DOWNES, born 17 Sep 1832 in Calais (VR, bowhis:678). Bapt. 8 Dec 1833 in Calais (congo). Graduated in class of 1853 from Bowdoin College in Brunswick ME, studied law at Harvard. Practiced in Sioux City, Iowa and then moved to Presque Isle in 1858 (bowhis:678). He was an attorney, Selectman, Treasurer and Clerk of Presque Isle and Judge of Probate in Aroostook County. Died 24 Oct 1883 in Presque Isle (obit, bowhis:678, alumni file, adv, g.s.). Buried in Calais Cemetery. Census: 1850 in Calais. He married 4 June 1862 (his obit, bowhis:678) VASHTI HARRIET WHIDDEN, born Mar 1833 in Canada (1900 census) of Presque Isle, Me at time of marriage. Census: 1900 in Houlton, ME. They resided in Presque Isle (bowhis:678).

vii. ELIZABETH PIKE DOWNES, born 6 Mar 1834 in Calais, died 20 Mar 1834 in Calais (VR:1:237). Bapt. 18 Mar 1834 in Calais (congo). Buried in Calais Cemetery.

viii. EDMUND MONROE DOWNES, born 24 Aug 1835 in Calais, died 10 Apr 1852 in Calais (adv - drowned, g.s.). Bapt. 15 Nov 1835 in Calais (congo). Buried: 12 Apr 1852 in Calais Cemetery. Census: 1850 in Calais.

ix. JOHN DOWNES, born 12 Jan 1837 in Calais, died 14 Jan 1837 in Calais (VR:1:237). Buried in Calais Cemetery.

x. DANFORD DOWNES, born 30 Jan 1838 in Calais, died 1 Feb 1838 in Calais (VR:1:237). Buried in Calais Cemetery.

xi. LEMUEL GROSVENOR DOWNES, born 26 Oct 1839 in Calais (VR, bowhis:747). Bapt. 19 Jan 1840 in Calais (congo). Graduated in class of 1860 from Bowdoin College, in Brunswick ME, was admitted to the bar in 1863 (bowhis:747). He was an attorney and Judge of Probate. Elected Mayor of Calais in 1876, served in the State Executive council in 1874, 1878, 1890-94, Treasurer of City in 1889. He also served as President of the Calais National Bank, President of the St. Croix Shoe Co., President of the Maine Water Co. and Treasurer of the Ferry Point Bridge Co. (RMM:23, biorev:337). In partnership with Mr. George A. Curran he established an insurance business in Halliday's building on Union Street in Calais (CEV:30). Died 5 Dec 1895 in Calais (VR, obit, times). Census: 1850, 60 & 80 in Calais. He married 28 Jun 1866 (RMM, bowhis:747). AUGUSTA HALE WADSWORTH, born ca 1840 in Pembroke, daughter of LEWIS L. & MARIE H. WADSWORTH of Pembroke (wads:219). She died 31 May 1888 in Calais (g.s., adv.). Buried in Calais Cemetery. Census: 1880 in Calais.

xii. MARTHA HELEN TRASK DOWNES, born 17 Apr 1842 in Calais, died Oct 1858 in Calais (congo, g.s.). Bapt. 11 Sept 1842 in Calais (congo). Buried: 18 Oct 1858 in Calais Cemetery. Census: 1850 in Calais.

xiii. CHARLOTTE LOUISA GROSVENOR DOWNES, born 3 Dec 1842 in Calais, died 9 May 1846 in Calais (VR:1:237, union age 16). Buried in Calais Cemetery.

- Note: father and 3 sons graduated from Bowdoin College and became lawyers.

WILLIAM & MARY DOYLE, p. 205

WILLIAM DOYLE, born circa 1810 in Ireland. Census: 1840, 50 & 60 in Calais.
He married MARY (_____) , born circa 1819 in Ireland. Died 12 Jan 1876 in Calais (congo). Census: 1850 & 60 in Calais. Children:

i. CAROLINE 'Carrie' A. DOYLE (twin), born circa 1838 in St. Stephen, NB (1850 census). Census: 1850 in Calais. She married 31 Dec 1859 by Rev. S. H. Keeler in Calais (VR:3:174, stack:237 = 1 Jan 1860) CHARLES^6 STACKPOLE, born 15 Feb 1835 in Durham, Me, son of SAMUEL O.^{5} & SARAH ROBINSON, JOHN^4, JAMES^3, PHILIP^2, JAMES^1, he was a farmer and he died 3 Dec 1913 (stack: 2nd edition:237, 1st edition:150).

ii. WILLIAM DOYLE Jr., (twin), born circa 1838 in St. Stephen, NB (1850 census). Served in Civil War in Co. D 6th Maine, he died 25 May 1864 in Andersonville, GA, buried there in National Cemetery grave #1359 (cwcard, NRMS:239). He was a meat cutter. Census: 1850 & 60 in Calais. He married (int.) 2 Apr 1861 (VR) ADELAIDE CLEAVES .

iii. JOHN DOYLE, born circa 1841, died 11 Jun 1846 age 5 years in Calais (VR).

iv. EDWARD DOYLE, born circa 1842 in Calais (1850 census). Census: 1850 & 60 in Calais.

v. MARGARET DOYLE, born 7 May 1845 in Calais (VR). Census: 1850 & 60 in Calais.

vi. JAMES DOYLE, born circa 1849 in Calais (1850 census). Census: 1850 & 60 in Calais.

WILLIAM & NANCY DRUGAN, p. 195

WILLIAM C. DRUGAN, Sr., born circa 1817 at Termoine, County of Tyrene in Ireland. Left Ireland in 1836 arrived in Calais in Aug 1841, applied for citizenship 26 Mar 1844 (SJC:8:47) Naturalized 7 Oct 1852 (irmch). He was a merchant & tailor. Died 10 Jul 1865 age 70y 2m 12d in Calais (VR:3:312, Probate of estate has date of death 8th July). Census: 1840 (name spelled Dougan 4 males, 2 females), 50 & 60 in Calais.

He married 8 Aug 1835 in St Andrews, NB (CCMR, he of St. Andrews she of St. Stephen), NANCY ANN TOPPING, born circa 1820, on Atlantic Ocean (1850 census), daughter of ROBERT TOPPING AND MARTHA FALES, both born in Ireland. She died 25 Apr 1892 in Milltown, NB (obit, adv, MSA). Census: 1850, 60 & 70 in Calais. Children:

i. JOHN DRUGAN, born 20 Jun 1837 in Calais (VR). Died before 1865 (not mentioned in father's will). Census: 1850 in Calais.

ii. WILLIAM C. DRUGAN, Jr., born 17 May 1839 in Calais (VR). He was a tailor. Died after 1865 (administrator of father's will, as eldest son). Census: 1850 & 60 in Calais. He married (___?___) and his wife died of TB 28 Mar 1876 in Calais (adv).

iii. JAMES DRUGAN, born 3 May 1841 in Calais (VR). Died 1 Jun 1857 age 16 in Calais (obit). Buried: 25

Jun 1857 in Calais Cemetery. Census: 1850 in Calais.

iv. REBECCA ANNIE DRUGAN, born 20 Jun 1843 in Calais (VR). She was a tailoress. Census: 1850 & 60 in Calais. She possibly married twice – 1st 20 Sept 1865 by Rev. Edwin R. Murray in Calais GEORGE C. McALLISTER of St. Stephen (VR:3:214) and 2nd, 24 Nov 1879 by Rev. A. J. Padleford in Calais (VR:3:329) NORMAN COX.

v. MARTHA 'MATTIE' MARY DRUGAN, born 7 Oct 1847 in Calais (VR). Died 29 Dec 1887 age 34y 2m in Milltown, NB (SSC, times). Census: 1850 & 60 in Calais. She married (_____) POTTER (her name at death).

vi. MATILDA JANE DRUGAN, born Apr 1850 in Calais. Census: 1850, 60 & 70 in Calais. She married 16 May 1869 in St Stephen, NB (CCMR) ALBION K.P. RICH b. ca 1839. Census: 1870 (age 31a seaman, living with her mother).

WILLIAM & AMELIA DUNCAN, p. 211

WILLIAM DUNCAN, born circa 1790 in Scotland. He died before 1870. Census: 1840 (6 males, 3 females), 50, 60 & 70 in Calais.

He married before 1833 AMELIA GRACE (_____), born circa 1798 in NB. She died 24 Oct 1881 age 84 in Calais (adv). Census: 1860 thru 1880 in Calais. Children:

i. MARGARET A. DUNCAN, born circa 1834 in NB, died 8 Sept 1876 in Boston, MA (adv). Census: 1860 & 70 in Calais.

ii. DAVID DUNCAN, born 16 Jul 1837 in Calais (VR). He was in Civil War (1862-63) Co F 22nd Regt. Maine Inf. 5'9" with blue eyes and light hair (cwcard). Died 10 Apr 1878 at residence of his mother in Calais (adv). Census: 1870 in Calais. He married 4 Dec 1864 by Rev. E. W. Murray in Calais (VR) Mrs. JENNIE C. WRENTON born in St. Stephen, NB. Census 1870 in Calais.

iii. CHARLES DUNCAN, born 21 Feb 1839 in Calais, died 16 Jan 1840 in Calais (VR).

iv. FREDERICK DUNCAN, born 18 Nov 1840 in Calais (VR). Died after 1901 (Inmate at poor farm 1901 directory). Possibly died 19 Jan 1926 age 86 (MSA record faint hard to see). Census: 1860, 70 & 1880 (in poor farm) in Calais.

JAMES B. & MARY DUNN, p. 192

JAMES B. DUNN, born in 1810 in Kilenard, Queans Co., Ireland, left Ireland 1831/2, arrived at Eastport May 1831/32 settled in Calais, filed int. to be naturalized on 1 Mar 1844 (SJC:9:257). Naturalized 18 July 1848 [record in Machias has no entry date, born in Great Britain /Ireland no date].

He married MARY (_____). Children:

i. BERNARD EMMET DUNN, born 8 Oct 1842 in Calais (VR).
ii. MARY JANE DUNN, born 1 Feb 1845 in Calais (VR).
iii. HENRY GRATTON DUNN, born 17 Nov 1847 in Calais (VR).

WILLIAM & MARY DUREN, p. 222

WILLIAM DUREN, born circa 1812, possibly in Waterville ME, both parents b. Mass. He was merchant and carpenter in business with James S. Hall in 1836 & 38 when they were involved in many court cases (SJC). He came to Calais from Waterville, Me about 1827; engaged in lumbering and trade; served a representative and senator in the State Legislature in 1856, 1857 & 1863, and as Mayor of Calais (beg.:122). He died 21 Oct 1888 age 77y 4m in Calais (g.s., SCC). Buried in Calais Cemetery. Probate of Estate: 1888 (will dated 21 Aug 1866 prbt, Machias). Census: 1840 (6 males, 3 females), 50 thru 1880 in Calais.

He married (int) 1 Feb 1835 in Calais (cal2:38) MARY CALIFF DUTCH, born 16 Feb 1815 in Calais (Eastport VR, g.s.), daughter of Capt. JOHN CALIFF DUTCH AND MARGARET 'PEGGY' TODD (see DUTCH). Children:

i. EDWARD KENT DUREN, born 8 Jul 1838 in Calais (VR). Died 10 Aug 1855 age 17 in Calais (g.s.). Buried in Calais Cemetery. Census: 1850 in Calais.

ii. MARY 'ADDIE' ADELAIDE DUREN, born 11 Oct 1840 in Calais (VR). Resided in Cambridgeport, MA in 1875 (beg:123). Died 20 Apr 1885 age 43y 6m in Cambridge, MA (obit, times, g.s.). Census: 1850, 60 & 70 (with her parents) in Calais. She married on 13 Sep 1860 by J. J. Burgess in Calais (VR) ENNIS (Enos) D. SAWYER, born 9 Feb 1839 in Augusta, Me, son of EBENEZER SAWYER & LUCY W. HAMBLIN of Steuben and Augusta, Me (sawofne: 420). He died 16 Sept 1907 in Cambridge, MA (sawofne:459]. Census: 1860 (age 15 in household of Ephraim Spring) &70 (with her parents) in Calais. Soon after marriage they resided in Cambridge. He married 2nd in 1890 Lucy R. (Smith) Duer in Cambridge (sawofne:459).

iii. FRANCES PARTHENA DUREN, born 8 Aug 1846 in Calais (VR). Died 20 Jun 1859 age 13 in Calais (obit, adv, g.s.). Buried: 21 Jun 1859 in Calais Cemetery. Census: 1850 in Calais.

iv. JED FRYE DUREN, born 30 Dec 1850 in Calais, died 5 July 1919 age 68 in Calais (MSA). He was a merchant and prop. of St Croix Exchange Hotel (dir 1891.). Buried in Calais Cemetery. Census: 1860, 70 & 80 in Calais. He married 12 Sep 1876 in Calais (adv) CARRIE M. KING, born 28 Sept 1850 in Calais (MSA), daughter of WILLIAM TROTT KING & HENRIETTA BAKER (both buried in Calais Cemetery). She died 7 May 1927 age 70y 8m in Bangor, ME (adv, MSA). Buried in Calais Cemetery.

WALTER & ELIZABETH DURGIN, p. 208

WALTER DURGIN, born circa 1800 in Ireland. He was a ship carpenter. Census: 1850 in Calais.
He married ELIZABETH (_____), born circa 1803 in Ireland. Census: 1850 in Calais. Children:

i. ELIZA J. DURGIN, born circa 1833 in Lubec Me. Census: 1850 in Calais.
ii. JAMES DURGIN, born 6 Oct 1834 in Calais (VR). Census: 1850 in Calais.
iii. SYLPHIA DURGIN, born circa 1838 in Calais. Census: 1850 in Calais.
iv. ELIZABETH R. DURGIN, born circa 1840 in Calais. Census: 1850 in Calais.
v. CHARLOTTE C. DURGIN, born circa 1845. Died 27 Jan 1875 age 30y 10m 18d in Calais (adv). Census: 1850 & 70 in Calais. She married (int.) 4 Nov 1865 in Calais (VR:1:118) CHARLES EDGAR THURSTON, son of DAVID THURSTON AND JANE G. McNEIL (see THURSTON).

JOHN C. & MARGARET DUTCH, p. 204

{births of this family are recorded in Steuben, Eastport and Calais, place of birth varies in each record. John C. Dutch not listed in 1840 census of Calais, tenth child born in 1841 is probably the only one born in Calais}

Capt. JOHN CALIFF DUTCH, born 4 Jul 1788 in Ipswich, MA (Eastport VR), son of Capt. JOHN DUTCH & MARY ANN CALIFF. Died 4 Aug 1872 age 83y 1m (east:265, drum:123 = (1873), calef:13). Buried in Calais Cemetery. Census: 1840 (3 males, 5 females) in Charlotte, 1850, 60 & 70 in Calais.

He married 7 Apr 1814 by Jonathan Weston, JP in Eastport, ME (VR) MARGARET 'PEGGY' TODD born 10 Sep 1796 in Steuben Me (VR, 1850 census & drum:126 = Steuben, Eastport VR:90), daughter of JOHN CAMPBELL [Camel] TODD and ABIGAIL 'Nabby' NICHOLS (VR). She died 23 May 1880 (drum:126, Mortality Schedule 1880 census). Census: 1850, 60 & 70 in Calais. Children: (births are all recorded in drum:126)

i. MARY CALIFF DUTCH, born 16 Feb 1815 in Calais (Eastport VR). Died 14 Jan 1900 in Calais (VR, g.s., times, probate, g.s.). Census: 1850 thru 1880 in Calais. She married WILLIAM DUREN (see DUREN).
ii. SUSAN ELIZA DUTCH, born 16 May 1817 in Calais (Eastport VR). Died 5 Sep 1857 age 40 in Calais (stick:279, adv). Buried in Calais Cemetery. Census: 1850 in Calais. She married 20 Dec 1838 ROBERT CLARK STICKNEY, son of BENJAMIN STICKNEY and ANNA POOR (see STICKNEY).
iii. JOHN PARSONS DUTCH (see BELOW).
iv. MARGARET ELIZABETH DUTCH, born 28 Oct 1822 in Eastport ME (VR, Calais VR). Census: 1860 & 70 in Oshkosh, WI. She married (int.) 17 Sep 1844 in Calais (VR) JOHN PATTERSON McALLISTER (see McALLISTER).
v. ABIGAIL TODD DUTCH, born 21 Mar 1825 in Eastport ME (VR). Census: 1850 in Calais. Census: 1860 in Oshkosh, WI. She married 1846 (int.)22 Aug 1846 in Calais (VR) EPHRAIM WHITNEY (see WHITNEY).
vi. MARIA HAYCOCK DUTCH, born 28 Oct 1828 in Eastport (VR). Probably died in Minn. Census: 1850 & 60 in Calais. She married 15 Jan 1850 in Calais WILLIAM LOVEJOY KELLEY (see KELLEY).

vii. ROBERT SHAW DUTCH, born 30 Jun 1831 in Eastport (VR). Enlisted in Civil War at age 31, in Co F 22nd Me Inf. had blue eyes and dark hair (cwcard). Census: 1850 & 60 in Calais. He married 6 Mar 1853 in Calais (VR) HENRIETTA JAMESON, born ca 1833 in NB. Census: 1860 (age 27 with his parents).

viii. HANNAH SOPHIA DUTCH, born 14 Feb 1834 in Eastport ME (VR). Died 24 Sep 1862 (VR). Census: 1850 in Calais.

ix. WINSLOW STICKNEY DUTCH, born 1 Jan 1838 in Eastport or Calais ? (VR in both places, death rec. has Eastport). He enlisted 1 May 1861 in Co d 6th Me Inf. res. in Calais (cwcard, no other info on card). He was a railroad conductor and later operated a laundry. Died 21 Nov 1909 age 70y 10m 21d in Calais (MSA, sfh:1:223, adv). Buried: Calais Cemetery. Census: 1850 thru 1900 with her parents in Calais. He married 2 Aug 1865 in Calais (VR) by Rev. B.M. Mitchell EMILY C. CLEAVES, born ca 1844 in Saco, ME, daughter of JAMES CLEAVES & MARIA McDONALD of Saco. She died 8 July 1909 at age 64y 7m 3d in Calais (MSA, sfh:1:189). Census: 1880 with her parents & 1900 in Calais. Buried: Calais Cemetery.

x. FRANCIS AUGUSTUS DUTCH, born 4 Mar 1841 in Calais (VR). Died 11 Jan 1842 age 10 months in Calais (VR, obit gaz). Buried in Calais Cemetery.

JOHN P. & AMANDA J. DUTCH, p. 223

JOHN PARSONS DUTCH, son of Capt. JOHN CALIFF DUTCH AND MARGARET 'PEGGY' TODD, born 30 Jul 1819 in Eastport (VR, 1850 census). Died 4 Sep 1860 age 41 in Calais (g.s., adv). Buried: 7 Sep 1860 in Calais Cemetery. Census: 1850 & 60 in Calais.

He married circa 1843, (int) 3 Sep 1843 in Calais AMANDA J. HALL, born circa 1824, in St. Stephen, NB (1850 census). She married 2nd 24 Dec 1863 by Rev. H.A. Philbrick in Milltown, NB, JAMES WHITNEY of Milltown, ME (CCMR). She died 8 Jul 1876 age 53y 1m 26d in Calais (g.s.). Buried in Calais Cemetery. Census: 1850 & 60 in Calais. Children:

i. EMMA SOPHIA DUTCH, born 1 Jun 1845 in Calais (VR). Died 1 Jul 1861 age 16y 1m in Calais (g.s.). Buried in Calais Cemetery. Census: 1850 & 60 in Calais.

ii. M. GERTRUDE DUTCH, born 1855 in Calais (g.s.). Died 8 Feb 1859 age 4y 3m in Milltown ME (g.s.). Buried: 9 Feb 1859 in Calais Cemetery.

SAMUEL & MARGARET DYER, P. 218

SAMUEL DYER, born 29 Jun 1790 in Calais (g.s., 1850 census), son of JAMES DYER, Sr. He was a lumberman and farmer. He was in the War of 1812, served 27 days in Capt. Keen's Co. Mass. Militia, he had brown hair and blue eyes (pension rec NADC). In May 1876 at age 87 he sold his farm and moved to Minnesota to live with his step-daughter (adv)(pension rec says lived there one year). Died 13 Sept 1883 age 93y 2m 10d in Calais (g.s.). Buried in Calais Cemetery. Census: 1820 (1 male, 3 females), 30 (4 males, 5 females), 40 (4 males, 8 females), 50, 60 & 70 in Calais.

He married 1st ca 1813 MARGARET DOAK/DOKE/DUKE, marriage intentions 5 Dec 1813 her name DUKE (cal2:20) (maiden name DOKE in his obit, DUKE on his pension rec.), born circa 1797. Died 28 May 1843 age 46 in Calais (FJ, pension rec NADC, g.s.). Buried: 30 May 1843 in Calais Cemetery. Children:

i. WILLIAM MCLEAN DYER, born 19 Jan 1815 in Calais, died 29 Sep 1817 in Calais (VR).

ii. MARY JANE DYER, born 5 Sep 1816 in Calais (VR). Died 27 Jan 1861 in Calais (g.s.). Buried in Calais Cemetery. Census: 1850 & 60 in Calais. She married JOHN H. GOODWIN (see GOODWIN).

iii. SARAH DYER, born 28 Oct 1818 in Calais (VR).

iv. MARTHA ANN DYER, born 17 Feb 1821 in Calais (VR). Died 4 Apr 1882 in Calais (times). She married 16 Aug 1846 by Rev. Eaton in Dennysville Me (Pembroke VR, wilder) BENJAMIN SINCLAIR, b. 20 Sept 1820 in Dennysville (wwcf). He deserted his family and went to California (wldr).

v. WILLIAM SAMUEL DYER, born 14 Dec 1823 in Calais (VR). He was a sailor. Died 19 Oct 1871 age 50 (obit adv, aboard schooner "John McAdam" off Gay Head). Census: 1850 & 60 in Calais.

vi. HARRIET ELIZABETH DYER, born 26 May 1826 in Calais (VR), born (2): 27 May 1827 in Calais (Bucksport ME VR). Died 6 May 1914 in Evanston, IL (adv). She married 23 May 1847 in St. Stephen, NB (Bucksport VR) ABNER H. HALL born 19 Feb 1820 in Nobleboro, ME (Bucksport VR).

vii. GEORGE WASHINGTON DYER, born 28 Jul 1828 in Calais (VR, 1850 census). Died after 1883 when

father died. Census: 1850 & 60 in Calais. He <u>possibly</u> married by Rev. Drummond in Oroville, Calif. 1 May 1878 JENNIE JONES (adv, times).
viii. SOPHRONIA ABIGAIL DYER, born 3 Jan 1831 in Calais (VR). Died 23 Jun 1851 age 20y 6m 20d in Waldoboro, ME (FJ). She married HARRISON BAKER (her obit).
ix. MARIA NANCY DYER, born 25 Dec 1833 in Calais (g.s.). Died 31 Jan 1934 age 100 in Calais (VR, MSA). Buried in Calais Cemetery. Census: 1850 thru 1900 in Calais. She married 10 Oct 1861 in Calais THOMAS E. WHARFF (see WHARFF).
x. JOHN HAMPDEN DYER, born 2 Jun 1836 in Calais (VR, 1850 census). Died after 1883 when father died. Census: 1850 & 60 (age 26 listed as James H.) in Calais.
xi. MARGARET MATILDA DYER, born 19 Nov 1839 in Calais (VR). Died after 1883, she may be one of the children in the West mentioned in father's obit. Census: 1850 in Calais.

SAMUEL DYER married 2nd 19 Oct 1851 JANE M. CHRISTIE by James S. Hall, JP in Calais (VR:1:150), she born 29 Mar 1816 in Grafton, VT, daughter of JAMES C. CHRISTIE & MARY MORRISON (christie). After her Samuel's death she moved to Eureka, CA to live with her son, Mr. Christie, in March 1884 (adv). Died 30 July 1887 in Eureka, CA (her widow's pension rec NADC). Census: 1860 [with them are Charles J. Christie age 19, Mary C. (Christie) Dyer age 15 and Margaret J. (Christie) Dyer age 13, her children by former marriage to John McDiarmid Christie in St. Stephen, NB, he died 1847 (christie)] & 70 in Calais. [Machias union has death for Margaret J. Dyer on 2 Mar 1861 in Calais age 13, daughter of Mrs. Samuel Dyer].

JEDEDIAH & ELLEN EILLS, p. 217

JEDEDIAH EILLS, born circa 1814 in Cornwallis NS (1850 census). Census: 1850 in Calais. He was a millman.

He married ELLEN (_____), born circa 1824 in Cork, Ireland (1850 census). Census: 1850 in Calais. Children:

i. CATHERINE EILLS, born circa 1842 in St. John, NB (1850 census). Census: 1850 in Calais.
ii. MARY ANN EILLS, born 21 Feb 1843 in Calais (VR). Census: 1850 in Calais.
iii. GEORGE ALBERT EILLS, born 27 Dec 1845 in Calais (VR). Census: 1850 in Calais.
iv. THOMAS EILLS, born circa 1848 in Calais (1850 census). Census: 1850 in Calais.
v. ELLEN EILLS, born circa 1848 in Calais (1850 census). Census: 1850 in Calais.
vi. JAMES EILLS, born circa 1850 in Calais (1850 census). Census: 1850 in Calais.

MOSES & LUCY ELLSMORE, p. 191

MOSES ELSEMORE, Sr. born ??, died 13 Mar 1892 (this date copied from stone may be an error and 1842 is more likely the date he died since he married LYDIA ANDREWS on 12 Aug 1785 (DJA), died ca 1855 (MOCA). They are buried in Elsemore Family Cemetery East Machias. Their son, Moses Elsemore, Jr. lived in Calais for a few years.

MOSES ELSEMORE Jr., born 31 Aug 1789 in Machias, Me (VR). Census: 1830 in Plantation # 18, 1840 (3 males, 3 females) & 1850 (age 65) in Calais.

He married 16 Jul 1814, in Machias Me (VR), LUCY FOSTER, born circa 1799 in E. Machias, Me (1850 census), daughter of JOHN WOODEN FOSTER, Jr. & 1st wife LUCY CHASE or 2nd wife MEHITABLE MESERVE (memcen:161). Died 9 Sep 1851 age 52 in Calais (g.s.). Buried in Calais. Census: 1850 in Calais. Children:

i. SOPHIA ELSEMORE, born ca 1816, died June 1828 age 12y in E. Machias (east:92).
ii. BETHIAH L. or Martha ELSEMORE [possible daughter] born ca 1821, died 26 Sept 1847 in Calais (VR). She married 29 Oct 1843 in Calais WILLIAM KEENE (see KEENE).
iii. PHEBE ABIGAIL ELSEMORE, [possible daughter] born ca 1826 in Machias, married ca 1845 SAMUEL CALLAGHAN, Jr. (see CALLAGHAN).
iv. SOPHIA ELSEMORE, born circa 1828 in E. Machias, Me (1850 census). Census: 1850 in Calais. She married 14 Dec 1850 JOHN ASH in Calais (VR).
v. GEORGE STILLMAN ELSEMORE, born 4 Nov 1840 in Calais (VR). Enlisted in Civil War 12 Jan 1864 in 9th Maine Inf. Co A (enlist). He was a clerk & lumberman. Died after 1880. Census: 1850 thru 1880 in

Calais. He married 13 Aug 1859 in Calais (VR) CLARA A. WOODMAN born ca 1840 in Canada (poss. d/o JOHN & ANN (CHASE) WOODMAN). Census: 1860 (Geo. & Clara living with John & Ann Woodman), 1870 & 80 in Calais.

MARK & ELIZA JANE ELLSWORTH, p. 191

JACOB[4] ELLSWORTH & SARAH TODD were married 13 June 1785 in Rowley, MA (VR:291) Jacob born 22 Aug 1764 in Rowley son of Nathaniel[3] Ellsworth, Jeremiah [2-1]. Jacob d. 20 Sept 1842 in Bridgton, ME. Sarah d. 9 Apr 1833 in Bridgton (VR:79). Sarah[5] Todd born 7 Nov 1766 in Rowley, daughter of David[4] TODD & Sarah HASKELL, Jeremiah[3] Todd, James[2] & John[1] (rowley:392). The first seven of their eleven children were born in Rowley, the others in Bridgton. For child number eight, Mark and child number ten, Reuben who moved to Calais see below.
* There are two sets of records for Bridgton one is hand written copy (not original) the other a typed copy some dates differ.

MARK[5] ELLSWORTH, born 23 Feb 1801 in Bridgton, ME (VR). In Nov of 1850 he went to California (see Charles Waite). Died 3 May 1887 age 86 in Oshkosh, WI (obit, wife, 3 dau & 2 sons survive, wdr). Census: 1840 (3males & 3 females), 1850 in Calais, 1870 in Oshkosh, WI. Buried: Riverside Cemetery, Oshkosh (north).

He married ELIZA JANE CHENEY born 10 Feb 1812 in Eastport ME (VR), daughter of AMASA CHENEY & NANCY CAMPBELL TODD. She is the sister of Mary Clark (see Amos Clark). Her great-great grandfather, William Cheney (1750-1802) served in Rev. War (DAR #42638). She probably died in Oshkosh after 1887. Census: 1850 in Calais, 1870 in Oshkosh, WI. Children:

i. ALBERT E. ELLSWORTH, born 6 Apr 1832 in Calais (VR). He was a painter, cashier and bookkeeper. Died 5 Feb 1899 in Oshkosh, WI (wdr). Census: 1860 & 70 in Oshkosh, WI. Resided in Escanaba, MI at time of 2nd marriage. He married 1st 9 June 1857 (wmr) LYDIA FRANCES CONLY, born ca 1838. Census: 1860 & 70 in Oshkosh. He married 2nd 11 Sept 1890 by Rev. W. W. Warner in Utica, WI (wmr) CORA ESTELLA MILLAR, born in Utica, WI, daughter of GEORGE MILLAR & MARY ESTEY of Wisconsin..

ii. NANCY MARIA ELLSWORTH, born 19 Jul 1834 in Calais (VR). Census: 1850 in Calais. She died between 1891 when she visited Calais and before 1907 in Oshkosh (sister Sarah's obit). She married (int.) 6 Jan 1853 in Calais (VR) E. W. TILTON of Calais.

iii. EDWIN TODD ELLSWORTH, born 29 Apr 1838 in Calais (VR). He was a Sgt. in Co. E 2nd Regt Wis. Vol. Inf. in Civil War. In 1868 he was listed as a civil engineer in Oshkosh. He is listed in the Oshkosh city directories of 1857-68-76-82. Died after 1899 when he was listed as residing in Marshfield, Wood Co. WI. (cwWI:239). Census: 1850 in Calais, 1880 & 1900 in Oshkosh. He married 26 Oct 1865 by Rector F. R. Wolff in Winnebago County, WI (wmr), MARTHA D. SHERWOOD, born 13 May 1877 in Oshkosh, WI. (cwWI:239). She was the daughter of GILBERT & CYNTHIA SHERWOOD (wmr). They visited Calais in Aug 1891 with his sister, Mrs. Tilton, they left Calais 37 years ago (adv). Census: 1880 & 1990 in Oshkosh.

iv. GEORGIANNA ELLSWORTH, born 19 Apr 1840 in Calais (VR). At age 12, she moved to Oshkosh in 1856 with her mother and sister, a year after her father and two brothers had moved there (obit, north). She was for many years a teacher in the public schools in Oshkosh, she was a member of the DAR (#42638, obit). Died 3 Jan 1923 age 83 in Oshkosh, WI (wdr, obit north). Census: 1850 in Calais, 1870 in Oshkosh.

v. SARAH JANE ELLSWORTH, born 3 May 1843 in Calais (VR). She was for many years a teacher in the public schools of Oshkosh. Died 7 Jul 1907 in Oshkosh, WI (obit north) Census: 1850 in Calais, 1870 in Oshkosh.

vi. CAROLINE 'Carrie' ELLSWORTH, born 29 May 1845 in Calais, died 13 Oct 1846 in Calais (VR). Buried: 15 Oct 1846 in Calais Cemetery.

REUBEN & ELIZABETH M. ELLSWORTH, p. 214

Reuben J.[5] Ellsworth, born 2 Mar 1807 (sic, his brother, Nathan T. b. 15 May 1807 sic) in Bridgton, ME (VR:3:88, rowley:117 has Nathan b. 1809). He was a cabinet maker. Census: 1840 (2 males & 3 females), 1850 in Calais.

He married (int) 16 Nov 1834 (cal2:38, mrwc:14) ELIZABETH M. HARMON, born 15 Feb 1813, Bapt 11 Apr 1813 in St. Stephen, NB (kmc), daughter of NATHANIEL HARMON and LYDIA McALLISTER (harm: 32). Census: 1850 in Calais. Children:

i. HENRY BYRON ELLSWORTH, born 21 Jan 1838 in Calais (VR, 1850 census = b. in St. Stephen). Census: 1850 in Calais.

ii. ADELIA ELLSWORTH, born 8 Mar 1840 in Calais, died 11 Apr 1847 in Calais (VR), buried: 12 Apr 1847 in Calais Cemetery.
iii. GORHAM ELLSWORTH, born 21 Mar 1843 in Calais (VR). Census: 1850 in Calais.
iv. EDGAR ELLSWORTH, born 11 Oct 1846 (sic) in Calais (VR). Died 11 Oct 1846 age 2 years (sic) in Calais (VR:I:239). Buried: 14 Oct 1846 in Calais Cemetery.

- There may be another female child who died before 1850 census.

SETH & MARY EMERSON, p. 216

WILLIAM EMERSON & ELIZABETH MYRICK/MERRICK married 22 June 1769 in Methuen, MA (VR:183). William b. 15 June 1748 in Haverhill, MA d. 25 Nov 1827 in Bridgton, ME (VR:36). Elizabeth b. 19 Feb 1751 in Methuen (Bridgeton VR:36). There were 13 children: first two b. in Methuen the rest in Bridgeton. They moved to Bridgton between 1771 and 1773. The youngest child of 14, Seth moved to Calais (see below).

Capt. SETH EMERSON, born 18 Apr 1796 in Bridgeton, ME (VR:36). Before coming to Calais he became an Ens. on 20 Aug 1821, a Lt. on 3 Aug 1822 and a Capt. on 31 May 1823 in the 1st Brig. 5th Div of the Militia in Bridgton (milit). Came to Calais about 1825 (beg:123). In 1832 he was a trader when he appeared in court (SJC) later he was a millwright. In 1844 he was an officer in St. Croix Lodge No. 46 (lodge:20). He was a Representative to the Legislature, deputy revenue collector, cashier in Washington Co. Bank and a member of the Masons (obit adv). Died 3 Oct 1881 age 85 in Calais (obit). Probate of Estate: 4 Oct 1881 in Machias Me. Buried in Calais Cemetery (foot stone only). Census: 1830 (3 males, 1 female) 40 (5 males, 3 females), thru 70 in Calais.

He married (int) 22 Sept 1827 in Calais (cal2:26) MARY W. KNIGHT, born circa 1807, daughter of PAUL KNIGHT {son of JONATHAN KNIGHT} and HANNAH WHITNEY {daughter of JOEL WHITNEY}. Died 5 Mar 1883 age 76 in Calais (obit, times). Buried in Calais Cemetery (foot stone only). Census: 1850, 60 & 70 in Calais. Children:

i. EDWIN EDWARD EMERSON, born 10 Mar 1831 in Calais (VR). He was a millwright. Died 11 Oct 1878 age 48y 2m in Milltown ME (obit, g.s.). Census: 1850, 60 & 70 in Calais. Buried: Calais Cemetery. He married before 1863 HARRIET (_____), born ca 1837. Census: 1870 in Calais.
ii. ELIZABETH EMERSON, born 31 Mar 1833 in Calais (VR). Died at her residence 20 May 1883 in Calais (adv, times). Census: 1860, 70 & 80 in Calais. She married (int.) 28 Jan 1856 in Calais (VR) REUBEN BRADDOCK LOWELL, son of REUBEN N. LOWELL AND SARAH 'SALLY' SMITH (see LOWELL).
iii. SON EMERSON, born ca 1840, died 26 Feb 1844 age 3 ½ (sext).

- Note – There are possibly other children – 2 males in 1830 census and 2 males 1 female in 1840 census.
- S. James Emerson who died 26 Oct 1864 age 29 who died in Columbia, GA formerly of Calais (union). He may be one of the sons.

DAVID & JUDITH ESTABROOKS, p. 220

DAVID E. ESTABROOKS, born circa 1791 in St. John, NB (esta:63, 78, 1850 census), son of EBENEZER ESTABROOKS AND MARIA FLETCHER.. In 1814 he owned land in Wakefield, NB until he moved to Calais in late 1820's (lesko). On 14 Aug 1838 he appeared in Superior Judicial Court to file intentions to become a citizen. He stated he was born in Parish of Lincoln,{Sunbury Parish} Province of New Brunswick in 1794. He left NB 15 Jan 1822 arrived in Houlton, ME 18 Jan 1822 and then to Calais 22 May 1826, where he has since resided (SJC). Naturalized 19 July 1844. He was a house carpenter. Died after 1870. Census: 1830 (8 males, 3 females), 1840 (8 males, 4 females), 50, 60 & 70 in Calais.

He married before 1813 in Wakefield, NB (esta:63) JUDITH FLETCHER, born circa 1794 in Cornwallis NS (1850 census). Died 30 Apr 1876 age 82 in Princeton Me (obit). Buried in Calais Cemetery. Census: 1850, 60 & 70 in Calais. Children:

i. MARY ANN ESTABROOKS, born 30 May 1813 in St John, NB, died 10 Dec 1888 in Biddeford, ME , buried there in Greenwood Cemetery (lesko). She was a dressmaker. She married 1st 30 May 1836 by Rev James Huckings (wcmr20) in Calais ISAIAH SMITH born ca 1810, died ca 1848 (lesko). She married 2nd ca 1839 ANGUS McDONALD, born ca 1813 in Scotland, he went west and presumed died ca 1861 on trip back home. After his death Mary Ann moved to Biddeford and established a dressmaking business (lesko, Biddeford city directories 1870-80).
ii. NANCY J. ESTABROOKS, born circa 1814 in St. John, NB (1850 census). Died after 1870. Census:

1850 in Calais, 1860 & 70 in Princeton Me. She married ca 1832 ALBY KEENE/KEEN Sr. (see KEENE).

iii. THOMAS ESTABROOKS, born circa 1818, probably in NB, died 29 Apr 1837 age 19 in Calais (VR:32:239).

iv. SARAH ESTABROOKS, born ? (esta:78). Estimate 1820

v. JUDITH ELIZA ESTABROOKS, born circa 1823 (1850 census) Died 26 Nov 1847 age 24 in Calais (VR:3:239). Buried: 28 Nov 1847 in Calais Cemetery.

vi. DAVID N. ESTABROOKS, born 4 Feb 1825 (g.s.). Died: 13 Jan 1883 in Old Town, ME (g.s.). Married and lived in Bangor (esta:79). Census: 1840 (male age 15-25 in David's household) in Calais, 1860 & 70 in Old Town, Me. Married before 1848 (a son died 1850 age 2) MARY A. (_____), born ca 1829, died 9 Jan 1893 age 64 (g.s., MSA parents unk.). Both are buried in Forest Hill Cemetery in Old Town (in same lot with Ira & his wives and children).

vii. REUBEN L. ESTABROOKS (probable son), born ca 1826. Census: 1850 (age 24) in Calais, (with wife, Almira (age 22), and son Rufus (age 2) living next door to David with Ira). Married 9 Jan 1848 by Rev. H.V.Dexter in Calais ALMIRA DEBORAH McCURDY (MSA) born ca 1828. Census: 1850 in Calais.

viii. CHARLES ESTABROOKS, (probable son), born ca 1827 (fits male 0-4 in 1830 census, not in 40, in 1850 census age 26 married, wife Elizabeth I. age 20, living with James Simmons, in Calais)

ix. JULIA ANN ESTABROOKS, born 14 Nov 1829 in Calais, died 29 Dec 1830 in Calais (VR:3:239).

x. MELVIN ESTABROOKS, born ? (esta:79). Estimate 1830

xi. IRA SIDNEY ESTABROOKS, born 20 Jan 1831in Calais (VR). He worked in a sawmill. Died ca 1889 (g.s.). Buried in Forest Hill Cemetery in Old Town. Census: 1850 in Calais, 1860 & 70 in Old Town ME. He married 1st 25 Aug 1855 in Old Town (VR) RUTH K. COLLEY, born ca 1833, died ca 1856 (g.s.). Buried: Forest Hill Cemetery, in Old Town. He married 2nd 12 Apr 1857 by Rev. Isaac C. Knowlton in Old Town (VR), ANN E. HALL born ca 1830, died ca 1902 (g.s.). Buried: Forest Hill Cemetery in Old Town. Census: 1860 & 70 in Old Town. All three are buried in Forest Hill Cemetery in Old Town (MOCA).

xii. ELVIRA ADALINE ESTABROOKS, born 20 Sep 1833 in Calais. Died before 1857, when her husband remarried. She married 3 Sep 1848 in St. Stephen, NB (CCMR). WYATT DICKERMAN Jr., born 15 Mar 1814, son of WYATT DICKERMAN & LOIS ALLEN (dick:48). He was an artist, house decorator and singing teacher. He died 5 Dec 1895 at Calais (adv). They resided in Calais. Census: 1850 & 60 in Calais. He married 2nd 11 Oct 1857 ABIGAIL TORREY REED of St. David, NB, daughter of JOSEPH REED & MERCY COLLINS (dick:48). Census: 1850 (living with David & Judith), 1860 & 70 in Calais.

xiii. DANIEL SYLVESTER ESTABROOKS, born 20 Sep 1835 in Calais (VR). Census: 1850 (age 16) a lumberman in Calais.

LEONARD & NANCY EYE, p. 208

GEORGE & MARIA EYE, both probably born in Halifax, NS, of German descent, had two sons who immigrated to Calais in the 1830's: Leonard A. Eye and Philip Edward Eye.

LEONARD A. EYE, christened 19 Jul 1807 St. Paul's Church, in Halifax, NS (church records at Halifax Arichives). Came to Calais with his brother ca 1833. He was a carpenter. Died ca 1855 in Calais. Buried: 4 Apr 1855 in Calais (sext). Census: 1840 (2 males, 2 females) & 50 in Calais.

He married 7 Jan 1837 in Calais (WCMR:114) NANCY McLELLAN /McCellan (name Mary on Margaret's death rec.) born 1818 in Antium, Ireland (1850 census), daughter of WILLIAM & MARY McLELLAN. Died 18 Jan 1865 in Calais (VR). Buried: 18 Jan 1865 in Calais (sext). Census: 1840, 50 & 60 in Calais. Children:

i. MARIA JANE EYE, born 5 Oct 1837 in Calais (VR). Died 13 Mar 1913 in Calais (MSA). Buried in Calais Cemetery. Census: 1840 thru 1900. She married MITCHELES SILVERSTONE 19 Nov 1857 in Calais (adv of 26 Nov 1857, p2) [CCMR married same date Michaeles Magnus by Rev. John B. Brownell in St. Stephen, NB] *Note magnus is stone in German. Mitcheles born, Feb 1834 in Germany or Prussia. He began a tailoring business in 1857, he organized the Calais City Band about 1867 and for 32 years was its instructor, leader and director (times: 25 Oct 1900). Died 13 Jan 1908 in Calais (MSA). Buried in Calais Cemetery. Census: 1860 thru 1900.

Michelis Silverstone was the most picturesque leader that the Calais Band ever had. He, his wife, Maria L., and his daughter, Ophella, lived on Washington street. His vocation was that of tailor, with a store where Grearson's is now. His avocation was leading the Calais Band. He was a German, and splendidly educated in music. He was the band's good angel. He led the Band, he furnished a room for them to meet in, he made their uniforms, and he taught many of them to play. Those uniforms had the Civil War touch. High plume in a Civil War cap, epaulets on the shoulders, long coat, wide belt with brass buckle. Mr. Silverstone was a small man, but when he used his right hand to play that E flat cornet, and gave the time to the rest of the band with his left, he looked about three times as big as he was. That band was not only a street band but was a concert band besides, and could play the most difficult music. Mr. Silverstone organized, what he called the Vicopia Orchestra consisting of himself, Herbert Bernard and Charles W. Bennett. The name was made from their instruments <u>Violin</u> - <u>Cornet</u> - <u>Piano</u>. <u>Vicopia.</u> (Clipping from Calais Advertiser undated).

ii. GEORGE WILLIAM EYE, born 19 Apr 1839 in Calais (VR). In 1864 he established his business as a manufacturer and dealer of coffins, caskets, etc., and undertaker's materials; funeral director and practical embalmer. The business was located on Main Street in Calais with all out-of-town orders promptly attended to (CEV:30). He later moved his undertaking business to Bangor Me where he died 22 Dec 1916. Buried 25 Dec 1916 in Calais Cemetery. Census: 1840, 50, 60, 80 &1900 in Calais. He married (int.) 3 Nov 1862 in Calais (VR) ELIZABETH A. COOK, born June 1842, daughter of JAMES WARREN COOK and ELIZA NICKERSON. Elizabeth, died 11 Nov 1910 (MSA). Buried in Calais Cemetery. Census: 1880 & 1900 her mother, Eliza, age 84 with her in Calais.

iii. LEONARD ALEXANDER EYE, born 3 Sept 1842 in Calais (VR). He was a sailor. He was in U.S. Navy during the Civil War (MSA). Died before 1914 in Greenland (according to statement by brother in the Civil War pension record of his brother James L. Eye). Census: 1850 & 60 in Calais. He married 9 Mar 1870 in Tremont (VR) SARAH JANE MARIA DIX, born Mar 1849 in Tremont, ME (g.s.), daughter of Capt. GEORGE & SALLY DIX of Tremont. She was a dressmaker. She died in 1947 (g.s.). Buried in Hillcrest Cemetery in Tremont. Census: 1860 & 1880 in Tremont, 1900 in Boston Mass. with daughter and family, 1920 in Tremont.

iv. MARGARET LOUISA EYE, born 15 Dec 1844 in Calais (VR). She was a seamstress, worked for and lived with her brother-in-law, M. Silverstone. Died 24 Dec 1910 age 66y 9d in Calais (MSA). Census: 1850, 60, 70 (with sister, Maria), 1880, 1900 (with son Herbert) in Calais

v. JAMES LESLIE/LASLEY EYE, born 9 Feb 1847 in Calais (VR). In the Civil War he was in the Coast Guard at age 21 on 1 Feb 1865, he was 5' 10" with gray eyes and black hair (enlist). His pension application record at the National Archives has a discrepancy in his age. He claims to be born in 1844 and tried to use his cousin, James B. Eye's civil war record to get his pension. Moved to Waverly IA in the Spring of 1866, to Albert, MN in 1877 and to Lamberton, MN in 1899 (pensrec). He was a janitor. Died 14 July 1927 in Wabassa, MN (g.s.). Buried in Lamberton, MN. Census: 1850 (age 3) & 60 (age 14) in Calais, 1900 in Lamberton, MN, 1910 in Wabassa, MN. He married 30 June 1881 in North Star Twp, Redwood Co, MN (pensrec) AUATHUSIA GORY born Apr 1862 (1900 census). Died circa 1907 in Wabassa, MN (pensrec). Census: 1900 in Lamberton, MN.

vi. CHARLES EDWARD SWAN EYE, born 23 July 1850 in Calais (copy of bible in brother, Jim's pension record). He was a hose cart driver for the Calais Fire Dept. He was probably named for Dr. Charles Edward Swan. He died 26 Jan 1915 in Calais (MSA, obit). Buried in Calais Cemetery. Census: 1860, 80 & 1900 in Calais. He married 11 June 1871 in Calais EMMA ELZORA WILSON born 13 May 1850, daughter of WILLIAM & MARY WILSON of Tower Hill, NB. She died 18 Jan 1929 in Calais (obit). Census: 1880, 1900 & 20 in Calais.

vii. CLARA A. EYE, born circa 1853 in Calais. She died 10 July 1923 in Ithaca, NY (obit ithaca), where she was living with her son, who was a professor at Cornell University. Buried: 14 July 1923 Calais Cemetery (sext). Census: 1860, 70 & 80 (with sister, Maria) in Calais, 1900 in Eastport. She married circa 1888 MILLARD 'MEL' O/D. LAWRENCE, born 7 Sept 1851 in Lubec, ME (lubec:55), son of SAMUEL A. LAWRENCE & CHRISTINA WATT [alive in 1900 census] both born Eastport (pensrec of James Eye). He was an

Express Agent and Customs Clerk. Died 13 Jan 1914 in Eastport (MSA). Buried Calais Cemetery. Census: 1870 & 80 (with his parents in Calais), 1900 in Eastport.

PHILIP E. & ELLEN EYE, p. 206

PHILIP EDWARD EYE, born, circa 1811 in Halifax, NS (1850 census). He applied 25 Sept 1852 for citizenship stating he was born in 1811 in Halifax, and left Halifax Nov 1832 for Calais where he has since resided (SJC:9:511). He was a carpenter. Died 21 May 1879 in Calais (pensrec, g.s.). Buried in Red Beach ME. Census: 1840 (2 males, 4 females), 50, 60 & 70 in Calais.

He married in Halifax, NS, before coming to Calais ca 1833, ELLEN /ELEANOR McKENNEY born ca 1811 in Nova Scotia. Died 13 Apr 1876 in Calais (Red Beach) ME (g.s.). Buried: 1876 in Red Beach Cemetery. Census: 1840 & 50 (name Eleanor E. age 38), 60 & 70 in Calais. Children:

i. ELIZABETH SARAH EYE. born 9 Aug 1834, in Halifax, NS (Calais VR) (1856 lived in Charlestown, Ma. unmarried). Died 1871 in Red Beach ME (g.s.). Buried in Red Beach ME. Census: 1850, 60 &70 in Calais. She married 19 Jul 1866 (her sister's widower) ELIAS STUART LANE (see below).

ii. EDWARD WILLIAM WHITEWALL EYE, born 17 Mar 1835 in Calais (VR). Served in Civil War in Co K 1st Maine heavy artillery from 17 Jun 1861 to 30 Nov 1861, Corp'l. (pensrec). (Guardian app. 26 May 1891). Died 17 Nov 1899 in Pembroke ME (adv). Buried in Forest Hill Cemetery Pembroke. Census: 1850 in Calais, 1860 in Pembroke. He married 6 Nov 1854 LUCY S. REYNOLDS, born 1836 (g.s.), daughter of BENJAMIN & JERUSHA REYNOLDS. She 24 Nov 1871 age 44y 11m in Pembroke (east:258, g.s.). Buried in Forest Hill Cemetery in Pembroke ME. Census: 1850 & 60 in Pembroke.

iii. MARGARET ELLEN EYE, born 9 Jun 1837 in Calais (VR). Census: 1840 & 50 in Calais, 1860 in Pembroke. She married Jan 1857 in Pembroke (VR:156) GEORGE GILLIS, Jr. born ca 1834 (possibly in Pembroke), son of GEORGE GILLIS, Sr. Census: 1860 in Pembroke.

iv. MARTHA MARIA EYE, born, 12 Mar 1839 in Calais (VR). Died 1864 (g.s.). Buried in Red Beach ME. Census: 1840, 50 in Calais. She married 21 Jul 1858 in Calais (VR:3:172) ELIAS STUART LANE, born 1837 in Red Beach ME, son of CLEMENT LANE (jr.) and MARGARET PENDELTON YOUNG. He was in Civil War Co G 22nd Me Inf. a farmer 5'5" with black eyes and black hair (cwcard). He was a mail carrier. Died 13 Dec 1915 age 75y 5m in St. Stephen, N B (Calais VR, adv). Buried in Red Beach ME. Will proved in Machias ME (prbt # L-4-369). Census: 1870 in Calais.

v. FREDERICK EYE, born 7 Oct 1841 in Calais (VR). Census: 1850 & 60 in Calais. He married before 1874 AGNES (_____). In Apr 1874 Agnes E. Eye sued Frederick W. Eye for divorce but case was dismissed (SJC docket # 199). Same term of court docket # 269 Agnes Eye sued Elias S. Lane for six months wages for housekeeping.

vi. JAMES BALL EYE, born 31 Aug 1842 in Calais (VR). Census: 1850 thru 1880 in Calais. Military in Civil War from 12 Aug 1862 to 16 June 1865 (pensrec). He enlisted 12 Aug 1862 age 20, he was 5'5" with gray eyes and black hair (enlist). Died 20 Dec 1903 age 63 in Machias (VR, obit adv). Buried: Red Beach Cemetery, Calais. Census: 50, 60, 70 & 80 in Calais. He married 14 Aug 1879, in Robbinston ME (pensrec) REBECCA LOUISE CRAIG, born 18 Nov 1858 in Robbinston ME, divorced 28 Apr 1891(pensrec). Died after 1927. Census: 1900 in Calais (with 2nd husband, Ellsworth Brigham Garnett).

vii. HENRY AUGUSTUS EYE, born 7 Sep 1844 in Calais (VR). Enlisted in Civil War 29 Mar 1865 in Co. F 22 Regt, 5'6". (enlist). Census: 1850 & 60 in Calais.

viii. SAMUEL WADE EYE, born 7 Jul 1846 in Calais (VR). Enlisted in the Civil War 15 Feb 1965 at age 18, 5'7" dark eyes and hair, both father and mother (Eleanor) signed enlistment paper (enlist). Census: 1850, 60 & 70 in Calais. He married 22 Nov 1872 in Calais (VR:3) MARGARET BROWN [This may be the Margaret Eye who d. Dec 1875 age 18 (adv 10 Feb 1875 p. 2)].

ix. FRANKLIN C. EYE, born 1848 in Calais. Census: 1850 & 60 in Calais.

x. MARY E. EYE, born 22 Dec 1851 in Calais (VR). Died 30 Aug 1931 in Red Beach (sfh:6:100, b. & d.). Buried in Red Beach, ME (1852-1931, g.s.). Census: 1860, 70, 80 & 1900 in Calais. She married ca 1872 GEORGE WARREN COOK, born May 1852 (1900 census) in Red Beach, son of JAMES WARREN COOK & ELIZA NICKERSON. He was a farmer. Died 28 Feb 1916 in Calais. Buried in Red Beach. Census: 1880 & 1900 in Calais.

xi. FANNY STUART EYE, born 14 Mar 1854 in Calais (ps). Died 4 Oct 1894 age 40y 6m 20d in Calais (MSA, adv). Buried in Red Beach ME. Census: 1860, 70 & 80 in Calais. She married 4 Dec 1875 in St. Stephen, NB (CCMR) Capt. WILLARD BROWN, born 21 Mar 1853 in Red Beach, ME (MSA), son of DAVID BROWN & FRANCES BOHANAN. He was a master mariner. Died 14 Nov 1918 in So Bristol ME (MSA). Buried in Red Beach Cemetery in Calais. Census: 1880 in Calais.

JOHN & DIANIA FERRIS, p. 181
(Sometimes FARRIS)

JOHN FERRIS Jr., born circa 1808 in Lisburn, Ireland, immigrated 1 Jun 1820 in Eastport ME, naturalized 18 Sept 1833, of Charlotte, witnesses to establish his residence: Warren Gilmor, Cooper, ME and Peter Mallow, Pembroke, ME (irmch). His parents, JOHN & SARAH FERRIS, living in Charlotte in 1830 ages between 60 & 70. He was a house carpenter. Died after 1860. Census: 1830 (1 male, 2 females) in Charlotte, 40 (2 males, 5 females), 50 & 60 in Calais.

He married DIANNAH ZELMA, born circa 1812 in Charlotte ME (1850 census). Bapt. 20 June 1852 in Calais (saint). Probably the daughter of AUGUSTUS & AMELIA ZELMA. Died 24 May 1891 age 82y in Calais (adv, east:461, SSC). Census: 1850, 60 & 80 in Calais. Children:

i. MARY KILBY (Kelly) FERRIS, born 11 Nov 1829 in Charlotte ME (VR). Bapt. 7 June 1857 in Calais (saint). Died 25 May 1892 age 62y 6m 15d in Calais (MSA, east:484). Buried in Calais Cemetery. Census: 1870 in Calais. She married (int) 8 June 1850 in Calais (VR:1:40) BENJAMIN SMITH, born ca 1824 in NB, Bapt. 7 June 1857 in Calais (saint). He died 22 June 1908 at the home of his daughter in Vanceboro, ME (obit adv, MSA). Census: 1870 in Calais.

ii. MARTHA ZILMA FERRIS, born 11 May 1831 in Charlotte ME (VR). She probably died before 1860 when Nathaniel age 28 was living with his parents. Census: 1850 in Calais. She married 10 Aug 1851 by Rev. George Durell in Calais (VR: 3:160, FJ), NATHANIEL WHITE, son of DANIEL & BATHSHEBA WHITE (see WHITE).

iii. NANCY FERRIS, born 11 Dec 1832 in Charlotte ME (VR). Census: 1850 in Calais.

iv. JOHN WESLEY FERRIS, born 10 May 1835 in Charlotte ME (VR, Calais VR). Died 15 Sep 1836 age 1y 4m 7d in Calais (VR:1:227, g.s.). Buried in Calais Cemetery.

v. WESLEY FERRIS, born 9 Feb 1837 in Calais, died 2 May 1837 age 2m 22d in Calais (VR:1:228, g.s.). Buried in Calais Cemetery.

vi. CELINDA ELIZABETH FERRIS, born 20 Mar 1838 in Calais, died 14 Dec 1852 age 15 y in Calais (VR, g.s.). Buried in Calais Cemetery. Bapt. 22 June 1851 in Calais (saint). Census: 1850 in Calais.

vii. THOMAS COKE FERRIS, born 9 Apr 1840 in Calais (VR). Bapt. 13 Jan 1860 in Calais (saint). Census: 1850 & 60 in Calais.

viii. AMELIA E.{1} FERRIS, born 19 Apr 1842 in Calais, died 15 Mar 1843 age 11mos in Calais (VR:1:228). Buried: 16 Mar 1843 in Calais Cemetery.

ix. AMELIA E.{2} FERRIS, born circa 1844. Bapt. 13 Jan 1860 in Calais (saint). Census: 1850 & 60 in Calais.

x. HORTENCE ISADORE FERRIS, born circa 1846. Bapt. 12 Feb 1851 in Calais (saint). Census: 1850 & 60 in Calais.

xi. JOHN AUGUSTUS FERRIS, born Jun 1850, died 2 Sep 1851 age 14m in Calais (FJ, g.s.). Bapt. 12 Feb 1851 in Calais (saint). Buried 4 Sept 1851 in Calais Cemetery (saint). Census: 1850 in Calais.

SAMUEL & SARAH FIELD, p. 216

SAMUEL FIELD, born circa 1805 in Brunswick ME (1850 census). He was a teamster. Died circa 1861 in Calais (g.s.). Buried: 9 Apr 1861 in Calais Cemetery. Census: 1850 & 60 (living in boarding home) in Calais.

He married SARAH (_____), born circa 1805 in St. David, NB (1850 census). Probably died before 1860. Census: 1850 in Calais. Children:

i. HANNAH ELIZABETH FIELD, born 27 Mar 1844 in Calais (VR). Died 9 Nov 1853 Calais (VR, g.s.). Buried: 11 Nov 1853 in Calais Cemetery. Census: 1850 in Calais.

WILLIAM & MARGARET FINTON, p. 206

WILLIAM FINTON, born circa 1813 in Ireland. Immigrated about 1844-45 from NB (irmsa). He worked as a gardener. Died 16 Jan 1877 age 62 in Calais (g.s.). Buried in Calais Cemetery. Census: 1860 & 70 in Calais.

He married in Ireland, MARGARET (_____), born circa 1804 in Ireland. Died 31 Jul 1868 age 64y 5m in Calais (g.s.). Buried in Calais Cemetery. Census: 1860 in Calais. Children:

i. WILLIAM FINTON, Jr., born circa 1837 in Ireland. Served in Civil War, enlisted 14 Sept 1861 at age 23 in Co A 9th Me Inf., he was 5' 7 ¾" with blue eyes and light hair, left service 22 Dec 1864, died of disease (cwcard). Census: 1860 in Calais.

ii. MARY FINTON, born circa 1839 in Ireland. Census: 1860 (age 21 with parents) in Calais. [1860 census Mary J. Finton age 19 living with James Farling (sp ?) family as servant]

iii. EUGENE OWEN FINTON, born circa 1843 in Ireland. He was blind from age 2 (1880 special census). Died 13 Mar 1905 age 62 in Calais (MSA, g.s.). Unmarried. He was buried 14 Mar 1905 in Calais Cemetery. Census: 1860, 70 & 80, 1900 (in Alms House age 61) in Calais.

iv. MARGARET FINTON, born circa 1844 in NB. Census: 1860 (age 16) in Calais.

v. ANN/ANNIE FINTON, born (1) 25 May 1845 in Calais (VR), born (2) 16 Mar 1846 Calais (VR:3: 249). Census: 1860 (age 15), 1870 (age 25 with brother, Michael) in Calais.

vi. MICHAEL FINTON, born (1) 10 Sep 1846 in Calais (VR), born (2) 1 Jan 1847 Calais (VR:3:249). He was a teamster. Census: 1860 (age 12) & 70 (age 23) in Calais.

vii. HELLEN/ELLEN FINTON, born 2 Jan 1850 in Calais (VR:3:249). Census: 1860, 1870 (age 20 with brother, Michael) in Calais.

He married 2nd on 16 Oct 1868 in Calais (VR:3) CATHERINE GOOD born ca 1816-1822 in Ireland. She died 11 Sept 1893 age 78 in Calais (adv). Census 1870 (age 48), 1880 (age 63, granddaughter, Maggie E. Courtney age 4 living with her) in Calais.

EDWARD & MARY FITSGERALD, p. 201

EDWARD FITSGERALD, born ca 1814 Kilbenny, Limerick Co. Ireland. Left Ireland 10 Apr 1838, arrived St. Andrews, NB 12 June 1838, left NB in 1840 and arrived in Sept in Calais applied for citizenship 24 Sept 1852 (SJC 10:509). Naturalized 4 Oct 1854, witness: George B. Burns (irmch, no birth date or port of entry given).

He married MARY (_____). Children:

i. WILLIAM FITSGERALD, born 24 Feb 1843 in Calais (VR).

ii. BRIDGET FITSGERALD, born 5 May 1845 in Calais (VR).

iii. PATRICK H. FITSGERALD, born 14 Mar 1846 in Calais. Died 24 Jan 1926 age 82 in Minneapolis, MN survived by wife and 2 sons, also two nieces in Calais, Mrs. Thompson and Miss Nellie Casey (obit adv). Buried in St. Mary's Cemetery in Minneapolis.

iv. JOHN FITSGERALD, born 3 Feb 1848 in Calais (VR). Enlisted in Civil War at age 18y 4m in Co A. 1st Batt. Inf. a laborer 5'5" with gray eyes and brown hair (cwcard). Died 26 Apr 1913 age 65 in Milltown, NB (obit).

BENJAMIN M. & ANN FLINT, p. 208

Deacon ADDISON[6] FLINT, born 23 May, 1782 in North Reading, MA, 2nd son, 6th child, of Benjamin[5], Ebenezer[4-3], George[2], Thomas[1], he married 1st 10 June 1804 SALLY UPTON, she was born in Charlesmont, MA, 15 Jan 1785 died 4 Dec. 1830. He married 2nd 3 Oct 1833 MRS. MARY E.(FOSTER) BURRILL (flint:95-6). The 4th child of Addison & Sally Flint, BENJAMIN MILTON FLINT, settled in Calais.

BENJAMIN MILTON FLINT, born 6 Mar 1812 in North Reading, MA (VR, flint:122). Came to Calais ca 1840 (obit). Served in Civil War as Captain of Home Guards, Co. G 6th Regiment, also 1st Maine. He was a postmaster and Fire Insurance Agent. He was a member of the Calais Band, played the French horn. Died 3 Sep 1890 age 79 in Calais (VR:3:314, obit, times, prbt, g.s.). Census: 1840 (1 male, 5 females), 50 thru 1880 in Calais.

He married 11 Jun 1838 by Rev. Jason Whitman in North Reading, MA (VR, flint:122), ANN S. SPARROW, born circa 1807 in Mass (1850 census = Portland). Died 30 Jun 1890 age 83 in Calais (obit, times, SSC, g.s.). Buried in Calais Cemetery. Census: 1850 thru 1880 in Calais. Children:

i. ELLEN SPARROW FLINT, born 19 Sep 1839 in Calais, died 27 Dec 1856 age 17y 3m in Calais (VR, flint:122, g.s.). Buried in Calais Cemetery. Census: 1850 in Calais.
ii. CHARLES MILTON FLINT, born 3 Sep 1841 in Calais (VR, flint:122). Served in Civil War, Co. B 6th Regt., Died 10 May 1864 age 22 (missing in action Battle of Spotsylvania, NRMS:232). His father signed permission on his enlistment paper (MSA). He was a clerk, 5' 11" with blue eyes and brown hair (cwcard). Grave stone in Calais Cemetery (age 22). Census: 1860 in Calais.
iii. JULIA GREENWOOD FLINT, born 3 Oct 1843 in Calais (VR, flint:122). Died after 1890 (sole heir of father). Census: 1850, 60 & 70 in Calais. Married 28 Dec 1865 by Rev. J. Caldwell in Calais (VR) Dr. EDWIN /EDWARD S. LAUGHTON, born ca 1839 in Bangor, ME. He was a dentist (1879 Maine Register). Census: 1870 (age 31) in Calais.

JOHN & PRISCILLA FLOOD, p. 200

JOHN FLOOD, died after Priscilla, who was his wife when she died in 1839. He does not appear in 1840 or 50 census of Calais.

He married PRISCILLA MOSHER, born circa 1817 in St. John's River (sic), NB (1850 census). Died (see note below). Buried 10 Oct 1839 in Calais Cemetery (sext). Children:

- Note – There is confusion with date of death of Priscilla. [1st]daughter, Priscilla Waite's death record says her mother is Priscilla.[2nd] obit in FJ, 8 Oct 1839, Mrs. Priscilla Flood age 23 wife of John died in Calais, Mon. last, daughter of DANIEL MOSHIER of Newport, NS. [3rd] grave stone agrees Oct 8 1839 death date. [4th] three children born after 1839.

i. LOUISA JANE FLOOD, born 22 Sep 1837 in Calais (VR). Census: 1850 (Louisa J. Flood age 12 living with James Irving family). She married 26 Aug 1856 in Calais by Rev. S. H. Keeler (union), HENRY E. BRADLEY of Calais (VR:1:169).
ii. PRISCILLA W. FLOOD, born 16 Sep 1844 in Calais (VR, sfh:112, MSA has 16 July). Died 28Oct 1931age 87y 11m 12d in Calais (sfh:6:112, union, MSA). Buried in Calais Cemetery. Census: 1850 (with Mary Ann Hersey in boarding home of Eliza Flood) & 60 (with Freeman Hersey), 70 & 80 in Calais. She married (int.) 12 May 1864 FREDERICK TOWNSLEY WAITE, son of BENJAMIN FRANKLIN WAITE AND HANNAH TODD (see WAITE).
iii. UNNAMED CHILD FLOOD, born circa 1845. Died Aug 1847 in Calais (g.s.). Buried: 15 Aug 1847 in Calais Cemetery.
iv. JOHN FLOOD, (jr.), born circa 1848. Census: 1850 (age 2 with Mary Ann Hersey in boarding home of Eliza Flood), 1860 (age 12 with Freeman Hersey and sister Priscilla) in Calais.

MICHAEL & ELIZA FOLAY, p. 205
(also Foley)

MICHAEL FOLEY/FOLLAY, born circa 1810, in Ireland. Census: 1850 (age 40) & 60 (age 55) in Calais.
He married before 1839 ELIZA F. (_____), born circa 1820 in Ireland. Census: 1850 (age 30) & 60 (age 40) in Calais. Children:

i. MARY FOLEY, born circa 1839 in St. John's River (sic), NB (1850 census). Census: 1850 (age 11) & 60 (age 18) in Calais. Married (int.) filed 14 Nov 1861 to JOHN PHINNEY in Calais (VR:1:98).
ii. ANDREW FOLEY, born circa 1841, in St. John's River (sic), NB (1850 census). Census: 1850 (age 9) & 60 (age 17) in Calais.
iii. JOHN FOLEY, born circa 1843 in Calais (1850 census). Census: 1850 (age 9) & 60 (age 14) in Calais.
iv. JAMES FOLEY, born Aug 1846 in Calais (VR). Census: 1850 (age 4), & 1860 (age 10) in Calais.
v. EDWARD FOLEY, born Sep 1849 in Calais (1850 census). Census: 1850 (age 10mos) & 60 (age9) in Calais.

*Note: Notice the ages in the 50 & 60 census, none of the children 10 years older than previous census. None appear in 70 census.

WILLIAM & ELLEN FOLAY, p. 198

WILLIAM FOLEY/FOLAY/FOLLAY, born in British Empire, no date, of Eastport, naturalized 1 Mar 1849 (irmch *no port of entry or witnesses given*).
He married before 1846 ELLEN (_____). Children:

i. STEPHEN FOLEY, born 2 Sept 1846 in Calais (VR).

EDMUND & ELIZABETH FOSS, p. 219

EDMUND FOSS, born circa 1802 in Lisbon ME (1850 census), (his 2 youngest sons' death records list his birthplace as Michigan). He was a surveyor and in 1860 he was the Poor Farm Overseer. Died 26 Apr 1863 age 60 in Calais (VR:3:303, g.s.). Buried: 28 Apr 1863 in Calais Cemetery. Census: 1850 & 60 in Calais.

He married 1st ELIZABETH S. (_____), born circa 1822 in NB. Died 28 May 1848 age 42 in Calais (g.s.). Buried in Calais Cemetery. Children:

i. MARY LOVEJOY FOSS, born 8 Jul 1835 in St. Stephen, NB (Calais VR). Census: 1850 in Calais.
ii. JULIA ELIZABETH FOSS, born 10 Nov 1837 in Perry ME (Calais VR). Census: 1850 in Calais.
iii. MARTHA FOSS, born 25 Dec 1839 in Calais (VR). Census: 1850 in Calais.
iv. MINERVA FOSS, born 12 Aug 1843 in Calais (VR). Census: 1850 in Calais.
v. CHARLES HENRY MCFARLAND FOSS, born 22 Jan 1846 in Calais (VR). Served in Civil War. Resided in So. Omaha, Neb. (after Civil War, MSA). Census: 1850 & 60 in Calais.
vi. HIRAM STICKNEY FOSS, born 3 Oct 1847 in Calais (VR). Census: 1850 & 60 in Calais.

He married 2nd 16 Jun 1849 in Calais (VR:1:145) ANN MARIA KIDD (name from son's death rec.), born in Moores Mills NB. Died 24 Oct 1886 age 64 in Calais (g.s.). Census: 1860 in Calais. Children:

vii. HOLMAN D. FOSS, born 29 Apr 1850 in Calais (obit). He was a traveling salesman, died 3 Aug 1917 at age 67y 3m 5d in Houlton Me (obit, adv, MSA). Census: 1850 & 60 in Calais, 1900 in Houlton. He married May 1872 in Upper Mills, NB (adv) T. BERRANGA THOMPSON, born 23 Mar 1851 in St. Stephen, NB, daughter of WILLIAM & REBECCA THOMPSON, died 17 Oct 1915 in Houlton, ME (MSA, his obit). Census: 1900 in Houlton.
viii. GEORGE EVERETT FOSS, born circa 1859. He was a horse dealer. Died 16 June 1924 age 59y 9m 11d in Danforth, Me (obit adv, MSA). Census: 1860 in Calais. He married MILLIE OUTHOUSE (from son's death record).

GILBERT & ELLEN C. FOSTER, p. 201

ROBERT FOSTER, b. ca Dec 1773 in NB, d. 24 Apr 1854, son of JOHN FOSTER. He married 1st MARY CAMPBELL, b. ca 1770 in Steuben, d. 12 Feb 1803, no children. He married 2nd JANE ALLINE, b. 13 Aug 1786, d. at Cherryfield after 1854. They had eleven children, the oldest was Gilbert Foster of Calais (prf:211).

GILBERT FOSTER, born 16 Apr 1804 in Steuben (prf: 211) in Cherryfield, ME (1850 census). He was a tinsmith & merchant, in 1871 owned a meat shop. Died 8 Apr 1880 in Calais (times). Census: 1840 (3 males, 3 females), 50, 60 & 70 in Calais.

He married July 1830 in Calais, by Rev. Mr. Church (light of 28 July 1830) ELLEN COBB JONES, born circa 1808 in Ellsworth Me, daughter of THEODORE JONES & (C)KATHERINE WINTHROP SARGENT (prf:211). Died 6 Apr 1893 age 86 in Calais (obit, MSA, east:497). Buried in Calais Cemetery. Census: 1850, 60 & 70 in Calais. Children:

i. GILBERT HENRY FOSTER, born 30 Mar 1831 in Calais (VR). He was a bookkeeper. Died 16 May 1899 age 68 in Calais (MSA). Census: 1850 thru 1880 in Calais. He married 1st 26 Oct 1858 in Calais (union) HELEN AUGUSTA PIKE, daughter of WILLIAM CORNELIUS PIKE JR. AND FRANCES CAMPBELL

TODD (see PIKE). He married 2nd 15 Aug 1871 (east:255) in Calais MARIA LOUISA PIKE, sister of his first wife, all three buried in Calais Cemetery (see PIKE).

ii. MARY ELLEN FOSTER, born 9 May 1835 in Calais (VR). Census: 1850 & 60 in Calais. She married 11 Feb 1868 (union, jord:258) in Calais HENRY COBB JORDAN, born 15 July 1827, son of SAMUEL JORDAN of Ellsworth, ME and CLARISSA BLUNT of Trenton, Me (jord:257, 8). He died 24 June 1875 (jord:258). Resided Ellsworth.

iii. HENRIETTA BREWER FOSTER, born 29 Nov 1836 in Calais (VR). Henrietta is a lineal descendant of John Winthrop and Thomas Dudley (mop:196). Died after 1911. Census: 1850, 60, 70 & 1900 in Calais. She married 30 Aug 1859 by Rev. S.H. Keller in Calais (biorev:29:330, east:173, union), (VR has date 27 Aug) FRANK NELSON, born 4 Jan 1837 in Bangor, ME (mop:195-6), son of SAMUEL NELSON & CYNTHIA ALDRICH, descendant of Thomas Nelson, immigrant, and Moses Aldrich (biorev:29:326). He was of Boston at time of marriage where he was an accountant. He moved to Calais in 1860 where he became active in public affairs of the City of Calais (mop:196). In 1870 he was a bank cashier. He died 14 Apr 1911 in Bangor (MSA). Census: 1860, 70 & 1900 in Calais.

iv. WILLIAM BREWER FOSTER, born 21 Apr 1838 in Calais (VR), born (2): 6 Apr 1835 (sfh:7:90). He was a sheriff. Died 3 Feb 1928 age 92y 9m 28d in Calais (MSA, sext, sfh, g.s. = 1837-1929). Buried in Calais Cemetery. Census: 1850 thru 80 in Calais. He married HANNAH EMMA HALL, daughter of JAMES SULLIVAN HALL AND MARY E. SPRING (see HALL).

BENJAMIN & SARAH FRENCH, p. 189

BENJAMIN W. FRENCH, born circa 1814 in Livermore ME, son of WARREN FRENCH b. ca 1793 (MSA). He was a watchman. Died 26 Sep 1896 age 82y 7m 9d in Calais (MSA, obit times). Census: 1840 (1 male, 1 female), 50, 60 & 70 in Calais.

He married (int.) 21 Mar 1840 in Calais (VR:1:5, FJ), SARAH HALKSHAW born circa 1822 in Ireland. Died 31 Mar 1889 age 70y 2m 8d in Calais (east:420). Census: 1850, 60 & 70 in Calais. Children:

i. DAUGHTER FRENCH {adopted}, born circa 1835, died Apr 1846 age 11 in Calais (sext). Buried: 9 Apr 1846 in Calais Cemetery.

ii. LUCY ANN FRENCH, born 23 Jan 1842 in Calais. Census: 1850, 60 & 70 in Calais. She married 6 Jul 1864 by Rev. E. W. Murray in Calais (VR) JAMES MCFARLANE, born ca 1823. He was a lumberman. Census: 1870.

iii. WARREN ALBERT FRENCH,{twin} born 24 Nov 1844 in Calais (VR). Died 14 Apr 1846 age 17m in Calais (VR, sext). Buried: 17 Apr 1846 in Calais Cemetery.

iv. THOMAS WILLIAM FRENCH, {twin} born 24 Nov 1844 in Calais (VR). Died 8 Jun 1846 age 19m in Calais (VR, sext). Buried: 10 Jun 1846 in Calais Cemetery.

v. WARREN FRENCH, born 7 May 1847 in Calais (VR). Census: 1850 & 60 in Calais.

vi. MARGARET E. FRENCH, born 15 July 1850 in Calais (VR:3:255). Census: 1850 & 60 in Calais.

vii. ONETTA FRENCH, born 23 Jul 1852 (VR). Census: 1860 & 70 in Calais.

viii. ALBERT H. FRENCH, born 31 Aug 1854 in Calais (VR). He was a guide and in 1907 a policeman (adv). Died 12 June 1911 38y 10m in Calais (MSA). Census: 1860, 70 & 1900 in Calais. He married before 1881 JENNIE MAE L. GAGE, born 6 Mar 1857 in St. George, NB (MSA), daughter of KENNEDY GAGE (b. Ire) & ISABELLA EVANS (b. St. John, NB). Died 24 May 1943 age 86y 1m 18d in Calais (MSA). Census: 1900 & 1920 (age 63 living with Joseph Doyle and family) in Calais.

ELI & CYNTHIA FROST, p. 215

ELI FROST, he was in Calais by 1837 when he was a defendant in a court action, he was a lumberman (CCP:16:178). Not listed in 1840 census of Calais.

He married (int) 5 July 1835 in Calais (cal2:39) CYNTHIA NASH. (poss d/o Joseph Nash) Children:

i. ANGELINE SOPHIA FROST, born 9 Feb 1836 in Calais (VR). Census: 1850 (age 14 with Joseph Nash) in Calais.

ii. ELY R. FROST, born circa 1840, died Jul 1848 age 8y in Calais (g.s.). Buried: 18 Jul 1848 in Calais

Cemetery.

*Note. Is it possible that Eli died or moved away from Calais before 1850 census? Did Cynthia die in childbirth when Ely R. was born? At age 14 Angeline living in another household.

THOMAS J. D. & ELIZABETH D. FULLER, p. 215

MARTIN[6] FULLER, son of THOMAS[5], JOHN[4-3-2], MATTHEW[1] (FULLER), married LETITIA DUNCAN their son Thomas lived in Calais (fuller:88).

THOMAS JAMES DUNCAN[7] FULLER, born 17 Mar 1808 in Hardwick, VT (biodir:976). In 1841 he was a Div. Advocate in the State Militia. He was an Attorney with a practice in Calais. He was elected to four terms as a representative to Congress (4 Mar 1849 to 3 Mar 1857); appointed by President Buchanan as Second Auditor of the treasury and served from 15 Apr 1857 to 3 Aug 1861; engaged in the practice of law before the U S Supreme Court and the Court of Claims in Washington, DC (biodir:976). Died 13 Feb 1876 age 68 in Upperville, VA (fuller:88), while on a visit to his son. Buried Oak Hill Cemetery, Washington, DC (biodir). Census: 1840 (3 males, 2 females), 50 in Calais.

He married 1st 6 Jun 1836 in Calais (mrwc:21, fuller:81), ELIZABETH DORDIN[7] TITCOM born circa 1809 in NH (1850 census), daughter of PEARSON[6] TITCOMB AND ANNE MARIA DE LES DERNIER, granddaughter of JOHN[5], SAMUEL[4], JOHN[3], PENUEL[2], WILLIAM[1] TITCOMB Died 13 Sep 1864 in Washington, DC (titcomb:86-87). Census: 1850 in Calais. Children:

i. WILLIAM DE LES DERNEIR FULLER, born 22 May 1837 in Calais (VR). Graduate of West Point Military Academy, served in the Civil War, received rank of Major at Gettysburg (fuller:86). Died 11 Mar 1886 (fuller:86). He died in Sedalis, MO and was called 'Major' in his obit, he left $50,000 to charity and nothing to his step-mother and her son (adv). Resided in Upperville, VA & Florida. Census: 1850 in Calais.

ii. UNNAMED CHILD FULLER, born circa 1839 in Calais, died 19 Aug 1840 age 1y in Calais (g.s.). Buried in Calais Cemetery.

iii. UNNAMED CHILD FULLER, born circa 1841 in Calais, died 19 Aug 1842 age 11m in Calais (g.s.) Buried in Calais Cemetery.

iv. LYDIA JANE FULLER, born circa 1846 in Calais, died 17 Oct 1847 age 18m in Calais (FJ, g.s.). Buried in Calais Cemetery.

He married 2nd 25 Jul 1869 (fuller:86) JENNIE ELIZABETH DOLITTLE. Died after 1886 (when step-son died). Children:

v. THOMAS JAMES DUNCAN FULLER, Jr., born 18 Aug 1870 (fuller:81). Died after 1886. He married 2 Nov 1892 ELIZABETH ASHMEAD SHAEFFER, born 1 Feb 1872 in Ithaca, NY (fuller:88).

SAMUEL & ABIGAIL FURLONG, p. 178 & 222

THOMAS W. FURLONG, possibly the son of PATRICK FURLONG & ANN SWEET, he married ELIZABETH JORDAN they lived in Greenwood, Me (lime). Their son Samuel moved from Greenville to Calais.

SAMUEL FURLONG, born 17 July 1800 in Norway, ME (1850 census). Resided in Greenwood, Me. before moving to Calais. He was a lumberman and farmer, in 1850 he was a member of the State Legislature, served as Calais City Tax Collector and was a Deputy Sheriff under Benjamin Farrar in 1866, the year he died of a heart attack after subduing a robbery suspect, Thomas McKay (NRMS:22, SCC). In testimony given in court Oct 1857 he stated he has been tax collector for 9 years and assessor for 5 years, lived in Calais for last 39 years (SJC:14:516). Died 22 Nov 1866 age 66y 4m in Calais (g.s., prbt). Buried in Calais Cemetery. Census: 1840 (3 males, 3 females), 50 & 60 in Calais.

He married before 1833 ABIGAIL DOW, born 22 Mar 1811 in Whitefield ME (VR), daughter of JEREMIAH DOW & REBECKAH GLIDDEN, sister of Jonathan Dow (see DOW). Died 8 Mar 1867 age 56y 9m in Calais (east:227). Probate of Estate in Machias Me (dau., Hannah Furlong exec.). Buried in Calais Cemetery. Census: 1850 & 60 in Calais. Children:

i. ALONZO FURLONG, born 2 Apr 1834 in Calais (VR). Died 22 Mar 1843 age 28y 11m 19d in Calais

(sext, g.s.). Buried in Calais Cemetery.
ii. REUEL WILLIAMS {1} FURLONG, born 23 Nov 1834 in Calais, died Nov 1834 in Calais (VR).
iii. REUEL WILLIAMS {2} FURLONG, born 23 Nov 1835 in Calais (VR) in Whitefield ME (1850 census). Before entering the service he was a schoolmaster. He died 19 Nov 1863, killed in action in the Battle of Rappahannock, VA Civil War, Capt. of Co. D 6th Maine (NRMS:155). He was 6' 2" and known as 'The Calais giant' and was found surrounded by the bodies of his enemies (NRMS:238). Census: 1850 in Calais. He married 7 Mar 1863 in St. Stephen, NB (CCMR). FANNIE BILLINGS HIGGINS, born 6 Apr 1843 in Eastport, daughter of SIMEON & MARGARET HIGGINS (Eastport VR).
iv. LOUISA AMANDA FURLONG, born 10 Oct 1837 in Calais (VR). Died 31 Jan 1864 20y 2m 23d in Calais (g.s.). Buried in Calais Cemetery. Census: 1850 in Calais. She married before 1859 JOSEPH HUBBARD.
v. MINERVA ABIGAIL FURLONG, born 17 Oct 1839 in Milltown ME (Calais VR). She was a teacher. Died 7 Jan 1924 in Meddybemps ME (MSA). Buried: Round Pond Cemetery, Charlotte. Census: 1850 & 60 in Calais, 1870 in Charlotte. She married (int.) 2 Oct 1860 in Charlotte, ME (VR) MOSES L. DAMON, born 12 Feb 1833 in Charlotte (VR), son of ISAIAH DAMON AND MARY BRIDGES. Died 10 Nov 1913 age 80y 9m in Charlotte (MSA, adv). Buried: Round Pond Cemetery, Charlotte. Census: 1870 in Charlotte.
vi. MELISSA PEASLEE FURLONG, born 1842 in Calais (fur:54). She was a dressmaker. Census: 1850 & 60 in Calais. She married 1st 7 Apr 1864 in Calais (VR) RUFUS D. PHIPPS who enlisted in Co F of 6th Maine at age 22 on 14 June 1861. Discharged for disability on 16 Oct 1862, had blue eyes and brown hair, was a farmer (cwcard). He died before 1867. She married 2nd (as Malissa P. Phipps) 20 Oct 1867 in Calais (VR) CHARLES M. HOLMES, born ca 1833, son of JAMES & TEMPERANCE HOLMES (see HOLMES). She married 3rd (as Malissa P. Holmes) 16 Dec 1873 by Rev. I. C. Knowlton in Calais (VR:3:238), B. F. OSGOOD of Prentis, ME.

* In a news article {not dated} found at CFL about the Furlong family there is mentioned a Mrs. Melissa P. Osgood of Prentis formerly Melissa Furlong oldest daughter of Samuel Furlong.

vii. HANNAH REBECCA [1] FURLONG, born 21 Jan 1844 in Calais (VR:1:222). Died 15 Apr 1845 age 1y 2m in Calais (VR:1:240).
viii. HANNAH REBECCA [2] FURLONG, born ca 1846. Census: 1850 (age 4) & 60 (age 14) in Calais. She married 17 Aug 1874 in Calais (VR:3:239) JAMES A. PHELPS.
ix. SAMUEL FURLONG, born 23 Jan 1846 in Calais, died 23 Jan 1846 in Calais (VR).
x. SAMUEL AUGUSTUS FURLONG, born 1848 in Calais (fur:54). Died 10 Feb 1876 age 27y 9m in Milltown, Me (adv, g.s.). Buried in Calais Cemetery. Census: 1850 (age 2) & 60 in Calais.
xi. CHARLES L. FURLONG, born ca July 1850, died 22 Sept 1851 age 1y 2m (g.s.). Buried in Calais Cemetery.
xii. WILLARD FRANKLIN FURLONG, born circa 1854 in Calais. Died after 1885. Census: 1860 in Calais. He married 4 Apr 1873 in Lewiston, ELIZABETH L. (_____) she left him 1 Dec 1876, he divorced her in Apr 1885 (SJC docket #27).

SAMUEL & MARY GALLAGHER, p. 197

SAMUEL J. GALLAGHER, born 12 May 1813 in Donegal, Ire. (1850 census, obit). Entered U. S. 28 June 1836 at Eastport, born in County of Donegal, Ireland in 1813, naturalized 24 Feb 1852 (irmch, no witnesses). After his marriage he lived for short periods in St. John, NB, Machias, Me, and St. Stephen, NB before moving to Calais where he resided for the rest of his life. He was a house painter by trade and a deacon in Congregational church from 1875 to 1883. Died 18 Nov 1883 age 70 in Calais (adv, congo). Probate of Estate in Machias Me. Buried in Calais Cemetery. Census: 1840 (1 male, 3 females), 50 thru 1880 in Calais.

He married ca 1837 in St. John, NB, MARY THOMPSON, born circa 1814 in Scotland (1850 census = Derry, Ire.), daughter of JAMES THOMPSON AND MARGARET FURGASON (both b. in Scotland). Died: 9 Nov 1896 age 77y 6m in Calais (obit adv, survived by 7 children, MSA, congo). Census: 1850 thru 1880 in Calais. Children:

i. JAMES WILLIAM GALLAGHER, born 16 Jul 1838 in Calais (VR). Died 16 Oct 1839 in Calais (VR:1:235).
ii. CATHERINE 'Kate' HALL GALLAGHER, born 3 Oct 1839 in Calais (VR). Bapt. 17 Nov 1839 in Calais (congo). Died after Aug 1896 (she survived her mother adv). Census: 1850 & 60 in Calais. She married

      (int.) 28 Oct 1863 in Calais JOSEPH BYRON, Jr. of Jamaica Plain, MA (VR 1:107).
- iii. MARGARET 'Maggie' FERGUSON GALLAGHER, born 26 Mar 1841 in Calais (VR). Bapt. 18 July 1841 in Calais (congo). Died 19 Mar 1875 age 32 in Calais (obit adv, congo). Census: 1850, 60 & 70 in Calais.
- iv. SAMUEL JAMES GALLAGHER, born 6 Apr 1842 in Calais (VR). Bapt. 23 Oct 1842 in Calais (congo). Served in Civil War enlisted at age 19 Co F 22nd inf., as Pvt., then Sgt., then was a Lt. in Co E of 14th Inf., he had blue eyes and dark hair. Resided in Augusta, ME 1872 when he married and in 1884 when he was exec. of father's will. In Dec 1894 he was appointed Commissary and Quartermaster of the Soldier's Home at Togus (SCC). Died 3 Apr 1910 age 68 at the Soldiers Home, in Chelsea, Ma (cwcard, post Civil War addresses at MSA, obit). Buried in Calais Cemetery. Census: 1850, 60 & 70 in Calais. He married 1st 24 July 1860 by Rev. Burt at Minneapolis, MN (VSNB:25:1634) ADELAIDE E. CROSBY born 1845 in Bangor (fini), daughter of CHARLES WILLIAM CROSBY & SARAH STONE PARSONS, she died 3 Mar 1868 age 23 in Jamaica Plain, MA (VSNB:27:223, fini). Buried: In her father's lot at Mt. Hope Cemetery, Bangor, ME (cem. rec.). He married 2nd 27 Sept 1872 in Calais by Rev. William Carruthers (union) MARIA/EMMA YOUNG of Calais, born ca 1851, daughter of WILLIAM HARRISON YOUNG [born in Waterford, Vt. he was the proprietor. of the St. Croix Exchange Hotel in Calais. He died 1889 in Calais at age 74 (adv)] & his wife MARGRET. Census: 1870 in Calais (with her parents).
- v. ROBERT JOHN GALLAGHER, born 10 Sep 1843 in NB (VR). Bapt. 30 June 1844 in Calais (congo). Died 20 Jun 1918 age 73 in Wollaston, MA (obit, adv). Census: 1850 & 60 in Calais.
- vi. MARY ELIZABETH GALLAGHER, born 10 Feb 1845 by Rev. William S. McKeller in Calais (VR:3:221). Died possibly before mother. Census: 1850, 60 & 70 in Calais. She married 13 Aug 1866 in Calais (VR:1:122, fini). ALPHEUS H. WARD of Calais, born ca 1841. He was a trader. Census: 1870 in Calais.
- vii. MARTHA GALLAGHER, born 20 Aug 1846 in Calais (VR, fini). Died 12 Oct 1915 age 68y 3m in Calais (MSA). Census: 1850, 60, 70 & 1900 in Calais. She married JOHN A. SEARS, born ca 1843 in Canada. He was a fancy job painter. He died after 1920. Census: 1870, 1900 & 1920 (age 77) in Calais.
- viii. JANE GALLAGHER, born circa 1849 in Calais. Died after 1896 (she survived her mother). Resided Boston 1896. Census: 1850 in Calais. She married 15 May 1873 (VR:3) RODNEY P. WOODMAN of NH.
- ix. JOSEPH GALLAGHER, born circa 1851 in Maine (fini). Census: 1860 & 70 in Calais. He resided in Black Hills, Col. in 1890 when he visited his family in Calais after a 15-16 year absence (adv).
- x. EUGENIA GALLAGHER, born circa 1852 in Maine (fini). Died: possibly before mother. Census: 1860 in Calais.
- xi. ANNIE ISABEL GALLAGHER, born ca 1854, died ca 1860 (deaths of 1860 age 6, union has age 7y 1m).
- xii. JESSIE F. GALLAGHER, born circa 1857 in Maine (fini). Died Mar 1906 in St. Stephen, NB (obit adv). Census: 1860, 70 & 80 in Calais.

NATHANIEL & NANCY GARDNER, p. 207

NATHANIEL GARDNER, born 5 Sep 1793 in Paris ME ? (Calais book at LDS no ref., unable to confirm). Died before 1846 (Nancy was a widow 1846). Census: 1830 (1 male, 1 female), 40 (5 males, 15 females) in Calais.
    He married ca 1830 NANCY (_____). Died after May 1846 (sext, buried Mrs. Gardner's child). Children:

- i. SAMUEL GARDNER, born 29 Jul 1831 in Calais (VR).
- ii. NATHANIEL GARDNER, [jr.], born 16 Jan 1835 in Calais (VR).
- iii. CAROLINE GARDNER, born 14 May 1839 in Calais (VR).
- iv. EMELINE L. GARDNER, born, 10 Jan 1841 in Calais (VR).
- v. ANGELINE GARDNER, born 15 Mar 1843 in Calais (VR). Died: May 1846 age 2y 6m in Calais (sext). Buried: 17 May 1846 in Calais Cemetery.

SALMON & LUCY GATES, p. 221

SALMON P. GATES, born 30 Aug 1783 in Hubbardston, MA (VR, beg:123, gate:143) son of JONATHAN GATES [1746-1808) served in Rev. War (DAR #159724)] & HEPZIBAH STONE (1747-1818). He came to Calais from Hubbardston, Ma in 1807 and didn't bring his family until 1822, he built a mansion in Milltown where he lived and died (daughter, Lucy's obit). He was Treasurer of Proprietors of Middle Bridge Corp in 1836 (SJC:3:376). He was an owner of a mill on St. Croix when in court June 1836 (SJC:3:367). Died 9 Apr 1845 age 61 in Calais (VR, gate:143, prbt, g.s.). Buried: 12 Apr 1845 in Calais Cemetery. Census: 1830 (10 males, 5 females), 40 (4 males, 3 females).

He married 28 May 1804 in Hubbardston, MA (VR) LUCY CHURCH born 5 Dec 1782 in Hubbardston, MA (VR), daughter of ASA CHURCH & RACHEL NEWTON. Died 10 Aug 1844 age 61 in Calais (obit adv, g.s, congo). Buried: 12 Aug 1844 in Calais Cemetery. Children:

i. EMELINE G. GATES, born {1} 4 Aug 1804 in Hubbardston, MA (VR), born {2} 4 Sept 1804 (kimb:663). Died 26 Aug 1892 age 87y 11m 20d in Calais (VR, MSA, gate:143). Buried in Calais Cemetery. Census: 1850 thru 1880 (living with son in law, Charles King) in Calais. She married 19 Sept 1830 JAMES GORHAM KIMBALL in Calais (see KIMBALL).
ii. CAROLINE GATES, born 25 Dec 1805 in Hubbardston, MA (VR). Died 30 Sep 1808 in Hubbardston (VR).
iii. HARRIET THURSY GATES, born 5 Nov 1807 in Hubbardston, MA (VR). Died 16 May 1883 (adv), in Calais, probate filed 16 Sept 1884. Buried in Calais Cemetery. Census: 1850 (with sister Emeline), 60 (with sister Lucy) & 70 in Calais. Never married.
iv. MARTHA GATES, born 11 Aug 1813 in Hubbardston, MA (VR). Died 7 Jan 1894 age 60y 5m in Calais (MSA). Buried in Calais Cemetery. Census: 1850 (with James Kimball), 70 & 80 (with Charles King) in Calais. Never married.
v. ASA CHURCH GATES, born 17 Apr 1815, in Hubbardston, MA (VR). Resided in Weymouth, NS in 1875 (beg:124). Died 1893 age 77y in Weymouth, NS (obit adv). He married (_____) Wentworth (gate:143).
vi. EPHRAIM CHURCH GATES, born 28 Mar 1817 in Hubbardston, MA (VR). Came to Calais in ca 1823. Graduated from Calais Academy. He was in the lumbering business, from 1847 to 1882 known as Gates & Wentworth, in 1889 he sold his business in Calais and bought another in Mott Haven, NY (adv). Died 25 Oct 1897, age 80 in New York, NY (obit adv, times, g.s.). Buried in Calais Cemetery. Census: 1850 thru 1880 in Calais. He married 1 Dec 1839 VASHTI RANDALL PICKENS, daughter of LEONARD PICKENS AND VASHTI RANDALL (see PICKENS).
vii. LUCY CAROLINE GATES, born 2 Oct 1819 in Hubbardston, MA (VR:272). Bapt. 2 Apr 1920 in Hubbardston. Came to Calais at age 3 (obit). Died 18 May 1896 in Providence RI, she left the bulk of her estate to charity (times, obit adv). Buried in Calais Cemetery. Census: 1850, 60 & 70 in Calais. She married 9 Jun 1846 by Rev. S. H. Keeler in Calais GILES MERRILL WENTWORTH, son of TAPPAN WENTWORTH AND ELIZABETH BRADBURY (see WENTWORTH).
viii. SALMON STEPHEN GATES, born 28 May 1827 in Calais (VR). Died 8 Apr 1883 age 55y 10m in Milltown ME (obit, times). Buried in Calais Cemetery. Census: 1850, 1860 (living with James Kimball) in Calais. Never married.

JOHN & MARGARET GOOD, p. 194
(sometimes GOODE)

JOHN GOOD, born circa 1805 in Roscommon, Ireland (casey). Census: 1860 in Calais. Immigrated to U. S. in 1850, naturalized 9 Oct. 1856 (irmch, no port of entry or birth date given). He was a grocer. Died 19 Oct 1869 age 65 in Calais (obit).

He married 29 Nov 1846 in St. Stephen, NB (his obit, cath) MARGARET TRACEY born 3 May 1827 in Galway, Ireland, daughter of THOMAS S. & MARY TRACEY, immigrated in 1843 (casey). Died 3 Sep 1900 age 73y 4m in Calais (MSA). Buried: 5 Sep 1900 in St. Stephen, NB. Census: 1860, 70, 1900 (with son Joseph) in Calais. Children:

i. MICHAEL GOOD, born 7 Sep 1847 in Calais (VR). Died circa 1848 in Calais.
ii. MARY GOOD, born circa 1849 in Maine. Resided in E. Boston, MA. 1908 when she was a survivor of her brother, William. Census: 1860 & 70 in Calais. She married 19 Dec 1871 in Calais (VR) HUGH MCMULLEN.
iii. THOMAS GOOD, born 23 Jan 1855 in Calais (VR). Died 1 Feb 1894 (cath). Census: 1860 & 70 in Calais.
iv. JOHN GOOD [jr.], born 5 Apr 1857 in Calais (cath). Died circa 1860 (g.s). Buried in Calais Cemetery.
v. WILLIAM JOHN GOOD, born 14 Mar 1860 in Calais (cath, sfh). He was a cabinet maker. He resided in E.

Boston, MA for thirty years prior to his death (obit). Died 19 May 1908 age 48y 2m in St. Stephen, NB (sfh:1:76, obit adv). Buried in St. Stephen, NB. Census: 1860 & 70 in Calais.

vi. JOSEPH M. GOOD, born 30 Nov 1862 in Calais (MSA). Died 3 Dec 1920 age 58y 3d in Calais (MSA, obit). Census: 1870, 1900, 10, 20 (name James) in Calais. He married circa 1891 (from his obit) HENORA 'NORA' AGNES CROWLEY, born 12 July 1861 in Cork Station, NB, daughter of CORNELIUS CROWLEY & NANCY WINSTON, died 23 Dec 1951 in Calais (MSA). Census: 1900, 10 & 20 in Calais.

vii. MARTIN J. GOOD, born Apr 1864 in Calais, died 22 Mar 1907 age 41y 11m 3d in Calais (MSA, adv). He was a shoemaker. He played in the Calais City Band (SCC). Census: 1870 & 1900 in Calais. He married circa 1890 MARGARET M. GOULDRICH (McGouldrick) b. Feb 1866 (1900 census) in Union, NB (from his obit). Census: 1900, 1910 & 1920 (Margaret age 52 b. Canada, became citizen in Nov 1890) in Calais.

CALVIN R. & ELIZA ANN GOODENOW, p. 200
C. R. & SARAH GOODENOW, p. 200

CALVIN RICE GOODNOW, born 2 Jun 1807 in Bucksport, ME (VR), son of CALVIN GOODENOW & SALOME PHILLIPS. Calvin was of St. John, NB when he appeared in court in Apr 1854 (SJC:12:169). In 1870 he was a shingle merchant. Died 23 Jan 1873 age 66 in Calais (obit, came to Calais 1834, east:271). Buried in Calais Cemetery. Probate of Estate: 1873, in Machias Me (wife & 4 children survive, his signature on will has no 'e'). Census: 1840 (7 males, 3 females), 50, 60 & 70 in Calais.

He married 1st before 1837 ELIZA ANN (_____). Died 16 Sep 1841 in Calais (g.s.). Buried: 18 Sep 1841 in Calais Cemetery. Children:

i. HENRY KENT GOODNOW, born 9 Mar 1839 in Calais (VR). Died 3 Nov 1865 age 26 in Calais (VR:3:312, g.s., union). Buried in Calais Cemetery. Census: 1850 & 60 in Calais.

He married 2nd 29 Jul 1843 by Rev. Seth H. Keeler in Calais (mrwc:39, gaz) SARAH ELIZABETH ARNOLD, daughter of BENJAMIN & MARY ARNOLD (see ARNOLD)

ii. ELIZA MARIA GOODNOW, born 12 Apr 1844 in Calais (VR). Died 18 Dec 1920 in Chicago, IL (g.s., congo). Buried in Calais Cemetery. Census: 1850, 60 & 70 in Calais. She married 12 Sep 1866 by Rev. H. Keeler in Calais (VR:3:216, mop:233, congo) Dr. EDWARD HOWARD VOSE, born 20 Aug 1838 in Robbinston, son of PETER THACHER VOSE AND LYDIA CUSHING BUCK (mop:233). He was a teacher in Calais 1858-60 (mop:233). He graduated from Maine Medical school of Bowdoin College, in class of 1864. Served as U.S. Navy surgeon from 2 Dec 1863 to 22 Mar 1864 (mop:233). He was interested in genealogy (vose:480). They resided in Gorham and Calais. Died 27 June 1909 age 70y 10m 27d in Calais (sfh:1:184, vose:480, bowcat:481, g.s.). Buried in Calais Cemetery. Census: 1870 in Calais.

iii. CALVIN GOODNOW (jr.), born 7 Aug 1847 in Calais, died 7 Aug 1847 in Calais (g.s.). Buried in Calais Cemetery.

iv. BENJAMIN GOODNOW, born 7 Aug 1847 in Calais, died 7 Aug 1847 in Calais (g.s.). Buried in Calais Cemetery.

v. EDWARD CALVIN GOODNOW, born circa 1852 in Calais. He was a lumber dealer and shingle manufacturer, a city councilman in 1877, member of House of Representatives in 1883-85 (biosk:1883:9). Died 16 Feb 1891 age 39 in Calais (obit adv, SCC). Census: 1860 & 70 in Calais. He married 18 Feb 1874 in Calais (adv) ELIZABETH ELLEN 'NELLIE' PIKE born 31 July 1851, daughter of SAMUEL G. PIKE [b. 6 Nov 1811] & ELLEN TRICKEY [b. 16 May 1818] (biorev:140). Died: 23 Dec 1874 age 23 in Calais (adv, obit).

vi. WALTER R. GOODNOW, born circa 1855. He was a jeweler and watchmaker. In 1889 he resided in Boston MA. Died: 12 Aug 1917 age 62 in Boston (adv). Census: 1860 & 70 in Calais. He married 26 Oct 1881 by Rev, S.J. Stewart in Bangor ME (VR, times) NELLIE A. STRICKLAND, born 13 Dec 1860 in Bangor (VR:vol.3), only daughter of PHILO & MARY E. STRICKLAND Esq. of Bangor (adv).

vii. WILLIAM NELSON GOODNOW, born circa 1858. In 1888 he was in Calais from Boston, with is brother (adv). Died after 1891 (survived brother Edward). Census: 1860 & 70 in Calais.

JOHN H. & MARY J. GOODWIN, p. 218

JOHN H. GOODWIN, born circa 1813 in St. Stephen, NB (1850 census). He was in the 1st Brigade, 7th Div. Maine Militia as a Pvt. in 1832 (mil). He was a river driver. Died 23 Dec 1879 age 66 in Calais (obit adv, g.s.). Buried in Calais Cemetery. Census: 1850, 60 & 70 in Calais.

He married (int) 26 Apr 1836 married 5 June (cal2:41, 49) MARY JANE DYER, daughter of SAMUEL DYER & MARGARET DOAK/DOKE, born 5 Sep 1816 in Calais (VR). Died 27 Jan 1861 age 45y 2m 22d in Calais (g.s.). Buried in Calais Cemetery. Census: 1850 & 60 in Calais (see DYER). Children:

i. AMAZIAH NASH GOODWIN, born 16 Dec 1837 in Calais (VR). He was a Lieut. In Co. A, 9th Me Inf. In Civil War also Co. C 6th Mass Vol. Militia, he was a machinist 5'8" with hazel eyes and brown hair, he was wounded and taken prisoner 18 July 1863 at Fort Wagner, S.C.; died of wounds, 29 July 1863 (cwcard, mss: I:378). Buried in Calais Cemetery. Census: 1850 & 60 in Calais.
ii. AUGUSTA JANE GOODWIN, born 14 Jul 1839 in Calais (VR). She was a teacher. Died 2 Dec 1895 age 55 in Calais (MSA, congo, g.s.). Buried in Calais Cemetery. Census: 1850 & 60 in Calais.. She married between Apr 1863 & Apr 1864 by Rev. Keeler in Calais, JOSIAH LYSANDER HUME, son of JOSIAH HUME & REBECCA S. STOCKWELL (see HUME).
iii. JOHN GRANVILLE GOODWIN, born 28 Sep 1842 in Calais (VR). Died 21 Aug 1843 age 10m 24d in Calais (VR:1:239, g.s.). Buried in Calais Cemetery.
iv. ABBY HOOPER GOODWIN, born 11 Jul 1844 in Calais (VR). Died 15 Jan 1883 age 37 in New York (times, g.s.). Buried in Calais Cemetery. Census: 1850 & 60 in Calais. She married EUGENE KEITH born ca 1845, died 22 Jan 1885 in New York City, buried in Calais Cemetery (obit adv).
v. HARRIET HALL GOODWIN, born 13 Aug 1847 in Calais (VR). Census: 1850, 60 & 70 in Calais. She married 27 May 1869 in Calais (VR:3:233) JOHN WADE, born in Canada. Census 1870 in Calais.
vi. GEORGE W. GOODWIN, born circa 1849. He enlisted in Civil War in Co G Coast Guard he was a laborer 5'5" with blue eyes and light hair (cwcard). From Calais adv of 30 Sept 1903: Capt. George W. Goodwin has presented to the St. Croix Club, a handsome painting of the ship *Dirigo*, of which he is master. Died 14 Jan 1916 age 67 in Brighton, MA, buried in Mt. Auburn Cemetery (obit adv). Census: 1850, 60 & 70 in Calais.
vii. FRANK ALLEN GOODWIN, born circa 1851. Died 22 Dec 1888 age ca 35 in Shanghai (obit). Census: 1860 & 70 (blacksmith) in Calais.
viii. MINNIE M. GOODWIN, born circa 1853. Census: 1860 & 70 in Calais. She married 15 Dec 1874 by Rev. William Carruthers in Calais (VR, adv) BYRON McALLISTER, born ca 1852. Census: 1870 (age 18, seaman, with mother Rachel age 50) in Calais.
ix. SARAH E. GOODWIN, born circa 1859. Census: 1860 & 70 in Calais.

JAMES W. & HANNAH GRAHAM, p. 219

JAMES GRAHAM born 1809 in Quit-Hill Island, County of Ceva, Province of Leicester, Ireland. Left Ireland 1812, arrived St. Johns, Newfoundland and stayed until September 1831, went to Halifax, NS until November 1833, then to Eastport and then to Calais. Filed naturalization intentions 11 August 1838. Witnesses to establish his residence were WILLIAM L. McALLISTER of Calais and PATRICK E. DONWORTH of Machias. Signed by George Downes, J. of P. He was naturalized 18 Sept 1840 [*from Naturalization Papers in the Sept. 1840 term of the Washington County District Court records at MSA*]. [*Records at Machias have birth place as: Lusk Hill, Cavan County, Ireland*]. He was a tailor. Census: 1840 (4 males, 2 females) & 50 in Calais.

He married (int) 1 Dec 1836 in Calais (cal2:43) HANNAH BOYDEN born circa 1819 in Robbinston Me (1850 census). Census: 1850 in Calais. Children:

i. CATHARINE WHITELY GRAHAM, born 28 Sep 1837 in Calais (VR). Census: 1850 in Calais.
ii. ZIBA ROYDEN GRAHAM, born 19 Apr 1839 in Calais (VR). Census: 1850 in Calais.
iii. ISABELLA JANE GRAHAM, born 2 Dec 1840 in Calais (VR). Census: 1850 in Calais.
iv. MINERVA LOUISE GRAHAM, born 28 Aug 1841 in Calais (VR). Census: 1850 in Calais.
v. JAMES MADISON GRAHAM, born 28 Apr 1844 in Calais (VR). Census: 1850 in Calais.

vi. MARY ANN GRAHAM, born 7 Oct 1846 in Calais (VR). Census: 1850 in Calais.
vii. EMMA L./S. GRAHAM, born circa 1849 in Calais. Census: 1850 (age 1) in Calais.

ELIJAH D. & HANNAH GREEN, p. 210

ELIJAH DIX GREEN, born 22 Mar 1799 in N. Yarmouth, ME (1850 census) (poss. s/o Rev. Thomas & Salome Green). In 1824 he was a merchant in Eastport (SJC). He was a merchant & businessman in Calais 1837 in business with Charles Copeland (SJC). He was a deacon in the Second Baptist Church. Died 6 Mar 1867 age 68y in Calais (obit SCC, union). Buried in Calais Cemetery. Census: 1840 (1 male, 4 females), 50, & 60 in Calais.

He married 1st 9 Nov 1823 in Eastport ME (east:53) HANNAH CLAFLIN HAYDEN born 4 May 1804 in Eastport ME (VR), daughter of AARON HAYDEN & RUTH RICHARDS JONES (bhm:7:134). Died 18 Jul 1864 age 60y 2m in Boston MA (g.s., east:206). Buried: 20 Jul 1864 in Calais Cemetery. Census: 1850 in Calais. Census: 1860 in Calais. [Her brother, Charles Henry Hayden, married Caroline M. Boardman (see BOARDMAN)]. Children:

i. MARY HAYDEN GREEN, born 30 Nov 1824 (bhm:1678) in Eastport, moved to Calais when very young. (obit). She was a novelist, her first novel was published in 1854, her favorite subject was the anti-slavery movement (speak), three of her books were: *Ida May, Caste, and Agnes* (obit). She died 15 Jan 1908 age 83 at the home of her niece, Mrs. H. T. Oudesluys in Baltimore, MD (obit adv, g.s.). Census: 1860, 70 & 80 in Calais. She married 28 Sept 1846 in Calais (VR:3:140) FREDERICK AUGUSTUS PIKE. Both buried in same lot with her parents in Calais Cemetery (see PIKE).
ii. EMELINE CARLTON GREEN, born 10 Oct 1827; d. 1 Mar 1829 (bhm:1678, east:90 = age 17m, paper date 8 Mar 1828).
iii. EMMA SOPHIA GREEN, born 1 Aug 1829 (bhm:1678) in Eastport ME (1850 census). Died after husband's death in 1895 poss. in Baltimore, MD. Census: 1850 & 60 in Calais. She married 9 Oct 1851 in St. Stephen, NB (adv) CHARLES HART SMITH, son of NOAH SMITH JR. AND HANNAH DRAPER WHEATON (see SMITH).
iv. KATHERINE JEWETT GREEN, born 24 June 1835 (bhm:1678) in Calais. Died 22 Oct 1837 age 2y 4m in Calais (g.s.). Buried in Calais Cemetery.
v. SARAH BROOKS GREEN, born 8 Aug 1837 (bhm:1678) in Calais. Died 28 Nov 1838 age 1y 2m in Calais (g.s.). Buried in Calais Cemetery.
vi. THOMAS HENRY GREEN, born 31 Mar 1842 in Calais (VR). He graduated from Calais Academy. Served in the regular army in the Civil War as a Capt. He was killed in action 9 Aug 1862 at Cedar Mt., VA, where he fell on the front (g.s., cwcard). Unmarried. Buried in Calais Cemetery. Census: 1850 & 60 in Calais.

- Note. Possible Elijah married 2nd Margaret A. Robinson of Vassalboro, int. filed 29 Nov 1866 in Calais (VR), also (int) 19 Nov 1866 in Vassalboro (VR). [no marriage record found, he died Mar 1867].

GEORGE & LUCY ANN GREENLAW, p. 190

GEORGE C. GREENLAW, born circa 1814 in St. Andrews, NB (1850 census). Died 6 Oct 1865 49y 5m in Calais (VR:3:312, g.s.). Buried in Calais Cemetery (buried in same lot as John P. Greenlaw, see below). Census: 1850 (age 36) & 60 in Calais.

He married in Nov 1840 by Lemuel H. Jones in Calais (demo, of 3 Nov 1840) LUCY ANN ELLSMORE born circa 1825 in E. Machias, Me (1850 census) (possible daughter of Moses & Lucy Ellsmore). Census: 1850 & 60 in Calais. Children:

i. GEORGIANNA {1} GREENLAW, born 29 Jul 1841 in Calais, died 2 Feb 1843 in Calais (VR:1:233). Death (2): 8 Jan 1843 age 1y 6m in Calais (g.s.). Buried in Calais Cemetery.
ii. GEORGIANNA {2} GREENLAW, born 19 Mar 1843 in Calais (VR). Census: 1850 & 60 in Calais.
iii. LORENZO DOW GREENLAW, born 14 Jun 1845 in Calais (VR). Died 6 Feb 1859 age 13y 8m (g.s.) in Calais. Buried: 8 Feb 1859 in Calais Cemetery (sext). Census: 1850 in Calais.
iv. CHARLES E. S. GREENLAW, born circa 1850 in Calais (VR). Died 26 Jan 1859 age 9y 8m in Calais (sext, g.s.). Buried in Calais Cemetery. Census: 1850 in Calais.
v. MARY J. GREENLAW, born circa 1852 in Calais, died 21 Apr 1852 age 3 weeks in Calais (g.s., sext = of

smallpox). Buried in Calais Cemetery.
vi. LUCY GREENLAW, born circa 1855 in Calais. Census: 1860 in Calais.

JOHN P. & MARIA GREENLAW, p. 187

JOHN P. GREENLAW, born circa 1814 in St. Andrews, NB (1850 census). Died 25 Dec 1854 in Calais (sext). Buried in Calais Cemetery (buried in same lot as George C. Greenlaw, above). Census: 1850 (age 36) in Calais.
He married MARIA (_____), born circa 1818 in St. Andrews, NB (1850 census). Died after 1870. Census: 1850, 60 & 70 in Calais. She married 2nd 19 May 1855 by Rev. George W. Durell in Calais (VR) WILLIAM LOGAN. They had a child who died 20 Feb 1862 age 3, in Calais (VR:1:243). Census 1860 & 70 in Calais. Children:

i. ISABELLA GREENLAW, born circa 1839 in St. Andrews, NB (1850 census). Census: 1850 in Calais.
ii. JOHN A. GREENLAW, born circa 1841 in St. Andrews, NB (1850 census). Enlisted in Civil War in 9th Maine Co A, 2nd enlistment on 1 Jan 1864 (enlist). He was a farmer 5'4" with blue eyes and brown hair (cwcard). Census: 1850, 60 (with step-father William Logan) & 70 in Calais. He married before 1866 KATE (_____) born ca 1848. Census: 1870 in Calais.
iii. AUGUSTUS SALOMON GREENLAW, born 2 May 1845 in Calais (VR). He enlisted in Civil War in Co C 1st Maine Cavalry (cwcard). Died 13 Oct 1917 age 73 at State Hospital in Bangor Me (obit, adv, MSA, sfh:2:139). Buried in Calais Cemetery. Census: 1850, 70 & 80 in Calais, 1900 in Robbinston. He married ca 1874 SUSAN ANNA MITCHELL, born 26 Aug 1851 in Old Ridge, NB, daughter of THOMAS MITCHELL & JULIA BARNES (both born Old Ridge), died 8 Jan 1930 age 79y 4m 12d in Calais (MSA).
iv. WILLIAM FREDERICK GREENLAW, born 2 Jan 1848 in Calais (VR). Census: 1850, 60 & 70 (with step-father William Logan) in Calais.
v. DANIEL S. GREENLAW, born circa 1849, died 2 Apr 1849 age 2m in Calais (g.s.). Buried in Calais Cemetery.
vi. DAVID GREENLAW, born 1850 in Calais, died 1850 in Calais (1850 census deaths, age 1 mo.). Buried in Calais Cemetery.
vii. CHARLES GREENLAW, born circa 1853 in Calais, died 28 Sep 1853 age 3m in Calais (g.s.). Buried in Calais Cemetery.

- Note. 1860 census also has a Maria G. Greenlaw age 9 in the family of William Logan poss. another daughter.
- Note. It is possible that George C. and John P. were brothers {both age 36 in 1850 twins??} the families are buried in same lot in Calais Cemetery.

STEPHEN & ALICE GROVER, p. 219

STEPHEN GROVER. Census: 1830 (2 males, 2 females). Not in 1840.
He married ALICE (_____).Children:

i. WILLIAM GROVER, born 14 Jun 1825 in Calais (VR).
ii. ELIZA ELLIOT GROVER, born 15 Jul 1827 in Calais (VR).
iii. MALINDA ADALINE GROVER, born 20 Aug 1832 in Calais (VR).

JOSEPH & MARY GUBBINS, p. 211

JOSEPH B. GUBBINS /GIBBINS, born circa 1818 in Ireland. Died after 1871. Census: 1850 (name listed as John) in Calais, 1861 & 71 (name as Joseph B.) in St. Stephen, NB.
He married MARY (_____), born circa 1826 in Ireland. Census: 1850 in Calais, 1861 & 71 in St. Stephen, NB. Children:

i. WILLIAM GUBBINS, born 1 Apr 1847 in Calais (VR). Census: 1850 in Calais. 1861 & 71 in St. Stephen, NB.
ii. GEORGE GUBBINS, born circa 1849 in Calais. Census: 1850 in Calais, 1861& 71 in St. Stephen, NB.

iii. JAMES GUBBINS, born circa 1852. Census: 1861 & 71 in St. Stephen, NB.
iv. JOHN GUBBINS, born circa 1856. Census: 1861 & 71 in St. Stephen, NB.

JAMES S. & MARY E. HALL, p. 212

JAMES SULLIVAN HALL, born circa 1809, son of JOHN HALL (came to Calais 1821, beg:124, with James age 74 in 1850). He served the town as representative in the Legislature of Maine, captain and quarter-master in the army against the Rebellion (beg:124). He was a merchant and carpenter in business with William Duren in 1836-38 involved in many court cases (SJC) and in 1854 he was a lumberman in the trading business with partners, James M. & Jacob Hall under the name of James S. Hall & Co. (SJC). He was mayor of Calais 1869, he also was a Representative to the Legislature and Executive Council (obit). Died 15 Jul 1879 age 70 in Calais (g.s., Mortality Schedule 1880). Probate of will in Machias. Buried in Calais Cemetery. Census: 1840 (3 males, 3 females), 50, 60 & 70 in Calais.

He married (int) 12 July 1835 in Calais (cal2:38) MARY E. SPRING born 6 May 1816 in Hubbardston, MA (VR), daughter of EPHRAIM SPRING AND HANNAH S. MORSE. She died 20 Apr 1908 age 92 in Calais (obit adv, sfh:1:66, MSA). Buried in Calais Cemetery. Census: 1850 thru & 80 in Calais (see SPRING). Children:

i. ELVIRA L. HALL, born 24 Jun 1836 (VR). Died 11 Apr 1837 in Calais (VR, g.s., name Alvira). Buried in Calais Cemetery.
ii. HENRY SULLIVAN HALL, born 14 Feb 1838 (VR). Died 29 Dec 1838 age 11m in Calais (VR, g.s.). Buried in Calais Cemetery.
iii. MARY CAROLINE HALL, born 4 Jan 1840. Census: 1850 in Calais. She married 25 Oct 1858 in Calais NATHANIEL I. WILSON of Bangor (union).
iv. HANNAH EMMA HALL, born 30 Aug 1842 in Calais (VR). Died 27 Mar 1928 in Calais (adv, MSA, g.s. = 1843-1929). Census: 1850 thru 1880 in Calais. She married WILLIAM BREWER FOSTER, son of GILBERT FOSTER & ELLEN C. JONES (see FOSTER). [Note - His g.s. = 1837-1929 both stones one year different than records]
v. WILLARD SULLIVAN HALL, born 25 Mar 1845 in Calais (VR). He was a surveyor. Died 17 Sep 1921 age 77 in Calais (MSA, sfh:3:254). Buried in Calais Cemetery. Census: 1850, 60, 70 & 1900 in Calais. He married 1st (int) 20 or 24 Apr 1872 in Calais (VR:3) EVA SOMES, born ca 1849, died 27 Apr 1885 age 35 in Robbinston (east:374). He married 2nd 18 Feb 1890 in St. Stephen, NB (east:437) MARY HELEN DOW born 12 Mar 1965 in Robbinston (sfh:7:279), daughter of ORION S. DOW & CATHERINE CARMODY. She died 13 July 1930 (adv, sfh:7:279). Buried in Calais Cemetery. Census: 1900 in Calais. They were in NH in 1894 when their 1st child was born but returned to Calais by 1896 when 2nd child was born (1900 census).
vi. FREDERICK H. HALL, born circa 1850. Died in May 1917 in Cottage Grove, OR (obit, adv). Census: 1850, 60 & 70 in Calais. He married before 1877 ANNIE MURCHIE, born ca 1848 in St. Stephen, NB, daughter of JAMES MURCHIE & MARY ANN GRIMMER (mop:195). She died after 1917. Census: 1851 (age 3) in St. Stephen, NB. [a daughter of Fred & Annie Hall buried in Rural Cemetery St. Stephen with grandparents (rural:150)].
vii. FRANK C. HALL, born circa Nov 1854. Died 23 Jan 1922 age 67 (adv) in Calais. He graduated from Calais Academy. He owned a stable. Census: 1860, 70 & 1900 (living with William Foster) in Calais. He married 5 Oct 1908 in Calais (MSA) JESSIE HUTCHINS born ca 1872, daughter of GEORGE W. HUTCHINS & MARY HELEN BELMORE (see BELMORE & HUTCHINS).
viii. CHARLES D. HALL, born circa 1858. Died 27 Jul 1858 age 4m in Calais (g.s.). Buried in Calais Cemetery.

CHARLES W. & SUSAN HAMMOND, p. 207

WILLIAM[7] HAMMOND, Jr., born 27 Jan 1772 in Newton, MA (VR:88), son of Capt. WILLIAM[6] HAMMOND (born in Newton MA) & MARY LIVERMORE, (born in Waltham MA), [grandson of JOSHUA[5], JOHN[4], THOMAS[3-2-1], WILLIAM[-1], JOHN[-2]], married 3 Aug 1796 SUSANNA CAMPBELL, daughter of Capt. Thomas Campbell of Bangor (hamm:123). Charles W. the son of William & Susanna resided in Calais for a short time.

CHARLES WILLIAM[8] HAMMOND, born Aug 1820 in Bangor Me, died in Calais (hamm:124). He married in Jan 1845 in Calais (FJ of 27 Jan 1845, m. Thurs. last) SUSAN LOUISE AMES, daughter of JOHN AMES AND DELILAH DODGE of East Boston, MA (hamm:162). Children:

i. CHARLES FREDERICK HAMMOND, born 26 Oct 1846 in Calais (VR, hamm:221). Died after 1904

when he resided in Dorchester, MA. He married 24 Jun 1869 ABBIE FRANCES HUNT, born 8 Aug 1850, daughter of REUBEN S. HUNT & ABBIE W. CLAPP of E. Boston, MA. (hamm: 222).
ii. CARRIE MCDONALD HAMMOND (hamm:162).
iii. EDITH HAMMOND (hamm:162).
iv. WALTER D. HAMMOND, born 24 Jan 1867, in 1904 he resided in Boston MA, married with one child (hamm:162).

CHARLES & REBECCA HAPGOOD, p. 177 & 179 & 195

EBER[5] HAPGOOD, son of SETH[4], THOMAS[3-2], SHADRACK[1], married DOLLY GROUT, daughter of Honorable Jonathan Grout, a colonel in the Revolutionary War (hap:203). Their son, Charles settled in Calais.

CHARLES HAPGOOD, born 11 Oct 1807 in Petersham, MA (VR, hap:269). He was a merchant in Calais in 1834 (SJC). In 1841 he was a Deputy Sheriff in Calais (adv). In 1857 he resided in Levenworth, KS, died 25 Aug 1886 in Red Bluff, Ark. (hap: 269). Census: 1840 (3 males, 2 females).

He married 9 May 1839 in Waterford, VT (hap:204) REBECCA HIBBARD born 22 Sep 1816 in Littleton, NH, daughter of LYMAN HIBBARD AND REBECCA CHARLTON (hap:269). Died 4 Nov 1859 of small pox, in Boston Ma (hap:269). After death of his wife he married 2nd 19 Sept 1863, at Levenworth, Mrs. STREETER from MA, who survived him, no issue (hap:270). Children by 1st wife:

i. GEORGE GROUT HAPGOOD, born 20 May 1840 in Calais (VR, hap:270). Went to Boston and worked in the produce business; contacted small pox which killed his mother, he recovered and in 1861he went to Oil City, Pa and later to Colorado then to Butte, Mont. with no further trace of him (hap:270).
ii. WILLIAM CHARLTON HAPGOOD, born 14 Dec 1841 in Calais, died 29 Aug 1844 in Calais (VR, hap:270). Buried in Calais Cemetery.
iii. CHARLES FRANCIS HAPGOOD, born 27 Nov 1845 in Calais (VR, hap:270). Died 21 Apr 1852, in Morrisania, NY (hap:270).
iv. MARY ELIZABETH HAPGOOD, born 3 Nov 1848 in Calais (VR, hap:270). After the death of her mother she lived with relatives in Boston and then to Nova Scotia where she married on 29 Dec 1874 CHARLES WENTWORTH UPHAM HEWSON, born 28 Feb 1844, at Jolcum, NB, graduated from U of PA with a degree in medicine in 1872, they settled in Amherst, NS where he practiced his profession, he died after 1907 (hap:270).

DANIEL & ELEANOR HARMON, p. 213

DANIEL[5] HARMON, Jr., born 9 Feb 1778, son of DANIEL[4] HARMON & SARAH YORK, grandson of JOHN[3], SAMUEL[2], JOHN[1],(harm:18) he was a soldier in the War of 1812 and a politician, holding offices in the town of Durham, Me and the state, died 26 Nov 1848, he married Mary True, born 28 Oct 1781 in Salisbury, MA. They had nine children, their sixth child, Daniel 3rd resided in Calais before moving to Oshkosh, WI. (durh:196).

DANIEL HARMON 3rd, born 11 Jul 1811 in Durham ME (durh:196). He came from Calais to Amity, ME in 1837 and taught school, lived there six years, where he was town clerk and moved to Portland (aroos:I:45). Moved to Oshkosh, WI in 1855 (wife's obit). Died 10 Jun 1862 in Oshkosh (harm: 78). Census: 1850 in Calais.

He married 8 Dec 1836 in Calais (mrwc:20) ELEANOR LAMB born 30 Sept 1819 in Calais (1850 census), daughter of JAMES & BETSEY (?DUNN?) LAMB, sister of Robert & Nathaniel Lamb (see LAMB). She died 29 Jan 1887 in Oshkosh (obit north). Census: 1850 in Calais. She married 2nd 8 Oct 1867 Carlos D. Church in Oshkosh (oshlib, record lists mother as Betsey). Children:

i. MARIA COBB HARMON, born 30 Apr 1838 in Amity, ME (VR). Died before her mother. Census: 1850 in Calais.
ii. LORENZO DOW HARMON, born 21 Jan 1841 in Hodgdon Me (VR). He was an insurance agent. Died after his mother (mother's obit). Census: 1850 in Calais.
iii. AMANDA ALLEN HARMON, born 23 May 1843 in Calais (VR). Died Jun 1849 in Calais (sext). Buried: 21 Jun 1849 in Calais Cemetery.
iv. NATHANIEL LAMB HARMON, born 5 Sep 1845 in Calais (VR). Resided in Two Lakes, Iowa in 1887 (mother's obit). Died after 1887. Census: 1850 in Calais.

v. HORACE M. HARMON, a painter who survived his parents (mother's obit).
vi. FLORA HARMON, a bookkeeper at the Union National bank in Oshkosh, died after her mother (mother's obit).

HENRY & LUCY HARMON, p. 213

NATHANIEL[4] HARMON, born 12 Aug 1784 in Machias, son of BENJAMIN[3] HARMON AND SARAH HILL, grandson of NATHANIEL[2], JOHN[1]. He married in 1809 at St. Stephen, NB LYDIA MCALLISTER, of St. David, NB. She died Aug 1835 (harm: 32). Children:

1. HANNAH HARMON, born 21 May 1811, married James Martin (see MARTIN).
2. ELIZABETH HARMON, born Feb 1814, married Reuben Ellsworth (see ELLSWORTH).
3. HENRY HARMON (see BELOW).
4. SARAH ANN HARMON, born June 1818, married Eben Martin of Calais.
5. WILLIAM P. HARMON, born Sept 1820, died 8 Dec 1864 age 42 in Waverly, IA (union) married 1854 Abzina Reaves of Iowa.

HENRY HARMON, born 1 Feb 1815 in St. Stephen, NB, Bapt 2 Sept 1815 in St. Stephen (kmc, harm:32). Died.
He married 30 Sep 1841 by Phenneas Higgins in Calais (mrwc:36) LUCY G. WADSWORTH, she may be the daughter of AARON WADSWORTH & LUCY STEVENS, sister of Aaron (Jr.) (see WADSWORTH). Children:

i. ABNER WADSWORTH HARMON, born 12 Apr 1845 in Calais (VR). Died 19 Apr 1916 (adv).

ISAIAH/JOSIAH & MARY JANE HARRIS, p. 186

ISAIAH HARRIS, born circa 1818 in NS. He was a carpenter. [?Died 24 Oct 1885, age 68 in Calais (times & g.s. ? have name Isaiah)]. Buried in Calais Cemetery. Census: 1850 in Eastport (name Josiah), 70 (name Josiah), 1880 (name Isaiah) in Calais.

ISAIAH of Eastport married 14 Sep 1843 by Benjamin Shattuck, JP in Calais (VR:1:131,mrwc:40) MARY JANE EDWARDS born circa 1830 of St. Andrews, NB. [? Died 6 Sept 1887 age 61y 3m (g.s. = Jane)]. Buried in Calais Cemetery. Census: 1850 (name Mary Jane) in Eastport, 1870 (name Jane), 1880 (Jane) in Calais. Children:

i. JAMES BENJAMIN HARRIS, born 25 Nov 1844 in Calais (VR). Died 15 May 1846 age 2 ½ y in Calais (VR:1:231, g.s. has 18th). Buried in Calais Cemetery.
ii. EMMA JANE HARRIS, born 23 Jan 1845 in Calais (VR). Died 1928 (g.s.). Buried in Calais Cemetery. Census: 1850 in Eastport, 70 in Calais. She married 2 Sept 1865 by Rev. Edwin Murray in Calais (VR:3:214, union) STEPHEN SPINNEY, born ca 1842, s/o NATHANIEL SPINNEY & MARY LOWE (see SPINNEY).
iii. JOSIAH WELLINGTON HARRIS, born 22 Sep 1847 in Calais (VR). Census: 1850 (James W. age 3) in Eastport, 1870 (James W. age 20), 1880 (James 31) in Calais. [Died: James A. Harris 29 Aug 1918 age 71y 9m 20d in Calais, single, born 20 Nov 1839 in Calais s/o Josiah & Jane (Edwards) Harris buried in Calais].

- Note: unable to find confirmation on the names of the father, mother and son James, names and dates on records were inconsistent.

WILLIAM P. & BASHEBA HARRISON, p.196

WILLIAM P. HARRISON, born circa 1820, in Penna. He had a baker-confectionary business. Died 12 Aug 1883 in Calais (obit union, times). Census: 1850, 60 & 70 in Calais.
He married BATHSHEBA R. (_____), born circa 1813 in Nova Scotia. Died 30 Sep 1872 age 60 in Calais (obit, union). Census: 1850, 60 & 70 in Calais. Children:

i. WILLIAM (PUIMOSE ? sp) HARRISON, born 20 Mar 1845 in Calais (VR). Died after 1870. Census: 1850, 60 & 70 in Calais.
ii. MARIA ANN HARRISON, born 7 Jun 1847 in Calais (VR). Died after 1860. Census: 1850 & 60 in Calais.
iii. EDWARD S. HARRISON, born circa 1848 in Maine. Died after 1870. Census: 1850, 60 & 70 in

Calais.

iv. CAROLINE. A. HARRISON, born, circa Jan 1850 in Maine. Died Feb 1851 age 1y 1m in Calais (adv). Buried: 2 Mar 1851 in Calais Cemetery (sext). Census: 1850 in Calais.
v. CHARLES P. HARRISON, born ca Mar 1852 in Maine. Died 11 Jan 1854 age 22m in Calais (g.s.). Buried in Calais Cemetery.
vi. IDA M. HARRISON, born circa 1855 in Maine. Died after 1870. Census: 1860 & 70 in Calais.

MATHEW & REBECCA A. HASTINGS, p. 218

MATTHEW HASTINGS, born 7 Apr 1796 in Sidney ME (1850 census, rey), son of MOSES HASTINGS & HANNAH MARSH. Baptized 21 Jun 1840 in Calais (lord:11). He served as a Pvt. in the War of 1812 in Capt. Lovejoy's Co. of Mass. from 24 Sept to 10 Nov 1814, Company raised at Sidney with service at Wiscasset (massv, pension rec. NADC). He was a member of the staff of Gov. William King, Maine's first Chief Executive, in 1820 and served as State senator form Washington Co., also represented Calais in the House several times (2nd wife's obit). He served as a Lt. in the 2nd Brig. Art. Regt. 2nd Div. of the Militia in Sidney from 8 Apr 1820 to & July 1824, then in Calais was a Capt. on 1 Apr 1826, a Major on 17 Sept 1827 and Lt. Col. on 2 May 1829 in the 1st Brig. 7th Div. (milit). He was a member of the Masons and in 1826 was elected the first Senior Steward of St. Croix Lodge No. 46 in Calais and was Master in 1844-1849-1850-1855 (lodge:15, 43). In 1841, he was a Brig. General in State Militia; he was also a collector of customs; representative and state senator from Calais. Died 17 Oct 1878 in Calais (obit, pension rec. NADC). Probate of estate 18 Jan 1879. Census: 1830 (2 males, 2 females), 40 (4 males, 2 females), 50, 60 & 70 in Calais.

He married 1st 20 Jan 1828 in Calais by A. G. Chandler, JP (cal2:45) REBECCA ANN GILLMOR born 1806, daughter of ARTHUR HILL GILLMOR AND MARY KNIGHT. Died 5 Jan 1840 in Calais (VR:1:239). Buried: 8 Jan 1840 in Calais. Children:

i. ALBERT GALLATIN HASTINGS, born 11 Nov 1828 in Calais, died 15 Aug 1829 in Calais (VR:1:239).
ii. GORHAM KIMBALL HASTINGS, born 7 Feb 1830 in Calais (VR). He enlisted in Civil War in Co K 26th Inf. as a 2nd Lieut., a seaman 5'9 ½" with blue eyes and brown hair (cwcard). Died 18 Mar 1921 age 91y 1m 11d, in Sidney ME (MSA). Census: 1920 in Sidney. He married 1st 5 Aug 1855 (rey) MARY LUCINDA PARK, daughter of Capt. JONATHAN GREEN PARK & SARAH BLACK, He married 2nd 30 Jul 1865 (rey) LINDA ANN PARK, born in Searsport, ME, sister of his first wife, died 25 Aug 1893 in Sidney, buried in Sidney (MSA). He married 3rd 27 Sep 1894 in Sidney (rey), ANNETTE 'NETTIE' G. MACK, born in Sidney, daughter of LUTHER J. MACK & MATILDA J. BLAISDELL, died 10 Dec 1913 age 53y 9m 4d in Sidney (MSA). Census: 1920 in Sidney.
iii. GEORGE ALBION HASTINGS, born 12 Aug 1831 in Calais (VR). Died Dec 1854 in Calais (sext). Buried: 15 Dec 1854 in Calais Cemetery.
iv. ANN MARIA HASTINGS born 12 Oct 1833 in Calais (VR). Resided in Menonomee, MI. She had children Nellie & Dorothy Lee (rey).
v. EDGAR P. HASTINGS, born 18 Dec 1834 in Robbinston Me (VR, wiscnh:210, has b. 1835 in Calais). Resided in Seattle, WA. In Oct. 1856 he went to Chippewa Falls, WI, where he was a bookkeeper and Lumber Inspector then in 1880 was elected County Treasurer (wiscnh:210). Census: 1850 in Calais. He married in 1875, MARY KIMBALL, who was born in Wellsboro, Pa (wiscnh:210).
vi. ADALAIDE HASTINGS, born 20 Sep 1836 in Calais, died 24 Aug 1837 in Calais (VR:1:239).
vii. MATHEW HASTINGS, born 7 May 1838 in Calais, died 5 Sep 1838 in Calais (VR:1:239). Buried: 6 Sep 1838 in Calais Cemetery (sext).
viii. MARY HELEN HASTINGS, born 5 Jul 1839 in Calais, died 27 Feb 1840 in Calais (VR:1:239).

MATHEW married 2nd 21 Mar 1842 in Westbrook, ME (rey, widow's pension rec. = 20 Mar). ANN GRAFFAM CUTTER, born circa 1815 in Cape Elizabeth, Me (1850 census, MSA), daughter of SIMON CUTTER [veteran of War of 1812] & CHRISTINA DYER. Resided 1889 in Merrimac, Ma. Died 9 Dec 1902 age 87 at Portland, Me (SSC, Mach, MSA). She resided with daughter, Jenny Tyler in Portland (obit adv). She received a widow's pension from the War of 1812 of $12 (copy of pension record). Census: 1850, 60 & 70 in Calais. Children:

ix. SIMON CUTTER HASTINGS, born 5 May 1843 in Calais (VR). He served in Civil War, Co H, 21st ME Inf. as a corporal in Co H of 21st Me Inf. and Co H of 1st Cav. A farmer 5'6" with blue eyes and brown hair (cwcard). He was state commander of the GAR in 1931. He was a selectman in Sidney for five years. Died 15 July 1938 age 95 in Portland, ME (MSA). Resided with his sister, Jennie Tyler, in Portland at time of his death (obit adv). Buried: Sibley Cemetery, in Sidney. Census: 1850, & 60 in Calais, 1900 & 20 in Sidney. He married 30 Sep 1873 in Auburn ME (rey), ELLEN FAUGHT, born ca Mar 1845 (1900 census) in Sidney, daughter of ELIJAH FAUGHT (1787-1852) & OLIVE HAMLIN (1804-1884). She died 19 Jan 1912 age 66y 10m in Sidney (MSA), Buried: in the Sibley Cemetery, in Sidney. Census: 1900 in Sidney.

x. SOPHIA REBECCA HASTINGS, born 8 Jan 1845 in Calais, died 31 Oct 1847 in Calais (VR:1:239).

xi. CHRISTINA D. HASTINGS, born circa 1850 in Calais, died 23 Dec 1854 in Calais (sext). Buried: 24 Dec 1854 in Calais Cemetery. Census: 1850 in Calais.

xii. FRANK PIERCE HASTINGS, born 21 May 1852 in Calais (rey). He was the U.S. Vice & Deputy Consul-General at Honolulu in 1889 when he was visiting in Calais (adv). Died 28 June 1897 in Washington, DC, he became ill while attending a reception at the White House on May 19th (obit adv). Resided: 1874 in Honolulu, HI. Census: 1860 in Calais. He married ALICE C. MAKOE /MAKER, daughter of Capt. JAMES & ALICE MAKER/MAKOE of Hawaii, 4 Oct 1881 in New York, NY (times). She died 12 Mar 1913 in Portland, ME (MSA) (her death rec. has Maker, times has Makoe).

xiii. GEORGE OSMAN HASTINGS, born 31 Mar 1857 in Calais (rey). Died Jan 1937. Resided in Deer River, MN (rey) also resided in Euclair, Wis. in 1890 (adv). Census: 1860 & 70 in Calais.

xiv. MARY 'MAE' DOW HASTINGS, born 21 Feb 1863 in Calais (rey). She was single and residing in Merrimac, MA in 1888 when she was visiting in Calais (adv). Census: 1870 in Calais. She married 2 Apr 1889 in Denver, by Rev. G. N. Eldridge Col. DANIEL HENDERSON of Kimball Neb (adv) .

xv. JENNIE CUTTER HASTINGS, born 21 Feb 1863 in Calais (rey). Died after 1938. Resided in Portland Me in 1938. Census: 1870 in Calais, 1900 & 20 in Portland. She married 19 Feb 1885 in Portland (adv) JOSEPH TYLER, born ca Jan 1845 (1900 census). Census: 1900 & 20 in Portland.

SAMUEL W. & MARY R. HAYCOCK, p. 220

SAMUEL WATTS HAYCOCK, born 24 Jul 1815 (hay) in Milltown, NB (son's death rec), son of RALPH HAYCOCK JR. AND ELSIE WATTS, (grandson of RALPH HAYCOCK b. Shropshire, Eng. & MARTHA BRUNEL / SAMUEL WATTS & ELSIE WATTS)(hay). Died 3 Jun 1846 age 33 in Calais (VR:1:239, drowned, hay, prbt, g.s.). Buried: 4 Jun 1846 in Calais Cemetery. Census: 1840 (4 males, 3 females).

He married 9 Nov 1834 in Calais (mrwc:13, hay) (copy of bible record in bhm: 6:144 has 9 Nov 1833) MARY BALL FARRAR, born Nov 1812 in West Moreland, NH, daughter of GEORGE FARRAR AND REBECCA PRICE (both born Townsend, MA), (obit). She was executive of husband's estate 1846 (prbt). Died 17 Aug 1905 age 92y 8m 29d in Calais (obit adv, MSA, g.s.). Buried in Calais Cemetery. Census: 1850, 60 & 70, 1900 (alone) in Calais. Children:

i. FRANCES MARY HAYCOCK, born 12 Nov 1835 in Calais (VR). Died 22 Jan 1886 age 50 in Washington, DC (times). Census: 1850 & 60 in Calais. She married 9 Nov 1853 by Rev. H. V. Dexter in Calais (VR:3:156, east:131, FJ) SULLIVAN CLARK SWETT, born ca 1832. He was a cabinet maker. Census: 1860 in Calais.

ii. JOHN L. HAYCOCK, born circa 1836. Census: 1860 in Calais.

iii. SAMUEL WALLACE HAYCOCK, born 7 Aug 1837 in Calais (VR). He enlisted a Corp'l in Civil War in Co F 22nd Me Inf. an engineer 5'9 1/2" with blue eyes and light hair (cwcard). During the Civil War in the swamps of Louisiana he contracted the disease which ended in his death (obit did not mention what disease). He was a RR mechanic. Died 20 Mar 1905 age 67y 7m 13d in Calais (obit adv, MSA). Buried in Calais Cemetery. Census: 1850, 60, 70 & 80 in Calais. He married 5 Jan 1865 in Calais (VR:3:208) MARTHA C. HENRY, born ca 1845, daughter of WILLIAM HENRY & MARY O. SMITH. She died after her husband. Census: 1870 & 80.

iv. ELSIE WATTS HAYCOCK, born 7 Oct 1839 in Calais (VR). Died after 1888. Census: 1850 & 60 in Calais. She married 3 Nov 1859 in Calais by I. J. Burgess, JOHN L. WOODCOCK of Calais (VR: 3:182). They visited Calais in Aug 1888 from Chicago. He was son of JOHN T. & HARRIET WOODCOCK, he was in the hotel business and died at age 80 on 12 June 1916 in Oak Park, Ill (obit adv).

v. JOHN WARREN HAYCOCK, born 22 Aug 1841 in Calais (VR). Census: 1850, 60 & 70 in Calais. He married EMMA C. (_____), born ca 1851. Census: 1870 (age 19) in Calais.

vi. KIMBALL CHASE HAYCOCK, born 22 May 1844 in Calais (VR). He was a member of "Society of the Sons of the State of Maine" in Chicago (DEA:3:4:26). Visited Calais with his wife (her name not mentioned) in Aug 1888 from Chicago (adv). He was residing in Fort Fairfield in Mar 1905 when his brother died and in Houlton in Mar 1905 when his mother died. Census: 1850 & 60 in Calais.

vii. NANCY JANE HAYCOCK, born 7 May 1846 in Calais, died 28 Aug 1847 age 16m in Calais (VR:1:239, g.s.). Buried: 29 Aug 1847 in Calais Cemetery.

SETH & CAROLINE HEAL, p. 179

SETH HEAL, born 17 Mar 1802 in Linconville, ME, son of JOHN HEAL & JOSEPHINE ELIZABETH HINCKLY (heal:10-7, devo). He was in the 1st Brigade, 7th Div Maine Militia as a 1st Lieut. 1828, 1829, 1831 (mil). He became a Lt. on 8 Apr 1824 (milit). Census: 1840 (4 males, 4 females) & 50 in Calais. [Seth Heal arrived at San Francisco, 18 Sept 1849, after a passage of 215 days, starting by sailing vessel from New York by way of Cape Horn. His wife, his daughter, Caroline, and his son arrived later on a mail steamer, the *John L. Stevens*, 14 Nov 1855, coming across the Isthmus by rail (sanbay:127,128)].
* Note - His date of arrival, stated in the article, may be off by a year or two as he is listed in census of Calais in 1850.

He married Nov 1830 by George Downes in Calais (east:111), (int.) 20 Nov 1830 in Portland ME (heal:10-7) CAROLINE B. WARREN born circa 1824 in Portland ME (1850 census). Census: 1850 in Calais. Children:

i. JOSEPH WARREN HEAL, born 10 Oct 1831 in Calais (VR). In 1875-77 he was living in San Francisco, CA (devo). Died 6 Dec 1885 age 50 near Antelope, OR (obit call:6, devo). Census: 1850 in Calais.

ii. JULIET HEAL, born 27 Feb 1834 in Calais (VR). Died 6 Sep 1848 age 14y 7m in Calais (g.s.). Buried: 8 Sep 1848 in Calais Cemetery.

iii. ADELAIDE HEAL, born 6 May 1836 in Calais (VR). Died 21 Jan 1845 age 8 in Calais (FJ, g.s.). Buried in Calais Cemetery.

iv. LEONIDAS HEAL, born 7 May 1840 in Calais (VR). Census: 1850 in Calais. Possibly died before family moved west (not mentioned in (sanbay) article, only dau., Caroline and one son mentioned).

v. CAROLINE ELIZABETH HINCKLEY HEAL, born 19 Feb 1843 in Calais (VR). Died 4 Feb 1880 in San Francisco, CA, buried there in Cypress Lawn Cemetery (devo). Census: 1850 in Calais. She married 25 Dec 1856 (sanbay) FRANCIS JOSEPH GRACIER, Jr., son of FRANCIS JOSEPH GRACIER, Sr. & Mrs. SABRA ATHERTON (WILLIAMS) HASACK (sanbay), Buried at Cypress Lawn (devo).

ZIMRI B. & HANNAH HEYWARD, p. 183
also JANE P. & REBECCA, p 183

ZEMRI BREWER[4] HEYWARD, born 24 May 1803 in Winslow, ME (VR), son OF SAMUEL[3] HEYWARD & ELIZABETH FAXTON HAYDEN, grandson of ZIMRI[2], NATHANIEL[1]. In 1833 he arrived in Calais and engaged in the lumbering business (obit). In 1841 he was a tax collector (adv). He went to California by way of Cape Horn, in Sept 1849 and arrived in San Francisco 6 Apr 1850 (obit, note: he is listed in 1850 census of Calais, perhaps he came back for his family). In 1857 he resided in San Francisco, CA when Gorham G. Kimball of Calais made contact with him when he arrived in California (kimb:952). In 1867 he was an owner in the Gualala Mill Company of Mendocino County, CA and became a wealthy man, he died 31 July 1879 age 76 in Berkeley, CA, survived by wife and her 4 children, and 4 sons by previous wives (obit adv). Buried in Laurel Hill Cemetery, San Francisco, CA. Census: 1840 (6 males, 4 females) & 1850 in Calais, 1870 (age 67) in San Francisco, CA.

He married 1st 9 Dec 1827 in St. Stephen, NB (CCMR) HANNAH COOPER, born 13 May 1805, in Robbinston Me (Calais VR). Died 10 Jul 1835 in St. Stephen, NB (Calais VR:1:230). Buried in Calais Cemetery. Children:

i. WILLIAM D. HEYWARD, born, 19 Apr 1829, in St. Stephen, NB (Calais VR). Died 31 Aug 1830 in St. Stephen, NB (CalaisVR:1:230). Buried in Calais Cemetery.

ii. WILLIAM BREWER HEYWARD, Jr., born 15 Aug 1830 in St. Stephen, NB (Calais VR). Died after 1887 when he wrote a letter to the Calais Advertiser from California where he moved during the gold rush. He married 28 Apr 1859 (VR:3:176) in Calais SALOME BRADFORD, daughter of PEREZ BRADFORD, JR. AND DEBORAH DAVIS (see BRADFORD).

iii. CHARLES WARREN HEYWARD, born 28 Mar 1832, in St. Stephen, NB (Calais VR). Went to California with his father and probably survived him. Census: 1850 in Calais.
iv. SAMUEL B. HEYWARD, born 16 Nov 1833, in St. Stephen, NB (Calais VR). Went to California with his father and probably survived him. Census: 1850 in Calais. He married 14 May 1874 in San Francisco, CA (adv) EMMA FRANCES DINGLEY (adv).

He married 2nd circa 1835 JANE P/T. SCOTT born 19 Feb 1812 in St. James, NB (Calais VR:1:183). Died 28 Mar 1841 in Calais (VR:1:230). Buried: 30 Mar 1841 in Calais Cemetery. Children:

v. FRANKLIN 'Frank' HEYWARD, born 29 Jan 1837 in Calais (VR). Died after 1882 when he was visiting Calais from Calif., where he moved ca 1852 (adv). Census: 1850 in Calais.
vi. ALBERT HEYWARD, born 27 Dec 1838 in Calais (VR). Died: probably before his father. Census: 1850 in Calais.
vii. HELEN JANE VICTORIA HEYWARD, born 25 Sep 1840 in Calais (VR). Died: probably before her father. Census: 1850 in Calais.

He married 3rd 12 Mar 1842 in Calais (VR) REBECCA SCOTT, born 18 Apr 1818 in St. James, NB (Calais VR:1:183). Died 30 Mar 1845 in Calais (VR:1:230). Buried: 1 Apr 1845 in Calais Cemetery. Children:

viii. WESLEY HEYWARD, born 28 Oct 1843 in Calais (VR). Died: probably not one of the 4 sons who survived their father. Census: 1850 in Calais.
ix. EDWARD HEYWARD, born 16 Feb 1845 in Calais (VR). Died 14 Nov 1846 in Calais (VR:1:230). Buried in Calais Cemetery.

He married 4th after 1845 (she is his wife in 1850 census) ANN (_____), born circa 1818 in St. George NB (1850 census). She went to California with her husband, and was the surviving wife with 4 children (his obit). Died probably in CA after 1879. Census: 1850 in Calais, 1870 (age 50) in San Francisco, CA. Children:

x. HARRIET GRANGER HEYWARD, born Mar 1850 in Calais. Died after 1879. Census: 1850 in Calais, 1870 (age 20) in San Francisco. She married 20 Aug 1874 in San Francisco, CA. CLARENCE M. HUNT (adv).
xi. WALTER HEYWARD, born ca 1854 in CA, 1870 census (age 16) in San Francisco.
xii. GEORGIANNA HEYWARD, born ca 1858 in CA, 1870 census (age 12) in San Francisco.
xiii. HARRY HEYWARD, born ca 1862 in CA, 1870 census (age 8) in San Francisco.

WILLIAM & BRIDGET HICKEY, p. 205

WILLIAM HICKEY, born circa 1815, in Ireland. Born in Great Britain / Ireland, naturalized 26 Apr 1861, (irmch, no birth date or port of entry given, witnesses: C. R. Whitten and C. W. Porter). Came to Calais between 1844 -45. Died 19 Apr 1866 (g.s.). Buried in Calais Cemetery. Census: 1850 & 60 in Calais
He married before 1839 BRIDGET MORRISCY /MORICY born circa 1818, in Ireland, daughter of TIMOTHY MORICY AND MARY KATYING. Died 24 Mar 1910 age 92y 7m, in Calais (sfh:1:263, MSA). Census: 1850 thru 1880 & 1900 in Calais. Children:

i. TATE / TIMOTHY HICKEY, born circa 1839, in Ireland. Census: 1850 (age 11, Tate) & 60 (age 21, Timothy) in Calais.
ii. JOHN {1} HICKEY, born circa 1842, in Ireland. Served in Civil War in Co A 9th Maine Inf. (g.s., MSA). A lumberman described as 5" 4' with brown hair and blue eyes, enlisted 30 Aug 1861 (cwcard). He died Jun 1875 in Calais (g.s.). Buried: 6 Jun 1875 in Calais Cemetery (sext). Census: 1850 & 60 in Calais.
iii. PATRICK HICKEY, born circa 1844, in Ireland. Served in Civil War in Co F 22nd Maine Inf. (g.s.). Described as 5' 5 1/2", hazel eyes, dark hair enlisted 10 Sept 1862 (cwcard). Died 30 Apr 1887 age 44 in Calais (SCC, g.s.). Buried: 2 May 1887 in Calais Cemetery. Census: 1850 & 60 in Calais.
iv. WILLIAM HICKEY, Jr., born 18 Dec 1845 in Calais (VR). Died Nov 1902 age 59. Buried: 18 Nov 1902 in Calais Cemetery. Census: 1850, 60 & 70 in Calais.

v. MICHAEL JOSEPH HICKEY, born 20 Aug 1847 in Calais (VR). Served in Civil War in Co G Coast Guard (g.s., cwcard). Described as 5' 5" with light hair and blue eyes, enlisted 1 Feb 1865 (cwcard, enlist, father signed permission). Died 27 Jan 1897 age 48y 6m in Calais (MSA, east:560, g.s.). Census: 1850, 60 & 80 in Calais. He married before 1880 MARTHA ANN IRVIN born ca 1848 in St. Andrews, NB, daughter of JOHN & CATHERINE IRVIN. Died: 5 Mar 1920 age 71 in Calais (MSA). Census: 1851 (age 4) in St. Andrews, NB, 1861 (age 13) in St. Stephen, NB, 1880 (living with his mother and brother) in Calais.

vi. THOMAS HICKEY, born Sep 1849, in Calais. Died May 1874 age 24 in Calais (g.s.). Buried: 29 May 1874 in Calais Cemetery (sext). Census: 1850 & 70 in Calais.

vii. JOHN {2} or JERE HICKEY, born circa 1852, in Maine. Census: 1860 & 70 (name Jere) in Calais.

viii. MARY HICKEY, born circa 1854 in Maine. Census: 1860 & 70 in Calais.

ix. JAMES HICKEY, born circa 1856 in Maine. Died 29 May 1904 age 43 of self administrated poison in Calais (obit adv, MSA, SSC). From his obit: he was the youngest of 11 sons of Mrs. Bridget Hickey, all of whom are deceased, mother and sister only survivors. [Note: names of only 8 sons located in Calais] Census: 1860, 70, 80 & 1900 in Calais. He possibly married before 1887 MARY (_____), born ca Apr 1848. Census: 1900 (James, Mary & son, living with Bridget Hickey) in Calais.

x. BRIDGET HICKEY, born circa 1860 in Calais. Census: 1860 in Calais.

HARRIS & ANN HILL, p. 198

HARRIS HILL, born circa 1814 in Hills Point, NB (son, George's death rec.). In 1883 he resigned as night watchman (adv). Died 9 Mar 1891 age 74y 11m 25d in Calais (east:457, adv). Census: 1850 thru 1880 in Calais.

He married ANN KELLEY, born circa 1822 in Ireland (1850 census, son's death rec. = St. Andrews, NB). Died 23 Aug 1886 in Calais (times). Probate of Estate filed 3 Aug 1888 in Machias Me. Census: 1850 thru 1880 in Calais. Children:

i. MARGARET 'Maggie' HILL, born 23 Jun 1845 in Calais (VR). She was a seamstress. Died 25 Dec 1919 in Winchester, MA (death cert. SRW). Census: 1850 & 60 in Calais. She married 20 Sept 1868 in Chelsea, MA HENRY NEWELL WENTWORTH born 6 June 1837 in Bristol, ME, son of ABIAL WENTWORTH (s/o James & MARY ANN WENTWORTH(d/o Samuel) (went:388-389). He was a business man in Chelsea, and died 7 Aug 1896 in Chelsea, MA (SRW).

ii. NANCY ANN HILL, born 10 Mar 1847 in Calais (VR). Bapt. 8 Sept 1856 Calais (saint). Census: 1850 & 60 in Calais.

iii. CHARLES HENRY HILL, born circa 1851 in Calais. Bapt. 8 Sept 1856 Calais (saint). Census: 1860 (age 9) in Calais 1870 (age 18 name Charles), 1880 (name John H. age 28 ??, brickmason) in Calais. dir 1891. (Charles H. Hill police res. Munroe St.) Calais. John married ISABEL (_____), born ca 1853. Census: 1880 in Calais.

iv. GEORGE FREDERICK HILL, born between 1853-1855 (census ages, not in 1850 or 1900) in Calais. He died 16 Nov 1934 age 85y 5m 10d in Calais (MSA gives birth date 6 June 1849, parents as Harris & Ann). Buried Calais Cemetery (stone = 1849-1934) Census: 1860 (Frederick age 7), 1870 (Fred age 15, rope maker), 1880 (Fredrick G. 26 blacksmith), dir 1891. George F. (blacksmith, Belmore St./ now Garfield St), dir 1901. (George F. & Priscilla Garfield St) in Calais, 1920 (age 64 with Priscilla age 59 and son George F. 24, Garfield St) in Calais. He married PRISCILLA F. CARVER, born 20 May 1856 in Birch Harbor, ME (MSA), daughter of JOSEPH HENRY CARVER & LUCY ARLEY, died 7 Oct 1939 age 84y 4m 17d in Calais (MSA). Buried Calais Cemetery (stone = 1855-1939).

v. ALICE M. HILL, born circa 1861 in Calais. She was a dressmaker. Census: 1870 & 80 in Calais.

vi. JEFFERSON HILL, born circa 1864 in Calais. Census: 1870 in Calais.

SAMUEL & ESTHER HODSDON, p. 188

SAMUEL HODSDON, born 14 Dec 1806 (acsh, 1850 census = b. Waterville, son's death rec. b. Berwick). Died 5 Dec 1890 in Topsfield, ME (g.s.). Buried in Town Cemetery, in Topsfield. Census: 1840 (6 males, 3 females), 50 (with wife & children in home of Michael Cary/Carey) in Calais, 1860 in Waite & 70 in Topsfield.

He married (int) 12 July 1835 in Calais (cal2:39) ESTHER W. JONES, born Nov 1815 in NB, daughter of CALVIN JONES & (_____) STILES both b. NB (MSA). Died 22 Apr 1910 in Princeton (MSA, g.s.). Buried in Town Cemetery in Topsfield. Census: 1850 (b. Calais) in Calais, 1860 in Waite, 70 & 1900 in Topsfield. [could she be a daughter of Calvin & Frances Jones, see JONES, VR:1:213] Children:

i. JONES C. HODSDON, born 14 Apr 1837 in Calais (VR). Died 17 Oct 1837 age 7m 25d, in Calais (VR:3:232, g.s.). Buried in Calais Cemetery.
ii. SARAH PRISCILLA HODSDON, born 7 Jul 1838 in Calais (VR). Died ca 1879 in Topsfield (daveh), buried Topsfield Cemetery. Census: 1850 in Calais. She married 20 Nov 1854 at Crawford (daveh) CHARLES COX.
iii. WEBSTER HODSDON, born 23 Jan 1841 in Calais (VR). Died 20 Jun 1842 age 17m, in Calais (VR:3:232, g.s.). Buried in Calais Cemetery.
iv. HENRY WEBSTER HODSDON, born 25 Mar 1843 in Calais (VR). Served in Civil War in Co A, 31st Maine, was wounded in the right arm, which left him impaired (daveh). Died 21 Mar 1907 age 67 in Limestone, ME (MSA, daveh). Census: 1850 in Calais, 1860 in Waite, 1870 in Topsfield, 1900 in Caribou. He married 11 Feb 1866 in Topsfield HARRIET B. JEWELL, born 21 Feb 1848 in Topsfield (VR:12), daughter of JOHN & CLARRASSA JEWELL both born in Industry, ME (VR:41, daveh). Died after 1907. Census: 1870 in Topsfield, 1900 in Caribou.
v. ISAIAH HODSDON, born 14 Mar 1845 in Calais (VR). Served in Civil War in Co. A, 31st Maine. Died in action in 1864 in Cold Harbor, VA (daveh). Census: 1850 in Calais, 1860 in Waite.
vi. JOSIAH HODSDON, born 23 Nov 1847 in Calais (VR). He was a farmer. Census: 1850 in Calais, 1860 in Waite, 1870 in Topsfield, 1880 in Plantation #14, 1900 in Princeton.. He married 4 Jul 1871 in Crawford ME AMANDA SPRAGUE, born 18 Mar 1848, in Princeton, daughter of JOSEPH SPRAGUE & EUNICE FICKETT (MSA, achs). Mar. cert. 4 July 1871 in Princeton (VR). She died 16 Oct 1921 age 73y 7m 2d in Princeton. Census: 1880 in Plantation #14, 1900 & 20 in Princeton.
vii. HARDY HODSDON, born ca July 1852 in Calais, died 13 Apr 1853 age 21 m 18d in Calais. Buried in Calais Cemetery.
viii. CHARLES HARDY HODSDON, born 9 Apr 1858 in Crawford ME (MSA, daveh). He was a farmer and blacksmith. Died 7 Jun 1901 age 48y 1m 28d in Topsfield (MSA). Census: 1860 in Waite, 1870 & 1900 in Topsfield. He married 18 Mar 1882 in Topsfield (VR) MARY JOSEPHINE HODGMAN, born Feb 1860, in Canada (1900 census), daughter of SAMUEL HODGMAN & JANE E. GREENLAW (she died 10 Mar 1905, daveh). Census: 1900 in Topsfield.

JAMES & TEMPERANCE HOLMES, p. 221

JAMES HOLMES Jr., born 14 May 1804 in Machias Me (VR, g.s.), son of JAMES HOLMES Sr. & SARAH BERRY. He was a farmer. Died 2 May 1874 age 70 in Milltown ME (obit). Buried in Calais Cemetery. Census: 1830 (2 males, 1 female) in Machias, 1840 (4 males & 2 females) in Machiasport, 1850 & 60 in Calais.

He married (drisko:467) TEMPERANCE CLARK, born circa 1807 in Machias Me (g.s., 1850 census). daughter of WILLIAM CLARK & SARAH 'SALLY' CROCKER (m. ca 1780, Bristol Me VR). Died 17 May 1864 age 56 in Calais (VR:3:309, sext, g.s.). Buried in Calais Cemetery. Census: 1850 & 60 in Calais. Children:

i. JAMES FRANCIS HOLMES, born Apr 1830, in Machias Me (jeff, g.s. has 1829). Served in Civil War (Co. I State Guards). He was a lumberman. Died 11 May 1904 age 79y 6m in Calais (MSA). Census: 1850 thru 1880 in Calais. He married 29 Oct 1856 in Calais (jeff) MARY EMELINE SMYTH, born ca 1833, daughter of STEWART & CHARITY SMYTH (see SMYTH).
ii. CHARLES M. HOLMES, born circa 1833 (?) in Machias Me. He probably died before 1874 when wife, Melissa remarried. Census: 1850 & 60 in Calais. He married 1st 6 May 1853 (int VR:1:52) in Calais MARY JANE ABBOTT (drisko:467 no dates given for the 3 marriages), born ca 1836, daughter of JACOB & SARAH A. ABBOTT. She died before 1859. Census: 1850 (age 14 with her parents) in Calais. He married 2nd 9 Aug 1859 by Rev. S. Wentworth in Calais (VR:1:174) EMILY/ EMMA S. SPOONER, who died 1866, daughter of PAUL SPOONER AND SERENA PRICE (see SPOONER). He married 3rd 20 Oct 1867 in Calais (VR) MELISSA P. (Furlong) PHIPPS (she was the widow of Rufus Phipps {see FURLONG}).
iii. GILBERT A. HOLMES, born 16 Apr 1835 in Machias Me. He was a grocer. Died 18 Jun 1911 age 76 in Calais (obit adv, g.s., MSA, prbt). Buried in Calais Cemetery. Census: 1850 60 & 70 in Calais. He married 23 Nov 1865 in Calais (VR) HENRIETTA SPOONER, sister of Emily, above (see SPOONER)
iv. LENORA A. HOLMES, born circa 1839, died 17 Sep 1842 age 3y 6m in Calais (g.s., name spelled Leenora). Buried in Calais Cemetery.

- v. ANN LOUISA HOLMES, born 2 Jul 1844 in Calais (VR), died circa 1866 in Calais (g.s.). Buried in Calais Cemetery. Census: 1850 & 60 in Calais.
- vi. SALEM LAFLIN HOLMES, born 25 Jun 1847 in Calais (VR). Died Oct 1848 age 16m in Calais (sext, g.s.). Buried: 24 Oct 1848 in Calais Cemetery.
- vii. EVERETT HOLMES, born circa 1849 (g.s. has 1851), died circa 1870 (g.s.). Census: 1850 (age 8/12) & 60 (age 11) in Calais.

JOB & VESTA HOLMES, p. 207

JOB HOLMES, born 17 Oct 1797, in Hebron ME, son of Capt. JAMES HOLMES AND JERUSHA RAWSON. (norw:533, paris:632, Oxford:207 has birth 1799). Moved to Calais in 1834 Graduated: 1826, Bowdoin College Maine Medical School (bowcat:440). He was a physician with offices in Paris 1826-34 and in Calais 1834-64 (bowcat:440). In Sept 1862 he examined the men from Washington County to determine eligibility to serve in the Civil War (CW records at MSA). Died 3 Mar 1864 in Calais (VR). Buried in Calais Cemetery. Census: 1840 (2 males, 5 females), 1860 in Calais..

He married 1 Jan 1833 in Paris ME (VR, liver:81, paris:632) VESTA HAMLIN born 6 Jun 1808 in Paris, daughter of CYRUS HAMLIN AND ANNA LIVERMORE, granddaughter of ELEAZER & LYDIA HAMLIN and ELIJAH & HANNAH LIVERMORE (paris:622, haml:193). Died 7 May 1885 76y 11m in Calais (obit, times). Buried in Calais Cemetery. Census: 1850 thru 1880 in Calais. Children:

- i. AGNES HOLMES, born 12 Apr 1837 in Calais (VR). Died 28 Aug 1884 age 47 in Calais (adv, g.s.). Buried in Calais Cemetery. Census: 1850 thru 1880 in Calais. She married 10 Aug 1865 in Calais EDWARD[5] MOORE, son of JOHN WARREN[4] MOORE & MARY LOUISA DEWOLFE, TRISTRRAM[3], WILLIAM[2-1] MOORE (haml:193, mhl:28). Born 11 Sep 1838, in St. Stephen, NB (obit, g.s.). He was Vice President of St. Croix Club and trustee of the Calais Academy (obit). Died 17 Jul 1905 age 66y 10m in Grand Manan, NB while on a trip (obit adv, g.s.). Buried in Calais Cemetery. Census: 1880 (age 41), 1900 (age 63) in Calais.
- ii. ANNA LIVERMORE HOLMES, born 3 Nov 1838 in Calais (VR). Graduated from Calais Academy 1857 (adv). In 1872 she was a piano teacher. Died 16 Oct 1921 age 82y 11m 13d in Calais (sfh:3:266, g.s.). Buried in Calais Cemetery. Census: 1850 thru 1900 in Calais.
- iii. ELLEN 'NELLIE' VESTA HOLMES, born 14 Mar 1840 in Calais (VR). Graduated from Calais Academy 1857 (adv). Died 6 Feb 1920 in Calais (g.s., probate rec). Buried in Calais Cemetery. Census: 1850 thru 1900 in Calais. She married 22 Oct 1863 in Calais (VR) Capt. JOSEPH S. CONY. He was lost at sea by burning of the Steamer *City of Bath*, of which he was Commander, off Cape Hatteras, 10 Feb 1867 (haml:193).
- iv. CYRUS HAMLIN HOLMES, born 1 Dec 1841 in Calais (VR). Died 3 Oct 1842 in Calais (VR, g.s.). Buried in Calais Cemetery.
- v. FRANK PIERPONT HOLMES, born 14 Aug 1843 in Calais (VR). Graduated from Calais Academy (adv). Served in Civil War, a Sgt. in Co. A 6th Maine, he was a student with blue eyes and light brown hair (cwcard). Died: 3 May 1863 killed in action, in Fredericsburg VA (NRMS:228). Buried in Calais Cemetery (date on family stone). Census: 1850 & 60 in Calais.
- vi. WALTER HAMLIN HOLMES, born 23 Jun 1854 in Calais (VR, bowcat:141). Graduated from Calais Academy 1871 (adv). He graduated from Bowdoin College in class of 1875 and Harvard Medical School in class of 1878 (haml:192, bowhis:850). He was a physician in Waterbury, CT, died 27 Nov 1898 in Waterbury (bowcat:141, obit, adv of 1 Dec 1898 no date of death given). Census: 1860 & 70 in Calais. He married 6 Apr 1881 in Waterbury MEDORA CAROLINE PLATT (bowhis: 850, haml:192), only daughter of Dr. GIDEON PRATT of Waterbury, CT (adv). She died after her husband.

ZEBADIAH & SARAH HOLT, p. 207

ZEBADIAH SHATTUCK HOLT, born 11 May 1797 in Antrim, NH, son of Deacon BARACHIAS HOLT & ELIZABETH SHATTUCK, he moved to Maine around 1820 (antr, phill). He was a defendant in court Apr 1859 for non payment of land rent for 1854-58 (SJC:16:241). He was a brick mason. Died before 1897. Census: 1850 & 60 in Calais, 1871 in St. Stephen, NB.

He married 1st 17 Nov 1821 by Rev. Joseph Osgood, in Exeter, ME (VR:200) ABIGAIL ATKINS, she died before 1844. Children:

    i. AMBROSE HOLT, born 16 June 1822 in Exeter (VR:31).
    ii. HANNAH HOLT, born 25 Feb 1824 in Exeter (VR:31).
    iii. ELIZA (D?) HOLT, born 5 May 1826 in Exeter (VR:31)
    iv. ABIGAIL HOLT, born ca 1829. Census: 1850 (age 21) in Calais. Probably the daughter of a first wife.
    v. EMILY J. HOLT, born ca 1834, in Exeter ME (1850 census). Died 28 Dec 1851 age 17 in Calais, daughter of Z.C. & A. Holt (g.s.). Buried in Calais cemetery.

He married 2nd before 1844 SARAH C. SPINNEY, born circa 1819 in St. George NB (1850 census), daughter of JONATHAN SPINNEY & MARY TROKE/TROAT (phill, fran). Died 23 Nov 1891 age 73y 6m in Calais (VSNB:79:951). Census: 1850 & 60 in Calais, 1871 in St. Stephen, NB. Children:

    vi. CHARLES MELVILLE HOLT, born 15 Jan 1844 in Calais (VR). He was a baker & candy maker. Census: 1850 & 60 in Calais, 1871 in St. Stephen, NB (with 3 children b. NB). He married 1 Oct 1866 by Rev. W. S. McKeller in Calais (VR:3:221) MARGARET J. McCARTNEY born ca 1838. Census: 1871 (age 33) in St. Stephen.
    vii. ADALINE A. HOLT, born 1 Feb 1847 in Calais (VR). Census: 1850 & 60 in Calais, 1871 in St. Stephen, NB. Possibly she is the Addie Holt who married John Caldwallder, Esq. on 23 May 1871 in Calais by Rev. E. W. Murray, both of St. Stephen (adv).
    viii. ZEBADIAH SHATTUCK HOLT, Jr., born circa July 1850 in Calais. He was a stevedore and a member of the Salvation Army. Died 8 July 1903 age 53y 3d in Calais (obit adv, MSA). Census: 1850 & 60 in Calais, 1871 in St. Stephen, NB. He married 1 Oct 1897 in Calais by Rev. W. J. Coyens of Boston Salvation Army, SUSAN C. GIBSON, born ca 1863, daughter of JAMES GIBSON (born in NB) & ELIZABETH LANGFORD (born in NB), she was a member of the Salvation Army (MSA).
    ix. FRANK P. HOLT, born circa 1853 in Calais. Census: 1860 in Calais, 1871 in St. Stephen, NB.
    x. GEORGE HOLT, born circa 1856 in Calais. Census: 1860 (age 4) in Calais. Possibly he is the male Holt who was buried 15 June 1862 age 6 years (sext).
    xi. ABBIE HOLT, born circa 1858. Census: 1871 in St. Stephen, NB.

PHILANDER & MARIAM HOPKINS, p. 192

PHILANDER HOPKINS, born 12 Aug 1808 in Montpelier, VT (1850 census, IGI), son of DAVID HOPKINS & POLLY FELLOWS. He resided in Antrim, NH before living in Calais. Died ca 1875 in Chichester (antr:547). Census: 1850 in Calais (with Patrick Welch).

He married 1st MARIAM R. GIBSON of Hampden, ME (antr:547), born circa 1819. Died 17 Jul 1849 in Calais (FJ, mortality schedule 1850). Buried in Calais Cemetery. Child:

    i. SARAH MARIA HOPKINS, born 18 Apr 1846 in Calais (VR).

Philander married 2nd CAROLINE E. RAND of Chichester (NH?) (antr:547).

WILLIAM D. & MARIA HOSKINS, p. 191

WILLIAM D. HOSKINS.

He married MARIA (   ). Children:

    i. MELISSA LOUISA HOSKINS, born 4 Apr 1840 in Calais (VR).
    ii. ROBERT MILES HOSKINS, born 21 Feb 1842 in Calais (VR).
    iii. WILLIAM HENRY HOSKINS, born 10 Nov 1844 in Calais (VR).
    iv. ICYVINDA HOSKINS, born 3 Nov 1847 in Calais (VR).

ALEXIS (ELECTUS) & LYDIA ANN HOYT, p. 194

ELECTUS HOYT, born 23 Jun 1768, son of JUSTUS HOYT AND ELIZABETH FITCH (hoyt:421). Resided in New Canaan, CT, before coming to Maine. He was of Robbinston when he appeared in court Sept 1824 (CCP:4:133). Died

14 Oct 1842 age 72 in Calais (VR:3:234). Buried: 17 Oct 1842 in Calais Cemetery. Census: 1820 (4 males, 5 females) & 1830 (4 males, 3 females) in Robbinston, 1840 (5 males, 4 females, he listed as Justus) in Calais.

He married 1st ABIGAIL E. KNIGHT. Died ca June 1820 in Robbinston Me (east:14). Children:

    i. HENRY P. HOYT. Resided: 1850, in California. Died circa 1862 in California (hoyt:503). He married EMILY KISSAM.
    ii. Capt. MOSES HOYT, born 4 Apr 1809 in Calais ? (hoyt:503). Died 8 Sep 1862, in Brooklyn, N Y (hoyt:503). He married 4 Sep 1833 SARAH COTTNAM WILSON, daughter of Hon. JOHN WILSON, of Hunterdon Co., NJ (hoyt:503). Resided in NJ (hoyt:503).
    iii. FITCH HOYT (hoyt:504), born before 1820.
    iv. GEORGE HOYT (hoyt:504), born before 1820.
    v. ABIGAIL HOYT (hoyt:504), born before 1820.
    vi. ALIDA HOYT (hoyt:504), born before 1820.

* Note – Three of the sons command vessels sailing from New England ports (hoyt:504).

He married 2nd Apr 1824 in Robbinston Me LYDIA ANN MORRISON (star: of 29 Apr 1824), born circa 1806 in Robbinston (he age 64 she age 18 at marriage) (congo member in 1840). Died after 1850. Census: 1850 in Calais. Children:

    vii. ALEXANDER HOYT, born circa 1825 in Robbinston Me (1850 census). He was a ship's master. Census: 1850 in Calais.
    viii. BENJAMIN F. HOYT, born circa 1829 in Robbinston Me (1850 census). Census: 1850 in Calais. He was a ship master. He married 1854 – 1855 by Rev. S. H. Keeler in Calais ANN M. PIKE (VR:1:158).
    ix. GEORGE B. HOYT, born circa 1831 in Robbinston Me (1850 census). Census: 1850 in Calais.
    x. SARAH I. HOYT, born circa 1833 in Robbinston Me (1850 census). Census: 1850 in Calais.
    xi. WILLIAM E. HOYT, born circa 1835 in Robbinston Me (1850 census). Census: 1850 in Calais.
    xii. UNNAMED FEMALE HOYT, born circa 1835, died Mar 1841 age 5 ½ (g.s.). Buried: 27 Mar 1841 in Calais Cemetery.
    xiii. MARGARET HOYT, born circa 1837, died circa 1839 age 2 in Calais (g.s.). Buried: 29 Sep 1839 in Calais Cemetery.
    xiv. ANN MARIA HOYT, born 13 Mar 1841 in Calais (VR). Census: 1850 (age 9) in Calais.

ROBERT & CATHARINE HUDSON, p. 205

ROBERT HUDSON, born ca 1802 in Ireland (dau's death rec). They probably left Calais between 1848 Edwards birth and 1849 Mary's death. Resided in Portland, ME. Died: 12 Mar 1872 age 70 in Portland (MSA). Census: 1850, 60, & 70 in Portland.

He married CATHARINE McCARTHY born ca 1810 in St. Stephen, NB (dau's death rec). She died ca 1886 age 76 and is buried in Calvary Cemetery in Portland, ME (diane). Census: 1850, 60 & 70 in Portland. Children:

    i. WILLIAM H. HUDSON, ca 1833. Census: 1850 in Portland. He was a mariner. He married 1854 in Portland CATHERINE BUTLER (diane).
    ii. CATHERINE HUDSON, born ca 1834 in St. Andrews, NB, died 3 Mar 1914 age 80y 8m at home of her daughter in Portland (MSA, obit argus). Census: 1870 in Portland. She married in 1853 in Portland (diane) RICHARD O. FULLER, born in Nova Scotia, died 29 Nov 1909 age 87 in Portland, he was a stevedore (MSA). Both parents born in NS but not named on the death certificate. Census: 1870 in Portland.
    iii. JANE HUDSON, born ca 1836 in St. Stephen, NB, died 24 Jan 1925 age 89 in Portland (MSA). She married in 1857 in Portland (diane) JOSEPH TOWLE.
    iv. ELIZABETH HUDSON, born ca 1838 in St. Stephen, NB, died 13 Feb 1897 age 58 in Portland (VR:9:33, MSA). Buried Calvary Cemetery in Portland. Census: 1850 & 60 in Portland. Married JOHN MARTIN (diane), born 24 Mar 1838 in Norway, Europe, son of JACOB MARTIN (MSA). Died: 12 July 1934 in Portland (MSA).
    v. ROBERT HUDSON, born ca 1841, died 9 Feb 1866 age 25y 7m in Portland, buried Calvary Cemetery in Portland (diane, MSA). Census: 1850 in Portland.

vi. MARY HUDSON, born ca 1844. Died: 1849 age 5, buried in Western Cemetery, Portland (grave rec.)
vii. EDWARD HUDSON, born 1 Mar 1848 in Calais (VR). He was a clerk in boot store. He died 12 Sept 1882 age 34 in Portland, buried Calvary Cemetery in Portland (diane, MSA). Census: 1850, 60 & 70 in Portland.

DAVID & MARY ANN HUME, p. 194

JOHN HUME born ca 1770, in Boston, he married NANCY WEBB born ca 1786 in Boston. He died 15 Jan 1830, she died 15 Apr 1847 (LDS)(Me Farmer of 6 May 1847, widow of John Hume formerly of Waterville). Children:
1. WILLIAM HUME, born 1794 in Boston.
2. JOHN HUME, Jr., born 1797 in Boston, died 13 Oct 1866 in Robbinston. He married LUCY B. BROOKS born ca 1799 (LDS) In Calais in 1830 & 40 census.
3. JOSIAH HUME, born 1799 (see BELOW).
4. DAVID W. HUME, born 1807 (see BELOW).
5. MANSON HUME, born 1808, in Boston. Married HANNAH C. BROOKS.
6. ORRA HUME, born 1810.
7. MARY HUME, born 1813.
8. NANCY HUME, born 1813.
9. NANCY HUME, born 1816, m. 24 Dec 1837 in Calais, Thomas Johnson, Jr..

DAVID W. HUME, born circa 1807, in Boston Ma., son of JOHN HUME AND NANCY WEBB. Came to Calais about 1827 (obit). He was a shoemaker & farmer. Died 22 May 1877 age 70 in Calais (g.s., adv). Buried in Bog Brook Cemetery in Calais. Census: 1860 & 70 in Calais.

He married 8 Feb 1837 by Rev. Ashal Moore in Calais (mrwc:20) MARY ANN LANE born circa 1809, daughter of WILLIAM & MARY LANE (sister of Almira (Lane) Huntley). Died before 1870. Census: 1860 in Calais. Children:

i. SABRA/SABRIA HUME, born 14 Jan 1838 in Calais (VR). Census: 1860, 70 & 80 in Calais. She married 20 May 1865 in Calais (VR) WILLIAM LANE HUNTLEY, son of GIDEON G. HUNTLEY AND ALMIRA LANE (see HUNTLEY)
ii. AMANDA HUME, born 5 Aug 1840 in Calais, died 22 Aug 1840 in Calais (VR:1:234). Buried: 24 Aug 1840 in Calais Cemetery.
iii. AMELIA HUME, born 11 Jan 1847 in Calais (VR). Census: 1860 & 70 (age 23 with father) in Calais. She married 22 Aug 1870 in Calais by Rev. H.A. Philbrook (adv) JOHN H. KNIGHT, born ca 1844, son of JEROME H. KNIGHT & MARIA ANN ELWELL. Census: 1860 & 70 (age 26 with mother, Ann) in Calais.

JOSIAH & REBECCA HUME, p. 198

JOSIAH HUME, born circa 1799, in Boston Ma, son of JOHN HUME AND NANCY WEBB (LDS). Came to Calais after War of 1812 (obit). He was a trader & toll man. Died 12 Feb 1872 age 72 in Perry, Plymouth Co. IA, while visiting his son (obit adv, union, east:261). Census: 1840 (2 males, 1 female), 50, 60, & 1870 (age 72) in Calais

He married 1st 27 Sept 1827 in Calais (cal2:45) MA(E)LINDA KNIGHT d/o PAUL KNIGHT & HANNAH WHITNEY (pkjdt). Died before 1831.

He married 2nd (int) 2 Feb 1832 SABRA LOW (LDS). Died before 1837.

He married 3rd 17 Sep 1837 by Rev. James Huckins in Calais (mrwc:24) Mrs. REBECCA S. (COOPER) STOCKWELL, born circa 1814 in Livermore ME (1850 census), daughter of WILLIAM COOPER & DELIVERANCE LOVELL (liver:91, sister of Columbus Cooper). Died 2 Feb 1889 age 75 in Calais (times, east:417, g.s.). Buried in Calais Cemetery. Probate of Estate: Apr 1889, in Machias Me (will dated 29 Oct 1886). Census: 1850 thru 1880 in Calais. Children:

i. JOSIAH LYSANDER HUME, born 5 Apr 1839 in Calais (VR). He was a 1st Sergt. and 2nd Lieut. in Co K of 6th also Co K in 19th Mass Inf.; wounded 13 Dec 1862 at Fredericksburg, VA; prisoner 22 June 1864 at Petersburg, VA; exchanged 14 Dec 1864; mustered out 30 June 1865 (Hist. of 19th Mass Inf. 1906:392, mss:II:483). Died 11 Mar 1874 age 34y 11m in Calais (obit adv, g.s. = Capt.) (guardianship for dau. filed 28 Mar 1881, prbt). Census: 1850 & 60 in Calais. He was Lieut. Hume when he married (int.) 28 Jan 1863 in Calais (VR:1:103) AUGUSTA JANE GOODWIN, daughter of JOHN H. GOODWIN AND MARY JANE DYER (see

  GOODWIN).
ii. REUBEN STOCKWELL {1} HUME, born 1 Dec 1842 in Calais, died 10 Jan 1844 in Calais (VR:1:235).
iii. REUBEN STOCKWELL{2} Hume, born circa 1851 in Calais. He was a shoemaker. Died after 1880. Census: 1860 thru 1880 in Calais. Probably resided in Perry, IA when father died 1872.

GIDEON G. & ALMIRA HUNTLEY, p. 197

DANIEL[6] HUNTLEY, born 1778, in Cornwallis, NS, son of FREDERICK[5], JABEZ[4], MOSES[2-3], JOHN[1], married RACHEL GARDNER, b. 5 May 1782, daughter of DAVID GARDNER & ZERIAH HUNTLEY, 20 July 1801, in Machias, by George Stillman, Esq. (hunt:101). Their son, Gideon G. Huntley settled in Calais.

  GIDEON G. HUNTLEY, born circa 1805, in E. Machias, Me (1850 census, hunt:191). He was in the 1st Brigade, 7th Div Maine Militia as a Pvt. 1829-32 (mil). He was a fisherman. Resided in Mass. Died 10 Oct 1873 age 66 in Calais (obit adv, union). Census: 1840 (2 males, 2 females), 50 & 60 in Calais.
  He married (int) 26 Oct 1834 in Calais (cal2:38) ALMIRA LANE born circa 1812 in Calais (1850 census), daughter of WILLIAM & MARY LANE (sister of Mary Ann (Lane) Hume). Died 8 Dec 1889 in Somerville, MA (obit). Buried: 12 Dec 1889 in Calais Cemetery. Census: 1850 thru 1880 in Calais. Children:

i. WILLIAM LANE HUNTLEY, born 12 Apr 1837 in Calais (VR). He was a mariner. Census: 1850, 60, 70 & 80 in Calais. He married 20 May 1865 in Calais (VR) his cousin, SABRIA HUME, daughter of DAVID W. HUME AND MARY ANN LANE (see HUME). Census: 1870 & 80 in Calais.
ii. HELEN M. HUNTLEY, born 10 Jul 1839 in Calais (VR). Died 25 Jan 1872 age 34y 6m in Princeton Me (kidd:313, east:261, union, g.s.). Buried in Princeton Cemetery. Census: 1850, 60 in Calais, 1870 in Princeton Me. She married 19 May 1860 in Calais JONATHAN KIDDER, son of JOSEPH CALVIN KIDDER Sr. & MARY WILKINS (see KIDDER).
iii. AMANDA HUNTLEY, born 30 Nov 1841 in Calais, died 27 Oct 1844 in Calais (VR:1:235).
iv. MARY HUNTLEY, born 5 Oct 1843 in Calais, died 10 Aug 1844 in Calais (VR:1:235).
v. ALMIRA HUNTLEY, born 28 Jan 1845 in Calais (VR). Bapt. 2 Mar 1851 in Calais (saint). Died after 1880. Census: 1850, 60 & 80 (with mother and 1 child age 1y) in Calais. She married 20 July 1873 in Calais (VR:3) EDWARD BOYD. Probably died before 1880 not with wife & child.
vi. ALBERT C/G. HUNTLEY, born 10 May 1847 in Calais (VR). Died 19 Feb 1886 age 38y 9m 9d (hunt:191). Census: 1860 in Calais. He married 26 Jul 1868 in Boston Ma (VSNB:27:317, hunt:191) EMMA SAWIN PATTEN of Boston, died 6 Nov 1887 age 42y, 10m 16d (hunt:191).
vii. SOPHIA (Hugens?) HUNTLEY, bapt. 3 May 1853 in Calais (saint).

SAMUEL & LOUISA HUSON, p. 193

  SAMUEL HUSON /HUSTON, born circa 1802, in NB. He was a house carpenter. In 1841 he resided in NB. Census: 1850 in Calais, 1860 & 70 in Princeton.
  He married 22 Apr 1832 in St. George, NB, LOUISA ANN SPINNEY born circa 1811 in St. George NB. Census: 1850 in Calais, 1860 & 70 in Princeton. Children:

i. CHARLOTTE E. HUSON, born circa 1834 in St. George NB (1850 census). Census: 1850 in Calais. She married 17 Jul 1852 in Calais (int. VR:1:46) AMOS CASWELL.
ii. SARAH A. HUSON, born circa 1836 in St George NB (1850 census). Census: 1850 in Calais. She married 7 Oct 1854 in Calais by Edward C. Mitchell (VR:1:159) JAMES FALEN (this may be Phelan).
iii. PHEBE HUSON, born circa 1839, died 23 Aug 1845 in Calais (VR:1:234). Buried in Calais.
iv. JAMES A. HUSON, born circa 1841, in St George, NB (1850 census). Died after 1917. Census: 1850 in Calais, 1860 in Princeton. He married SARAH A. STEWART, born 30 June 1847 in Parrsboro, NS, daughter of CHARLES STEWART & CAROLINE MAURICE (both b. NB), died 12 Dec 1917 age 70y 5m 13d in Calais (MSA).
v. GEORGE K. HUSON, born 16 Jul 1844 in Calais (VR). He was a carpenter. Died 28 Apr 1934 age 78y 4m 11d, widowed, in Calais (MSA= b. 17 July 1845 in Upper Mills, NB, widowed). Census: 1850 (age 5) in Calais, 1860 (age 16) in Princeton. [1900 census of Calais has a George Huson age 51 born July 1848 with wife Sarah b. Aug 1848 and two children.]

vi. THOMAS ALBERT HUSON, born 19 Nov 1847 in Calais (VR). Census: 1850 (age 3) in Calais, 60 (Albert age 13), 70 (age 23) in Princeton, 80 (age 34) & 1900 (has Thomas age 50 born Nov 1844) in Calais. He married (int.)12 Nov 1867 in Princeton (VR) VICTORIA ELIZABETH KEEN, daughter of ALBY KEEN, Sr. & NANCY J. ESTABROOKS (see KEENE).

vii. CHARLES CRAWFORD HUSON, born circa 1850 in Calais. Bapt. 4 June 1852 in Calais (saint). Died ? Census: 1850 in Calais, 1860 & 70 in Princeton.

viii. MELVINA HUSON, bapt. 4 June 1852 in Calais (saint) (not in 1860 census).

ix. PHEBE ELLIS HUSON, born ca 1854. Bapt. 28 Sept 1854 in Calais (saint). Census: 1860 (age 6) & 70 in Princeton.

JOSEPH & MARY ANN HUTCHINS, p. 195

JOSEPH W. HUTCHINS, born circa 1818, in Minot, ME (1850 census, CEV), son of JONATHAN HUTCHINS & MARY YORK. In 1841 he established a business making sails for ships, located in Porter's Building, on Depot Street in Calais. The business occupies two floors each 85 X 70 feet, making all kinds of sails, there are four employees (CEV: 27). Died 22 Mar 1892 age 72y 9m 23d in Calais (MSA, obit SCC). Buried in Calais Cemetery. Census: 1850 census (includes Mary Gardner, age 58 born in Portland, Benjamin Hutchings age 28, born in Westbrook and Margaret Hutchings age 23. These are possibly his mother and siblings). Mary still with him in 1860 in Calais.

He married MARY ANN MANSFIELD (surname from dau's death rec), born circa 1818 / 22, in Portland ME (1850 census). Died 6 Sep 1851, age 27y in Portland ME (FJ, sext). Buried: 20 Sep 1851 in Calais Cemetery. Census: 1850 in Calais. Children:

i. JONATHAN HUTCHINS, born 27 Sep 1841 in Calais (VR). Died 26 Feb 1842 age 4 ½ in Calais (VR:1:234, sext).

ii. GEORGE WASHINGTON HUTCHINS, born 23 Feb 1843 in Calais (VR). Enlisted in Civil War on 1 Feb 1865, he was 5'8" with black eyes and black hair, no unit mentioned on his enlistment paper (MSA). He was a sail maker. Died before 1892. Census: 1850 thru 1880 in Calais. He married 15 Nov 1865 in Calais (VR:3:208) MARY HELEN BELMORE, daughter of JAMES M. BELMORE & ANNIE COLSON (see BELMORE).

iii. MARY ANN (HELEN) HUTCHINS, born 28 Feb 1845 in Calais (VR, mid. name Helen). Died 1 Oct 1924 age 76y 7m 3d in Fairfield (VR, name Mary Ann). Buried: Pine Grove Cemetery, Waterville, ME (name Mary Ann) Census: 1850 (name Mary E.), 1860 (name Mary E.) & 70 (name Mary A.) in Calais, 1880 in Fairfield, ME. She married STILLMAN OSGOOD SAWYER, son of WARREN SAWYER AND SARAH SWIM, 12 Feb 1866 (see SAWYER)

iv. ABBY ANN HUTCHINS, born 15 Jan 1847 in Calais (VR). Died 6 Sep 1847 age 8m in Calais (VR:1:234, FJ). Buried: 8 Sep 1847 in Calais Cemetery.

v. UNNAMED CHILD HUTCHINS, born 22 Aug 1848 in Calais, died 22 Aug 1848 in Calais (sext). Buried in Calais Cemetery.

vi. STILLBORN HUTCHINS, born Aug 1850 in Calais, died Aug 1850 in Calais (sext). Buried in Calais Cemetery.

He married 2nd 19 May 1867 in Calais (union) VESTA H. NEVERS, born Mar 1840, daughter of NATHAN & MARY NEVERS (see NEVERS).

JAMES & ANN ARVINE (IRVIN), p. 199

JAMES ARVINE/ARVIN/ IRVING, born circa 1824 in Ireland (1850 census). Census: 1850 in Calais. Possibly went to California.

He married ANN/NANCY McLELLAN, born 12 Feb 1822 in St. Andrews, NB, daughter of MARTIN McLELLAN & MARGARET LESLIE, both born and married in Ireland (presSA). Census: 1850 in Calais. (possible 2nd marriage) Married 30 May 1876 by J. A. Freiday in Calais John T. Kildea and Mrs. Anna Irvin both of Calais (VR:3:236).
Children:

i. MARGARET IRVING, born 27 May 1846 in Calais (VR). Census: 1850 in Calais.

JOHN & ELIZABETH ANN JACKSON, p. 225

JOHN JACKSON, born circa 1815, in Toronto (then Little York), Ont., son of JAMES JACKSON & MARTHA SAUNDERS (James was a soldier, both b. England). Applied for citizenship 26 Mar 1844; stated he was born in Toronto, 1814, left there at age 2 to NH, back to Canada; in Jan 1834 to Calais where he now resides (SJC:8:41). Naturalized 23 Sept 1848 (irmch, no witnesses given). He founded the Calais Advertiser in 1841 and was editor and publisher until his death, also was town clerk in Calais, died 2 Nov 1892 age 78y 9m 6d in Calais (obit adv, MSA). Buried in Calais Cemetery. Census: 1850, 60 & 70 in Calais.

He married 27 Sep 1846 in St. Stephen, NB (CCMR) ELIZABETH ANN CHRISTOPHER, born circa 1818 in Calais (1850 census), daughter of GEORGE CHRISTOPHER (b. Minot ME) & BETSEY GILMORE. Died 27 Jan 1893 age 75y 5m in Calais (obit adv, MSA). Buried in Calais Cemetery. Census: 1850, 60 & 70 in Calais. Children:

i. ELIZABETH 'LIZZIE' CHANDLER JACKSON, born 17 Jul 1848 in Calais (VR). Graduated from Calais Academy (adv). She became editor of Advertiser after father's death. Died 13 Jul 1924 in Calais (MSA). Buried in Calais Cemetery. Census: 1850, 60, 70 & 1900 in Calais.
ii. JAMES FREDERICK JACKSON, born 13 Jan 1850 in Calais (VR) [g.s. in Calais Cemetery has a Fred died 27 Dec 1881 age 29y]. Census: 1850, 60 & 70 in Calais.
iii. EDGAR C. JACKSON, born 9 Jan 1852 in Calais (VR), born (2) 8 Jan 1854 (sfh:6:210). Died 23 Jan 1933 age 79y 15d in Calais (MSA, sfh:6:210). Buried in Calais Cemetery. Census: 1860, 70 & 1900 in Calais.
iv. JOHN SAUNDERS JACKSON, born 10 Oct 1854 in Calais (VR:3:241). Died 8 Oct 1855 in Calais (VR:3:301).
v. HERBERT SAUNDERS JACKSON, born 26 Jul 1856 in Calais (VR:3:241). Died 20 May 1859 age 3y in Calais (VR:3:301, east:168). Buried in Calais Cemetery (sext).
vi. UNNAMED CHILD JACKSON, born May 1857, died 20 Nov 1857 in Calais (sext). Buried in Calais Cemetery.
vii. MARTHA 'Mattie' DOWNES JACKSON, born 13 Feb 1858 in Calais (VR:3:241). Died 12 Jun 1880 age 21y 4m in Calais (adv). Buried: 14 Jun 1880 in Calais Cemetery. Census: 1860 & 70 in Calais.

ARTHUR & MARY L. JONES, p.189

ARTHUR JONES Jr., born 9 Mar 1809 (?) in Unity, ME (VR). Died 20 Mar 1848 age 39 in Calais (VR:1:232, Adv, g.s.). Buried: 22 Mar 1848 in Calais Cemetery. Probate of Estate: 6 Apr 1848, in Machias Me (died intestate, petition to sell property filed 2 Oct 1849). Census 1840 (7 males, 5 females including 4 adult males and 2 adult females).

He married before 1833 MARY L. (_____), born 3 May 1811 in St. Stephen, NB, (Calais VR). Died 23 Oct 1848 age 38 in Calais (g.s.). Buried in Calais Cemetery. Children:

i. MARY JANE JONES, born 6 Oct 1833 in St. Stephen, NB (Calais VR:1:232). Died 16 Mar 1836 age 3y 5m in Calais (VR:1:232, g.s.). Buried in Calais Cemetery.
ii. GEORGE WASHINGTON JONES, born 5 May 1835 in Calais, died 1 Oct 1836 age 1y 5m in Calais (VR:1:232, g.s.). Buried in Calais Cemetery.
iii. ROXANNA JONES, born 9 Jul 1837 in Calais (VR). Died after 1848 (age 12 father's probate). Census: (Roxanna Jones age 13 living with James Belmore family).
iv. ANN MARIA JONES, born 16 Jun 1839 in Calais (VR). Died 9 May 1852 age 13 in Calais (g.s.). Buried in Calais Cemetery.
v. ADELAIDE VICTORIA JONES, born 2 Jun 1842 in Calais, died 20 May 1847 age 6 in Calais (VR:1:232), buried 22 May 1847 in Calais Cemetery.
vi. UNNAMED CHILD JONES, born Jun 1844 in Calais, died Jun 1844 age 1d in Calais (sext). Buried: 21 Jun 1844 in Calais Cemetery.
vii. JAMES DALLAS JONES, born 16 May 1845 in Calais, died 31 Aug 1847 in Calais (VR:1:232).
viii. UNNAMED CHILD JONES, born circa 1845, died Aug 1846 age 15m in Calais, buried: 23 Aug 1846 in Calais (sext).
ix. ANGELINA HATCH JONES, born 1 Oct 1847 in Calais (VR). Died 14 Sep 1848 age 1y in Calais (sext, dau of widow, Jones).

CALVIN & FRANCES JONES, p. 213

CALVIN JONES, born between 1791-1800. He was in court in 1833 for payment on land in Milltown 10 years past due. Possibly died before 1840. Census: 1830 (9 males, 3 females) in Calais.

He married before 1831 FRANCES (_____), born between 1801-10. Children (there may have been other older children):

i. FRANCES OLIVE JONES, born 13 Sep 1831 in Calais (VR).
ii. EDWARD DIMSEY JONES, born 13 Sep 1833 in Calais (VR).

- Note. This family does not appear in the 1850 census. [Poss. Calvin died and Frances remarried, John Butler (see BUTLER].

ISAAC & SALOME JONES, p 205

Capt. ISAAC N(ICHOLS?) JONES, born 28 Feb 1808, in Anapolis, NS (jones 3rd, 1850 census), son of NICHOLAS JONES and CATHERINE DITMARS. Served in Civil War, enlisted in USN 2 Nov 1864 disc. 22 Apr 1865. His War Record on grave card at MSA lists: Vandalis, Ohio; Lackawana; Kanawha; and Naval Hospital, Chelsea, MA, as places of service. He was a master mariner. Died 20 Nov 1879 age 72 in Calais (adv, bibj). Buried Calais Cemetery, no date on military stone U.S. Navy. Census: 1850 & 60 in Calais.

* 1880 mortality list has Isaac Jones age 72 b. NS (parents both born Wales), Sail maker, died Nov.

He married 20 Nov 1832 (bibj) SALOME HINES, born 28 Nov 1810 in Digby, NS, daughter of RICHARD HINES and SARAH SYPHER (jones 3rd). Died 5 Apr 1867 age 56y 4m in Calais (g.s.). Buried in Calais Cemetery. Census: 1850 & 60 in Calais. Children:

i. NICHOLAS T. JONES, born 28 Aug 1833, in Digby, NS (bibj). He was a sailor. Died 17 Mar 1874 age 40y 5m 11d, in Japanese Sea (lost from steamship "Manchu", bibj, adv). Census: 1850 & 60 in Calais.
ii. CHARLES HENRY JONES, born 22 Aug 1835, in Nova Scotia (jones 3rd). He was a ship captain and pilot. Died 22 Aug 1902 in Port Townsend, WA (jones 3rd). Census: 1860 in Calais.
iii. SOPHIA TERESA JONES, born, 30 Dec 1838 in Calais (VR, bibj). In 1856 she was a teacher in Calais. Died 28 Aug 1904 in Robbinston Me (jones 3rd). Buried in Brewer Cemetery, Robbinston. Census: 1850 in Calais, 1860, 70 & 80 in Robbinston. She married 21 July 1858 by George D. Strout (VR:3:173) in Calais (jones 3rd) ELBRIDGE JOSEPH GERRY, born 25 June 1825 in Robbinston (bibj), son of SETH & GERRY & MARY STETSON. He was a farmer & blacksmith. Died 31 Jan 1898 in Robbinston, ME (times, g.s.). Buried Brewer Cemetery in Robbinston. Census: 1850 thru 80 in Robbinston.
iv. SALOME A. JONES, born 30 Dec 1838 in Calais (VR, bibj). Died circa 1916 (jones 3rd). In 1856 she was a teacher in Calais. Resided: 1870 in Colorado in 1891, later in Wyoming. Census: 1850 & 60 in Calais. She married 11 Nov 1860 at home of Isaac N. Jones, Sr. in Calais (adv, union) JAMES JOHN ARMSTRONG of Worcester, MA.
v. GEORGE KEENE JONES, born 14 Jan 1843 in Calais (VR, bibj). He was a dealer in Stoves, Ranges & furnaces doing business as G.K. Jones & Co (CEV:18). Died 22 Jun 1915 age 72y 5m 8d in Calais (adv, sfh:2:184). Buried in Calais Cemetery. Census: 1850 thru 1910 in Calais. He married 23 Nov 1870 (bibj) in Calais, MARY A. O'BRIEN, born 15 May 1844 in Fredericton, NB, daughter of Thomas A. O'Brien (b. Ireland) (MSA). Died 15 May 1923 age 79y 11m 29d (MSA, jones 3rd). Census 1900 in Calais.
vi. ISAAC N. JONES, Jr., born 7 Jul 1846 in Calais (VR, bibj). Resided in Springfield, MA (jones 3rd). Died 18 Sep 1917 (adv). Census: 1850 & 60 in Calais. He was married by Aug 1891 when visiting in Calais after 20 years absence (adv). [Calais Advertiser dated 16 Sept 1908, Dr. Frank H. Moore and Mr. Isaac N. Jones left Wednesday morning by boat for New York City for consultation and treatment with an eminent oral surgeon for an injury to Mr. Jones' jaw caused by the difficult removal of a wisdom tooth by a Boston dentist, some weeks since]. [adv of 25 Nov 1908 – Samuel Harris died, one of his daughters is Mrs. I. N. Jones].

LEMUEL H. & RACHEL JONES, p. 187

LEMUEL HOWE JONES, born 8 May 1789 in Robbinston Me (1850 census, bhm:131), son of SAMUEL JONES, Jr. & MARY RICHARDS (bhm:7:130). He was a house carpenter. Died 1 May 1868 age 79 in Calais (obit union, first white child born in

Robbinston). Census: 1840 (3 males, 3 females), 1850 & 60 in Calais.

He married 1st Margaret McNeill of St. John, NB (mefam:4:143). She died ca 1824 age 28 in Robbinston (Eastern Star, newspaper dated 9 Dec 1824). Children:

    i. BARTLETT JONES, born between 1820-25 (1840 census, bhm:131).
    ii. HENRY JONES, born between 1825-30 (1840 census, bhm:131).

He married 2nd 18 Dec 1830 by Rev. Bennett Roberts in Perry (VR, mrwc:3, Lemuel is listed as Samuel, Northern Light has Lemuel) Mrs. RACHEL (LORING) SWETT, born 31 May 1798 in Perry ME (VR:38), daughter of PETER LORING. She was previously married to Daniel Swett of Perry [their daughter, Rachel Swett married Solomon Pool (see POOL) and daughter Lydia Swett married William Rogers (see ROGERS)]. Died 26 Aug 1872 age 74 in Calais (union, adv). Census: 1850, 60 & 70 in Calais. Children:

    iii. JOHN ALDEN {1} JONES, born 10 Oct 1831 in Perry ME (VR:91). Probably died before 1837.
    iv. JOHN ALDEN {2} JONES, born 17 Dec 1837 in Calais (VR). Census: 1850 & 60 in Calais.
    v. MARY RICHARDS JONES, born 6 Jul 1841 in Calais (VR). Census: 1850 & 60 in Calais. She married 27 Aug 1863 in Calais (VR) BENJAMIN D. WYATT.

SETH H. & MARY KEELER, p. 224

SETH[6] KEELER, born 12 Jan 1777 in Brandon, VT, son of (SETH[5], JOSEPH[4], JOSEPH[3], SAMUEL[2], RALPH[1]) He died there 13 Sept 1850. He married 1st 22 Aug 1799 in Brandon, VT FANNY CARVER, born 16 Dec 1781, daughter of RUFUS CARVER and PRISCILLA CUMMINGS. She died 15 June 1820 in Brandon. Seth married 2nd, 6 Sept 1821 in Brandon LAURA HALE, she died 15 Aug 1824, Seth married 3rd 14 Apr 1825 in Brandon, REBECCA HYDE. The first child of the 1st marriage was SETH HARRISON KEELER, who lived in Calais in 1839 and stayed until 1867 (keeler:148).

SETH HARRISON[7] KEELER Sr. born 24 Sept 1800, in Brandon, VT (keeler:149). He was appointed the minister of the Congo Church in Calais on 20 Nov 1839 and left in 1867. Before coming to Calais he was the minister in South Berwick, ME from 1829 to 1836. From Calais he went to Mt. Vernon, NH. Died 26 Dec 1886, in Sommerville, MA. Census: 1850 & 60 in Calais (keeler:243).

He married 26 Nov 1829 (newip:405) MARY F.[6] FELT, born 21 Feb 1808 in New Ipswich, NH (newip:405), daughter of PETER[5] FELT and POLLY FLETCHER, (granddaughter of PETER[4], AARON[3], MOSES[2], GEORGE[1]). Died after 1893 when she resided in Somerville, MA (felt:196). Census: 1850 & 60 in Calais. Children:

    i. MARY PRISCILLA KEELER, born 30 Sep 1830 in S. Berwick, ME (felt:197). Died 7 Jul 1839 in Amesbury, MA (keeler:243).
    ii. CAROLINE F. KEELER, born 23 Feb 1832 in S. Berwick, ME, died 31 Dec 1833 in S. Berwick, ME (keeler:243, felt:197).
    iii. FRANCES REBEKAH KEELER, born 21 Nov 1834 in S. Berwick, ME (keeler:243, felt:197). Resided: 1863 in Boston Ma. She was a music teacher. Died after 1893. Census: 1850 & 60 in Calais. She married 31 May 1865 in Calais (VR:3:213) WILLIAM BRADSHAW BYRNES, son of WILLIAM M. BYRNES & ELIZABETH BAILEY of Medford, MA (felt:197).
    iv. MARTHA LEIGH KEELER, born 14 Nov 1837 in Amesbury, MA (felt:197). Died 17 Sep 1842 in Calais (obit gaz). Buried: 20 Sep 1842 in Calais Cemetery.
    v. SETH HARRISON {1} KEELER, born 27 Jul 1840 in Calais (felt:197). Bapt. 3 Jan 1841 in Calais (congo). Died 29 Nov 1841 in Calais (obit gaz, g.s.). Buried: 1 Dec 1841 in Calais Cemetery.
    vi. SETH HARRISON KEELER, Jr., born 8 Nov 1845 in Calais (VR). Bapt. 3 May 1846 (congo). Died 9 May 1849 in Calais (felt:197, g.s.). Buried: 11 May 1849 in Calais Cemetery.
    vii. CHARLES WELLINGTON KEELER, born 12 Jul 1849 in Calais (felt:197). Graduated from Calais Academy (adv). Occupation: Bookkeeper. Died after 1893. Resided: 1893 in Somerville, MA. Census: 1850 & 60 in Calais. He married 7 Jan 1879 in Melrose, MA (felt) JENNIE FLORENCE MORSS Jennie, daughter of WILLIAM MORSS & JANE GOSS (keeler: 243, felt:197).

ALBY & NANCY KEENE, p. 190

ALBY KEENE/KEEN Sr., born circa 1808, (?) in Belfast, ME (1850 census = Nobleboro). Died 20 Feb 1890 age 83y 10m in Calais (east: 437). Census: 1840 (2 males, 3 females) in Perry, 50 in Calais, 1860 & 70 in Princeton Me.

* Note. Records show he used the name Keen without the '<u>e</u>'. This family had records in Calais and in Perry but there is a difference in many dates, all dates found have been noted.

He married (int) 29 Mar 1834 in Calais (cal2:37) NANCY J. ESTABROOKS, born circa 1814 in St John, NB (1850 census). daughter of DAVID E. ESTABROOKS & JUDITH FLETCHER. Census: 1850 in Calais, 60 & 70 in Princeton Me (see ESTABROOKS) Children:

i. THOMAS EDWARD KEEN, born <u>11 Sep 1833</u> in St. Stephen, NB (Calais VR), born (2) <u>11 Sep 1834</u> in St. Stephen, NB (Perry VR:167). Census: 1850 in Calais.

ii. AMANDA JANE KEEN, born (1) <u>6 Apr 1835</u> in St. Stephen, NB (Calais VR), born (2) <u>6 Apr 1837</u> in St. Stephen, NB (Perry VR). Census: 1850 in Calais. She married, 2 Dec 1853 in Calais (VR). HENRY SEDERQUIST.

iii. HARRIET ELIZABETH KEEN, born (1) <u>7 Jan 1837</u> in St Stephen, NB (Calais VR), born (2) <u>5 Jan 1838</u> in Perry (VR). Died (1) 8 Sep 1838 in Calais (VR:I:233), died (2) 11 Sept 1839 (g.s.), died (3) 15 Sep 1839 in Perry (VR:167).

iv. JUDITH ELIZA KEEN, born 6 Apr 1839 in Calais (VR, Perry VR:167). Census: 1850 in Calais.

v. VICTORIA ELIZABETH KEEN, born (1) <u>22 Apr 1841</u> in Calais (VR), born (2) <u>19 Apr 1841</u> in Perry (VR:167). Died 19 Nov 1911 age 67y 6m in Calais (MSA). Census: 1850 in Calais, 1860 in Princeton Me, 1900 in Calais. She married in 1867 THOMAS ALBERT HUSON, son of SAMUEL & LOUSIA HUSON (see HUSON).

vi. NANCY JANE KEEN, born 22 Jun 1843 in Calais (VR). Census: 1850 in Calais, 1860 in Princeton Me. She married (int.) 28 May 1862 in Princeton Me (VR) JOHN WHITE.

vii. HARRIET L. KEEN, born 22 Mar 1845 in Calais (VR). Died 7 Mar 1848 in Calais (g.s.). Buried: 10 Mar 1848 in Calais Cemetery.

viii. DELIA JANE KEEN, born 8 Dec 1846 in Calais (VR). Died 3 May 1848 in Calais (g.s.). Buried: 7 May 1848 in Calais Cemetery.

ix. PERTHENIA KEEN, born circa 1849. Census: 1850 in Calais, 1860 & 70 in Princeton.

x. ANNA G. KEEN, born circa 1852. Census: 1860 & 70, in Princeton.

xi. ALBY KEEN, Jr., born Jun 1853 (1900 census). He was a shingle maker. Census: 1860, 70, 80 in Princeton, 1900 in Kingman, ME. He married (int.) 5 Dec 1874 in Princeton (VR). LIZZIE CRAFTS. Census: 1880 in Princeton, 1900 in Kingman.

xii. WILLIAM D. KEEN, born circa 1856. Census: 1860 & 70 in Princeton.

xiii. NEIL KEEN, born circa 1857. Died 6 Oct 1858 in Calais (g.s.). Buried: 7 Oct 1858 in Calais Cemetery.

xiv. ELVINA KEEN, born Jan 1860. Census: 1860 (age 5/12) in Princeton Me.

JARIUS & MARY KEEN, p. 198

JARIUS KEEN Jr., born 16 July 1802 in Duxbury, MA (cal2:1), son of Capt. JARIUS KEEN Sr. (beg:125) [died 8 Dec 1844 (g.s., prbt)] & LUCY KNIGHT [died 17 Jan 1866 (g.s.)]. His grandfather, Isaac Keen and great grandfather, Jonathan Knight both served in the Rev. War. Like his father he was a ship carpenter. He died 17 Aug 1868 age 66y 1m in Calais (g.s., union). Buried in Calais Cemetery. Census: 1830 (2 males, 3 females), 40 (2 males & 5 females), 1850 & 60 (with his mother, Lucy age 75) in Calais.

He married (int) 10 Dec 1825 in Calais (cal2:24), married circa Jan 1826 in Robbinston Me (east:72, no date) MARY B. BROOKS, born circa 1802 in St. Andrews, NB. Died 27 Oct 1859 age 58y 9m in Calais (g.s.). Buried: 29 Oct 1859 in Calais Cemetery. Census: 1850 in Calais. Children:

i. ADALINE H. KEEN, born 31 Mar 1827 in Calais (VR). Census: 1850 (age 23) in Calais.

ii. ELIZABETH KEEN, born 2 Dec 1829 in Calais (VR).

iii. MARY B. KEEN, born 6 Mar 1831 in Calais (VR). Died after her husband. Census: 1850, 60, 70 & 1900 in Calais. She married (int) 22 Jan 1848 in Calais (VR:I:33) DAVID GORDON, born ca May

1821 in Henneker, NH, son of DAVID GORDON & MARY HART, died 21 July 1907 age 85 in Calais (MSA). He was a shoemaker. Census: 1850 (living with her parents), 60, 70 & 1900 in Calais.

ii. ISAAC KEEN, born 10 May 1833 in Calais, died 31 Mar 1842 age 9 in Calais (VR, g.s.). Buried: 2 Apr 1842 in Calais Cemetery.

iii. LUCY H. KEEN, born 23 Apr 1835 in Calais (VR). Census: 1850, 60 & 70 in Calais. She married (int) 1 May 1850 in Calais (VR:1:58) WILLIAM B. TAYLOR, born ca 1826. He was a tinsmith. Census: 1860 & 70 in Calais.

iv. MARIA T. KEEN, born 2 Apr 1838 in Calais (VR). Census: 1850 in Calais.

WILLIAM & BATHIA KEENE, p. 192

WILLIAM KEENE, born 1816 (g.s.) in Waldoboro (son's death rec). He worked in a mill, filing saws. Died 12 Feb 1884, in Milltown ME (times, g.s.). Buried in Calais Cemetery. Census: 1840 (4 males, 4 females), 60, 70 & 80 in Calais.

He married 1st 29 Oct 1843 in Calais by Nathaniel Whitman (VR:1:132) BETHIAH L. ELLSMORE born circa 1821 (poss. she is the daughter of Moses & Lucy Ellsmore), her name sometimes written as Martha. Died 26 Sep 1847 age 26 in Calais (VR:3:233). Buried: 28 Sep 1847 in Calais Cemetery. Children:

i. LUCY ADLA KEENE, born Mar 1845 in Calais (VR). Census: 1860 & 70 in Calais.

He married 2nd (int.) 14 Apr 1850 in Calais (VR) ZOA ANN WOODMAN, born Feb 1832 in St. David, NB (1900 census), daughter of JOHN WOODMAN (b. Dedham, Ma) & ANN McCANN (b. St. David). Died age 77 on 14 Jun 1909 in Calais (obit, MSA, g.s.). Buried in Calais Cemetery. Census: 1860 thru 1900 in Calais. Children:

ii. MARY O. KEENE, born circa 1850. Census: 1860 (age 10) & 70 in Calais.

iii. ANNA E. KEENE, born circa 1852. Census: 1860 (age 8), 70 & 80 in Calais. She married 13 Apr 1877 by S.D. Wardwell in Calais (VR:3:329, date ?) FRANK McDONALD.

iv. LUCY B. KEENE, born 15 Dec 1856 in Milltown, Me, died 8 Nov 1941 in Omaha, NE, buried ?? in Millinocket, Me (obit adv). Buried: Rural Cemetery St. Stephen, NB (rural:41). Census: 1860 & 70 in Calais. She married 28 Dec 1881 by Rev. W.L. Brown in Calais (VR:2:13) ARTHUR F. INNESS, born 25 Aug 1852 (g.s.) of Milltown, NB, son of _____ & MARTHA INNESS (with him age 66 in 1871 census). Died 7 July 1938 (g.s., rural:41). Census: 1871 (age 20) in St. Stephen, NB. Buried in St. Stephen, NB.

v. MINNIE C. KEENE, born circa 1858. Census: 1860 (age 2) thru 1880 in Calais.

vi. WILLIAM H. KEENE, born 4 Jul 1861 in Calais (MSA). He was a lumberman and weaver. Died 26 Dec 1942 age 81y 5m 22d in Calais (MSA). Census: 1870 thru 1900 in Calais. He married 3 July 1886 in Calais (VR:2:59) NELLIE A. McBRIDE of Calais.

vii. CHARLES EDWARD KEENE, born Mar 1873 (1900 census). Died circa 1949 (g.s.). Buried in Calais Cemetery. Census: 1880 &1900 in Calais.

MICHAEL & CATHARINE KELLY, p. 224

MICHAEL KELLY, born circa 1794. He applied for citizenship on 14 Aug 1838, stating he was 44 years of age, born at Scotland, Tipperary, Co. Ireland in 1794, left Ireland 4 June 1819, arrived Baring 20 Nov 1821, and then to Calais on 22 May 1829 where he now resides. (CCP:16:376). Immigrated to U. S. 20 Nov 1821, born in Sollohead, Tipperary, Ireland naturalized 19 Sept 1840, witnesses: Thomas J. D. Fuller and Bion Bradbury (irmch). Died 7 May 1865 in Calais, probate of will dated 30 Apr 1864 in Machias Me. [Survived by wife and 2 daughters, Nancy Barritt and Mary Lawler]. Census: 1840 (2 males, 3 females), 50 & 60 in Calais.

He married before 1825 CATHERINE 'Kate' (_____), born circa 1794 in Tipperary, Ireland (1850 census). Died after 1880. Census: 1850, 60 & 80 [with 3 grandchildren named Crangle] in Calais. Children:

i. JAMES KELLY, born circa 1826 in Baring ME (1850 census). Died before 1865 (not mentioned in father's will). Census: 1850 in Calais.

ii. SARAH JANE KELLY, born circa 1829 in Baring ME (1850 census). Died 27 Sep 1851 in Milltown ME

(FJ). Census: 1850 in Calais.

iii. MARY KELLY, born 5 Aug 1831 in Calais (VR). Census: 1850 in Calais. Possible mother of Crangle grandchildren.

SAMUEL & MARY KELLY, p. 209

SAMUEL KELLY, born 2 Aug 1796 in Northwood, NH (VR, g.s. has 1897), son of BENJAMIN KELLY & MARY GILE. Came to Calais in 1821, he was a Justice of Peace in 1829, in 1838 he was treas. of Temperance House, and a farmer. In 1826 he was a partner in the firm of Kelley & Kimball with James G. Kimball & David Kimball (CCP:4:330). His property on Main Street later became the site of the Memorial Park. Died 22 Apr 1885 age 88y 8m 20d in Calais (g.s., east:375). Buried in Calais Cemetery. Census: 1830 (8 males, 6 females), 40 (4 males, 6 females), 50 thru 1880 in Calais.

He married 1st Jan 1826 in Calais (beg:124, east:72, no mar date) MARY DANFORD, born 28 Nov 1800 in Wiscasset, ME (VR), daughter of PAUL DANFORD & MARY COTHRAN. Died 1 Dec 1859 age 60 in Calais (east:173). Buried: 3 Dec 1859 in Calais Cemetery. Census: 1850 in Calais. Children:
* Note. Mary was a sister of Betsey (Danford) Downes and Emeline (Danford) Lowell.

i. CHARLES H. KELLY, born 2 Nov 1826 in Calais (VR, g.s. has 22 Nov). He was a merchant Died 4 Mar 1866 in Calais (g.s., east: 219). Buried in Calais Cemetery. Census: 1850 & 60 in Calais.

ii. MARY ELIZABETH SHAW KELLY, born 10 Mar 1828 in Calais (VR, g.s.). Died 15 Dec 1863 in Calais (VR:3:305, g.s.). Buried: 19 Dec 1863 in Calais Cemetery. Census: 1850 & 60 in Calais. She married 7 Sep 1848 in Calais (VR:3:142) GEORGE WASHINGTON DYER, born 11 Jan 1824 in Calais, son of JONES DYER, Jr. & LYDIA KNIGHT. He graduated from Bowdoin College in class of 1843, was a lawyer, member of State Legislature, moved to Washington, DC following the Civil War and died there 13 Apr 1889 (bowcat:82). Census: 1850 & 60 in Calais. He married 2nd KATE HUNTRESS ca 1868 daughter of Leonard Huntress & Lydia McKinnon.

iii. EMELINE DANFORD KELLY, born 24 Feb 1830 in Calais (VR). Census: 1850, 60, 70 & 80 in Calais. She married 27 Sep 1853 in Calais (VR:1:155) GEORGE GILMAN KING born ca 1830 in Upper Mills, NB. son of GILMAN D. KING (b. Chester, NH) & HANNAH W. HAYCOCK (b. Jonesport). He was a merchant, & grocer. Died: 17 Mar 1895 in Calais (MSA). Census: 1860, 70 (age 40), & 80 in Calais. He possibly had first marriage 1848 to Susan H. Stevens age 23 in 1850 census.

iv. BENJAMIN FRANKLIN KELLY, born 8 May 1831 in Calais (VR). He was a lumberman. Census: 1850, 60 & 70 in Calais. He married 19 May 1860 in St. Stephen, NB (union). MARY TOWNSEND COPELAND, born 11 Apr 1834 in Norridgewock, Me, daughter of THOMAS JEFFERSON COPELAND & JULIA ELVIRA TOWNSEND of Norridgewock (cope:500). Census: 1860 (with Henry C. & Julia E. Copeland) & 70 in Calais.

v. ANN MARIA JUDSON KELLY, born 15 Jan 1834 in Calais (VR). She was a teacher. Died 18 Jan 1894 in Calais (MSA). Buried in Calais Cemetery. Census: 1850, 60 & 70 in Calais. She married 13 Jun 1861 in Calais (VR, wads:219) LEWIS LUMBER WADSWORTH Jr., born ca 1832 in Plymouth, MA, son of LEWIS LUMBER WADSWORTH, SR. & MARIA HALL, moved to Maine when 10 years old (wads:219). He was a relative of the poet Longfellow (obit). He was a merchant and lumber manufacturer, a Maine State Senator 1864-65, president of Calais City Council 1867 (biosk:18). Resided in MA in 1874. Died: 29 Dec 1905 at The Revere House, Boston, MA (obit adv, g.s. has 15 Feb). Buried in Calais Cemetery. Census: 1850 in Pembroke,1870 in Calais.

vi. SUSAN ABBOTT KELLY, born 19 Mar 1836 in Calais (VR). Died 11 May 1858 in Calais (obit adv, g.s.). Buried: 13 May 1858 in Calais Cemetery. Census: 1850 in Calais.

vii. SAMUEL KELLY, Jr., born 27 May 1837 in Calais (VR, beg:125). He was a lumberman. Died 22 Mar 1883 age 45y 9m 21d in Calais (times, g.s.). He was shot by Herbert Eaton on 20 March and died of peritonitis two days later, Eaton was a rich man and was charged with murder but ended up with a fine of only $1000 (article in Calais Advertiser Mar 1 & 8, 2001). Census: 1850, 60 & 70 in Calais. He married 2 May 1865 in Calais (beg:128, east:213). HELEN MARIA WAITE, daughter of BENJAMIN FRANKLIN WAITE & HANNAH TOWNSLEY TODD (see WAITE).

viii. FREDERICK AUGUSTUS PIKE KELLY, born 14 Dec 1838 in Calais (VR, beg:125). Graduated Colby College in class of 1859 (colby). Died 15 Dec 1860 in Calais (g.s., east:180). Buried in Calais Cemetery.

Census: 1850 & 60 in Calais.

ix. EMMA/EMILY SOPHIA GREEN KELLY, born 11 Oct 1840 in Calais (VR, beg:125). Died 14 Oct 1921 age 81 in Calais (MSA, sfh:3:264). Census: 1850, 60 & 70 in Calais. She married 11 Dec 1890 (biorev:256, times, married at home of G. G. King) as his 2nd wife, in Calais JOHN PRESCOTT, born 23 Feb 1831 in Pennfield, NB, son of JESSE PRESCOTT & SARAH KNIGHT [d/o Joshua Knight of Philadelphia] (biorev:255). He died 2 May 1917 in Calais, moved to Calais from NB 41 years ago, he was a real estate agent (MSA, obit). Buried in Calais Cemetery with both wives. His 1st wife was SARAH G. DINSMORE (1835-1888 g.s.).

x. HANNAH DANFORD KELLY, born 31 Aug 1842 in Calais (VR, beg:125). Graduated from Calais Academy. Died 18 June 1873 age 30y 10m in Calais (union, g.s.). Buried in Calais Cemetery. Census: 1850, 60 & 70 in Calais.

Possible that Samuel married 2nd 2 Sept 1861 Mrs. ABIGAIL POTTER in Pittsfield NH (union). She died 16 Dec 1868 in Pittsfield, NH (union, wife of Deacon Samuel Kelley of Calais).

Samuel married 3rd 22 Nov 1871, at residence of D. Thompson, by Rev. J. E. Hopper (SCC) LYDIA R. (_____) THOMPSON, widow of Rev. A. D. Thompson, born circa 1810. Died 2 Aug 1889 at her residence on Germain St. in Calais age 81, her remains were taken to St. Andrews and buried with her first husband, Rev. Duncan Thompson (obit adv). Census: 1880 in Calais.

WILLIAM & CORDELIA KELLY, p. 222

WILLIAM KELLY, born Aug 1794 in Conway, NH (love:120). He was a farmer, surveyor & lumberman. He was in business with Sumner Waldron in 1837 when he was in court (SJC). Died 15 Mar 1874 age 80y 6m in Calais (love:120, g.s.). Buried in Calais Cemetery. Census: 1840 (5 males, 5 females), 50, 60 & 70 in Calais.

He married 5 May 1822 in St. Stephen, NB (CCMR, love:120) CORDELIA LOVEJOY, born 12 Sep 1801 in Wayne, ME (love:120, MSA), daughter of WILLIAM LOVEJOY AND ATTAI LOVEJOY. Died 30 May 1896 age 94y 8m 14d in Milltown ME (times, g.s., MSA). Buried in Calais Cemetery. Census: 1850 thru 1880 in Calais. Children:

i. AMANDA JANE KELLY, born 19 Dec 1822 in St. Stephen, NB (1850 census). Died 11 Feb 1886 age 63y in Calais (times, g.s.). Buried in Calais Cemetery. Census: 1850 thru 1880 in Calais.

ii. FRANCES MARIA KELLY, born 3 Aug 1824 in Calais (1850 census). Died 5 Apr 1889 in Calais age 64y 5m (obit adv). Census: 1850 & 60 (with her parents age 34) in Calais. She married 27 Oct 1846 in St. Stephen, NB (CCMR) JACOB B. HALL, born ca 1820. Probably died before 1860. Census: 1850 (age 30, living with her parents).

iii. WILLIAM LOVEJOY KELLY, born 13 Aug 1826 in Calais (VR). He was a surveyor of lumber. Died 26 May 1885 in Minneapolis, MN (times). Census: 1850 (living with John C. Dutch), 60 & 70 in Calais. He married 15 Jan 1850 in Calais (mrwc:53) MARIA HAYCOCK DUTCH, daughter of Capt. JOHN CALIFF DUTCH & MARGARET 'PEGGY' TODD (see DUTCH).

iv. CHARLES LORING KELLY, born 12 Mar 1828 in Calais (VR). He was a grocer. Died 6 Oct 1903 age 25y 7m in Calais (MSA, obit adv, g.s.). Buried in Calais Cemetery. Census: 1850 thru 1900 in Calais. He married 23 Nov 1862 in St. Stephen, NB (CCMR) VICTORIA A. FROST, born 23 Feb 1838 in St. Stephen, NB (MSA), daughter of OLIVER R. FROST & ELIZABETH HILL. She died 18 Dec 1900 in Calais (g.s.). Buried in Calais Cemetery. Census: 1870, 80 & 1900 in Calais.

v. ATTIA CORDELIA KELLY, born 19 Aug 1830 in Calais (VR). She died 21 Nov 1888 in Milltown ME age 58y (east:414, g.s., adv). Buried in Calais Cemetery. Census: 1850, 60 & 70 (A. C. Traynor age 30 & son, George W. age 9 with Wm. & Cordelia Kelly) in Calais. She married 24 Mar 1861 in Calais (union) [int. his name William Trainer 16 Mar 1861(VR:3:94)] WILLIAM W. TRYNOR, born ca 1840. He died 27 Jan 1862 (g.s.), buried in Calais Cemetery.

vi. STEPHEN A. KELLY, born, circa 1832 (love:120).

vii. HENRIETTA C. KELLY, born circa 1833 (love:120).

viii. STEPHEN BROWN KELLY, born 11 Jun 1835 in Calais (VR). He was a lumberman & clerk. Died 25 Sep 1918 age 83 in Calais (sfh:3:20, MSA has previous res. as Nova Scotia). Buried in Rural Cemetery in St. Stephen (1835-1813 rural:214). Census: 1850, 60 & 70 in Calais. He married 12 Jun 1861 in St. Stephen, NB (CCMR) [?? they were in Calais with 2 kids in 1860] LAVINIA HILL of St. Stephen, b. ca 1844.

Died: 21 Jan 1906 age 68, buried Rural Cemetery St. Stephen in same lot with Stephen & Elizabeth Hill (rural:214). Census: 1860 & 70 in Calais. [possibly she is the Lavinia age 13, daughter of Stephen & Elizabeth Hill in 1851 census of St. Stephen, NB].

ix. ANN ELIZABETH KELLY, born 9 Sep 1837 in Calais (VR). Died Mar 1926 age 88 (obit adv of 14 Mar 1926, g.s.). Buried Rural Cemetery, St. Stephen (rural:197). Census: 1850 & 60 in Calais. She married 14 Sept 1865 (union) WILLIAM TODD, Jr. of St. Stephen, NB, born ca 1836, died 1918 (g.s.), buried Rural Cemetery, St. Stephen (rural:197).

x. MARY PLUMMER KELLY, born 19 Aug 1839 in Calais (VR). Died 29 July 1901 in St. Stephen, NB (adv). Census: 1850 & 60 in Calais, 1871 in St Stephen, NB.. She married 31 Oct 1861 in St. Stephen, NB (CCMR) LUCIUS STILLMAN SPRING, born 10 Sept 1836, son of EPHRAIM & HANNAH SPRING (see SPRING).

xi. LUCY CAROLINE KELLY, born 22 Jun 1842 in Calais (VR). Died after 1889 (mentioned in sister, Frances' probate, unmarried). Census: 1850, 60 & 70 in Calais.

xii. MARTHA EMELINE KELLY, born 22 Jun 1842 in Calais (VR). Died after 1926 (sister, Ann's obit, unmarried). Census: 1850, 60 & 70 in Calais.

ISAAC & CAROLINE A. KELSEY, p. 182

ELIAS KELSEY & EMELINE M. CRAFTS, were in Calais by 1830 with 7 males and 4 females, in 1840 there were no female over age 20, his wife died 1 Sept 1831 (g.s. in Calais Cemetery). From the VR the following marriages were probably his children: Harriet E. Kelsey who married George B. Preble in 1852; Lysander W. Kelsey who married Elizabeth A. Osborn in 1856; Mary Kelsey who married James Pine in 1855; and Samuel Kelsey who married Mrs. Eleanor Turner in 1842; and Isaac who married Caroline Bugbee in 1844 (see BELOW). Elias born ca 1800 in NH, died 10 Dec 1866 in Milltown (union). Census: 1830 thru 1860 in Calais.

ISAAC STEARNS KELSEY, born 17 Sep 1821 in Portland ME (VR). Died - Isaac S. Kelsey age 30 at the mines on Stanislaus River, CA [Me Farmer of 1 Aug 1850]. Census: 1850 (with Elias Kelsey age 60 b. NH) in Calais. He must have left Calais shortly after the census was taken.

He married 15 Aug 1844 in St. Stephen, NB (gaz, CCMR:B:104), CAROLINE A. BUGBEE born circa 1824 in St. Stephen, NB. She married 2nd 3 Aug 1871 by Rev. E.W. Murray in Calais (adv) Hon. CHARLES PERLEY of Woodstock, NB (SCC). Died after 1871. Census: 1850 in Calais. Children:

i. EMELINE MOWBRY KELSEY, born 25 May 1845 in Calais, died 28 Feb 1847 in Calais (VR). Buried: 2 Mar 1847 in Calais Cemetery.

ii. ANNA CAROLINE KELSEY, born 2 Dec 1846 in Calais (VR). Died after 1871. Census: 1850, 1860 (with Elias Kelsey) in Calais. She married 6 May 1867 in Calais by Rev. H.A. Philbrook (VSNB:25:1606) WILLIAM AUGUSTUS GRANGER, born 10 Oct 1839 in Calais (LDS), son of JOSEPH & HARRIET (GRANGER) GRANGER. He died 6 May 1871 (prbt). Census: 1850 & 60 (with parents), in Calais.

iii. SARAH CAROLINE KELSEY, born circa 1849 in St. Stephen, N B (1850 census). Census: 1850, 1860 (with Elias Kelsey), & 70 in Calais. She married 20 Feb 1865 in Calais (VR). CHARLES T. ESTABROOK Census: 1870 in Calais. [possible - death in Edmunds, ME 4 Dec 1879, Rev. Charles T. Estabrook age 34, pastor of M.E Church in Edmunds & S. Pembroke (east:330)]

CALVIN & MARY KIDDER, p. 186.

CALVIN^5 KIDDER born 22 Aug 1765 in New Ipswich, NH son of JOSEPH^4 KIDDER and REBECCA WILDER, (THOMAS^3, JOHN^2, JAMES^1). Died by drowning in St. Andrews Bay, NB about 1799. He married, probably in New Brunswick. Name of wife unknown (kidd:79). [possible marriage found in records of All Saints Anglican Church, St. Andrews, NB of Calvin Kidder to Mrs. Mary Greenlaw 1 July 179?]. Their only child was Joseph Calvin.

JOSEPH CALVIN^6 KIDDER Sr. He was born circa 1799 in St. Stephen, NB (kidd:160, 1850 census = St. Andrews). He was a hardy lumber man and river man, a man of marked industry and integrity. During a great fire which devastated wide stretches of territory in New Brunswick, he was in the deep woods at Miramichi, where he narrowly escaped death from the flames, and later from starvation, owing to the loss of all nearby settlements with their stores of provisions (kidd:160). In 1829 he was of Baileyville when he appeared in court (SJC:3:323). Died 19 May 1891 in Princeton Me age 92y 3m 21d (adv, kidd:160). Census: 1850 in Calais 1860, 70 & 80 in Princeton.

He married 12 Oct 1834 by Rev. Abel Alton (mrwc:14), MARY WILKINS born circa 1813 in Amity, ME (kidd:160). Died circa 1880 in Princeton Me (kidd:160). Census: 1850 in Calais, 1860 & 70 in Princeton

Me. {1880 Mortality schedule has a Mary J. Kidder age 65 in Princeton died Jan 1880}. Children:

i. JONATHAN 'John' KIDDER, born 18 Jul 1835 in Amity, ME (Calais VR). Died circa 1887 (kidd:313, called John, drowned at sea). Census: 1850 & 60 in Calais, 1870 in Princeton Me. He married, 1st 19 May 1860 by Rev. S.H. Keeler in Calais (adv, union) HELEN M. HUNTLEY, daughter of GIDEON G. HUNTLEY & ALMIRA LANE Census: 1870 in Princeton (see HUNTLEY). He married, 2nd JANE CALLAHAN KILLMAN, a widow of Frederiction, NB, after 1873 (kidd:313).

ii. CHARLES KIDDER, born 4 Apr 1837 in Amity, ME (Calais VR). He died 22 Dec 1860 age 22 in Princeton (union). Died unmarried, aged 24 years, circa 1860 (kidd:160). Census: 1850 in Calais [the Machias union has a marriage in Calais 2 April 1860 of Charles Kidder of Princeton and Amanda Bradford of Calais.]

iii. JOSEPH KIDDER, born 4 Jul 1839 in Amity, ME (Calais VR, death rec., 1850 census = Orient). Served in Civil War, a private in Co. A 9th Me Vol. Inf. For nearly four years. He was badly wounded at St. Mary's, LA in 1862 (kidd:314). He was a millman 5'5" with blue eyes and light hair (cwcard). He was a seaman & farmer. Died at age 76 on 21 May 1915 in Princeton Me (VR, MSA has both parents born in Nova Scotia). Census: 1850 in Calais, 1860, 70 & 80 in Princeton. He married (int.) 7 Dec 1869 in Princeton (VR) CLARISSA 'Clara' WILKINS (name also from son's death rec.) (kidd:314 has her name Clara Wilson of Canterbury, NB), born ca 1850. Died 7 Feb 1885, buried in Princeton Cemetery (g.s.). Census: 1870 (age 20) in Princeton.

iv. JOSEPH CALVIN KIDDER, Jr., born 16 Feb 1842 in Amity, ME (Calais VR, MSA has 10 Aug 1842, Calais). He was a lumberman & mill worker. Died 26 Oct 1915 age 73y 8m 26d in Waite, ME (MSA has father born in Scotland mother in Amity, Me, prinvr:30,31). Resided in Princeton Me. Census: 1850 in Calais, 1860 & 70, in Princeton, 1900 in Indian Township. He married (int.) 21 Aug 1866 to Mira M. McLauflin in Princeton (VR), MARINDA 'Mira' MCLAUGHLIN (kidd:314), born 18 Feb 1846 (1900 census, MSA = 1844, Tower Hill, NB) in Oak Bay, NB, daughter of J. McLAUGHLIN (b. Boston) & MILDRED SCRIPPS (b. Bath, ME) died 30 Dec 1924 age 80y 10m 12d in Baileyville, ME (MSA, sfh:4:280). [In 1851 census of St. David, NB there is a Melranda age 8, daughter of LAUGHLIN McLAUGHLIN & AMELIA WALKER (her father was 64 when she was born the 19th child)]. Census: 1870 in Princeton, 1900 in Indian Township (Princeton).

v. MARY ANN KIDDER, born 20 Jul 1844 in Amity, ME (Calais VR, 1850 census = Orient). Died 8 June 1861 age 17 in Princeton (union), died ca 1860 in Princeton, aged 16 years (kidd:160). Census: 1850 in Calais 1860 in Princeton.

vi. JAMES THOMPSON KIDDER, born 21 Mar 1847 in Calais (VR) [perhaps he died young, not mentioned in kidd].

vii. MERCY E. KIDDER born Jan 1850 in Calais. Census: 1850 in Calais 1860 & 80 in Princeton, 1900 in Waite, ME. She married (int.) 15 Mar 1870 Princeton (VR) HIRAM T. DAVIS (kidd:160) born Aug 1849 in MA. Census: 1880 in Princeton, 1900 in Waite.

JAMES G. & EMILINE G. KIMBILL, p. 221

JAMES KIMBALL, born 9 Aug 1770, in Ipswich, MA, son of NATHANIEL KIMBALL AND ELIZABETH LOW, grandson of John[4], Caleb[3-2], Richard[1], married MARY ESTABROOK, born 19 Sept 1778 in Lunenburg, MA, died 30 April 1851, in Augusta, ME. They resided in Ispwich, until 1801, Newburyport, MA until 1821, then in Eastport, ME where he died 16 April 1828 (VR). Their oldest child, James Gorham Kimball, settled in Calais (kimb:363)

JAMES GORHAM KIMBALL, born 4 Sep 1800 in Ipswich, MA (VR). He was a merchant. He was a partner in firm of Kelley & Kimball in 1829 (SJC:3:474). Died 6 Jan 1870 age 69 in Calais (g.s., congo, prbt, east:241 = 8th). Buried in Calais Cemetery. Census: 1840 (2 males, 3 females), 50 & 60 in Calais (kimb:663).

He married 19 Sep 1830 in Calais (kimb:663), EMELINE G. GATES, born (1) 4 Aug 1804, in Hubbardston, MA (VR), born (2): 4 Sep 1804 daughter of SALMON GATES AND LUCY CHURCH, (kimb:663). Died 26 Aug 1892 age 88 in Calais (MSA, SCC, g.s.). Buried in Calais Cemetery. Census: 1850, 60 & 70, 1880 (living with Charles King) in Calais (see GATES). Children:

i. LUCY CAROLINE KIMBALL, born Apr 1831 in Robbinston ME (Calais VR), born (2): 29 Jan 1832 in Robbinston (kimb:663). Died 8 Feb 1835 age 3y 10m in Calais (VR:1:239, g.s.). Buried in Calais Cemetery.

ii. JAMES SALMON KIMBALL, born 18 Apr 1833 in Calais (VR). Died 26 Sep 1833 in Calais (VR:1:239, g.s.), died (2): 27 Oct 1833 (kimb:663). Buried in Calais Cemetery.

iii. HARRIET EMELINE KIMBALL, born 18 Jan 1836 in Calais (VR). She was a teacher. Census: 1850 thru 1880 in Calais. She married 20 Jan 1862 by Rev. McColly in Calais (VR, kimb:951) CHARLES WILLARD KING born 7 May 1839 in St. Stephen (kimb:951), son of HEZEKIAH KING & JERUSHA COLE (both born in NB), he died 13 July 1911 age 71 in Princeton (MSA). Census: 1870 (with parents), 80 in Calais.

iv. GORHAM GATES KIMBALL, born 5 Apr 1838 in Calais (VR). He went to California in 1857, landed in San Francisco in October 1857, his first work was piling lumber for Zimri Heyward, formerly of Calais, an old friend of his father. He became a wealthy man (kimb:951-954). The Kimball Genealogy gives 24 Jan 1877 as a marriage date but does not give name of his wife. Died in Calif. Census: 1850 & 60 in Calais.

v. JAMES READ/Reed KIMBALL, born (1) 26 Dec 1841 in Calais (VR), born (2): 26 Dec 1842 (kimb:663). He was a hotel prop. He bought the Barker House in 1878 from H.H. King with the help of his brother, Gorham, who sent a gift of $600 (adv). Died 28 Jul 1896 age 55y 7m in Calais (VR, MSA, adv). Buried in Calais Cemetery. Census: 1850 thru 1880 in Calais. He married 24 Oct 1866 (kimb:663), AUGUSTA L. SWETT, born ca 1845 in St. Stephen, NB. Died 14 May 1930 in St. Petersburg, FL at age 86 at home of her daughter (obit adv). Census: 1870 & 80 in Calais.

LUTHER B. & SARAH A. KNIGHT, p. 210

LUTHER B. KNIGHT son of WESTBROOK KNIGHT & MARY ATKINS of Calais. Bapt. 26 Apr 1840 in Milltown, ME (lord:12). [adv of 19 Dec 1871 Rev. Luther Knight, one of our Calais boys, was in town last week after an absence of 15-16 years. Came to attend funeral of his sister, widow Herald, but arrived too late].

He married 13 Sep 1843 by Rev. Artemus N. Whittier in Cornville, ME (VR, gaz) SARAH A. WHITTIER born 6 Dec 1820 in Cornville, the daughter of ARTEMUS WHITTIER, (b. 4 Jun 1795) and ALICE CASS (b. 4 Jan 1796) in Cornville, ME (VR, whit:134). Children:

i. UNNAMED CHILD KNIGHT, stillborn 2 Aug 1844 (sext). Buried in Calais Cemetery.
ii. ARTIMUS WESTBROOK KNIGHT, born Jun 1845, died 23 Jan 1847 in Calais (FJ). Buried: 25 Jan 1847 in Calais Cemetery.
iii. ALICE WHITTIER KNIGHT, born 10 Aug 1847 in Calais (VR).
iv. UNNAMED CHILD KNIGHT. Died circa 1847 (sext). Buried: 1 Jul 1847 in Calais Cemetery.

NATHANIEL & ELMIRA LAMB, p. 215

NATHANIEL LAMB, born 11 Jul 1803 in Cornish/Waterboro, ME (Alexander VR, 1850 census = Hollis, howell = Waterboro) son of JAMES & BETSEY (?DUNN?) LAMB (howell, sister in law's 2nd marriage rec.) [He lived with them in Calais in 1850 age 76, died 4 Mar 1853 age 78, buried in same lot in Calais Cemetery]. He was in Calais by 1826 when he incurred debts and was in court in Aug 1839 (SJC). He was in partnership with William L. McAllister in 1837 in Calais (SJC). He was a lumberman and farmer. Died 4 Jun 1880 age 78 in Waite, Me (VR, adv, g.s.). Buried in Calais Cemetery. Census: 1840 (3 males & 2 females) in Alexander, 1850, 60 & 70 in Calais.

He married 13 Jul 1830 (Alexander VR), ELMIRA/ALMIRA CARLE, born 16 Nov 1812 in Waterboro Me (VR), daughter of PETER CARLE AND ABIGAIL HAMILTON. Died 10 Dec 1887 age 75y 25d in Milltown, NB (SSC, times, g.s.). Buried in Calais Cemetery. Census: 1850, 60 & 70 in Calais. Children:

i. SETH TURNER LAMB, born 26 Apr 1831 in Calais (VR, Alexander VR:97). He was a farmer. Died 12 Nov 1912 age 81y 7m in Robbinston Me (MSA). Buried in Brewer Cemetery in Robbinston. Census: 1850 in Calais, 60 in Alexander, 70, 80 & 1900 in Robbinston. He married 16 Nov 1853 by Rev. Mr. Sewell at Robbinston (MSA, g.s.). HARRIET BRACKETT born {1} 9 Oct 1833 in Robbinston (Alexander VR), born {2} 9 Oct 1832 (death record), daughter of JOHN BRACKETT AND NANCY JOHNSON (see BRACKETT). She died 25 Mar 1921 age 85 in Robbinston (MSA).
ii. ALBERT LAMB, born 25 Jan 1835 in Calais (VR). He was a lumberman. He died 30 Dec 1864 age 30 in Calais (g.s.). Buried: 1 Jan 1865 in Calais Cemetery. Census: 1850 & 60 in Calais. He married 11 Oct 1854 in Calais (VR:1: 157) SARAH ANN WALDRON, daughter of SUMNER T. WALDRON AND CATHARINE HAMILTON (see WALDRON).
iii. BETSEY LAMB, born 14 Nov 1836 in Calais. Probably died young not in 1850 census.
iv. PETER CARLE LAMB, born 20 Jul 1840 in Alexander ME (VR). Enlisted in Civil War 1862 a Sargent in Co F 22nd Me Inf., a sawyer 5'10" with blue eyes and light hair (cwcard). He was a surveyor of lumber and farmer. Died 7 Nov 1892 age 52y 3m 1d in Indian Township (prinvr:2,3), in Baileyville ME (times,

g.s.). Buried in Calais Cemetery. Census: 1850, 60 & 70 in Calais. He married 21 May 1873 by Rev. A. S. Townsend in Milltown ME (adv) SARAH GRIGGS MANSON, daughter of ROBERT MANSON & HANNAH BARCLAY (see MANSON).

v. JAMES LAMB, born 21 May 1843 in Calais (VR). He was a farmer and grocer. Died circa 1934 in Calais (g.s.). Buried in Calais Cemetery. Census: 1850, 60 & 70 in Calais, 1880 & 1900 in Robbinston Me. He married 7 Jan 1870 in Calais (VR: 3) NANCY C. MITCHELL born ca Oct 1844, died 1933 (g.s.). Buried in Calais Cemetery. Census: 1870 in Calais, 1880 & 1900 in Robbinston.

vi. ANNA C. LAMB, born circa 1849 in Calais. She was a music teacher. Census: 1850, 60 & 70 in Calais.

ROBERT J. & LYDIA W. LAMB, p. 203

ROBERT JAMES LAMB, born circa 1817 in Calais (1850 census), son of JAMES & BETSEY (?DUNN?) LAMB and brother of Nathaniel Lamb & Eleanor (Lamb) Harmon. Bapt. 26 Apr 1840 in Milltown ME (lord:13). He was a teamster. Died 2 Mar 1889 in Milltown, Me (adv). Will dated 29 Jan 1889, probated 28 May 1889, left a trust for son, Oramendal and grandchildren (prbt). Buried: 4 Mar 1889 in Calais. Census: 1850 thru 1880 in Calais.

He married 4 May 1842 by Phenneas Higgins in Calais (mrwc:36) LYDIA W. PICKENS, born circa 1822 in Wilton, ME (1850 census), daughter of LEONARD PICKENS AND VASHTI RANDALL (see PICKENS) Baptism: 26 Apr 1840 in Milltown ME (lord:15). Died circa 1878. Buried: 1 Mar 1878 in Calais Cemetery. Census: 1850, 60 & 70 in Calais. Children:

i. ORAMENDAL D. LAMB, born 19 Jan 1844 in Calais (VR). He was a lumber surveyor. Died May 1921 age 80 in Calais (MSA) Buried: 26 May 1921 in Calais Cemetery. Census: 1871 in St. Stephen, NB. Census: 1850, 60, 80, 1900 & 1910 in Calais, 1871 in St. Stephen, NB. He married 1st 20 Oct 1867 in Calais (VR:3) EMMA L. STROUT of Alexander. She died 25 Jan 1890 in Calais (MSA), buried in Calais Cemetery. Census: 1871 in St. Stephen, 1880 in Calais. He married 2nd 26 Nov 1891 in Calais (VR:3:125, times) Mrs. ADDIE M. (WHITNEY) HINDS born 10 Jan 1845 in Westbrook, ME, daughter of JAMES B. WHITNEY & JULIA A. DOOR (MSA, wtny:364 has Martha Whitney b. 10 June 1848). She died 21 Oct 1915 in Calais (MSA). Census 1900 & 1910 in Calais.

ii. LEONARD PICKENS LAMB, born 5 Mar 1845 in Calais, died 26 Mar 1846 in Calais (VR:1:236).

iii. MARY ARABELLA LAMB, born circa 1851. Graduated from Calais Academy. Died circa 1887. Buried: 4 Aug 1887 in Calais Cemetery. Census: 1860, 70 & 80 in Calais.

ISAAC & ORELIA LANE, p. 178

ISAAC LANE, born ca 1790. In 1823 he was one of 14 who petitioned to establish a Lodge in Calais. He was an officer in Lodge No. 46 in 1826 and again in 1844 (lodge:15,18). Died after 1844 before 1875. Buried in Calais Cemetery - (no dates). Census: 1830 (6 males, 4 females), 40 (3 males, 4 females) in Calais.

He married ORELIA (_____), born between 1801-10. Buried in Calais Cemetery (no dates on stone). Children:

i. ISAAC EATON LANE, born 4 May 1824 in Calais (VR).
ii. ANN TRUMAN LANE, born 30 Dec 1827 in Calais (VR).
iii. MARY HELEN LANE, born 28 Oct 1829 in Calais, died 30 Jul 1840 in Calais (VR:1:227). Buried 1 Aug 1840 in Calais Cemetery (sext).
iv. EUNICE MARIA LANE, born 8 Feb 1833 in Calais (VR).

- Note: none of this family appears in the 1850 census.

PATRICK & MARY ANN LAVY, p. 203
(various spellings)

PATRICK LEVI /LAVY/LEVY, born circa 1818 in Ireland. He was a lumberman and worked in a mill. He is listed in 1901 directory as Patrick Lavey. Died after 1901. Census: 1850 thru 1880 & 1900 in Calais.

He married MARY ANN FERGERSON, born circa 1827 in Machias Me (1850 census). Died after

1880, before 1900. Census: 1850 thru 1880 in Calais. Children:

i. MARGARET ANN LEVI, born 17 Sep 1847 in Calais (VR, sfh & MSA =27 Sept 1848). She was a seamstress. Died 1 Mar 1929 in Milltown ME (sfh:7:167, MSA). Buried in Calais Cemetery. Census: 1850, 60, 70 & 1900 (with father) in Calais. She married (int.) 6 Jun 1867 in Calais (VR) DAVID McCARTY. He died before his wife.

ii. MARY ANN LEVI, born circa 1850 in Calais. Died 3 Oct 1865 age 15 in Calais (VR:3:312). Census: 1850 in Calais.

iii. ELIZABETH LEVI, born circa 1851 in Calais. Census: 1860 in Calais.

iv. JOHN LEVI, born circa 1854 in Calais. He was a millman. Census: 1860 & 70 in Calais.

v. HUGH LEVI, born 8 Jul 1856 in Calais (MSA). He was a teamster, who drove a six horse team from Milltown to the wharf in Calais (as:18). Died 12 Oct 1929 in Calais (MSA, sfh:7:221, name LAVY). Census: 1860, 70, 80 & 1900 in Calais. He married 18 Dec 1883 in Calais (VR:2:35) Mrs. ESTHER S. SCOTT, born ca Apr 1845 (1900 census). She died before her husband, both are listed in the 1901 Directory. Census: 1900 in Calais.

vi. ELLEN 'Sis' LEVI, born circa June 1859 in Calais. She was a dressmaker. Died 3 May 1893 age 33y 11m in Calais (MSA). Buried in Calais Cemetery. Census: 1860 in Calais, (name male Allen 1860- Ellen 1870, Mary E.1880). She married (int) 20 Sept 1882 in Calais (VR:2:18) THOMAS J. O'HARA, born 10 Feb 1858 in Calais (VR:3:257), son of JOHN O"HARA (b. ca 1820) & MARY McLAUGHLIN (both born in Ireland). He sang bass in a male quartette (as:18). Died 27 May 1920 age 64y 3m 17d in Calais (MSA, sfh:3:151). Census: 1900 (age 42 in Calais with father, John & son, John), 1920 (with Agnes Lavy) in Calais.

vii. WILLIAM J. LEVI, born circa 1861 in Calais. Census: 1870 in Calais.

viii. AGNES LEVI, born circa May 1864 (1900 census) in Calais. Died after 1929 when she was informant of Margaret's death. Buried in Calais Cemetery. Census: 1870 (age 7), 80, 1900 & 1920 (with brother in law) in Calais. In 1901 Calais Directory Miss Agnes Lavey was housekeeper for Thomas O'Hara.

ix. JAMES LEVI, born circa 1863 in Calais. Died 21 Feb 1879 age 16 in Milltown, ME (times). Census: 1870 (age 7) in Calais.

WILLIAM & LYDIA LAWRENCE, p. 188

WILLIAM LAWRENCE, born 8 Apr 1782 (brack:319), [in 1900 census, daughter, Lucinda's father born Mass]. Died 7 Feb 1848 age 65y 10m in Calais (VR:3:328, adv). Buried: 9 Feb 1848 in Calais Cemetery.

He married 2 Feb 1823 in Vassalboro, ME (VR, brack:319) LYDIA BRACKETT, born 24 Jan 1796 in Vassalboro, ME (VR), daughter of JAMES BRACKETT, JR. AND BATHULA BEAL. Died 13 Sep 1867 (VR). Census: 1850 in Calais (see BRACKETT). Children:

i. SAMUEL BRACKETT LAWRENCE, born 31 Jan 1824 in Vassalboro, ME (brack:319, wissnh:1153). He was a lumberman and logger. Left Calais shortly after 1854 when he appeared in Court (SJC) and became a pioneer of Oshkosh, WI and began lumbering in winter of 1855-56 and retired about 1888 (north:1153). Died 26 Jan 1897 age 74 in Oshkosh, WI (obit north, wdr). Census: 1850 in Calais, 1860 & 70 in Oshkosh. He married 15 Nov 1843 in Springfield, ME (his obit has 16 Nov - north, wiscnh:1153) NANCY A. CRAIG, born 12 Sept 1825 in St. Stephen, NB. She died 11 Jan 1901age 75 in Oshkosh (obit north). Census: 1860 & 70 & 1900 in Oshkosh.

ii. BETSEY 'Bessie' MARIA LAWRENCE, born 27 Jun 1826 in Calais (brack:319). Died 20 Oct 1903 (brack:319). Census: 1850 (age 24) in Calais. She married 26 Dec 1852 in Calais by Rev. H.V. Dexter (VR:3:155, east:124) CONRAD CLINCH. Resided in Sacramento, CA in 1897 (Samuel B.'s obit).

iii. GEORGE WASHINGTON LAWRENCE, born 4 Sep 1828 in Calais (VR, brack:319). Died 28 Sep 1828 in Calais (VR:1:232, brack:319).

iv. JOSEPHINE LAWRENCE, born 12 Feb 1830 in Calais (VR, brack:319). Died 16 Apr 1851 in Calais (times). Buried: 19 Apr 1851 in Calais Cemetery. Census: 1850 in Calais.

v. ANGELINE LAWRENCE, born 12 Feb 1830 in Calais (VR, brack:319). Died 3 Mar 1840 in Calais (VR:1:232). Buried: 5 Mar 1840 in Calais Cemetery.

vi. GUSTAVUS A. LAWRENCE, born 12 Apr 1832 in Calais (VR, brack:319). He was a lumberman. He resided in Watertown, ND (brack:319) and was in Troy, SD in 1897 (Samuel's obit). Died 26 Feb 1899 in

Wisconsin (wdr). Census: 1850 in Calais, 1870 in Oshkosh. He married 2 Sep 1858 in Calais (VR:3:171, adv) SARAH JANE COY, daughter of SOLOMON COY AND JANE MORRISON (see COY).

vii. THADDEUS BRACKET LAWRENCE, born 7 Mar 1835 in Princeton Me (Calais VR, brack:319). Census: 1850 in Calais, 1870 in Oshkosh, WI. Resided in Iron Mountain, MI in 1897 (Samuel's obit). He married 31 Oct 1864 in Oshkosh (winn:1:262, brack:319) SOPHIA F. LULL, born ca 1834 in VT. Census 1870 in Oshkosh. Both resided in Troy, Mont. in 1907(brack:319).

viii. LUCINDA BRACKETT LAWRENCE, born 27 Jun 1838 in Princeton Me (Calais VR, brack:319). Resided in Neenah in 1897 (Samuel's obit) and resided 1907 in Oshkosh, WI (brack). Died after 1907. Census: 1850 in Calais, 1870, 1900 & 1905 in Neenah, WI. She married 24 Jan 1861 in Oshkosh, WI (brack:319, winn) DANIEL WEBSTER BARNES, born 13 Jul 1836 in Steuben, NY, son of ETHELBERT BARNES & ZILPHIA TRIPP (brack:319). He was a contractor and builder and resided in Neenah, WI (brack:319). Died after 1905. Census: 1870, 1900 & 1905 in Neenah.

WILLIAM D. & NANCY A. B. LAWRENCE, p. 197

Capt. WILLIAM DWIGHT LAWRENCE, Sr., born 28 May 1811 (cwWI:437), son of WILLIAM LAWRENCE (son, Frank's obit). Bapt. 3 May 1840 in Calais (congo). He was a clerk when he appeared in court Mar 1831(SJC). In Oct 1856 he was a lumberman in the firm of W. D. Lawrence & Co. his partner was Samuel Lawrence. From 1855 to 1858 he was Mayor of Calais and also a blacksmith. He was a member of the Calais Band, played the trombone. His family left Calais on 17 June 1872 aboard steamer *Belle Browne* in route to their new home in Oshkosh (adv). Died 31 Jan 1897 age 87 in Oshkosh (otime obit) [adv of 11 July 1888, they celebrated their 50th wedding anniversary in Oshkosh]. Census: 1840 (2 males, 2 females), 50, 60 in Calais & 70 in Oshkosh, WI.

He married 27 May 1838 by J.P.Vance, Esq. in Calais (cal2:50, gaz) NANCY ANN B. POOL, born 22 May 1817 in Edgecomb, ME (cwWI:437), daughter of WILLIAM POOL AND LYDIA BURNHAM and sister of Solomon Pool (see POOL). Bapt. 3 May 1840 in Calais (congo). Died 31 Jan 1905 age 87 in Oshkosh at home of her daughter, Maggie (otime obit). Buried at Ellenwood Cemetery in Oshkosh. Census: 1850, 60 & 70 in Calais, 1900 in Oshkosh. Children:

i. LYDIA ANNA 'Annie L.' LAWRENCE, born 24 Apr 1839 in Calais (VR). They celebrated their 20th wedding anniversary in Oshkosh 22 Mar 1888 (adv). Died 1 Oct 1924 at the Wisconsin Masonic home at Dousman, WI (obit north). Buried in Riverside Cemetery in Oshkosh. Census: 1850 & 60 in Calais, 1900 in Oshkosh. She married 22 Mar 1868 at home of bride's mother by Rev. Joseph Beal in Calais (VR:3:226, VSNB:27:238) SOLON PARKER FARNSWORTH, born 24 Mar 1843 in Pembroke, son of JONAS FARNSWORTH & ABI GARDNER (farn:271), of Pembroke, ME. They moved to Oshkosh in 1868. He died 25 Aug 1926 age 84 at the Wisconsin Masonic home at Dousman, WI. (wldr, obit north). He is a brother of Abi & Mary Farnsworth who married Morey brothers (see MOREY). Buried in Oshkosh. Census: 1900 in Oshkosh.

ii. WILLIAM DWIGHT LAWRENCE, Jr., born 4 Jan 1842 in Calais (VR). He was a lumberman. Died after 1892 (when he was mentioned in his bro. Frank's obit as living in Dakota). Census: 1850 in Calais, 60 & 70 in Oshkosh, WI.

iii. ELIZABETH 'LIZZIE' POOL LAWRENCE, born 1 Sep 1845 in Calais (VR). Died before 1892 (Frank's obit). Census: 1850, 60 & 70 in Calais.

iv. FRANK H. LAWRENCE, born 16 Dec 1847 in Calais (VR, cwWI:437). He served in Civil War as a Pvt. in Co. G, 5th Regt of the Maine Vol. Inf., after his discharge at age 19 he moved to Oshkosh with his father and brother (cwWI: 437). He was 5'7" with black eyes and dark hair (cwcard, obit). He was a lumberman and grocer. Died 18 Jan 1892 age 44 in Algoma, WI. Census: 1850 & 60 in Calais, 1870 in Oshkosh, WI. In 1885 in Wis. state census. He married 22 Oct 1879 in Wisconsin CORNELIA S. BRADLEY, born 8 May 1856 in Connetville, PA, daughter of CHRISTOPHER C. BRADLEY & MARGARET MAYHER (obit, cwWI:437).

v. HARRIET E. LAWRENCE, born circa 1854 in Calais. Her name Mrs. WILLIAM A. FREEBORN living in Cecil, WI in 1931 (sister's obit). Died after 1931. Census: 1860 in Calais.

vi. MARTHA 'MATTIE' L. LAWRENCE, born 10 Feb 1856 in Calais (obit). Went to Oshkosh at age 15 (obit). Died 1 June 1931 age 75 in Oshkosh, WI (obit, north). Census: 1860 & 70 in Calais, 1900 in

Oshkosh. She married 25 Dec 1874 in Oshkosh, WI (winn). HARVEY C. SAWTELL, born 8 Apr 1848 in Annsville, NY, went to Oshkosh with his parents in 1853, died 8 June 1930 in Oshkosh (obit, north). Census: 1900 in Oshkosh.

vii. MARGARET 'MAGGIE' P. LAWRENCE, born circa 1858 in Calais. Census: 1860 & 70 in Calais, 1900 in Oshkosh. Resided in Madison, MN in 1892 (Frank's obit), and in Portland OR in 1924 (Lydia's obit). She married 28 May 1880 (copy of marriage certif.) in Algoma, WI. WILLIAM C. LAWRENCE, born in Oshkosh, son of GUSTAVUS A. & SARAH J. LAWRENCE (see previous family above). They lived in Dakota in 1882 when their first child was born. Census: 1870 & 1900 in Oshkosh.

viii. FRED LAWRENCE, born circa 1870 in Calais. Census: 1870 (age 2/12) in Calais.

JOHN & HANNAH LEDDY, p. 201

JOHN LEDDY born about 1812 in the Parish of Killmore, County of Cavan, Ireland. He left Ireland 15 July 1832, arrived in Calais 20 Oct 1832. Lived between Calais and St. Stephen, NB until 25 Oct 1836 when he fixed his residence at Calais. Witnesses to knowledge of John Leddy's residence in Calais were: Thomas J. D. Fuller and Bion Bradbury both of Calais. John signed with an 'X'. He was naturalized 17 Sept 1840. [From Naturalization Papers in the Sept. 1840 term of the Washington County court records at MSA]. Died 14 July 1863 age 54 in Calais (VR:3:304). Census: 1850, & 60 (living with Thomas Royal family) in Calais.

He married before 1838 HANNAH (SULLIVAN?) BURK (on dau. Hannah's death cert.) born circa 1822, in Ireland (rilla). Died 26 July 1854 at age 32 (rilla). Census: 1850 in Calais. Children:

i. JOHN LEDDY, Jr., born 17 Oct 1838 in Calais (VR). Enlisted 4 Aug 1862 in Civil War in Co. I in 6th Maine (NRMS:264, cwcard, enlist). He was 5'8 ½" with gray eyes and brown hair (cwcard). Died: 17 May 1864 of wounds (NRMS:264, cwcard), at Harwood Hospital, Fredericksburg, VA (milnat). Buried: Arlington National Cemetery, Washington, DC. Census: 1850 & 60 in Calais. He married before 1860 PHEBE ANN KERR (rilla), born ca 1838. [possible daughter of John & Sarah Kerr] Census: 1860 in Calais.

ii. MARY E. LEDDY, born 20 Nov 1840 in Calais (VR). She was a teacher (rilla). Census: 1850 & 60 (with bro. John Jr.) in Calais.

iii. EUGENE LEDDY, born 19 Oct 1842 in Calais (VR). Served in Civil War in Co D 51st Mass. Inf. Enlisted at Worcester, 28 Aug 1862, he came to the home at Togus from Philadelphia 21 Aug 1901 (death notice ppress, rilla). He was a stock broker (rilla). Died 26 May 1925 age 80y 5m 2d at Togus, ME (obit KJ). Buried in cemetery at Togus (rilla, MSA has him listed as a widower). Census: 1850 & 60 (with bro. John Jr.) in Calais.

iv. ANN JANE LEDDY, born 20 Dec 1844 in Calais (VR). Died 20 Jan 1847 in Calais (VR:1:236). Buried: 1 Feb 1847 in Calais Cemetery (sext).

v. MARGARET JANE LEDDY, born 12 Mar 1847 in Calais (VR). She died 28 Feb 1937 age 90y 11m 16d in Brockton, MA (from death cert. rilla). Census: 1850, 60 (with John Murray family) & 1870 in Calais. She married 26 June 1864, by Rev. D. F. Smith in Calais (VR) ROBERT DOHERTY, born ca 1840. He died 6 Dec 1902 (rilla). Census: 1870 in Calais.

vi. HANNAH LEDDY, born 4 Jan 1849 in Calais (death cert.). She owned a Tea Room in Ogunquit, ME which she ran in the summertime (rilla). Died Jan 1944 age 95y 4d in St. Petersburg, FL (death cert., rilla). Census: 1850 in Calais. She married FREDERICK DEARBORN who died before his wife (rilla).

JOSEPH A. & MARY L. LEE, p. 202

JOSEPH LEE, fifth of the name, who was born at Royalston in 1773 and died in 1861, he was a merchant, and traded in different towns in Maine. He married 19 Sept 1800 PRISCILLA SPARHAWK, born 13 May 1777 (water:547, leigh:279) daughter of the Rev. EBENEZER SPARHAWK & NAOMI HILL of Templeton, MA. They had eight children (biorev:315). Their 4th child was Joseph Appollas, who resided in Calais.

JOSEPH APOLLAS LEE, born, 19 Jul 1808, in Bucksport, ME (VR, leigh:279, biorev:314), the sixth generation named Joseph, (biorev:315). Came to Calais in 1833 (beg:125). In 1841 he was a Notary Public. When the Calais Bank was organized, Mr. Lee became its cashier and became president in 1866 until his death. He served in the city government and in the Legislature. He also was an Insurance Agent under the name of Jos. A. Lee & Son established in 1848 (CEV:31). Died 4 Jan 1880 in Calais (obit times, g.s.). Buried in Calais Cemetery. Census: 1840 (1 male, 4 females),

50, 60 & 70 in Calais.

He married 1st 22 Aug 1837 in Calais (gaz) MARY L. SAWYER, born 16 Jan 1814 in Winchendon, MA (biorev:315, leigh:342), daughter of ABNER SAWYER (b. 26 July 1786, Templeton, Ma. son of SILAS SAWYER & MARY ROSS) & PHOEBE COLE (b. 16 Nov 1808 in Phillipston, MA). Died 29 Sep 1849 in Calais (sawofne:237-295-392, biorev:315, FJ). Children:

i. PHOEBE SAWYER LEE, born 4 Jun 1838 in Calais (VR). Died 18 July 1871 age 33 in Calais (SCC, adv, g.s.) Buried in Calais Cemetery. Census: 1850, 60 & 70 in Calais. She married 30 Nov 1865 in Calais (VR, beg:125, biorev:179) as his 2nd wife, Col. WILLARD BANCROFT KING, born 27 Mar 1830 in Baring, NB, son of GILMAN D. KING & HANNAH HAYCOCK (biorev:179). He was in the mercantile business on both sides of the St. Croix river, he died 2 Apr 1897 (g.s., biorev). His 1st wife was Elizabeth 'Lizzie' Veazie who died 4 June 1865 age 34 (union. g.s., see VEAZIE). His 3rd wife was Fannie E. Hayden (1842-1926 g.s.). All three wives buried with him in Calais Cemetery. Census: 1870 (with Phoebe) in Calais.

ii. ELIZABETH SPARHAWK LEE, born 16 Aug 1839 in Calais (VR). Died 10 Nov 1922 in Dorchester MA (obit). Buried in Calais Cemetery. Census: 1850 thru 1880 in Calais. She married 16 Apr 1863 in Eastport ME (east:194) CHARLES HARRISON NEWTON. He was born 5 Aug 1830 in Templeton, (obit has Fitchburg) MA, son of HORACE NEWTON & ABIGAIL BURRAGE (biorev:257). He worked in a store in Boston, as a bookkeeper & clerk in Portland, Me and back to his former employers in Boston. The firm acquired a plaster mine in Calais and Mr. Newton, along with Henry A. Willis & George R. Tarbox, made a survey of the property in Red Beach, and started business as George R. Tarbox & Co. In 1858 the Red Beach Plaster Company was organized, with Mr. Newton as manager. He became president of the Company in 1878. In 1875 he became treasurer of the new Red Granite Co. He was also a director of the Calais National Bank for 18 years. In 1888 he was elected to the State legislature (biorev:258). He died 2 Dec 1897 in Red Beach (adv).

iii. MARY ELLEN LEE, born 21 Nov 1840 in Calais (VR). Resided in Minneapolis, MN. Died 28 Nov 1868 age 28 in Minneapolis (union, SCC). Census: 1850 & 60 in Calais. She married 11 Dec 1867 in Calais by Rev. H.V. Dexter (SCC, union) in Calais (VR:3;227) CHARLES CARROLL LADD of Ellsworth & St. Anthony, MN, born 7 Mar 1834, son of JOSEPH WARREN LADD, of Providence, RI who was born 24 May 1801, the son of CALEB LADD (ladd:308, biorev:315).

iv. JOSEPH WOOD LEE, born 21 Mar 1842 in Calais (VR). Graduated from Calais Academy. He served in the Civil War in several units of the 1st Cavalry, 5'8" with gray eyes and dark hair, also served in Mass. Cavalry (cwcard). He was an Episcopalian clergyman at Bristol., PA (biorev:315, leigh:342). Died after 1898 when he resided in Bristol, PA (brother's obit). Census: 1850 & 60 in Calais.

v. ALMEIDA TOWNSEND LEE, born 22 Oct 1843 in Calais (VR). Died 6 May 1845 age 19m in Calais (gaz). Buried in Calais Cemetery 8 May 1845 (sext).

vi. WILLIAM HOWARD LEE, born 15 Feb 1845 in Calais (VR). Resided: 1898, in Augusta, ME (bro.'s obit). He was a farmer. Died 1926 in Augusta, ME (MSA, film faint, can't read date). Census: 1850 thru 1880 in Calais, 1900 & 20 in Augusta. He married 9 Oct 1869 (leigh:387) HEPSIBAH 'HEPSIE' PICKARD, born 5 Apr 1847 (leigh:387) in Petitcodac, NB, daughter of VALENTINE PICKETT (MSA). Died 15 Oct 1923 age 76y 9m 10 d in Augusta, Me (MSA). Census 1880 in Calais, 1900 & 20 in Augusta.

vii. ALMEDA SALOME LEE, born 20 Jul 1846 in Calais (VR, g.s.). Died 16 Aug 1861 in Calais (g.s.). Buried: 17 Aug 1861 in Calais Cemetery. Census: 1850 & 60 in Calais.

viii. CLARA JANE GREENLEAF LEE, born circa 1848 in Calais. Resided: 1898, in Napa, CA (biorev:316). Died after 1898 (bro.'s obit). Census: 1850, 60 & 70 in Calais. She married 25 Dec 1877 by Rev. McCully in Calais (VR:3:226, adv, east:314). FREDERICK K. SMYTH(e), of Lancaster, PA. [An item in the Calais Advertiser of 1 Sept 1880 says Prof. & Mrs. Smythe would soon move to California].

Joseph A. married 2nd 28 Aug 1856 (biorev:316) in Wiscasset (union) ISABELLA A. THEOBALD, born 14 Nov 1818 in Wiscasset, ME, daughter of Dr. PHILIP ERNST THEOBALD, Jr. of Wiscasset & NANCY PAYSON. Died 9 May 1899 in Calais (MSA, obit adv), her death followed by just a few months that of her only son and her only sister (obit adv). Buried in Calais Cemetery. Census: 1860, 70 & 80 in Calais. Dr. Philip Theobald Jr. was the son of Dr. PHILIP THEOBALD a surgeon in Burgoyne's army (biorev:316). Children:

ix. ERNST THEOBALD LEE, born 20 Sep 1861 in Calais (biorev:316). He was a bank clerk and a member of Calais Fire Dept. He served in Co. K in State Militia. Died 22 Aug 1898 age 36 in Calais (biorev:316, from a fire extinguisher explosion, MSA = 23 Aug). Buried in Calais Cemetery. Census: 1870 & 80 in Calais. He married 26 Sep 1883 in Calais (VR:2:31, biorev:316, times) ANNIE LAURIE WASHBURN, born 25 Nov 1858 in Calais (VR:3:260), daughter of CHARLES FRANCIS WASHBURN (1826-1890, g.s.) & SOPHIA McKENZIE (1830 – 1881, g.s., daughter of George McKenzie of St. George, NB). Died 8 Sept 1933 in Calais (MSA, g.s., china). Buried in Calais Cemetery. Census: 1860, 70 & 1900 (with bro. Frank), 1910 (a widow) in Calais.

BENAJAH & SALLY LESUER, p. 179

BENIAH LESUER, born 30 Nov 1796 in Perry, ME, died 18 May 1854 in Calais (stan). Census: 1830 (3 males, 4 females) in Perry, 40 (5 males, 7 females) in Robbinston, 50 in Calais. [married in Eastport Benjah Lashure & Miss Fanny Patterson Sept 1795 both of Plantation #1, poss. parents of Beniah (Eastport VR)]

He married 9 Nov 1817 (stan) SARAH `SALLY' E.^{6} STANHOPE, born 28 Dec 1797 in Mass (stan), daughter of PETER^5 STANHOPE, SAMUEL^4, JONATHAN^3, JOSEPH^2, JONATHAN^1. Died 1Nov 1869 in Calais (stan). Census: 1850, 60 & 70 in Calais. Children:

i. MEDORAH LESUER, born 27 Sep 1818 in Perry ME (VR:53).
ii. SARAH ELIZA LESUER, born 22 May 1821 in Perry (VR:53).
iii. ALFRED C. LESUER, born 14 Oct 1823 in Perry (VR:53, came to Calais 1840 with father). Died 11 Jun 1884 in Calais (stan, times). Census: 1850, 60 & 70 in Calais. He married 30 May 1847 in Calais ELIZA JANE NOBLE, born 13 May 1829 in Calais (stan, TWB), daughter of JOHN NOBLE & SUSAN PALMER (TWB). She died 21 Jan 1912 age 83y 8m in Calais (MSA, adv). Census: 1850, 60 & 70 in Calais.
iv. BENJAMIN LEWIS LESUER, born 19 Sep 1826 in Perry (VR:53). He was a school janitor in 1880. Died 28 Apr 1885 in Calais (times, g.s.). Buried Calais Cemetery. Census: 1850 thru 1880 in Calais. He married 3 Mar 1857 in Calais (VR) ANNA MARIA TOWERS, born 3 Feb 1835, daughter of JOHN TOWERS AND MARTHA `HATTIE' GRIMMER. (see TOWERS)
v. MARY G. LESUER, born 8 Apr 1829 in Perry (VR:53). Died 12 Jan 1838, in Robbinston Me (FJ).
vi. HARRIET GLEASON LESUER, born 18 Apr 1831 in Perry (VR:53).
vii. BENNETT ROBERT LESUER, born 9 Nov 1833 in Perry (VR:53, MSA). He was a truckman & teamster. Died 30 Jul 1906 in Calais (MSA). Buried: 1 Aug 1906 in Calais Cemetery. Census: 1860 thru 1900 in Calais. He married (int.) 11 Jan 1854 married by Rev. S. H. Keeler in Calais MATILDA M. NEVENS, born Jul 1836 in Calais (1900 census), daughter OF JONATHAN NEVENS & LYDIA A. LANE. Died 25 Oct 1914 78y 4m in Calais (MSA, adv). Buried in Calais Cemetery. Census: 1850 thru 1900 in Calais.
viii. HANNAH /ANNA M. LESUER, born circa 1836 in Robbinston Me (1850 census). Census: 1850 (age 14) & 60 (age 23) in Calais.
ix. MARY S. LESUER, born circa 1838 in Robbinston Me (1850 census). Census: 1850 in Calais (age 12).
x. IRA LESUER, born 14 Mar 1841 in Calais (VR). Served in Civil War, Co. K 6th Maine (NRMS:268). He was a laborer with light blue eyes and brown hair (cwcard). Census: 1850 & 60 in Calais. He married 1st 23 Dec 1861 by Rev. D. F. Smith in Calais LYDIA CLAXTON of St. David, NB (VR:3:185). Lydia A. Lesuer was granted a divorce Oct 1864 states they were married 23 Dec 1862. He married 2nd 13 Dec 1865 by Rev. W.S. McKellar in Calais CHARLOTTE CARVER of Calais (VSNB:23:97:#1245).

DAVID & JANE LINSCOTT, p. 203

DAVID LINSCOTT, born circa 1809 in Palermo, ME (1850 census). He was a teamster. Died 3 Jul 1875 in Perry ME (VR). Census: 1840 (1 male, 3 females), 50 & 60 in Calais, 1870 in Perry.

He married JANE MOONEY/ MAHONEY, born circa 1817 in Oak Bay, NB (1850 census = St. Stephen). Died 9 May 1884 in Perry (VR, times). Census: 1850 & 60 in Calais, 1870 & 80 in Perry. Children:

i. EMELINE LINSCOTT, born 8 Nov 1836 in Oak Bay, NB (Perry VR). She was a teacher. Died 28 Mar 1874 in Perry (VR). Census: 1850, 60 & 70 in Calais. She married 8 Mar 1861 in Calais (VR:1:94, union) MARCELLUS WALKER born ca 1836. He was a lumberman. Census: 1870 in Calais, 1880 (living with new wife, Margaret, and children by 1st wife) in Houlton.
ii. MARGARET 'Maggie' E. LINSCOTT, born circa 1840 in St. David, NB (1850 census). She worked in a

factory in 1860. Census: 1850 & 60 in Calais, 1880 in Houlton. She married her sisters' widower 12 Jan 1876 by Rev. R. D. Porter in Calais (VR:3:239) MARCELLUS WALKER, born ca 1839. Census: 1880 in Houlton, Me.

iii. HENRIETTA 'ETTA'/ HARRIET LINSCOTT, born 16 Jan 1844 in St. David, NB (Calais VR). She was a milliner. Died 29 Jul 1864 age 22 in Calais (VR:3:309, g.s.). Buried: 31 Jul 1864 in Calais Cemetery. Census: 1850 & 60 in Calais.

iv. WILLIAM CHARLES LINSCOTT, born 2 May 1850 in Calais (Perry VR). Died 1 Sep 1851 in Calais (VR & Perry VR). Census: 1850 in Calais.

v. EVA JANE LINSCOTT, born 1 Nov 1853 in Milltown ME (MSA), born 1 Nov 1852 (VR Perry). Died 28 Jun 1935, in Perry ME (VR MSA). Census: 1860 in Calais, 1870 & 80 in Perry, 1900 in Calais. She married, 17 Aug 1881, in Perry ME (times & adv) married 10 Aug 1881, in Eastport (east:343) WILLIAM MELVIN SMALL, son of ALEXANDER NICHOLAS SMALL AND ALMIRA HITCHINGS (see SMALL).

vi. ANNA AUGUSTA LINSCOTT, born 7 Jul 1859 in Milltown ME (Perry VR). Died 2 May 1942 age 92y 9m 25d in Perry (MSA). Census: 1860 in Calais, 1870, 80, 1900 & 20 in Perry. Married before 1876 FERDINAND McPHAIL, born Jan 1850 (1900 census), son of JOHN & MARTHA McPHAIL. Died after 1900 before 1942. Census: 1860 (age 8, with parents), 80, 1900 & 1920 in Perry.

- Note. VR of Perry were recorded 19 Mar 1878 except for Jane's death.

RUFUS & MARIA LORD, p. 217

RUFUS LORD, born circa 1812 in N H. He was a store manager. Died before 1870. Census: 1850 & 60 in Calais. [Possible son of Jacob Lord in 1830-40 census of Calais].

He married 4 Dec 1844 in Milltown ME (mrwc:44, gaz), LUCRETIA MARIA LOVEJOY, born 30 Jan 1825 in Dennysville, ME (VR), daughter of THOMAS ODIORNE LOVEJOY & RUBY WOODWORTH. Died in Calais. (see LOVEJOY). Children:

i. UNNAMED CHILD LORD who died 11 Mar 1846, aged 1 year (sext).

ii. WILLARD LORD, born 16 Apr 1847 in Calais. Census: 1850 thru 1880 in Calais.

iii. EMMA LORD, born Jun 1849 in Calais, died 21 Dec 1850 (sext). Buried in Calais Cemetery. Census: 1850 in Calais.

iv. CHARLES H. LORD, born, circa 1851 in Calais. Census: 1860 & 70 in Calais.

v. CLARA E. LORD, born, circa 1854 in Calais. Census: 1860 & 70 in Calais.

vi. NELLIE LORD, born circa 1859 in Calais. She was a dressmaker. Died after 1880. Census: (not in 1860), 1870 (age 11), 1880 age 22 in Calais.

vii. RUBY M. LORD, born, circa 1859/60 in Calais. Census: 1860 (age 1) in Calais.
[Child of Rufus aged 2 years, died 27 Mar 1862 in Calais (VR:1:243)].

- Note. {1860 census has Ruby M. age 1 no Nellie; 1870 census has Nellie age 11, no Ruby}
- Note. "One son burned to death, one son killed by falling from team at Calais, one son robbed and murdered 'in the provinces'" and there were also two daughters, one of whom lived in Bath, Me (love:158).

JOHN L. & ANN M. LOVEJOY, p. 223

WILLIAM[3] LOVEJOY, born 4 Aug 1778 in Vassalboro, son of Capt. ABIEL[2] LOVEJOY, grandson of HEZEKIAH[1] LOVEJOY, died 6 July 1872 in Minneapolis, MN, married ca 1801 ATTAI LOVEJOY his second cousin. They had three children: Cordelia Lovejoy who married WILLIAM KELLEY (see KELLEY); JOHN LORING LOVEJOY (see BELOW); and Stephen Brown Lovejoy born 17 Sept 1805, in Wayne, ME; died 26 June 1835 in Milltown, NB of lead poisoning. (love:120).

JOHN LORIN[4] LOVEJOY, born 11 Jul 1803 in Wayne or Fayette, ME (love:120, 1850 census = Wayne). He was a lumberman. Died 16 Oct 1860, in Minneapolis, MN (love:165), death(2): 10 Oct 1860, in St. Anthony's, Falls, MN (union, adv). Census: 1840 (6 males, 4 females), 50 in Calais.

He married 8 Feb 1828 in St. Stephen, NB (love:165, CCMR:247 = 1829) ANN MARPLE ALBEE, born 9 Feb 1810 in St. Stephen, NB, daughter of JAMES DELLAWAY ALBEE AND HANNAH MARPLE, she was a descendant of Lieutenant William Albee, a Revolutionary War officer who served as commandant of Fort Machias, ME (DAR #98199 & 90918). She died 7 Nov 1897 in Osceola, WI (wdr, love:165 = 1847). Census: 1850 in Calais, 1870 in St. Anthony, MN. Children:

i. JAMES ALBEE LOVEJOY, born 29 Apr 1831 in St. Stephen, NB (love:165, Calais VR). He was a lumberman. Died 29 Jul 1886 in Santa Cruz, CA (love:165). Census: 1870 in St. Anthony, MN. Census: 1850 in Calais. He married 30 Jul 1853 by Rev. S. H. Keeler in Calais (love:232) HANNAH EMMA/AMY SPRING, daughter of EPHRAIM SPRING & HANNAH S. MORSE (see SPRING).
ii. LORING FULLER LOVEJOY, born 28 Oct 1833 in Calais (VR, love:166 = 29 Oct 1832). Died 19 Feb 1835 in Calais (VR:1:240, love:166).
iii. ANN MARIA LOVEJOY, born 16 Jul 1837 in Calais (VR, love = 15 July). Died 18 Oct 1837 in Calais (VR:1:240, love:166).
iv. MARY CORDELIA LOVEJOY, born 31 Aug 1839 in Calais (love:166= 21 Aug). Died 11 Nov 1842 in Calais (VR:1:240, love). Buried: 13 Nov 1842 in Calais Cemetery.
v. JULIA NORRIS LOVEJOY, born 11 Apr 1842 in Calais (VR, love:165, DAR # 98199). Census: 1850 in Calais. She married 12 Sep 1861, in Minneapolis, MN (love:165) Rev. WILLIAM WALLACE KING, born, ca 1824, resided in Chicago, IL (love:165).
vi. EMMA GERTRUDE LOVEJOY, born 16 Mar 1844 in Milltown ME (love:166, DAR # 90918). Census: 1850 in Calais, 1870 in St. Anthony, MN. She married 15 Sep 1863 in Minneapolis, MN, JOSEPH WARREN LADD, Jr., born 24 Mar 1841 in Phenix, RI, son of JOSEPH W. LADD & ALMY WICKS SPENCER (ladd:306, love:166). Died ca 1917 in Minneapolis (ladd:308, love:166). Census: 1870 in St. Anthony, MN.
vii. WILLIAM LORING LOVEJOY, born 4 Jul 1846 in Calais, died 3 May 1848 in Calais (VR, love:166, adv). Buried: 7 May 1848 in Calais Cemetery.
viii. STEPHEN BROWN LOVEJOY, born 19 Jan 1850 in Livermore ME (VR). He went to Minneapolis when a boy and became a leading business man there, prominent in local and state politics. He was named postmaster of Minneapolis in 1898 and reappointed in 1902. He graduated from Penn. Military Academy, in Chester, PA. In 1895 he was elected to the Minnesota State Legislature, he died 5 Jul 1902, in Minneapolis, MN (love:232). Census: 1850 in Calais, 1870 in St. Anthony, MN. He married 13 Oct 1872 in Minneapolis, MN (love:232) ERECTA LOUISE MORGAN, born 23 Aug 1853 in St. Catherine's, Ont., daughter of Gen. GEORGE NELSON MORGAN & ELIZABETH WARNER. She died Dec 1917 in Minnesota (love:232).

THOMAS O. & RUBY LOVEJOY, p. 219

THOMAS ODIORNE[4] LOVEJOY, born 27 Jan 1792 in Vassalboro, ME, son of NATHANIEL[3] LOVEJOY & MARY ROBERTS, grandson of Capt. ABIEL[2], HEZEKIAH[1] (love: 158). Died 24 Mar 1845 age 53 in Calais (VR:1:239, love:158). Buried: 26 Mar 1845 in Calais Cemetery. Census: 1830 (2 males, 4 females) in Dennysville, ME.
    He married 13 Nov 1817, in Cornwallis NS (IGI= St. John's Anglican Church) RUBY WOODWORTH, born ca 1800, daughter of WILLIAM WOODWORTH, Jr. & MARCEY PINEO of Lebanon, CT, they married 8 Jan 1778 in Cornwallis, NS (VR, love:158, chute:127). She died ca 1885 in Calais (love:158, chute:268). Census: 1880 (with her daughter, Maria Lord and children, in household of Cordelia Peabody) in Calais. Children:

i. MARY ANN LOVEJOY, born 23 Feb 1821 in Dennysville, ME (VR). Died in Calais (love158). She married 29 Aug 1841 by M. B. Townsend, Esq. in Calais (gaz) SAMUEL H. COFFIN, resided in Calais.
ii. SARAH PERSIS LOVEJOY, born 1 Aug 1823 in Dennysville (VR). She married EZRA L. HERSEY (chute:268). Resided in E. Boston, MA (love:158).
iii. LUCRETIA MARIA LOVEJOY, born 30 Jan 1825 in Dennysville (VR, 1850 census = Pembroke). Died in Calais. Census: 1850 thru 80 in Calais. She married 1st 4 Dec 1844, in Milltown, ME RUFUS LORD (see LORD). She married 2nd 22 Oct 1894 in Calais (times, MSA) Capt. IRA F. MITCHELL, born ca 1823 in Harrington, ME, died 10 Dec 1907 in Pembroke, ME, son of JEROME MITCHELL & RUTH CUSHING (MSA). His 1st wife was Corilla N. Blackwood.
iv. WILLIAM ODIORNE LOVEJOY, born (1) 7 July 1827 in Dennysville (VR), born (2) 7 Jul 1828 in Pembroke Me (love:222). He was a carpenter. Died in Seattle, WA (love:158). Census: 1870 in St. Anthony, MN. He married 27 Oct 1850 in Dover, NH (love:222). ELLEN VAUGHAN of Fredericksburg, VA.
v. CHARLES NORMAN LOVEJOY, born 6 Nov 1830 in Dennysville, ME (VR). Resided in E. Boston, MA. Died in E. Boston, MA (of effects of accidental dose of poison, love:158). Census: 1850 (with sister, Maria Lord) in Calais.

vi. LEONARD HIRAM LOVEJOY, born 1 Mar 1833 in Vassalboro, ME (VR, birth also recorded in Pembroke VR). Probably served in Civil War and in 1900 resided at Soldiers Home in Minneapolis, MN (love:158).
vii. AMANDA ELIZABETH LOVEJOY), born 6 Aug 1837 in Calais (VR). Census: 1850 (with sister, Maria Lord) in Calais (poss. mar. a WOODCOCK and lived in Minn. MN, love:158).
viii. JAMES LORING LOVEJOY, born 6 Apr 1840 in Calais (VR).
ix. RUBY MELVINA LOVEJOY, born 6 Nov 1842 in Calais. Resided in Portland ME (love:158).
x. HENRY AUGUSTUS LOVEJOY, born 20 May 1845 in Calais, died 24 Sep 1847 in Calais (VR). Buried: 28 Sep 1847 in Calais Cemetery.

- Note – Two daughters died in infancy in Calais (chute:268).

LEVI L. & EMELINE M. LOWELL, p. 211

JOSEPH^8 LOWELL AND LYDIA NASH, (son of JOSEPH^7, JOHN$^{6-5}$, GIDEON^4, PERCIVAL^3, RICHARD^2, PERCIVAL^1, Old Families of Salisbury & Amesbury:234), they lived in Wiscasset, ME where their children were born. Joseph died 1886 obit in Calais Advertiser 2 June 1886. Their 5th child was Levi L. Lowell who settled in Calais.

LEVI LINCOLN^9 LOWELL, born 11 Apr 1805 in Wiscasset, ME (low: 463) He moved from Wiscasset, to Calais 1828 (beg:125) where he became a merchant and insurance agent and after 1830 he had charge of the Munroe estate embracing large tracts of land in and about the city of Calais; for a time he was a U.S. Custom officer; a Mason and member of the Congregational Church (low:463). He was a member of the Calais Band, played the clarinet. Died 9 Aug 1880 age 75 in Calais (low:463, g.s.). Buried in Calais Cemetery. Census: 1840 (3 males, 3 females), 50 thru 1880 in Calais.

He married 18 Dec 1832 in Calais (low:463, news item in demo) EMELINE MOWBRAY DANFORD, born 30 Jan 1808 in Wiscasset, ME, daughter of PAUL DANFORD AND MARY COTHRAN (low:463). Died 24 Feb 1896 88y 26d in Calais (VR, MSA, adv, g.s.). Buried in Calais Cemetery. Census: 1850 thru 1880 in Calais. Children:

i. DANFORD L. LOWELL, born 26 Apr 1837 in Calais, died 27 Apr 1837 in Calais (low:568, VR:1:238 g.s.). Buried in Calais Cemetery.
ii. JOSEPH KENDALL LOWELL, born 6 Apr 1838 in Calais (VR, low:568). Died 6 Apr 1857 age 19 in Calais (VR, low, g.s.). Buried: 8 Apr 1857 in Calais Cemetery. Census: 1850 in Calais.
iii. HELEN LOWELL, born 4 Apr 1840 in Calais, died 5 Apr 1840 in Calais (VR, low:568, g.s.). Buried: 6 Apr 1840 in Calais Cemetery.
iv. LEVI LOWELL, born 28 Mar 1841 in Calais, died 30 Mar 1841 in Calais (VR, low:568, g.s.). Buried: 31 Mar 1841 in Calais Cemetery.
v. WALTER LINCOLN LOWELL, born 12 Apr 1842 in Calais, died 12 Aug 1842 age 4m in Calais (VR, low:568, g.s., gaz). Buried: 13 Aug 1842 in Calais Cemetery.
vi. CHARLOTTE GROSVENOR LOWELL, born 13 Jan 1844 in Calais (VR). Graduated from Calais Academy (adv). Died after 1896, she survived mother. Census: 1850 & 60 in Calais. She married 12 Sep 1866 by Rev. S.H. Keeler in Calais (VR:3:216) FRANK A. KENNEDY of Cambridge, MA (beg:125, low:568), he was (1889) retired as proprietor of the Kennedy Cracker Manufactory (low:568). They resided in Cambridge, MA.
vii. HENRY DOWNES LOWELL, born 9 Dec 1846 in Calais, died 15 Jul 1847 age 7m in Calais (VR, low:568). Buried: 16 Jul 1847 in Calais Cemetery.
viii. ALICE BRADBURY LOWELL, born 9 Dec 1848 in Calais. Died after 1896, she survived mother and resided in Boston. Census: 1850, 60 & 70 in Calais. She married 28 Oct 1873 by Rev. William Carruthers at home of the bride in Calais (union) DAVID NELSON SKILLINGS Jr. he was a lumber merchant in Boston and resided in Winchester, MA (low:568).

REUBEN & SARAH LOWELL, p. 223

REUBEN N.^{8} LOWELL born 31 Dec 1794 in Buckfield, ME (low:397), son of THOMAS^7 LOWELL & JUDITH FARRAR, STEPHEN$^{6-5}$, GIDEON^4, PERCIVAL^3, RICHARD^2, PERCIVAL^1. He moved from Buckfield to Litchfield in 1815, and to Calais 1825 (low:397). He was a merchant. He died 18 May 1837 age 42 in Calais (VR:1:240, low:397, prbt, his mother, Judith left $50.00 per year in his will). Buried in Calais Cemetery. Census: 1830 (5 males, 3 females) in Calais.

He married 28 Feb 1820, in Litchfield ME (litch:209, 311, obit) SARAH `SALLY' SMITH, born, 28 Nov 1795, in Litchfield ME, daughter of JOSEPH SMITH & MARTHA ROBINSON, (granddaughter of ELIPHALET & JANE SMITH, and JABEZ ROBINSON & MARTHA MEIGGS). They moved to Calais 1 Jan 1825 (her obit). She died 1 Mar 1884 age 88 in Calais (obit, adv, g.s.). Buried in Calais Cemetery. Census: 1850 thru 1880 in Calais. Children:

i. MINERVA LOWELL, born 24 Dec 1820 in Litchfield ME (low:488, obit). She died 6 Feb 1869 age 48 in Calais (low:488, obit CFL hand written date 1869, g.s.) Buried in Calais Cemetery. Census: 1850 & 60 in Calais. She married 1st 2 Dec 1838 in Calais (cal2:51, Bangor VR) HORACE HAMILTON, born ca 1812 in Baring, ME. He died age 30 in 1842 (gaz of 7 Sept 1842 on Thurs. last). She married 2nd 4 Sept 1843 in Calais by Rev. Mr. Hitchings (gaz) Hon. DANIEL KIMBALL CHASE, he was a mayor of Calais (1859-61), he died 1 Apr 1876 (prbt, low:488). His 2nd wife, Janet Cameron survived him, will dated 18 Oct 1875 (prbt). Census: 1850, 60 & 70 in Calais.

ii. SARAH TRUE LOWELL, born 16 Oct 1822 in Litchfield ME (low:488, litch:209). Died circa 1823 in Litchfield ME (litch).

iii. EGBERT LOWELL, born 6 Jun 1824 in Litchfield ME, died circa 1824 in Litchfield (litch:209, low:488).

iv. REUBEN LOWELL, born 22 Aug 1825 in Calais, died circa 1825 in Calais (low:488).

v. REUBEN BRADDOCK LOWELL, born 8 Mar 1827 in Calais (VR). In 1849 he went to California, via Cape Horn, with his brother, George, but after two years returned to Calais. Upon returning from Calif. he became a customs officer in Milltown where he remained until retirement (obit CFL). He died 23 Jun 1910 age 83 in Brooklyn, NY, while visiting his daughters (sfh:1:283, obit, prbt). Buried in Calais Cemetery. Census: 1860, 70, 80 & 1900 in Calais. He married 1st Jan 1856 (int.) 28 Jan 1856 in Calais (VR, low:488) ELIZABETH EMERSON, daughter of Capt. SETH EMERSON AND MARY W. KNIGHT (see EMERSON). He married 2nd 25 Sep 1884 in Calais (times) ARISTINE H. ABELL, she died before 1900 census. Census: 1860 & 70 in Calais.

vi. FREDERICK AUGUSTUS LOWELL, born 6 Aug 1828 in Calais (VR, low:488). Died 9 Jul 1854 age 25 in San Francisco, CA (low:488). Buried in Calais Cemetery (obit). Census: 1850 in Calais. Never married.

vii. GEORGE ALBERT LOWELL, born 6 May 1831 in Calais (VR, low:488). During the gold fever in 1849 he and his brother Reuben B., went (1849) to in California but two years later returned to Calais where he entered the retail store business; in 1879 he became the treasurer of the Calais Savings Bank; in 1882 he was elected city treasurer and held that office for 8 years; a member of the Universalist Church (low:488, obit). Died 29 May 1907 age 76y 23d in Calais (obit adv, sfh:1 MSA). Census: 1870 & 1900 in Calais. He married 26 Sep 1856 Calais (low:488) SARAH E. HILL, born 8 Nov 1833 in Upper Mills, NB, only child of HORATIO N. & PHEBE WHITNEY (WHITNEY) HILL. She died on their annual trip to Florida in New York City 19 Nov 1905 (obit CFL). Buried 21 Nov 1905 Calais Cemetery. Census: 1870 &1900 in Calais.

viii. SARAH LOWELL, born 30 Dec 1833 in Calais (VR, low). Died 9 Jan 1916 in Cambridge, MA (obit, adv, g.s.). Census: 1850 thru 1880 in Calais. She married 15 Dec 1858 (low:489, VR:3:171) HENRY CLAY COPELAND, born 7 Jan 1832 in Norridgewock (obit, g.s.), son of THOMAS JEFFERSON COPELAND (b. Boston, editor of Somerset Journal before moving to Calais in 1843) & JULIA ELVIRA TOWNSEND b. Norridgewock, Me (cope: 500). Henry, died 7 Nov 1912 in Calais (g.s., obit CFL, sfh:2:2). Bottom of grave stone in Calais Cemetery says buried in Forest Hills Cemetery, Boston, MA. Census 1850 & 60 in Calais.

MICHAEL & MARGARET MAGUIRE, p. 199

MICHAEL MAGUIRE/McGUIRE, born circa 1807 in Ireland, came from NB to Calais between 1844-1845. He was a trader. Census: 1850 (age 47 name McGuire, insane) in Calais.

He married 6 Oct 1834, in St. Stephen, NB (CCMR) MARGARET GLEASON, born circa 1818 in Ireland (1850 census). Census: 1850 in Calais. Children:

i. MARY MAGUIRE, born circa 1836 in St. Stephen, NB (1850 census). Census: 1850 in Calais.
ii. JOHN MAGUIRE, born circa 1837 in St. Stephen, NB (1850 census). Census: 1850 in Calais.

    iii. MICHAEL MAGUIRE, Jr., born circa 1838 in St. Stephen, NB (1850 census). Census: 1850 in Calais.
    iv. CATHERINE MAGUIRE, born circa 1840 in St. Stephen, NB (1850 census). Census: 1850 in Calais.
    v. MARGARET MAGUIRE, born circa 1842 in St. Stephen, NB (1850 census). Census: 1850 in Calais.
    vi. JAMES MAGUIRE, born circa 1844 in St. Stephen, NB (1850 census). Census: 1850 in Calais.
    vii. EDWARD ROBERT MAGUIRE, born 4 Sep 1845 in Calais (VR, 1850 census = St. Stephen). Census: 1850 in Calais.
    viii. ANN MARIA MAGUIRE, born 2 Jul 1847 in Calais (VR). Census: 1850 in Calais.

ROBIE & HANNAH MANSON, p. 203

ROBERT 'ROBIE' TAPPAN MANSON, born circa 1807, in Limerick ME, son of MARK MANSON b. 1772 in Kittery & CATHERINE COX born 1775. *'A minor child when his father gave him his time 3 Aug 1826'* (lime:90-91). Died 21 Mar 1889 age 83 in Calais (g.s.). Buried in Calais Cemetery. {Calais Adv. reported death of Robie Manson of Milltown on 26 Sept 1883, which was retracted in next issue, his quote 'it's a gd lie'}. Census: 1840 (4 males, 4 females), 50 thru 1880 in Calais.

He married 28 Mar 1833 in Calais by T. Q. Kettle, JP (cal2:48) HANNAH BARTLETT, born circa 1801 in Whitefield ME (1850 census, daughter's death rec. = b. NB). Died 5 May 1884 age 83y 9m (adv, g.s.) in Calais. Buried in Calais Cemetery. Census: 1850 thru 1880 in Calais. Children:

    i. MARY C. MANSON ?, born circa 1830 in Calais. Census: 1860 (works in factory) in Calais. Born before marriage, appears only in 1860 census, may be a relative and not daughter.
    ii. HARRIET A. MANSON, born 29 Aug 1834 in Calais (VR). Census: 1850 & 60 (works in factory) in Calais.
    iii. CHARLES FREDERICK MANSON, born 20 May 1836 in Calais (VR). He worked in a mill. Died 15 Sep 1911 age 71y 4m in Calais (MSA). Buried in Calais Cemetery. Census: 1850, 60, 70 & 1900 in Calais.
    iv. GEORGE FRANKLIN MANSON, born 21 Aug 1838 in Calais (VR). Died in Calais. Buried in Calais Cemetery- (no dates on stone). Census: 1850 in Calais.
    v. SARAH GRIGGS MANSON, born 15 Jan 1840 in Calais (VR). Died 12 Jun 1910 age 69 in Calais (MSA, g.s.). Buried in Calais Cemetery. Census: 1850, 60 (works in factory) & 1900 (age 56 with brother, Fred) in Calais. She married 21 May 1873 by Rev. A.S. Townsend in Milltown ME (adv) PETER CARLE LAMB, son of NATHANIEL LAMB AND ELMIRA/ALMIRA CARLE (see LAMB).
    vi. MARINDA GRIGGS MANSON, born 22 May 1842 in Calais, died 30 Aug 1843 in Calais (VR:1:236). Buried: 31 Aug 1843 in Calais Cemetery.
    vii. ANNA M. MANSON, born circa 1846 in Calais. Died 12 Apr 1916 in Calais (MSA). Census: 1850, 60, 70 & 1900 (age 50 with brother, Fred) in Calais. Unmarried.

BRADFORD & ELLEN MARSHALL, p. 225 + 226

BRADFORD MARSHALL, born 1816, in Bangor Me (cwcard). Enlisted in Civil War age 48 in 1st Batty Light Artillery, he was a merchant with hazel eyes and black hair (cwcard). He also was an expressman. Died 6 Aug 1888 in Augusta, ME (times). Census: 1850 thru 1880 in Calais.

He married ELLEN SHEEHAN, born Apr 1825 in Waterford, Ireland (1850 census), daughter of RICHARD & MARGARET SHEEHAN (MSA). After her husband's death she moved to Portland to live with her son, Walter (adv). Died 26 Oct 1910 age 85 in Portland, buried in Calais Cemetery (MSA, obit argus). Census: 1850 thru 1880 in Calais, 1900 in Portland. Children:

    i. ALFRED B. MARSHALL, born 12 Apr 1846 in Calais (VR). Died 28 Oct 1846 age 6m in Calais (VR). Buried: 29 Oct 1846 in Calais Cemetery.
    ii. HELEN ELIZABETH MARSHALL, born 8 Oct 1847 in Calais (VR). Died 25 Nov 1869 age 22y 1m in Lowell, MA (obit, SCC). Census: 1850 & 60 in Calais. She married (____) CARR (from her obit).
    iii. ANNA ELIZA MARSHALL, born 23 Nov 1849 in Calais. Resided in St. Paul, MN in 1888. Census: 1850 & 70 in Calais. She married 12 Feb 1874 in Calais (adv) ASHER BENJAMIN BASSFORD Jr., son of ASHER & LUCY JANE BASSFORD (see BASSFORD).
    iv. HARRIET CALL MARSHALL, born 4 Feb 1852 in Calais (VR). Census: 1860 & 70 in Calais. She married 2 Mar 1873 by Rev. I. C. Knowlton in Calais (adv) WILLIAM O. JONES (mar int. has his name as

Wilmot S. Jones).

v. FANNY PRESTON MARSHALL, born 28 Dec 1854 in Calais (VR). Died 20 Mar 1865 age 11 in Calais (VR:3:311). Census: 1860 in Calais.

vi. CHARLES FREEMONT MARSHALL, born 14 Jun 1856 in Calais (VR). He was a sign painter. Died 9 Mar 1930 age 73y 8m in Malden, MA (sfh:7:254, adv). Buried in Calais Cemetery. Census: 1860, 70 & 80 in Calais. He married 1 Feb 1883 in Calais (VR:2:25, times) LAURA McFARLAND, born ca 1860, died ca 1933 (g.s.), buried in Calais Cemetery.

vii. WALTER BION MARSHALL, born 4 May 1858 in Calais (VR). Died after 1920. Census: 1860, 70 & 80 in Calais, 1900 & 20 in Portland. He married EDITH CALDERWOOD, born 17 May 1868 in Portland, ME, daughter of SAMUEL CALDERWOOD & MARY SHAW (MSA). Died 22 Dec 1947 in Portland (MSA). Census: 1900 & 20 in Portland.

viii. LEONICE S. MARSHALL, born 6 June 1864 in Calais, died 27 May 1944 in Portland (MSA). Died at home for aged women, buried in Evergreen Cemetery, Portland (obit ppress). Census: 1870 & 80 in Calais, 1900 & 20 (with brother Walter) in Portland.

JAMES & HANNAH MARTIN, p. 214

JAMES MARTIN, born circa 1811. Died 18 Oct 1891 age 80y 14d in Calais (times, SSC). Buried: 20 Oct 1891 in Calais Cemetery. Census: 1840 (3 males, 2 females) in Calais.

He married 8 Apr 1838 (harm:32, mrwc:24) in Calais HANNAH HARMON born 21 May 1811 in Calais, bapt 19 June 1812 St. Stephen, NB (kmc), daughter of NATHANIEL HARMON & LYDIA McALLISTER. (see HARMON). Children:

i. ELMIRA McALLISTER MARTIN, born 8 Mar 1840 in Calais (VR).
ii. GEORGE DAVIS MARTIN, born 4 Apr 1842 in Calais (VR).
iii. WILLIAM HENRY MARTIN born 7 Sep 1844 in Calais, died 11 Apr 1845 in Calais (VR:1:238).
iv. ELIZABETH ANN MARTIN, born 7 Sep 1844 in Calais (VR). Died Jul 1845 in Calais. Buried: 18 Jul 1845 in Calais Cemetery (sext).
v. NATHANIEL HARMON MARTIN, born 16 Jul 1847 in Calais (VR).

JOHN P. & MARGARET McALLISTER, p. 216

JOHN PATTERSON McALLISTER, born circa 1822 in St. Stephen, NB. He was a lumberman. He was of Calais when in court Oct 1854 at Machias (SJC:12:251). Died: 6 Jan 1903 age 80 in Eldsvold, MN (obit adv, dated 21 Jan 1903). Census: 1850 in Calais, 1860 & 70 in Oshkosh, WI. Moved to Oshkosh between 1854 & 1855. To Minnesota in 1878 (obit).

He married 17 Sep 1844 in Calais (VR:1:134) MARGARET ELIZABETH DUTCH, daughter of Capt. JOHN & MARGARET DUTCH (see DUTCH). Children:

i. EMMA McALLISTER, born Jul 1845, died 21 Aug 1846 in Calais (sext, g.s.). Buried: 23 Aug 1846 in Calais Cemetery.
ii. MARIA LOUISA McALLISTER, born 29 Oct 1847 in Calais (VR). Died before 1903. Census: 1850 in Calais.
iii. MARGARET E. McALLISTER, born 1847, died 1 Jun 1849 age 1y 7m (g.s.). Buried in Calais Cemetery. [was she a twin of Maria?]
iv. GEORGE F. McALLISTER, born circa 1851. He worked in the National Bank in Oshkosh. Died: 20 Apr 1874 in Oshkosh (otime & north). Census: 1860 & 70 in Oshkosh.
v. JOHN WINSLOW McALLISTER, born circa 1855 in Oshkosh, WI. Died after 1903 (only survivor of father). Census: 1860 & 70 in Oshkosh. Married: 4 Jan 1877 in Winnebago Co. WI (winn) HATTIE ADELICA RICHARDS.
vi. JENNIE McALLISTER, born circa 1865 in Oshkosh, WI. Died 19 Nov 1870 age 5y 8m in Oshkosh (north). Census: 1860 & 70 in Oshkosh.

WILLIAM L. & ALMIRA McALLISTER, Sr., p. 222

WILLIAM LEONARD McALLISTER, Sr., born 25 Jun 1806, in St. Stephen, NB (Alexander, Me VR). He was of Alexander in 1837, a partner in business with Nathaniel Lamb, when in was in a court action (SJC). He was an owner of a meat shop. Died 30 May 1864 age 58 in Calais (VR, union, g.s.). Buried in Calais Cemetery. Census: 1840 (3 males, 3 females) in Alexander, 1850 & 60 in Calais.

He married 2 Jun 1830 in Calais by Rev. Josiah Eaton (Alexander VR, cal2:47) ALMIRA LAMB, born 29 Jan 1812 in Calais (Alexander VR). (possible daughter of James & Betsey Lamb and sister of Nathaniel & Robert Lamb). Died 15 Feb 1868 age 56 (g.s.) in Calais. Buried in Calais Cemetery. Census: 1850 & 60 in Calais. Children:

i. ALMIRA McALLISTER, born 31 Mar 1831 in St. Stephen, NB (Alexander VR).
ii. WILLIAM LEONARD McALLISTER, Jr., born 28 Sep 1833 in St. Stephen, NB (Alexander VR). Census: 1850 in Calais.

* From Aroostook Times of Wed. 19 May 1909: William McAllister of Orient died on Thursday last in Houlton, lumberman, age 74, survived by daughter and son. Remains to Calais for burial. [This William s/o Ellis McAllister & Ann Ames (MSA)].

iii. ANN MARIA McALLISTER, born 30 Aug 1838 in Calais (VR). Census: 1850 in Calais. She married 20 Apr 1860 in Calais by Rev. S. H. Keeler (VR:3:174) CALVIN HORTON.
iv. CLARA PHINNEY McALLISTER, born 13 Mar 1844 in Calais (VR). Died 2 Oct 1914 in Houlton, Me (adv). Census: 1850 & 60 in Calais, 1870 & 1900 in Houlton, Me. She married 21 Feb 1867 by Rev. J. Caldwell in Calais (VR:3:224) HUDSON TOWNSEND FRISBIE, born 26 July 1839 in Houlton, ME (VR), son of TIMOTHY & MARY E. FRISBIE. He was a merchant. Died Feb 1908 (wife's obit). Census: 1860, 70 &1900 in Houlton.
v. MARY C. McALLISTER, born circa 1851 in Calais. Census: 1860 in Calais.

JAMES & LOUISA McCURDY, p. 211

CHANDLER McCURDY, Sr. born 1812 in Maine, and married 3 Mar 1834 by Rev. Alexander MacLean in St. Andrews, NB (CCMR:742) RACHEL SIMPSON of Maine. They arrived in Oshkosh, WI, with their children (seven in all, not known if they were all born in Maine) arriving on 10 Oct. 1850. Chandler served in the Civil War as a Pvt. In Co. B, 37th Regt., Wis. Vol. Inf. He died at the Soldiers' Home at Milwaukee, WI, April 1885. His brother was James McCurdy, Sr. (see below) and he had a sister, Lucy who married John Buckstaff, Sr. of St. Andrews. NB. They moved to Oshkosh also (cwWI:2:483-484).

JAMES McCURDY, Sr., born circa 1809 in Camden, ME (1850 census). He moved Oshkosh, WI, arriving on 10 Oct. 1850, the same day as his brother, Chandler. They probably traveled together. Died before his wife in Oshkosh WI. Census: 1850 (Louisa W. McCurdy age 68 living with them, possibly his mother) in Calais, 1860 (a boarding house operator) & 70 (a carpenter) in Oshkosh, WI.

He married 7 Mar 1832 in St. Stephen, NB (CCMR) LOUISE VICTORIA WHITTIER, born 12 Oct 1814 in St. Patrick, NB (1850 census, obit). Died 3 Nov 1903 age 89 at home of daughter, Lucy in Oshkosh, WI (wdr, obit north). Buried in Boyd Cemetery near Oshkosh. Census: 1850 in Calais. Census: 1860, 70 & 80 (with dau. Lucy) in Oshkosh. Children:

i. DANIEL McCURDY, born circa 1832 in St. Patrick, NB (1850 census). He was a sailor. Census: 1850 in Calais.
ii. JAMES H. McCURDY, born 13 Feb 1834 in St. Patrick, NB (1850 census, obit). Served in Civil War and is described as 5' 4" brown hair and gray eyes on the muster rolls, was a Pvt. in Co. F 11th Regt. Wis. Vol. Inf. (cwWI: 2: 484). He was a boatman & lumberman. In 1868 he was listed as a river man boarding in Oshkosh. Died 7 July 1902 age 68 in Oshkosh, WI (obit north). Census: 1850 in Calais, 1860, 70 & 80 (with sister Lucy) in Oshkosh, WI.
iii. LYDIA McCURDY, born circa 1838 in St. Patrick, NB (1850 census). Census: 1850 in Calais. She married, born ca 1838 (LDS) OLIVER ELLSWORTH.
iv. LUCY H. McCURDY, born 6 June 1840 in St. Patrick, NB (1850 census, obit). Went to Oshkosh with parents in 1851 (obit). Died 15 Oct 1905 age 65 in Oshkosh, Winnebago County, WI (wdr, obit north). Census: 1850 in Calais. Census: 1860 & 80 in Oshkosh, WI. She married 3 June 1864 by Rev. H.G. McArthur in Oshkosh (obit, wmr:Oshkosh Library) BENJAMIN DOUGHTY, born 27 Mar 1828 in NB, son of DAVID DOUGHTY & MARTHA LORD, he was a lumberman, a member of the Masons, he died 25 Nov

1911 age 83y 7m 28d in Oshkosh and is buried in Riverside Cemetery, Oshkosh (atlas:32, death rec.). He went to Maine as a child then to California, back to Maine before moving to Oshkosh in 1855 where he remained (obit). Census: 1880 in Oshkosh.

v. LOUISA VICTORIA McCURDY, born 6 Jun 1842 in St. Patrick, NB (1850 census). She was a teacher. Died 17 Jan 1923 in Eagle Gorge, WA (LDS). Census: 1850 in Calais, 1860 & 70 in Oshkosh, WI. She married 25 Dec 1862 by J. H. Morrison in Oshkosh (marriage cert.) CHARLES STEVENSON, born 2 Sept 1840 in St. Andrews, NB, son of CHARLES STEVENSON & REBECCA SIMEZ. He was a shoemaker. He died 13 Jan 1921 in Oshkosh (LDS). Census: 1860 & 70 in Oshkosh. They resided in Oshkosh, WI.

vi. MARY McCURDY, born circa 1845 in St. Patrick, NB (1850 census). Census: 1850 in Calais, she does not appear in 1860 in Oshkosh with rest of family.

vii. WILLIAM HENRY McCURDY, born 15 Apr 1847 in Calais (VR). He does not appear in 1850 census in Calais with rest of family.

viii. SARAH A. McCURDY born circa 1850 in Calais. Died probably before 1878 when husband remarried. Census: 1850 in Calais, 1860 & 70 in Oshkosh, WI. She married 29 Dec 1870 by W.H. Whitelaw in Oshkosh, WI (marriage cert.) DARIUS DeFOREST HERSEY, born 23 Jan 1841 in Pembroke, Me, son of CALEB HERSEY & ELIZABETH DeFOREST of Pembroke, he was a carpenter, he died 22 Feb 1925 in Oshkosh, WI (wldr, obit north). He married 2nd 16 July 1878 in Oshkosh Mary E. Jackson, daughter of S. B. & Abigail P. Jackson (obit, marriage rec.).

JOHN & MARGARET A. McCURDY, p. 211

JOHN McCURDY, born circa 1810. He was a shoemaker. Died 15 Jun 1881 in San Diego, CA (bunnell). Census: 1850 in Calais.

He married MARGARET A. (_____), born circa 1802 in Columbia, ME (1850 census). Census: 1850 in Calais. Children:

i. SARAH A. McCURDY, born circa 1833. Died 10 May 1844 age 11y 8m in Calais (gaz, g.s.).

ii. LYDIA E. McCURDY, born, circa 1835 in Robbinston Me (1850 census). Died before 1856 when her husband remarried. Census: 1850 in Calais. She married 2 Mar 1853 in Calais (FJ, VR:3:160 has date 25 Mar). JAMES DAVIS SAWYER, born 5 Oct 1830 in Portland, ME, son of CHARLES & SARAH SAWYER, died 9 July 1892 (sawofne:604)

iii. GEORGE W. McCURDY, born circa 1838 in Robbinston Me (1850 census). Census: 1850 in Calais.

iv. SAMUEL A. McCURDY, born circa 1839 in Robbinston Me (1850 census). Census: 1850 in Calais.

v. JOHN R. McCURDY, born May 1842, died 24 Jan 1843 age 8m 19d in Calais (FJ, adv, g.s.). Buried in Calais Cemetery.

vi. JOHN RANDOLPH McCURDY, born 28 Mar 1845 in Calais (VR). Census: 1850 in Calais.

vii. ALBERT MADISON McCURDY, born 3 Sep 1847 in Calais (VR). Census: 1850 in Calais.

viii. JAMES FREDERICK McCURDY, (poss. son) born ca 1851 in Calais, married 30 Sept 1874 in Ophir, CA, CAROLINE ELLEN RHOADES, daughter of DANIEL & MARY RHOADES (LDS anc. file).

WILLIAM & DEBORAH M. McDONALD, p. 215

WILLIAM McDONALD, born circa 1826 in Topsham, ME (1850 census), son of MAJOR McDONALD b. Gardiner & MARGARET WELLS (MSA). He enlisted in Civil War at age 37 in Co D 6th Me Inf. a laborer with blue eyes and brown hair b. New Brunswick (cwcard, NRMS:241). He worked in a sawmill and was a machinist. Died on 3 June 1894 age 77 in Milltown, ME (east:516, MSA, Adv). Buried in Calais Cemetery. Census: 1850, 60 & 70 in Calais.

He married 10 Nov 1844 by Charles L. Browning in Calais (mrwc:44) DEBORAH M. WADSWORTH, daughter of ABNER WADSWORTH AND JENNETT H. TOWERS (see WADSWORTH). Children:

i. FRANCES JENNETTE McDONALD, born 29 Nov 1845 in Calais, died 19 Jun 1853 in Calais (VR:3:302). Buried in Calais Cemetery. Census: 1850 in Calais.

ii. WILLIAM RANDOLD McDONALD, born circa 1848 in Calais. Died after 1913. He was called home when his father died (obit 1894), had been away many years. Census: 1850 & 60 in Calais. He married 1st (int.) 21 Apr 1854 in Calais (VR:1:58) LYDIA ELTHEA CALLAGHAN (see CALLAGHAN). He possibly

married 2nd (int) 3 June 1872 LILLIAN K. BENNETT of Houlton, ME (VR)
iii. JAMES M. McDONALD, born circa 1850 in Calais. Died 26 Jul 1913 in Calais (MSA). Census: 1850, 60 & 70 in Calais.
iv. LUCY McDONALD, born circa 1852 in Calais. Census: 1860 & 70 in Calais.
v. ARMELIA/ARZELIA McDONALD, born circa 1856 in Calais. Died after 1908 when she was mentioned in a clipping of W.W. Smith, her uncle. Census: 1860 & 70 in Calais.
vi. HELEN McDONALD, born circa 1861 in Calais. Census: 1870 in Calais.
vii. JENNIE McDONALD, born circa 1864 in Calais. Census: 1870 in Calais.
viii. GRACE McDONALD, born circa 1869 in Calais. Census: 1870 in Calais.

THOMAS & CATHARINE McGERRY, p. 200

THOMAS McGERRY/ McGARRY, born in Ireland. He was a customs agent. Died 17 Aug 1846 in Calais (VR:1:229).

He married CATHERINE (_____), born circa 1815 in Ireland (1850 census). Died 9 Feb 1887 age 79 in Calais (SCC). (prbt: will dated 8 Feb 1887). Census: 1850 & 60 in Calais. Children:

i. NOAH SMITH McGERRY, born 25 Dec 1840 in Calais (VR). Served in Civil War, Co. B 6th Maine, he was wounded at Rappahannock Station, lost his right arm (NRMS:232, enlist, trib). He was a stonemason, policeman and customs agent. Died 25 Sept 1906 in Calais (MSA). Census: 1850, 60, 70 & 1900 in Calais. He married 1st 26 Feb 1868 by Rev. Seth Beal in Calais (VR:3:226) ELIZABETH 'LIZZIE' MONDIE of St. Stephen, NB, born in NB, died 16 Aug 1879 (times), resided US 12 years (Mortality Schedule 1880 census). He married 2nd on Friday, 15 Sept 1882 in Calais, by Rev. Charles McCully (times) ANNIE DORCAS DAVIDSON, daughter of GEORGE & SARAH DAVIDSON. Census: 1870 (she was a dressmaker) in Calais (see DAVIDSON).
ii. JOHN EDWARD McGERRY, born 25 Dec 1840 in Calais (VR). Died 21 Nov 1842 in Calais (VR:1:235)
iii. JOHN McGERRY, born 11 May 1844 in Calais (VR). Died 14 Oct 1847 in Calais (VR:1:235).
iv. GRACE ENNIS McGERRY, born 27 May 1846 in Calais (VR). Died between 1887 and 1900 census. She and three children mentioned in mother's will. Census: 1850 & 60 in Calais. She married ca 1870 JEREMIAH E. FITZPATRICK born Apr 1850 in NB. Census: 1900 (with his three youngest children).

ALBERT & JOANNA McGLAFFLIN, p. 194
{This name has various spellings from the original McLochland}

JOHN McGLAUFLIN, born in Charleston, NH 11 Oct 1798, son of JAMES McGLAUFLIN, died 6 Dec 1850 in Charlotte, Me. John, a farmer in Charlotte, married HANNAH SMITH ca 1819. She was born in Dennysville, Me, 11 Feb 1805, died Presque Isle, Me 5 Jan 1880. Their two oldest children of 18, Albert and Lewis lived in Calais for a short time (cutter:1:171).

ALBERT McGLAFFLIN, born, 31 Dec 1819 in Plantation # 3, ME (Charlotte, Me VR). He was a blacksmith and a Baptist Minister (cutter:171, goffs:306). Died 24 May 1891 in Mapleton, Me (adv). Census: 1850 in Calais.

He married 1st 7 Feb 1841 in Calais (mrwc:31) JOANNA NOBLE, born 20 June 1820 in Charlotte (VR), daughter of ROBERT NOBLE & HANNAH GREENLAW (TWB).

- note: article from Adv of 22 Jan 1873 p. 2 – *A daughter of Elder Albert McGlaufin of Franklin, NH, died about five o'clock Sunday afternoon, Jan 5, probable from an injury received in a mill in that place on Thursday last; and Mrs. McGlauflin died during Sunday night, the nature of her disease not having been determined on Saturday. The daughter was about fifteen years old, and the mother about fifty.*

Census: 1850 in Calais. Children:

i. LOUISA/LORENA McGLAFFLIN, born 6 Dec 1841 in Calais, died 27 Dec 1842 age 1y 21d in Calais (VR:1:234, obit gaz, adv).
ii. CLARINDA McGLAFFLIN, born 28 Mar 1843 in Calais. Census: 1850 in Calais.
iii. ERASTUS McGLAFFLIN, born 9 Jan 1845 in Calais. Census: 1850 in Calais.
iv. ORELLIA McGLAFFLIN, born 21 Nov 1846 in Calais.
v. ALBERT F. McGLAFFLIN, born 20 Oct 1849 in Calais (goffs:306). He was a blacksmith. Census: 1850

in Calais. He married 17 May 1882 CLARA MARTHA MURPHY of Garland, Me., b. 20 Sept 1853, daughter of SAMUEL MURPHY & MARTHA MAXFIELD. They resided in Maine, Massachusetts and in May 1905 moved to Goffstown, NH (goffs:306, name spelled MacGlauflin).

vi. WILLARD McGLAFFLIN, born ca 1852, died 10 Feb 1852 in Calais (adv, inf. son of Albert & Joanna McLauflin).

Albert married 2nd 8 June 1874 in Charlotte, Me MARGARET E. (GRIFFIN) McGLAUGHLIN (sic), both of Charlotte by Rev. Samuel Woodbury (east:284). {adv Mrs. Margaret E. McGlauflin widow of late Thomas McGlaughlin, probably his brother who was killed in Civil War}. No children.

CHARLES & ANN McGLAUFFLIN, p. 185

CHARLES McGLAUFFLIN, born circa 1816, in Ireland. Census: 1850 (name McLaughlin) in Calais, 60 (name McLaughlin, no wife), & 70 (Charles McGlaufflin age 65, b. Ireland, living with him were CLEMENT & LAURA SALE) in Calais.

He married before 1839 probably in Ireland, ANN (_____) born circa 1821 in Ireland. Died: possibly before 1860 census. Census: 1850 in Calais. Children:

i. MARY McGLAFFLIN, born ca 1839 in Ireland (1850 census). Census 1850 in Calais. Marriage int. filed 19 Sept 1855 in Calais for Thomas Hancock & Mary McLaughlin (poss. this Mary).
ii. ROSANNE McGLAFFLIN, born circa 1842 in Fredericton, NB (1850 census). Census: 1850 (age 8), 60 (name Susan age 18) in Calais.
iii. JANE McGLAFFLIN, born circa 1844 in Fredericton, NB (1850 census). Census: 1850 in Calais.
iv. MICHAEL McGLAFFLIN, born (1): Nov 1844 in Calais (VR), born (2): 4 Sep 1846 in Calais (VR:3:259). Died after 1870. Census: 1850, 60 & 70 (age 26) in Calais. He married (int) 4 May 1866 in Calais (VR:1:120) MARY DONOHUE, born ca 1846 in Ireland. Census: 1870 (age 24) in Calais
v. ELLEN McGLAFFLIN, born 1 Mar 1852 in Calais (VR:3:259). Census: 1860 in Calais.
vi. BRIDGET McGLAFFLIN, born 2 Mar 1856 in Calais (VR:3:259). Census: 1860 in Calais.

HUGH & SUSAN McGLAFFLIN, p 215
(McGLOFLIN)

HUGH McGLAFFLIN, born _____ .
He married SUSAN (_____), born _____ . Child:

i. GEORGE HUGH McGLAFFLIN, born 8 Dec 1843 in Calais (VR).

LEWIS & EMELINE McGLAFFLIN, p. 208

LEWIS McGLAFFLIN, born 12 Feb 1821 in Plantation # 3, ME (Charlotte, Me VR), son of JOHN McGLAFFLIN & HANNAH SMITH. He was a wheelwright, farmer & broker. They transferred from the Congregational Church in Calais to the Methodist Church in Almeda CA 31 Oct 1855 (congo). They went to California in 1863 (Emeline's obit). Died before 1902 in Sacramento, CA. Census: 1850 in Calais.

He married 12 Feb 1842 in Pembroke Me (VR) by William Woodworth, JP, EMELINE WARD born circa 1820 in Wellington, NB (1850 census) (poss. d/o Elijah & Lydia Ward). Died 23 Jan 1902 age 82 in Alameda, CA (adv, survived by son, L.W. McGlauflin, 2 dau. F. D. Travellar and Mrs. Annie B. Jamison Bartlett, she resided with Mrs. Travellar). Census: 1850 in Calais. Children:

i. ARIALLAH BARKER McGLAFFLIN, born 14 Dec 1843 in Calais (VR). Census: 1850 in Calais.
ii. LEWIS WEBSTER McGLAFFLIN, born 26 May 1846 in Calais (VR). Died after 1902 Census: 1850 in Calais. [Adv of 10 May 1882 – Webster L. McGlauflin son of Lewis, formerly of Calais now of San Francisco, CA is in Calais visiting with his wife].

DANIEL & CLARISSA McLEAN, p. 203

DANIEL McLEAN, born circa 1809 in St. George NB (g.s.). Died circa 1868 (g.s.). Buried in Calais Cemetery. Census: 1850 & 60 in Calais.

He married CLARISSA (_____), born circa 1812 in St. George NB (g.s.). Died circa 1896 (g.s.). Buried in Calais Cemetery. Census: 1850, 60 & 70 in Calais. Children:

i. LORENZO McLEAN, born circa 1832 (g.s.). Died circa 1850 (g.s.). Buried in Calais Cemetery. Census: 1850 in Calais.
ii. ELIZA ANN McLEAN, born circa 1834 in Calais, died circa 1839 (g.s.). Buried in Calais Cemetery.
iii. LORINDA McLEAN, born circa 1836 in St. George NB (1850 census). Died circa 1904 (g.s.). Buried in Calais Cemetery. Census: 1850 & 60 in Calais.
iv. ELIZABETH VICTORIA McLEAN, born circa 1838 in St. George NB (1850 census). Died circa 1865 (g.s.). Buried in Calais Cemetery. Census: 1850 in Calais.
v. GEORGE W. McLEAN, born circa 1840 in St. George NB (1850 census). Died circa 1890 (g.s.). Buried in Calais Cemetery. Census: 1850 & 60 in Calais.
vi. ALWILDA ANN McLEAN, born 22 Aug 1844 in Calais. Census: 1850 & 60 in Calais.
vii. HENRY FRANKLIN McLEAN, born 8 Jul 1846 in Calais (VR). He was a truckman. Died circa 1908 (g.s.). Buried in Calais Cemetery. Census: 1850 & 60 in Calais. He married before 1879 ELIZABETH G. GAGE, born 18 Feb 1855 in St. George, NB, daughter of KENNEDY GAGE (b. Ireland) & ISABELLA HUNTER (b. St. George, NB), Elizabeth died 29 Dec 1933 age 78y 10m 11d in Calais (sfh:6:274).
viii. WINFRED S. McLEAN, born circa 1848 in Calais, died circa 1914 (g.s.). Buried in Calais Cemetery. Census: 1850, 60 & 70, a lumberman, in Calais.
ix. CLARA E. McLEAN, born circa 1857 in Calais, died circa 1875 (g.s.). Buried in Calais Cemetery. Census: 1860 & 70 in Calais.

JAMES L. & MARY ANN McLELLAN, p. 208

JAMES LESTER McLELLAN, born _____, son of WILLIAM & MARY McLELLAN, brother of Nancy McLellan Eye (see EYE). Sworn statement from Postmaster of Waverly, IA states: James resided in Waverly Iowa, left there for Kansas; going from there to Olympia, WA in 1871 (nephew in James Eye's Civil War Pension record).

He married MARY ANN (_____), born _____. Children:

i. DORCAS JANE McLELLAN, born 28 Dec 1846 in Calais (VR).

* Note - In 1857 they resided in Berlin, Marqueth County, WI, according to probate of sister, Nancy Eye's will.

EDWARD & HANNAH McMUNN, p. 202

EDWARD McMUNN, born circa 1820 in Dromard, Sligo Co. Ireland, left Ireland 21 May 1838, arrived St. John, NB, 21 August 1838, then to Calais Nov 1841 where he since resides (filed for citizenship 24 Sept 1852 SJC:10:503). Naturalized 9 Oct. 1856 (irmch, no port of entry given). He was a stevedore. He probably died before 1866 when wife Hannah filed mar. int. Census: 1850 in Calais.

He married 1st circa 1844 (int.) 20 Jul 1844 in Calais (VR:1:21) JANE McQUAY, born circa 1823. Died Aug 1846 age 24 (sext). Buried: 20 Aug 1846 in Calais Cemetery. Children:

i. EDWARD H. McMUNN, born 21 Nov 1844 in Calais (VR:1:121). (VR has Hannah listed as his mother ???). Went to Williamsport in 1860's, first worked as a sawyer in lumber business, in 1866 was appointed as a letter carrier and continued until his death (morin). Died 18 Jan 1908 in Williamsport, PA. Census: 1850 in Calais, 1870 in Williamsport, Lycoming Co, PA (morin). He married MARGARET SMALL, daughter of ROBERT SMALL, born 12 July 1840 in Glasgow, Scotland?, and died 28 Mar 1924 in Williamsport, PA (morin). Both are buried in Wildwood (Mt. Carmel) Cemetery, Williamsport.

Edward Sr. married 2nd 20 Jan 1847 in St Stephen, NB (CCMR) HANNAH SHEA, born circa 1827 in Ireland, daughter of DENNIS SHEA & MARY HONIGAN (both born in Ireland), she died 21 Mar 1895 age 65 in Bath (MSA).

Census: 1850 in Calais. She married 2nd Matthew McElroy, int. filed 21 July 1866 in Calais (VR:1:121) and is listed as Hannah McElroy on son, Thomas' death record. He died 29 Jan 1891 age 102 in Marion, ME (east:455). Children:

* Note: Somewhere between birth and children's marriages name changed to McMANN (rayt).

    ii. THOMAS BENJAMIN McMUNN/McMANN, born 12 Dec 1847 in Calais (VR). He served in Civil War in Co D of 9th Maine Infantry, had blue eyes and brown hair (cwcard). He was an Iron worker. He died 18 Nov 1907 age 61y 11m 9d in Bath (MSA, rayt). Census: 1850 in Calais, 1900 in Bath. He married (int) 23 Feb 1884 in Hallowell, ME (MSA) HATTIE GILBERT, born 8 July 1864 in Gardiner, ME (MSA), daughter of WILLIAM GILBERT & DIANTHIA LITTLEFIELD (both born in Kennebunk, ME). She died 3 Sept 1915 age 51y 2m 25d in Bath, Me (MSA). Census: 1900 in Bath.

    iii. JOHN HENRY McMUNN/McMANN, born Jun 1850 in Calais (VR, date on death rec. is 5 June 1857). He died 13 Apr 1922 65y 10m 8d in Bath (MSA, rayt). Census: 1850 in Calais, 1900 in Bath. He married 1st unknown. He married 2nd 18 May 1892 by Rev. A. A. Davis in Bath (MSA, age 35 a widower) MARY ETTA CRESSEY, daughter of JOSEPH R. CRESSEY & AMELIA B. (Hatchen ?sp). Census: 1900 in Bath.

THOMAS McNEAR, p. 221

THOMAS McNEAR, born circa 1802 in Damariscotta, ME (1850 census = Bristol). He was a trader in 1838 when he appeared in court (SJC). He later operated a boarding home. Died 10 Sep 1867 (brack:322-324). Buried in Calais Cemetery. Census: 1840 (2 males, 2 females), 50 & 60 in Calais.

He married 26 Oct 1837 in Calais, by Rev. Mark Trafton (mrwc:23) MARY ANN BRACKETT, daughter of JOHN BRACKETT & NANCY JOHNSON (see BRACKETT). She married 2nd 6 Nov 1868 OLIVER DOW (see OLIVER DOW). Census: 1880 (living with Howard Brooks family). Children:

    i. RUTH AUGUSTA McNEAR, born 8 Oct 1840 in Calais (VR). Died after 1902 when son married. Census: 1850 in Calais. Census: 1850, 60, 70 & 80 in Calais. She married before 1862 JOSHUA C. DAMON born ca 1831. He was a truckman. Died before 1902 when son married. Census: 1870 & 80 in Calais.

    ii. THOMAS McNEAR, Jr., born 31 Jul 1843 in Calais (VR, brack:324). He served in Civil War in Co E 1st Inf.; Co H 5th Inf.; and in 20th Maine, a machinist 5'8" with blue eyes and brown hair (cwcard). Census: 1850 & 60 in Calais. He married (brack:324) FANNY LYONS.

    iii. BRACKETT McNEAR, born 31 Dec 1845 in Calais. Died: poss. before 1860. Census: 1850 in Calais.

    iv. HARRIET McNEAR, born 4 Nov 1849 in Calais (MSA). Died 13 Sep 1923 age 73y 10m 9d in Calais (MSA). Census: 1850, 60, 1900 & 1920 in Calais. She married HOWARD ALBERTUS BROOKS (brack:324), son of ALFRED BROOKS AND MARY CARPENTER (see BROOKS).

    v. MARY E. McNEAR, born ca 1856, died 29 Mar 1857 (g.s.) age 9m buried in Calais Cemetery (daughter of Thomas & Mary, in a Webb lot).

JOSEPH & NANCY MERCIER, p. 203

JOSEPH MERCIER, born circa 1822 in Canada. Census: 1850 (Sarah Christie 26, b. St. Stephen, NB and Francis Mercer 23 b. Canada living with him) in Calais.

He married 2 Jun 1844 by Rev. Josiah Eaton in Calais (VR:1:133, mrwc:43) NANCY SAMPSON. Died before 1850 (? not in census). Children:

    i. HARRISON MERCIER, born 19 Jan 1845 in Calais (VR). In 1868 resided in St. James NB. Census: 1850 (age 5) in Calais. He married 3 Jun 1868 in St. Stephen, NB (CCMR). MARY E. HALLIDAY, daughter of JOHN N. & ELIZABETH HALLIDAY. Mary, born ca 1847, died 23 Mar 1874 age 27y 3m St. Stephen (obit, adv). Buried in Rural Cemetery in St. Stephen, (rural:151 in same lot with her parents), JOHN N. HALLIDAY (1812 – 1897) & ELIZABETH HALLIDAY (1825 – 1908).

    [Harrison Mavel Mercer b. Calais, Me died 10 Nov 1909; married twice; married 2nd Clara L. FINCH, native of Atkinson, WI (DEA:15:28)].

    ii. JOSEPHINE MERCIER, born 24 Jan 1847 in Calais (VR). Census: 1850 (age 3) in Calais.

JOSEPH & CLARISSA MOHOLLAND, p. 194

JOSEPH MOHOLLAND, born circa 1829 in Perry ME (Eastport VR). He served in Civil War in Co K 18th Inf. wounded 16 June 1864, a joiner 5'8" with blue eyes and black hair, born in Perry, resided in Eastport (cwcard). Died 31 Jan 1891 age 65 in Eastport ME (VR, east:455). Probate of Estate: 24 Feb 1891 in Machias Me, daughter, Amanda J. Tucker was only survivor (Eastport VR says she died 1889). Buried Hillside Cemetery in Eastport. Census: 1880 in Eastport.

He married 1 Dec 1845 in Eastport (VR) CLARISSA DANBURY born 18 Apr 1827 in Eastport, daughter of JOHN & BATHSHEBA DANBURY of Eastport (VR). Died 19 Dec 1883 age 56 in Eastport (east:365). Census: 1880 in Eastport. Children:

i. HARRIET FURBUSH MOHOLLAND, born 18 Sep 1847 in Calais (VR, Eastport VR = 18 Oct 1846). Died before 1891. She possibly married – 30 Aug 1866 H. ALPHONCE BRUNYERBROECK (sp?) by Rev. Randall Smith (CCMR) and resided in Oswego when their son died (east:300).
ii. HENRIETTA MOHOLLAND, born 18 May 1849 in Calais (Eastport VR). Died Oct 1850 in Eastport (VR).
iii. ANN MARIA MOHOLLAND, born 9 May 1852 in Eastport (VR). Died Mar 1854 in Eastport (VR).
iv. ASA MOHOLLAND, born 13 Sep 1856 in Eastport, died 27 Sep 1856 in Eastport (VR).
v. AMANDA JANE MOHOLLAND, born 30 Sep 1858 in Eastport (VR:68). Died 19 Aug 1889 (Eastport VR). She married 18 Nov 1875 in Eastport (VR, east:297) WARREN A. TUCKER, born 24 Nov 1851 in Eastport (VR:68). Census: 1880 (both living with her parents in Eastport), 1900 (no wife) in Eastport.
vi. WILLIE MOHOLLAND, born 2 Nov 1858 in Eastport (VR). Died before 1891.

HUGH & CATHARINE MONAGHAN, p. 199

HUGH MONAGHAN, born ca 1811 in NB. Probably died before 1871, when wife & children were listed in Dumbarton, NB census. Census: 1861 (age 50, Irish) in Dunbarton, NB.

- Note - Possibly not the Hugh Monaghan of Whitneyville, born Ireland, entered U. S. in 1850 no port of entry or birth date given, naturalized, 11 Oct 1856 (irmch).

He married CATHERINE (_____), born ca 1813 in U.S. Census: 1861 (age 48, Irish) & 71 in Dumbarton, NB. Children:

i. HUGH MONAGHAN, Jr., born 10 Nov 1841 in Calais (VR). Census: 1861 in Dumbarton, NB.
ii. THOMAS MONAGHAN, born 11 Apr 1843 in Calais (VR). Census: 1861 & 71 in Dumbarton, NB.
iii. MARY MONAGHAN, born 1 Apr 1846 in Calais (VR). Census: 1861& 71 in Dumbarton, NB.
iv. SARAH MONAGHAN, born circa 1850 in U.S. Census: 1861 (age 11) & 71 (age 21) in Dumbarton, NB.
v. M-??-TON MONAGHAN, born circa 1853 in U.S. Census: 1871 (female age 18) in Dumbarton, NB.
vi. PHILIP J. MONAGHAN, born, circa 1856 in NB. Census: 1861 & 71 in Dumbarton, NB.
vii. SARAH ANN MONAGHAN, born circa 1867 in NB. Census: 1871 (age 4) in Dumbarton, NB.

NEWBEGIN H.& MARY MOONEY, p. 212

NEWBEGIN H. MOONEY, born between 1800-10 (possibly in Parsonsfield). He appeared in court actions in Sept 1831 and Mar 1833 when he stated he had been in Calais temporarily that he lived in Parsonsfield (CCP:8:167 & 7:96). Census: 1840 (3 males, 4 females) in Calais.

He married MARY (_____) born between 1811-20. Children:

i. ELIZABETH MOONEY, born 28 Nov 1834 in Calais (VR).
ii. ISAAC M. MOONEY, born in Calais. Died Jun 1836 in Calais (obit, dem, drowned).
iii. JOHN MOONEY, born 7 Apr 1837 in Calais (VR).
iv. BENJAMIN FRANKLIN MOONEY, born 5 Nov 1838 in Calais (VR).
v. STEPHEN EMERSON MOONEY, born 16 Aug 1842 in Calais (VR).
vi. ANNAH MOONEY, born 16 Apr 1844 in Calais (VR).
vii. CHEODATE MOONEY, born 25 Aug 1847 in Calais (VR).

Note * Two other female children from 1840 census ages bet. 5-10.

ALBERT & LUCRETIA MOORE, p. 219

ALBERT MOORE, born circa 1813 in Albion, ME (1850 census). He was a house carpenter. Census: 1840 (3 males, 3 females), 50 (wife's name Christianna age 39, b. Bay of Fundy, NB {1850 census}) in Calais, 1860 (no wife) & 1870 (wife Lucy L. age 43) in Calais.

He married 1st (int) 19 Oct 1834 in Calais (cal2:38) married by Rev. E. N. Harris (cal2:48 date missing) LUCRETIA McKAY, born circa 1811 in Maine. Died before ? 1850. Did he have 3 wives, Lucretia, Christianna & Lucy?? Possible: 1st 8 children born to Lucretia in Calais VR, 3 children born to Christianna from 1860 census and before he married Lucy and had 4 more children. Children:

i. GEORGE HENRY MOORE, born 17 Aug 1835 in Calais (VR). Census: 1850 in Calais.
ii. SAMUEL MOORE, born 21 Jan 1837 in Calais (VR). Census: 1850 & 60 in Calais.
iii. LYDIA MOORE, born 19 Aug 1839 in Calais (VR). Census: 1850 & 60 in Calais.
iv. MARY MARIA MOORE, born 5 Feb 1840 in Calais (VR). She was a seamstress. Census: 1850, 60 & 70 in Calais.
v. ALBERT MOORE, Jr., born 5 Feb 1840 in Calais. He served in Civil War, enlisted on 19 Oct 1861 in Co E 1st Maine Cavalry (MSA) also in Co M of 2nd Cav., he was promoted from private to Sgt. then to 1st Sgt. he died 2 Sept 1864 in hospital and is buried at Barrancas National Cemetery, FL, he was a carpenter 5'9" with gray eyes and brown hair (cwcard). Census: 1850 & 60 in Calais.
vi. BARBARA MOORE, born 28 Mar 1843 in Calais (VR). Census: 1850 & 60 in Calais.
vii. WILLIAM C. MOORE, born 10 Dec 1844 in Calais (VR). Served in Civil War in Co. D 6th Maine, deserted in 1862 (NRMS:241) He was a carpenter 5'7" with hazel eyes and brown hair (cwcard). Member of Joel Haycock GAR post of Calais, died 26 Nov 1915 age 73 at home of son, George W. Moore in Calais (obit adv). Buried in Calais Cemetery. Census: 1850 & 60 in Calais.
viii. LUCY MOORE, born 11 Jul 1846 in Calais (VR). Census: 1850 & 60 in Calais.
ix. RODNEY/LEVI MOORE, born circa 1849 in Calais. He was a house joiner apprentice in 1870. Census: 1850, 60 & 70 in Calais.
x. EMILY MOORE, born circa 1851. Census: 1860 & 70 in Calais.
xi. HARRIET L. MOORE, born circa 1854 in Calais. Census: 1860 & 70 in Calais.

He married 2nd (int.) 7 Aug 1860 in Calais (VR) LUCY L. BROWKER. born circa 1827. Census: 1870 in Calais. Children:

xii. CHARLES H. MOORE, born, circa 1862 in Calais. Census: 1870 in Calais.
xiii. ANNIE L. MOORE, born circa 1863 in Calais. Census: 1870 in Calais.
xiv. STEPHEN E. MOORE, born circa 1865 in Calais. Census: 1870 in Calais.
xv. M. (female) E. MOORE, born circa 1867 in Calais. Census: 1870 in Calais.

GIBBEON & ABI MOREY, p. 215

GIBBEON ELDEN MOREY, born 28 Dec 1815, son of WILLIAM & HANNAH MOREY (farns:270). Census: 1850, 60 & 70 in Machias Me.

He married 7 Aug 1836 (farns:270) ABI SARAH FARNSWORTH, born 21 Sept 1819 in Norridgewock, ME (farns), daughter of JONAS FARNSWORTH & his 2nd wife, ABI GARDNER. Census: 1850, 60 & 70 in Machias. Children:

i. HENRY S. MOREY, born, circa 1839. Census: 1850 & 60 in Machias.
ii. ROSWELL C. MOREY, born circa 1841. Census: 1850 & 60 in Machias.
iii. GEORGIANA MOREY, born circa 1844. Census: 1850 & 60 in Machias.
iv. PARKER FARNSWORTH MOREY, born 22 Oct 1847 in Calais (VR, Machias VR). Census: 1850 7 60 in Machias.
v. EDWIN L. MOREY, born 17 Mar 1852 in Machias (VR). Census: 1860 in Machias.
vi. FANNIE A. MOREY, born 28 Mar 1855 in Machias (VR). Census: 1860 & 70 in Machias.

vii. ELDEN G. MOREY, born 29 Mar 1859 in Machias (VR). Died in Mar 1864 age 5 in Machias (union). Census: 1860 in Machias.

- Note - Margaret Carmody Morey received a divorce from an Elden Morey both of Calais Apr 1894. She states they were married 28 May 1888 (SJC:30:346).
- Note - Farnsworth genealogy says there were 10 children but doesn't name them.
- Solon Farnsworth, brother of Abi & Mary, married Annie Lawrence (see LAWRENCE).

WILLIAM & MARY MOREY, p. 215

WILLIAM MOREY Jr., born 4 July 1816 (farns:), son of WILLIAM MOREY & HANNAH (_____). He was a machinist. Census: 1850 & 60 in Machias Me, 1880 in Calais

He married 6 Feb 1847 in Calais (VR, farns:270 says 1st Feb) MARY GARDNER FARNSWORTH, born 24 Feb 1826 (farns:270), sister of above Abi, who married his brother, Gibbeon. Census: 1850 & 60 in Machias, 1880 in Calais. Census: 1850 in Machias Me (VR).

- Note: William & Mary were divorced in Apr 1867. Mary states in her divorce action that they were married 21 Feb 1857 and lived together until 6 Mar 1862 when he deserted her and furnished no support. He has no known residence in this state and did not appear. Divorce was granted (SJC 20:318). Children:

i. HELEN MOREY, born 9 Nov 1847 in Calais (VR).
ii. WILLIAM FARNSWORTH MOREY, born 14 Sept 1849 (farns:270). Died 14 Oct 1888 age 38 in Calais (obit adv). Buried in Calais Cemetery (sext, CFL).

SAMUEL T. & ELIZABETH MORRISON, p. 205

SAMUEL T. MORRISON, born circa 1803, in Perry ME (VR). He was a seaman. Census: 1840 (5 males, 6 females), 50 in Calais, 60 in Perry.

He married ca Nov 1826 ELIZABETH T. CLARK, by Rev. Merriam (east:79) born 2 Aug 1803 in Eastport ME (Perry VR). Census: 1850 in Calais, 1860 in Perry. Children:

i. GEORGE MORRISON, born 19 Feb 1827 in Robbinston Me (Perry VR). He was a sailor. Census: 1850 in Calais.
ii. MARGARET A. MORRISON, born 9 Sep 1832 in Eastport ME (Perry VR). Census: 1850 in Calais.
iii. ABIGAIL C. MORRISON, born Jan 1835 in Robbinston (Perry VR).
iv. ELVINA W. MORRISON, born circa 1836, died 8 Jan 1844 age 8y 4m in Calais (obit, gaz).
v. ELIZABETH MORRISON, born 1 Jan 1838 in Calais, died 28 Jan 1844 in Calais (VR:1:237).
vi. ALEXANDER MORRISON, born 9 Sep 1840 in Calais, died 8 Dec 1842 in Calais (VR:1:237).
vii. ELVINA ELIZABETH MORRISON, born 24 Jan 1844 in Calais (VR), born (2): 19 Jan 1844 in Calais (Perry VR). Died 20 July 1901 age 57y 5m 20d in Pembroke (MSA). Census: 1850 in Calais, 1860 in Perry. She married W. R. SMITH (her death rec.).
viii. SAMUEL P. MORRISON, born (1) 16 Dec 1847 in Calais (VR), born (2) 15 Jan 1848 in Calais (Perry VR). He served in Civil War at age 22 in Co C 6th Maine a seaman 5'6" with blue eyes and brown hair, born in Calais, resided in Pembroke, Me (cwcard). Census: 1850 (age 3) in Calais, 60 (age 11) in Perry. [Age difference or he lied about his age, may be a different Samuel in Civil War]

ROBERT & SARAH MUNSON, p. 226

ROBERT MUNSON, born _____ , died before 18 Oct 1869 when guardianship papers were filed for his heir, John, son of Robert Munson late of Keegan Gore, Aroostook Co.

He married 15 Mar 1856, by Rev. S. H. Keeler in Calais (VR:1:175) SARAH RIOX , born _____ . She died 1 Sept 1861 in Calais (VR :1: 245). Children:

i. JOHN MUNSON, born 14 May 1859 in Calais (VR). George B. Burns appointed guardian 7 Dec 1869 (prbt).

EDWARD & MARY MURPHY, p. 201

EDWARD D. MURPHY. Census: 1830 (there is an Edward Murphy age 40-50 living alone in Cooper). He married (int.) 17 Oct 1843 in Calais (VR) MARY BRENNAN. Children:

i. MARGARET MURPHY, born 29 Jul 1844 in Calais, died 11 Aug 1846 in Calais (VR:1:235).
ii. JAMES MURPHY, born 12 Jan 1846 in Calais (VR).

EZEKIEL & SARAH MURPHY, p. 212

EZEKIEL LEIGHTON MURPHY, born circa 1826 in Whitefield ME (1850 census). He was a teamster, and house carpenter. In 1856 he wrote a letter to the Maine Legislature asking for his name to be changed, because there were to many of that name in the area. His name was changed to LYMAN LEIGHTON KING. Census: 1850 in Calais, (living with him were James Murphy age 75 and Rebecca Murphy age 74 poss. his parents, making him a brother of George W. and Sawyer Murphy), 1860 (name King) in Calais.

He married 8 Nov 1845 by Rev. James G. Hennigan in St. Stephen, NB (CCMR) SARAH MORRIS, born circa 1827 in Halifax, NS (1850 census). Census: 1850 & 1860 (name King, family must have assumed the new name also) in Calais. Children:

i. MARYETTA MURPHY/ KING, born circa 1837 in Charlotte ME. Census: 1850 in Calais.
ii. SYLVESTER MUNROE MURPHY/ KING, born 21 Aug 1846 in Calais (VR). Census: 1850 & 60 (name King) in Calais.
iii. JOHN QUINCY MURPHY/ KING, born 3 Mar 1848 in Calais (VR). Census: 1850 & 60 (name Quincy A. King) in Calais.
iv. GEORGE W. MURPHY/ KING, born Oct 1849 in Calais (VR). Census: 1850 in Calais.
v. EDGAR MURPHY/ KING, born ca 1850 in Calais. Census: 1860 in Calais.
vi. JUDSON P. MURPHY/ KING, born ca 1851 in Calais. Census: 1860 in Calais.
vii. SILVIA MURPHY/ KING, born ca 1854 in Calais. Census: 1860 in Calais.

- Ezekiel Leighton Murphy of Calais changed his name to Lyman Leighton King on 9 Apr 1856 (Maine Genealogist May 1998:87).
- Maryetta and George do not appear in 1860 census. None of the family appear in 1870.

GEORGE W. & LYDIA MURPHY, p. 185

GEORGE WASHINGTON MURPHY, born 25 Jul 1802 in Whitefield ME (VR, obit has Castine, ME), son of JAMES MURPHY & REBECCA NORRIS, daughter of JEREMIAH NORRIS & HANNAH TOWLE. He was a carpenter and lumber surveyor. Died 1 Nov 1882 80y 3m 6d in Calais (times, g.s.). Probate of estate in Machias, he left property to daughter, Jane Sullivan, son, John B. and grand daughter, Annie Bovard. Census: 1850 & 60 (no wife with him, living in household of John & Deborah Sullivan), 1870 & 80 (alone) in Calais.

He married 1st 29 Jan 1828, by Rev. Peter McCullum (CCMR:124). LYDIA A. McCURDY, born in Red Beach Me. She died before 1850. Children:

i. DEBORAH JANE MURPHY, born circa 1827 in St. Patrick, NB (1850 census). Census: 1850, 60 & 70 in Calais. Her name Mrs. Jane Sullivan in 1882 (father's probate record). She married 8 Apr 1859 in Calais (VR:1:172, her name Deborah J.) JOHN SULLIVAN b. ca 1830 in NB (1850 census). Census: 1860 (her father with them), 70, & 80 in Calais.
ii. GEORGE F. MURPHY, born circa 1829 in St. Patrick, NB (1850 census). Census: 1850 in Calais.
iii. SAMUEL MURPHY, born circa 1831 in St. Patrick, NB (1850 census). Served in Civil War, Co. B 6th Maine, discharged from Cony Hospital. (NRMS:232). He was a millman 5'6" with blue eyes and brown hair (cwcard). Census: 1850 in Calais.
iv. JOHN B. MURPHY, born circa 1833 in St. Patrick, NB (1850 census). He served in Civil War, he was a lumber surveyor enlisted 17 Sept 1861 in Co H of 9th Me Inf. was 5'8" with blue eyes and auburn hair (cwcard). He served several terms as alderman in Calais and as Overseer of the Poor and Insane (obit). Died 25 Sep 1907 age 73y 3m 23d in Calais (sfh:1:24, MSA, obit adv). Buried in Calais Cemetery. Census: 1850, 1860 (there is a John Murphy age 27 living with John Crangle family), 70, 80 & 1900 in Calais. He married 3

Nov 1860 in Calais (VR, dea:13:78) FANNY STEPHENSON, born ca 1838 in St. Stephen, NB, daughter of JAMES STEPHENSON (MSA). She died 12 Apr 1915 age 77 in Calais (MSA, obit adv). Census: 70, 80, 1900 & 1910 in Calais.

v. ELISHA MURPHY, born circa 1840 in St. Patrick, NB (1850 census). He was a lumber surveyor. Died ? Census: 1850 & 70 in Calais. [Calais Adv of 8 Oct 1902, Elisha Murphy of Eureka, CA is visiting relatives in Calais, his 1st visit in 27 years, also from Calais Adv of 22 Sept 1915, Elisha Murphy died Sept 1915, funeral 17th Sept in Eureka, CA, where he resided for last 40 years. He was a veteran of the Civil War, a Lt. in the Cavalry, member of the Elks Lodge]. He may have married (int) 1 Nov 1866 (VR:1:124) HARRIET WOODBURY a dressmaker (age 25) in 1870 census (see WOODBURY).

vi. BRYON W. MURPHY, born 19 Jun 1844 in Calais (VR). He was a house joiner. He served in the Civil War as a sergeant in Co M 1st Maine Heavy Artillery He was wounded by a shot in the head 22 June 1864 (heavy:396). He was a laborer 5'7" with gray eyes and brown hair (cwcard). He was a house joiner and later a fisherman in Gloucester, MA (obit). He was admitted to Togus 24 Oct 1916 and died: 29 Jan 1933 age 88y 7m 10d at Togus Veterans Hospital (obit KJ). Buried Forest City Cemetery So. Portland (cwcard). Census: 1850, 60 & 70 in Calais, 1920 in Veteran's hospital in Augusta, ME. He was survived by a niece, Mrs. Frank Martin of South Portland, ME and was unmarried.

vii. JAMES R. F. MURPHY, born 14 Apr 1847 in Calais (VR). Census: 1850 in Calais.

viii. ALBION MURPHY, born circa 1849 in Calais (unable to determine if son of 1st or 2nd wife). Census: 1850 (age 10/12) in Calais. [is this name an error? Why isn't Georgianna listed in 1850?]

ix. GEORGIANNA H. MURPHY, born ca 1849 (age 11 in 1860 census, in household of John Sullivan). Died: 19 Sept 1920 in Augusta, Me (MSA). Census: 1860, 1880 (age 23), 1900 (age 44) in Calais. She married 10 Oct 1871 in Calais (VR:3:238, union) WILLIAM BOVARD, born ca 1842 in St. John, NB, son of JOSEPH BOVARD (b. Ire.). Died: 1 Apr 1822 age 80y 2m in Calais (MSA). Census: 1880, 1900 & 20 in Calais.

He married 2nd ELIZA BRADFORD second daughter of BENJAMIN BRADFORD of St. Andrews, born circa 1811 in St. Andrews, NB (1850 census). She died 19 Sept 1858 in Calais (VSNB:17:1633). Census: 1850 in Calais. Children:

x. MELBOURNE MURPHY, born circa 1851 in Calais. Died 15 Aug 1873 age 21y 3m 3d in Calais (g.s., fisher). Buried in Calais Cemetery. Census: 1860 & 70 in Calais. He married 31 Aug 1871 in St. Stephen, N B (CCMR) EMMA SARAH MCDONALD (or Marshall). She married 2nd 10 July 1878 Daniel Ferris, Jr. in Charlotte, Me (VR, fisher).

JOHN & CATHARINE MURPHY, p. 216

JOHN MURPHY, born circa 1817 in Ireland. Died before 1860 (not in census). Census: 1850 in Calais. [Sexton's record has a John Murphy buried 3 Mar 1887 age 69]. [a John Murphy b. ca 1770 in Ireland applied for citizenship 25 July 1836 may possibly be the father of this John Murphy (SJC:8:39)].

He married 7 Aug 1841 in St. Stephen, N B (CCMR) CATHARINE BARRY born circa 1817 in Ireland. Died after 1870. Census: 1850, 60 & 70 in Calais. Children:

i. PATRICK H. MURPHY, born 3 Jun 1842 in Calais (VR). He enlisted in Civil War 5 Jan 1863 in Co D 7th Me Inf. was a millman 5'8" with blue eyes and light hair, died of disease 24 May 1863 (cwcard). Census: 1850 & 60 in Calais.

ii. ROBERT MURPHY, born 12 Jun 1845 in Calais (VR). He worked in mills. Died 1 Jul 1906 age 61y 18d in Calais (MSA). Census: 1850, 60 & 70 in Calais. He married (1901 Dir. & his death rec.) MARY A. McGIBBON, born in NB, daughter of RICHARD McGIBBON (b. Ire) & ANN McGLINCHEY (b. NB). She died 21 Jan/June 1914 age 66 in Calais (MSA).

iii. MICHAEL MURPHY, born 17 Jan 1848 in Calais (VR). He worked in mills. Census: 1850, 60 & 70 in Calais.

iv. WINIFRED MURPHY, born circa 1851 in Calais. Census: 1860 in Calais.

v. CATHARINE MURPHY, born circa 1853 in Calais. Census: 1860 in Calais.

SAWYER & MARGARET MURPHY, p. 222

SAWYER W. MURPHY, born 4 Apr 1808 in Whitefield ME (VR), son of JAMES MURPHY & REBECCA NORRIS, and possible brother of Ezekiel & George W. He was a house joiner. Died 16 May 1862 age 55 in Calais (VR, east:189, killed when floor gave away in sawmill, g.s.). Buried in Calais Cemetery. Census: 1840 (3 males, 1 female), 50 & 60 in Calais.

He married 18 July 1836 by Rev. Alexander MacLean (CCMR:14) MARGARET McCONNEGHY of St. Patrick, NB born circa 1821 in Derry, Ireland (1850 census). Died 8 May 1899 age 72 in Calais (obit times, g.s.). Buried in Calais Cemetery. Census: 1850, 60 & 70 in Calais. Children:

i. SAMUEL ROBINSON MURPHY, born {1}10 Jan 1838 in Calais (VR:1:222), b. {2}10 Jan 1840 in Calais (VR3:259). Died 29 Jun 1864 age 24y 6m in Calais (VR:3:309, g.s.). Buried in Calais Cemetery. Census: 1850 & 60 in Calais.

ii. JAMES MADISON MURPHY, born {1} 1 Apr 1844 in Calais (VR), b. {2} 1 Apr 1845 in Calais (VR:3:259). He was a lumber surveyor. Served in Civil War, Co. I 6th Maine, made a corporal in 1863 (NRMS:264). He was 5'11 1/2" with hazel eyes and brown hair (enlist, mother signed permission). Member of G.A.R. Post in Calais. Died 17 Jul 1890 age 45y 9m in Calais (g.s., east:435, adv, probate of estate). Buried in Calais Cemetery. Census: 1850, 60 & 70 in Calais He married 3 Aug 1869 in Calais (VR:3:233, union) MARY ELLEN SPRAGUE, born May 1847 in Milltown, NB. daughter of (____) SPRAGUE (b. Calais) & HARRIET HILTZ (b. Milltown, NB). She was a teacher. Died 1 Nov 1909 age 63 in Calais (MSA, g.s.). Buried in Calais Cemetery. Census: 1870 & 1900 in Calais.

iii. ALWILDA ANN MURPHY, born {1}19 Jul 1845 in Calais (VR:1:222), b. {2} 19 July 1847 (VR:3:259). Census: 1850 & 60 in Calais.

iv. AMELIA G. MURPHY, born 8 Feb 1849 in Calais (VR). Census: 1850 & 70 in Calais.

v. LEORA/LELIA MURPHY, born 16 May 1856 in Calais (VR:3:259). Census: 1860 & 70 in Calais.

vi. BERTRAND MURPHY, born 4 Feb 1861 in Calais (VR:3:259).

vii. GERTRUDE MURPHY, born 1861 in Calais. Census: 1870 (age 9) in Calais. [unable to confirm if last two children were twins or name & sex on birth record or census was in error].

ISAAC W. & ELMIRA NASH, p. 216

ISAAC WILLIAM NASH born 29 June 1824 in Calais (MSA), son of AMAZIAH NASH (b. Addison, Me) & SARAH JACKSON (b. St. Stephen, NB), grandson of ISAAC NASH & JUDITH DOWNS (prf: 423) He was a tailor. Died 12 Nov 1896 age 72y 4m 14d in Robbinston Me (east:557, MSA, g.s.). Buried in Brewer Cemetery in Robbinston. Census: 1850 & 60 in Calais, 1870 & 80 in Robbinston.

He married 8 Dec 1846 in Perry (FJ) ELMIRA SWETT LORING, born 11 Feb 1825 in Perry (VR), daughter of PETER LORING, Jr. {born 20 July 1791 in Perry (VR), died 3 Nov 1831 in Perry (VR)} and SARAH McFARLAND {died 10 Jan 1870 in Perry (VR)}. Elmira died 13 Mar 1903 age 78y 24d in Robbinston (MSA). Buried in Brewer Cemetery in Robbinston. Census: 1850 & 60 in Calais, 1870 & 80 in Robbinston. Children:

i. GRANVILLE STEPHEN NASH, born 22 Sep 1847 in Calais (VR). Died 4 Jan 1849 age 1y 4m in Calais (g.s.). Buried in Calais Cemetery.

ii. WILLIAM ISAAC NASH, born 8 May 1849 in Calais (MSA, g.s. = b. 1850). Died 5 Apr 1921 in Robbinston (MSA, g.s.). Census: 1850, 60 in Calais, 1870, 80, 1900 & 1920 in Robbinston. Married 29 Sept 1876 in Robbinston MARY JANE SMITH, born 15 Sept 1852 in Eastport, daughter of JAMES SMITH (b. Pennfield, NB) & JANE BLACK (b. Eastport), died 26 Sept 1921 age 69 in Robbinston (MSA, g.s.). Census: 1880, 1900 & 1920 in Robbinston. Both are buried in Brewer Cemetery in Robbinston.

iii. SARAH A. NASH, born circa 1853 in Calais. Census: 1860 in Calais. She married ca 1873 JOHN DILLON (prf:423).

iv. EMELINE GERRY or ALMIRA E. 'Emma' NASH, born 15 Apr 1855 (prf:423) in Calais. Died 9 Oct 1941 (prf:423) in Belmont, MA (dyerf). Census: 1860 (name Elmira E) in Calais, 1900 (Emma G.) in Brunswick. Married WILLIAM ROGERS who died 18 July 1890, they resided in Belmont, MA (prf:423, dyerf). (In 1894 called Emma resided Brunswick on daughter's marriage rec.)

v. HELEN AUGUSTA NASH, born circa 1858 in Calais. Died after 1870. Census: 1860 in Calais, 1870 in Robbinston. Married (____) BURDICK (prf:423).

vi. ALBERT L or N. NASH, born circa 1862. Census: 1870 & 80 in Robbinston. Married EVA HUTCHINGS (prf:423).
vii. IDA G. NASH, born circa 1866. Census: 1870 & 80 in Robbinston.
viii. CLARA ESTELLE NASH, born 9 Aug 1873, daughter of Emeline brought up by grandparents (prf:423). Died (21/31) Mar 1950 in Robbinston (MSA). Census: 1880 in Robbinston. She married 14 July 1894 (MSA) WILLIAM ALLEN SHARMAN (g.s., census), born ca 1872 (g.s.), son of WILLIAM SHARMAN & RUTH ALLEN. Died ca 1959 (g.s.). Both buried in Brewer Cemetery, Robinston.

JOSEPH & SUSAN NASH, p. 215

ISAAC NASH, born 10 May 1763, in No. Yarmouth (prf:392, Columbia VR). He married JUDITH 'JUDE' DOWNS, in Yarmouth, born 17 Sept 1763, in Hebron, Me (prf:392). Shortly after their marriage they moved to Columbia, ME, where their eleven children were born, the 2nd child, Joseph (see below), and his brothers, Amaziah & Joshua settled in Calais.

JOSEPH NASH '3rd', born 5 Apr 1784 in Columbia, ME (VR, prf:392). He was a millwright. Died after 1850 in Calais. Census: 1850 in Calais.

He married ca 1810 SUSAN F. SCOTT (or Frost?), born circa 1791, daughter of JOHN SCOTT & FANNY THOMPSON (prf:403). She died 20 Mar 1849 in Calais (g.s.). Buried in Calais Cemetery. Children:

i. CYNTHIA S. NASH, born 1 Jun 1812 in Columbia, ME (VR). Died after 1820.
ii. JACOB T. NASH, born 31 Dec 1818 in Columbia, ME (MSA). Died 8 Oct 1832 age 14 in Calais (obit dem, drowned).
iii. JOHN N. SCOTT NASH, born 22 Oct 1820 in Columbia, ME (VR). Census: 1850 in Calais. He married before 1850 EUPHEMIA (_____), born ca 1828 in Pennfield, NB (prf:423). Census: 1850 in Calais.
iv. ROSELLA D. NASH, born circa 1828. Died 15 Apr 1832 age 4 in Calais (g.s.). Buried in Calais Cemetery.
v. SUSAN E. NASH, born 5 Sep 1833 in Calais (VR). Census: 1850 in Calais. Married 26 Mar 1854 by Rev. H. V. Dexter in Calais (VR: 1:156) CHARLES P. MOSHER of Calais.
vi. ANGELINE S. NASH, born circa 1836 in Calais. Census: 1850 in Calais.
vii. ALBERT JACOB TOWNSLEY NASH, born 12 Apr 1837 in Calais (VR). Census: 1850 in Calais.

NATHAN & MARY NEVERS, p. 212
(Sometimes written Nevens)

NATHAN NEVERS, born 17 July 1802 in Calais (cal2:4, 1850 census), son of ELISHA & CATHERINE NEVERS. Died Jun 1860 (1860 census deaths indicated he died before Census day June 1, 1860 but his is listed with family age 57 when census taken on 22 June 1860). Census: 1830 (8 males, 1 female), 40 (3 males, 3 females), 50 & 60 in Calais.

He married 20 Jan 1831 in Calais by Rev. Josiah Eaton (cal2:47) MARY DOE, born 5 Nov 1801, daughter of SIMON DOE & MARY WEYMOUTH (doe:180) in Gardiner ME (1850 census). Died Nov 1859 (1860 census deaths). Census: 1850 in Calais. Children:

i. THOMAS OWEN NEVERS, born 8 Jan 1832 in Calais (VR). Census: 1850 in Calais. He married 3 Apr 1857 in Calais (VR:3:168) SOPHIA EVERLINE SPRAGUE, daughter of CHARLES & BATHSHEBA SPRAGUE (see SPRAGUE).
ii. LOUISA GRIFFIN NEVERS, born (1) 21 Oct 1834 in Calais (VR), born (2) 21 Oct 1836 (doe:180). She died 1828 (MSA, film so faint rest of info unreadable). Census: 1850 & 60 in Calais, 1880 (age 41), 1900 (age 65) & 20 (age 83) in Brunswick. She married ca 1863 CHARLES HERBERT WAGG, born ca 1842 in Parkman, ME, son of ANDREW F. WAGG & SOPHRONIA WALKER, died 2 Mar 1896 age 54 in Brunswick, was accidentally drowned when a bridge gave away (MSA). Census: 1880 (age 36) in Brunswick. * Note [wife older than husband probably explains various ages]
iii. RENSELLAER NEVERS, born 2 Oct 1837 in Calais (VR) [Doe:180 has name Ramsdell]. He was a river driver. Census: 1850 & 60 in Calais.
iv. VESTA H. NEVERS, born 29 Mar 1840 in Calais (VR). Died after 1900. Census: 1850, 60, 80 & 1900 in Calais. She married 19 May 1867 in Calais (VR: 3:5) JOSEPH HUTCHINS (see HUTCHINS).

JOHN & ANN NICHOLS, p. 193

JOHN NICHOLS, born circa 1805 in Armagh, Ire (1850 census). He was a gardener. Died 11 Jan 1877 age 72 in Calais resided in Calais about 50 years (obit adv). Census: 1840 (4 males, 1 female), 50, 60 & 70 in Calais.

He married before 1826 ANN S. CARLTON (surname from Sunrise Co. Architecture:67), born circa 1810 in Down, Ireland (1850 census). Died 4 Feb 1888 age 87y in Calais (SSC, east:401= Ann E.). Census: 1850 thru 1880 in Calais. Children:

i. MATILDA NICHOLS, born 26 Jun 1826 in St. Stephen, NB (1850 census, Calais VR).
ii. HENRY BRADBURY NICHOLS, born 24 Oct 1836 in Calais (VR). Census: 1850 & 60 in Calais. Married (int.) 6 May 1857 in Calais (VR) NANCY ATCHISON of St. Stephen.
iii. JOSEPH BRADBURY NICHOLS, bapt. 3 June 1838 in Calais (congo, infant son of John & Ann).
iv. ANDREW McCULLOUGH NICHOLS, born 13 Oct 1839 in Calais (VR). Bapt. 17 Nov 1839 (congo). Census: 1850 & 60 in Calais.
v. JOHN NICHOLS, Jr., born 4 Aug 1843 in Calais (VR). Bapt. 17 Sept 1843 (congo). Served in Civil War, Co. D 6th Maine. – Musician (NRMS:238). Described as 5' 8" tall, hazel eyes, brown hair and light complexion (enlist). Died (poss. he is the John Nicholas Jr. formerly of Calais who died Boston 5 Mar 1870, adv). Census: 1850 & 60 in Calais.
vi. ELIZA ANN NICHOLS, born 17 Apr 1847 in Calais (VR). Bapt. July 1847 (congo). Census: 1850 & 60 in Calais. Married 25 Mar 1867 in Calais (VR) JOHN C. WARD, born ca 1847. He served in Civil War in 1st Me Calvary. He was 5'5" with hazel eyes and dark hair (cwcard). He was a prisoner at Libby prison, from which he escaped by tunneling under the walls, he died 7 Apr 1907 age 60 in Calais (obit adv).

JAMES & COZOMY NOBLE, p. 183

JAMES NOBLE, born circa 1807 in Calais (1850 census) son of JOHN NOBLE & JEMIMA PURDY (TWB). He was a doctor. Died 23 Jan 1868 age 61 in Minneapolis, MN (union). Census: 1840 (5 males, 4 females), 50 in Calais (moved to Minn. bet 1850 & 1860).

- *From Genealogy of Thomas Noble by Lucius M. Boltwood, 1878, p. 803. Mrs. Jemima Noble died in Calais 14 Jan 1876 age 96. A year or two prior to her death a new set of teeth grew in her mouth.*
- *Found at the Probate office in Machias: Vol. 4 p. 446 – I Nicholas Noble of Calais -- say that Jemima Noble late of Calais was my mother – she died at my house in Calais 14 June 1859 a widow of my father, John Noble who d. 16 years ago.*

He married COSOMY HARVELL, born 10 Oct 1808 in Grand Manan, NB (1850 census, family member says b. Madison, ME). Died 14 Feb 1879 in Minneapolis, MN (adv). Census: 1850 in Calais (went to Minn. between 1850 census and June 1860, from a letter written by her in June 1860 from St. Anthony, MN). Children:

i. JOHN HARVELL NOBLE, born 18 Aug 1833 in Calais (VR). He was a harness maker, chief of police, ass't chief of fire dept and belonged to the Masons, went to MN in 1852 (obit adv). Died 15 Mar 1897 in Minneapolis, MN (times). Buried in Lakewood Cemetery, Minneapolis. Census: 1850 in Calais. He married Jan 1876 in Minnesota HESTER A. CHURCH (TWB).
ii. MARGARET NOBLE, born 28 Jun 1835 in Calais, died 24 May 1836 in Calais (VR).
iii. ALBERT NOBLE, born 13 May 1837 in Calais, died 4 Dec 1837 in Calais (VR).
iv. MARY T. NOBLE, born 3 Jun 1839 in Calais (VR). Died 13 July 1848, buried Calais Cemetery (TWB).
v. HELEN A. NOBLE, born 30 Mar 1843 in Calais (VR). Died after 1867 in Minneapolis, MN. Census: 1850 in Calais (went to Minn. bet. 1850-60). She married DAVID WHITTIKER in Minn.
vi. BENTON NOBLE, born 5 Jun 1844 in Calais (VR). Died 26 Oct 1844 in Calais (VR).
vii. JAMES NOBLE, Jr., born 1 Nov 1845 in Calais (VR). Died after 1880 in Minn. (went to Minn. bet. 1850-60). Census: 1850 in Calais, 1880 in Minneapolis, MN (age 55, boarding with George O'Connor).
viii. UNNAMED CHILD NOBLE, born Dec 1847, died 26 June 1848, buried Calais Cemetery (TWB).
ix. UNNAMED CHILD NOBLE, born Apr 1851, died 26 June 1852, buried Calais Cemetery (TWB).

JOHN & JOANNA NOONAN, p. 195

JOHN NOONAN, he filed for citizenship 24 Sept 1852 stating he was born in 1822 in Limerick, Ireland, immigrated from Ireland, arriving in Calais in May 1849 (SJC), naturalized 4 Oct. 1854 [*Naturalization papers at MSA*]. He was a truckman. Died 9 Oct 1883 age 71 in Calais (times, g.s.). Buried in Calais Cemetery. Census: 1850 thru 80 in Calais.

He married 1st JOANNA (_____) , born circa 1830 in Ireland. Died before 1856. Census: 1850 in Calais. Children:

i. MARY NOONAN, born circa 1838 in Ireland (1850 census). Census: 1850 & 60 in Calais.
ii. LAWRENCE NOONAN, born circa 1842 in Calais (1850 census). Resided in San Francisco, CA in 1907 (brother James' obit). Census: 1850 & 60 in Calais.
iii. BRIDGET A. NOONAN, born, 15 Jun 1843 in Calais (VR). Census: 1850 & 60 in Calais.
iv. JOHN NOONAN, Jr., born 2 Jul 1847 in Calais (VR). Census: 1850 & 60 in Calais.
v. MARGARET NOONAN, born circa 1849 in Calais. Census: 1850 & 60 in Calais.

He married 2nd ca 1856 K(C)ATHERINE 'KATE' COYLE, born Feb 1825 (1900 census) in NB, daughter of HENRY COYLE, circa 1856. Died 22 Apr 1909 in Calais (MSA, g.s.). Buried in Calais Cemetery. Census: 1860, 70, 80 & 1900 in Calais. Children:

vi. ANNA/ANNIE NOONAN, born ca 1858. Died Jan 25 1920 age 61 in St. Stephen, NB (sfh:3:120, g.s.), buried in Calais Cemetery. Census: 1860, 70, 80 & 1900 in Calais. She married 12 June 1889 in Calais (VR: 2: 93) THOMAS HIGGINS born 21 Oct 1851 in Calais (sfh:3:158), son of PATRICK C. HIGGINS & CATHERINE McGARRITY. Died 11 Aug 1920 in Calais (MSA). Census: 1900 in Calais.
vii. ELLEN ELIZABETH LIZZIE NOONAN, born 5 Oct 1860 in Calais (VR). Died 20 Oct 1940 in Danforth, ME (MSA). Census: 1860, 70 & 80 in Calais. She married DAVID C. OSBORN, born 1864 (g.s.), died 7 Feb 1926 in Calais (MSA). Both are buried in Calais Cemetery. David was survived by a widow, Elizabeth Newnham (prob. a typo in paper) whom he married in 1910 (obit adv).
viii. JAMES HENRY or HARRY NOONAN, born June 1863 (1900 census, g.s.) in Calais. He was a truckman. Died 6 Jul 1907 age 44 in Calais (MSA, obit adv). Census: 1870, 80 & 1900 in Calais. He married 27 Feb 1889 in Calais (VR:2:91) JANE E. INCHES of St. Stephen, born 27 Jan 1867 in St. Stephen, NB, daughter of JAMES INCHES & CHARLOTTE WOFFENDALE (MSA). She died 27 June 1950 in Portland, ME (g.s., MSA). Census: 1871 (age 3) in St. Stephen, NB, 1900 & 10 in Calais.. Both buried in Calais Cemetery.
ix. THOMAS W. NOONAN, born circa 1863 in Calais. He was a customs inspector before he left Calais ca 1889, he died Feb 1916 age 52 in San Francisco, CA, survived by two sisters (obit adv). Census: 1870 & 80 in Calais.

JOHN & LAVINIA OTIS, p. 185 & 206

JOHN OTIS, born circa 1800. Died 4 July 1861 age 63 in Calais (union). Census: 1840 (6 males 4 females) in Calais.

He married (int) 11 Apr 1833 in Calais (cal2:34) FRANCES LAVINIA DAVIDSON. Died possibly in 1846 [Sexton's Journal: Buried Otises wife Lot 67, Feb 1846]. Children:

i. JOHN OTIS, Jr., born 17 Mar 1835 in Calais (VR).
ii. MALISSA OTIS, born (1) 6 Aug 1839 in Calais (VR:1:185), born (2): 16 Aug 1840 (VR:1:206).
iii. STEPHEN OTIS, born 11 Dec 1843 in Calais (VR). He was a blacksmith. Census: 1860 (living with Thomas Carter) in Calais.

JOSIAH & NANCY PAINE, p. 184

JOSIAH PAINE, born 15 July 1812, Calais (cal2:3), son of THOMAS PAINE & LYDIA BLAKE. Bapt. 15 Sept 1812

St. Stephen, NB (kmc). Died 8 Oct 1847 age 35 in Calais (obit adv, g.s.). Buried in Calais Cemetery.

He married 26 Nov 1840, in St. Stephen, NB (CCMR, SAS) NANCY MURPHY, born circa 1821 in St. David, NB (1850 census). She died 25 Sep 1874 age 54 in Calais (g.s.). Buried in Calais Cemetery. Census: 1850 in Calais. She married 2nd 14 July 1863 (VR) MILTON E. KNIGHT. [his 1st wife, Frances A. died 25 May 1857 age 30 in Calais (union)]. Children:

    i. STEPHEN FRANKLIN PAINE, born 14 Jan 1842 in Calais (VR). Census: 1850, 60 (age 18, a tailor, living with Silverstone family) in Calais. In July 1873 he moved his tailoring business next to Mr. Hastings meat shop (adv). After closing his tailoring business he opened a busheling (sic) shop, which he operated until shortly before his death (obit). Died: 4 Feb 1905 age 63 in Calais (obit adv, did not mention any survivors).

    ii. SARAH ABIGAIL 'Abbie' PAINE, born 8 Oct 1844 in Calais (VR). Died 7 May 1860 age 17 in Calais (1860 census deaths, union). Census: 1850 in Calais.

    iii. JOSIAH FREDERICK PAINE, born 20 Feb 1847 in Calais (VR). Died Jul 1850 in Calais (1850 census deaths). Census: 1850 in Calais.

THOMAS & NANCY PAINE, p. 184

JOHN PAINE, born 20 Aug 1749 in Truro, MA, son of JONATHAN PAINE AND HANNAH LOMBARD, grandson of JONATHAN PAINE AND MARY SNOW of Eastham, MA. He married ANNA PIKE of Truro, where he lived for a time after his marriage; but finally settled in Gorham, Me. Thomas, one of their nine children, born in Gorham but settled in Calais (gorh:700-701, 403).

THOMAS PAINE, born 2 July 1784 in Gorham, Me (gorh:700). He was the first shoemaker in Calais (pkjdt:15). Died 21 Dec 1869 in Calais (durh:215). Census: 1820 (4 males, 2 females), 30 (8 males, 3 females), 40 (5 males, 3 females [no wife]), 50 in Calais.

He married 1st 1 Dec 1808 in Gorham, Me (durh: 215) LYDIA BLAKE born 21 Aug 1790 in Gorham, daughter of JOSEPH BLAKE {a Revolutionary War Soldier} & HANNAH HOPKINS (gorh:700). Lydia was a sister of Mrs. Frank Pettygrove (pkjdt:15). Died between 1838 - 1840. Children:

    i. JOSIAH PAINE, born 15 July 1812 (see above).

    ii. SARAH PAINE, born 25 Jun 1814, Calais (kmc, cal2:3), bapt. 18 Nov 1814 St. Stephen, NB (kmc). Died 29 Jan 1855, she married (int) 28 Dec 1833 in Calais (cal2:36) SOCRATES HILL, born 22 July 1807 in Madbury (state not given), son of DAVID HILL & MARY HOOPER (durh:215). He died 20 June 1862 in Manitowoc, WI (durh:215).

    iii. FREEMAN PAINE, born (1) 27 Apr 1816 in Calais (cal2:4, 1850 census), bapt. 18 July 1816, b. (2) 23 Apr 1816, St. Stephen, NB (kmc,). He was a ship's master. Census: 1850 in Calais.

    iv. STEPHEN PAINE, born 25 Aug 1818 in Calais (cal2:4, 1850 census). He was a sailor. Census: 1850 in Calais. He is possibly the Stephen Paine age 44 listed in Eastport in 1860 census with wife Mary E. 34 and 5 children.

    v. JOHN PAINE, born 9 Dec 1820 in Calais (cal2:4), (male born between 1821 – 1825 in 1830 & 1840 census). Died: probably before 1850.

    vi. THOMAS OLIVER PERRY PAINE, born 6 Jan 1822 in Calais (cal2:4, 1850 census). Census: 1850 (living with Perez Bradford) in Calais, also listed as Oliver with parents (see Mary S. Bradford).

    vii. EZRA KELLOG PAINE, born, 10 Jan 1825 in Calais (cal2:8). Died 26 Jul 1848 age 23 in Staten Island, NY (g.s.). Buried in Calais Cemetery.

    viii. DANIEL B. PAINE, born 11 June 1829 in Calais (cal2:10). Died 5 Aug 1830 in Calais (VR:1:231).

    ix. LURENA/LURANA A. PAINE, born 12 Feb 1827 in Calais (cal2:10). Died 26 Mar 1850 age 23 in Calais (obit, FJ, g.s.). Buried in Calais Cemetery.

    x. MAHALA/ MEHALI ANN PAINE, born 17 Oct 1831 in Calais (cal2:10). Married 15 Oct 1849 by Reav. C. Scammon in Calais (VR:1:144) DONALD GRANT of St. Andrews, NB.

    xi. GEORGE LAFAYETTE PAINE, born 3 Aug 1834 in Calais (VR). Died 23 Nov 1848 age 15 in Calais (g.s.). Buried in Calais Cemetery.

    xii. MARY ELIZABETH PAINE, born 1 Oct 1838 in Calais (VR). Census: 1850 in Calais. [possibly she is the Mary Payne who filed mar. int 24 Aug 1869 to James Gillis in Calais (VR:3:21)].

Thomas married 2nd between 1840 - 1850 ABIGAIL BROWN, born circa 1802 in St. Stephen or Dufferin, NB (1850 census, durh: 215). Census: 1850 in Calais.

- NOTE. By using the 1820 thru 1850 census was able to establish that 1st wife died before 1840 and he married 2nd before 1850 and there were two other children not who did not appear in 1850.
- Newly discovered (2000) records of early Calais (cal2), states all the children were Abigail's. However with birth date ca 1802 she would probably have been too young to be the mother of the older children and the above note using the census and the History of Durham, Maine establishes that she was probably the step-mother when the records were recorded.

AARON & MARY PEABODY, p. 215

JOHN[6] PEABODY, born 2 Nov 1766, in Andover, MA, son of JOHN[5] PEABODY AND MARY PERLEY, {JOHN[4], WILLIAM[3], FRANCIS[2], AND JOHN[1]} (pea). He married ASENATH STEVENS she died 19 Apr 1840 in Bridgton, ME (VR:6). They resided in South Bridgton, ME. He was a deacon and contributed much to the building of the meeting house. He died 13 May 1838 in Bridgton. They had eleven children. Two of their sons, Charles and Aaron, settled in Calais (pea: 69).

AARON PEABODY, born 13 Mar 1812 in Bridgton, ME (VR, pea:70 & 149). Served in Civil War, Co. L 4th Iowa Cavalry, 25 Dec 1863 until 8 Aug 1865, he was 44 years old 5'7" with hazel eyes and dark hair, resided Morgan, IA (milnat). He was a blacksmith and Justice of the Peace (pea: 149). Died 17 Mar 1900 probably at Stultz, Texas Co. MO where he resided when he filed for pension (milnat). Census: 1850 in Calais, 1860 in Maysville, IA, 1880 in Cabool, MO.

He married 14 Dec 1842 in Bridgeton (milnat), Calais (pea) MARY ANN TYLER WHITNEY, born 4 Feb 1823 in St. Stephen, NB (pea: 149). Died Feb. 1884 in Pine, MO (pea: 149). Census: 1850 in Calais, 1860 in Maysville, IA. Children:

i. MARY ASENATH PEABODY, born 7 Jul 1844 in Calais (VR, pea:149). Died circa 1886 (pea). Census: 1850 in Calais, 1860 in Maysville, IA. She married ca 1864 EDWIN POPEJON CONNOR.
ii. ALBION PERLEY 'Pearl' PEABODY, born 23 Oct 1846 in Calais (VR, pea). He served in Civil War, Co. L 4th Iowa Cavalry, same dates as his father (pea: 287). He was 18 years old 5'4" with black eyes and black hair (milnat). He was a farmer. Died after 1928, of Phoenix, AZ in 1928 (brothers's obit). Census: 1850 in Calais, 1860 in Maysville, IA. He married 19 Jun 1886 in Cabool, MO, ELEANOR WISEGARVER, born 30 Oct 1860 (pea: 287). (Possibly went to California).
iii. AARON FILMORE 'Fill' PEABODY, born 28 Sep 1848 in Calais (pea: 287). He was a farmer and stock dealer. Died 1 Apr 1928 age 79y 6m 3d (obit, Gentry Journal-Advance, Gentry, AZ, milnat). Census: 1850 in Calais, 1860 in Maysville, IA, 1880 in Cabool, MO. He married 7 Jul 1875 in Holden, MO (pea: 287). SUSAN ISABEL SHELBY born 10 Apr 1857 (pea) in Shelbyville, IL, daughter of EVAN WILEY SHELBY & VIRGINIA ALMIRA SALLEE (obit). Died: 30 Dec 1939 age 82 in Fairmont, AZ (obit Gentry Journal-Advance). Census: 1880 in Cabool, MO.
iv. KATE PAULINE PEABODY, born 9 Jan 1860 in Maysville, IA, died 16 Jul 1862 (pea:287). Census: 1860 in Maysville, IA.

CHARLES C. P. & CORDELIA E. PEABODY, p. 215

CHARLES COLESWORTH PICKNEY PEABODY, born 13 Apr 1808 in Bridgton, ME (VR, pea:69 &148). He came to Calais alone in early manhood about 1831, was a blacksmith, later purchased a machine shop in partnership with late Levi Whitney (obit). He was in the 1st Brigade, 7th Div Maine Militia as a Pvt. in 1832 (mil) Died 14 Mar 1872 age 64 in Calais (adv). Probate of Estate: 1872 in Machias Me (Estate p-1, # 466). Census: 1840 (2 males, 1 female), 50, 60 & 70 in Calais.

He married 12 Jun 1840 in Calais (mrwc:34, pea:148, wtny:232 has 10 May) CORDELIA EVELYN[6] WHITNEY, born 28 Sep 1817 in St. Stephen, NB (pea, 1850 census, beg:129), daughter of PAUL[5] WHITNEY & CATHERINE BARKER /BARBOUR, granddaughter of JOEL WHITNEY & MARY WESTON (wtny: 232). Died 4 Oct 1892 age 75y 4m 6d in Milltown ME (times, MSA). Buried in Calais Cemetery. Census: 1850 thru 1880 in Calais. Children:

i. FLORA PEABODY, born 19 Mar 1841 in Calais (pea:148). Died young.
ii. CHARLES PEABODY, born 23 Oct 1842 in Calais (VR, pea:148). Graduated from Calais Academy He

was an attorney. Died after 1909. Census: 1850, 60, 70 & 1900 in Calais. He married 1st 1 Oct 1869 (pea:285) MARY ELIZABETH MORELAND, born, 27 July 1848 at Calais, died 3 Mar 1883 at Millbridge, ME (pea:286). Census: 1870 in Calais. He married 2nd 17 Mar 1885 in Calais MARY ANN BOIES TINKER daughter of FERDINAND TINKER AND HANNAH HILL PINEO (she married 1st (____?____) Todd) (see TINKER).

iii. ELIZABETH PEABODY, born 22 May 1845 in Calais (VR, pea:149). Census: 1850, 60 & 70 in Calais. She married by Rev. Merritt C. Beale 18 Sep 1875 in Milltown ME (adv) THOMAS JEFFERSON KNIGHT of Table Bluff, CA (adv). *Not married correction in Adv one week later.*

iv. CORDELIA PEABODY, born (1) 8 Sep 1847 in Calais (VR), born (2): 8 Feb 1848 (pea). Died 24 Feb 1854 (pea).

v. EDWARD PEABODY, born 9 Nov 1851 in Calais (pea). He was a general contractor for canals, bridges, dredging, etc. (pea: 286). Resided: 1909 in Oakland, Ca. Census: 1860 & 70 in Calais. He married 10 Nov 1872 (pea) IDA MAY EDGERLEY, born 22 Oct 1853 in Princeton, ME (pea).

vi. MARY EDNA PEABODY, born 7 Dec 1854 (pea). Died after 1901 (listed in city dir. 1901). Census: 1860, 70 & 1900 (age 45 living alone in Milltown) in Calais.

- Note: The 1840 census had one male child under age 5.

LEVI & CAROLINE PEARL, p. 184

LEVI PEARL, born 21 Aug 1799 in NH (pearl). He was a river boat captain in Troy, NY, later had a boat of his own, and also was a cooper (pearl). Died 24 Aug 1894 in Grand Rapids, MI. Buried in Oak Hill Cemetery in Grand Rapids (pearl). Census: 1830 (6 males, 2 females), 40 (4 males, 2 females) in Calais. Living in NY when 1850 census was taken and moved to Grand Rapids, MI by 1886 (pearl).

He married Nov 1829 (east:105, LDS), CAROLINE BRACKETT, daughter of JAMES BRACKETT & ABIGAIL FAIRFIELD, born 29 Feb 1808 in Augusta, Me. Died 27 May 1886 in Grand Rapids, MI. (see BRACKETT). Children:

i. LUTHER B. PEARL, born 17 Jan 1831 in Calais (VR). He was a butcher. Died 25 May 1907 in Grand Rapids, MI (pearl). He married 28 May 1860 ANNE E. PULLEN of Troy, NY, born Nov 1839 and died 26 May 1918, daughter of JOHN & PERMADIA PULLEN (pearl).

ii. MARIA PEARL, born 22 Mar 1832 in Calais (VR). She married 22 Feb 1857 by Rev. D. H. Gregory PHILLIP E. EDGE of Troy, NY. They probably both died in Grand Rapids (pearl).

iii. GEORGE PEARL, born 22 Jun 1834 in Calais (VR). Died 28 Oct 1903 in Grand Rapids (pearl). He was a farmer. He married ELIZABETH A. BURDICK, born ca 1836 in NY state and died 1 Jan 1903 in MI(pearl).

iv. FRANCES PEARL, born 17 Aug 1836 in Calais, died 20 Oct 1838 in Calais (VR:3:230).

v. ISAAC PEARL, born 22 Apr 1838 in Calais (VR). He served in the Civil War and was a carpenter and cabinet maker (pearl). Probably died in Texas (pearl). He married 1st name unknown, she and their child died and are buried in New York, he married 2nd JULIA MOSS, married 3rd and settled in Houston, TX (pearl).

vi. HARRISON PEARL, born 2 Apr 1840 in Calais (VR). He was a retail butcher and had a meat market (pearl). He died 3 Feb 1903 in Grand Rapids (pearl). He married AMELIA BURDICK, born Oct 1840 in NY state and died 10 Jan 1901 in Grand Rapids. She was the daughter of WILLIAM BURDICK of NY (pearl).

vii. HARRIET PEARL, born 1 Jun 1842 in Calais (VR). Died 12 Mar 1909 probably in Grand Rapids (pearl). She married DAVID JORDAN and lived in Grand Rapids (pearl).

viii. FRANKLIN PEARL, born 27 Oct 1844 in Calais (VR). He enlisted at Grand Haven, MI, 24 Sept 1864 at age of 20 for 3 years in Co. A. 3rd Reg't Michigan Inf. Made Corporal 19 Apr 1864 and according to official military records received by M. Arlene Pearl in 1967, Franklin died either 15 Jan or 18 June 1866 when he accidentally shot himself while on duty at San Antonio, TX (pearl).

ix. THADDEUS PEARL, born 12 Nov 1846 in Calais (VR). Died 15 Dec 1924 in Grand Rapids, MI (LDS). He married 28 July 1866 MARGARET JANE JACK (pearl, LDS), born 11 Feb 1848 and died 18 Mar 1922, both are buried in Oak Hill Cemetery in Grand Rapids (pearl).

x. LEVI PEARL, Jr., born 22 July 1849 in Troy, NY (pearl, brack:324). He was a butcher. He married 1st 2

Dec 1855 in Ohio, IRENA J. BARR, he married 2nd ALVINA (_____). He and both wives are buried in Oak Hill Cemetery in Grand Rapids (pearl).

CHARLES & ANN PERKINS, p. 209

CHARLES PERKINS, born 11 Jul 1802 in Durham, NH, son of ABRAHAM PERKINS & LYDIA NORTON, (durh:303). He was a grocer and a merchant in Calais when he appeared in court in 1835 (SJC) but does not appear in 1840 census. Died after 1880. Census: 1850 thru 1880 in Calais.

He married 1 Jan 1835 ANNA A. FOSTER, born 21 Feb 1813, in Columbia, ME (1850 census, prf:211), daughter of ROBERT FOSTER & JANE ALLINE (prf:211), sister of Gilbert Foster (see FOSTER). Died after 1900. Census: 1850 thru 1880 & 1900 (had grandson, Giles Field with her) in Calais. Children:

i. CAROLINE KING PERKINS, born 20 Mar 1836 in Calais (VR). Census: 1850 in Calais.
ii. GEORGIANNA BREWER PERKINS, born 22 Feb 1839 in Calais (VR). She was a music teacher. (From SCC 14 July 1892 – Calais, body of Mrs. Hay for burial Saturday from Woodstock, NB better known as Georgie Perkins 2nd daughter of Charles Perkins of Calais). Census: 1850 thru 1880 in Calais.
iii. EMILY/EMMA COPELAND PERKINS, born 8 Oct 1846 in Calais (VR). Died Jun 1860 in Calais (1860 census deaths). Census: 1850 & 60 in Calais.
iv. MARCIA PERKINS, born circa 1850. Census: 1850 thru 1880 in Calais. She was a music teacher. She married 19 Oct 1887 in Calais (east:396). FREDERICK FORD of Minneapolis, MN.

JOSHUA C. & ELIZA PERKINS, p. 194

JOSHUA C. PERKINS, born 20 July 1816 in Hampton Falls, NH (g.s.,1850 census). He was a merchant (g.s.). He died (1) 14 Dec 1866 age 50y 5m (g.s., prbt, minor children, Alice, Grace H. & Jessie C.), died (2) 14 Dec 1867 in Calais age 50y 4m (union). Census: 1850 & 60 in Calais.

He married in Sept 1845 by Rev. Adams in Cortlandville, NY, ELIZA S. HAYDEN born circa 1826 in Cortlandville, NY (g.s.) adopted daughter of Rev. OTIS WING of Hampton Falls, NH (gaz of 18 Sept 1845). Died 8 Nov 1859 age 33y 8m in Calais (g.s., 1860 census deaths). Census: 1850 in Calais. Children:

i. ALICE ELIZABETH PERKINS, born 21 Aug 1847 in Calais (VR). Died after 1900. Census: 1850 & 60 in Calais, 1900 in Perry. She married 18 July 1867 in Belvidere, IL (union) SAMUEL W. GOLDING of St. Stephen, NB, born ca Apr 1849. Census: 1900 (age 51) in Perry.
ii. JESSIE CHASE PERKINS, born Jun 1850 (twin) in Calais. Died 7 Feb 1879 in Denver, CO (obit, times). Resided: 1866 in Hampton Falls, NH (a minor child in father's probate). Census: 1850 & 60 in Calais.
iii. GRACE H. PERKINS, born Jun 1850 (twin) in Calais. Died after 1867 (a minor child in father's probate). Census: 1850 & 60 in Calais.
iv. HARRY H. PERKINS, born circa 1858 in Calais (1850 census). Died after 1875 when he requested his share of father's estate while residing in Bergen Point, NJ (prbt). Census: 1860 in Calais.

ANDREW & MARY PERRY, p. 186

ANDREW PERRY, born circa 1802 in Scotland. He was a stone cutter. Died after 1870. Census: 1850, 60 & 70 in Calais.

He married MARY FRAZIER born circa 1809 in St. Stephen, NB (1850 census). Died 7 Mar 1860 in Calais (union). Census: 1850 in Calais. Children:

i. ANDREW W. PERRY, Jr., born circa 1833 in St. Stephen, NB (1850 census). Enlisted in Civil War age 24 in Co K 12th Me Inf. a painter 5'8" with hazel eyes and dark hair, born St. Stephen resides in Calais (cwcard). Born 4 June 1837 St. Stephen, died 31 Aug 1899 in Bath, Me, buried Oak Grove Cemetery Bath, Me next of kin, Andrew Perry (cwcard). He was a painter. Died at age 62y 2m 27d in a RR accident, was married (MSA). Was struck by a train, both legs were cut off and he died from the injury (KJ). Census: 1850 & 60 (living with Nicholson family) in Calais. Possible that his wife is the Ellen Perry, a widow, who died 22 Apr 1903 age 70 in Bath, parents unknown (MSA).

ii. MARY PERRY, born circa 1835 in St. Stephen, NB (1850 census). Census: 1850 in Calais.
iii. WILLIAM PERRY, born circa 1837 in St. Stephen, NB (1850 census). Died after 1889. Census: 1850 & 60 (living with David McIntosh) in Calais. He married 4 Dec 1878 by Rev. G. N. Eldridge, SARAH A. SIMPSON of Calais, she divorced him for cruel & abusive treatment in Apr 1889 (SJC case # 220). Census: 1860 in Calais.
iv. BARBARY PERRY, born circa 1842 in St. Stephen, NB (1850 census). Census: 1850, 60 & 70 in Calais, 1900 (she may be the Barbara Perry an inmate in Insane Hospital in Augusta age 56). She married 22 Jun 1871 in Calais by Rev. W. G. Nowell (adv) JAMES BREEN. Census: 1900 soundex only James Breen listed is age 73, born Jan 1827 in Ireland at Soldiers Home Togus.
v. MARGERY PERRY, born 13 Aug 1843 in Calais (VR). Census: 1850 in Calais.
vi. JAMES CUMMINGS PERRY, born 18 Feb 1846 in Calais, died 16 Sep 1847 in Calais (VR:1:231).

LEONARD PICKENS FAMILY
(This family added to show relationships)

LEONARD PICKENS, born 13 Oct 1793 in Taunton, Ma (1850 census = Middlebury, MA) son of JOHN PICKENS & JOANNA CLARKE (LDS). He was a joiner. Paid poll tax in 1830 (cal2:321). Died 28 May 1863 in Calais. Buried in Calais Cemetery. Census: 1840 & 50 in Calais.

He married 10 Apr 1817 in Wilton, ME (VR Wilton) VASHTI RANDALL born circa 1794 in Easton, MA (g.s., 1850 census). Died 13 Jan 1881 in Calais (times, g.s.). Buried in Calais Cemetery. Census: 1850 thru 70 & 80 (with grandson Oramendal Lamb) in Calais. Children:

i. VASHTI R. PICKENS, born circa 1818 (g.s.). Died 3 Feb 1896 in Wilmington, Del (congo, times). Buried in Calais Cemetery. Census: 1860, 70 & 80 in Calais. She married Dec 1839 in Calais (VR Bangor) EPHRAIM CHURCH GATES, son of SALMON GATES AND LUCY CHURCH (see GATES).
ii. LEONARD PICKENS, Jr., born circa 1820, died at sea, 31 Apr 1851 aboard the bark *Clara C. Bell* on passage from Rio Janerio to New Orleans, he was the first officer (adv of 4 June 1851).
iii. LYDIA W. PICKENS, born circa 1822 in Wilton, ME (1850 census). Died circa 1878. Baptized: 26 Apr 1840, in Milltown ME (lord:15). Buried: 1 Mar 1878 in Calais Cemetery. Census: 1850, 60 & 70 in Calais. She married 4 May 1842 ROBERT JAMES LAMB (see LAMB),
iv. ADRONIRAM PICKENS, born circa 1830. Census: 1860 in Calais. He was a RR Conductor. He married Martha A. (_____), born circa 1834. Census: 1860 in Calais. Children:
  a. Franklin F. Pickens, born 22 July 1855 in Calais (VR). Census: 1860 in Calais.
  b. Fannie Pickens, born 14 May 1857 in Calais (VR). Census: 1860 in Calais.
  c. Betina Pickens, born 30 June 1859 in Calais (VR). Census: 1860 in Calais.

PIKE FAMILY

WILLIAM CORNELIUS PIKE, Sr., born 18 Aug 1775 in Portland, Me.[NEHGR April 1883:212], son of TIMOTHY PIKE AND ELIZABETH JONES (cumb:384). Came to Calais in 1804. He was elected Selectman of Calais at the first town meeting 31 July 1809. (beg:22). Census: 1810 (11 males, 3 females) in Calais. Died 1 July 1818, while in an open boat, fell overboard and was drowned (beg:21) [off Cranberry point in Robbinston (pkjdt)]. Buried in Calais Cemetery.

He married 1st 15 May 1798 (beg:126, howland) ELIZABETH CHRISTOPHER born 4 Nov 1777 in Wiscasset, Me. daughter of GEORGE & LYDIA CHRISTOPHER, Died 25 June 1805 in Calais. Children:

1. CHRISTOPHER PIKE, born 8 Jan 1799, died age 8 days (pkjdt:4).
2. LYDIA PIKE, born, 13 Jan 1800, died age 4mos 1d (pkjdt:4).
3. WILLIAM CORNELIUS PIKE, Jr. born 21 Aug 1801 (see BELOW).
4. ELIZABETH ANN PIKE, born 21 Feb 1803 (pkjdt:4), died 21 Nov 1847 in Calais (adv). Buried in Calais. She married ANSON GONZALO CHANDLER (see CHANDLER).

WILLIAM CORNELIUS PIKE, Sr. married 2nd 25 Aug 1808 (beg:126, howland). HANNAH SHEPERD, born 24 Nov 1785 in Jefferson, ME., daughter of JAMES SHEPERD & MRS. HANNAH (ROMINGEN) COCHRAN, a descendant of Davis Romingen of Germany (pkjdt:4). Died 10 Aug 1854 in Calais. Buried in Calais Cemetery. Census: 1820 (6 males, 5 females) in Calais. Children:

5. EDGAR PIKE, born 21 May 1809 (pkjdt:4, cal2:1), graduated class of 1829 from Bowdoin College (bowd, alumni file). Died in the summer of 1831at age 21 of lockjaw, induced by some slight injury (Northern Light of 18 May 1831). Died 21 Jan 1831 age 21y 8m (pkjdt:4).
6. JAMES SHEPHARD PIKE, born in Calais (see BELOW).
7. MARY CAROLINE PIKE, born 27 Aug 1813, died 18 Sept 1829 (pkjdt4).

8. CHARLES EDWARD PIKE, born 5 Apr 1816 (pkjdt:4, bowcat:73). Graduated class of 1837, Bowdoin College (bowhis:508). He was a lawyer. He resided in Washington, DC, Boston, Mass., & Oshkosh, WI. In 1859 in a letter to his brother, James to told of his trip from Boston to Oshkosh. In 1860 he established the Northwestern a newspaper in Oshkosh (wiscnh: 1160). Married MARY K. BOWLES, daughter of S. J. BOWLES, Esq. They had 7 children and reside in Oshkosh, WI (1882). He died 2 Oct 1886 in Oshkosh, WI (wdr).

9. FREDERIC AUGUSTUS PIKE, born 9 Dec 1817 in Calais (pkjdt:4, bowhis:508, g.s. has 1816). Attended schools in Calais and at Washington Academy in East Machias, graduated class of 1839, Bowdoin College, in Brunswick; admitted to the bar and practiced in Calais, 1840; was mayor of Calais in 1852/53; member of the State house of representatives 1858-60, served as speaker 1860; elected to U S Congress and served, 4 Mar 1861-3 Mar 1869; again state representative in 1870/71 (biodir:1545, obit times, bowhis:535, alumni file, speak). Died 2 Dec 1886 in Calais and is buried in Calais Cemetery. A copy of his will found in The Pike Papers, box 274 f. 490 (folg), one of his legacies was $5,000 for building the Calais Free Library. Married 1846 Miss MARY H. GREEN (see GREEN).

JAMES S. & CHARLOTTE PIKE, p. 204

JAMES SHEPHARD PIKE, born, 6 Sept 1811 in Calais (pkjdt:4). In 1841 he was a Notary Public in Calais. Ran for political office as a Whig in 1844 and 1850 but lost to the Democrats both times. During the Civil War he was our Minister at the Netherlands. Among his various occupations were a merchant and bank cashier. [NEHGR April 1883]. Died 29 Nov 1882 in Boston Ma (prbt). Buried in Laurel Hill Cemetery, Philadelphia, PA (jpike:184).

He married, 1st Oct 1837, in Boston MA, CHARLOTTE OTIS GROSVENOR born 30 Jan 1810 (jpike:184, g.s.), daughter of LEMUEL PUTNAM GROSVENOR, Esq. & CLARISSA DOWNES of Boston. Died 22 Oct 1847 in Calais (VR:1:136, obit FJ, g.s.). Buried in Calais Cemetery. [Clarissa is sister of George Downes of Calais]. Child:

i. MARY CAROLINE PIKE, born 8 Oct 1841 in Calais. Died 5 Nov 1912 in Milton, MA (pikej:185). Buried with her husband in Old Ship Cemetery, Milton, MA (pikej:185). She was married 30 Apr 1881 in Calais (jpike:185) JAMES HENRY ROBBINS in Pomfret, CT (adv). He was a physician, they resided in Hingham, MA (see ROBBINS).

JAMES S. PIKE married 2nd ca 1855 ELIZABETH ELLICOTT, daughter of THOMAS ELLICOTT & MARY MILLER, of Arundale, PA (howland, prbt, jpike:185). Elizabeth was exec. of James' will. She died 8 Nov 1891 age 71 in Philadelphia (jpike:185, prbt). Buried beside her husband in Laurel Hill Cemetery. James & Elizabeth both resided in Robbinston in 1880 census.

NEWELL & JOANNA PIKE, p. 187

NEWELL PIKE, born 23 Jul 1814 in Maine (Alexander VR:83). Census: 1840 (1 male, 4 females) in Calais, 50 in Alexander ME (moved from Calais to Alexander between 1847-1850) not found in 1860 or 70 census.

He married 15 May 1838 in Calais (cal2:50, FJ = 13th) JOANNA SULLIVAN, born 17 Jan 1822 in Maine (Alexander VR). Census: 1850 in Alexander ME. Children:

i. MARY ELIZABETH PIKE, born 6 Jun 1839 in Calais (VR). Census: 1850 in Alexander.
ii. RHODA AMELIA PIKE, born 8 Jan 1841 in Calais, died 16 Feb 1845 in Calais (VR:1:237).
iii. SARAH JANE PIKE, born 25 Feb 1843 in Calais (VR). Died 21 Sep 1853 in Alexander (VR). Census: 1850 in Alexander.
iv. CHANDLER G. PIKE, born 12 Feb 1845 in Calais (VR). He enlisted in Civil War 7 Aug 1861 in Co H 17th Me Inf. a farmer 5'8" brown eyes and dark hair, trans. to US Army 27 Feb 1863 (cwcard). Census: 1850 in Alexander.
v. NANCY MARIA PIKE, born 24 Apr 1847 in Calais (VR). Census: 1850 in Alexander
vi. FRANCES E. PIKE, born 24 Aug 1849 in Alexander (VR). Census: 1850 in Alexander.
vii. GEORGE F. PIKE, born 12 May 1852 in Alexander (VR).

WILLIAM & FRANCES PIKE, p. 177

WILLIAM CORNELIUS PIKE, Jr., born 10 Aug 1801 in Calais (pkjdt, drum:128=18). He was a merchant. Died 21

Nov 1863 (on his daughter's birthday and his sister, Elizabeth's, letter in J. S. Pike file, Orono) age 62 in Calais (VR:1:305, g.s.). Buried in Calais Cemetery. Census:1830 (1 male, 6 females), 40 (4 males, 7 females), 50 & 60 in Calais.

He married 6 Aug 1826 (drum:128, cal2:44) FRANCES CAMPBELL TODD born 30 Apr 1799 in Columbia, ME (drum:128), daughter of JAMES TODD AND MERCY FOSTER. Died 14 Feb 1872 in Calais (drum:128, prbt, g.s.). Buried in Calais Cemetery. Census: 1850, 60 & 70 in Calais. Children:

i. FRANCES ELIZABETH PIKE, born 21 Nov 1827 in Calais (VR). Died 5 Jan 1887 age 59y in Calais (SCC, times). Buried 7 Jan 1887 in Calais Cemetery (sext). Census: 1850, 60 & 80 in Calais. She married 18 Oct 1861 CHARLES WAITE (see WAITE).

ii. HELEN AUGUSTA PIKE, born 1 Feb 1829 in Calais (VR). Died 2 Mar 1868 age 39y in Calais (g.s. & SCC, union). Buried in Calais Cemetery. Census: 1850 & 60 in Calais. She married 26 Oct 1858 GILBERT HENRY FOSTER (see FOSTER).

iii. MARIA LOUISA PIKE, born 30 Jun 1830 in Calais (VR, cal2:9). Died 11 Nov 1881 age 51 in Calais (times, g.s.). Buried in Calais Cemetery. Census: 1850 & 70 in Calais. She married 15 Aug 1871 GILBERT HENRY FOSTER (see FOSTER).

iv. MARTHA PRESCOTT PIKE, born 30 Dec 1832 in Calais (VR). Died 2 Mar 1901 at the home of her daughter, Mrs. Percy L. Lord at age 68, in Calais (adv, MSA). Buried in Calais. Census: 1850 thru 1880 in Calais. She married 26 Aug 1858 by Rev. Mr. Jackson in Calais (adv) GEORGE EDWARD DOWNES (see DOWNES). Divorced Oct 1879 in Machias Me (east:329).

v. WILLIAM HENRY PIKE, born 5 Feb 1834 in Calais (VR). Died 26 Apr 1859 age 25 in Calais (VR, east:167 aboard steamer "Queen" of consumption). Buried in Calais Cemetery. Census: 1850 in Calais.

vi. ALICE WILLIAMS {1} PIKE, born 7 Nov 1836 in Calais, died 9 Sep 1837 age 10 months in Calais (VR). Buried in Calais Cemetery.

vii. ALICE WILLIAMS {2} PIKE, born 16 Apr 1839 in Calais (VR). She was a housekeeper. Died 8 Oct 1907 at her home on Hinckley Hill in Calais (MSA, obit adv). Buried in Calais Cemetery. Census: 1850, 60 & 70 in Calais. Unmarried.

DAVID & AMELIA PINEO, p. 203

DAVID PINEO, Sr. b. 17 July/Feb 1774 in Machias married 13 Dec 1797 PRISCILLA HILL b. 28 July 1780, daughter of JAPHET HILL & HANNAH KNIGHT (beg:124, howland). Three of their children David Pineo, Jr., Hannah (Tinker) and Mary Ann (Bois) settled in Calais.

DAVID PINEO Jr., born 25 Sep 1803 in Machias Me (VR, biorev:375). He was in Calais by 1830 when he appeared in court (SJC). He was a lumberman and merchant. Died 4 Oct 1862 in Calais (VR:1:242). Census: 1850 & 60 in Calais.

He married 6 Feb 1832 (biorev:377, howland) AMELIA (HALL) SEDGLEY, born 9 Mar 1807 in St. Stephen, NB (biorev:377), daughter of JOHN HALL and widow of Stephen Sedgley. Died 3 May 1890 in Milltown ME (obit times). Will probated 8 July 1890 (prbt). Buried in Calais Cemetery. Census: 1850, 60 & 80 in Calais. Children:

i. JULIA ANN PINEO, born 16 Mar 1834 in Calais, died 13 Sep 1840 age 6y in Calais (VR:1:236, notice in demo, lord:37).

ii. JOSIAH HILL PINEO, born 6 Jan 1836 in Calais (VR). Served in Civil War in Co. K 12th Maine an engineer 5'8" with hazel eyes and black hair, he was wounded (cwcard). He was employed in the customhouse in Milltown. Died 5 Feb 1920 age 84 in Calais (g.s., MSA). Buried in Calais Cemetery. Census: 1850 thru 1900 in Calais. He married 1st 6 Jul 1858 in Calais (VR:3:171, howland) VICTORIA E. MCLEAN. She died 7 May 1864 at age 26 in Calais (VR:3: 311). Census: 1850, 60, 70 & 1900 in Calais. He married 2nd 6 Apr 1868 in Calais (VR:3:226, union) SOPHIA ANN CHASE, born 16 Jan 1849 in St. Andrews, NB, daughter of JAMES M. CHASE & CHARLOTTE EARL, died 5 Apr 1916 67y 2m 20d in Calais (sfh:2:223, MSA). Census: 1870 & 1900 in Calais.

iii. GEORGE WASHINGTON PINEO, born 23 Nov 1837 in Calais (VR). He was a mechanic and a painter. Died 11 Nov 1926 age 89y 11m 13d in Calais (MSA, adv). Buried in Calais. Census: 1850, 60 & 1900 in Calais. He married 19 Apr 1867 by Rev. B. M. Mitchell in Calais (VR:3:220) MARY AUGUSTA ROBBINS, born ca Feb 1843 in Northport, who died in Calais 26 Feb 1910 age 66 wife of George Pineo, daughter of (___) ROBBINS & (___) DENHAM (MSA). Census: 1900 (age 57) in Calais.

iv. EBBINE LIBBY PINEO born 7 Oct 1841 in Calais, died 5 Sep 1842 in Calais (VR:1:236). Buried in Calais Cemetery.

v. AMELIA PINEO born 12 Dec 1846 in Calais, died 5 Oct 1847 in Calais (VR:1:236). Buried in Calais Cemetery

vi. MINERVA MINNIE PINEO, born (1) 27 Nov 1847 in Calais (VR), born (2) 27 Nov 1843 in Calais (mayf:304). [Note * VR film clearly has 1847 as her date of birth but she is listed between Ebbine and Amelia which would indicate the 1843 date may be the correct one, also the census ages]. Died 1 Oct 1883 in Buffalo, NY (mayf:305, little:3:1642, howland). Buried in Calais Cemetery. Resided: 1898 in Buffalo, NY (biorev::377). Census: 1850 (age 6) & 60 (age 17) in Calais. She married 29 Jun 1871 in Calais by Rev. E. L. Foster (SCC) JAMES ARTHUR ROBERTS, born 8 Mar 1847 in Waldoboro, ME, son of JEREMIAH & ALMA ROBERTS (mayf:304, biorev:377). James was a teacher and lawyer. Established a law business in Buffalo, NY (biorev:377). He died 19 Nov 1922 in New York City, NY (mayf:305). (Their daughter is a member of the Mayflower Society)

vii. DAVID PINEO, III, born 16 Apr 1848 in Calais (VR). (b. 16 Mar, bible rec mayf:304). He was a RR Engineer. Resided: 1898, in Moncton NB (biorev:377). Census: 1850 in Calais. [in 1860 census there is a Josiah age 13 – this may be an error Josiah was married and had a family in 1860, probably should be David 13]

viii. STEPHEN SEDGLEY PINEO, born 10 Feb 1850 in Milltown ME. Educated in schools of Milltown, until the age of fifteen when he began working upon the boom, at eighteen was placed in charge of the boom, a position he held until 1872. The next year he became a clerk in the store of James G. Smith. In October 1877 he established his own business, which became one of the largest general stores in Washington County, also a meat market and five storehouses. He also was a member of the firm of Pineo & Brown, dealers in boots and shoes. He was a member of the Knights of Pythias and resided at the old homestead on Main Street, which his family occupied since 1832 (biorev:377). Died 20 Jun 1925 in Calais (MSA). Buried in Calais Cemetery. Census: 1850, 60, 80 & 1900 in Calais. He married 30 Jun 1876 in Calais ANNIE TRAFTON BROWN, born 10 Feb 1850 in Fredericton, NB, daughter of ALEXANDER BROWN & SARAH ROGERS, (both born Fredericton, NB). She died 16 June 1896 age 39y 5m in Calais (biorev:377, MSA).

SOLOMON B. & RACHEL POOL, p. 197

SOLOMON B. POOL, born circa 1820, son of WILLIAM POOL & LYDIA BURNHAM [marriage int. 19 Dec 1816 in Edgecomb VR]. In 1837 he was working in the firm of Isaac Pool & Son when he appeared in court (SJC, Pool & Son were in Calais in 1833) He was a merchant & brick maker. Died 25 Aug 1884 age 66y in Calais (prbt, obit times, g.s.). Census: 1860, 70 & 80 in Calais.

He married 14 Feb 1841 by J.P. Washburn, JP in Calais (VR:1:126, mrwc:34) RACHEL SWETT, born 7 Apr 1820 in Perry, ME (VR:38), daughter of DANIEL SWETT AND RACHEL (LORING)(SWETT)JONES (swett:90). Died 1 Jan 1899 age 78 in Calais (MSA, obit times, g.s.). Buried in Calais Cemetery. Census: 1860, 70 & 80 in Calais, she was a widow in the 1890 city directory. She is sister of Lydia Rogers (see Rogers). Children:

i. LAURA ANN POOL, born 21 Aug 1842 in Calais. Died 7 Aug 1881 age 38y 11m 15d in Calais (obit Times, g.s.). Census: 1860 & 70 in Calais. She married 2 Oct 1865 by Rev. E. W. Murray in Calais (VR:3:214) CLEMENT S. SALE, born in England. He was a merchant. In June 1884 he was visiting his ailing father-in-law in Calais from Oregon (adv). Census: 1870 (a dry goods merchant living with Charles McLaughlin) in Calais.

ii. WILLIAM PITT POOL, born 18 Jul 1845 in Calais (VR). He was a merchant and had a restaurant and billiard room. On 17 June 1872 he and his wife left Calais aboard the steamer *Belle Browne* in route to their new home in Oshkosh, WI (adv). Died after his mother. Census: 1850 in Calais, 1871 in St. Stephen, NB, 1900 living with James Clendinon in Meddybemps. He married 4 Mar 1868 in Calais (VR:3:229) by Rev. Edward W. Murray (SCC) EMMA G. CROWELL born ca 1847 in St. Stephen, NB, daughter of GARRISON & NANCY W. CROWELL. Died 18 Feb 1875 age 27y (adv, g.s.). Census: 1851 (age 3) & 71 in St. Stephen, NB. In 1880 census their three children were living with her parents in Calais. He married 2nd REBECCA (_____) who was his wife mentioned in his father's will in 1884.

CHARLES C. & SOPHIA PORTER p. 207

ZACCHEUS PORTER, born 25 Oct 1780 Peterboro, NH, son of JAMES PORTER. He moved to Belfast, Me about 1813, a lawyer; and died 9 Nov 1824. He married on 4 Oct 1811 RACHEL CUNNINGHAM, dau. of SAMUEL CUNNINGHAM AND SUSAN CURTIS; she was born 10 May 1788; died 16 June 1861. They had seven children the oldest being Charles Curtis Porter of Calais (belf:388).

CHARLES CURTIS PORTER born 20 Mar 1813 in Peterboro, NH (port:309). Graduated: class of 1832, Bowdoin Med. School, Brunswick, Me in 1836 and the Univ. of Pa 1851. He was a physician in Calais from 1836-1853 and 1855 to 1875, and was a surgeon at the Marine Hospital in Lahaina, in the Sandwich Islands from 1853 - 1855. (bowhis:435). Died 14 Dec 1875 age 62 in Calais (port:309, prbt, obit bowd). Census: 1840 (2 males & 4 fem.) thru 1870 in Calais.

He married before 1837 SOPHIA B. DYER born circa 1817, daughter of JONES DYER JR. & LYDIA KNIGHT (one of the first families to settle in Calais). She was exec. of husband's estate. Died 16 Feb 1890 age 73 in Portland (adv). Census: 1850, 60 & 70 in Calais. Buried in Calais Cemetery. Children:

i. GEORGE THATCHER PORTER, born 23 Sep 1837 in Machias Me. Graduated in 1857 from Bowdoin Med. School in Brunswick, Me. and Columbia 1859 (bowcat:475, alumni file). He was a physician with offices in Cherryfield and Calais. Died 21 Jan 1876 age 38 (bowcat:475, g.s.). Buried in Calais Cemetery. Census: 1870 in Calais. He married 25 Jun 1863 in Calais (VR) HARRIET LARKIN BARNARD, daughter of EDWARD AUGUSTUS BARNARD & MARY ANN SHEPPARD (see BARNARD).

ii. ANNIE C. PORTER, born 1 Jul 1840 in Calais (VR). She was an artist. In 1913 she had an art exhibit in Portland (adv of 12 Feb 1913). She was the only surviving child of her mother. Died after 1913. Census: 1850, 60 & 70 in Calais.

EBER & ELIZABETH PORTER, p. 188

EBER PORTER, born 3 Oct 1808 in Cornwallis NS (gengbr. daughter's mar, 1850 census = Bridgeton, ME), son of DAVID PORTER, born in NS, who died 11 Nov 1847 age 94 in Calais (VR:3:238) & HULDAH KIMBALL. He was in the 1st Brigade, 7th Div Maine Militia as a Pvt. in 1832. Eber died 7 Sept 1892 at age 83y 11m 4d in Princeton (VR + MSA has birth in Denmark, ME, adv of 7 Sept 1892 has death 2nd Sept). Buried West St. Cemetery in Princeton. Census: 1840 (1 male, 3 females), 50 & 60 in Calais, 1870 in Princeton.

He married 4 Nov 1838 in Calais (cal2:51) ELIZABETH H. BATES, born 28 Jan 1819 in St Andrews, NB (daughter's mar, gengbr) daughter of AMBROSE BATES & MERCY GREENLAW (MSA, family tradition, geng). Died 22 Nov 1910 at age 92y 9m 27d in Princeton (MSA). Buried in Princeton. Census: 1850 & 60 in Calais, 1870 & 1900 in Princeton. [Mercy Bates d. 29 Aug 1841 age 65 in Calais (VR:3:238)]. Children:

i. JOHN PORTER, born 2 Aug 1840 in Calais, died Jun 1841 in Calais (VR;1:232). Buried in Calais Cemetery.

ii. EBER PORTER, born 21 Oct 1841 in Calais, died 3 Oct 1850 age 11 in Calais (VR, g.s.). Buried in Calais Cemetery. Census: 1850 in Calais.

iii. ERASTUS BATES PORTER, born 1 Jun 1842 in Calais (VR). Served in Civil War Co H, 9th Maine, he was 5'8" with blue eyes and dark hair, wounded 1 June 1864 at Cold Harbor, VA, never married (geng, cwcard). Died at age 22 on 2 June 1864 of wounds at Cold Harbor, VA (g.s., geng, cwcard). Buried West St. Cemetery in Princeton. Census: 1850 & 60 in Calais.

iv. MARY AMANDA PORTER, born 8 Jun 1843 in Calais {poss. a twin of John K.}. Died 25 Apr 1911 in Bucksport, Me (MSA). Buried East Ridge Cemetery Wesley (geng). Census: 1850 (name Amanda Bates age 6), 1860 (name Amanda Porter age 17) in Calais, 1870 in Wesley, ME. She married 1 Oct 1864 by Rev. B. R. Rackliff in Wesley (mrwc:78) EBEN SMITH HAYWARD, born ca Aug 1843 in Wesley, son of ALLEN HAYWARD (born Sussex, NB) & THANKFUL SMITH (born in St David, NB). Served in Civil War in Co C, 6th Maine Inf. he had hazel eyes and brown hair and was 5'8 ½ " tall, he was wounded on right wrist (cwcard). Died 16 Jan 1899 age 56y 5m in Wesley (MSA). Buried in Wesley. Census: 1870 in Wesley.

v. JOHN K. PORTER, born, circa 1843, died 17 Jul 1844 age 11m, in Calais (g.s.). Buried in Calais Cemetery.

vi. HULDAH ANN PORTER, born 16 May 1845 in Calais, died 16 Sep 1846 in Calais (VR:1:232, g.s. broken).

Buried in Calais Cemetery.

vii. OLIVIA MARIA B. PORTER, born 25 Jan 1847 in Calais (VR). Died 11 July 1912 in Princeton (MSA). Buried West St. Cemetery in Princeton. Census: 1850 & 60 in Calais, 1870, 80 & 1900 in Princeton. She married 1 Sept 1867 in Princeton Me (pkbib) WILLIAM FRANKLIN 'FRANK' PIKE, born 23 Feb 1845, in Baring, ME (pkbib), son of ALVIN PIKE & NANCY JANE WOODCOCK/WOODMAN (name is woodman in prinvr:36,37) of Baring, ME (MSA death rec has Woodman, mar int Calais (VR:1:16, pkbib) has Woodcock). He served in the Civil War in Co H of 9th Maine Inf., he was 5' 6" (cwcard). He died 6 July 1917 age 72y 4m 13d in Oakland, ME (MSA, g.s.). In his death record he had lived in Oakland only 3 weeks and worked as a janitor. Census: 1870, 80 & 1900 in Princeton.

viii. GEORGE K. PORTER, born circa 1848 in Calais, died 16 Apr 1850 age 1y 7m, in Calais (g.s.). Buried in Calais Cemetery.

ix. LAURA H. PORTER, born, circa 1851 in Calais, died 16 Aug 1852 age 1y 8m, in Calais (g.s.). Buried in Calais Cemetery.

x. CHILD INFANT PORTER, born ca Oct 1854 in Calais, died ca Sept 1855, buried 14 Sept 1855 in Calais Cemetery (sext).

xi. UNNAMED CHILD PORTER, born ca Feb 1857 in Calais, died ca Feb 1859 in Calais, buried 5 Feb 1859 in Calais Cemetery (sext).

xii. CHARLES EBER PORTER, born circa May 1860 in Calais, died ca Oct 1860, buried 11 Oct 1860 in Calais Cemetery (sext). Census: 1860 (age 3/12) in Calais.

xiii. BENJAMIN PORTER, he is possibly a son and twin of Charles, 1860 census deaths has him age 7/12 died in Aug.

JOSEPH N. & SARAH J. PRESCOTT, p. 177, 181, 182

JOSEPH NEWMARCH PRESCOTT, born 19 Jun 1807 in Newburyport, MA (presc:99), son of WILLIAM PEPPERELL PRESCOTT & HARRIET DE LESDERNIER. In 1834 he was a Brig. Major in 1st Brigade of 7th Div. Maine Militia. He was a lawyer. In 1850 he resided in Oregon where he was Mayor of Oregon City (pres:99). Died 26 Jan 1881, at the family home called Deer Island in Newburyport, MA (pressp:114). Census: 1840 (1 male, 7 females) in Calais.

He married 18 Dec 1833 (pres:139, pressp:13), SARAH JANE BRIDGES (sister of Otis L. Bridges), daughter of JOHN BRIDGES & ANNA LIVINGSTONE HITCHINGS, born 19 Jan 1807 in Charlotte, Me (obit, Bridges Family Notes). Died 1 Apr 1883 at Deer Island, Newburyport (pressp:114, adv). Census: 1850 in Meddybemps ME with her parents. Children:

i. HARRIET ELIZABETH PRESCOTT, born 3 Apr 1835 in Calais (VR, presc:139). Resided in Massachusetts after 1850. She was a noted author and teacher. Died 14 Aug 1921 at Deer Island-in-the-Merrimack (pressp:221). Census: 1850 in Meddybemps ME. She married 19 Dec 1865 in Newburyport, MA (pres:189, pressp:104). RICHARD SMITH SPOFFORD Jr., born 15 Feb 1833, son of Dr. RICHARD S. SPOFFORD & FRANCES MARIA MILLS, grandson of Dr. AMOS SPOFFORD and IRENE DOLE (pressp:104). He died Aug 1888 at Deer Island, Newburyport.

ii. ANNIE LIVINGSTON PRESCOTT, born 21 Dec 1836 in Calais (VR, presc:139). Died Aug 1838 age 20m in Calais, buried 21 Aug 1838 in Calais Cemetery (sext).

iii. MARY NEWMARCH PRESCOTT, born 2 Aug 1839 in Calais (VR, presc:139). Like her sister she was an author. Died 14 Jun 1888 at Deer Island, in Newburyport, MA (pressp:189). Census: 1850 in Meddybemps.

iv. WILLIAM PEPPERELL PRESCOTT, born 11 Jun 1842 in Calais (VR, pressp:23). Died 8 Jun 1843 in Calais (FJ).

v. KATHERINE MONTAGUE PRESCOTT, born 5 May 1844 in Calais (VR has name as Catherine Frazier, pressp:23 & presc:140 as above). Census: 1850 in Meddybemps ME. She married EDWARD A. MOSELEY. He was Secretary of the Interstate Commerce Commission. They had one daughter who never married (pressp:114).

vi. OTIS LIVINGSTONE BRIDGES PRESCOTT, born 5 Oct 1846 in Calais (VR, presc:140, pressp:23). Resided: 1910, in Boston Ma (harv:546). Graduated 1868 from Harvard College. He was a lawyer. Never married, died 25 Mar 1922 at Deer Island, Newburyport where he is buried (pressp:207). Census: 1850, in Meddybemps ME.

vii. EDITH JOSEPHINE PRESCOTT, born 14 Oct 1849 in Calais (VR, presc:140, pressp:27). Census: 1850, in Meddybemps ME. Died 24 June 1924 in Newburyport. She married ARTHUR ST. CLAIR RICHARDSON who died in 1899, they had no children (pressp:114).

WILLIAM & MARGARET PRIDE, p. 203

WILLIAM PRIDE, born ca 1810 in Cornwallis NS (1850 census, of St. George NB at time of marriage). Census: 1850 in Calais. He was in Calais by 1826 when he appears on tax list (cal2:153,165,174).

He married 8 May 1835, by Rev. Thomson in St George, NB (CCMR, anglch), MARGARET BURNS, born circa 1820 in Machias (1850 census, of St. Patrick, NB at time of marriage). Census: 1850 in Calais. Children:

i. JOHN PRIDE, born circa 1838 in St. Stephen, NB (1850 census). Census: 1850 in Calais.
ii. ISABELLA PRIDE, born 9 Jul 1843 in Calais (VR). Died 26 Aug 1848 age 5y in Calais (g.s.). Buried in Calais Cemetery.
iii. ELIZA PRIDE, born ca 1845. Died 9 Jan 1846 age 10m in Calais (g.s.). Buried in Calais Cemetery.
iv. GEORGE PRIDE, born ca 1846. Died 5 Oct 1847 age 20m in Calais (g.s.). Buried in Calais Cemetery.
v. ELIZA A. PRIDE, born circa 1849 in Calais (1850 census). Census: 1850 in Calais.

JOHN & CATHARINE QUINN, p. 200

JOHN QUINN
He married CATHERINE (_____). Children:

i. MARY QUINN, born 24 Aug 1847 in Calais (VR).

SAMUEL H. & ELIZABETH RAIRDEN, p. 224
(Name Rairden in Calais VR changed to Redding in Cherryfield VR & Cemetery)

SAMUEL H. RAIRDEN /REDDING, born circa 1798 in Maine. He was in the 1st Brigade, 7th Div Maine Militia as a Pvt. in 1832 (mil). [He is poss. the Samuel Redding Bapt. 26 Apr 1840 (lord:16)]. He died 7 Oct 1870 in Cherryfield, ME (g.s.). Buried in Pine Grove Cemetery in Cherryfield. Census: 1840 (2 males, 4 females) in Calais, 50, 60 & 70 in Cherryfield (name Redding). He moved to Cherryfield between 1848 and 1850.

He married (int) 12 Oct 1828 in Calais (cal2:28) ELIZABETH 'Betsey' TOURTELOTT, born circa 1813 in Orono, ME (Cherryfield VR) daughter of REUBEN TOURTELLOTT & LUCY MANSELL. Died after 1870. Census: 1850, 60 & 70 in Cherryfield. Children:

i. ELISHA TOURTELLOTTE REDDING, born 12 Sep 1830 in Calais (VR). Died 12 Feb 1906 in Augusta, ME (MSA, at State Hosp.). Census: 1850 thru 1880 in Cherryfield. He married 25 Jul 1860 in Lowell, MA (Cherryfield VR mar. cert. #301) LOUISE R. ROMAIS, born ca 1839 in England, daughter of JOHN S. & JANE ROMAIS of England. They resided in Gouldsboro, ME in 1893 when son, George, was married.
ii. PHOEBE ABIGAIL REDDING, born 22 Sep 1833 in Calais, died 2 May 1847 in Calais (VR:1:240).
iii. MARY ELIZABETH REDDING, born 22 Feb 1836 in Calais (VR). Census: 1850 in Cherryfield.
iv. MATILDA ANN REDDING, born 18 Jan 1838 in Calais (VR). Died circa 1903 (g.s.). Buried in Pine Grove Cemetery in Cherryfield. Census: 1850 thru 1880 in Cherryfield. She married. (int.) 3 Oct 1858 in Cherryfield (VR) HENRY C. SHOPPEE born 1830 in Cherryfield, son of JAMES RUPERT SHOPPEE & BETSEY MESERVE (shop). Died 1898 (g.s.). Buried in Pine Grove Cemetery in Cherryfield. Census: 1860, 70 & 80 in Cherryfield.
v. SUSAN CAROLINE REDDING born 31 Dec 1840 in Calais (VR). Census: 1850 & 70 in Cherryfield. (Poss. married Samuel H. Whitaker).
vi. DAVID ANDREWS REDDING, born 21 May 1845 in Lincolnville, ME (Calais VR). Census: 1850, 60 & 70 in Cherryfield.
vii. EMMA PHEBE REDDING, born 1 Jan 1848 in Calais (VR). Died 29 Jan 1942 age 94y 28d in

Harrington, ME (MSA). Buried in Pine Grove Cemetery in Cherryfield. Census: 1850 thru 1900 in Cherryfield. She married 7 Jul 1863 in Cherryfield (IGI). (int.) 26 Jun 1863 in Cherryfield (VR) JOSEPH W. SHOPPEE, born ca 1836 in Cherryfield, son of JAMES RUPERT SHOPPEE & BETSEY MESERVE (shop). Died 21 Apr 1894 in Cherryfield (MSA). Census: 1870 & 1900 in Cherryfield.

viii. ORAMITTA REDDING, born circa 1850 in Cherryfield (1850 census). Census: 1850 in Cherryfield.

ix. FRANK P. REDDING, born circa 1851 in Cherryfield (1860 census). Census: 1860 & 70 in Cherryfield.

x. RHODA R. REDDING, born circa 1853 in Cherryfield (1860 census). Died 6 Dec 1863 age 9 in Cherryfield (g.s., union). Buried in Cherryfield in a Private cemetery on Shoppee property. Census: 1860 in Cherryfield.

JOSEPH & MARY REDDING, p. 215

JOSEPH REDDING/REDING, born 22 Jan 1817 in Calais (cal2:4, 1850 census), son of EBENEZER 'MAJOR' REDDING & REBECCA HILL (daughter of Samuel Hill) [Rebecca married 2nd Thomas Hill (her obit, times)]. He worked on RR and was a farmer. Died 28 May 1907 age 90y 3m 6d in Calais (MSA). Buried in Calais Cemetery. Census: 1850 thru 1880 & 1900 in Calais.

He married 14 Nov 1843 in Topsfield, ME (VR:1:142) MARY JANE FOSTER, born circa 1821 in Industry, ME (1850 census). Died 24 Mar 1890 in Calais (obit times, g.s.). Buried in Calais Cemetery. Census: 1850 thru 1880 in Calais. Children:

i. GEORGE EDWIN REDDING, born 11 Sep 1844 in Calais (VR). Died 7 Jan 1847 age 2y 4m in Calais (VR:1:238, g.s. = 16 Jan 1846). Buried in Calais Cemetery.

ii. FANNIE M. REDDING, born ca Apr 1846 (1900 census, her name Wheaton, with 2 children living with father, listed as daughter & grand ch.). Census: 1900 in Calais. (not in 1850 census?)

iii. NICHOLAS BURNHAM REDDING, born 4 Aug 1847 in Calais (VR). He was a machinist. Burnham served in the Civil War, he enlisted 5 Feb 1864, in the 9th Maine. He is described as having blue eyes, brown hair, and 5'6" (enlist). Died ca 1925 (g.s.). Buried in Calais Cemetery. Census: 1850 thru 1880 & 1900 in Calais. He married 3 Mar 1886 in Calais (VR:2: 57) CLARA A. FOWLER, born ca Feb 1854 in Blackville, NB,, daughter of JOHN FOWLER {settled in Calais in 1857} & HANNAH SOMERS (both born in NB) (biorev:618). She died 13 Mar 1909 in Calais (MSA). Census: 1900 in Calais.

iv. CHARLES E. REDDING, born Jun 1854. Died 1 Sep 1855 age 15m in Calais (g.s.). Buried in Calais Cemetery.

v. ANNA C. REDDING, born circa 1856. Census: 1860, 70 & 80 in Calais. She married 27 Dec 1882 in Calais (VR:2:23, times) ISREAL J. ANDREWS of Milltown, NB.

vi. HARRY H. REDDING, born circa 1858. Census: 1860 & 70 in Calais.

ALBERT & HANNAH M. REED, p. 202

ALBERT REED, born 14 May 1815, in St. George NB (whidd), son of ELEAZOR REED AND SARAH MARIE CLINCH. Bapt. 5 June 1817 in St. Andrews, NB (clinch:26). Entered U. S. Nov 1831, naturalized 22 Sept 1847 (irmch). He was a trader and innkeeper. Died 18 Nov 1898 age 83 in Milford, MA (clinch:26, adv, g.s.). Buried in Calais Cemetery. Census: 1840 (4 males, 1 female), 50, 60 & 70 in Calais.

He married 19 Sep 1837 in Calais (mrwc:24) HANNAH MILLER BOYD, born 14 Sept 1814, in Wiscasset, ME (clinch:26) [mother poss. Jane (1784–1856, g.s. in Calais Cemetery)]. Died 3 Sep 1874 age 60 in Calais (obit adv, g.s.). Buried in Calais Cemetery. Census: 1850, 60 & 70 in Calais. Children:

i. THOMAS BOYD REED, born 22 Jul 1838 in Calais (VR). In 1850 he was a clerk. Died 14 Feb 1862 age 23 in Calais (east:187, union, g.s.). Buried in Calais Cemetery. Census: 1850 & 60 in Calais.

ii. SARAH WHIDDEN REED, born 27 Jul 1841 in Calais (VR). Graduated from Calais Academy and was a teacher. Died 13 Feb 1919 in Calais (clinch:27). Census: 1850, 60 & 70 in Calais. She married 13 Oct 1875 by Rev. M. Jamison in East Medway, MA at home of M. H. Collins, Esq. (adv) A. W. HUSSEY of Boston (adv).

iii. MARIA CAMILIA REED, born 27 Jul 1841 in Calais (VR). Died 16 Aug 1841 in Calais (g.s., clinch). Buried: 18 Aug 1841 in Calais Cemetery.

iv. INEZ ALBERTI REED, born 31 Jul 1844 in Calais (VR). Graduated from Calais Academy and was a music teacher. Died 6 Apr 1929 in Millis, MA, buried in Milford, MA (clinch:27). Census: 1850, 60 & 70 in Calais. She married by Rev. E. R. Eddy 6 Oct 1875 in Calais AUGUSTUS LYMAN WARE (adv), born 14 Oct 1838, son of JOSIAH H. WARE, in E. Medway, MA (VR:127, clinch:26).

- v. HANNAH MARIA REED, born 21 Aug 1846 in Calais (VR). Graduated from Calais Academy and was a teacher. Died 2 Sept 1902 in Milford, MA (clinch:27). Census: 1850, 60 & 70 in Calais. She married by Rev. F.B. Allen 24 Aug 1875 in Calais ARTHUR PERKINS of Portland (adv).
- vi. MARY HILTON REED, born 16 Sept 1849 in Calais, died 20 Feb 1894 in Calais (g.s., clinch:27 has died and buried in Milford). Buried in Calais Cemetery. Census: 1860 & 70 in Calais.
- vii. UNNAMED SON REED, born circa 1850 in Calais. Census: 1850 [poss. the male age 8/12 is female, Mary H. who is age 10 in 1860] in Calais.

EZEKIEL H. & SABRINA K. RICHARDSON, p. 193

EZEKIEL H. RICHARDSON, of Boston, Ma.

He married, 24 Nov 1844 by Japheth Coombs Washburn, JP, in Calais (VR:1:135, mrwc:45, gaz) SABRINA K. WYMAN. Children:

- i. EDWIN WYMAN RICHARDSON, born 15 Mar 1846 in Calais (VR).

MARTIN & FRANCES RICKER, p. 221

MARTIN RICKER, born circa 1807 in St. John's River, NB (1850 census). Census: 1850 in Calais.
He married before 1831 FRANCES (_____), born circa 1812 in York Co., NB (1850 census). Census: 1850 in Calais. Children:

- i. JEMIMA RICKER, born circa 1832 in York Co., NB (1850 census). Census: 1850 in Calais.
- ii. JOSEPH RICKER, born circa 1833 in York Co., NB (1850 census). He was a millman. Census: 1850, 60 & 70 in Calais. He married 18 Oct 1857 in St. Stephen, NB (CCMR) SARAH JOHNSON, born ca 1833. Census: 1860 in Calais.
- iii. GEORGE RICKER, born circa 1835 in York Co., NB (1850 census). Census: 1850 in Calais.
- iv. JERUSHA RICKER, born circa 1836 in York Co., NB (1850 census). Census: 1850 in Calais.
- v. JOHN RICKER, born circa 1838 in York Co., NB (1850 census). Census: 1850 in Calais.
- vi. RHODA ANN RICKER, born circa 1840 in St. John, NB (1850 census). Census: 1850 in Calais.
- vii. SAMUEL RICKER, born 2 Aug 1847 in Calais (VR). Probably died before 1850 (not listed in 1850 census).

JAMES & MARY A. ROBBINS, p. 208

JAMES ROBBINS, Jr. born circa 1777. Died 19 June 1812 Concord, MA (VR:3:332) age 35. He married Anna (_____), born circa 1772. Died 20 July 1823 age 51 in Concord, MA (VR:3:341). Their son, James married in Concord then settled in Calais.

JAMES ROBBINS, born 6 Feb 1803 in Concord, MA (VR:3:287). He was a shoe merchant and a deacon in Congo Church from 1850 to 1873. He was a member of the Calais Band, played the trombone. Died 13 Dec 1873 age 70y 10m in Calais (congo, adv, union, g.s.). Buried in Calais Cemetery. Probate of Estate 1873 in Machias Me (will dated 13 June 1873). Census: 1840 (3 males, 3 females), 50 thru 1870 in Calais.

He married 15 Dec 1829 by Rev. Daniel S. Sothm in Concord, MA (VR:3:377) MARY AUGUSTA PARKMAN, born circa 1807 in Boston Ma (1850 census), daughter of JOHN A. & MARY PARKMAN (the mother, Mary with them age 75 in 1860 census, died 17 Feb 1864, g.s.). The wife, Mary, died 14 Oct 1887 age 80y 11m in Calais (east:396, times, prbt will dated 16 May 1881, g.s.). Buried in Calais Cemetery. Census: 1850 thru 1880 in Calais. Children:

- i. MARY JANE ROBBINS, born 23 May 1837 in Calais (VR). Bapt 26 Nov 1837 in Calais (congo). Died 1 Oct 1842 age 5y 4m (g.s.). Buried in Calais Cemetery.
- ii. JAMES HENRY ROBBINS, born 22 Jul 1839 in Calais (VR, bowhis:485). Bapt 10 Nov 1839 in Calais

(congo). Graduated from Bowdoin Medical School 1865, Harvard 1867; he practiced medicine in Machias 1867-76; Calais 1876-81; Hingham, MA 1881-1900; he died 22 Aug 1900 in Hingham (bowcat:485). Census: 1850, 60 in Calais, 1870 in Machias & 1880 (with his mother & his son no wife) in Calais. He was mentioned in fathers probate. He married 1st 16 Sept 1868 in Calais (union), (int.) 9 Sept 1868 in Calais (VR) LAURA DAILEY, daughter of ANSEL & MARY DAILEY. She died 14 Dec 1875 (see DAILEY). Census: 1870 in Machias. He married 2nd 20 Apr 1881 MARY CAROLINE PIKE, who survived her husband (his obit) (see PIKE)

iii. JOHN AUGUSTUS ROBBINS, born 25 Oct 1841 in Calais (VR). Bapt 1 May 1842 in Calais (congo). Died 29 July 1892 age 51y (congo, g.s.). Buried in Calais Cemetery [inscription on stone- In memory of John Augustus Robbins, victim of an avalanche at Grindelwald, Switzerland where he is buried]. Census: 1850 thru 1880 in Calais.

iv. ANN ELIZA ROBBINS, born 6 Sep 1843 in Calais (VR). Died 1920 in Calais (g.s.). Buried in Calais Cemetery. Census: 1850, 60 & 70 in Calais. She married 25 Jan 1888, in Hingham, MA (times, Calais VR:3:285) GEORGE REYNOLDS GARDNER, born 14 Jan 1852, in Dennysville (gard:16), son of AARON LEEMAN RAYMOND GARDNER (son of EBENEZER & SARAH GARDNER) & ABBIE WILDER REYNOLDS (daughter of BELA R. REYNOLDS). He was admitted to the bar 1880, judge of probate, Washington Co. in 1888 thru 1896 (biorev:658). Died 14 Feb 1937 in Calais (MSA). (see also WHARFF)

v. CHARLES PARKMAN ROBBINS, born 29 Jan 1846 in Calais (VR). He was a boot & shoe merchant, in business with his father, Robbins & Son and took over as proprietor upon the death of his father (CEV:24). Died 4 Jan 1896 age 50 in Calais (MSA, adv, g.s.). Buried in Calais Cemetery. Census: 1850 thru 1880 in Calais.. He married 1st 19 Sept 1872 in Farmington, ME (VR, union) CARRIE G. SEWALL in Calais (VR:3), born ca 1853 (1880 census in Calais), daughter of C. D. SEWALL of Farmington. Died 17 Apr 1886 age 34 (SSC, g.s.). Buried in Calais Cemetery. He married 2nd 18 July 1894 in Indianapolis, IN by Rev. Frederick Dewhurst LULU BELLE WILDES of Indianapolis (adv).

- Samuel Robbins, a sea captain, age 40 in 1870 census of Calais may be another son.

THOMAS H. & BATHIAH ROBINSON, Sr., p. 210
(Name spelled Robitson in VR.)

THOMAS HENRY ROBINSON, Sr., born circa 1799 in Ireland. He was a ship carpenter and farmer. Died 23 Sept 1867 (g.s). Buried in Calais Cemetery. Census: 1840 (1 male, 1 female?, there should be one son) in Calais. Census: 1860 in Calais.

He married MARTHA/BATHIAH (_____), born circa 1802 in Calais (1850 census). Died 28 Apr 1852 (g.s. name Martha). Buried in Calais Cemetery. Census: 1850 in Calais. Children:

i. THOMAS HENRY ROBINSON, Jr., born 11 Oct 1834 in Calais (VR). He was a mariner. During the Civil War he was a seaman in Co. D, 6th Maine, died 24 Jan 1863 in hospital of disease (NRMS:242). He enlisted 23 Nov 1861 and was 5'8" with dark eyes and black hair (cwcard). Census: 1850 & 60 in Calais.

ii. GEORGE DOWNES ROBINSON, born 1 Mar 1842 in Calais (VR). Census: 1850 & 60 in Calais.

LORENZO & CAROLINE ROCKWOOD, p. 211

LORENZO D. ROCKWOOD, born circa 1797 in Haverhill, MA (son's death rec., g.s. has 1796 in Northfield MA). In Sept 1826 he was a merchant when he appeared in court (CCP:4:413). He was an Adj. in the Maine Militia in the 1st Brig. 7th Div. received his rank on 21 Apr 1827 and discharged 20 Feb 1832 (milit). Later he was a teacher. Died 19 Jun 1861 age 65 (g.s.). Buried in Calais Cemetery. Census: 1830 (6 males, 5 females) in Calais, 1840 (4 males, 4 females) in Baring, 1850 & 60 in Calais.

He married (int) 10 Sept 1825 (cal2:24) CAROLINE CHRISTOPHER, born circa 1800 in Wiscasset, ME. Came to Calais about 1816 with her mother Lydia and sister Mary. Died 21 Feb 1871 age 72 in Calais (g.s., union). Buried in Calais Cemetery. Census: 1850, 60 & 70 in Calais. Children:

i. FEMALE ROCKWOOD, born between 1816-1820 (1830 census), does not appear in 1840 she perhaps died young or married before 1840.

ii. LORENZO D. PARMETER ROCKWOOD, born 15 Jul 1826 in Calais (VR). He served in the Navy during the Civil War (obit). He was a mariner and a member of the Joel A. Haycock Post GAR. Died 19

Sep 1907 age 81y 2m 1d in Calais, he has been an invalid for several years and survived by a widow (obit adv, sfh:1:23, MSA). Buried in Calais Cemetery. Census: 1850 in Calais. He married 11 Nov 1882 by Rev. Padleford in Calais (VR:2:21) MARY ELLA STANHOPE, born ca 1851, died ca 1887 age 36y, buried 9 Jan 1887 in Calais Cemetery (sext).

iii. SARAH CAROLINE ROCKWOOD, born 28 Apr 1828 in Calais (VR). She was a teacher. Died 19 Aug 1871 age 43 in Calais, at home of sister, Mrs. Samuel King (east:255, adv, g.s.). Buried in Calais Cemetery. Census: 1850 in Calais. She married circa 1847 (congo) HENRY K. PURPLE, died 18 Nov 1861 (g.s.). Buried in Calais Cemetery.

iv. ELIZABETH ANN CHANDLER ROCKWOOD, born 27 Mar 1830 in Calais (VR). In 1856 she was a teacher in Calais. She was a milliner. Died 7 May 1915 in Toronto, Ont. (obit adv). Census: 1850 & 60 in Calais. She married as his second wife, 18 Sept 1860 in Calais (union) SAMUEL TYLER KING, born 9 Jan 1811 (g.s.). He was Mayor of Calais in 1868. In 1883 they resided in St. John, NB. Died 11 Jan 1891 in Chicago where they had been spending the winter, he married 1st Miss Ricker (obit adv). Ann G. King died 12 Aug 1859 age 47 (g.s.). [Anna Garland Ricker, born 18 June 1812 (rock:70) in Upper Mills, NB, daughter of Gershom Ricker and Ann Garland (rick:221)].

v. LUCY ADELAIDE ROCKWOOD, born 19 May 1832 in Calais (VR, g.s.). She was a teacher. Died 3 Aug 1883 in St. John, NB, at residence of brother-in-law, Samuel T. King (times, g.s.). Buried in Calais Cemetery. Census: 1850, 60 & 70 in Calais.

vi. JOSEPH CHRISTOPHER ROCKWOOD, born 4 May 1834 in Robbinston Me (VR, g.s.). He served in 28th Maine Reg't, Home Guards during Civil War (obit). He was a builder, carpenter, City Marshall and tax collector (brief:222). He was a deacon of the Congo Church 1884-1926. Some of the buildings which he constructed: Opera House, City Building, National Bank, Congo church, and the Catholic Church (obit). Died 6 Oct 1926 age 92y 5m 2d at his home in Calais (MSA, obit adv, congo, sfh:6:16, g.s.). Buried in Calais Cemetery. Census: 1850 thru 1880 in Calais. He married 19 Jan 1876 in Calais (VR:3:236, adv) CAROLINE `CARRIE' G. LAMBE, 29 Oct 1851 (g.s.), daughter of SAMUEL LAMBE (b. Athol MA) & MARY WHITNEY (b. Machias). She graduated from Calais Academy. She died 21 Oct 1921 age 69y 11m 21d in Calais (MSA, sfh:3:269, g.s.). Census: 1910 in Calais.

vii. THEODORE JELLISON ROCKWOOD, born 7 Sep 1836 in Calais, died 5 May 1842 in Calais (g.s.). Buried in Calais Cemetery.

HUGH & HANNAH ROGERS, p. 186

HUGH ROGERS, born circa 1815 in Ireland. Census: 1840 (5 males 4 females) & 1850 in Calais. [Maine Farmer Death Notices - Calais Advertiser of 21 Oct 1847 - Hugh Rogers of Calais shockingly mutilated on Tuesday last while blasting rock in the field belonging to George Downes, Esq. at Calais. ?? There is a Hugh is listed in 1850 census].

He married 3 Jun 1837 in Calais (mrwc:23) HANNAH HALLIDAY, born circa 1812 in Ireland. Census: 1850 in Calais. Children:

i. MARGARET ROGERS, born 25 Feb 1837 in Calais (VR). Census: 1850 (age 12 - with Archibald Holliday) in Calais.

ii. MARY SOPHIA ROGERS, born 3 Dec 1839 in Calais (VR). She married 21 Aug 1868 by Rev. H. V. Dexter in Calais (VR:3:229) MELVILLE W. MYRICK of Williamsport, PA.

iii. ANN JANE ROGERS, born 25 Aug 1840 in Calais (VR). Census: 1850 in Calais.

iv. THOMAS ROGERS, born 25 Mar 1842 in Calais (VR). He enlisted in Civil War on 19 Oct 1861 in Co D 1st Cavalry, described as 6' tall with blue eyes and brown hair, he deserted then enlisted in the 1st Batt. Heavy Artl. in Nov 1861 and failed to appear (cwcard). Census: 1850 in Calais. [Possible that he is the Thomas who married Sarah J. Spinney, daughter of Nathaniel] (see SPINNEY).

v. JAMES ROGERS, born 3 Mar 1844 in Calais (VR). Census: 1850 in Calais.

vi. ARCHIBALD ROGERS, born 17 Jun 1846 in Calais (VR). Census: 1850 in Calais.

vii. ELLEN ROGERS, born circa 1848 in Calais. Census: 1850 in Calais.

LEROY & CYNTHIA ROGERS, p. 207

LEROY ROGERS, born circa 1806 in Sedgwick, ME (1850 census). [Born Leroy Rogers, son to Polly Fly b. 16

Jan 1805 in Sedgwick, ME (VR no other info)]. He was a ship master. Census: 1850 in Calais.

    He married CYNTHIA (_____), born circa 1810 in Sedgwick, ME (1850 census). Census: 1850 in Calais. [There is a Cynthia Cole b. 10 Sept 1810 d/o Benjamin & Lucy Cole in Sedgwick VR, possibly wife of Leroy]. Children:

    i. LEROY MELVILLE ROGERS, born 28 Aug 1836 in Calais (VR, 1850 census = Sedgwick). Census: 1850 in Calais.

WILLIAM & LYDIA ROGERS, p. 188

WILLIAM ROGERS. Died possibly in WI.

    He married 31 Aug 1843 by Rev. Alley in St. Andrews, NB (gaz, CCMR:90) LYDIA G. SWETT, born 19 May 1821 in Perry (VR:38), daughter of DANIEL SWETT & RACHEL (LORING) (SWETT) JONES. Resided: 1887 in Morristown, WI. (swett:90). Children:

    i. WILLIAM HENRY ROGERS, born 1 Jun 1844 in Calais (VR). He enlisted in Civil War as a Private in Co K 15th Inf. on 27 Dec 1861, a clerk 5' 3 ½", with blue eyes and brown hair, he died of disease on 19 July 1862 (cwcard). Census: 1860 (with Solomon & Rachel Pool) in Calais.
    ii. GEORGE BYRON ROGERS, born 21 Feb 1847 in Calais (VR). Died: 23 Mar 1847 in Calais (VR:3:327).
    iii. ANGELINE ROGERS, born circa 1851 in Calais. Census: 1860 (with Solomon & Rachel Pool) in Calais. She married 21 Sept 1868 in Calais by Rev. H. V. Dexter (VR:3:228) ROBERT ROGERS.

*Note—Rachel Pool was a sister of Lydia Rogers, it is possible that William & Lydia moved west before 1860 census and left their children with the Pool's.

DAVID & ALICE RUTHERFORD, p. 204

DAVID RUTHERFORD, he applied for citizenship on 24 Sept 1852 stating he was born 1812 in County Down in Ireland, left Ireland Mar 1825, arrived in St. Andrews in May 1825 and to Calais in April 1833 where he since resides (SJC). Died: between 1850 and 1870. Census: 1850 (age 38) in Calais.
* Note: there were no Rutherfords found in 1860 census of Calais.

    He married 5 Dec 1836 (?), in St George NB (CCMR:834 her name Alice Hurley) ELSIE/ Alice HURLEY/ Huntley, born circa 1812 in St George NB (1850 census), daughter of WILLIAM HENRY HUNTLEY, born in Ireland & MARY WILLIAMS, born in France (MSA). Died 9 Aug 1896 age 91 in Calais (MSA maiden name Elsie Hurley). Buried in Calais Cemetery. Census: 1850 (Alice age 38), 1870 (Alice age 60) & 1880 (age 72) in Calais. Children:

    i. WILLIAM RUTHERFORD, born circa 1840 in St George NB (1850 census). Census: 1850 in Calais.
    ii. DAVID H. RUTHERFORD, born 9 Apr 1843 in St George, NB (1850 census, MSA= b. Calais). He was a stevedore. Died 26 Mar 1926 age 82y 11m 14d in Calais (VR, MSA, mother's name Elsie Huntley, sfh:5:71). Census: 1850 (age 8), 70 (age 28), 80 & 1900 (age 55 b. Apr 1845), 1910 (age 66) & 1920 (age 75) in Calais. He married (int.) 25 Oct 1869 (VR:3) CLORLINDA or Curlinda ROLFE, born ca 1848 in Eastport, daughter of STEPHEN ROLFE & MARGARET CAHILL (both born in NS). Died 27 Apr 1912 in age 64y 1m 3d Calais (VR). Census: 1870, 80 & 1900 in Calais. [Possibility he married first A. Balk who is listed as the mother of his son William, born ca 1864, on his death certificate].
    iii. SUSAN C. RUTHERFORD, born 29 May 1844 in Calais (VR). Died 11 May 1850 in Calais (adv). Buried: 13 May 1850 in Calais Cemetery.
    iv. ALICE RUTHERFORD, born 1 Apr 1846 in Calais (VR). Census: 1850 in Calais.
    v. JAMES RUTHERFORD, born 8 Sep 1847 in Calais (VR), born (2): 15 Sep 1850 (MSA, obit). He was a carpenter. Died 17 May 1940 age 89y 8m 2d in Calais (obit, adv). Buried in Calais. Census: 1850 (age 2), 70 (age 22), 80 (age 28), 1900 (age 48) & 1910 (age 58) in Calais. He married 21 Feb 1876 in Calais (adv) EMMA W. GIBSON born 3 Jan 1853 in England, daughter of EDWARD GIBSON (born in England), died 7 Oct 1917 age 64y 10m in Calais (MSA, adv). Census: 1880, 1900 & 1920 in Calais.
    vi. JOHN RUTHERFORD born ca Jan 1849 (age 10/12 1850 census) in Calais, born (2): 15 Sep 1850 (MSA, obit). Died 11 Feb 1915 age 64y in Eastport (MSA, mother's name Alice Hurley). Census: 1850 in Calais. He possibly married HANNAH (_____) (1850 census).

DANIEL & MARY RYAN, p. 207

DANIEL RYAN, born circa 1808 in Ireland. He was a gardener. Died after 1860. Census: 1840 (2 males & 4 females) thru 1860 in Calais.

He married MARY BREEN, born circa 1809 in Ireland. Census: 1850 & 60 in Calais. Children:

i. MARY RYAN, born circa 1836 in Calais (1850 census). Census: 1850 in Calais.
ii. DANIEL B. RYAN, born 24 May 1838 in Calais (VR, obit born 1839). He worked for Frontier Steamboat Co. for 35 years as Capt. on the *Belle Brown* (obit SCC, adv). Died 16 Apr 1907 in Calais (MSA, obit). Buried in Calais Cemetery. Census: 1850 thru 1880 in Calais. He married (int.) 16 Nov 1872 in Calais (VR:3) MARY ELLEN McVAY, born ca 1841 in St. Stephen, NB, daughter of JOHN McVAY & BRIDGET LANNIGAN both born in Ireland, died 14 Oct 1914 age 73y (g.s., MSA). Buried in Calais Cemetery. Census: 1880 & 1910 in Calais.
iii. ELIZABETH RYAN, born 14 Oct 1841 in Calais (VR). Census: 1850, 60 & 80 in Calais. She married (_____) GARVEY (her name in 1880, living with brother Michael).
iv. BRIDGET RYAN, born 10 May 1844 in Calais (VR). Died after 1870. Census: 1850, 60 & 70 in Calais.
v. JOHN RYAN, born 3 Sep 1847 in Calais (VR). There is no John in 1850 census.
vi. MICHAEL RYAN, born circa 1849. Census: 1850 thru 1880 in Calais. He married ANN (_____), born ca 1840 in MA. Census 1880 in Calais.

LEMUEL D. & LOVE M. SAWYER, p. 183

NATHAN[4] SAWYER b Feb 1771 in Cape Elizabeth, ME (son of EBENEZER[3], JOSEPH[2], JOHN[1]) d. 20 June 1838 in Cape Elizabeth; married 1st ABIGAIL DYER born 24 July 1776 in Steuben, ME dau of HENRY DYER & BETTY SIMONTON. She died 1 Jan 1807. Nathan died 20 May 1828 and is buried in Pleasant Hill Cemetery in South Portland, ME. Their 2nd child was Lemuel D. Sawyer (sawofne:392) who resided in Calais.

LEMUEL DYER SAWYER, born 8 May 1801 in Cape Elizabeth, Me (sawofne:392, Steuben, ME VR). Came to Calais in 1836, he was in the harness making business, he served several years on the City Council, and was a member of the Masons (obit adv). Died at age 83 in July 1883 (obit adv, g.s.). Buried in Calais Cemetery. Census: 1840 (2 males & 2 females) thru 80 in Calais.

He married 1st SOPHRONIA (_____), born circa 1808. Died 13 May 1841 age 33 in Calais (g.s.). Buried in Calais Cemetery. No known children.

He married 2nd 16 Nov 1841 by Rev. Joshua Millet in Cherryfield, ME (mrwc:35, gaz) LOVE M. PATTEN, born 24 Nov 1815 in Cherryfield, ME, daughter of JOHN PATTEN AND PERMELIA LEIGHTON (wwcf). Died 20 Jul 1893 age 77y 8m in Calais (wwcf, obit times). Buried in Calais Cemetery. Census: 1850 thru 1880 in Calais. She married 2nd 9 Sept 1884 in Calais (VR:2:39) JAMES C. BRACKETT of E. Corinth, Me. Children:

i. SARAH WAITE SAWYER, born 29 Nov 1845 in Calais (VR). Died 16 Dec 1870 in Calais (sawofne:392). Buried in Calais Cemetery (g.s. = lost at sea). Census: 1850, 60 & 70 in Calais. She married 14 Mar 1868 by Rev. H. V. Dexter in Calais (VR:3:227) WILLIAM T. HILL, born ca 1845. Census: 1870 sea Capt. living with her parents in Calais.

THOMAS & MARIA SAWYER, p. 180, 182

THOMAS SAWYER, born 12 Jan 1801 in Phillipston, MA (VR:40, sawofne:295, g.s.), son of SILAS SAWYER AND MARY ROSS. Graduated from Middlebury College in Vermont. He came to Calais ca 1826 and was a clerk in the general store of his brother, Abner Sawyer, then started his own mercantile business (biorev:149). Died 14 Aug 1862 age 61y 7m, in Calais (VR, congo, prbt:4:1-36). Buried in Calais Cemetery. Census: 1840 (2 males, 6 females), 50 & 60 in Calais.

He married (int) 9 Sept 1832 in Calais (cal2:33) MARIA DYER, born circa 1806 (g.s.) in Calais, daughter of JONES DYER JR. (1775-1860) & LYDIA KNIGHT the daughter of Capt. EPHRAIM KNIGHT who is said to have fired the first shot in the capture of the British gunboat, *Marguerite* off Machias harbor in the Revolution (biorev:147). In Sept 1883 she and 2 daughters, Caroline & Mary, moved to Boston (adv). Died 17 Apr 1896 at age 90 in Boston Ma (adv, congo, g.s.). Buried in Calais Cemetery. Census: 1850 thru 1880 in Calais. Children:

i. ABBA MARIA SAWYER, born 4 Jan 1834 in Calais, died 3 Sep 1843 age 9y 8m in Calais (VR:1:241, gaz, g.s.). Buried in Calais Cemetery.

ii. ALBERT HENRY SAWYER, born 15 Aug 1835 in Calais (VR, biorev:149). Graduated from Middlebury College, in Vermont and Hampden Academy. He started working for his father, after 1873 he was in the lumbering business, owned lumber mills in Benton, Woodstock and Hartland, NB (biorev:149), also a wholesale lumber business in Calais (CEV:29). Died 21 Nov 1907 age 72y 3m 6d in Calais (MSA, obit adv, g.s.). Buried in Calais Cemetery. Census: 1850 thru 1900 in Calais. He married 15 Oct 1868 in St. Stephen, NB (CCMR) ELIZA A. McADAM, born July 1845 in Milltown, NB, daughter of Hon. JOHN McADAM (born in Ireland) & JANE A. MURCHIE (born St. Stephen). She died 18 Jan 1904 age 58y 6m in Calais (MSA, g.s., SSC). Census: 1870, 80 & 1900 in Calais.

iii. CAROLINE DYER SAWYER, born 25 May 1837 in Calais (VR, sawofne:295). Resided: 1898 in Boston Ma. Died 1904 (g.s.). Buried in Calais Cemetery. Census: 1850 thru 1880 in Calais. Unmarried.

iv. EMILY DYER SAWYER, born 19 Oct 1840 in Calais, died 23 Dec 1856 age 16y 2m 4d in Calais (VR:1:241, g.s.). Buried in Calais Cemetery. Census: 1850 in Calais.

v. MARY ATKINS SAWYER, born 3 Feb 1846 in Calais (VR:180). Resided 1898 in Boston Ma. Died 10 Oct 1903 age 50 in Boston, MA (obit adv, g.s.). Buried in Calais Cemetery. Census: 1850 thru 1880 in Calais. Never married. [VR:182 has Mary Elizabeth, born 3 Feb 1846 in Calais, this is possibly an error, Mary A. appears in census records and father's will, Mary E. does not, or they could have been twins, sawofne:295 also has Mary Elizabeth].

WARREN & SARAH SAWYER, p. 199

JONATHAN SAWYER, born 5 Nov 1772 Danvers, MA (VR:324), son of JONATHAN SAWYER, Revolutionary soldier at Lexington, and SARAH FLINT (sawofne:203). Died 1845 Levant, ME (sawofne:247). He married 23 Dec 1803 in Boothbay, ME (sawofne:247) MARTHA REED, b. 26 Oct 1770, daughter of JOSEPH REED AND SARAH WYLIE. Their son, Warren Sawyer settled in Calais.

WARREN SAWYER, born circa 1811, in (?)Belfast, ME (1850 census), Levant, ME (sawofne:305), Camden, ME (son's death rec.). He was a house carpenter. Died 29 Feb 1876 age 65y 6m in Calais (obit). Census: 1850 & 60 in Calais.
He married 29 Jul 1832 by Rev. Samuel Sawyer in St. George, NB (anglch), SARAH SWIM born circa 1814 in St. George NB (possibly a sister of Maria (Swim) Bassett). Died 21 Sep 1852 age 38 in Calais (FJ, g.s. = 34y). Buried in Calais Cemetery. Census: 1850 (age 36) in Calais. Children:

i. LORINDA SAWYER, born 20 Jul 1832 in St. George NB (Calais VR). Bapt. 7 Jan 1851 in Calais (saint). Died 11 Jan 1851 age 16y 6m in Calais (FJ dated 15 Jan 1851, g.s.). Buried 13 Jan 1851 in Calais Cemetery (saint). Census: 1850 in Calais.

ii. ANN MARIE SAWYER, born 20 Aug 1834 in Calais (VR). Died 15 May 1852 age 17y 9m in Calais (g.s.). Buried in Calais Cemetery. Census: 1850 in Calais.

iii. JOSEPH WARREN SAWYER, born 20 Aug 1834 in Calais (VR). Served in Civil War a Private in Co. F 22nd Me Inf., 5' 5" with blue eyes and brown hair, he was a carpenter (cwcard). Died 30 Jan 1888 in Calais age 55 (east:400, mil. g.s.). Buried Calais Cemetery (cwcard). Census: 1860 & 70 in Calais. He married 4 Apr 1857 in Calais (VR:1:169, sawofne:345) ELLEN (Helen) JOY, born May 1831 in Ireland (1900 census), daughter of ROBERT & MARGARET JOY (both born in Ire). Died 16 Dec 1902 age 72y 8m in Calais (MSA). Census: 1860, (Helen age 25), 70 & 1900 in Calais.

iv. PHOEBE SAWYER, born 12 Jan 1838 in Calais (VR). Census: 1850 in Calais. She married 11 Oct 1855 by William H. Tyler, HARRISON B. LEIGHTON in Calais (VR:3:163).

v. ALFRED SAWYER, born 8 May 1841 in Calais (VR, sawofne:305). He enlisted in Civil War on 27 Nov 1861, left 17 June 1865, a private in Co M 3rd Battery of Light Artillery, 5' 6" with blue eyes and dark hair, he was a house carpenter (cwcard). Census: 1850 in Calais.

vi. STILLMAN OSGOOD SAWYER, born 5 Dec 1842 in St. Stephen, NB (Calais VR, death rec. Fairfield VR has birth 19 Oct 1847). He enlisted in Civil War on 10 Sept 1862, left 14 Aug 1863, he was a carpenter 5' 3" with blue eyes and black hair (cwcard). Moved to Fairfield, ME before 1880. Died 30 Nov 1917 age 70y

1m in Fairfield, ME (sawofne:345, MSA). Buried in Pine Grove Cemetery, Waterville, ME. Census: 1850, 60 (age 17 with bro. Joseph), 70 in Calais, 1800 in Fairfield. He married 12 Feb 1866 in Calais (VR, sawofne:345). MARY ANN HUTCHINS, daughter of JOSEPH HUTCHINS AND MARY ANN MANSFIELD (see HUTCHINS).

vii. TRUNZINA SAWYER, born 8 Apr 1845 in Calais (VR). Died before 1850.

viii. MARTHA ELLEN SAWYER, born 10 Dec 1847 in Calais (VR). Died after 1880. Census: 1850 in Calais. Census: 1880 in Harrington, ME. She married 18 Nov 1865 (sawofne:305) GEORGE W. TURNER, born ca 1842. Census 1880 in Harrington.

JAMES & MARY SCOTT, p. 201

JAMES SCOTT, born circa 1813 at (Keluska?) Co of Temanock in Ireland. He left Ireland 13 May 1832 arrived in Calais 4 July 1833 where he has since resided when he applied for citizenship on 27 Mar 1844 (SJC 8:46). Died Aug 1849 in Calais (1850 census deaths).

He married MARY (_____), born circa 1821. Census: 1850 in Calais (with Michael Higgins).
Children:

i. MARY SCOTT, born 12 Aug 1844 in Calais (VR). Census: 1850 (with Michael Higgins) in Calais.
ii. JAMES SCOTT, born 25 Jan 1846 in Calais (VR). Census: 1850 (with Michael Higgins) in Calais.

JESSE & ELIZA M. G. SCOTT p. 187

JESSE SCOTT. [There is Jesse Dorman Scott b. 22 Apr 1820 in Machias (VR) s/o Levi & Lacy Scott who may possibly be this Jesse. Levi is a brother of Jesse Bracy Scott].
He married ELIZA M. G. (_____) before 1846. Children:
i. ROSEMA DELPHINA SCOTT, born 25 Jun 1847 in Calais (VR).

JESSE B. & RUXBY SCOTT, p. 191

JESSE BRACY SCOTT, born 14 Jul 1797 in Machias Me (VR), son of JESSE SCOTT & BETHIAH BRACY, who were married 26 Nov 1786 in Machias (VR). He was in the Maine Militia received rank of Ensign on 29 May 1822 in Cooper, 1st Brig, 7th Div. (milit). Died: before 1870, before his wife left Calais or in Oshkosh, WI, where the family moved. Census: 1830 (5 males, 2 females) in Cooper, ME, 40 (9 males & 1-2 females), 1850 & 60 in Calais.

He married before 1829, RUXBY (_____), born circa 1802 in Shepherdy, NS (1850 census). Died: 15 Oct 1883 age 81 in Oshkosh, WI (times, obit north). Census: 1850 & 60 in Calais, 1870 in Oshkosh.
Children:

i. ALBERT LEWIS SCOTT, died 20 Jun 1834 in Calais (VR:233).
ii. JULIA P. SCOTT, born, circa 1829, in Cooper (1850 census). Died 16 Sep 1850 in Calais (g.s.). Buried in Calais Cemetery. Census: 1850 in Calais.
iii. JESSE R. SCOTT, born 30 Apr 1830 in Cooper ME (1850 census, north). He moved to Wisconsin in Aug 1855 (1882 Dir. of Oshkosh). He was a lumber manufacturer in Oshkosh. Died 8 Dec 1903 age 73 at home of his son, Frank, in Oshkosh (obit north). Census: 1850 in Calais, 1860 & 70 in Oshkosh, WI. He married in Calais Mar 1852 CHARLOTTE A. WHITE, born 22 Feb 1834 in St. John, NB daughter of JOHN W. T. & EMMA (alive 1889 when daughter died) WHITE. Died 27 June 1889 in Oshkosh, WI. (obit north). Census: 1860 & 70 in Oshkosh.
iv. SARAH SCOTT, born circa 1832 in St. David, NB (1850 census). Census: 1850 in Calais.
v. WINFIELD SCOTT, born circa 1833 in Cooper ME (1850 census). Died after 1883 when he resided in Oshkosh. Census: 1850 & 60 in Calais. Appears in 1876 & 1882 Oshkosh City Directories.
vi. ANDREW JACKSON SCOTT, born 3 Sep 1835 in Calais (VR). Died: before 1883 (not mentioned in mothers death notice). Census: 1850 in Calais.
vii. GEORGE FRANCIS SCOTT, born 21 May 1839 in Calais (VR). He served in Civil War Co F, 22nd Regt. Me. Vols. also 25th Maine as a member of brigade band, moved to Oshkosh 1864, where he worked as a mill foreman (wisch). He was 5' 7" with gray eyes and black hair (cwcard). Died after 1883 when he

resided in Oshkosh. Census: 1850 & 60 in Calais. He married 16 Nov 1858 in Washington Co. Maine IDA A. KNIGHT (wisch).

viii. JOHN CHALONER SCOTT, born 21 Aug 1843 in Calais (VR). He enlisted in Civil War on 6 Aug 1862 in Co I 6th Me Inf. and was missing in action 10 May 1864, a lumberman 5'9" with dark blue eyes and dark brown hair, died 1910 (cwcard, enlist, father signed permission). [But not mentioned in his mothers death notice with his brothers] Census: 1850 & 60 in Calais.

MILTON JOHN & MARY JANE SEELEY, p. 199

MILTON JOHN SEELEY, born circa 1821 (possible b. in Perry son of Joseph and Fanny Seeley). Died 17 Mar 1864 age 43 in Calais (VR:3:308). Buried in Calais Cemetery (only initials, no dates on stone).

He married (int.) 25 Oct 1845 in Calais (VR) MARY JANE CRAIG born circa 1823. Died 14 Aug 1846 age 22 in Calais (sext, VR:1:235). Buried in Calais Cemetery. Children:

i. CHARLOTTE SOPHIA SEELEY, born 9 Mar 1846 in Calais (VR).

ROBERT & MARGARET SHEEHY, p. 205

ROBERT SHEEHY, born circa 1818 at Limerick in Ireland (1850 census) He left Ireland 10 Apr 1840, arrived St. Andrews 16 May 1840 came to Calais in fall of 1840 where he has since resided when he applied for citizenship on 7 Oct 1852 (SJC). Census: 1850 in Calais.

He married MARGARET (_____), born circa 1820, in Ireland (1850 census). Census: 1850 in Calais. Children:

i. JOHN SHEEHY, born 27 Apr 1841 in Calais (VR, 1850 census = Portland). Census: 1850 in Calais.
ii. WILLIAM SHEEHY, born 11 Oct 1843 in Calais (VR). Census: 1850 in Calais.
iii. MARY SHEEHY, born 23 Mar 1845 in Calais (VR). Census: 1850 in Calais.
iv. ELLEN SHEEHY, born 8 Jun 1847 in Calais (VR). Census: 1850 in Calais.
v. JAMES SHEEHY [twin], born Dec 1849 in Calais (1850 census). Census: 1850 in Calais.
vi. JOSEPH SHEEHY [twin], born Dec 1849 in Calais (1850 census). Census: 1850 in Calais.

WILLIAM & SARAH SHERMAN, p. 220

WILLIAM^6 SHERMAN, born ca 1775 Marshfield, MA, son of JOSEPH^5, WILLIAM^4, EBENEZER^3, WILLIAM$^{2-1}$. He died probably in Camden, ME after 1810. His wife's name is unknown but thought to have died shortly after birth of the two sons, Joseph S. who married but had no children and William who settled in Calais (shergen:176).

WILLIAM SHERMAN, born 1 Feb 1809 in Marshfield, MA (sherdir:2531). Died 13 Oct 1883 age 77 from a fall in the street in Milltown (shergen:285, obit has birth 1806). Buried in Calais Cemetery (g.s. has b. 1806). Census: 1830 (1 male, 1 female), (no 1840), 50, 60 & 70 in Calais.

He married 29 Apr 1838 by Rev. James Huskins in Calais (mrwc:24) SARAH E. SMITH, born circa 1816 in Fredericton, NB (1850 census). Died 10 Dec 1875 age 60 in Calais (shergen:286, adv, g.s.). Census: 1850, 60 & 70 in Calais. Children:

i. CHARLES WILLIAM SHERMAN, born 21 Mar 1839 in Calais (VR, shergen:286). He enlisted in Civil War 15 Oct 1861, left 7 Dec 1864, a private in Co K 12th Inf., he was a lumberman 5' 3" with gray eyes and lt. brown hair (cwcard). Died probably after 1883 in Boseman, Mont. (shergen:286). Census: 1850 (age 11) & 60 (age 21) in Calais.
ii. DANIEL WEBSTER SHERMAN, born 21 Mar 1839 in Calais (VR, shergen:286), born (2): 27 Jan 1841 (shergen:370, sherdir:2531, g.s. has 1841, cwcard has 1841). [Daniel was a twin but records disagree if his twin was Charles or Willard, VR of Calais being the oldest are probably correct]. He enlisted 15 Oct 1861 and left 19

WILLIAM & CHARLOTTE SIMPSON, p. 197

WILLIAM SIMPSON, born circa 1807 in Maine. He was a Lt. in Militia 29 Mar 1831 1st Brig. 7th Div. (mil.). Died 20 Jan 1871 in Calais (adv. g.s.). Buried in Calais Cemetery. Census: 1840 (2 males & 3 females) in Princeton, 50, 60 & 70 in Calais.

He married CHARLOTTE A. BAILEY born circa 1810 (g.s.), in Maine, daughter of JOSIAH & CHARLOTTE BAILEY of Topsfield (MSA). She died 2 Nov 1888 in Brookton (times, g.s.). Buried in Calais Cemetery. Census: 1850, 60 & 70 in Calais. Children:

i. WILLIAM DELUE {1} SIMPSON, born 1 Sep 1833 in Calais, died 29 Oct 1833 in Calais (VR:1.235).
ii. MARY SOPHIA SIMPSON, born 25 Jan 1835 in Calais (VR). Census: 1850 in Calais.
iii. WILLIAM DELUE {2} SIMPSON, born 8 Jul 1837 in Princeton Me (Calais VR). He was a farmer. Died circa 1924. Buried in Calais Cemetery. Census: 1860 & 70 in Calais. He married 14 May 1862 in Calais (VR:3:193) ELIZABETH ROBINSON of Princeton, born ca 1838, died 1916 (g.s.). Buried in Calais Cemetery. Census: 1870 in Calais.
iv. GEORGIANNA BREWER SIMPSON, born 27 Oct 1839 in Waite, ME (Calais VR). Census: 1850 & 60 (living with his parents) in Calais. She married 11 Nov 1855 by T. S. Lathrop in Calais (VR:3:163) JOHN S/L. TYLER, born ca 1833, son of WILLIAM H. TYLER & HARRIET LADD [John's death record has mother's name Harriet Ladd, census of 1850, 60 & 70 has William's wife's name Rebecca]. He was an auctioneer like his father. Died 17 Apr 1896 in Calais (MSA, east:548). Buried in Calais Cemetery. Census: 1850 & 60 (living with his parents) in Calais.
v. HELEN AUGUSTA SIMPSON, born 20 Jun 1842 in Calais (VR). Census: 1850 & 60 in Calais.
vi. FRANK SIMPSON, born circa 1858 in Calais. Census: 1860 & 70 in Calais. He may be the Frank Simpson who died 30 Apr 1895 age 36 in Augusta (east:533).

- Note: Frontier journal – Died in Calais 7 Nov 1853 Charles H. Simpson age 3 years, adopted child of William & Charlotte Simpson. (g.s. has 1852-1853).
- Note: In 1870 census there is a Malissa Simpson age 25, that is not shown in earlier years.

138

May 1865, a private in Co K 12th Inf. and a Sgt. in Co A 1st Battery, a lumberman and clerk 5' 3" with blue eyes and lt. brown hair (cward). He served four years in Civil War, after his discharge he became a U. S. Customs Inspector in Calais (shergen:370). He died 11 May 1912 in Calais (g.s., MSA has age 70y 1 1m, shergen:370). Buried in Calais Cemetery. Census: 1850 (age 8), 60 (age 19) & 70 in Calais (ages in census show him to be twin of Willard). He married 3 Sep 1865 by Rev. I. J. Burgess in Calais (VR:3:214, shergen:370, union) ADA MARIA ALBEE, born 22 Aug 1840 (MSA, g.s. has 1843), died 24 Oct 1932 (MSA, g.s.), daughter of ARTHUR D. ALBEE & SARAH HUNTLEY. She is buried in Calais Cemetery.

iii. WILLARD 'Billy' GRIGGS SHERMAN, born 27 Jun 1841 in Calais (VR, shergen:286 has 27 Mar 1839). Died 17 May 1895 age 53 death was result of suicide by hanging, in Oshkosh, WI, he was depressed because of worry over his work as an Assessor (obit, times). Census: 1850 (age 8) & 60 (age 19) in Calais, 1880 in Oshkosh, WI. He married in 1872 RUTH JULIA BUCKSTAFF (shergen:286 is uncertain of name, records were found in Oshkosh her name is Buckstaff). She was born Aug 1843 in Dumbarton, NB, daughter of JOHN BUCKSTAFF and LUCY McCURDY. She moved to Oshkosh with her parents in 1850. In 1900 she was living with her father in Oshkosh. She died Feb 1927 in Oshkosh is buried in Ellenwood Cemetery (obit north).
iv. JULIA HELENA SHERMAN, born 26 Jun 1843 in Calais (VR). Died 22 Nov 1874 in Calais (g.s. shergen:286). Census: 1850 & 60 in Calais. Buried in Calais Cemetery. She married 23 Jan 1869 by Rev. C. C. Long in Calais GEORGE GILLIS of Pembroke (VR:3:230).
v. JOSEPH SHERMAN, born 25 Jul 1846 in Calais (VR). He enlisted in Civil War 27 Feb 1865 as a musician in Co A 1st Battery left 5 Apr 1866, 5' 6" had blue eyes and light hair (cward). Resided in Alpena, Mich. (shergen:286). Died probably after 1883. Census: 1850, 60 & 70 in Calais.
vi. HORATIO NELSON S. SHERMAN, born circa 1850 in Calais. Died 19 Mar 1888 in Boston Ma (shergen: a suicide). Census: 1850, 60, & 80 in Calais. He married 10 Jan 1874 in Boston Ma (shergen:370) EVA HANNAH GALLEGHER, born in Ireland, daughter of PATRICK & ROSE HANNAH GALLEGHER. She died 24 Oct 1924, age 70 (shergen:370).
vii. ANNA SHERMAN, born ca 1854, died 1854 age 8mos (g.s.). Buried in Calais Cemetery.

JOHN & MARTHA SLATER p.188

JOHN SLATER, born circa 1805 in Ireland. Census: 1850 (also with him were ROBERT DUNCAN 21 & MARTHA J. DUNCAN 12 both born Ireland), & 60 (also Robert Duncan 27 & Martha J. Duncan, 21 a teacher) in Calais. (Unknown if there is a relationship to the Duncans, possibly Martha's siblings).

He married MARTHA (_____) in Ireland, born circa 1809 in Ireland. Died 3 Jan 1862 in Calais (VR:1:242). Census: 1850 & 60 in Calais. Children:

i. ANDREW DUNCAN SLATER, born circa 1834 in Ireland, died 8 May 1846 in Calais (VR:3:238), in a house fire. Buried: in Calais Cemetery.
ii. JOHN SLATER, Jr., born circa 1835 in Ireland. Census: 1850 & 60 (living with Edwin Bates and Jonathan Kidder) in Calais. [There was a John Slater age 22 who enlisted in Civil War 21 Sept 1861 in Co A 9th Inf., 5' 10" with gray eyes and brown hair, born in St. David, NB, was a lumberman and resided in Princeton and was killed at Bermuda, VA (cwcard) may possibly be this John Slater].
iii. WILLIAM ALEXANDER SLATER, born circa 1843 in Calais, died 8 May 1846 in Calais (VR:3:238), in a house fire. Buried: in Calais Cemetery.
iv. EMELINE SLATER, born 23 Mar 1846 in Calais (VR).

Bones of two children, ages 12 and 3, of John Slater were buried after a house fire 1846 (sext).

ALEXANDER N. & ALMIRA SMALL, p. 191

TIMOTHY SMALL, whose wife's name is unknown, was the son of Jonathan Small. Timothy was possibly the father of Alexander N. SMALL.

ALEXANDER NICHOLAS SMALL, born circa 1811 in Cherryfield, ME. He was in the 1st Brigade, 7th Div Maine Militia as a Pvt. in 1832 (mil). He worked in a mill. Died before 1860. Census: 1850 in Calais.

He married 25 Sep 1842 by Rev. M. K. Beals in St. David, NB (gaz, CCMR) A(E)LMIRA HITCHINGS, born 9 Apr 1816 in St. David, NB (mhl:67-8), daughter of WILLIAM HITCHINGS & JANE HUMPHREY. She died after 1887 (a widow in Dir. 1887). Census: 1850, 60, 70 & 80 in Calais. Children:

i. GEORGE DALLAS SMALL, born 25 May 1845 in Calais (VR). Died 26 Jun 1846 in Calais (VR:1:233). Buried: 28 Jun 1846 in Calais Cemetery.
ii. GEORGIANNA SMALL, born 13 Jun 1847 in Calais (VR). Died 15 May 1918 in Calais (MSA). Census: 1850, 60, 70 & 80 (age 33 she and her son living with her mother) in Calais. She married 6 Dec 1869 in Calais (VR:3) FRANCIS 'FRANK' WOODS, born ca 1847 in Canada. He was a partner in the business of W. Woods & Co, Wholesale & Retail dealers founded in 1848 (CEV:25). Died: before his wife probably before 1880 census. Census: 1870 in Calais.
iii. WILLIAM MELVIN SMALL, born 30 Aug 1849 in Calais (VR). He was a clerk and customs officer. Died 14 Oct 1931 age 82y 1m 15d in Calais (MSA, sfh:6:107). Buried in Calais Cemetery. Census: 1850, 60, 70 & 1900 in Calais. He married 24 Aug 1881 in Perry ME (times, mhl:68). EVA JANE LINSCOTT, daughter of DAVID LINSCOTT AND JANE MOONEY (see LINSCOTT).

ANDREW & EUPHEMIA SMITH, p. 180 & 198

ANDREW I. or J. SMITH.
[Possibly the Andrew Smith, of E. Machias, born 1822 in Cootehill, Cavan County, Ireland, entered U.S. in 1836 at E. Machias, naturalized July 1844 (irmch)].

He married EUPHEMIA (_____). Children:

i. NEWMARCH PRESCOTT SMITH, born 23 Nov 1842 in Calais (VR).
ii. GEORGE MAFLIN DALLAS SMITH, born 13 Oct 1843 in Calais (VR).
iii. WORTH SMITH, born 24 Dec 1846 in Calais (VR).

GEORGE & HANNAH SMITH p. 208

GEORGE SMITH, born circa 1798 in Wiscasset, ME (1850 census). He was a house carpenter. Died after 1881. Census: 1850 in Calais, 1860 in Long Prairie, Todd County, MN.

He married (int) 18 Dec 1825 in Calais (cal2:24), married in Robbinston, ME, by John Brewer (east:72, paper date 14 Jan 1826), HANNAH NOBLE born circa 1802 in Calais (1850 census), daughter of JOHN NOBLE & JEMIMA PURDY (TWB). Died after 1881. Census: 1850 in Calais, 1860 in Long Prarie, MN. Children:

i. JOHN NOBLE SMITH, born 10 Apr 1827 in Calais, died 10 Oct 1828 in Calais (VR).
ii. JAMES HENRY SMITH, born 10 Apr 1829 in Calais (VR). He was a sailor. Died after 1881. Census: 1850 in Calais.
   Clipping from Calais Advertiser of 26 Oct 1881, p.2 (howland)
   We saw Mr. Jas. H. Smith of Forest City, in town to-day. He informed us that his father, Mr. George Smith, and his mother, live in west Union, MN, both hearty and well. His mother is the only survivor of the old Noble family, who were among the original settlers of this place. - There are but few of the old, original settlers in existence. They are 'Melting awa' like the snaw' (sic).
iii. MARY ELIZABETH SMITH, born 23 Aug 1831 in Calais (VR). Census: 1850 in Calais.
iv. GEORGE MUNROE SMITH, born 24 Sep 1833 in Calais (VR). He was a carpenter. Census: 1850 in Calais, 1870 in Forest City, ME, 1880 in Eaton, Me, 1900 in Danforth, ME. He married 17 Mar 1856 in Calais (VR:1:165) ELIZABETH SCHOOLS, born Sept 1835. Census: 1900 in Danforth, ME.
v. ROBERT NOBLE SMITH, born 19 May 1837 in Calais (VR). Census: 1850 in Calais.
vi. CHARLES BARNARD SMITH, born 2 Jun 1839 in Calais (VR). He was a painter. Census: 1850 in Calais, 1860 in Long Prarie, MN.
vii. THURSEY SOPHIA SMITH, born 22 Oct 1842 in Calais (VR). Died 21 Sep 1843 in Calais (VR).

GEORGE & ELIZABETH P. SMITH p. 193

GEORGE S. SMITH, born circa 1813 in Addison, Me (1850 census), son of JOSEPH OTIS SMITH [born Sandwich, Ma] & BETSEY COFFIN (drisko:544), grandson of STEPHEN SMITH & DEBORAH ELLIS (Sandwich, MA VR:179a). Died 12 Sep 1850 age 37 in Calais (g.s.). Buried in Calais Cemetery. Census: 1850 in Calais.

He married (int) 26 June 1836 in Calais (cal2:42) ELIZABETH P. BRADLEY born circa 1817, in Westbrook, ME (1850 census) (poss. d/o William C. Bradley of Portland). Census: 1850 in Calais. Children:

i. SARAH BRADLEY SMITH, born 26 Apr 1837 in Calais (VR). Bapt. 26 Nov 1837 in Calais (congo). Died 6 Apr 1851 age 14 in Portland ME (FJ, at res. of William C. Bradley, adv, g.s.). Buried in Calais Cemetery. Census: 1850 in Calais.
ii. LEONICE HOWARD SMITH, born 13 May 1839 in Calais (VR). Bapt. 15 Sept 1839 (congo). Census: 1850 in Calais. She married EDGAR WAYE (drisko:545).
iii. BRADLEY SMITH, born circa 1841 in Calais (1850 census). Bapt. 18 July 1841 (congo). He enlisted in Civil War age 21 on 26 Aug 1861, left 5 Dec 1864, he was in Co G & A in 9th Me Inf. a Sgt., 2nd Lieut. & 1st Lieut. A farmer 5' 6" with hazel eyes and light hair, resided in Hodgdon, Me (cwcard). Census: 1850 in Calais.
iv. HARRIET ELIZABETH SMITH, born circa 1843, died 28 Jun 1843 age 5m in Calais (VR:1:234, g.s., gaz). Buried in Calais Cemetery.
v. BREWER {1} SMITH, born circa 1844, died 8 Oct 1844 age 9 m in Calais (VR:1:234, g.s.).
vi. BREWER {2} SMITH, born circa 1846 in Calais (1850 census). Census: 1850 in Calais. Possibly married MARY S. _____ (drisko:545).
vii. FRANK Y. SMITH, born circa 1847 in Calais. Died ca 1899 (g.s.). Buried in Calais Cemetery. Census: 1850 in Calais. He married ELLEN (_____), born 1848, died 1897 (g.s.). Buried in Calais Cemetery.
viii. EMILY B. SMITH, born circa 1849 in Calais (1850 census). Census: 1850 in Calais.

JOHN & DORCAS SMITH p. 193

JOHN B. SMITH, born circa 1800 in N B. He was a house carpenter. Census: 1840 (7 males, 5 females),

1850 in Calais.

He married circa 1820 DORCAS (_____), born circa 1803 in NB. Died 21 Dec 1850 age 48 in Calais (g.s.). Buried in Calais Cemetery. Census: 1850 in Calais. Children:

i. JOHN W. SMITH, born circa 1822 in NB. Census: 1850 in Calais.
ii. WILLIAM H. SMITH, born ca 1824 in St. David, NB (cwcard). He was in Civil War in Co K of 12th Reg't Inf., he had blue eyes and red hair was 5' 9 ½" (cwcard). He was a lumberman. Died 3 Oct 1893 age 70y 1m 2d (MSA, g.s.). Buried in Calais Cemetery. Census: 1850, 60 & 70 in Calais. He married ca 1851 AMY (_____), born ca 1827. Died 3 Apr 1878 age 51y 9m (g.s.). Buried in Calais Cemetery.
iii. THOMAS SMITH, born circa 1826 in NB. He was a sailor. Census: 1850 in Calais. [poss. he is the Thomas Smith who married in 1850 or 1851 by Rev. Keeler, Hannah Greenlow in Calais (VR:1:147)]
iv. JOSEPH SMITH, born circa 1828 in NB. Died 14 Mar 1861 at age 32 in Port Huron, MI (union). Census: 1850 in Calais.
v. DAVID SMITH, born circa 1830 in NB. Census: 1850 in Calais. [poss. He is the David Smith who married Elizabeth Woodman bet. Apr 1856 and Apr 1857 by Rev. S. H. Keeler (VR:1:169)]
vi. LUCY SMITH, born circa 1832 in NB. Census: 1850 in Calais. [poss. she is the Lucy Smith who filed int. to marry Frederick P. Walker 18 Oct 1852 in Calais (VR:1:47)]
vii. JAMES E. SMITH, born circa 1834 in NB. Census: 1850, 60 & 70 in Calais. He married 9 July 1859 in Calais (VR:3:174, union) HENRIETTA HAM, born ca 1836, daughter of RUFUS HAM & JANE SPENCE, (sister of Rufus, Jr. see SPENCER, Martha) . Census: 1850 (age 13), 60 & 70 in Calais.
viii. ANN SMITH, born circa 1836 in St. Stephen, NB (1850 census). Census: 1850 in Calais. [poss. she is the Ann Smith who married 5 Jan 1857 by Rev. C. M. Freeman , William Lamb in Calais (VR:1:168)]
ix. HANNAH SMITH, born circa 1839 in Calais (1850 census). Census: 1850 & 60 in Calais. She married 1 Oct 1858 in Calais (VR:3:172) ABIAH McPHAIL, born ca 1832. Census: 1860 in Calais.
x. STEPHEN SMITH, born 5 Apr 1843 in Calais (VR). Census: 1850 in Calais.
xi. GEORGE HARRISON SMITH, born 21 Jan 1846 in Calais, died 2 Jan 1847 in Calais (VR:1:234).

MOSES A. & ELIZABETH SMITH p. 211

MOSES A. SMITH, born circa 1808 in Solon, ME (1850 census). Census: 1850 in Calais.

He married (int.) 16 May 1843 in Calais (VR) ELIZABETH 'BETSEY' BACON born circa 1812 in Calais ME (1850 census). Census: 1850 in Calais. Children:

i. LEWIS SMITH, born 22 Mar 1844 in Calais (VR). Census: 1850 in Calais.
ii. LORAINNEY/LAVINA SMITH, born 11 May 1846 in Calais (VR). Census: 1850 in Calais.
iii. CYRUS W. SMITH, born circa 1848 in Calais (1850 census). Census: 1850 in Calais.

NOAH & HANNAH SMITH, Jr. p. 200

NOAH SMITH, Sr. b. 1775 the son of Capt. DAVID AND MARY (SMITH) SMITH. He was a captain in the cavalry, a selectman, justice of the peace and a representative. He married 1st in 1799 MARY SWEETSER, daughter of PAUL & MARY SWEETSER born ca 1774 died 1816. (History of Reading MA. P.353). Their oldest child was Noah Smith, Jr. who settled in Calais.

NOAH SMITH, Jr., born 21 Aug 1800 in Wakefield, MA (VR, 1850 census, g.s. has S. Reading MA). He was an agent for the St. Croix Manufacturing Co. of Calais in 1838 when he was involved in a court case (SJC). He came to Calais in 1832 where he was a deacon in the Baptist Church; Insurance agent; speaker of the Maine House of Representatives 1850-1854; secretary of the U.S. Senate 1858-1860; ran for governor for the Whig party but lost the nomination to Isaac Reed, who lost the election to Anson P. Morrill (History of Reading MA, Biographies of Speakers of the House, MSA). He is said to have been one of the last people who had official business with President Lincoln before his assassination; at that time he received the President's signature to a pardon granted to a young Calais soldier who had been convicted of treason (American Guide Series 1969:200). He died 14 Jan 1868 age 67 in Philadelphia, PA at home of his son, James (obit, adv, g.s.). Census: 1840 (8 males, 4 females), 50 in Calais. In 1860, while speaker of the house he resided at the Augusta House Hotel in Augusta, ME.

He married 6 Sep 1821 in 1st Baptist Church of Providence RI (fish) HANNAH DRAPER WHEATON born 8 Jul 1800 in Providence, RI (g.s.), daughter of JAMES WHEATON & ABIGAIL ROBINSON of

Rehoboth, MA (VR). Died 22 May 1849 age 48y 10m 14d in Calais (obit adv, g.s.). Buried in Calais Cemetery. Children:

i. MILA FRANCES SMITH, born 25 Aug 1825 in Providence. She died 9 June 1905 at home of daughter, May Gibson in Germantown, PA (whidd:c7). Buried in Calais Cemetery. Census: 1850 thru 1880. She married CHARLES RANDOL WHIDDEN (see WHIDDEN).

ii. SETH WHEATON SMITH, born 24 Feb 1826 in RI (g.s.). As an Indian agent he was a signer of a peace treaty with the Passamaquoddy Indians (pst of 2/16/1958). He was a customs collector. He died 15 Feb 1886 age 59y 11m 22d in Calais (obit times, g.s.). Buried in Calais Cemetery. Census: 1850 thru 1880 in Calais. He married CHARLOTTE EATON WRIGHT b ca 1828 in NB, daughter of DAVID WRIGHT & CHARLOTTE SMITH. She died 7 Nov 1892 age 65y 6m in Calais (MSA, SCC, adv, g.s.), buried in Calais Cemetery. Census: 1850, 60 & 70 in Calais.

iii. JAMES WHEATON SMITH, born probably in Providence, RI. He was a Baptist minister. Resided: 1875 in Philadelphia, PA (beg:127).

iv. ELLEN SWEETSER SMITH, born probably in Providence, RI. Died Mar 1888 in Portland, Ore (adv). Resided: 1865 in Iowa. She married 11 Dec 1843 in Calais (VR:1:131), by Japheth C. Washburn, Esq. (adv, gaz, beg:127). ALLEN TUPPER, of Houlton

v. ROBERT NOAH SMITH, born circa 1829 in RI (beg). Attended Brown University in RI 1846-50 (non-graduate, brown:622). Did not attend Bowdoin or Harvard as stated in daughter's autobiography. He was an attorney. Died 29 Dec 1860 at age 32 in a RR accident in Springfield, IL (obit adv, union). Census: 1850 in Calais. He married 1 Oct 1852 by Rev. G. W. Durrell in Calais (VR, FJ, SJC) HELEN ELIZABETH DYER, born Sept 1830 in Calais daughter of JONES DYER Jr. & LYDIA KNIGHT. She died 20 Feb 1921 at age 91 in ME. Helen filed for divorce from Robert in Sept 1858 "her husband was living in adultery with a prostitute in Bangor and he was drunken in his habits and at times abusive and quarrelsome." Divorce was granted in Oct Term of Supreme Judicial Court 1858. They were the parents of KATE DOUGLAS WIGGIN noted author.

vi. CHARLES HART SMITH, born circa 1832. He was a house carpenter. Resided: 1875 in Baltimore, MD (beg:127). Died 29 June 1895 in Baltimore, MD (adv). Census: 1860 (with her parents), 70 & 80 in Calais. He married 9 Oct 1851 in St Stephen, NB (CCMR, adv) EMMA SOPHIA GREEN, daughter of ELIJAH D. GREEN AND HANNAH C. HAYDEN (see GREEN).

vii. WALTER NEIL SMITH, born 12 May 1833 in Calais. Resided: 1875 in Iowa (beg:127). Census: 1850 in Calais.

viii. AMY ELLEN SMITH, born 22 May 1846 in Calais (VR).

THOMAS & HARRIET SMITH, p. 224

THOMAS SMITH, born between 1811–1820. Census: 1840 (2 males, 3 females) in Calais. [possible he is brother of Stuart Smyth below and they married sisters, his third child named Stuart].

He married May 1832 by Elias Kelsey, JP in Calais (cal2:48) HARRIET CALDWELL born between 1811-1820, daughter of WILLIAM CALDWELL AND ABIGAIL BAILEY. Children:

i. ELIZABETH JANE SMITH, born 26 Jun 1834 in Calais (VR).
ii. CORDELIA MARIA SMITH, born 8 Aug 1836 in Calais (VR).
iii. STUART SMITH, born 22 Dec 1838 in Calais (VR).
iv. MARY ABIGAIL SMITH, born 3 Apr 1841 in Calais (VR).
v. JOHN SMITH, born 3 Jun 1843 in Calais (VR).
vi. HARRIET EMELINE SMITH, born 25 Jul 1845 in Calais (VR).
vii. GEORGE ALBERT SMITH, born 6 Sep 1847 in Calais (VR).

URIAH & HOPESTILL SMITH, p. 211

URIAH SMITH, son of SETH & MARY SMITH, born 6 Aug 1783, in Stoughton, MA (VR:121). He was a potter and cemetery sexton. He moved from Robbinston to Calais 22 Nov 1835 (congo). Died 14 Jul 1865 age 82 in Calais (VR:3:312, g.s., union). Buried in Calais Cemetery. Census: 1830 (3 males, 7 females) in Robbinston, 1840 (2 males, 5 females), 50 & 60 in Calais.

He married before 1812 HOPESTILL (_____) , born circa 1786 (g.s.). Died 14 Jan 1858 at age 72 in Calais (union, g.s.). Buried in Calais Cemetery. Census: 1850 in Calais. Children:

i. SUSAN SMITH, born circa 1812. Died 16 Aug 1892 age 79y 11m in Calais (SSC). Census: 1850 (age 37), 60, 70 & 80 (living with sister, Chloe Smith) in Calais. She married before 1827 JAMES DYER, born ca 1798, son of JAMES DYER, Sr. & MARTHA BAILEY, and brother of Samuel Dyer (see DYER). He was a farmer. Died 8 May 1876 age 77 in Calais (obit adv). Census: 1850 (age 51), 1860 & 70 (age 72) in Calais. [1850 census has oldest child age 23, Susan must have married at 14 or 15 or she is his second wife].

ii. CHLOE ANN SMITH, born circa 1815 in Dorchester MA (1850 census). She was a tailoress. Died 16 Dec 1880 age 65 in Calais (g.s., east:338). Buried in Calais Cemetery. Census: 1850 thru 80 (living with sister, Susan Dyer) in Calais.

iii. URIAH ROBBINS SMITH, born circa 1822, died 15 Apr 1838 age 16 in Calais (VR:3:238, g.s.). Buried 17 Apr 1838 (sext).

iv. ANN MARIAH SMITH, born ca 1826 (1860 census). She married 27 Feb 1845 by Rev. Josiah Eaton EZRA ALDRICH, born ca 1815 (1860 census) of Baring. He was an axe manufacturer. In his Journal her father mentions going to her wedding. Census: 1840 (alone) in Baring, 1860 (with 4 children) in Calais.

v. ABIGAIL T. SMITH born circa 1827 in Robbinston Me (1850 census). Died 8 Sep 1870 age 43 (g.s.). Buried in Calais Cemetery. Census: 1850 & 60 in Calais.

vi. GEORGE W. SMITH, born circa 1830 in Robbinston Me (1850 census). Census: 1850 in Calais.

vii. LOUISA EMMA SMITH, born 28 Nov 1834 in Calais (VR). Died 8 Oct 1907 in Burrillsville, RI (obit, adv). Census: 1850, 70 & 80 in Calais. She married 6 June 1855 in Calais (VR:3:164) JOHN B. BURNHAM a blacksmith of Newfield, ME. Census: 1860 (with her parents), 70 & 80 in Calais. [he may be the John B. Burnham who died 23 Jan 1892 in Deering, Me, age 59y 6m a blacksmith (MSA)]

- Note – there were 2 females age under 5 in the 1830 census that do not appear in 1840, possibly they died young.

WILLIAM & MARGARET SMITH, p. 214

WILLIAM SMITH, born circa 1811 in Fredericton, NB (1850 census). Census: 1850 in Calais. [He is not the William S. Smith of Calais, born in British Empire, no date given, no entry date, naturalized on 17 July 1844 (irmch)].

He married 16 Nov 1843 by Benjamin Shattuck, JP in Calais (VR:1:131, mrwc:40) MARGARET BROWN, born circa 1820 in St. Andrews, NB (1850 census). Census: 1850 in Calais. Children:

i. EVELINE SMITH, born 14 Sep 1844 in Calais (VR). Census: 1850 in Calais.
ii. ALFRED WILLIAM SMITH, born 6 Feb 1848 in Calais (VR). Census: 1850 in Calais.

STUART & CHARITY SMYTH, p. 204
{Smith in 1860 census and on grave stone}

STUART/STEWART SMYTH/SMITH, born 6 Aug 1802 in Clonmain, Co Armagh, Ireland, left Ireland 6 May 1817-18 arrived St. Andrews, NB July 1817-18 the following Jan. he went to St. Stephen stayed six months then to Calais, naturalized July 1844 (irmch, name, Stewart Smith, naturalization records at Machias, SJC, brownj, 1850 census = Greenoak, Scotland). He was a tailor. Died 28 Nov 1865 age 67 in Calais (VR:3:312, brownj, union has 25 Nov). Buried in Calais Cemetery (g.s. has SMITH). Census: 1830 (4 males, 2 females), 40 (3 males, 4 females), 50 & 60 in Calais.

He married 9 Mar 1828 in Calais by Rev. Josiah Eaton (brownj, cal2:45) CHARITY CALDWELL, born 18 Jan 1805 in Baileyville ME, daughter of WILLIAM CALDWELL AND ABIGAIL BAILEY (brownj, from Smyth Family Bible, bail:70, 1850 census). Baptism: 8 Jul 1840 in Calais (lord:17). Died 28 Nov 1868 in Calais (brownj). Buried in Calais Cemetery. Census: 1850 & 60 in Calais. Children:

i. ELIZABETH JANE SMYTH, born 4 Mar 1829 in Calais (VR, brownj). Died 30 Mar 1831 in Calais (VR:1:236, brownj).

ii. WILLIAM HENRY SMYTH/ Smith, born 16 Sep 1830 in Calais (VR, brownj). He left Calais ca 1855, went to St. Anthony, MN and in 1858 to Eau Claire, WI, where he established a grocery business (wiscnh:333). Died 19 Feb 1922 in Eau Clair, WI (brownj). Census: 1850 in Calais. He married 8 May 1862 in Eau Claire KATHERINE 'Kate' FOX a native of Wisconsin (wiscnh:333).

iii. ELIZA JANE SMYTH, born 1 Apr 1832 in Calais (VR, brownj). Died 25 Sep 1832 in Calais (VR:1:236).

iv. MARY EMELINE SMYTH, born 8 Jul 1833 in Calais (VR, brownj). Died 23 Apr 1886 in Calais (brownj, g.s.). Census: 1850 thru 1880 in Calais. She married 29 Oct 1856 by Rev. C. M. Freeman in Calais (VR:1:168, brownj) JAMES FRANCIS HOLMES, son of JAMES HOLMES JR. AND TEMPERANCE CLARK (see HOLMES).

v. ADELAIDE COLWELL SMYTH, born 15 Mar 1836 in Milltown ME (VR, Alexander VR film at MSA). Died 26 Aug 1913 in Alexander ME. Census: 1850 in Calais. She married 22 Mar 1860 by by George H. Strout in Calais (VR:1:173). SOLOMON OBADIAH STROUT Jr., born 8 Apr 1827 in Alexander, son of SOLOMON O. STROUT & LYDIA BAILEY (bail:56, 70, achs). He died 28 Dec 1885 in Alexander (acsh). Both are buried in Alexander (achs).

vi. LUCINDA SMYTH, born 23 Mar 1838 in Calais (VR, brownj). Bapt. 16 May 1840 in Milltown, ME (lord:16). Died circa 1925 (brownj). Census: 1850 & 60 in Calais.

vii. ISAAC WESTLEY SMYTH, born 15 Jun 1840 in Calais (VR, brownj). Bapt. 8 July 1840 in Calais (lord:17). Resided in Caladonia, PA (brownj). Census: 1850 & 60 in Calais.

viii. STEPHEN EMERSON SMYTH/ Smith, born 14 May 1842 in Calais (VR, brownj). Left Calais for Eau Claire, WI in 1865 where he was a salesman for his brother, W. H. Smith, he owned two grocery stores "Union Grocery" and "Chicago Grocery" which he sold and retired in 1881 (wiscnh:333). Died 7 Apr 1907 in Eau Clair, WI (brownj). Census: 1850 & 60 in Calais.

ix. JULIA ELMY SMYTH, born 13 Mar 1844 in Calais (VR, brownj). Resided in Durand, WI. Probably died in Wisconsin. Census: 1850 & 60 in Calais. She married (_____) DORWIN (brownj).

x. JAMES STILLMAN SMYTH/ Smith, born 15 Sep 1847 in Calais (VR, brownj). He went to Wisconsin in the fall of 1867, he was in the grocery business (nwisc:333). Died 21 Sept 1883 in WI (wdr). Census: 1850 & 60 in Calais. He married 4 Sept 1878 in Monroe, WI, HELEN D. MORRISON a native of NJ (nwisc:333).

xi. CLARA H. SMYTH, born circa 1850. Census: 1860 in Calais. She married (int.) 16 Mar 1881 in Princeton (VR) FRANK ROLFE (brownj).

A. F. & C. E. SPAULDING, p. 226

AMOS FLETCHER[7] SPAULDING born 12 Jan 1821 in Boston Ma (brownu:212, spauld:313), son of AMOS[6] SPAULDING, who was a teacher and deacon in the Baptist church, & MARY WARREN, grandson of JOHN[5-4-3], ANDREW[2], EDWARD[1] (spald). He graduated in class of 1847 from Brown University and in class of 1850 from Newton Theological Seminary. He was ordained in Montreal, Que. remaining there until 1852; from there he moved to the Second Baptist church, in Cambridge, MA until 1856; from there to Calais until 1860; Chaplain in Civil War (1862-63) then to Warren, RI, Norwich, CT, and Needham, MA (spald:561, brownu:212). Died 30 Nov 1877 in Chelmsford, MA (brownu:212, spald:561).

He married 7 Oct 1852 (spald:561) CAROLINE ELIZABETH SANDERSON, born in Brookline, MA. Children:

i. EMMA CAROLINE SPAULDING, born 17 Oct 1853 in Brookline, MA, died 5 Jul 1855 in Brookline, MA (spald:561).

ii. MARY ELLEN SPAULDING, born 24 Nov 1857 in Calais (VR, spald:561).

JOSEPH & CLARA ANN SPAULDING, p. 217

JOSEPH[6] SPAULDING b. 5 August 1791 in Ashburnham, MA., son of James[5-4], Andrew[3-2], Edward[1]. He married 1st BETSEY HASTINGS; 2nd REBECCA NICHOLS, ca 1810; she died in 1856. Two children by 1st wife died young. About 1824 he moved to New Brunswick, where he soon died. He was a brick maker. His widow became insane, and the family was entirely dependent on the oldest son, who was Joseph Stillman, who moved to Calais.

Unless otherwise stated information on this family came from "The Spalding Memorial" by Charles W. Spalding, A.M., Chicago, 1897.{p. 292-293-515-755-756}

JOSEPH STILLMAN SPAULDING, born 30 Apr 1811 near Milford, NH (spald:293). He was a farmer. In 1863 he moved to California with his family. Died circa 1883 in Mayfield, CA. Census: 1850 & 60 in Calais.

He married circa 1832 CLARA ANN CHASE, born circa 1809 in St. David, NB (1850 census). Probably died in Calif. Census: 1850 & 60 in Calais. Children: the 1850 census shows the first six children born in St. David, NB.

i. JOSEPH STILLMAN SPAULDING, Jr., born 9 Sept 1833 in St. David, NB. Moved to Santa Clara Co. CA by way of San Francisco in 1866, he was a miner, lumberman and farmer (DEA 12:2:52). Died after 1897 probably in CA. Census: 1850 & 60 in Calais. He married after 1860, ELIZA (_____) she died 3 Apr 1895 in Mayfield, CA (spald:755).

ii. ROGER SHERMAN SPAULDING, born 29 Dec 1834 in St. David, NB. Census: 1850 & 60 in Calais. In 1897 they resided in Palo Alto, CA where he was a Constable. He married 11 Aug 1864 ABBIE A. NICHOLS.

iii. LYDIA F. SPAULDING, born circa 1837 in St. David, NB. Census: 1850 & 60 in Calais. She married 19 June 1853 in Calais by B.B. Byrne (VR:3:153) GEORGE WASHINGTON SHIRLEY of Calais. Both died in Calif.

iv. MEHITABLE S. or L. SPAULDING, born circa 1839 in St. David, NB. Died after 1897, prob. in NH. Census: 1850 & 60 in Calais. She married circa 1861 WALTER B. NICHOLS, he died before 1897 when she was a widow residing in Manchester, NH.

v. COLIN SYLVANUS V. SPAULDING, born circa 1841 in St. David, NB. In 1897 he resided in Monroe, WA (spald:756). He was one of the best known landowners and farmers in Scohomiah County. He and his brother, Thomas, having purchased the Salem Woods place about 13 years ago, known as the Hazel Farm of about 300 acres. He grew up on his father's farm in Maguerrawock{Calais} (obit). Died: 10 Dec 1905 age 63 in Monroe WA (obit adv, taken from Monroe Monitor). Census: 1850 & 60 in Calais.

vi. JANE EMELINE SPAULDING, born circa 1845 in St. David, NB. Died: in CA. Census: 1850 & 60 in Calais. She married ZACH STAFFORD. In 1897 they resided in Redwood City, CA.

vii. THOMAS WILLIAM PERLEY SPAULDING, born 13 Oct 1846 in Calais (VR, spald:756 has 14 Oct 1847]). Census: 1850 & 60 in Calais. He married 16 Jun 1888 NELLIE JAKIN, a talented musician and a descendant of the Fossetts of Maine. They resided in Monroe, WA 1897 (spald:756), still there when his brother died 1905. No children.

viii. BENJAMIN SHEPPARD SPAULDING, born 31 Jan 1850 or 51 in Milltown ME. Census: 1850 (age 4m), 1860 age 10 in Calais (spald:756 has him b. 1851). In 1863 he sailed from New York to San Francisco, CA, in company with his parents, brothers and sisters. He has been a teamster in the Redwoods, and for twenty-two years he drove a nine-yoke oxen team, and for two years drove a twelve-horse team. He resided in Washington and Oregon and finally in Arcata, CA (spald:756). Died after 1897. He married 12 Dec 1876 EUNICE CLARK, born 12 Jan 1856, daughter of WILLIAM CLARK & MARY RICHARDS.

ix. ANNA I. or Q. SPAULDING. Died 30 Apr 1854 in Calais (VR:3: 301).

x. MARY E. SPAULDING, born circa 1852. Census: 1860 in Calais.

- Note The two youngest children not mentioned in Spaulding Genealogy.

ROBERT TAYLOR & ELIZA ANN SPENCER, p. 189

ROBERT TAYLOR SPENCER born circa 1815, in Fredericton, NB (1850 census) (possibly he is the son of David D. Spencer who d. Calais 19 Mar 1845 age 63y). Died before 1870. Census: 1840 (3 males, 2 females), 1850 & 60 in Calais.

He married 1 Sept 1838 by John Sargent, Esq. (cal2:50, gaz, adv of 12 Sept 1838) ELIZA ANN GREENLAW, born circa 1816 in St Andrews, NB (1850 census), probable daughter of SOLOMON GREENLAW & MARGARET COOKSON. Died 7 May 1877 age 60y 9m in Calais (adv). Census: 1850, 60 & 70 in Calais. Children:

i. MARGARET JONES SPENCER, born 23 Jan 1840 in Calais (VR). Census: 1850 & 60 in Calais. She married 5 Oct 1868 by Rev, H.V. Dexter in Calais (VR:3:228, union) SAMUEL GREENLAW, born ca 1839.

ii. MARTHA ALMENA SPENCER, born 29 Jul 1841 in Calais (VR). Census: 1850 in Calais. She married 30 July 1859 in Calais (VR:3:173) by George D. Strout RUFUS HAM, Jr., born ca 1829 I NB, son of RUFUS & JANE HAM & bro. of Henrietta (Ham) Smith, (see James E. SMITH) He was a merchant. Census: 1850, 60 & 70 in Calais.

iii. BARTLETT RICHARD SPENCER, born 6 Aug 1842 in Calais (VR). He enlisted in Civil War 4 Aug 1862 in Co D & C 6th Me Inf., he was lumberman 5' 6" with blue eyes and brown hair (cwcard). Census:

1850, 60 & 70 (Margaret Tufts age 55 with them poss. mother of Elizabeth) in Calais, 1880 in Kossuth. He married 1st 13 May 1867 by Rev. H.V. Dexter in Calais (VR:3:217) ELIZABETH TUFTS born ca 1845 in Canada (1870 census). Census: 1870 in Calais. He married 2nd before 1875 (census Topsfield) ALICE ROSALIND WHITE, born ca 1856 in Kossuth, Me. Census: 1880 (age 24) in Kossuth.

iv. DAVID DELESS SPENCER, born Apr 1845 in Calais (VR). He enlisted in Civil War 1 Feb 1865, left 6 July 1865, Co G of Coast Guard, 5' 6" with blue eyes and brown hair (cwcard). He was a carpenter. Died 4 Nov 1905 age 60y 7m in Calais (MSA). Census: 1850 thru 1900 in Calais. He married 15 Dec 1870 by Rev. E. B. Eddy in Calais (VR:3:32, adv, union) JOSEPHINE 'Josie' V. GREENLAW born ca May 1846 (1900 census) in Calais, daughter of GILBERT H. GREENLAW (b. St Stephen) & ELIZABETH JAMES. Died 3 Jan 1907 in Calais (MSA, adv). Census: 1870 (age 20 with her father), 80 & 1900 in Calais.

v. SOLOMON FRANKLIN SPENCER, born 24 Mar 1847 in Calais (VR). Census: 1850 & 60 in Calais.

vi. FRANCES R. SPENCER, born circa 1850 (VR). Census: 1850, 60 & 70 (living with sister, Almena Ham) in Calais. She married 22 June 1871 by Rev. E. B. Eddy in Calais (union) CHARLES H. CURRY of Calais.

vii. ROBERT HENRY SPENCER, born circa 1851. He was a clerk. Census: 1860, 70 & 80 (living with brother Deless) in Calais.

WILLIAM & PHEBE SPENCER, p. 193

WILLIAM SPENCER born ca 1817 in NB, 1851 census of Pennfield, NB (name Spence, age 34, a Block & Spar Maker absent from household. Shares house with Henry Young).

He married 15 Nov 1845 in Calais (VR) PHEBE YOUNG of Pennfield, NB, born ca 1820. Census: 1851 in Pennfield, NB. Children:

i. HENRY ALLEN SPENCER, born 19 Feb 1847 in Calais (VR). Census: 1851 in Pennfield.

ii. MARY SPENCER, born ca 1849, 1851 (age 2) census of Pennfield.

EDWARD & HANNAH SPINNEY, p. 206

CHARLES EDWARD SPINNEY, born circa 1821 in St. George N B (1850 census). Died 6 July 1884 age 62y in Calais (adv). Census: 1850, 60 & 70 in Calais.

He married 1st 18 Oct 1846 by Thomas D. Williams, JP in Calais (VR:1:139) HANNAH HOLT born circa 1822 in Dexter ME (1850 census). Died 26 Dec 1852 age 29 in Calais (g.s.). Buried in Calais Cemetery. Census: 1850 in Calais. Children:

i. ELIZA DUNBAR SPINNEY, born 11 Aug 1847 in Calais (VR). Died 15 Aug 1850 age 3y in Calais (g.s.). Buried in Calais Cemetery. Census: 1850 in Calais.

ii. AMBROSE A. SPINNEY, born May 1850 in Calais. Died 11 May 1876 age 26y 1m in Calais (obit adv). Buried in Calais Cemetery. Census: 1850, 60 & 70 in Calais.

iii. JASON ALBERT SPINNEY, born, circa 1852. Bapt. 11 Oct 1854 in Calais (saint). He went to sea at age 14 (phill). Died after 1920. Census: 1860 {age 8} & 70 {age 14} in Calais. Census: 1900 (Albert J. age 45), 1920 (Albert J. age 64, alone) in Calais.

Edward married 2nd 13 Aug 1853 by Rev. Jerome Alley in St. Stephen, NB (CCMR) JANE L. GOLDEN/GOLDING born circa 1839 in Dublin, Ireland (death rec.), daughter of PETER GOLDING & LUCY A. PARKS (both born in Ireland). Died 6 Jan 1912 in Calais (VR). Census: 1860, 70 & 1900 (age 64) in Calais. Children:

iv. HANNAH ELIZA SPINNEY, born circa 1855. Bapt. 1 Nov 1857 in Calais (saint). Died 18 Aug 1934I in Montreal, Que. (phill). Census: 1860 & 70 in Calais. She married 19 Feb 1885 in St. Stephen, NB, ROBERT THOMPSON STUART (phill).

v. CHARLES EDWARD SPINNEY, born circa 1860 in Calais, died 18 May 1865 age 4y 7m in Calais (g.s.). 'Little Eddie' struck by a train and died (phill). Bapt. 9 Feb 1861 in Calais (saint). Census: 1860 in Calais. Buried in Calais Cemetery.

vi. JESSIE MAUD SPINNEY, born circa 1864 in Calais. Census: 1870 in Calais. She married

FREDERICK BRADBURY APT, they resided in Eastport (phill, MSA).

vii. NELLIE M. SPINNEY, born circa 1865 in Calais. Census: 1870 in Calais. She married 14 Sept 1895 in Calais (VR, east:538, MSA) WILLIAM THOMPSON, son of JOSEPH THOMPSON & ANN STAPLES (both born in England). (MSA has Nellie M. age 33 her 1st marriage to William Thompson his 2nd).

viii. GEORGE F. SPINNEY, born 18 Nov 1868 in Calais (birth rec, phill). Died after 1901. Census: 1870 in Calais. He married 1st MARY E. JOHNSON, born ca 1868, daughter of ARCHIE JOHNSON (b. NB) & MAGGIE ANDERSON (b. Calais), she died 11 Aug 1901 age 33y 10m 5d in Calais (MSA). Buried in Calais. He married 2nd ELLEN SCULLIN, born ca 1866 in Rollingdam, NB, daughter of WILLIAM SCULLIN & AANNIE M. SHEAN (both born Rollingdam, NB). She died 13 Dec 1909 age 42 in Calais (MSA, sfh:1:229, phill).

ix. EDWARD C. SPINNEY, born circa Jan 1868. He was a carpenter. Census: 1870 & 1900 in Calais. He married 23 Jun 1906 in Calais (MSA) ANNIE MUSTARD, born 3 Jan 1879 in Scotland, daughter of ROBERT MUSTARD (a fireman) & JANE FURGERSON (both born in Scotland). She died 11 May 1931 in Portland age 52y 4m 8d. Census: 1900 in Calais.

x. FRANKLIN P. SPINNEY, born ca 1869/75 in Calais (age 22, in 1895 at marriage, record has Jane as mother but she d. 1870). Died 18 Aug 1948 age 79y 5m 28d in Bangor (MSA). Census: 1900 (age 25 b. Feb 1875) in Calais. He married 27 Jul 1895 in Calais (MSA) CASSIE FELICA GARNET, born ca June 1875 in Perry, daughter of JAMES C. GARNET & MARY McPHAIL (both born in Perry). She died 9 July 1937 age 67y 1n 4d in Bangor (MSA). Census: 1900 in Calais.

xi. LOUISE 'Lucy' PARKS SPINNEY, born ca 1879, died 28 Nov 1957 age 78y 14d in Malden, MA, buried in Oak Grove Cemetery, Malden (copy of death cert. phill). She married 20 Aug 1894 in Calais (VR, MSA) ALEXANDER BARRY MILLS, born in Boston, MA, son of JAMES MILLS (b. St. John, NB) & MARY L. CAMPBELL (b. P.E.I.).

xii. CAROLYN B. SPINNEY, born 14 Apr 1879 (birth rec.). Died 24 Feb 1961 age 81y 10m 10d in Newton, MA, buried in Newton (copy of death cert. phill). She married 17 May 1913 in Calais as his 2nd wife (his age 56 her age 34 MSA, phill) FRANK H. BARCLAY, son of ANDREW BARCLAY & ELIZA ARMSTRONG, he died before his wife.

JOHN & EMILY SPINNEY, p. 196

JOHN SPINNEY, born circa 1820 in Kittery, ME (Etta's death rec.). He was a truckman. Died 25 Apr 1879 age 63y in Calais (adv). Census: 1860 & 70 (born in NB) in Calais.

He married 10 Nov 1844 by J. P. Washburn, JP in Calais (VR, mrwc: 45) EMILY R. WAKEFIELD, born 9 Mar 1826 in Lubec (lubec:14), daughter of CYRUS WAKEFIELD AND MAHALA McDONALD. Died 12 Oct 1909 in Calais (MSA). Census: 1860 thru 1900 in Calais (see WAKEFIELD). Children:

i. MARY ELLEN SPINNEY, born 30 Jul 1845 in Calais, died 7 Jan 1847 in Calais (VR:1:235).

ii. CHARLES ALBERT SPINNEY, born 21 Jun 1849 in Calais (VR). Census: 1860, 70 & 80 in Calais. He married 10 Sep 1873 in Calais (VR:3:235). MARGARET E. CALDWELL, born ca 1851. Census: 1880 in Calais.

iii. JOHN HENRY SPINNEY, born circa 1849-51 in Calais. He enlisted in Civil War at age 17 (?lied about age? Father may have lied also when he signed enlistment paper), on 16 Nov 1864, left 23 June 1865, a teamster 5' 6" with blue eyes and brown hair, resided in Bath, Me at enlistment (cwcard). He was a stevedore. Died 30 Jul 1899 age 50y 5m in Calais (MSA). Died in the office of the City Clerk, he was a member of GAR post of Calais (obit adv). Buried in Calais Cemetery, (military stone no dates). Census: [not in 1850], 1860 (age 9) & 70 (age 21) in Calais. He married (int.) 10 Dec 1869 in Calais (VR:3) ANGELINE ESTEY, born ca 1848 in Woodstock, NB, daughter of CHARLES ESTEY & MARY A. KITCHEN. She died 8 Apr 1896 in Calais, buried in Calais (MSA). Census: 1870 in Calais.

iv. CLARA AUGUSTA SPINNEY, born circa 1854. Bapt. 11 Oct 1854 in Calais (saint). Census: 1860 & 70 in Calais. She married 12 Oct 1872 in Calais (VR:3:326) WILLIAM H. EDERSON of New York.

v. AARON T. SPINNEY, born circa 1856 in Calais. He was a stevedore. Died 3 Apr 1896 in Calais (VR). Buried in Calais Cemetery. Census: 1860, 70 & 80 in Calais. He married 3 Nov 1880 in Calais (VR:3:88, CCMR) MARTHA MOWATT, born 29 July 1885 in Oak Bay, NB, daughter of HENRY MOWATT, (a shipbuilder born in Scotland) & MARGARET WILLIAMS (b. Ire). She died 30 June 1919 age 62 y 11m 2d in St. Stephen, NB (Calais VR).

vi. MAY E. SPINNEY, born circa 1858. Census: 1860 in Calais.

vii. LILLIAN A. SPINNEY, born circa 1860. Census: 1870 & 80 in Calais. She was a dressmaker. She married (_____) KING [her name Lillian King in Etta's will].

viii. ETTA M. SPINNEY, born circa 1864. Died 16 Aug 1923 age 59 in Calais (MSA, prbt). Buried in Calais Cemetery. Probate of Estate in Machias Me (will # R 5-253). Census: 1870 & 80 in Calais. She married 1st (_____) COLLINS, 2nd WILLIAM JOHN RUTHERFORD, born ca 1864 in Calais, son of DAVID RUTHERFORD & A. BALK (parents names on death record). Died 13 Oct 1922 in Calais (MSA). Census: 1870, 80, 1900, 10, & 20. He married 1st Annie Morris (see RUTHERFORD).

ix. FREDERICK W. SPINNEY, born 22 Sep 1869 in Calais (MSA). He was a shoemaker, then a restaurant owner & merchant. Died 11 Dec 1933 in Calais age 65y 2m 19d (MSA). Census: 1870, 80 & 1900 in Calais. He married 1st 21 Sept 1890 in Calais by Rev. A.W.C. Anderson LIZZIE IRVING of Calais (adv). He married 2nd 7 Jul 1896 in Calais (MSA) MARY GRAY, born Sept 1874, daughter of GEORGE GRAY & ELLEN HURLEY (both born in NB). They were divorced. Census: 1900 in Calais. He married 3rd 6 Mar 1912 TRESSA L. MARSHALL, daughter of JOHN M. MARSHALL & ANNIE MURRAY (both born Halifax, NS). She died after 1933. Census: 1900 in Calais.

NATHANIEL & MARY SPINNEY, p. 186

NATHANIEL SPINNEY, born circa 1806, son of JONATHAN SPINNEY AND MARY (TROTE ?/TROTT), in St George, NB (1850 census). He was a truckman. Died 5 Jan 1892 age 77y 11m in Calais (g.s., east:475, MSA). Buried in Calais Cemetery. Census: 1850, 60 & 70 in Calais.

He married 1 Dec 1834 in St George NB (angch), MARY LOWE born circa 1819 in St George NB (1850 census). Died 14 Mar 1879 age 61 in Calais (times, g.s.). Buried in Calais Cemetery. Census: 1850, 60 & 70 in Calais. Children:

i WILLIAM L. SPINNEY, born circa 1835 in St George NB (his death rec.). He was a stevedore. Died 10 Oct 1915 age 80y 6m in Calais (MSA). Buried in Calais Cemetery. Census: 1850 thru 1880 & 1900 in Calais. He married 7 June 1860 in Calais (VR), 9 June 1861 (saint) SARAH A. CONNORS, born ca 1837 (g.s.) in St. George, NB, daughter of PATRICK CONNORS, (a teacher, b. Ire) & JANE McCLUSKEE (b. NB) (MSA). She died 28 Oct 1896 in Calais, buried in Calais Cemetery (MSA). Census: 1851 in St. James, NB, 1870 & 80 in Calais.

ii NANCY SPINNEY, born circa 1840 in St George NB (1850 census). Died 1934 (g.s.). Buried in Calais Cemetery. Census: 1850 & 60 in Calais. Married 3 May 1863 by D. F. Smith in Calais (VR) HUGH CONNORS of St. Stephen, born ca 1836, son of PATRICK CONNORS (a teacher, b. Ire) & JANE McCLUSKEE (b. NB). Died 1874 (g.s.), buried in Calais Cemetery. Census: 1851 in St. James, NB.

iii STEPHEN ALEX SPINNEY, born Jun 1842 in St George NB (1850 & 1900 census). Bapt. 29 Mar 1851 in Calais (saint). He enlisted in Civil War 25 Oct 1861 Co K 12th Me Inf. and failed to appear, a hostler 5'9" with red hair and blue eyes (cwcard). He was a stevedore. Died 8 Dec 1914 age 72y 3m in Calais (MSA, g.s.). Buried in Calais Cemetery. Census: 1850 thru 1910 in Calais. He married 2 Sept 1865 in Calais (phill, VR). EMMA J. HARRIS, born 1844, died 1928 (g.s.), daughter of ISAIAH & MARY JANE HARRIS. Buried in Calais Cemetery. Census: 1870, 1900 [born Jan 1846] & 1910 in Calais (see HARRIS).

iv SARAH JANE SPINNEY, born 10 May 1845 in Calais (VR). Bapt. 29 Mar 1851 in Calais (saint). Died 28 Nov 1895 age 49y 7m in Calais (MSA). Buried in Calais Cemetery. Census: 1850 & 60 in Calais. She married 7 Nov 1867 in Calais by Rev. H.V. Dexter (VR:3:227) THOMAS ROGERS.

v ZEBEDIAH or Zebulon D. SPINNEY, born 10 Jan 1848 in Calais (VR). Bapt. 29 Mar 1851 in Calais (saint). He was a stevedore. Died 6 Sep 1893 in Calais (MSA). Buried 8 Sept 1893 in Calais Cemetery (saint). Census: 1850 thru 1880 in Calais. He married 16 Aug 1872 in Calais (VR:3:240) ANNE M. RAIRDEN / REDDING / REARDON born ca 1855. Census: 1880 in Calais.

vi SHUBIEL T. SPINNEY, born circa 1849. Bapt. 29 Mar 1851 in Calais (saint). In 1881 he was injured while helping to fight a house fire and never fully recovered, died 24 Mar 1889 in Calais age 37y 2m (east:420, adv). Census: 1860, 70 in Calais. He filed mar. int. 22 June 1872 in Calais (VR :3) EMERLINE COX, married 19 Apr 1873 EVELYN COX (union).

vii CATHARINE SPINNEY, Bapt. 29 Mar 1851 in Calais (saint).

vii MARY ANN SPINNEY, Bapt. 29 Mar 1851 in Calais (saint).

ix GEORGE ALBERT SPINNEY, born circa 1853. Bapt. 12 May 1854 in Calais (saint). Died 19 May 1854 age 10m in Calais (g.s.). Buried in Calais Cemetery.

x MARY E. SPINNEY, born circa 1855, died 22 Mar 1863 age 8 in Calais (VR:3:303, g.s.). Bapt. 13 Mar 1856 in Calais (saint). Census: 1860 in Calais.

xi ZEB/LEB SPINNEY, born ca 1857, died 25 Mar 1863 age 6y (a son of Nathaniel & Mary) (VR:3:303) (not listed in 1860 census).

xii GEORGE F. SPINNEY, born circa 1858, died 21 Mar 1863 age 5 in Calais (g.s.). Bapt. 22 Sept 1858 in Calais (saint). Buried in Calais Cemetery. Census:1860 in Calais.

xiii NELLIE SPINNEY, born circa 1862. Census: 1870 in Calais. She married 28 Oct 1882 in Calais GEORGE A. JOHNSON (phill).

WILLIAM & ANNA SPINNEY, p. 186

WILLIAM SPINNEY, born circa 1805 in Eastport ME (1850 census). Census: 1850 in Calais.

He married Dec 1825 in Eastport by J. D. Weston (east:72) HANNAH/ANNA L. STAMP, born circa 1808 in St George NB (1850 census). Census: 1850 in Calais. [There was a William Spinney buried 30 Apr 1851 age 58 and Mrs. William (no dates given) in Calais Cemetery records in same lot as Nathaniel & Mary Spinney, could William be a brother of Nathaniel?]. Children:

i. JOHN SPINNEY, born circa 1829 in St George NB (1850 census). Died after 1850. Census: 1850 in Calais.

ii. HORATIO NELSON SPINNEY, born Aug 1833 in St George NB (1850 census). Died after 1900 before 1920. Census: 1850 in Calais, 1871 in St. George, NB, 1880 & 1900 in Danforth, ME. He married 1st 12 July 1859 in Topsfield (VR:1:27, both of Jackson Brook, ME) MARGARET ANN ELLIOT (daughter, Annie's death rec.). He married 2nd (after 1863 before 1870 census) MARY R. CORNING (son's death rec.). He married 3rd MARGARET C. (_____), born ca 1840 (1900 census), died after 1900.

iii. SARAH C. SPINNEY, born circa 1835 in Cooper ME (1850 census). Census: 1850 in Calais.

iv. LOUIZA J. SPINNEY, born 1838 in Cooper ME (1850 census). Census: 1850 in Calais.

v. LAVINIA SPINNEY, born 1841 in Cooper ME (1850 census). Census: 1850 in Calais.

vi. CHARLES W/M. SPINNEY, born circa 1843 in Baring ME (1850 census). He served in Civil War in Co F 7th Me Inf. Mar 1864 to June 1865 a laborer 5'9 ½" with gray eyes and brown hair (cwcard). Census: 1850 in Calais. He married 14 July 1868 by Rev. H. V. Dexter in Calais (VR:3:228) ELIZA J. THOMPSON.

vii. WILLIAM A. SPINNEY, born circa 1845 in Baring ME (1850 census). He served in Civil War enlisted at age 19 on 24 Mar 1864 in Co F 7th Me Inf. a laborer 5'8" with gray eyes and brown hair, left 28 Jan 1865 (cwcard). Census: 1850 in Calais. He married 20 Aug 1870 by Rev. E. B. Eddy in Calais (VSNB:29:1359) MARY ELLEN BULLOCK of St. George, NB, daughter of CHARLES BULLOCK & ELEANOR 'ELLEN' HURLEY. They resided in St. George, NB and had 7 sons.

viii. REUBEN DOUGLAS SPINNEY, born 30 Dec 1847 in Calais (VR). Census: 1850 in Calais.

PAUL & SERENA SPOONER, p. 217

PAUL SPOONER, born circa 1801 in Miramichi, NB (dau death rec.), (1850 census = Sangerville, ME, son's death rec. = Eddington, ME). He is possibly the son of Stevens Spooner & Sally Hodgkins (lit:1333). The census says he was a house carpenter, biography of son, Saunders, says he was a mechanic and a miller, came to Calais in 1835 and operated a grist mill, moved to Princeton in 1857, built another mill and he died at age 86 (biorev:488). Died 12 Mar 1887 in Princeton Me (times). Buried in Calais Cemetery. Census: 1830 (1 male age 20-30 & 1 male age 50-60) in Cooper,1840 (4 males, 4 females) & 50 in Calais, 1860, 70 & 80 in Princeton Me.

He married SERENA or Cyrena PRICE, born circa 1809 in Boiestown, NB (biorev, son's death rec.). Died 13 Feb 1878 age 69y 11m 13d in Princeton Me (times, adv = 1879, biorev:488). Buried in Calais Cemetery. Census: 1850 in Calais, 1860 & 70 in Princeton Me. Children:

i. LUCRETIA SPOONER, born ca 1829, in NB. She died before 1898. Census: 1850 (with parents & husband) in Calais. She married 7 Oct 1845 in Calais by Rev. Allen Barrows (VR:3:136, gaz) LORENZO

HUNTLEY born ca 1820. Census: 1850 (a carpenter) in Calais.

ii. RICHARD P. SPOONER born 1830 in NB, died 4 Jul 1848 age 18 in Calais (g.s.). Buried in Calais Cemetery.

iii. ABIGAIL SPOONER, born circa 1832 in Miramichi, NB (1850 census). Census: 1850, 60 & 70 in Calais. She married 29 Nov 1855 in Calais (VR:3:165), DAVID LEIGHTON, born ca 1829, he was a house joiner. Census: 1860 & 70 in Calais.

iv. CHARLES LECHMERE SPOONER, born 14 Feb 1834 in Ludlow, NB. He was a carriage maker and carpenter. Died 7 Feb 1911 age 76y 11m 21d in Princeton Me (prinvr:22,23). Buried in Princeton. Census: 1850 in Calais, 1860, & 80 in Princeton. He married 1st 4 Nov 1854 in Eastport by Nathaniel Butler (east:139); (int.) 25 Oct 1854 in Calais (VR) MARY ALICE SCOTT born 1833, daughter of DANIEL & ELIZABETH SCOTT (g.s.). Mary A. died 15 Aug 1873 in Princeton. Buried in Princeton Cemetery. Census: 1860, in Princeton. He married 2nd after 1873 MARY ELLEN 'Nellie' POOLE, born 6 Sept 1849 in Pennfield, NB, daughter of ENOS POOLE & KATHERINE JUSTASON, Mary E. died 1 June 1923 age 73y 8m 25d in Princeton (MSA, g.s.). Buried in Princeton. Census: 1880 & 1900 in Princeton.

v. SAUNDERS GILL SPOONER, born 9 Apr 1836 in Calais (VR). During Civil War he enlisted in Co. A of the 9th 1 Jan 1864, also was in Co. H, he served as hospital steward. Upon his return to civil life he had many interests and occupations: drug business, practiced medicine, Selectman, Town Treasurer, Postmaster, County Commissioner and Justice of the Peace (biorev:488). Enlistment paper at MSA describes him as 27 years old, blue eyes, dark hair, and 5' 8 ½" tall. He was a dealer in drugs, medicines, confectionery, cigars, tobacco, teas, coffees, spices, books and stationery, fancy baskets and Indian novelties, etc. and in 1892 was the town librarian in Princeton (CEV:84). Died 3 Aug 1906 in Princeton Me (MSA). Buried in Calais Cemetery. Census: 1850 in Calais, 1860, 70, 80 & 1900 in Princeton Me. He married 20 Mar 1864 in Milltown ME (VR) ALICE DODGE CLARK, daughter of AMOS CLARK AND MARY ANN CHENEY (see CLARK).

vi. SARAH JANE SPOONER, born 6 Sep 1838 in Calais (VR). Census: 1850 in Calais. She married 18 Mar 1860 in Princeton (union) EBEN C. VARNUM of Princeton. [Mar. int 26 Aug 1874 Mrs. Sarah Varnum and Joseph Edgett both of Grand Lake Stream, Me. (Princeton VR)].

vii. EMMA/EMILY SPOONER, born 17 Feb 1840 in Calais (VR). Died 28 Nov 1866 in Calais (sext). Buried in Calais Cemetery. Census: 1850 & 60 in Calais. She married 9 Aug 1859 in Calais (VR) CHARLES HOLMES, son of JAMES HOLMES, Jr. and TEMPERANCE CLARK (see HOLMES).

viii. HENRY ALLEN SPOONER, born 21 May 1842 in Calais (VR). Census: 1870 in Topsfield, ME. Census: 1850 in Calais, 1860 in Princeton Me, 1870 in Topsfield. He married 5 Jan 1867 by Rev. Evan Powell in Topsfield (VR) CORDELIA TRACY, born 19 June 1847 in Topsfield (VR:9), daughter of WILLIAM & JANE TRACY. Census: 1870 in Topsfield.

ix. HENRIETTA SPOONER, born 21 May 1842 in Milltown ME (VR). Died 30 Jan 1933 in Milltown ME (MSA). Census: 1850 & 70 in Calais, 1860 in Princeton Me. She married 23 Nov 1865 GILBERT A. HOLMES, son of JAMES HOLMES Jr. & TEMPERANCE CLARK (see HOLMES).

x. CLARISSA SPOONER, born 19 Jun 1844 in Calais (VR). Died after 1870. Census: 1850 in Calais, 1860 & 70 in Princeton Me.

xi. IDA SPOONER, born circa 1848 in Calais (1850 census). Died 2 Nov 1910 age 62y 1m 26d in Princeton (prinvr:22,23). Census: 1850 in Calais, 1860, 70, 80 & 1900 in Princeton Me. She married WILLIAM PORTER PLAISTED, (prinvr:84.85, on son's marriage record 1915), born ca Oct 1842 in Gardiner, ME, son of WILLIAM P. PLAISTED & MARIETTA FORBES (both born Jefferson, NH), died 19 Mar 1902 age 59y 5m 14d in Princeton (death record MSA). He was a Trial Justice. Census: 1900 in Princeton.

xii. LAURA FIDELLA 'FLORA' SPOONER, born 4 Oct 1852, in Milltown ME (LDS). She died after 1884 when son was born and before 1898. Census: 1860, 70 & 80 in Princeton Me. She married (int.) 22 Jul 1872 in Princeton Me (VR) SETH HENRY GREENLAW, born 14 July 1847 age 82y 9m 8d in Princeton, son of CHARLES HENRY GREENLAW & MARTHA GREENLAW (both born in NB) (MSA). Died 22 Apr 1931 in Princeton (MSA). Census: 1880 & 1900 in Princeton.

Note * Biographical Review:487 article written in 1898 on Saunders, lists two other siblings: Price & Aaron H., who were deceased probably died as infants, also deceased by then were: Lucretia, Richard, Emma and Della.

CHARLES & BATHSHEBA SPRAGUE p 220

JAMES[6] SPRAGUE, son of JAMES[5], ABIEL[4], SAMUEL[3], JOHN[2], AND FRANCIS[1], was born ca 1777 in Machias, ME. He married, PRISCILLA NOBLE born ca 1782, in NB, died after 1860, daughter of JOHN NOBLE & JEMIMA PURDY (TWB). James died ca 1859 and is buried in Machiasport, ME. From *"Supplement to Sprague Families in America", by W. V. Sprague, 1941*: "[James] Sprague was extensively engaged in the lumber trade. After cutting the timber from his land in Red Beach, he secured land in Charlotte, and made a road to it. He then moved his equipment and built the first saw mill on the Moosehorn Stream, near Charlotte station, a few steps from Sprague road [on 20 Oct 1845] he and Priscilla sold and moved to Machiasport." (TWB). Their 1st child was Jonathan whose wife was Anna and they resided in Calais (mead, TWB). Their 1st child, Jonathan resided in Calais (see below) and their 5th child was Charles who married Bathsheba Bridges and resided in Calais (mead, TWB). (see BELOW)

CHARLES FRANK SPRAGUE, born 25 July 1808 in Calais (1850 census). Bapt. 25 Feb 1809 (kmc). He was a farmer and butcher. Died before 1884 in Minneapolis, MN (mead). Census: 1830 (2 males, 2 females) in Charlotte, ME, 1840 (3 males, 6 females), 50, 60 & 70 in Calais.

He married 30 Jul 1827 by Ebenezer Fisher in Charlotte ME (VR) BATHSHEBA BRIDGES, born circa 1810 in Charlotte ME (1850 census), daughter of THOMAS BRIDGES AND BATHSHEBA WILDER. Died in Dec 1884 in Minneapolis, MN (mead) Census: 1850, 60 & 70 in Calais. Children:

i. HEMAN N. SPRAGUE, born 22 Sep 1828 in Charlotte ME (VR). Died 3 Nov 1909 in Calais (MSA). Census: 1850 in Calais, 1860 in Crawford, 1871 in St. Stephen, NB, 1880 & 1900 in Calais. He married 30 May 1852 by Rev. C. H. Johnson in Calais (VR:3:153) HANNAH 'ANNA' JORDAN, born ca 1829 in NB, daughter of ASA JORDAN (b. Charlotte, Me) & MAGGIE JORDAN (b. NB) (spragf). Census: 1860 in Crawford, 1871 in St. Stephen, NB, 1880 in Calais.

ii. EUNICE SPRAGUE, born circa 1831 in Charlotte ME (1850 census). Census: 1850 in Calais. She married 7 Dec 1851 in Calais by Mathew Hastings, JP (VR:3:201, mead) LEVI T. or F. HANSON.

iii. LYDIA SPRAGUE, born circa 1833 in Charlotte ME (1850 census) born Apr 1843 (1900 census). Died 24 Nov 1903 Milltown, ME age 71y 3m 2d (MSA). Census: 1850 & 1900 in Calais. She married 25 Sept 1850 in Calais (VR:3:146) BENJAMIN BABB, Jr. of St. James, NB (mead), born Aug 1813 (1900 census), son of BENJAMIN BABB (a sea captain b. in NB) & PERLEY McKENZIE (b. Scotland) (MSA). Census: 1900 in Calais. Died 20 June 1906 in Calais age 88y 10m 11d (MSA).

iv. THOMAS SPRAGUE, born circa 1835 in Charlotte ME (1850 census). Census: 1850 & 60 in Calais. He married 13 Aug 1854 by Mathew Hastings in Calais (VR:3:161) MARY ANGELINE HIGGINS. They resided Baileyville (spragf). She died 12 Mar 1888 (TWB). Census: 1860 in Calais. No children.

v. MARY ELIZA DAMON SPRAGUE, born 22 Feb 1836 in Charlotte ME (VR). Died 1 Dec 1862 in Calais (stack:115, union). Buried 4 Dec 1862 in Calais Cemetery. Census: 1850 in Calais. Married 12 Aug 1854 in Calais by M. D. Mathews (VR:3:157) JAMES H. STACKPOLE, born 11 Apr 1822 in Lewiston, Me, son of CORNELIUS STACKPOLE & MARY RICHARDSON, died 24 Dec 1897 age 75 in Calais (stack:114, 115, adv, MSA). Buried Calais Cemetery.

vi. SOPHIA EVELINE SPRAGUE, born Oct 1839 (spragf) in Charlotte ME (1850 census). Census: 1850 in Calais. Married 3 Apr 1857 in Calais (VR:1:168, mead) THOMAS OWEN NEVERS (see NEVERS).

vii. COZOMY N. SPRAGUE, born 15 Oct 1839 (TWB) in Charlotte ME (1850 census). She died 17 Apr 1919 in Santa Cruz, CA (TWB). Census: 1850 & 60 in Calais. She married THOMAS PHIPPS, born Feb. 1838 in Wesley, ME, son of WILLIAM PHIPPS & ELIZA HOWE (TWB). They resided in Minneapolis, MN (spragf).

viii. ISAAC 'Ike' LORD SPRAGUE, born 25 Jul 1841 in Calais (VR). He enlisted in Civil War at age 20 in Co K 12th Me Inf. on 21 Oct 1861, a butcher 5'8" with blue eyes and black hair, left service 17 May 1866 (cwcard). He owned a butcher shop. Died 17 Jan 1913 age 71 in Bangor (MSA, adv, sfh:2:23). Buried in Calais Cemetery. Census: 1850 thru 1900 in Calais. He married (int.) 3 May 1864 in Calais (VR) MARTHA LOUISA STEPHENS/STEVENS born ca 1846. Died before 1900. Census: 1870 & 80 in Calais.

ix. CHARLES SPRAGUE, born 4 Mar 1846 in Calais, died 24 Nov 1847 in Calais (VR). Buried 25 Nov 1847 in Calais Cemetery (sext).

x. HARRIET M. SPRAGUE, born circa 1848 in Calais (1850 census). Died 28 Jan 1920 in Greenacres, WA (sdow). Census: 1850 & 60 in Calais.

xi. JULIETTE/JULIA E. SPRAGUE, born circa 1850. Census: 1850, 60 & 70 in Calais. She married ABNER R. HOWE (mead).

xii. CHARLES FRANK SPRAGUE, Jr., born circa 1853. Census: 1860, 70 (age 17) in Calais, 1880 in

Minneapolis. He married before 1880 GEORGIA (_____), and resided in Minneapolis, MN (mead). Census 1880 in Minneapolis.

* Note - [Charles Sprague first son of Charles & Bathsheba born ?, was a member of an emigrant train on its way to Oregon. An Indian who was hidden in a stand of trees shot him. The bullet carried a piece of red underwear into the wound and Charles died from an infection that it caused on 24 Nov 1847 (sprag:202).] This sounds like a fabricated story, since the Calais Vital records show a Charles Sprague died as a baby on 24 Nov 1847 and Charles was not the 1st son.

JONATHAN & ANNA SPRAGUE, p. 190

JONATHAN SPRAGUE, born circa 1800, son of JAMES SPRAGUE & PRISCILLA NOBLE (TWP, mead). Probably died before 1840 census. Census 1830 (3 males, 3 females).

He married ANNA CHAMBERLAIN (mead), born circa 1802 in St Stephen, NB (1850 census). Census: 1850 in Calais. Children:

i. UNICE/EUNICE SPRAGUE, born 4 Jan 1819 in St David, NB (Calais VR). Died 13 Jul 1833 in Calais (VR:1:233).
ii. ELIZABETH S. SPRAGUE, born 9 Aug 1820 in St David, NB (Calais VR). She married 29 Mar 1842 by Joseph A. Prescott, JP in Calais (VR:1:127) REUBEN B. KNOWLES of Calais.
iii. CALVIN SPRAGUE, born 14 May 1824 in Robbinston Me (Calais VR). Census: 1850 in Calais.
iv. EDWARD T. SPRAGUE, born 1 Oct 1826 in Robbinston Me (Calais VR). He served in Civil War at age 37 enlisted in Co G 2nd Cav., a millman 5'4 1/2" with dark eyes and dark hair, born in Calais resided in Veazie, Me (cwcard). Died 1867 (g.s.). He married 4 Nov 1849 in Calais (VR:3:144). HEPSIBETH SAMPSON, born ca 1830, died 1926 (g.s.). Both are buried in Fairview Cemetery in Veazie. Census: 1870 in Veazie.
v. DANIEL SPRAGUE, born 26 Sep 1830 in Calais, died 20 Jul 1833 in Calais (VR:3:144).
vi. JOHN T. SPRAGUE, born 25 Jun 1834 in Calais (VR). He served in Civil War at age 28 enlisted in Co I of 28th Inf. a millman 5'7" with black eyes and black hair, born in Calais resided in Veazie, Me (cwcard). Census: 1850 in Calais, 1870 in Veazie. He married before 1858 (when a child was born in Veazie) MARY E. (_____), born ca 1832 (1870 census in Veazie).
vii. CYRENE SPRAGUE, born 8 Mar 1837 in Calais (VR, 1850 census = St Stephen). Census: 1850 in Calais.

EPHRAIM & HANNAH SPRING, p. 216

EPHRAIM AUGUSTUS SPRING, born 16 Mar 1794 in Hubbardston, MA (VR:93), son of SAMUEL & SARAH SPRING. He was of Calais in 1823 when he appeared in Court (SJC). He was a stone mason. Died 3 Jun 1868 age 74 in Calais (g.s.). Buried in Calais Cemetery. Census: 1830 (4 males, 3 females), 40 (6 males, 3 females), 50 & 60 in Calais.

He married 8 Feb 1816 in Hubbardston, MA (VR:165), HANNAH S. MORSE, born 27 Jun 1796 in Hubbardston (VR:72), daughter of WILLIAM MORSE AND HANNAH RICHARDSON. Died 28 Nov 1863 age 67 in Calais (VR:3:305, g.s.). Buried in Calais Cemetery. Census: 1850 & 60 in Calais. Children:

i. MARY E. SPRING, born 6 May 1816 in Hubbardston (VR). Died 20 Apr 1908 age 91y 11m 4d in Calais (sfh:1:66, MSA). Buried in Calais Cemetery. Probate of will, Washington Co. # H-2-35. Census: 1850, 60 & 70 in Calais. She married JAMES SULLIVAN HALL (see HALL).
ii. EPHRAIM AUGUSTUS SPRING, Jr. born 30 Jul 1827 in Calais (VR). Died 11 Jan 1870 age 42 in Calais (g.s., obit SCC). Buried in Calais Cemetery. Probate of estate, Washington Co. # S-2-35, executor, his widow, Keziah H. Spring. Guardianship filed 14 Sept 1876 for children of Keziah H. Stratton, mother, of children of Ephraim Spring. Abner McAllister of Milltown, NB to be guardian. Census: 1850 & 60 in Calais. He married 8 Jan 1859 by Rev. H. A. Philbrook in Calais (VR:3:181, adv). KEZIAH HILL McALLISTER of St. Stephen, NB, born ca 1840. Census: 1860 & 70 in Calais, 1871 in St. Stephen. [Keziah married 2nd ca 1874 George Stratton of Machias, son of Joseph Stratton & Cordelia Cates (drisko:549-550). He died 8 Feb 1888 in Machias (east:401).
iii. HANNAH EMMA/AMY SPRING, born 6 Dec 1833 in Calais (VR, love:232 = Nov 1834). Died 21 Jul 1894 in Minneapolis, MN (love:232). Census: 1850 in Calais, 1870 in St. Anthony, MN. She married 30 Jul

1853 JAMES ALBEE LOVEJOY, son of JOHN LORIN LOVEJOY AND ANN MARPLE ALBEE (see LOVEJOY).

iv. LUCIUS STILLMAN SPRING, born 10 Sep 1836 in Calais (VR, 1850 census). He was a RR Engineer on the Canadian Pacific RR. Died 4 June 1903 age 66y 9m in St. Stephen, NB (obit adv). Census: 1860 in Calais, 1871 in St. Stephen, NB. He married 31 Oct 1861 in St. Stephen, NB (CCMR) MARY PLUMMER KELLY, born 19 Aug 1839 in Calais daughter of WILLIAM & CORDELIA KELLEY. Res. on Prince St. in St. Stephen, 1896 directory. Died 29 July 1901 in St. Stephen, NB (adv) (see KELLEY).

JOHN R. & MARIA STANCHFIELD, p. 215
Also Stinchfield

Capt. ROGERS M. W. STINCHFIELD, born 9 Feb 1781, the first male white child born in Leeds, Me., the son of Rogers Stinchfield and Sarah Babson. He married 5 June 1799 MARY 'POLLY' LINDSAY, daughter of WILLIAM LINDSEY AND HANNAH LEADBETTER, and settled in Wayne, Me. He later moved to Milo; thence to Robbinston; thence to Marion, Iowa, where his wife died 10 June 1819. He subsequently married Fannie Allen. He returned to Robbinston, Me., and there died 31 May 1862. He adopted the name Stanchfield very late in his life. Rogers and Polly had nine children, the 8th child was John R. who resided in Calais (stinch:148, 150, leed:23, 126).

JOHN ROGER STANCHFIELD, born 20 Jan 1814 in Greene, ME (stinch:150). He was a lumberman. Died 3 Aug 1860 in New Gloucester, ME (stinch:150). Census: 1850 in Calais.

He married 3 Aug 1844 in St Stephen, NB (stinch:150, CCMR, leed:126), MARIA L. FOSTER born circa 1825 in Machias Me (1850 census). Census: 1850 in Calais. Children:

i. ROSE EMMA STANCHFIELD, born 26 May 1845 in Calais (VR). Died 31 Aug 1917 in Detroit, MI. Census: 1850 in Calais. She married JAMES B. McMAHAN, a judge, born in Michigan, son of JAMES McMAHAN & THEDBOLIA MAMBURG, died 15 Mar 1901 in Ludington, MI, both are buried in Ludington (Burial records of Ludington at LDS, stinch:156). They resided in Ludington, MI (stinch:156).

ii. EDWARD FOSTER STANCHFIELD, born 22 May 1847 in Calais (VR). Died 6 Feb 1888 in Ludington, MI (stinch:156). Census: 1850 in Calais. He married NELLIE F. WOODWARD (stinch:156). She was born, ca 1848 in Augusta, ME, daughter of DANIEL WOODWARD & MARY WINTER, she died 15 Aug 1922, both are buried at Ludington (burial records of Ludington at LDS).

iii. FANNIE FOSTER STANCHFIELD, born circa 1849, died 1849 age 3m (stinch:156, g.s.) in Calais. Buried in Calais Cemetery.

JOHN & JULIA C. STEARNS, p. 179
JOHN G. & JANE M. STEARNS, p. 209

ELIJAH & MARY STEARNS. Elijah died at residence of his son, J. G. Stearns in Brooklyn, NY, on Monday, 21 May 1872 (adv) They had two children born in Eastport (VR), Salome Bastow Stearns, b. 23 Nov 1809 [who married 1 Jan 181827 William H. Tyler (cal2:26)]. and William Henry Clark Stearns, b. 6 Dec 1811 (see BELOW). The record of the birth of their son John G. is not recorded in Eastport or Calais. The family was in Calais by 1835 (SJC).

JOHN G. STEARNS. Resided: in Calais between 1841 and 1847 when children were born and in 1872, in Brooklyn, NY when his father died, and where he probably died.

He married 1st 21 Nov 1840 in Calais (VR) JULIA CAROLINE WASHBURN, born 16 Sept 1820 in China, ME (china), daughter of JAPHETH COOMBS WASHBURN & SARAH BLISH. She died 7 Aug 1842 age 22 in Calais (VR:1:227, obit gaz). Children:

i. MARY SALOME STEARNS, born 17 Sep 1841 in Calais (VR). Died 15 Dec 1841 age 3m in Calais (VR:1:227, obit, gaz, only child).

He married 2nd 10 Jan 1844 in Eastport ME (gaz) JANE M. BELL of Eastport, ME, daughter of PHILIP Y. BELL. She died 16 Feb 1892 in New York (east: 480). Children:

ii. UNNAMED CHILD STEARNS, born circa 1844, died circa 1846 age 19m, buried: 10 Aug 1846 in Calais Cemetery (sext).

iii. DELIA STEARNS, born 18 Feb 1847 in Calais (VR).

WILLIAM H. C. & MARY STEARNS, p. 207

WILLIAM HENRY CLARK STEARNS, born 6 Dec 1811, in Eastport ME (VR), son of ELIJAH (see above), born (2) circa 1812 in Sullivan, ME (1850 census). He was a clerk. Died before 1860. Census: 1850 in Calais.

He married 1st 29 Sep 1841 in Calais (VR, gaz) MARY SOPHIA GLEASON VEAZIE, born 13 Sep 1822 in Eastport ME (VR) daughter of JOSHUA VEAZIE & ELIZABETH DELUE. She died 21 Nov 1844 age 22 in Calais (obit gaz) (see VEAZIE). Children:

i. HENRY V. STEARNS, born 4 Oct 1842 in Calais (VR). Census: 1850 & 60 in Calais.
ii. MARY SOPHIA G. STEARNS, born 4 Oct 1844 in Calais (VR). Census: 1850 in Calais.

He married 2nd 10 Jun 1846 in Sullivan, ME, by Rev. R. S. Watson (VR Sullivan), (int.) 9 May 1846 in Calais (VR:1:28) MARY H. HILL, born circa 1814 in Sullivan, ME (1850 census), daughter of SAMUEL HILL & MARY HOBBS. She died 27 Aug 1892 age 78y 11m in Calais (MSA, obit adv, prbt). Probate of Estate: 1 Nov 1892, in Machias Me. She left $500. to each of her grandchildren and balance to children Sarah & Fred. Census: 1850 thru 1880 in Calais. Children:

iii. SARAH ARCHIBALD STEARNS, born 16 Aug 1847 in Calais (VR). Died after 1892. Census: 1850 thru 1880 in Calais. She married 8 Dec 1873 by Rev. Mr. Carruthers in Calais (adv, at res. of Hon. F.A. Pike). AUGUSTUS EBEN SAWYER, born ca 1848 in Sedgwick, ME, son of NATHANIEL SAWYER AND SOPHIA H. WATSON (sawofne:426). He was of Jacksonville, FL at time of marriage, still resided there in 1891 when wife was visiting Calais (adv).
iv. WILLARD STEARNS, born circa 1849 in Calais. Died before 1860 (?). Census: 1850 in Calais.
v. FREDERICK PIKE STEARNS, born circa 1851 in Calais. Graduated from Calais Academy. In 1905 he was a member of the Consulting Board of Engineers of the Isthmian Canal in Washington, DC (news clipping dated 27 Sept 1905 in alumni file at Bowdoin College). Died after 1905. Census: 1860 in Calais.

JAMES & JANE STEEN, p. 223

JAMES STEEN /STEIN, born circa 1794 in Tyrone, Ireland (1850 census, came to Calais circa 1829). Died 28 Oct 1876 (g.s.). Buried in Calais Cemetery. Census: 1850, 60 & 70 in Calais.

He married 18 Oct 1829 by Rev Peter McCallum (CCMR Book A) JANE MITCHELL, born circa 1803 in Derry, Ireland (1850 census). Both of St. Andrews, NB at time of marriage. Died 6 May 1884 age 84y 9m in Calais (times, g.s.). Buried in Calais Cemetery. Census: 1850 thru 1880 in Calais. Children:

i. JANE STEEN, born ca 1826 in St Andrews, NB (1850 census). Census: 1850 & 60 (living with Jane Tuttle) in Calais.
ii. ALEXANDER STEEN, born circa 1833 in Rollingdam, NB (1850 census = St. Andrews, came to Calais age 6). He worked in a sawmill. Died 10 Feb 1916 at age 84y 5m 28d in Calais (MSA, SCC). Census: 1850, 60, (living with Jane Tuttle), 70, 80, 1900 in Calais. He married (int.) 13 Jun 1859, both of St. Andrews (PANB film # F6717) JANE BOYD, born 12 Oct 1829 in NB (sfh:2:33, MSA), daughter of JOHN BOYD & ELIZA KELLEY both born in Ireland. She died 9 Feb 1913 age 83y 5m in Calais (MSA, sfh:2:33). Census: 1850, 70, 80, 1900 in Calais.
iii. GEORGE M. STEEN, born 11 Feb 1835 in Rollingdam, NB (MSA, 1850 census = St Andrews, came to Calais at age 4). He worked in a sawmill. Died 28 Aug 1919 age 84y 6m 17d in Calais, unmarried (MSA, sfh:3:92). Probate of estate, Washington Co. # S-4-637, estate left to his nephew, James McClaskey, son of sister. Census: 1850 thru 1880 & 1900 in Calais.
iv. JAMES STEEN, born circa 1838 in St Andrews, NB (1850 census). Enlisted at age 23 in Civil War in 9th Maine Inf. Co A (enlist), promoted to Cpl. and Sgt. he was 6' tall with blue eyes and brown hair, resided in Wesley, Me at enlistment (cwcard). Died after 1919, he resided in Willliamsport, PA (brother George's obit). Census: 1850 in Calais.
v. MARGARET STEEN, born circa 1838 in St Andrews, NB (1850 census). Died 8 Apr 1896 age 55 in Princeton (MSA her name Smith). Buried in Princeton. Census: 1850 in Calais.

vi. MARY STEEN, born 20 Sept 1839 in St Andrews, NB (1850 census, MSA). Died 6 Dec 1921 age 82y 2m 16d in Calais (MSA, sfh:3:284). Census: 1850 thru 70 in Calais. She married 23 Aug 1876 in Calais (VR:3:234) JAMES MCCLUSKEY of St. Stephen, NB. He died before his wife.

vii. ISABELLA STEEN, born 10 Sep 1842 in St Andrews, NB (VR). She was a nurse. Died 11 Feb 1916 in Calais (SCC). Probate of will: 13 Jun 1916 in Machias. Census: 1850 thru 1880 in Calais. Unmarried.

viii. ELIZABETH STEEN, born 25 Mar 1845 in Calais (VR, 1850 census). Died before brother, George. Census: 1850 & 60 in Calais.

ix. ELLEN STEEN, born 10 May 1847 (VR). Census: 1850 (age 3) in Calais. (not in 1860 census)

ROBERT C. & SUSAN E. STICKNEY, p. 202

BENJAMIN STICKNEY, born 13 June 1767 in Newburyport, MA. He married 5 June 1793 in Newbury, ANNA POOR daughter of JONATHAN POOR & SARAH DOLE. He was a Major in the Militia as early as 1798 and in 1821 elected Major-General and held that office until his death on 19 July 1846 in Newbury. His will was dated 2 Mar 1844 and proved August 1846 (stick:178). They had nine children, the seventh being Robert C. who settled in Calais.

ROBERT CLARK STICKNEY, born 1 Sep 1808 in Newbury, MA (VR:495, Stick:279), died after 1871. In a court action in 1837 he was a merchant, a partner, in the business, John Stickney & Co (SJC). He represented Calais in the State Legislature, was a Commissary during the Civil War in the Army of the Potomac, in 1869 he was employed by Government at Washington, DC (stick:279). He and his wife (not named) visited Calais in 1871 (adv). Census: 1840 (1 male, 2 females), 50 & 60 in Calais.

He married 20 Dec 1838 by Rev. William A. Whitwell in Calais (MRWC:27, stick:279) SUSAN ELIZA DUTCH, born 16 May 1817 in Calais (Eastport VR), daughter of Capt. JOHN CALIFF DUTCH AND MARGARET 'PEGGY' TODD. Died 5 Sep 1857 age 40y in Calais (stick:279, adv). Buried in Calais Cemetery. Census: 1850 in Calais (see also her brother John C. Dutch).

He married 2nd 6 Sept 1869 in Washington, DC, Mrs. C. B. HERON of Detroit, MI (union). Children by 1st wife:

i. UNNAMED SON STICKNEY, born and died 21 Jan 1841 in Calais (stick: 279). Buried in Calais Cemetery.

ii. JOHN MARCUS MORTIN STICKNEY, born 29 Jan 1843 in Calais (VR, stick: 279). Census: 1850 & 60 in Calais. Resided in Boston, MA in 1869. In Aug 1887 he and his wife (not named) visited in Calais from Boston (adv).

iii. UNNAMED SON STICKNEY, born and died 18 May 1845 in Calais (stick: 280). Buried in Calais Cemetery.

iv. ANNA CAROLINE STICKNEY, born 20 Oct 1846 in Calais (VR, stick: 280). Died 12 Sep 1851 age 4y 11m in Calais (g.s., FJ). Buried in Calais Cemetery. Census: 1850 in Calais.

v. CHARLES EDWARD STICKNEY, born 22 Feb 1853 in Calais (stick:280). Resided: 1869 in Pittsfield, ME (at school). Census: 1860 & 70 in Calais. He possibly is the Charles Stickney who married 24 Dec 1874 by Rev. C. Haskell Mary O. Nordstrom in Calais (VR:3:239).

vi. UNNAMED SON STICKNEY, born and died on 28 Aug 1857 in Calais (stick:280). Buried in Calais Cemetery.

BENJAMIN & SUSAN STODDARD, p. 214

NATHANIEL STODDARD, born 18 June 1758 in Hingham, MA, son of NATHANIEL STODDARD & ELIZABETH SPRAGUE, he married 1ST in 1779 JANE GARDNER, he married 2nd 21 Oct 1802 in Perry HANNAH TODD, daughter of SAMUEL TODD & RUTH LINCOLN. (Me Fam 3:267). His son Benjamin Stoddard by his 2nd wife resided in Perry and by 1844 was in Calais.

BENJAMIN STODDARD, born 19 Jul 1810 in Perry ME, son of NATHANIEL STODDARD & HANNAH or Sally TODD, died 23 Sep 1869 age 59 in Perry ME (VR, mefam:3:268, 4:226, union obit). Buried in Gleason Rd. Cemetery in Perry. Probate, Washington Co., #S-2-24, only paper in the file is will dated 15 June 1869. Census: 1840 (1 male, 3 females), 50 & 60 in Calais.

He married 21 May 1839 by Rev. William Davenport in Perry ME (mrwc:29, pott:12) SUSAN H. POTTER, born 1 May 1818 in Perry (VR), daughter of SOLOMON POTTER Jr. & SUSAN HODGE (pott:12). Died 18

Jul 1889 in Calais age 71y 2m (east:425). Census: 1850 thru 1880 in Calais. Children:

i. SARAH JANE STODDARD, born 5 May 1840 in Perry ME (VR:153, pott:12). Died 11 Oct 1879 (pott:12). Census: 1850, 60 & 70 in Calais. She married 5 Dec 1874 JAMES SMYTH (pott:12).
ii. HENRY AUGUSTUS STODDARD, born 10 Feb 1844 in Calais (VR, pott:12). He enlisted in Civil War in Co A 1st Battery Inf., he had gray eyes and light hair (cwcard). He was a wheelwright and in 1870 he established a factory which manufactured carriages in Milltown (CEV: 39). Died 17 Jul 1904 in Calais (MSA). Buried in Calais Cemetery. Census: 1850 thru 1900 in Calais. He married 8 Dec 1874 SERENA A. McBEAN, born in NB, daughter of DONALD A. McBEAN & FANNY or Nancy R. BOIES/Boice (pott:12). She died 6 Apr 1910 age 54 in Calais (MSA). Census: 1900 in Calais

JEREMIAH & SOPHIA STUART, p. 224

JEREMIAH STUART/STEWART, born circa 1812 in St George, NB (1850 census). Census: 1850 in Calais.

He married 8 May 1842 by Phineas Higgins in Calais (VR:1:129) SOPHIA A. FARRISH, born circa 1823 in St George NB (1850 census), daughter of JOHN FARRISH. Died 10 Apr 1854 age 33y 8m in Calais (g.s.). Buried in Calais Cemetery. Census: 1850 in Calais. Children:

i. JAMES CLARENCE STUART, born 20 May 1843 in Calais (VR). Died circa 1850 (1850 census deaths).
ii. JOANNA STUART, born 31 Mar 1845 in Calais (VR, 1850 census = Baring). Census: 1850 & 60 (age 15 in household of Ephraim Spring) in Calais. She married 12 Oct 1866 in Milltown, NB by Rev. Philbrick SAMUEL G. GRAVES of St. Stephen, NB (CCMR).
iii. WILLIAM STUART, born 27 May 1847 in Calais (VR). Census: 1850 (age 3) in Calais.
iv. HANNAH E. STUART, born ca Nov 1849 in Calais. Census: 1850 (age 8/12) in Calais.
v. MARY E. STUART, born, circa 1852. Died 28 Apr 1854 age 2y in Calais (g.s.). Buried in Calais Cemetery.

THOMAS & LORINDA STUART, p. 215

THOMAS S. STUART/STEWART, born circa 1819 in Ireland. He was a farmer. Died 28 Sept 1885 age 67 in Calais (adv). Buried in Calais Cemetery. Census: 1850 thru 1880 in Calais.

He married LORINDA (in VR & 60 census) – MALINDA (in '50 & '70 census) McCANN born circa 1822 in St David, NB (1850 census)(her death rec. says b. Salem, MA, daughter of RODNEY McCANN [born NB] & ANNIE McLAUGHLIN [born NB]). Died 3 Feb 1898 age 83y 10m in Calais, buried in Calais Cemetery (MSA & g.s. = Melinda 1814-1898). {Her father was a Sea Captain perhaps she was born on ship in Salem birth not found in Salem records}. Census: 1850 thru 1880 in Calais. Children:

i. JOHN AUGUSTUS STUART, born circa 1841 in St David, NB (1850 census). Died 3 Feb 1921 age 79y 8m (g.s.) in Calais. Census: 1850 thru 1880 in Calais. He married 8 Oct 1866 by Rev. W. S. McKellar in Calais (VRNB:24:2228, TWB) MARY C. NOBLE, born ca Apr 1836, daughter of NICHOLAS NOBLE (born Calais) & SARAH POMROY (born NB) (TWB). She died 24 Jan 1899 age 62y 10m (g.s.) in Calais, buried in Calais Cemetery (MSA).
ii. MARY ANN STUART, born 14 Feb 1845 in Calais (VR). Census: 1850 thru 1880 in Calais. She married 17 May 1869 in Calais (union) SHEPPARD BOHANNAN, son of DANIEL & MARTHA BOHANNAN. He died 15 June 1872 age 33 in Calais (adv) (wife & 2 children with her parents in 1880).
iii. HUGH AUGUSTUS C. STUART, born Jun 1850 in Calais (1850 census first name Hugh, name on daughter's marriage & g.s. is Augustus C.). Died 1938 (g.s.). Buried in Calais Cemetery. Census: 1850 (female age 1/12), 60 (Hugh A. 10) & 70 (Augustus 20) in Calais. He married circa 1873 (1880 census) EMMA A. PRESCOTT, born ca 1853 in Jonesport, daughter of ALBION P. PRESCOTT & E. FARNSWORTH, she died 28 Aug 1897 age 44y 5m in Calais, buried in Calais Cemetery (MSA, g.s.).
iv. WILLIAM STUART, inf. son on grave stone no dates.

FRANCIS K. & EMILY B. SWAN, p. 210

FRANCIS [7] SWAN, born, 26 June 1785 Groton, MA, son of WILLIAM [6-5]; EBEN [4]; THOMAS [3-2]; HENRY[1]. Died 13 June 1862 in Calais (g.s.). He married HANNAH CHILD, born 2 Mar 1795 in Augusta (g.s.), daughter of JAMES CHILD and HANNAH CUSHING. She died 20 May 1869 in Calais (obit SCC). Both are buried in Calais Cemetery. They had six children: SARAH PORTER SWAN, born 6 Feb 1816 m. RICHARD MANNING (bradb:184); JAMES CHILD SWAN (see BELOW); WILLIAM HENRY SWAN born 13 Jan 1819, unmarried (bradb, p. 184); FRANCIS KEYES (see BELOW); CHARLES EDWARD SWAN (see DOWNES); and EUGENE SWAN born 23 July 1824, died 30 Mar 1890 (g.s.), buried in Calais Cemetery. Unmarried.

FRANCIS KEYES SWAN born 20 Oct 1820, in Winslow, ME (mop: 85), son of FRANCIS SWAN & HANNAH CHILD. In 1836 he was owner of a mill on St. Croix when he appeared in a court case June 1836 (SJC:3:367). Later he was a banker. Attended Colby College 1836-37 (colby). Moved from Calais in 1865 to Portland ME (bradb:184). Died 28 May 1896 in Portland ME (MSA, obit ppress). Census: 1840 (5 males, 3 females), 50 & 60 in Calais.

He married 16 Sep 1843 by Rev. S. H. Keeler in Calais (gaz, bradb) EMILY BRADBURY, born 18 May 1821 in Alfred, Me (bradb:114) daughter of JEREMIAH BRADBURY (a lawyer from Alfred, ME) & MARY LANGDON STORER, granddaughter of SETH STORER & OLIVE JORDAN (d/o Col. TRISTRAM JORDAN). Resided: after 1865 in Portland ME (bradb:184). She died 4 Dec 1877 in Portland ME (obit times, bradb:184). Census: 1850 & 60 in Calais. Children:

i. HENRY STORER SWAN, born 8 Dec 1844 in Calais (VR, bradb:185). Resided in Mamoroneck, NY at marriage. He was a physician in Bristol, RI (bradb:185). Died 29 Jan 1929 in Portland ME (obit adv). Buried in Bristol. Census: 1850 & 60 in Calais. He married 7 Apr 1877 in Portland ME (bradb:185, adv) ANNIE C. (CODMAN) SHAW, daughter of RANDOLPH A. L. CODMAN of Portland. She died 11 Oct 1891 in Bristol, RI (obit adv)

ii. EMILY MANNING SWAN, born 24 Oct 1846 in Calais (VR, bradb:185). Died 14 May 1931 in Portland ME (MSA). Buried in Evergreen Cemetery in Portland ME. Census: 1850 & 60 in Calais, 1900 & 20 in Portland ME. She married 31 Dec 1879 in Portland ME (bradb:185) FREDERICK HENRY GERRISH, born 21 Mar 1845 in Portland, ME, son of OLIVER GERRISH & SARAH LITTLE., he died 8 Sept 1920 in Portland (MSA). He was a physician. Census: 1920 in Portland.

iii. MARCIA BRADBURY SWAN, born 31 May 1853 (bradb:185) in Calais. Census: 1860 in Calais. Resided: 1900 in Portland ME (uncle's probate).

iv. FLORENCE WAINWRIGHT SWAN, born 20 Aug 1857 (bradb:185) in Calais. Census: 1860 in Calais, 1900 & 20 (with sister Emily) in Portland ME.

JAMES C. & HELEN SWAN, p. 225

JAMES CHILD SWAN, born 4 Aug 1817 (g.s.) in Winslow, ME, son of FRANCIS SWAN AND HANNAH CHILD. Resided: 1842 in Texas. Died 15 Oct 1853 (g.s.). Buried in Calais Cemetery. Census: 1850 in Calais.

He married 9 Sep 1845 in Calais (VR 1: 26) HELEN S. TRASK, born circa 1824 in Portland ME. Died 18 Feb 1887 in Somerville, MA (times). Census: 1850 & 60 (living with Mary Stearns) in Calais. Children:

i. HELEN LOUISA SWAN, born 21 May 1846 in Calais (VR). Died 29 Mar 1851 (g.s.). Buried in Calais Cemetery. Census: 1850 in Calais.

ii. SARAH P. SWAN born 25 Apr 1848 in Calais (death rec.). Resided with sister, Anna in Portland. Died after 1920. Died: 18 Aug or June 1931 age 87y 1m 23d in Portland (MSA). Census: 1850 & 60 (living with Mary Stearns) in Calais, 1900 & 20 in Portland ME.

iii. ANNA C. SWAN born Mar 1850 in Calais (1900 census). Resided with sister, Sarah in Portland. Died after 1920. Census: 1850 & 60 (living with Mary Stearns) in Calais, 1900 & 20 in Portland ME.

iv. AGNES MINOT SWAN, born 25 Sept 1852, died 31 Aug 1854 in Calais (g.s.). Buried in Calais Cemetery.

EDWARD B. & EMILY B. TAYLOR, p. 204

EDWARD B. TAYLOR, born circa 1820. Died 27 Nov 1845 age 25 in Calais (VR:1:229, gaz).

He married Aug 1842 in Calais (gaz) EMILY B. WASHBURN, born 9 May 1822 in China, ME (china) daughter of JEPHETH COOMBS WASHBURN & SARAH BLISH, sister of Julia Washburn Stearns). She died 10 Oct 1850 age 28y 6m in Calais (FJ, funeral at home of brother George Washburn). Census: 1850 (with parents) in Calais. Children:

i. CHARLES EDWARD TAYLOR, born 16 May 1843 in Calais (VR). Died 2 Sep 1850 in Calais (FJ). Census: 1850 (with grandfather Japheth C. Washburn) in Calais.
ii. WILLIS WASHBURN TAYLOR, born 14 Nov 1844 in Calais, died 16 Feb 1846 in Calais (VR:1:236).

CHARLES W. & MALINDA C. THOMPSON, p. 195

CHARLES WHEELER THOMPSON, born 14 Dec 1817 in St. Stephen, son of JAMES THOMPSON & PATRICE BRADFORD (obit, arnie, MSA). He was in the retail boot & shoe business in Lynn, MA, moving to Ferry Village in Cape Elizabeth, ME (now South Portland) in 1860 as a clerk for the Portland Steam Packet Co., then into the grocery & dry goods business in 1866 (obit argus). In 1870 he was a Ferry Agent. Died 14 Jan 1894 age 78y 1m in South Portland, Me (MSA, obit argus). Buried in Mt. Pleasant Cemetery in South Portland. Census: Does not appear in 1850 census of Calais or Cape Elizabeth, 1860 & 70 in Cape Elizabeth.

He married 3 Jan 1841 in St. Stephen, NB (CCMR) MALINDA C. HARVEY. Died between 1848 when son was born in Calais and 1860 when Charles is recorded with wife, Caroline in census. Children:

i. JAMES LEONARD THOMPSON, Sr. born 15 Oct 1842 in Calais (VR). He worked on steamboats and went to New York in 1905 (obit). Died 8 Jan 1925 age 82y 3mos New York City (obit SCC). Census: 1870 & 1900 in Calais. He married FRANCES `FANNIE' (_____), born ca May 1847. Census 1900 in Calais.
ii. MARY LOUISA THOMPSON, born 5 Feb 1845 in Calais (VR). She married WILLIAM F. JAMES, he was a secretary of NY fire department (father's obit).
iii. CHARLES F. THOMPSON, born 11 Feb 1848 in Calais (VR). [May have died young because another Charles F. age 4 appears in 1860 census of Cape Elizabeth].

CHARLES W. married 2nd before 1856 CAROLYN A. KNIGHT, born ca 1824-27. Died: 23 Feb 1905 age 80y 5m in S. Portland, daughter of BENJAMIN KNIGHT & MARY HUTCHINSON (MSA). Census: 1860 & 70 in Cape Elizabeth, ME.

iv. CHARLES FREDERICK THOMPSON, born 19 May 1856 in Cape Elizabeth, ME (VR:22). He was in the grocery business in South Portland, ME (father's obit). Died: 28 May 1933 age 77y 9d in South Portland (MSA). Buried in Mt. Pleasant Cemetery in South Portland. Census: 1860 & 70 in Cape Elizabeth.
v. BENJAMIN K. THOMPSON, born 6 Mar 1858 in Cape Elizabeth (VR:22). He was in the grocery business in South Portland (father's obit). He was an alderman in South Portland (obit). Died: 5 Mar 1935 age 76y 10m 24d in South Portland at time of death he was a clerk in Portland Steam Packing Co. (MSA, obit argus his widow was Elizabeth K.). Buried in Mt. Pleasant Cemetery in South Portland. Census: 1860 & 70 in Cape Elizabeth, 1900 in Portland, ME. He married before 1885 EMMA S. (_____), born ca Feb 1860 (1900 census).
vi. CAROLINE 'Carrie' A. THOMPSON, born 24 Nov 1860 in Cape Elizabeth (VR:22). She resided in Bridgeton when brother Ben died in 1935. She married 18 Nov 1880 by Rev. Charles A. Hayden in Cape Elizabeth (VR:48, father's obit) JOHN F. MERRIMAN, he was a postmaster and grocer in Portland (cityd:1891).
vii. PATIENCE A. THOMPSON, born 7 Feb 1863 in Cape Elizabeth (VR:22). Unmarried and resided in South Portland in 1894 (father's obit). Died: 24 July 1942 age 79y in South Portland (MSA). Buried: Mt. Pleasant Cemetery in South Portland. Census: 1870 in Cape Elizabeth.
viii. SUMNER R. THOMPSON, born 15 Feb 1867 in Cape Elizabeth (VR:22). He married before 1883 CATHERINE CONNELLY (son, Joseph's death rec.). Census: 1870 in Cape Elizabeth.

*Note – Charles's obit states that he had six sons but only named 3 of them.

DAVID & JANE THURSTON, p. 191

DAVID THURSTON, born Apr 1824 in Waterville ME ? Quebec ? (1850, 1900 census), son of ROBERT THURSTON & PHEOBE TOWNS. He was a teamster in the 1887 directory. He was also a lumberman. Died 12 May 1913 age 91y 5m 12d in Calais (sfh:2:57, MSA, adv). Census: 1850 thru 1900 in Calais.

He married 1st on 29 Jul 1843 by Rev. E. B. Harris in Eastport ME (gaz) JANE G. McNEIL, born circa 1825 in Majorville, NB (resided in Eastport at marriage). Died 11 Oct 1853 age 28y 5m (g.s.) in Calais. Buried in Calais Cemetery. Census: 1850 in Calais. Children:

i. CHARLES EDGAR THURSTON, born 21 May 1845 in Calais (VR). Served in Co G 1st Maine Cavalry in Civil War. He was 5'9" with black eyes and brown hair (cwcard). Died: Aug 1926 at the Veterans' Home Youngsville, Napa Co., CA, until 1924, Charles led the missionary life, living in Oakland and holding his services in a large tent that became noted among religious circles (obit from Humbolt Standard reprint in adv). Census: 1850, 60 & 70 in Calais. He married 4 Nov 1865 in Calais (VR) CHARLOTTE C. DURGIN born ca 1845, daughter of WALTER & ELIZABETH DURGIN. Died after 1926. They moved to Eureka, CA in 1875. Census: 1870 in Calais (see DURGIN)

ii. ADALAIDE ELIZA THURSTON, born 24 Aug 1847 in Calais (VR). Census: 1850 & 60 in Calais. She married 17 Apr 1866 by Rev. S. H. Keeler in Calais (VR:3:216) JOSEPH McNELLY of Calais. Census: 1860 (age 10 with parents Matthew and Hannah McNelly, both born in Ireland).

iii. FREDERICK THURSTON, born Apr 1850 in Calais (g.s.). Died 4 May 1850 age 1m in Calais (1850 census, g.s.). Buried in Calais Cemetery.

iv. JOHN C. THURSTON, born circa 1853 (?). Bapt. 29 Sept 1855 in Calais (saint, record has Eliza as mother). He resided in Humbolt, CA in 1926 and survived his brother, Charles (adv). Died after 1926. Census: 1870 in Calais.

He married 2nd 14 May 1854 (VR:3:160) ELIZA CLENDENING, born ca July 1843 (1900 census), in St David, NB, daughter of ANDREW & MARY CLENDENING (b. in St. David). She died 17 Sep 1906 in Calais (MSA). Census: 1851 in St. David, NB, 1870, 80 & 1900 in Calais. Children:

v. ANDREW THURSTON, born circa 1855. Bapt. 29 Sept 1855 in Calais (saint). He worked in a saw mill. Census: 1860 & 70 in Calais.

vi. EMMA THURSTON, born circa Apr 1858 in Calais. Died 11 Dec 1908 age 49 in Calais (sfh:1:131= parents both born St. David, NB). Buried in Calais Cemetery. Census: 1860 thru 1900 in Calais. Emma married 30 June 1888 by Rev. A.W.C. Anderson in Calais (VR:2:81, adv) THOMAS McNAMARA, son of THOMAS McNAMARA & ELIZA MILLS both born in Ireland. He was a fireman. He died 24 Apr 1896 age 38 in Calais (MSA).

vii. DAVID FRANK THURSTON, born 18 July 1863 in Calais (MSA). Died 29 June 1915 age 52y 11m 11d in Calais (MSA, adv, sfh:2:185). Census: 1870 thru 1910 in Calais. He married after 1880 JENNIE (_____), born ca Aug 1866 in Canada. Died: after 1920. Census: 1900 (age 36), 1910 & 1920 (age 54 living alone) in Calais.

FERDINAND & HANNAH TINKER p. 214

JOHN TINKER, born between 1752 & 1757, died between 1842 & 1847, a sea captain. He served in the Revolutionary Was as a private in the 10th company, 1st Reg't, also in Captain Lewis' Company, 5th Battalion, Wadsworth's Brigade in 1776 (tink:28-30). He married MARY HASLEM. They had ten children and resided in Ellsworth, ME. Their son, Ferdinand raised a large family in Calais.

FERDINAND TINKER, born 28 Feb 1801 in Ellsworth, Me (tink:28-30, album:278), son of JOHN TINKER (Rev. War) & MARY HASLEM. He was a millwright. Died 9 Aug 1875 age 75y 5m in Calais (obit adv, g.s.). Buried in Calais Cemetery. Census: 1840 (5 males, 6 females), 50, 60 & 70 in Calais.

He married 28 Sep 1828 in St. Stephen, NB (tink) HANNAH HILL (PINEO) SMITH, born 7 Nov 1806 in Machias Me (tink:28, album:278, g.s. = 1805), daughter of DAVID PINEO AND PRISCILLA HILL, and widow of NATHAN SMITH. Died 21 May 1887 in Milltown ME (adv, g.s.). Buried in Calais Cemetery. Census: 1850 thru 1880 in Calais. Children:

i. FERDINAND G. TINKER, born 2 Jul 1829 in St. Stephen, NB (tink:28). He served in the Civil War in Co F 21st Maine, he was a carpenter, 5'11" with blue eyes and brown hair (cwcard). Died 28 Apr 1904 in Winthrop, ME (VR). Buried in Readfield Corner Cemetery, Readfield, Me (MOCA). Census: 1850 in Calais, 1900 (living alone) in Winthrop, ME. He married 1st 11 Aug 1852 in Calais (tink) ALMIRA J. SKOFIELD, of Baring, born 14 Oct 1833 (MOCA). She died 15 May 1865, Mt. Vernon, ME (tink:28). Buried in Readfield Corner Cemetery, Readfield (MOCA) He married 2nd 7 Mar 1867 by Rev. Parker Jaques in Winthrop, ME (VR, tink:29). Mrs. ALVIRA SHAW or SNOW. She died 7 Mar 1886 (tink:29).

ii. ELIZA S. TINKER, born 15 Nov 1830 & died 7 Dec 1831 in St Stephen, NB (tink:29, g.s.). Buried in Calais Cemetery.

iii. ALMEDA S. TINKER, born 14 Feb 1832 in St Stephen, NB (boy:204, tink:29). Resided in Washington, D.C. in 1900. Died ca 1906 (DAR). Census: 1850 in Calais. She married 10 Oct 1852 in Milltown ME (boy:204, tink:29, DAR:96486) STEPHEN ARNOLD BOYDEN, born 11 July 1831 in Robbinston, ME, son of PHILIP BOYDEN & JANE MASON (boy:204, tink:29). He enlisted in the 39th Regt. Mass. Vols. in the Civil War, and was promoted to the captain of Co. F, 1st U. D. colored troops; he was discharged in 1864 for disability; he was then appointed to service in the Capitol, where he has been employed ever since. Resided in Washington, DC. (tink:29, boy: 204). His great-great grandfather, Jacob Boyden (1744 -1818) served in Rev. War, Stephen died ca 1907 (DAR # 96486), probably in Washington.

iv. JOHN T. TINKER, born 12 Sep 1833 in St Stephen, NB (tink:29, album:278). He went West in 1858 and settled in Eau Clair, WI, appointed postmaster in 1861, he enlisted in Co H. of the 16th Wisconsin Infantry and was a 1st Lieutenant, and mustered out Aug 1865. He was a member of Eagle Post No. 52 in Eau Clair. After the war he became a millwright and bridge builder (album:278). Captain Tinker resided in Eau Claire for 40 years, was a 72 year member of GAR, and was a postmaster in Eau Claire, and celebrated his 50th wedding anniversary on 3rd of June (obit). Died 7 Nov 1905 in Eau Clair (wdr, obit adv). Census: 1850 in Calais. He married 3 Jun 1855 by Rev. Keeler in Calais (VR:3:164, tink:29, album) SARAH D. JONES, born 1 Jan 1835 in Pembroke, ME, daughter of JOHN Y. JONES & MYRA VOSE, sister of Almeda M. Clapp. Died 18 July 1906 in Eau Clair (wdr, album:278).

v. GEORGIANNA TINKER, born 6 Jun 1835 in St Stephen, NB (tink:29). Died 22 May 1848 in Calais (tink, g.s.). Buried in Calais Cemetery.

vi. HANNAH H. TINKER, born 20 Jul 1837 in St Stephen, NB (tink:29). Died circa 1898 in Hermosa, Dakota (tink). Census: 1850 in Calais. She married 2 Aug 1857 in St. Stephen, NB (CCMR, tink) JOSEPH A. BOYDEN (he may be a brother of Stephen who married Almeda Tinker [boy:153]).

vii. GEORGE W. TINKER, born 9 Jun 1839 in St Stephen, NB (tink:29). Died 1 Jan 1880 in Bath, NB (tink). Census: 1850 & 60 in Calais. He married 27 Nov 1863 in Dearfield (sic), ME, ISABELLA M. BRIDGES born, 19 Aug 1843 (tink: 29).

viii. JANE SMITH PINEO TINKER, born 25 Jun 1841 in Calais (VR, tink:30). In 1870 she was a teacher. Died before 1918, her children mentioned in brother, Henry's will. Census: 1850 thru 1880 in Calais. She married 25 Dec 1871 in Milltown ME (tink:30), as his 2nd wife ANDREW S. McCATHERINE, he was born 12 Apr 1839 in Richibucto, NB, son of CHARLES McEACHERN & MARY STUART, (both born in Scotland). He filed saws in the mill. He died 14 March 1895 age 53y 11m (MSA, adv). Census: 1880 in Calais. The name McCatherine changed from the old Scotch name McEachern (tink:30) (see also Mary Townsend his 1st wife).

ix. HENRY CLAY TINKER, born 1 Oct 1843 in Calais (VR, tink:30). He was a policeman and a mechanic. Died 27 Sep 1918 in Calais (VR, MSA, g.s.). Buried in Calais Cemetery. Probate of his will, Washington Co. # T-4-352. He left money for a monument in cemetery for his father, mother and siblings who died young. Census: 1850 thru 1910 in Calais. He married 13 Mar 1884 in Milltown, ME (tink:30, VR:2:35) PRISCILLA B. SCOTT of Elmsville, NB, born ca 1848, buried in Calais Cemetery (g.s. no date). Census: 1910 in Calais.

x. HELEN TINKER, born 25 Apr 1845 in Calais, died 18 Mar 1847 in Calais (VR:1:238, tink:30). Buried in Calais Cemetery.

xi. MARY ANN BOIES TINKER, born 22 Nov 1846 in Calais (VR, tink:30 has 1845). Died 15 May 1916 age 76y 6m 7d in Millbridge, ME (VR, MSA). Buried in Millbridge (probate of will, Washington Co. # P-4-407). Census: 1850, 60, 70 & 80 in Calais. She married 1st (___?___) TODD, 2nd 17 Mar 1885 in Calais (tink:30) CHARLES PEABODY, son of CHARLES C. P. PEABODY & CORDELIA EVELYN WHITNEY (see

PEABODY).

xii. FRANKLIN W. TINKER, born 8 Feb 1850 in Calais (VR, tink:30). Died after 1900 when he was residing in Lowell, MA (tink p. 30). Census: 1850, 60 & 70 in Calais. He married 2 Dec 1874 (VR, tink) MARY LOUISE SCOTT, born 14 Sept 1952 in Pennfield, NB. In 1900 they resided in Lowell, MA (tink:30).

xiii. CHARLES TINKER, born 25 Apr 1852 in Calais (VR, tink:30). Died in Calais (tink = 15 Apr 1853 but alive age 8 in 1860 census). Buried in Calais Cemetery. Census: 1860 in Calais.

JOHN CAMPBELL TODD FAMILY

JOHN CAMPBELL [Sometimes pronounced Camel] TODD, born 17 Apr 1767 in Georgetown, son of JOHN TODD & NANCY TODD, he died in Calais 9 June 1828 (drum:123). He married at Steuben 2 Dec 1790 ABIGAIL 'NABBY' NICHOLS who died 22 Nov 1832 in Steuben (VR). They resided in Steuben, Eastport and Calais. Census: 1830 Abigail head of household (10 males & 4 females) in Calais. They had nine children:

1. JOHN NICHOLS TODD, b. 27 Oct 1791 (see BELOW)
2. NANCY CAMPBELL TODD b. 19 Nov 1793, died 17 Dec 1878 in Oshkosh, WI. She married AMASA CHENEY who died 30 June 1827. Their daughter, Mary Ann TODD, married AMOS CLARK of Calais (see CLARK).
3. MARGARET 'PEGGY' TODD, b. 10 Sept 1796, married JOHN CALIFF DUTCH (see DUTCH).
4. ALEXANDER TODD, b. 31 Mar 1799 (see BELOW).
5. WILLIAM TODD, b. 14 Aug 1801 (see BELOW).
6. MARY ANN TODD, b. 3 June 1804, d. 20 Apr 1855, unmarried. Census: 1850 (with brother, John N. Todd) in Calais.
7. HANNAH TOWNSLEY TODD, b. 27 May 1817, she married BENJAMIN F. WAITE (see WAITE).
8. ELIZABETH JANE TODD, b. 23 Aug 1810, married 1832 in Calais (cal2:33), JAMES THEODORE MAYVILLE.
9. ABIGAIL TODD, b. 30 Dec 1812, married LUTHER BRACKETT (see BRACKETT) [Abbie died 24 Apr 1891 in Farmington, ND age 79 (adv)]

The above information on John Todd Family, from the Alexander Drummond Genealogy pages 123-128. Unless otherwise noted.

ALEXANDER & HANNAH TODD, p. 178

ALEXANDER TODD, born 31 Mar 1799, in Eastport or Steuben ME (VR Eastport, BHM) son of John C. Todd (see above). He was a Lt. in the Militia 13 May 1826 and Capt. 10 Nov 1828 in 1st Brig. 7th Div. (milit). He was a druggist, the City Clerk of Calais until his death and he was the first master of St. Croix Lodge #46 F. & A. M. to die in office (lodge:22, 43). Died 23 May 1852 age 53 in Calais (VR, g.s.). Buried in Calais Cemetery. Probate of Estate: 1852 in Machias Me. Census: 1830 (1 male, 3 females), 40 (3 males, 3 females), 50 in Calais.

He married 26 Nov 1826 in Eastport ME (VR) HARRIET J. LITTLE, born 11 Feb 1807 in Eastport (VR), daughter of ROBERT & ELIZABETH LITTLE. Died 19 Apr 1886 age 79y 2m in Calais (VR, obit times, g.s.). Probate of estate, Washington Co. (# T-1-196). Census: 1850 thru 1880 in Calais. Children:

i. CHARLOTTE HAWKS TODD, born 14 Mar 1829 in Calais (VR). Died 2 May 1848 age 19 (g.s.) in Calais. Buried in Calais Cemetery.
ii. HARRIET ELIZABETH TODD, born 23 Feb 1835 in Calais (VR, father's will b. St. Stephen, NB). She was a teacher. Never married. Died 14 May 1886 in Calais. Probate of estate, Washington Co. # T1-196. Her only heir A.W. Todd. Census: 1850 thru 1880 in Calais.
iii. ALEXANDER WINSLOW TODD, born 19 Aug 1837 in Calais (VR, father's will = b. St. Stephen, NB). Died after 1886, mentioned in both mother & sister's probates. He must have married, his children are mention in mother's probate. Census: 1850 & 60 in Calais.
iv. STEPHEN HILL TODD, born 12 Feb 1840 in Calais (VR). Died 21 Jan 1866 age 26 in Calais (union, g.s.). Buried in Calais Cemetery. Census: 1850 & 60 in Calais.

* In the 1880 census there were three grandchildren living with Harriet J. and unmarried daughter, Harriet E. The middle child was born in Cape Breton ca 1870. Alexander W. not in the 1870 census of Calais, perhaps these are his children.

JOHN N. & LYDIA TODD, p. 184

JOHN NICHOLS TODD, born 27 Oct 1791 in Steuben ME (VR: 90, Eastport VR, drum:125) son of John C. Todd (see above). He was a lumber surveyor. He was in the 1st Brigade, 7th Div Maine Militia, Sgt. In 1828-1831 and Capt. in 1832 (mil). Died 26 Apr 1862 age 70 in Calais (VR:1:243:244, east:188 = 23 Apr age 79, g.s. = 23 Apr). Buried in Calais Cemetery. Census: 1820 (3 males, 1 female) in Eastport, 1830 (12 males, 4 females) in Baring, 50 & 60 in Calais.

He married 12 Jun 1817 in Eastport ME (VR) LYDIA DOWNES, born 4 Jul 1799 in Calais (VR, cal2:1), daughter of SHUBIEL & TEMPERANCE DOWNES. She died 27 Jan 1875 age 75y 6m in Eastport (adv, g.s., drum:125). Buried in Calais Cemetery. Census: 1850 & 60 in Calais. Children:

i. WILLIAM TYLER TODD, born 23 Apr 1818 in Eastport ME (VR, Calais VR). Attended Colby College 1845-48 did not graduate (colby).
ii. SHUBIEL DOWNES TODD, born 28 Jan 1820 (see BELOW)
iii. TEMPERANCE LUCINDA TODD, born 16 Feb 1822 in Eastport ME (VR). Died 23 Jan 1874 unmarried (drum:125). Census: 1850 in Calais.
iv. HARRIET DOWNES TODD, born 10 Apr 1824 in Eastport ME (VR, Calais VR). Died 27 Oct 1903 in Eastport ME (MSA). Census: 1860 in Eastport. She married 2 Nov 1845 in Calais (mop:198), (int.) 12 Oct 1845 in Calais (VR) NOEL BYRON NUTT born 11 June 1824 in Perry (VR), son of JAMES NUTT & SARAH BROWN. He was a teacher, deputy collector of customs at Eastport, and treasurer of Eastport Savings Bank (mop:197). They resided in Eastport. Also was editor of Eastport Sentinel. Died 10 May 1898 at age 74 in Eastport (east:578, adv). Census: 1860 in Eastport.
v. JOHN CAMPBELL TODD, born 20 Aug 1826 in St Stephen, NB (Calais VR). Died 16 Apr 1859 age 32 in Shaw's Flat, CA, unmarried (drum:125, east:168).
vi. CHARLOTTE DOWNES TODD, born 15 Jul 1829 in Calais (VR). Died 24 May 1860 (drum:125). Census: 1850 in Calais. She married 23 Nov 1851 by Rev. Mr. Barrett in St. Stephen, NB (adv, FJ) TOBIAS DELUE, he filed for citizenship on 27 May 1852 stating he was born 1809 in St. John, NB, left St. John in 1833 and arrived same year in Calais (SJC). Census: 1860 in Calais.
vii. GEORGE EDWARD TODD, born 7 Feb 1832 in Calais. He was a sailor. Died after 1873 when he was injured in an accident (adv). Census: 1850 in Calais.
viii. JACOB LEROY TODD, born 25 Sep 1834 in Dyer Township, ME (VR). Died 4 Jun 1852 (drum:125). Census: 1850 in Calais.
ix. HELEN LEROY TODD, born 26 Jan 1837 in Dyer Township, ME (VR). Census: 1850 in Calais.
x. LYDIA LOUISE TODD, born 10 Aug 1839 in Dyer Township, ME (VR). Died 18 Sep 1842 age 3 in Calais (VR, drum:125).
xi. MARY ABBY TODD, born 6 Apr 1842 in Calais (VR). Census: 1850 & 60 in Calais.
xii. JULIA T. TODD, born circa 1846 in Calais (1850 census). Census: 1850 in Calais.
xiii. DANIEL D. C. TODD, born circa 1848 in Calais (1850 census). Census: 1850 in Calais.

SHUBIEL D. & CLEMENTINA TODD, p. 195

SHUBIEL DOWNES TODD, born 28 Jan 1820 in Eastport ME (VR), son of JOHN C. TODD (see above). In 1846 he was in business with Benjamin F. Waite, as Waite & Todd (SJC court action in July 1848 term).
Note *   He was not in 1850 census where did he and children go after wife died?

He married 31 Jul 1845 by Rev. Desbow in St Stephen, NB (CCMR, adv) CLEMENTINA E. CROCKER of Charlotte, ME. She died 5 Sep 1848 age 27 in Calais (VR:1:240). Children:

i. JULIA FLORENCE TODD, born 24 Nov 1846 in Calais (VR).
ii. DANIEL DUNHAM TODD, born 16 Jul 1848 in Calais (VR).

WILLIAM & MARY ANN TODD, p. 180

WILLIAM TODD, born 14 Aug 1801 in Eastport ME (VR) son of JOHN C. TODD (see above). Died 16 Feb 1862 in Cherryfield, ME (drum:126, union has 2 Feb 1862 age 62). Buried in Pine Grove Cemetery in Cherryfield, ME. Census: 1850 & 60 in Cherryfield, ME.

He married 23 Dec 1831 in Cherryfield (drum:126), (int.) 11 Oct 1831 in Cherryfield (VR) MARY ANN NICKELS (his cousin), born circa 1819 in Cherryfield, daughter of ALEXANDER NICKELS AND MARTHA HOLWAY. She died 30 Jul 1869 in Cherryfield (drum:126). Buried in Pine Grove Cemetery in Cherryfield. Census: 1850 & 60 in Cherryfield. Children:

i. SARAH SHAW TODD, born 24 Jun 1835 in Calais, died 11 Sep 1837 age 2y 2m 19d in Calais

(VR:1:227, drum:126). Buried in Calais Cemetery.

ii. WILLIAM EDGAR TODD, born 28 Jul 1837 in Calais, died 16 Jan 1841 age 3y 5m 21d in Calais (VR:1:227, drum:126, g.s.). Buried in Pine Grove Cemetery in Cherryfield.

iii. BENJAMIN FRANKLIN TODD, born 28 Sep 1839 in Calais (VR). He was a clerk. Died 16 Jul 1860 (drum:126, g.s.). Buried in Pine Grove Cemetery in Cherryfield. Census: 1850 & 60 in Cherryfield, ME.

iv. MARTHA NICHOLS TODD, born 23 Sep 1842 in Calais (VR). Died 8 Apr 1862 (drum:126, g.s.). Buried in Pine Grove Cemetery in Cherryfield. Census: 1850 & 60 in Cherryfield, ME.

v. WENDALL PHILIPS TODD, born 2 Oct 1846 in ? Cherryfield, ME. Died 27 Oct 1868 (drum:126, g.s.). Buried in Pine Grove Cemetery in Cherryfield. Census: 1850 & 60 in Cherryfield, ME.

JOHN & MARTHA TOWERS, p. 187

JOHN TOWERS, applied for citizenship Mar 1832 stating he was born 1793 in Tower Hill, St. David Parish, NB, son of WILLIAM TOWERS AND ANNIE STAPLES, entered U.S. at Calais 3 July 1826 (CCP docket # 251). Naturalized 18 Sept 1834 (irmch). Bapt. 17 Sept 1793 (presSA). He was a millwright. Died 1 Jan 1868 age 74 (union, presSA, will filed 19 Mar 1866). Buried: 3 Jan 1868 in Calais Cemetery. Census: 1830 (17 males [10 between ages 20 to 30], 4 females), 40 (10 males, 4 females), 50 & 60 in Calais.

He married 6 Aug 1816 in St. Stephen, NB, at home of her parents (bruce), MARTHA 'HATTIE' GRIMMER, born circa 1794 in Old Ridge, NB (bruce), bapt. 25 May 1794 (presSA, bruce), daughter of THOMAS GRIMMER of Philadelphia, PA & LYDIA WAY of NY [Loyalists who fled NY for Port Matoon, NS (bruce)]. She died 25 May 1862 age 68 in Calais (VR:1:242, g.s., union). Buried in Calais Cemetery. Census: 1850 & 60 in Calais. Children:

i. JESSE TOWERS, born 26 Nov 1816 in Tower Hill, NB (bruce). He was a millwright. Died 10 Apr 1864 (bruce) killed in pit of gang saw (bruce). He married 9 Sept 1838 in Calais, by Rev. William A. Whitwell, MARY ANN JANE MURPHY (cal2:50, mrwc: 27=23 Sept). She was born 1818 (g.s.). Died 20 July 1902 (g.s.). Both are buried Rural Cemetery in St. Stephen, NB (rural:39). Census: 1871 in St. Stephen, NB.

ii. FREDERICK TOWERS, born circa 1818 prob. In Tower Hill. Died 30 Oct 1846 age 28 in Calais (VR:1:231). Buried in Calais Cemetery. He married (int) 23 Oct 1841 (VR:1:12) EUNICE E(liza) BECKWITH. [ELIZA E. MAXWELL, born ca 1847, died 7 Sept 1889 (g.s.). Buried in Towers lot in Calais Cemetery could this be a daughter?].

iii. LYDIA TOWERS, born ca 1820, [according to Jesse Towers (1869-1948) there was a daughter named Lydia in this family (bruce)]. In the Gazette of 3 June 1841 a Lydia Ann Towers daughter of John of Calais married Tuesday last, James Thompson. He was born 17 Oct 1817 in Nova Scotia (bruce). Died: 24 May 1847 (arnie).

iv. MERCY TOWERS, born circa 1822 in St. David, NB (1850 census). Died 25 Feb 1901 age 78y 11m in Calais (g.s.). Buried in Calais Cemetery. Census: 1850 thru 1880 in Calais. She married 1st 6 Dec 1842 in Calais AUGUSTUS L. TOWNSEND (see TOWNSEND). She married 2nd 6 Jun 1858 in Calais (rey, adv) WILLIAM BARBER born between 1819 - 21 in NB. Died 12 Sep 1892 age 73 in Calais (MSA, obit times). Census: 1860, 70 & 80 in Calais.

v. MILES TOWERS, born circa 1823 in Tower Hill, NB. He was a millwright. Died 19 Nov 1865 age 47y 7m in Calais (VR, bruce, VSNB:23:567, g.s.). Buried in Calais Cemetery. Census: 1860 in Calais. He married 1st LUCINDA P. RUNELLS 2 Dec 1847 in St Stephen, NB (CCMR). She died 24 Oct 1850, buried in Calais Cemetery (g.s.). He married 2nd 15 Jan 1853 in Calais (VR:3:155) by Rev. H.V. Dexter, SUSAN Y. DICKEY born ca 1821, daughter of THOMAS DICKEY (bruce). Census: 1860 in Calais.

vi. EDWARD TOWERS, born 27 Dec 1827 in Calais (VR). He was a member of the Masons. Died 6 Sep 1874 at age 46 in Calais (adv, bruce, SCC). Buried in Calais Cemetery. Census: 1861 & 71 in St. Stephen, NB. He married 23 Sep 1849 by Rev. William C. Crawford in Calais (VR:3:145, mrwc:53) MARY JANE FLEMING born ca 1828 in Ireland. She died 5 July 1890 age 68y in Baring (g.s., adv). Buried in Calais Cemetery. Census: 1861 & 71 in St. Stephen, NB.

vii. ALBERT TOWERS, born 25 Feb 1829 in Calais (VR). Died circa 1885 in Calif. (bruce), had a sheep farm near Los Angeles CA. Census: 1850 (age 19) in Calais. He married 18 Sep 1853 in Calais (VR). MARGARET A. LULL.

viii. ALFRED TOWERS, born 25 Feb 1829 in Calais (VR, death rec. has 1832). Died 25 Jan 1918 age 88y 11m in Calais (MSA, adv). Probate of will, Washington Co. (# T-4-517). Will mentions a brother-in-law, William

Pike and niece, Ethel Pike. Census: 1850, 60 & 70 in Calais. He married 1st 4 Dec 1852 by Rev. Mr. Johnson in Calais (VR:3:153, east:124) MARY ANN STAPLES of Baileyville. She born 1827, died 3 Oct 1880 age 55 in Calais (adv, g.s.). Census: 1860 & 70 in Calais. He married 2nd 2 Nov 1881by Rev. Howard Sprague in Old Ridge NB (times) JANNET 'JENNIE' P. FRASEUR/FRAZER, born 1842 in Old Ridge, daughter of WILLIAM FRASEUR [b. Scotland] & AMY GRIMMER [b. St. David, NB]. She died 19 May 1910 in Calais (MSA, sfh:1:278, g.s.). Probate of will in Machias Washington Co. (# T-4-14). All three buried in Calais Cemetery.

ix. ELMIRA/ALMIRA'MYRA' TOWERS, born 9 Oct 1833 in Calais (VR). Died before brother, Alfred. Census: 1850 (age 16) in Calais. She married 1st 18 Sept 1853 by Rev. H. V. Dexter in Calais (VR:3:155) WILLIS N. HAVERSTOCK. She married 2nd 2 June 1870 WILLIAM WEBSTER in Lewiston, Me (bruce).

x. ANNA MARIA TOWERS, born 3 Feb 1835 in Calais (MSA). She was a dressmaker. Died 8 Nov 1931age 96y 4m 4d in Calais (MSA, sfh:6:117). Census: 1850, 60, 70 & 1910 in Calais. She married 3 Mar 1857 in Calais BENJAMIN LEWIS LESUER (see LESUER).

xi. WILLIAM H. TOWERS, born 17 Jul 1838 in Calais (VR). He was a millwright. Served in Civil War, Co. G 16th Maine, he was 5'7" with black eyes and black hair (cwcard). Died 1 Jan 1863 in Fairfax, Va. (bruce). Buried National Cemetery, Alexandria, VA (cwcard). Census: 1850 & 60 in Calais. He married 14 May 1859 by Rev. I.J. Burgess in St. Stephen, NB (CCMR, Calais VR:3:183) ABBIE L. BACON. Census: 1860 in Calais.

AUGUSTUS & MERCY TOWNSEND, p. 189

AUGUSTUS L. TOWNSEND, born circa 1818 in Sidney ME (1850 census), son of DAVID TOWNSEND AND MARY 'POLLY' ROLLINS. He worked in a mill. Died 2 May 1852 age 36 in Calais (g.s., poss. d. in St. Stephen). Buried in Calais Cemetery. Census: 1850 in Calais.

He married 6 Dec 1842 by J. C. Washburn, JP in Calais (mrwc:36, gaz) MERCY TOWERS, born circa 1822 in St. David, NB (1850 census), daughter of JOHN TOWERS & MARTHA 'HATTIE' GRIMMER. She died 25 Feb 1901 age 78y 11m in Calais (g.s.). Buried in Calais Cemetery Census: 1850, 60 & 70 in Calais. She married 2nd WILLIAM BARBER (see TOWERS) Children:

i. MARY AMANDA TOWNSEND, born 30 Nov 1843 in St Stephen, NB. Died 19 Jan 1869 in Calais (g.s.). Buried in Calais Cemetery. Census: 1850 & 60 in Calais. She married 28 Jun 1862 by Rev. H. V. Dexter in Calais (VR) ANDREW S. McCATHERINE /McEACHERN, born ca 1840, son of CHARLES McEACHERN & MARY STUART. Census: 1870 in Calais.

ii. FREDERICK A. TOWNSEND, born Oct 1848 in Calais. Graduated from Calais Academy. Served in Civil War in Co E 12th Inf., he was a sailor 5'2 ½" with blue eyes and light hair (cwcard). Called Captain in wife's obit. Died 21 Dec 1913 in Calais (MSA). Buried in Calais Cemetery. Census: 1850 thru 80 & 1900 in Calais. He married 10 Jun 1871 by Rev. E. B. Eddy in Calais (adv) ANGELINE 'ANGIE' V. TRAFTON, born ca 1847 in Oak Hill, NB, daughter of THEODORE TRAFTON & ELIZA BARBOUR (both born in Oak Hill, NB). She died 23 Oct 1905 age 57 in Calais (obit adv, MSA, rey). Buried in Calais Cemetery. Census: 1860 & 80 in Calais.

ASA E. & CATHARINE TOZIER, p. 220

ASA E. TOZIER, born circa 1805 in Waterville ME (1850 census). He worked in a mill. In Oct 1833 he was a lumberman in a court action (SJC). He was in the 1st Brigade, 7th Div Maine Militia as a Pvt. In 1832 (mil). Died 18 Apr 1877 age 76y in Waterville (MOCA). Buried in Pine Grove Cemetery Waterville. Census: 1840 (2 males, 3 females), 50 in Calais, 60 & 70 a farmer in Waterville.

He married 29 Aug 1836 in Milltown by Rev. Mr. Clark (gaz of 1 Sept 1836) CATHERINE CHANDLER born circa 1816 in Fredericton, NB (1850 census). She was a seamstress. Died 1 Dec 1893 in Waterville (MOCA). Buried in Pine Grove Cemetery Waterville. Census: 1850 in Calais, 60 & 70 in Waterville. Children:

i. HENRY THOMAS TOZIER, born 18 May 1837 in Calais (VR). He served in Civil War in Co I 8th Inf., a

Captain, he was a paper maker 5'8" with gray eyes and black hair. He was killed in action 10 Dec 1864 at Petersburg, VA and is buried in Pine Grove Cemetery, Waterville, ME (cwcard, MOCA). Census: 1850 in Calais, 60 in Waterville.

ii. MARY ELIZABETH TOZIER, born 21 Aug 1839 in Calais (VR). Died 17 Nov 1898 age 59y 2m 27d in Waterville (MOCA, MSA). Buried in Pine Grove Cemetery Waterville. Census: 1850 in Calais, 60 & 70 in Waterville. Unmarried.

iii. HARRIET SOPHIA TOZIER, born 19 Apr 1846 in Calais (VR). Census: 1850 in Calais, 60 in Waterville.

JOHN & MARY TRACEY, p. 200

JOHN TRACEY, born circa 1814, in Kelmatherry, Ireland, left Ireland 4 Apr 1829, arrived Halifax 1 May 1829, to Eastport Sept 1833, and to Calais Sept 1833. Naturalized 2 Sept 1840 (Nat. papers MSA). He was a ship rigger and operated a Boarding Home. Census: 1850, 60 & 70 in Calais. [In 60 there was living with him Ann Hastings age 70, she may be his wife's sister or mother].

He married MARY `HASTY' HASTINGS, born circa 1812 in Ireland. She possibly died before 1860. Census: 1850 in Calais. Children:

i. HUGH TRACEY, born 27 Jun 1838 in Calais (VR). Census: 1850 & 60 in Calais.
ii. JANE TRACEY, born 7 Feb 1840 in Calais (VR). Census: 1850 & 60 in Calais.
iii. JOHN TRACEY, Jr., born 5 Apr 1842 in Calais (VR). He was a Shiprigger. Died 9 Dec 1910 in Calais (MSA). Census: 1850 thru 1900 in Calais. He married 6 Sep 1862 by Rev. H. V. Dexter in Calais (VR) REBECCA CHAMBERS, born June 1843 in NB. Census: 1870, 80 & 1900 in Calais.
iv. ANN TRACEY, born 30 May 1844 in Calais (VR). Census: 1850 & 60 in Calais.
v. THOMAS TRACEY, born 12 Jan 1846 in Calais (VR). Census: 1850 & 60 in Calais.
vi. MARY A. TRACEY, born, circa 1848 in Calais. Died 26 Oct 1893 in Calais (VR, MSA). Buried in Calais Cemetery. Census: 1860, 70 & 80 in Calais. She married JOHN COFFRON born ca 1848 in NB. Census: 1880 in Calais.
vii. JAMES TRACEY, born circa 1850 in Calais. Census: 1860 in Calais.

THOMAS & SARAH TRACEY, p. 195

THOMAS TRACEY and his wife SARAH are listed in VR with one child:

i. MARY TRACEY, born 21 Oct 1847 in Calais (VR).

RICHARD & JANE TRIMBLE, p. 205

RICHARD TRIMBLE, he stated in his application for naturalization that he was born in 1800 (g.s. has 1803), in Kern-Kill, County Down, Ireland, left Ireland July 1828, arrived in Calais Sept 1828 (SJC:8:50). Naturalized 29 Apr 1859 (irmch). Served in Civil War enlisted Sept 1863, Co B in 16th Maine also served in Co G. of 20th Maine, is described as 5' 8", with gray eyes and brown hair (MSA). Died 10 Dec 1872 age 73 in Calais (g.s., obit). Buried in Calais Cemetery. Census: 1840 (4 males, 3 females), 50 & 60 in Calais.

He married before 1830 JANE McBRIDE, born circa 1801, in Ireland (1850 census, g.s., her maiden name from son, William's death rec.). Died 27 Sep 1852 age 50 in Calais (FJ). Buried in Calais Cemetery. Census: 1850 in Calais. Children:

i. MARY ANN TRIMBLE, born circa 1831 in St David, NB (1850 census). Census: 1850, 60 & 70 in Calais. She married 1856 or 1857 by Rev. S. H. Keeler in Calais (VR:3:169) BENJAMIN WHEELER, born ca 1823, in NB. Census: 1860 & 70 (a caulker), in Calais.
ii. ALEXANDER TRIMBLE, born 27 Jan 1834 in Calais (VR). He was a sailor. Census: 1850 & 60 in Calais.
iii. SARAH TRIMBLE, born 21 July 1835 in Calais (VR). Died 18 Nov 1901 at Amityville, Long Island, NY (obit adv has birth 21 July 1836, also that her brother, William, is the last survivor of a family of 3 sons and 2 daughters).

Census: 1850 & 60 in Calais. She married 5 Dec 1864 in Calais (VR) JOHN LOUDEN, born ca 1820, son of WILLIAM & LYDIA LOUDEN, he died after his wife. Census: 1860 (age 20 with parents) in Calais.

iv. WILLIAM TRIMBLE, born 16 Jul 1838 in Calais (VR). He served in the Civil War as a saddler in Co C of 1st Maine Cavalry. He was 5' 10 ½" with hazel eyes and black hair (cwcard). He worked as a carriage trimmer and harness maker. Died 5 May 1908 age 69y 9m 19d in Calais (MSA, g.s.). Buried in Calais Cemetery. Census: 1850, thru 80 & 1900 in Calais. He married 4 Nov 1866 in Calais (VR:3:223) ISABELLA ANDERSON, born 30 Apr 1842 in Calais, daughter of JOHN ANDERSON & ISABELLA MC (?) CELLAN both born in Ire. (MSA). Died 20 Feb 1924 age 81y 2m 20d in Calais (MSA, sfh:4:169). Buried in Calais Cemetery. Census: 1860 (with parents), 70, 80 & 1900 in Calais.

JAMES & MAHALA TROTT, p. 204

JAMES TROTT, born ca 1808 in Perry ME (1850 census). He was a millman. Died before 1870. Census: 1850 (age 42) & 60 (age 54) in Calais. [Perry VR:68 has Benjamin & Elizabeth Trott with a son, James b. 23 Jan 1806 and d. 1808, is it possible this death date is in error? Or are his parents other than Benjamin?]

He married (int.) 14 Jul 1832 in Perry ME (VR) MAHALA LORING, born 19 Sep 1813 in Perry ME (DEA:8:217), daughter of ZACHEUS & ELIZABETH 'BETSEY' LORING (both alive in 1850 census living with John Loring in Perry). Died 25 Mar 1903 age 88 in Calais (MSA). Census: 1850 thru 1900 in Calais, (in 70 she living with daughter, Julia). Children:

i. PETER G. TROTT, born 11 Jun 1834 in Perry ME (VR). Died 13 Nov 1835 in Perry (VR:121).
ii. BENJAMIN FRANKLIN 'Frank' TROTT, born 5 Apr 1836 in Perry (VR:121, Calais VR, b. in Milltown, NB on death rec.). He enlisted at age 24 in 1861, a laborer 5'4" with hazel eyes and brown hair (cwcard). (Frank Trott age 21 deserted Co D 6th Maine NRMS:241). He worked in a mill. Died 21 May 1903 in Orono, ME (MSA). Census: 1850 & 60 in Calais. He married 19 Mar 1864 in St Stephen, NB (CCMR) ALTHEA A. LEIGHTON. [Mary wife of Frank Trott died 5 Apr 1860 in Calais age 25 (union) possibly his first wife].
iii. THOMAS MELVIN TROTT, born 18 July 1840 in Robbinston Me (MSA). He was a barber. Died 30 Apr 1916 age 75y 9m 12d in Pembroke, ME (MSA). Buried in Pembroke. Census: 1850 & 60 in Calais, 1900 in Pembroke. He married LAVINIA B. CAREW, born ca July 1841 (1900 census) in Perry, daughter of JOHN CAREW & BARBARA TROTT both born in Perry (MSA). Died 9 Aug 1909 in Pembroke (MSA). Census: 1900 in Pembroke.
iv. JULIA A. TROTT, born 9 Nov 1843 in Robbinston Me (Calais VR, 1850 census). Died 17 Feb 1917 in Calais (VR, MSA). Census: 1850 thru 1900 in Calais. She married (int.) 7 Sept 1863 in Calais JOHN CONREY born May 1840 in Perry, son of _____ CONREY & SARAH PATTERSON. He worked for the RR. Died 25 Jun or Jan ? 1912 in Calais (MSA). Census: 1870 & 80 (her mother with them) & 1900 in Calais.
v. UNNAMED CHILD TROTT, born Mar 1846 (?). Died Aug 1846 age 5m. Buried: 23 Aug 1846 in Calais (sext).
vi. JAMES TROTT (jr.), born 4 Mar 1847 in Calais (VR).

JOHN & LAVINA TROTT, p. 199

JOHN TROTT, born, 3 May 1809 in Perry ME (VR:68), son of BENJAMIN TROTT & ELIZABETH 'BETSEY' NASON {(int.) 3 Apr 1805 in Eastport VR}. In 1860 he was a shingle inspector, he was also a carpenter. Died circa 1879 (g.s.). Buried in Calais Cemetery. Census: 1840 (1male, 5 females) in Perry, 1850 & 70 in Calais, 1860 in Princeton.

He married 19 Dec 1832 by Bennett Robert, in Calais (Perry VR:75, mrwc:7) LAVINIA S. PATTERSON born 9 Dec 1815 in Perry ME (VR:39, 1850 census, g.s.), daughter of ROBERT & HANNAH PATTERSON. Died 13 Jan 1891 in Calais (times, g.s.). Buried in Calais Cemetery. Census: 1850, 70 thru 1880 in Calais, 1860 in Princeton. Children:

i. HANNAH E. TROTT, born 25 May 1833, in Perry ME (VR:115). Died 13 Feb 1896 age 65y 9m in Calais (VR). Buried in Calais Cemetery. Census: 1850 in Calais, 60 (with her parents) in Princeton. She married (int) 26 Mar 1859 in Calais (VR:1:84) PETER WHEELER, born ca 1835 in NB (son's death rec.), he was a mail carrier. Census: 1860 in Princeton.
ii. CLARINDA MELISSA TROTT, born 3 Mar 1835 in Perry (VR:115). Census: 1850 in Calais.

iii. MATILDA P. TROTT, born 16 Mar 1837 in Perry (VR:115). Census: 1850 in Calais. She married 1854-55 by Rev. S. H. Keeler WILLIAM FINKLE (VR:1:158).
iv. BARBARA S. TROTT, born 19 Mar 1839 in Perry (VR:115). Died circa 1854 (g.s.). Buried 17 Sept 1854 in Calais Cemetery (saint). Census: 1850 in Calais.
v. LUCILLA STICKNEY TROTT, born 8 Apr 1841 in Perry (VR:115). She was a tailoress. Census: 1850 in Calais, 1860 in Princeton.
vi. STEPHEN EMERSON TROTT, born 1 Oct 1843 in Calais (VR). He served in Civil War in Co I 13th Maine, a laborer 5'6" with blue eyes and brown hair resided in Princeton (cwcard). Census: 1850 in Calais, 1860 in Princeton.
vii. GEORGE JEFFERSON TROTT, born 1 Oct 1843 in Calais, died 24 Dec 1843 in Calais (VR).
viii. HENRIETTA TROTT, born May 1850 in Calais (1850 census). Died: 4 June 1897 age 48y 2m 13d in Calais (MSA). Buried: Calais Cemetery. Census: 1850 in Calais, 1860 in Princeton, 1870 in Calais. She married 18 Oct 1869, by Samuel Lambe in Calais (VR:3:232), DANIEL McNUTT, born ca 1844 in England, son of JOHN McNUTT [b. Scotland] & ELIZABETH GREGORY [b. Ireland] (parent's names from his 2nd marriage record 18 Nov 1899 to Nellie Fleming in Robbinston at MSA). He was a ship carpenter. Census: 1870 in Calais.
ix. JOHN H. TROTT, born circa 1853. He was a machinist. Census: 1860 in Princeton, 1870 & 80 in Calais. He married 10 Nov 1877 in Calais (VR:3:239, times) ELIZA S. MITCHELL born ca 1854, daughter of ____ & ALMIRA Y. (____) MITCHELL. Census: 1880 in Calais (living with her mother Almira Y. Mitchell age 55).
x. SARAH J. TROTT, born, circa 1853, died circa 1936 (g.s.). Buried in Calais Cemetery. Census: 1860 in Princeton , 1870 & 80 in Calais. She married ALBERT E. BENTON.
xi. JUNE LAVINIA TROTT, born ca 1855, died ca 1856, buried 13 June 1856 age 8mos (saint).

MICHAEL H. & SUSANNA TUOMY, p. 181

MICHAEL H. TOOMEY /TUOMY / TWOMY/TUMEY. {Several spellings found, most used TOOMEY}, born circa 1790 in Cary, Ireland (1850 census). Died before 1860. Census: 1850 in Calais. He was a ship carpenter.

He married SUSANNA MCKAY or MCVAY, born circa 1817 in Derry, Ireland (1850 census). Died after 1860. Census: 1850 & 60 in Calais. Children:

i. JAMES TOOMEY, born 28 Nov 1838 in Eastport ME (VR). Census: 1850 in Calais.
ii. SARAH TOOMEY, born 18 Feb 1840 in Eastport ME (VR). Census: 1850 in Calais.
iii. THOMAS H. TOOMEY, born 8 Dec 1841 in Calais (VR), birth (2): 6 Nov 1843 in Calais (VR:3:253). Served in Civil War in Co K 2nd Inf. and Co E 20th Maine, he was a lumberman 5'3 ¾" with blue eyes and brown hair (cwcard). Died 16 July 1926 84y in Calais (obit adv, name Toomey, sfh:5:107 name Tumey). Census: 1850 & 60 in Calais (dir 1901 with brother, Michael).
iv. MARGARET TOOMEY, born 28 Jan 1844 in Calais (VR:3:253). Died 3 Mar 1847 in Calais (VR:1:229).
v. MICHAEL TOOMEY, born 31 Mar 1848 in Calais (VR:3:253). Died 25 Apr 1920 age 60 in Calais (MSA unmarried, sfh:3:142). Census: 1850 & 60 in Calais (dir 1901 with brother, Thomas). Poss. marriage found in divorce action – Mary E. Toomey vs Michael Toomey married 5 June 1888 in Milltown, NB, lived together until 15 Oct 1893, cruel & abusive treatment, divorce granted Apr 1900 (SJC docket #150).
vi. JOHN TOOMEY, born 6 Jan 1851 in Calais (VR:3:253). In 1884 he established a tobacco store and restaurant on Main Street in Calais (CEV:27). Died 17 Jul 1892 42y 7m in St Andrews, NB (adv, VR, SCC an inquest was held – verdict accidental death by drowning).

- Note: the birth dates of Thomas and Margaret in VR book 3 are impossible so Thomas' date of birth in book one would likely be more accurate.

EBENEZER & JANE TUTTLE, p. 223

EBENEZER TUTTLE, born circa 1801. In 1829 he was in partnership with Robert E. Rumery as Tuttle & Rumery (SJC:1:346). Died 12 May 1846 age 45 in Calais (VR:3:229, g.s.). Buried: 14 May 1846 in Calais Cemetery. Census: 1830 (3 males, 2 females), 1840 (5 males, 2 females).

He married before 1829 JANE (_____), born circa 1806 in St. Stephen, NB (1850 census). Census: 1850 & 60 (Jane and Alexander Steen living with her) in Calais. Children:

i. JOHN HARRISON TUTTLE, born 24 Sep 1829 in Calais (VR). Died 11 Nov 1853 age 24 in Calais (VR). Buried in Calais Cemetery. Census: 1850 in Calais.
ii. MALE TUTTLE born before 1830 and alive in 1840 (1830 & 40 census).
iii. MOSES GRANT TUTTLE, born 30 Oct 1831 in Calais (VR). He was administrator of his father's estate, real estate sold to William H. Tuttle, final account, 16 Jan 1850 (prbt). Census: 1850 in Calais. [Canaan, ME VR has a Moses Tuttle of Calais married to Nancy Corson of Canaan on 5 Sept 1841]
iv. HARRIET ELIZA TUTTLE, born 30 Oct 1833 in Calais (VR). Died 24 Feb 1853 age 19y 5m in Calais (g.s.). Buried in Calais Cemetery. Census: 1850 in Calais.
v. THOMAS BENTON TUTTLE, born 12 Jun 1840 in Calais (VR). Census: 1850 & 60 in Calais. He married 7 Apr 1864 in Calais (VR:3:199) SARAH P. PALMER.

TINKER & HULDA TWITCHELL, p. 214

TINKER TWITCHELL born circa 1811 in Bethel, ME (1850 census), (possible he is Moses, son of Simeon Twitchell & Hannah Abbott in Bethel VR, bthl:.628). Census: 1840 (1 male, 2 females) & 50 in Calais.
He married HULDAH (_____) born circa 1812 in Bethel, ME (1850 census), (possible she is daughter of Nathaniel Swan & Mehitable Colby in Bethel VR, bthl:621) Census: 1850 in Calais. Children:

i. MARY HUNTER TWITCHELL, born 24 Aug 1839 in Calais (VR). Census: 1850 in Calais.
ii. HULDAH ANN TWITCHELL, born 28 Oct 1842 in Calais (VR). Census: 1850 in Calais.

LENDAL & MARY TYLER, p. 221

LENDAL TYLER, born 28 Aug 1805 in Gorham, Me (g.s., 1850 census), son of DANIEL TYLER & MARY ANN JORDAN (gorh:796). He was lumberman, farmer and he was owner of a mill on the St. Croix when in court in 1836 (SJC:3:367). He worked in the firm of Brooks & Waldron in 1837 (SJC). Died 21 Mar 1890 in Milltown ME (times, g.s.). Buried in Calais Cemetery. Census: 1840 (4 males, 3 females), 1850 thru 1880 in Calais.
He married SARAH 'SALLIE' A. WHITNEY, born circa 1811 (g.s.) in Milltown NB, daughter of DANIEL WHITNEY AND MARY SPRAGUE. Died 8 May 1894 in Calais (MSA). Buried in Calais Cemetery. Census: 1850, thru 1880 in Calais. Children:

i. MARIA G. TYLER, born circa 1833 in Calais. Census: 1850 in Calais.
ii. EMMA TYLER, born 12 Oct 1836 in Calais (VR). She was a teacher and nurse. Died 31 Oct 1920 age 84y 19d in Calais (MSA, sfh:3:171). Buried in Calais Cemetery. Census: 1850 & 60 in Calais.
iii. HARRISON TYLER, born 12 Apr 1838 in Calais. He was a surveyor of lumber. Died: 10 Mar 1926 in Federalsburg, MD, he married ALICE AMANDA STOWELL who died in 1902, there were no children, he is survived by one female cousin in Calais (letter in Calais Adv. of 27 Mar 1926). Both are buried in Federalsburg. Census: 1850 & 60 in Calais.
iv. MARY TYLER, born 26 Sep 1840 in Calais (VR). Died 30 Aug 1841 in Calais (VR:I:240, g.s.). Buried in Calais Cemetery.
v. LENDAL TYLER, Jr., born 3 Jan 1842 in Calais (VR). He was a lumberman. Died 11 Aug 1888 age 46 in Milltown ME (times, SSC, g.s.). Buried in Calais Cemetery. Census: 1850 thru 1880 in Calais.
vi. ROBERT BUNTEN TYLER, born 13 Oct 1846 in Calais (VR). He was a customs officer. Died 3 Sep 1912 age 65y 10m 4d in Calais (g.s., MSA has parents Donald & Sallie Whitney). Buried in Calais Cemetery. Probate of Estate: 10 Dec 1912, in Machias Me. Census: 1850 thru 1900 in Calais. He married 13 Jun 1880 by W. W. Lovejoy in Calais (VR:3:332, times) MARY R. REDDING, born 10 Mar 1853 in Milltown, ME, daughter of OTIS REDDING & MARY EMELINE GETCHELL, died 26 June 1927 in Milltown, ME (MSA, g.s.). Buried in Calais Cemetery. Census: 1900 in Calais.

JOSHUA & ELIZABETH VEAZIE, p. 181

JOSHUA VEAZIE, born 10 Mar 1790 in Deerfield, NH (Eastport VR). He was in Calais by 1837 when he was in Court (SJC). In 1841 he was a Justice of Peace in Calais. He was Master of St. Croix Lodge, No. 46 in 1845-

1846-1854-1857 (lodge:43). He was a trader. Died 15 May 1858 in Calais (g.s.). He died intestate, he owed debts of over $1900.00 and his estate was sold for $2100+ (prbt). Buried in Calais Cemetery. Census: 1840 (3 males, 3 females), 50 in Calais.

He married in St. John, NB 14 July 1816 (Eastport VR) ELIZABETH DELUE, born 22 May 1796 in St. John, NB (Eastport VR), daughter of JACOB DELUE, a mariner of St. John, NB who died there in 1825, age 65 (New Brunswick Loyalist:40). She died possibly before 1850, not in census. Children:

i. GEORGE D. VEAZIE, born 7 Apr 1817 in Eastport, died in 1817 in Eastport (VR).
ii. ETHEL DELUE VEAZIE, born 2 Mar 1820 in Eastport (VR). Died 4 Oct 1853 in Calais (east:130).
iii. MARY SOPHIA GLEASON VEAZIE, born 13 Sep 1822 in Eastport (VR). Died 21 Nov 1844 age 22 in Calais (obit gaz). She married 29 Sept 1841 in Calais (VR, gaz) WILLIAM HENRY CLARK STEARNS (see STEARNS)
iv. GEORGE HAWKES VEAZIE, born 27 Mar 1824 in Eastport (VR). Died Mar 1826 age 21m (east:73).
v. JACOB VEAZIE, born 27 May 1826 in Eastport (VR). Died Mar 1827 age 10m (east:82).
vi. ELIZABETH VEAZIE, born ca May 1831. Died 4 June 1865 age 34y 10d (g.s.). Buried in Calais Cemetery. Census: 1850 in Calais. She married 14 Apr 1853 in Calais by Rev. H. V. Dexter (FJ) WILLARD BANCROFT KING, born 27 Mar 1830 in Baring (see LEE, Phebe his 2nd wife).
vii. EMMA ADELAIDE VEAZIE, born 2 Apr 1838 in Calais (VR). Census: 1850 in Calais. She married 10 Oct 1860 in Calais (union) GEORGE M. C. BRACKETT of Calais, born 21 Feb 1833, son of LUTHER BRACKETT & ABIGAIL TODD. Died Apr 1878 in Farmington, MN (brack:331).

PETER L. & REBECCA VERRILL, p. 198

DANIEL VERRILL b. 27 June 1781 in Poland, Me, d. 23 Dec 1852. He married 4 Dec 1800 EUNICE CORDWELL b. 21 July 1780 in Poland, d. 9 July 1859, both buried in Patch Mt. Cemetery. She was a daughter of William Cordwell (1755-1833) and Tryphosa Leach 1754-1844. His name was spelled Varriel on his birth and marriage records, Variell on many deeds in Oxford County, Varel in the 1850 census but Verrill on his gravestone. (varrell:173-174). Their son, Peter Verrill, resided in Calais after his 2nd marriage until his death.

PETER L. VERRILL, born 2 Mar 1801 in Poland ME, died 10 Oct 1853 in Calais (varrell:181). Census: 1830 (2 males, 2 females), 50 in Calais.

He married 1st 11 Apr 1822 in Greenwood, Aroostook, ME, MARY H. 'POLLY' YATES born 2 Oct 1803 in Greenwood (varrell:181). Polly, daughter of WILLIAM YATES & MARTHA MORGAN she married 2nd Newell Gammon (paris:775). Children:

i. MOSES YEATON VERRILL, born 18 Aug 1822, in Greenwood, Aroostook, ME (varrell:194). After his parents divorced he was raised by his mothers family (varrell:194). Died circa 1897 in West Paris, ME (varrell:194). He married MARTHA RICKER.

Peter married 2nd circa 1826 in St Stephen, NB (varrell:181), REBECCA McLAUGHLIN born 5 Aug 1805 in St David, NB (varrell:181). She married 2nd Mills Brown (varrell:181). Resided: after 1853 in Bethel, ME. Census: 1850 in Calais. Children:

ii. ABIGAIL L. VERRILL, born 4 Jun 1827 in St David, NB (varrell:194). Died 15 Dec 1881 age 53 in Bethel, ME (adv formerly of Calais). Census: 1850 in Calais. Unmarried.
iii. ARTHUR W. VERRILL, born 7 Jan 1829 in St David, NB (varrell:194). Resided: after 1853 in Biddeford, ME, where he worked in cotton mills. Census: 1850 in Calais. He married TEMPERANCE (_____), born ca 1829, resided in Biddeford in 1870 (varrell:194).
iv. ALMEDA S. VERRILL, born 9 Apr 1831 in St David, NB (varrell:194). Died 5 Nov 1916 in Calais (MSA). Census: 1850 thru 80 in Calais. She married 27 Jul 1851 by Rev. Mr. Bennett, in St Stephen, NB (FJ) HIRAM L. LAFLIN, born ca 1825 in Southbridge, MA, son of HIRAM LAFLIN & HELEN MABEE (both born in Southbridge, MA). He was a night watchman. Died 17 Feb 1901 age 75 in Calais (MSA). Buried in Calais Cemetery. Census: 1860, 70 & 80 in Calais.
v. DAVID GOLD VERRILL, born 22 Oct 1833 in St David, NB (varrell:195). He was a sailor and later Ship Capt. of Steamship *North America*. Died 7 Oct 1896 in Philadelphia, PA (varrell:195). Buried in Holy Cross Cemetery in Philadelphia, PA. Census: 1850 in Calais. He married circa 1856 at St. Augustine's

Church, in Philadelphia, PA, ELIZABETH CALLERY, she died 1897-8, buried with her husband (varrell:195).

vi. JULIA ELIZABETH W. VERRILL, born 7 Feb 1836 in St David, NB (varrell:195). Died 12 Jun 1858 (varrell:195). Census: 1850 in Calais. She married a Mr. PATTERSON, after 1850 (varrell:195).

vii. EUNICE VERRILL, born circa 1838 in Calais (varrell:195). Married and resided in St Stephen, NB (varrell:195).

viii. SALOME VERRILL, born circa 1841 in Calais (varrell:195). She worked in mills of Biddeford and met an early death, by an accident, unmarried (varrell:195).

ix. SYLVANUS OSGOOD BLAKE VERRILL, born 12 Aug 1845 in Calais. Served in Civil War Co. I 14th Maine, he was a millman 5'7 ½" with blue eyes and brown hair (cwcard, g.s.). Died in 1915 in Milford, ME. Census: 1850, 60 & 70 (living with Hiram Laflin) in Calais, 1900 in Houlton (living alone). He married MILLIE MARIE CORLISS, born 26 May 1855 in NB, daughter of CHARLES CORLISS AND PHEBE MILLER, both born in NB, died 5 Feb 1928 in Milford (MSA). They married 23 May 1875 in Auburn ME where they resided and later removed to Milford, ME (varrell:195). Both are buried in Milford Village Cemetery (MOCA).

HORACE & NANCY VERY, p. 185

HORACE VERY, born bet. 1801 – 1810. Census: 1840 (3 males 3 or 4 females) in Calais, family does not appear in later census.

He married NANCY (_____), born bet. 1801 - 1810. Children:

i. HORACE W. VERY, born 11 Nov 1830 in Westmoreland, NH (VR). Died 19 Jul 1837 in Calais (VR:1:231).
ii. CHARLES WILLIAM VERY, born 11 Jan 1837 in Calais (VR).
iii. NANCY SOPHIA VERY, born 10 Jun 1840 in Calais (VR).
iv. JAMES ORATUS VERY, born 9 May 1842 in Calais (VR).
v. MARY EMMA VERY, born 6 Sep 1846 in Calais, died 6 Oct 1846 in Calais (VR:1:231).

LEBBEUS S. & LOVINA VICKERY, p. 177, 181, 223

LEBBEUS SIMMONS VICKERY, Sr., born circa 1809 in Troy ME (1850 census, son's death lists Belfast, Me), son of DAVID VICKERY AND BETSEY SIMMONS. He was a carpenter. Died 20 Jan 1871 age 66 in Calais (obit, adv). Census: 1840 (3 males, 3 females), 50 & 60 in Calais.

He married 26 Jun 1834 by Rev. Edward N. Harris in Calais (mrwc:13), LOVINA J. STYLES, born circa 1814 in Marysville, NB (1850 census), daughter of JOHN STILES AND MARGARET M. GRANT. Died 18 Jan 1897 in Calais (VR, MSA). Buried in Calais Cemetery. Probate of Estate in Machias Me (will dated 2 Feb 1889 book 45 p 141-142). Census: 1850 thru 80 in Calais. Children:

i. MINERVA 'MINA' E. VICKERY, born (1) 9 Mar 1836 in Calais (VR:1:177), born (2) 9 Mar 1837 (VR:3:258). She died 26 Apr 1919 at age 88y 1m 17d in Calais (MSA, sfh:3:76). Census: 1850 age 13, 1860 (age 23), & 70 in Calais. She married before 1863 ROBERT GILLIS, born ca 1834. He died before his wife. Census: 1870 in Calais.

ii. PARKER N. S. VICKERY, born (1) 1 Sep 1838 in Calais (VR:1:177), born (2) 7 Sept 1839 (VR:3:258). He was a mariner. Died before 1889 (not in his mother's will). Census: 1850 (age 11) & 60 (age 22) in Calais.

iii. LEBBEUS SIMMONS VICKERY, Jr., born (1) 17 Sep 1840 in Calais (VR:1:177), born (2) 15 Oct 1841 (VR:3:258). He was a carpenter and house joiner. There is a Civil War grave card with birth date of 15 Oct 1841 and buried in Calais but no other info on card. Died 27 Dec 1916 age 77 in Calais (MSA). Census: 1850 (age 9), 1860 (age 19), 1870 (age 28), 1880, & 1900 (age 60 born Nov 1839), 1910 (age 69) in Calais. He married 1st 7 Jan 1865 by Rev. A. J. Padleford in Calais (VR) ADELIA 'DELLA' A. STILES, born ca 1844. She died Jan 1883, buried 9 Jan 1883 (sext). Her probate dated 12 June 1883. Census: 1870 & 80 in Calais. He married 2nd 16 Aug 1883 in Calais, by Rev. A.J. Padleford (VR:2:29), Mrs. LORANA/LAURINA (_____) BANGS {she married 1st (_____) BANGS}. She left him and he divorced her in Apr 1889 (SJC case #51). He married 3rd 3 July 1890 in Calais (VR:2:105, times) MARY ANN

(BARBER) WARR (tina), born Mar 1844. Census 1900 & 10 in Calais.

iv. VASHTI G. VICKERY, born (1) <u>14 May 1843</u> in Calais (VR:1:181), born (2) <u>22 Jan 1849</u> (VR:3:258). Graduated from Calais Academy (CFL). Died after 1889 (mother's will). Census: 1850 (age 4) & 60 (age 15) in Calais.

v. LAURA L(ovinia?). VICKERY, born (1) <u>6 Mar 1845</u> in Calais (VR:1:223), born (2) 7 Mar 1846 in Calais (VR:3:256). Died after 1897 (when she was admin. of mother's will). Census: 1850 (age 5), 1860 (age 17), 1870 (age 23), 1880 (age 39) in Calais ME. She married 31 Aug 1867 by Rev. H. V. Dexter in Calais (VR:3:226, union). JOSEPH MILLER. Census: 1870 in Calais (not in 1880 wife & children with her mother).

vi. CHARLES S. VICKERY, born (1) <u>2 Mar 1847</u> in Calais (VR:1:223), born (2) <u>22 Mar 1847</u> (VR:3:256, MSA = 22 Mar 1846). He served in the Civil War in Co I & Co G of the 1st Maine Cavalry, he was 5'6" with hazel eyes and black hair (cwcard, enlist, father signed permission). He was a stone mason. Died 22 Jan 1900 age 53y 10m in Calais (MSA, obit times). Buried in Calais Cemetery. Census: 1850, 60, &1880 in Calais. He married 24 Sep 1871by Rev. I. C. Knowlton in Calais (VR, adv, union) ELIZABETH TARBOX, born 19 July 1851 in Calais, daughter of GEORGE ROGERS TARBOX & MARY ELIZABETH SCRIPTURE, died 27 May 1928 in Red Beach, Me (sfh:7:106). Census: 1900 & 1910 (age 58 living with daughter, Nola Wentworth and husband, Vernon) in Calais.

vii. ALFRED W. VICKERY, born 15 Jul 1852 in Calais (VR:3:256). Died 3 Apr 1882 age 26y in Calais (g.s., stone erected by wife, Maggie, obit times). Buried in Calais Cemetery. Census: 1860 in Calais. He married 11 Dec 1880 MAGGIE VIOLETTE of Houlton, ME (VR).

viii. STILES H. VICKERY, born 22 Jul 1857 in Calais (VR:3:256). Died before 1897 (not mentioned in mother's will). Census: 1860 in Calais.

MATHIAS & MARY VICKERY, p. 207

MATHIAS VICKERY, born circa 1805 in Belfast, ME (1850 census). He was a merchant. In 1837 he was in partnership with Nathaniel Brown (SJC:3:482). In 1863 he was in partnership with his son, Albion, in A.K.P. Vickery & Co. (SJC:19:90). In Apr 1860 he was arrested and fined for running a gambling establishment (SJC:17:130). Died 20 Dec 1874 in St. Stephen at age 70y 7m (obit adv, g.s.). Buried in Calais Cemetery. Census: 1840 (4 males, 2 females), 50, 60 (customs inspector) & 70 in Calais, 1871 in St Stephen, NB.

He married 1 Jul 1838 in Perry ME (mrwc:25, FJ) MARY ANN^8 EATON, born 17 Sep 1813 in Newport NS (eaton:39, 40, 1850 census = Cornwallis, NS). daughter of DAN^7 EATON AND MARGARET BULMER, granddaughter of Elisha^6, David^5, James^4, Jonathan^3, Thomas^2, John^1. She died 12 Mar 1879 age 65 in St Stephen, NB (eaton:40, times). Census: 1850, 60 & 70 in Calais, 1871 in St Stephen, NB. Children:

i. ALBION KING PARIS VICKERY, born 13 Jul 1840 in Calais (VR). Served in Civil War, Drum Major in Co H 9th Regt. Me. Vols., he was a tinker 5'9 ½" with hazel eyes and brown hair, died 7 Aug 1863 age 23 in Folley Island, SC (cwcard, eaton:40, g.s.). Buried in Calais Cemetery. Census: 1850 & 60 in Calais.

ii. ADELAIDE MARY VICKERY, born 22 Aug 1842 in Calais (VR, LDS, eaton:40). Died 23 Jan 1886 in St Stephen, NB (SSC, adv). Census: 1850 & 60 in Calais. She married 19 Jun 1865 by Rev. R. V. Dexter in Calais (VR:3:209, eaton:40) BENJAMIN R. DeWOLFE.

iii. ALONZO VICKERY, born 15 Jun 1845 in Calais (VR:1:237, LDS). Died 11 Oct 1845 age 1y 6m in Calais (g.s., LDS). Buried in Calais Cemetery.

SAMUEL H. & MARGARET WADE, p. 205

SAMUEL HALE WADE, Sr., born circa 1803 in Anapolis, NS (1850 census). He was a ship carpenter. Died 12 Aug 1858 in Calais age 57 (union). Census: 1850 in Calais.

He married 21 Mar 1846 by Josiah Eaton in Calais (VR:3:140) MARGARET McWHINNEY, born circa 1813 in Halifax, NS (1850 census). Died after 1887 (when she was a widow in City Directory). Census: 1850, 60, 70 & 80 in Calais. Her brother, Thomas McWhinney, an invalid living with her in 1850, 60 & 70. Children:

i. ELIZABETH PATTEN WADE, born 23 Dec 1847 in Calais (VR). Bapt. 2 Aug 1858 in Calais (saint).

Died 24 May 1859 in Calais (east:168, union). Census: 1850 in Calais.
- ii. SARAH N. WADE, born circa 1849 in Calais. Bapt. 2 Aug 1858 in Calais (saint). She was a dressmaker. Census: 1850 thru 80 in Calais.
- iii. SAMUEL HALE WADE, Jr., born circa 1851 in Calais. Bapt. 2 Aug 1858 in Calais (saint). Census: 1860, 70 & 80 in Calais. He married 28 Nov 1877 in Calais (VR:3:239, times) MARY E. CREAMER, born ca 1856. Census: 1880 in Calais.

ABNER & JANE WADSWORTH, p. 213

ABNER WADSWORTH born 18 June 1801, in Litchfield ME (litch:374, IGI= b. Winthrop), son of AARON WADSWORTH & LUCY STEVENS, grandson of JOHN WADSWORTH & JERUSHA WHITE – JOSEPH & RACHEL STEVENS (wad:302). He was a millman. He was in the 1st Brigade. 7th Div. Maine Militia as a Sgt. 1828-1832 (mil). Died 1 Mar 1867 age 65y 9m in Cedar Rapids, IA (litch:374, east:227, of TB). Census: 1830 (7 males, 6 females), 1840 (7males, 7 females), 1850 in Calais.

He married ca 1820 (litch:375) JENNETTE H. TOWERS, born ca 1803 in St. David, NB (dau death rec, litch:375, 1850 census). She was a milliner. Died 28 Apr 1891 at home of her daughter, Mrs. W. W. Smith, in Minneapolis, MN (times). Buried in Calais Cemetery. Census: 1850 & 80 in Calais. Children:

- i. DEBORAH M. WADSWORTH, born ca 1824 (g.s.) in St. David, NB. Baptism: 5 July 1840 in Calais (lord:18). Died 3 Jan 1903 in Calais (MSA). Buried in Calais Cemetery. Probate of estate in Machias, ME (will dated 7 Aug 1894 her son James. M. exec.). Census 1850, 60 & 70 in Calais. She married 10 Nov 1844 in Calais (VR:1:134) WILLIAM McDONALD (see McDONALD).
- ii. ANNA TOWERS WADSWORTH, born 23 July 1827 in Calais. Baptism: 5 July 1840 in Calais (lord:18). Died after 1912 in Minneapolis, MN. She married 1 Jan 1845 in Milltown, ME (VR:1:134, adv) WILLIAM WALKER SMITH, 17 Apr 1820 in Windsor, NS,, son of WILLIAM S. SMITH & JANE COLWELL (clipping from Minneapolis Journal of Dec. 22 1907 reprinted in adv 1 Jan 1908). He enlisted as a 1st Lt. Co G. 24th Iowa Volunteer Inf., commissioned Capt. on 1 Oct 1862. He was in Libby prison. After discharge he was appointed postmaster of Cedar Rapids. In 1887 he moved to Minneapolis (adv, a biography of him can be found on the internet, Iowa in the Civil War). Died 3 June 1912 in Minneapolis (adv).
- iii. ARZELIA WADSWORTH, born 17 Sept 1829 in Calais (VR). Census: 1850 in Calais. She married (____) McDOUGHALD resided in Cedar Rapids (W.W. Smith's bio on internet).
- iv. MARY ANN S. WADSWORTH, born 11 Feb 1834 in Calais (VR). Census: 1850 in Calais. (Mrs. Sines, deceased 1855 in Cedar Rapids, bio on internet).
- v. ALFREDA HILLMAN WADSWORTH, born 21 Jan 1837 in Calais (VR). Died 27 June 1872 in Cedar Rapids, buried in Oak Hill Cemetery, Linn County IA. Census: 1850 in Calais. She married 7 Oct 1858 in Linn County, IA, OLIVER OTIS STINCHFIELD, born 16 Aug 1833 in Robbinston, ME, son of ROGER STINCHFIELD & FANNIE ALLEN (stinch:151, morris). He graduated from Univ. of Maine Law School, was a lawyer, businessman and legislator. He resided in Cedar Rapids, IA, Ludington MI, and Mitchell, S. D. (stinch:151). Died 12 Apr 1893 in Mitchell, SD (morris).
- vi. SUSAN DREW WADSWORTH, born 8 June 1841 in Calais (VR). Census: 1850 in Calais. She married (____) CAPRON of DeKalb County, IL (bio on internet).
- vii. ELIAS K. WADSWORTH, born 12 Nov 1843 in Calais (VR). Served in Civil War, in U.S. Navy. Died 3 Dec 1863 when he was lost aboard USS Sassacus (cwcard). Stone in Calais Cemetery.
- viii. MARTHA P. WADSWORTH, born 12 Nov 1843 in Calais (VR). Possibly died 22 Sept 1852.

Note * The bio on the internet says there were 8 daughters only 6 found.

BENJAMIN F. & HANNAH F. WAITE, p. 196

BENJAMIN FRANKLIN[6] WAITE, born 26 Dec 1801 in Hubbardston, MA (VR, beg:128), son of NATHANIEL[5] WAITE (1772-1846) & MERCY LAMSON (d. 1851), both died & buried in Calais. Grandson of NATHANIEL[4-3-2], JOHN[1] (wait:54). He was a lumberman and grocer. He came to Calais 1821and established a grocery business on Main Street in Calais in 1822, this business carried on by his son, Charles and later by his son, Frederick T. (CEV:19). Died 23 Feb 1875 age 73y 2m, in Calais (obit adv, east:290, g.s., prbt # W:4:152). Buried in Calais Cemetery. Census: 1840 (5 males, 4 females) 1850,

60 & 70 in Calais.

He married 1st 30 Apr 1826 in Calais (drum:126, wait:54) HANNAH TOWNSLEY TODD born 27 May 1807 in Eastport ME (VR), daughter of JOHN CAMPBELL [CAMEL] TODD AND ABIGAIL 'NABBY' NICHOLS (see TODD). Died 16 Dec 1855 age 48y 6m (g.s.,drum:126) in Calais. Buried in Calais Cemetery. Census: 1850 in Calais. Children

- i. CHARLES WAITE, born 1 May 1828 in St Stephen, NB (Calais VR, drum:126 has 21 May). On 1 Nov 1849 he along with Mark Ellsworth, Sam Thompson, John Hutton and James Hutton, left Calais on the brig B. M. Prescott for the gold mines in California, arriving at the Golden Gate 18 May 1850. After three years Charles returned to Calais and engaged in the grocery business for over 50 years. He was a tenor and enjoyed singing with coral groups (adv clipping dated 1908 at CFL). He died 22 Aug 1922 age 94y 3m 21d in Calais (MSA, adv). Census: 1850, 60, 80, 1900 (with bro., Fred), & 1910 in Calais. He married 18 Oct 1861by Rev. Philbrook in St. Stephen, NB (CCMR), FRANCES ELIZABETH PIKE, daughter of WILLIAM CORNELIUS PIKE Jr. and FRANCES CAMPBELL TODD, she died 5 Jan 1887 (see PIKE).
- ii. MARY ELIZABETH WAITE, born 26 Jan 1830 in St. Stephen, NB (Calais VR). Died 27 Jun 1886 in Winthrop, MA (times). Buried in Calais Cemetery. Census: 1850 &70 in Calais. She married 3 Nov 1852 in Calais (VR:1:152) WILLIAM DEMING Jr., son of WILLIAM DEMING & SARAH M. WILCOX (see DEMING).
- iii. HENRY HOYT WAITE, born 20 Sep 1832 in St. Stephen, NB (Calais VR, beg:128). He was a 1st Lieut. In Co. G 6th Me Infantry in the Civil War (NRMS:238). Wounded at Rappahannock Station and died at Armory Sq. Hospital on 19 Nov 1863 in Washington, DC (cwcard). Grave stone in Calais Cemetery reads: died 13 Nov 1863 age 31y, mortally wounded at battle of Rappahannock Station 7 Nov 1863 and interred there. Census: 1850 & 60 in Calais.
- iv. BENJAMIN FRANKLIN WAITE, Jr., born 30 Jan 1835, in St. Stephen, NB (Calais VR). Served in Co. D 6th Maine, during Civil War (NRMS:238). He was a lumberman 5'7" with blue eyes and brown hair (cwcard). Died after father's death in 1875. Census: 1850, 60 & 70 in Calais.
- v. JOHN CAMPBELL TODD WAITE, born 17 Jan 1837 in Calais (VR). He left Calais to winter in Florida (adv of 24 Jan 1871). Died 27 Jan 1871age 34 in Jacksonville, FL, remains brought from Florida 7 Feb. (SCC, adv, g.s.). Probate of Estate, Washington Co. # W-2-53 has death date 27 Dec 1870. Buried in Calais Cemetery. Census: 1850 & 60 in Calais. He married 2 Jun 1869 by Rev. Edgar L. Foster in Milltown, NB (CCMR) ELIZA McALLISTER, born in Milltown, NB. She died after her husband.
- vi. FREDERICK TOWNSLEY WAITE, born 11 Apr 1839 in Calais (VR). In 1878 he took over the family grocery business on Main St., started by his father in 1822, and his brother, Charles in 1846 (CEV:19). He was a city councilman for several years. Died 2 Oct 1912 in Calais (MSA). Buried in Calais Cemetery. Probate of Estate, Washington Co., # W-4-152. Census: 1850 thru 1910 in Calais. He married (int. VR:1:110) 12 May 1864 in Calais PRISCILLA W. FLOOD, daughter of JOHN FLOOD & PRISCILLA MOSHER (1870 census). She was born 16 Sept 1844 in Calais (VR). Died: 28 Oct 1931 in Calais (MSA, sfh:6:112). Buried in Calais Cemetery. Census: 1850 thru 1910 in Calais (see FLOOD)
- vii. HELEN MARIA WAITE, born 11 Jan 1844 in Calais. Graduated Calais Academy. In 1882 she went to Boston to live with brother, Horace (adv). Died after 1907 when she hosted a birthday party for brother, Charles (adv). Census: 1850, 60 & 70 in Calais, 1910 a widow living with brother, Charles in Calais. She married 2 May 1865 in Calais SAMUEL KELLY Jr. (see KELLY).
- viii. GEORGE EDWIN WAITE, born 3 Apr 1846 in Calais (VR). Died 3 May 1865 age 19y 1m, in Calais (VR:3:311, drum:127, g.s.). Buried in Calais Cemetery. Census: 1850 & 60 in Calais.
- ix. HORACE WAITE, born 11 Jan 1849 in Calais. He clerked in a store. He died 16 Apr 1940 in Winthrop, ME or MA ? (MSA) [article in Calais Adv. of 30 Dec 1914 states he was living in Boston formerly in California]. Census: 1850 thru 1880 in Calais. He married 2 Nov 1873 in Calais (VR, china) JULIA CAROLINE WASHBURN born 1 Feb 1853 in Calais (china), daughter of GEORGE WASHBURN & SARAH JANE EMERY (china). She was of Houlton at time of marriage. Census: 1880 in Calais. They resided in California in 1878 when a son was born (adv).

He married 2nd 1 Mar 1857 in Calais (VR:1:167, adv, east:153), NANCY FOLSOM[7] SHEDD /SHEAD, born 31 Jan 1805 in Eastport ME (VR, shed:245), daughter of NANCY YOUNG & OLIVER SHEAD[6-5], JAMES[4-3], ZACHARIAH[2], DANIEL[1]. She died 12 Mar 1875 age 70y 1m in Calais (obit adv, east:291, g.s.). Buried in Calais

Cemetery. Probate of estate, Washington Co. # W-2-52, death date 10 Mar 1875. Census: 1860 & 70 in Calais.

CYRUS & MAHALA WAKEFIELD, p. 199

SAMUEL[5] WAKEFIELD, born 15 Mar 1768 in Kennebunk, ME, son of SAMUEL[4] WAKEFIELD & RUTH BURBANK, grandson of SAMUEL[3], JAMES[2], JOHN[1.] He married ANNA COX, of Harrington. He was a farmer and they resided in Steuben, Me and had nine children. (wake:124). Their fourth child, Cyrus resided in Lubec and Calais.

CYRUS[6] WAKEFIELD, born 3 Jul 1798 in Steuben Me (VR, wake:130 = 3 Aug 1798). He was a fisherman. He died 17 Jan 1862 age 63 in Lubec Me (lubec:222). Census: 1850 in Lubec, 1860 in Calais.

He married 8 Jun 1820 by Solomon Thayer in Lubec (VR:154, east:13) MAHALA MCDONALD born circa 1798. Census: 1850 in Lubec, 1860 in Calais. Children:

i. NATHANIEL M. WAKEFIELD, born 28 Apr 1821 in Lubec (lubec:7, wake:130, MSL). He served in Civil War in Co K 12th Maine, he was a seaman 5'10" with gray eyes and dark hair, resided in Lubec (cwcard). Died 23 Apr 1892 age 74 in Calais (MSA, obit adv). Buried in Calais Cemetery. Census: 1850 in Lubec, 1870 & 80 in Calais. He married 1st 14 Oct 1845 by Japheth C. Washburn, JP in Calais (VR:3:138) CAROLINE WARD of Calais (WCMR:47). Census: 1850 in Calais. He married 2nd (int.) 7 Apr 1870 in Calais (VR:3) THERESA ANN PURRINGTON, born ca 1852. Census: 1870 & 80 in Calais.

ii. EMILY R. WAKEFIELD, born 9 Mar 1826 in Lubec (lubec:14, wake:130). Died 12 Oct 1909 in Calais (VR, MSA, 1901 Calais Dir. widow of John). Census: 1860 thru 1900 in Calais. She married 10 Nov 1844 JOHN SPINNEY (see SPINNEY).

iii. HANNAH WAKEFIELD, born 1 Jan 1831 in Lubec (lubec:22). Resided in Claremont, NH. Census: 1850 & 60 in Lubec. She married (int.) 15 Feb 1852 in Lubec (lubec:131) ANDREW JACKSON JOY, born 25 July 1830 in Lubec (lubec:30, wake:130), son of DANIEL JOY & MARTHA FINNEY of Claremont, NH. He was a fisherman. They resided in Lubec. Census: 1860 in Lubec.

iv. CYRUS WAKEFIELD, (Jr.), born circa 1837 (wake:130, MSL). Died Oct 1859 (1860 census deaths). Census: 1850 in Lubec Me.

v. AARON WEBBER WAKEFIELD, born circa 1838 (wake:130). He enlisted on 8 Feb 1864 in Civil War in Co K 15th Reg't at age 26, he was 5' 9 ¾", he was a moulder, with blue eyes and light hair (enlist). Census: 1850 in Lubec Me, 1860 in Calais. He married 9 Nov 1861 in Calais (VR) REBECCA LEEMAN, neither listed in 1870 census.

vi. JAMES FREDERICK WAKEFIELD, born 4 Aug 1842 in Calais (VR, wake:130). He enlisted on 8 Feb 1864 in Civil War in Co K 15th Reg't at age 21, he was 5'8 ½", he was a moulder, with blue eyes and light hair (enlist). Census: 1850 in Lubec, 1860 in Calais, not found in 1870.

vii. LOUISE WAKEFIELD, born circa 1845 (wake:130).

viii. KATHERINE WAKEFIELD, born circa 1847 (wake:130). Census: 1850 (with bro. Nathaniel). in Lubec Me.

SUMNER T. & CATHARINE WALDRON, p. 212

SUMNER T. WALDRON, born circa 1809 (g.s has age 53). He was in business with William Brooks in 1837 (SJC). He was in the 1st Brigade, 7th Div Maine Militia as a Pvt. 1829, 31, 32 (mil). He was a lumber surveyor. Died 24 Jan 1862 age 53 in Calais (VR:1:242, union). Buried in Calais Cemetery. Census: 1840 (2 males, 4 females), 50 & 60 in Calais.

- In the 1830 census there is a John D. Waldron with a male b. bet. 1811-1820 who could be Sumner.

He married 11 Nov 1834 by Rev. Joseph C. Aspenwall in Calais (mrwc:12) CATHARINE HAMILTON, born circa 1814. Died 2 Feb 1875 60y 11m in Calais (obit adv, g.s.). Buried in Calais Cemetery. Probate of estate, Washington Co., # W-2-73, death 3 Feb 1875. Census: 1850, 60 & 70 alone in Calais. Children:

i. SARAH ANNA WALDRON, born 9 Mar 1835, in Robbinston Me (1850 census). Died 9 May 1864 age 29 in Calais (VR). Buried in Calais Cemetery. Census: 1850 & 60 in Calais. She married 11 Oct 1854 in

Calais (VR:1:157). ALBERT LAMB, son of NATHANIEL LAMB & ELMIRA/ALMIRA CARLE (see LAMB).

ii. GEORGE WASHINGTON WALDRON, born 23 Aug 1836 in Calais (VR). Died 29 Mar 1858 age 21y 7m in Calais (g.s.). Buried in Calais Cemetery. Census: 1850 in Calais.

iii. ELIZA JANE TRAFTON WALDRON, born 16 Jun 1838 in Calais (VR). In 1856 she was a teacher in Calais. Died 28 Jan 1878 age 40 in Calais (obit, times). Buried in Calais Cemetery. Probate of estate, Washington Co. # S-1-180, husband, Horatio filed to be guardian for three minor children. Census: 1850, 60 & 70 in Calais. She married 9 Aug 1863 by Ed Fowler in Calais (VR:3:194). HORATIO NELSON SMITH, born ca 1827. Census: 1870 & 80 in Calais.

iv. SILAS DREW WALDRON, born 12 Apr 1842 in Calais (VR). He was a lumberman and clerk. Died 28 Feb 1865 age 23y 10m in Calais (g.s.). Buried in Calais Cemetery. Census: 1850 & 60 in Calais.

v. SUMNER T. WALDRON, Jr., born Sep 1844, died 5 Feb 1847 age 2y 5m in Milltown ME (FJ, g.s., Calais VR:1:229). Buried in Calais Cemetery.

JAMES & SARAH WATSON, p. 216

JAMES WATSON. Died before 1840. Census: 1830 (1male & 1 female age under 5, & wife).

He married Jan 1826 in Eastport ME (east:72, paper dated 14 Jan 1826), SARAH 'SALLY' W. EMERY, born 24 Sept 1794, Sandwich, NH d/o JOHN EMERY & PATIENCE COLE (EMERY:287,288). Died 23 June 1865 age 65 in Calais (VR:3:312, union, emery:288=30 June). Census: 1840 (widow with 1 son age bet. 10-15 years) in Calais. Children:

i. JULIAN ELIZABETH WATSON, born 19 Feb 1830 in Calais (VR). Died 16 Sep 1833 in Calais (VR:1:239).

ii. MALE CHILD WATSON, born circa 1832. Census: 1840 in Calais. Went to sea (emery:288). (Possible name Charles).

MARTIN & MARTHA WATSON, p. 217

MARTIN WATSON, born circa 1807 in Ireland. Census: 1850 in Calais.
He married MARTHA (_____), born circa 1822 in St Patrick, NB (1850 census). Census: 1850 in Calais. Children:

i. JAMES WATSON, born circa 1844 in St George NB (1850 census). Census: 1850 in Calais.

ii. MARTHA WATSON, born 15 Nov 1847 in Calais (VR). Census: 1850 in Calais.

iii. CATHERINE WATSON, born circa 1850 in Calais. Census: 1850 in Calais.

GILES M. & LUCY C. WENTWORTH, p. 223

TAPAN WENTWORTH, son of EVANS AND DOROTHY (WENTWORTH) WENTWORTH, born 16 Apr 1774; married, July 1804 ELIZABETH BRADBURY, daughter of THOMAS BRADBURY. They moved to Parsonsfield, ME, June 1806, where he died 21 June 1850 and she died 4 Nov 1849. They had 4 children (went:2:226). The third child, Giles M. Wentworth, was in Calais by 1836.

GILES MERRILL WENTWORTH, son of TAPPAN WENTWORTH AND ELIZABETH BRADBURY, born 17 Jun 1811 in Parsonsfield, ME (pars:412). Moved to Calais at age 24 (pars:305, went:578). He was Mayor of Calais 1870-71 and a State Senator in 1875 (legislative rec. at MSA). Died 19 Aug 1891 in Providence RI (adv). Buried in Calais Cemetery. Census: 1850 & 60 in Calais.

He married 9 Jun 1846 in Calais (pars:305, times,went:578) LUCY CAROLINE GATES, born 2 Oct 1819 in Hubbardston, MA (VR), daughter of SALMON GATES AND LUCY CHURCH (see GATES). She died 18 May 1896 in Providence RI (times, adv). Buried in Calais Cemetery. Census: 1850, 60 & 70 in Calais. Children:

i. LILLAH ELIZABETH WENTWORTH, born 27 May 1847 in Calais (VR, went:578). Died circa 1887 in Providence RI (pars:305, g.s.). Buried in Calais Cemetery. Census: 1850 & 60 in Calais. She married 7 Apr 1870 in Calais, by Rev. E. L. Foster (SCC, pars:305). ROBERT JOSEPH GILMORE, born 31 Mar 1845 in Calais (went 2:578). He died 9 July 1896 in Providence, RI (obit adv., g.s.). Buried in Calais Cemetery. He married 2nd 26 June 1896 MARY EMMA (BRITON) HOWARD in Providence just two weeks before his death (his obit).

ALEXANDER H. & BETHIAH WEYMOUTH, p. 210

ALEXANDER H. WEYMOUTH, born circa 1807 in Maine. In 1841 he was a Justice of Peace in Calais. He owned a jewelry store and an apothecary store (prbt: 4:266). He was a member of the Calais Band, played the bass. Died 15 Nov 1857 age 51 (g.s., obit in KJ, east:157 = age 56). Buried in Calais Cemetery. Census: 1840 (3 males & 4 females) & 1850 in Calais.

He married (int) 27 Aug 1833 in Calais (cal2:35) BETHIAH EMMELINE ATWOOD WILCOX, of New Bedford, MA, born circa 1808 in Dartmouth, Mass. Moved from Dartmouth to Calais as a young woman and married the following year, about 1869 she moved back to Mass. with her 3 surviving children (obit). Baptized 22 Aug 1830 in Calais (congo). Died 9 Mar 1894 age 85 in Boston MA (g.s.). Buried in Calais Cemetery. Census: 1850 & 60 in Calais. Children:

i. HENRY FULLER WEYMOUTH, born 20 June 1835 in Calais (cal2:11). Baptized 15 Nov 1835 in Calais (congo). Died 13 Feb 1858 age 22 in Greensboro, NC (g.s.). Buried in Calais Cemetery. Census: 1850 in Calais.

ii. EMELINE ATWOOD WEYMOUTH, born 16 Feb 1838 in Calais (VR, cal2:13). Baptized 3 Mar 1839 in Calais (congo). Died 11 May 1889 age 50 in Brooklyn, NY (g.s., prbt). Census: 1850 & 60 in Calais. Unmarried.

iii. FRANKLIN LEONARD WEYMOUTH, born 30 Nov 1839 in Calais (VR). Baptized 14 June 1840 in Calais (congo). Died 11 Sep 1859 age 19 (g.s.). Buried in Calais Cemetery. Census: 1850 in Calais.

iv. JANE (Jennie) WILCOX WEYMOUTH, born, circa 1841 in Maine. Baptized 4 July 1841 in Calais (congo). Died 25 Dec 1894 in Boston, the victim of an accidental shooting by a lodger at her residence. Buried in Brooklyn, NY (obit adv) In 1889 she resided in Brooklyn, NY (only surviving. sibling of sister Emeline). Census: 1850 & 60 in Calais. She married 31 May 1874 by Rev. N. Glover Allen (adv) PERRY M. LEDLARD of NY.

v. ALFRED LEONARD WEYMOUTH, born 2 Dec 1842 in Calais (VR). Baptized 7 July 1844 in Calais (congo). Died 27 Aug 1880 age 37 (g.s.) [Item in Calais Advertiser of 1 Sept 1880 says he died in Boston and was the former prop. of Weymouth Drug store in Calais, wife not mentioned]. Buried in Calais Cemetery. Census: 1850 & 60 in Calais. He married MELINE A. (_____). Census:

THOMAS E. & EDITH WHARFF, p. 208

CAPT. ELIPHALET WHARFF, born in Mass. married Sept 1816 by Rev. Edward Payson in Portland (MSA) SARAH DEAN CROSS b. 27 Oct 1794 daughter of Joseph Cross. Their son, Thomas E. Wharff was an early settler in Calais. Sarah, who was a widow in June 1835 in Calais when she appeared in Court (SJC:362), married 5 Nov 1837 in Portland, her sister's widower John Stickney and resided in Calais (stick:278).

THOMAS E. WHARFF, born 20 Oct 1816 in Portland ME son of ELIPHALET & SARAH WHARFF (g.s., MSA). In 1855, Mr. T. E. Wharff established an insurance business, agents for Fire, Marine and Life Insurance Companies, located on Main Street over Silverstone's tailoring establishment (CEV:25). Died 15 Jul 1892 age 76y 9m in Calais (g.s., MSA, obit adv). Buried in Calais Cemetery. Census: 1860, 70 & 80 in Calais.

He married 1st 26 Sep 1843 by Rev. S.H. Keeler in Calais (VR:1:130, gaz), EDITH ANNA JOHNSON, born circa 1820 in Robbinston Me (1850 census). Died 31 Jan 1860 age 42 in Calais (VR:3:130, g.s., congo). Buried in Calais Cemetery. Census: 1850 in Calais. Children:

i. THOMAS HOWARD WHARFF, born 20 Sep 1844 in Calais (VR). He enlisted at age 18 in 9th Maine Co. A, described as 5' 5 ½" with blue eyes and brown hair (cwcard). Calais Advertiser of 8 June 1887 published a letter from Dr. Howard T. Wharff, M.D. of Alhanbra, Ill., stating he was a member if Post 461 G.A.R. Edwardsville, Ill and unit of 9th Me Inf. Died after 1915 (he survived brother, Edward). Census: 1850 & 60 in Calais. He married 6 Nov 1873 in Edwardsville, IL (adv) MARY A. CARNEY.

ii. MONROE FOYE WHARFF, born 28 Nov 1846 in Calais (VR). Died 2 Nov 1870 age 24 in Quincy, IL (obit, adv). Census: 1850 & 60 in Calais.

iii. EDWARD DELAN WHARFF, born 15 Apr 1849 in Calais (VR). Died 5 Jan 1915 age 64 in Rochester

NY (adv). Census: 1850 & 60 in Calais. His wife (no name given) visited Calais in 1892 from Rochester, NY to see her father in law but he died before she arrived (adv of 20 July 1892). [Calais Advertiser of 5 June 1907 wife of Edward Delan Wharff died in NY, possible her name was Marietta B. , film is blurred]

iv. EMMA LINCOLN WHARFF, born 2 Aug 1854 in Calais (VR). Died 9 Sep 1875 age 21 in Calais (g.s., obit, adv). Buried in Calais Cemetery. Census: 1860 & 70 (in the household of John & Sarah Stickney [her grandmother] in Calais).

v. WILLIAM GAGE WHARFF, born 1 Nov 1856 in Calais (VR). Graduated Calais Academy 1875. Died 19 Aug 1886 age 29y in Calais (SSC, times, g.s.). Buried in Calais Cemetery. Census: 1860, 70 & 80 in Calais.

Thomas married 2nd 10 Oct 1861 in Calais (VR) MARIA NANCY DYER, born 25 Dec 1833 in Calais (g.s.), daughter of SAMUEL DYER AND MARGARET DOAK/DOKE (see DYER). She died on 31 Jan 1934 at age 100y 1m 6d in Calais (MSA, g.s.). Buried in Calais Cemetery. Census: 1850 thru 1920 in Calais. Children:

vi. EDITH MARIA WHARFF, born 16 Apr 1863 in Calais (VR). Died 3 Aug 1863 in Calais (VR). Buried in Calais Cemetery.

vii. FLORENCE BAILEY WHARFF, (1) born 4 Dec 1870 in Calais (obit adv) (2) born 12 Apr 1870 (g.s., MSA delayed return 1936). Bapt. Jan 1891 (congo). She was a piano teacher in 1892 (adv), and a dietitian. Died 4 Nov 1953 in Calais (obit, adv, MSA, g.s.). Buried in Calais Cemetery. Census: 1870 thru 1900 in Calais.

viii. HARRIET LOUISE WHARFF, born 22 Feb 1873 in Calais (MSA delayed return, 1950). Census: 1880, 1910 & 20 (with her mother) in Calais. She married on 28 Sept 1922 in Calais (MSA) as his 3rd wife, GEORGE REYNOLDS GARDNER, born 14 June 1854 in Dennysville (gard:16), son of AARON L. RAYMOND GARDNER & ABBIE WILDER REYNOLDS (both born in Dennysville) (biorev:656). Died ca 1950. Census: 1880 & 1900 in Calais (see also ANN ROBBINS).

CHARLES R. & MILA F. WHIDDEN, p. 200

RENDOL^6 WHIDDEN son of Ichabod$^{5-4}$, Samuel$^{3-2}$, Ichabod^1, born circa 1790 in NH, came to Calais 1831. In 1841 he was Major General in State Militia. Died circa 1887 after a terrible fall in Windsor, NS in his 97th year. Buried in Calais Cemetery. Census: 1840 (4 males, 5 females), 50, 60 & 70 in Calais. He married SARAH CLINCH daughter of PETER CLINCH & LETITIA HANDY of CT, born circa 1790 in NB. She married 1st ELEAZA REED, had one child, Albert (see REED). Died 17 Dec 1872 age 82y (obit times). Census: 1850, 60 & 70 in Calais. Two of their sons, Charles & Edgar, lived in Calais and raised large families. Also the child of Eleaza & Sarah Reed (whidd).

CHARLES RENDOL^7 WHIDDEN, born 22 May 1822 in St. George NB (colby). He was an Aid de Camp State Militia 1841. Graduated in class of 1843 at Colby College in Waterville ME (colby). He was an attorney; County Attorney; spent twelve years as a state legislature; collector of customs and mayor of Calais (1864-65) (colby). He was admitted to the bar 4 July 1844 (SJC). Died 3 Dec 1876 in Calais (colby, g.s.). Buried in Calais Cemetery. Census: 1850, 60 & 70 in Calais.

He married 19 Aug 1845 by Allen Barrows in Calais (mrwc:47) MILA FRANCES SMITH born 25 Aug 1825, in Providence RI, daughter of NOAH SMITH Jr. & HANNAH DRAPER WHEATON. She was an aunt of KATE DOUGLAS WIGGIN (see SMITH). She died 9 Jun 1905 at home of her daughter in Germantown, PA (whidd). Buried in Calais Cemetery. Children:

i. AMY ELLEN WHIDDEN, born 22 May 1846 in St. George NB. Graduated from Calais Academy. Died 5 Jul 1934 in Worcester, MA. Census: 1850 & 60 in Calais. She married 1 June 1870 in Calais, by Rev. E. B. Eddy (SCC). GEORGE CLARKSON WHITNEY of Worcester, born 19 Sept 1842, son of Deacon JOHN WHITNEY & LYDIA ALLEN (wtny:286,475). Died after 1895 when he resided in Worcester, MA.

ii. CHARLES RENDOL WHIDDEN, Jr., born 5 Oct 1848 in Calais (VR, colby has 1849). Graduated from Calais Academy and in 1870 from Colby College in Waterville ME (colby). He was editor of the *Calais Times* and a customs inspector. Died 26 Jun 1932 age 84y 8m 21d in Calais (MSA, sfh:6:171). Buried in Calais Cemetery. Census: 1850, 60 & 70 in Calais. He married 19 Nov 1877 by Rev. Padleford in Calais (times) PENOLIA 'NOLA' ALMASETTA MANNING. She died before 1932.

iii. ALBERT REED WHIDDEN, born 18 Aug 1850 in Calais. Graduated from Calais Academy about 1869. He was an attorney. Died 9 Apr 1911 in Calais (MSA, mental illness results of a high fever, g.s.). Buried in Calais Cemetery. Census: 1860 & 70 in Calais. Never married.

iv. MILA FRANCES WHIDDEN, born 5 Nov 1852 in Calais (VR). Died 30 Jan 1854 in Calais (VR:3:306). Buried in Calais Cemetery.

v. FLORENCE 'FLORRIE' MARIA WHIDDEN, born 16 Oct 1855 in Calais (VR). She was a personal shopper for Wanamaker's Department Store in New York, NY. Census: 1860 & 70 in Calais. She married 16 Oct 1875 in Calais CHARLES W. STOWELL of Worcester, MA (adv).

vi. LAURA SMITH WHIDDEN, born 4 Oct 1857 in Calais (VR). Resided in Worcester, MA. Census: 1860, 70 & 80 in Calais. She married 30 Dec 1881 by Rev. R. D. Marshall at home of George C. Whitney in Worcester, MA, GEORGE E. COLE (times, adv), son of GEORGE & OLIVA COLE (see COLE).

vii. ANNIE McCULLOUGH WHIDDEN, born 12 Sep 1860 in Calais (VR). She moved to Portland 1927 (obit). Died 9 Dec 1946 in Portland, Me (MSA, obit ppress). Census: 1870, 1900 & 1920 in Calais. She married 20 Oct 1881 by her uncle, Rev. J. Wheaton Smith of Philadelphia, in Worcester, MA (times) ALBION H. EATON, born 31 Mar 1856 in Milltown, NB (MSA), son of CHARLES H. EATON a lumber dealer (b. in Milltown, NB) & SARAH KEITH (b. in New Glochester, Me). He entered the country in 1869 and was naturalized in 1879 (1920 census). In 1887 dir. he is listed as a box manufacturer. He died 2 June 1936 in Portland (MSA). Census: 1900 & 1920 in Calais.

viii. MAY MERRILL WHIDDEN, born 14 May 1863 in Calais (VR). Census: 1870 & 80 in Calais. She married as his 2nd wife ALFRED C. GIBSON, a widower and a manufacturer of Philadelphia (whidd:c9).

ix. SARAH WHIDDEN, born circa 1866 in Calais. She went to Worcester, MA in 1886. Census: 1870 & 80 in Calais. She married circa 1879 FRANK L. SHEPARDSON. He was a teacher and professor at Colgate University (whidd:c10).

x. GUY CARLETON WHIDDEN, born circa 1867 in Calais. He went to Worcester ca 1886 and in 1899 he worked as a reporter for "Philadelphia Record" in Philadelphia, PA (whidd:c12). Census: 1870 & 80 in Calais. He married EDITH K. SMITH, daughter of CHANNING SMITH of Worcester, MA (whidd).

xi. FRANK B. WHIDDEN, born circa 1871. He moved ca 1886 to Worcester, MA. He was a newspaper reporter and later a chiropractor (whidd:c12). Census: 1880 in Calais.

EDGAR & HARRIET M. WHIDDEN, p. 225, 226

EDGAR WHIDDEN, born 30 Apr 1825 in St. George NB (colby, whidd:e5). He came to Calais in 1831 at age six with his parents. Graduated at age 19 in the class of 1844 at Colby College, in Waterville ME (colby). He was a teacher, postmaster, city councilor, judge and a U. S. Counsul at St. Stephen, NB (colby). Died 8 Feb 1904 age 78 in Worcester, MA (obit adv, g.s., family book, colby has 1 Feb 1904). Buried in Calais Cemetery. Census: 1850 thru 80 in Calais

He married 20 Oct 1853 in Boston Ma HARRIET N. MIRANDA FOSTER, born 26 Mar 1827 in E. Machias, Me, daughter of CYRUS WOODIN FOSTER & SALLY TURNER (dcf:412, drisko:416). Died 22 Mar 1876 age 48y 27d in Calais (g.s., adv). Buried in Calais Cemetery. Census: 1860 thru 70 in Calais. Graduated from Washington Academy in Machias Me. Children:

i. CAROLINE 'Carrie' FOSTER WHIDDEN, born 30 Sep 1854 in Calais (VR). She was a teacher. Died 19 Feb 1908 in Worcester, MA (obit). Census: 1860, 70 & 80 in Calais. She married 29 Aug 1882 in Windsor, NS (times, east:354). Rev. HEZEKIAH ALBERT SPENCER, born 18 Mar 1849 in Cape Breton Island, NS, graduated from Acadia College, Wolfville, NS, died 19 Oct 1887 in Milford, MA where he was pastor of Baptist Church (obit adv).

ii. HARRIET ELIZABETH WHIDDEN, born 1 Mar 1857 in Calais (VR, whidd:E5 has 19 Jan, 1857). She was a bookkeeper. Died 27 Jul 1936 (whidd:E5, g.s.) in Worcester, MA. Buried in Calais Cemetery. Census: 1860, 70 & 80 in Calais.

iii. EDGAR WHIDDEN, Jr., born 12 Dec 1859 in Calais (VR). Died 27 Sep 1938 in Worcester, MA (whidd:e5). Resided in Worcester, MA. Census: 1860, 70 & 80 in Calais. He married EDITH COOK, born 1871, died 1954.

iv. JAMES TALBOT WHIDDEN, born 3 Apr 1863 in Calais, died 24 Aug 1864 age 1y 4m 21d in Calais (VR:3:310, g.s.). Buried in Calais Cemetery.

v. UNNAMED DAUGHTER WHIDDEN. Died at birth (whidd).

vi. AMY HOBART WHIDDEN, born 31 Mar 1870 in Calais (VR). She was a bookkeeper. Died 10 Apr 1958 (VR, g.s.). Buried in Calais Cemetery. Census: 1870 & 80 in Calais.

* Note unless otherwise specified the information on this family was found in "The Story of Some Descendants of Rendol and

Sarah Whidden of Calais, Maine" by Foster C. Whidden, Rae M. Spencer and Amy W. Greene, their grandchildren, 1969. Manuscript found at the Calais Free Library.

DANIEL & BASHEBA (sic) WHITE, p. 198

DANIEL WHITE, born 26 Sept 1898 (biblew) in Fredericton, NB (1850 census), of Hodsdon, ME at marriage, son of ISAAC & SUSANNAH WHITE (biblew). Died 7 Nov 1863 in Calais (VR). Census: 1840 (4 males 3 females), 1850 & 60 in Calais.

He married 26 Oct 1830 by Joshua Putnam, Esq. in Houlton, ME (VR:425) BATHSHEBA SMITH, born circa 1806, in St. John's River, NB (1850 census). Died after 1870. Census: 1850, 60 & 70 (age 63 with daughter Joanna Greenlaw) in Calais. Children:

i. NATHANIEL WHITE, born circa 1831 in Hodgdon Me (1850 census). Bapt. 28 Apr 1857 in Calais (saint). Died 10 July 1875 in Charlotte (VR). Buried Damon Ridge Cemetery, Charlotte. Census: 1850, 60 & 70 in Calais. He married 1st 10 Aug 1851 by Rev. George W. Durrell in Calais (VR:1:160, saint, FJ) MARTHA ZILME FERRIS, born 11 May 1831, daughter of JOHN FERRIS & DIANNAH ZELMA (see FERRIS). She died before 1860, when he was living with his parents age 28. He married 2nd (int) 28 Apr 1863 in Calais (VR:1:104) ABIGAIL B. FERRIS, born 8 Feb 1843 in Charlotte, ME (VR), daughter of DANIEL FERRIS & HANNAH BLACKWOOD. Census: 1870 in Calais

ii. DORCAS WHITE, born circa 1833 in Houlton Me (1850 census). Census: 1850 in Calais. She married 15 Jan 1852 in Calais (VR) WILLIAM S. JUDKINS.

iii. SUSAN WHITE, born circa 1836, in Old Town Me (1850 census). She married 26 Nov 1855 in Calais (VR:1:70) by Rev. George W. Durrell (copy of page from family bible) ISAAC FENNEMORE (not in Calais 1860 census of Calais).

iv. WILLARD WHITE, born circa 1838 in Houlton Me (1850 census). Died 6 Feb 1872 of Small Pox in Calais (adv). Census: 1850 & 60 in Calais. He married 28 Mar 1858 by Rev. G. W. Durrell in Calais (VR:3: 172) LOUISA LEEMAN of Lynfield, NB. Census: 1860 in Calais.

v. ELIZABETH WHITE, born circa 1840. Died 17 Oct 1862 age 22 in Calais (VR:1:244). Census: 1860 in Calais.

vi. EDWIN WHITE, born 26 Oct 1841 in Calais (VR). Enlisted in Civil War in the 9th Maine Co A (enlist), he was 5' 4 ½" with hazel eyes and red hair (cwcard). He worked in saw mill. Died 12 Jul 1888 age 47 in Milltown, NB (east:407). Buried in Calais Cemetery. Census: 1850, 60 & 70 in Calais. He married (int) 4 Mar 1864 in Calais (VR:1:109) MARY J. BROWN, born ca 1843 in Canada. Census: 1870 (age 27) in Calais.

vii. ESTHER/ Hester WHITE, born 6 Aug 1843 in Calais (VR). Census: 1850 & 60 in Calais. She married 8 Mar 1862 by Solomon Coy, JP, in Calais (VR:3:184) ISAAC SCOTT.

viii. DANIEL WHITE (jr.), born 7 Dec 1845 in Calais (VR). He worked in a sawmill. Census: 1850, 60 & 70 in Calais. He married 10 Dec 1867 in Calais by Rev. H.V. Dexter in Calais (VR:3:227, VSNB:25:1715, union) NANCY CASSA CHRISTIE of Waweig, born ca 1849. Census: 1870 (name Cassa) in Calais.

ix. JOANNA/JOAN WHITE, born circa 1849. Possibly died before 1880. Census: 1850, 60 & 70 in Calais (VR). She married 15 Sept 1866 by Rev. H. V. Dexter in Calais (VR3:218) OTIS GREENLAW, born ca 1844. Census: 1870 (age 26) in Calais. [1880 census Otis 35, b. NB with wife, Emma D. 22 & 2 children].

SAMUEL & HANNAH WHITE, p. 205

SAMUEL WHITE, born ca 1791-1800. Census: 1830 (1 male, 1 female), 1840 (5 males, 2 females) in Calais. He married HANNAH (_____), born ca 1800. Children:

i. ELIZA MORTON WHITE, born 9 May 1831 in Calais (VR). She married 20 Jun 1850 in St. Stephen, NB (CCMR) ISAAC H. VARNEY.

ii. FRANCIS COOK WHITE, born 8 Feb 1839 in Calais (VR).

WILLIAM & MARIA WHITENECK, p. 206
(Whiteknact/Whitenack/Whitenect and various spellings)

WILLIAM F. WHITEKNACT, born circa 1817 in Pleasant Valley, NB (1850 census), son of JOHN WHITEKNACT AND ESTHER CULVER, [Esther age 80 buried in Calais Cemetery 16 Feb 1854 (saint)]. He was a ship carpenter. His signature on son's enlistment name spelled WHITEKNACT. Died 8 May 1887 in Calais (obit times). Buried in Calais Cemetery. Census: 1850 thru 1880 in Calais.

He married (int.) 23 Apr 1843 (knact:55) MARIA/MARIE DAVIDSON, born 19 May 1828 age 75y 11m in Calais (knact:55, MSA, adv), daughter of DANIEL DAVIDSON AND MARY ANN CAMPHOR, and sister of George Davidson. Died 16 Apr 1903 in Calais (knact:55, MSA). Probate of will, Washington Co. # W-3-127, surname is spelled Whiteknact, spelling used in this form since her signature on will was spelled this way. Census: 1850 thru 1880 in Calais (see DAVIDSON). Children:

- i. GEORGE WILLIAM WHITEKNACT, born 10 Feb 1845 in Calais (VR). Served in the Civil War in 1st Regt Calvary Maine Vols., described as 5' 8 ½" tall with blue eyes and light hair, died 4 May 1887 in Calais (cwcard). Census: 1850, 60 & 70 in Calais. He married 1 Sep 1871 by Rev. William Carruthers in Calais (VR3:233, obit, adv) JANE McDONALD of Calais.
- ii. JOHN NELSON WHITEKNACT (MSA name John W.), born 10 Mar 1847 in Calais (VR). He served in Civil War in Co. G 1st Maine Cavalry, transferred to Co A 14 Feb 1865, he was 5' 7" tall gray eyes and brown hair (cwcard, enlist, father signed permission). Died 17 Apr 1903 in Calais age 56y 1m 7d (MSA). Fred V. Pickard filed to be guardian to three minor children. Probate in Washington Co. # W-3-133. Census: 1850 thru 1880 in Calais. In 1887 Dir. he is listed as a seaman. He married 25 May 1867 by Rev. H. V. Dexter in Calais (VR:3:226, knact:56) MARGARET 'MAGGIE' A. RUSSELL born ca 1852 in NB, daughter of SOLOMON RUSSELL & MARGARET MARSHRALL, (both born NB). They were divorced Jan 1874 (copy of divorce). They remarried 30 Aug 1879 by Rev. Padleford in Calais (VR:3:329, times). She died 18 Apr 1898 in Calais (MSA). Census: 1870 in Calais.
- iii. ANN ELIZA WHITEKNACT, born 5 Mar 1849 in Calais (VR). Died before mother. Census: 1850 thru 80 in Calais. She married 1Nov 1869 in Calais (VR:3:240, knact:55) RANDOLPH GREENWOOD of Lowell MA.
- iv. JAMES HENRY WHITEKNACT, born 29 Jul 1851 in Calais (VR). Died before mother. Census: 1860 & 70 in Calais.
- v. BENJAMIN FRANKLIN WHITEKNACT, born 23 Dec 1853 in Calais (VR). Died before mother. Census: 1860 & 70 in Calais.
- vi. THOMAS E. WHITEKNACT, born 22 Aug 1857 in Calais (VR). Died after his mother, resided in Beechmont, MA (mother's will). Census: 1860 & 70 in Calais.
- vii. MARY H. WHITEKNACT, born 28 Jan 1862 in Calais (VR). Died 23 Feb 1881 in Calais (obit times). Mary E. buried 25 Feb 1881 (sext) in Calais Cemetery. Census: 1870, 1880 (Mary E.) in Calais.
- viii. CORA WHITEKNACT, born circa 1865. Died 30 Oct 1882 age 17y 4m in Calais (obit, times). Census: 1870 & 80 in Calais.
- ix. CHARLES A. WHITEKNACT, born, circa 1868. Died after 1903 when he resided in Newton Falls, MA. Census: 1870 & 80 in Calais.
- x. LUCY ORA WHITEKNACT, born Aug 1870 in Calais. Died after 1903. Census: 1880 & 1900 in Calais. She married 12 Oct 1887 by Rev. C. G. McCully in Calais (VR:1:73, east:396) GEORGE A. DeYOUNG born ca July 1853. He was a master mariner. Census: 1900 in Calais. They resided in Calais in 1903.
- xi. WILLIAM WHITEKNACT, Jr. born circa 1872 in Calais. Died after mother when he resided in Bermuda, ND. Census: 1880 in Calais.
- xii. ANNIE WHITEKNACT, born circa 1873 in Calais. Died after mother's death when her name was Annie Thomas of Greenhill, NB. Census: 1880 in Calais.

EPHRAIM & ABIGAIL WHITNEY, p. 220

EPHRAIM WHITNEY, born circa 1824 in St. Stephen, NB (1850 census), son of DANIEL WHITNEY (2nd marriage rec). He was a lumberman & carpenter. Probably died in Oshkosh, WI. Census: 1850 in Calais, 1860 & 70 in

Oshkosh, WI.

He married (int.) 22 Aug 1846 in Calais (VR), ABIGAIL TODD DUTCH, born 21 Mar 1825 in Eastport ME (VR), daughter of Capt. JOHN CALIFF DUTCH AND MARGARET 'PEGGY' TODD (see DUTCH). Probably died before 1878 when husband remarried, in Oshkosh. Census: 1850 in Calais, 1860 & 70 in Oshkosh. Children:

i. CHARLES HOWARD WHITNEY, born 25 Nov 1847 in Calais (VR). Census: 1850 in Calais, 1860 & 70 in Oshkosh (he was a store clerk). He married 27 June 1873 in Oshkosh MYRTLE R. WRIGHT, daughter of P. V. & HANNAH WRIGHT (mar. rec. Winnebago Co. vol.1867-73 p. 127).
ii. ELLA WHITNEY, born circa 1852. Census: 1860 (age 8) in Oshkosh.

Ephraim married 2nd 12 Oct 1878 in Oshkosh, Mrs. SALLY (Gallop) STARR, daughter of CHESTER & BETSEY GALLOP (mar. rec. Winnebago Co. WI :5:202).

LEVI & JANE WHITNEY, p. 218

AARON WHITNEY was a blacksmith, in Amherst, NH. About April 1819, he moved to Maine. He died in Calais 16 Feb 1845 at aged 74; he married 1st PHEBE DUNCKLEE 16 Nov 1797. She died 31 Jan 1800, age 21. He married 2nd OLIVE LUND (amher:828, wtny:202). The oldest child was Levi Whitney who lived in Calais.

LEVI WHITNEY, born 7 Jul 1798 in Amhurst, NH (amher:828, wtny:362). He was a machinist. Died 30 Jun 1863 age 65y in Calais (VR, union, wtny:362). Census: 1850 & 60 in Calais.

He married 1st 24 Aug 1824 in Watertown, MA, MARY JANE WHITNEY, born 13 June 1805 in Watertown, daughter of MOSES WHITNEY (wtny:362). Died 14 Jun 1843 age 41 in Calais (VR, obit, gaz). Children:

i. PHEBE JANE WHITNEY, born 18 June 1825, died 21 Oct 1826 in Saco (VR:231, wtny:362).
ii. LEVI F. WHITNEY, born 29 Oct 1827, died 3 Jan 1833 (wtny:362).
iii. ANGELINE WHITNEY, born circa 1828 in Saco ME (1850 census). Died 7 Jan 1868 age 41 (g.s.). Buried in Calais Cemetery. Census: 1850 & 60 in Calais. [Whitney Genealogy doesn't have her as a child].
iv. CHARLES HENRY WHITNEY, born, 3 Jan 1829 (wtny:362) in Biddeford, ME (1850 census). He was a machinist and merchant. He belonged to the Masons (obit). Died 1 Apr 1867 age 38 (g.s, wtny:550, union, SCC, prbt). His wife reported his death to probate office he left no will. Buried in Calais Cemetery. Census: 1850 & 60 in Calais. He married ca 1853 MARIA LOUISA (_____), born ca 1833 in NB, in 1860 (age 27) census of Calais. Died 23 Feb 1897 age 64 (g.s.), buried in Calais Cemetery.
v. HORACE WHITNEY, born 16 June 1830, died 30 Oct 1831 (wtny:362).
vi. GEORGE E. WHITNEY, born 20 Mar 1832, died 29 June 1833 (wtny:362).
vii. JULIA A. WHITNEY, born 1 Nov 1833, died 1849 (wtny:362).
viii. MARY OLIVE WHITNEY, born 15 May 1835, died 28 Apr 1836 (wtny:362).
ix. EDWARD LLEWELLEN WHITNEY, born 23 Sep 1837 in Calais, died 30 Aug 1838 in Calais (VR:1:239, wtny:362).
x. HARRIET EMELINE WHITNEY, born 18 Jan 1840 in Calais (VR). Census: 1850, & 70 in Calais. She married 19 Nov 1862 in Calais (VR) GEORGE BLAKE, born ca 1840 in Canada, he was a merchant. Census: 1870 census in Calais. [She married 18 Jan 1858 HENRY A. HILTZ, born 7 Feb 1831, died 18 Dec 1877, resided Somerville, MA (wtny:362)].
xi. WILLIAM HARRISON WHITNEY, born 22 Oct 1841 in Calais (VR, wtny:362). Died 6 Mar 1843 age 16y 12d in Calais (VR:1:239, obit gaz).
xii. JANE WHITNEY, born 26 May 1843 in Calais (VR, wtny:362). Died 6 Jun 1843 age 11d in Calais (VR:1:233, obit, gaz).
xiii. MARY WHITNEY, born 26 May 1843 in Calais (VR, wtny:362). Died 15 Sep 1844 in Calais (VR:1:239).

He married 2nd 5 Feb 1845 in Calais (VR, gaz) HANNAH E. W. MASON born circa 1812 in Eden, ME (1850 census). Died 4 Dec 1891 in Milltown, Me age 79y 3m (adv). Census: 1850, 60, 70 & 80 (with son, wife & children) in Calais.

* Note - Possible that she was previously married to a Ward, John Ward age 14 with them in 1860 census may be her son. Children:

xiv. EVERETT WHITNEY, born circa 1853 in Calais. He was a lumberman. Census: 1860, 70 & 80 in Calais. He married CA 1875 VIOLETTA (_____), born ca 1855. Census: 1880 (age 25) in Calais.

JOSEPH & LOUISA WHITTIER, p. 224

JOSEPH[6] WARREN WHITTIER, [JOSEPH[5], REUBEN[4-3], NATHANIEL[2], THOMAS[1]] born circa 1793 in Palermo, ME (1850 census). [Joseph Sr. died ca 1805 leaving a widow, Anna (clipping from Argus, [?14 Dec 1919?] at BPL)]. He was a teamster and carpenter. Census: 1840 (5 males, 3 females), 50 & 60 in Calais.

He married 1st PRISCILLA ROBINSON in Palermo 14 Dec 1812 by Timothy Copp, JP (pre 1892 VR at MSA)]. She was the daughter of CHASE & ELIZA ROBINSON (whit:121). Children:

i. JOHN COLBY WHITTIER, born 18 Sept 1813 in Palermo (whit:121, clipping from Argus, [?14 Dec 1919?] at BPL). He married REBECCA BURGESS (whit:121). Census: 1840 (2 males, 1 female) in Palermo.
ii. ELIZA WHITTIER, who possibly married Jeremiah James (whit:121, clipping from Argus at BPL).

Joseph married 2nd before 1821 LOUISA LEIGHTON, born circa 1800 in Palermo (1850 census). Died before 1860 (not in census). Census: 1850 in Calais. Children:

iii. MATILDA WHITTIER, born circa 1821 in St. David, NB (1850 census). Died 6 Jan 1913 age 91 in Calais (sfh:2:19, single, at Alms House, MSA, adv at Alms House since 9th Regt. left town). Buried in Calais Cemetery. Census: 1850, 60, 70 (age 49) & 80 (age 60) {pauper a resident in Poor Farm since June 1866} in Calais.
iv. JOSEPH WARREN WHITTIER, Jr., born circa 1823 in St. Patrick, NB (1850 census). He was a carpenter. Died 26 Jun 1894 in Calais (MSA, g.s.). Buried in Calais Cemetery. Census: 1850 (age 22, listed as James in the state copy of census, Joseph W. in the county copy), 60 (no wife, 3 children), & 80 in Calais. He married 1st Unknown, he filed intentions 26 Mar 1860 and married after 1860 census, JANE B. HANSON, born Sept 1828 (g.s.) in Milltown, NB, daughter of ELIJAH HANSON & ELIZABETH CROCKETT, she died 13 Mar 1901in Calais (MSA, g.s.). Buried in Calais Cemetery. Census: 1860 (in Joseph's household name Hanson, housekeeper age 34), & 1880 in Calais.
v. HENRY M. WHITTIER, born 21 Apr 1830 in St. David, NB (1850 census, g.s.). He was a cabinet maker. Died 22 Mar 1891age 61y 11m 1d in Calais (g.s., adv). Buried in Calais Cemetery. Census: 1850 & 60 & 1880 in Calais. He filed intentions 23 Oct 1855 and married between Apr 1855 – Apr 1856 by Rev. S. H. Keeler in Calais (VR:1:164) ELIZABETH ANN HUGHES, born ca 1840, she died between 1870 & 1880. Census: 1860 & 70 in Calais.
vi. JANE LEIGHTON WHITTIER, born 28 Feb 1833 in Calais (VR). Census: 1850 & 60 in Calais.
vii. LOUISA MELVINA WHITTIER, born circa 1836 in Calais. Died 19 Jan 1838 age 2y 8d in Milltown ME (FJ, g.s.). Buried in Calais Cemetery.
viii. CORDELIA EVELINE AUGUSTA WHITTIER, born 6 Sep 1840 in Calais. Census: 1850 in Calais.
ix. GEORGE MUNROE DALLAS WHITTIER, born 3 Jul 1844 in Calais (VR). Census: 1850 & 60 in Calais.

DANIEL O. & JULIA A. WIGHT, p. 220

JOEL WIGHT, the fifth in descent from Thomas Wight who settled in Dedham, MA, in 1637, married ELIZABETH TWITCHELL. They lived in Dublin, NH, Sherburne, MA and Gilead, ME. Their seventh child, SETH WIGHT, married LYDIA MASON, daughter of JOHN MASON of Gilead, .he later moved to Bethel where he died 29 Dec 1863. His widow died 8 Aug 1872. Seth and Lydia had fourteen children (bthl:642-43, wight:121). Their third child, DANIEL WIGHT, settled in Calais by 1844 when Daniel Wight, Jr. was born.

DANIEL ORMSBY WIGHT, Sr., born 1 Mar 1811 in Gilead, ME (MSA, bthl:643, wight:202). He was a mill man. Died 7 Jun 1872 age 61y 3m in Boston Ma, he became a Christian in Brunswick 1840, went to California, after several years he became ill of lung disease and moved back east, his mother's death quickly followed his (obit, adv). Census: 1850 & 60 in Calais.

He married 25 Jul 1833 in Gilead, ME (VR, bthl:643) JULIA ANN PEABODY, born 17 Apr 1811 in Gilead, ME, daughter of THOMAS PEABODY & MARY REED, she died 17 Nov 1873 (pea:71, wight:202). Census: 1850 & 60 in Calais. Children:

i. MARY ANN REED WIGHT, born 25 Nov 1833 (wight:202) in Gilead, ME (1850 census). Died before 1902. Census: 1850 & 60 in Calais.
ii. JULIA ANN PEABODY WIGHT, born 26 Dec 1835 (wight:202) in Bethel, ME (1850 census). Died before 1902. Census: 1850 & 60 in Calais.
iii. CELIA ANN PERKINS WIGHT, born circa 1839 in Topsham, ME (1850 census). Died after 1902 of Newton, MA (Walter's obit). Census: 1850 & 60 in Calais.
iv. DANIEL ORMSBY WIGHT, born 10 Dec 1840, died 14 Mar 1842 in Brunswick (wight:202).
v. DANIEL ORMSBY WIGHT, Jr., born 2 May 1844 in Calais (VR, wight has May 10). He enlisted in Civil War at age 19 on 22 Dec 1863 in 3rd Batt. Light Artillery, he was 5' 6 1/4" with blue eyes and light hair (enlist). He was employed in McNutt's Novelty Wood Works, Boston, where his children were born (wight:279). He visited Calais in 1892 from Somerville, MA, left Calais 30 years ago (adv). Died before 1902. Census: 1850 & 60 in Calais. He married 21 Sept 1868 LIZZIE McCURDY, born 6 Mar 1842, daughter of ALEXANDER McCURDY & ELLEN McQUADE, of Boston (wight:279).
vi. EDWARD AUGUSTUS WIGHT, born 2 Sep 1846 in Calais. Died before 1902. Census: 1850 & 60 in Calais.
vii. WALTER WIGHT, born 2 Apr 1850 in Calais (obit, 1850 census). He was a brick mason. Moved to Boston 1864, died 26 Apr 1902 age 52y 24d in Bethel, ME (obit adv, MSA). Census: 1850 & 60 in Calais. Married ADA A. TWITCHELL, born 18 Dec 1858 in Bethel, ME (VR:52), daughter of DANIEL A. & CYREN TWITCHELL. Died after 1902.
viii. FLORA ELLA WIGHT, born 14 Nov 1852 (wight:202). Died after 1902. Census: 1860 in Calais. She married WILLIAM G. WASHBURN of Beatrice, NE in 1902 (Walter's obit).
ix. JESSIE FREMONT WIGHT, born 1 Feb 1856 (wight:202). Died before 1902. Census: 1860 in Calais.

CALEB W. & GEOGIANNA WILEY, p. 204

CALEB W. WILEY, born circa 1825 in Lynn Ma (1850 census). He was an apothecary & trader. Died in 1852 in Calais, buried: 22 Nov 1852 in Calais Cemetery (sext). Census: 1850 with wife & children living with Abner Sawyer in Calais.

He married 19 May 1846 by Rev. S. H. Keeler in Calais (VR:1:139, gaz) GEORGIANNA NUTTING born circa 1826 in Boston Ma (1850 census). Census: 1850, 60 & 70 living with Henry & Rebecca King in Calais. She married 2nd STEPHEN B. BERRY in 1855 or 1856 by Rev. S. H. Keeler (VR:3:164). It is possible she m. 3rd JOSEPH WILSON. Children:

i. REBECCA ELIZA WILEY, born 7 Jan 1847 in Calais. Census: 1850, 60 & 70 in Calais. She married 5 Apr 1865 in Calais by Rev. S. H. Keeler in Calais (VR: 3:208, east:211, union) HENRY HARRISON KING, born ca 1841. He was a merchant. Census: 1870 in Calais.
ii. CALEB G. WILEY, born Jan 1849 in Calais (1850 census). Died Oct 1850 in Calais (FJ). Census: 1850 in Calais.

JAMES & NANCY WILLIAMS, p. 209

JAMES WILLIAMS, born circa 1805. Died 27 Oct 1843 in Calais (VR:3:237). Buried: 29 Oct 1843 in Calais Cemetery. Census: 1830 (3 males, 2 females) in Calais.

He married before 1828 NANCY (_____), born circa 1808 in Antrim, Ireland (1850 census). Census: 1850 & 60 in Calais. She married 2nd between Apr 1854 & Apr 1855 by Rev. S. H. Keeler in Calais ISAAC S. McBEAN, born ca 1826 in NB, a carpenter, 1860 census in Calais. Children:

i. JOHN WILLIAMS, born 6 Jan 1828 in Calais, died 27 Oct 1843 age 15y 10m (drowned) in Calais (VR:3:237). Buried in Calais Cemetery.
ii. MATILDA WILLIAMS, born 29 Jun 1829 in Calais (VR). She married 25 July 1848 in Calais Rev. E. H. HELMERSHAWSEN (VR:3:143).
iii. NANCY WILLIAMS, born circa 1832 in St. Stephen, NB (1850 census). Died probably before 1860 census [George Boyd age 4 living with her mother is possibly her son]. Census: 1850 in Calais. She married 1854-55 by Rev. S. H. Keeler in Calais (VR:3:158), GEORGE BOYD, Jr.

iv. EDWARD B. WILLIAMS, born circa 1835 in St. Stephen, NB (1850 census). Served in Co. D 6th Maine. A Sgt. promoted to 2nd Lieut. in 1863 (NRMS:238). He was 5' 10" with hazel eyes and brown hair, and was wounded 1 June 1864 (cwcard). Died before 1899 (sister's obit). Census: 1850 & 60 in Calais a surveyor of lumber. He married 11 May 1868 by Rev. H. V. Dexter in Calais (VR:3:228) SARAH E. PETTYGROVE, who died 15 Feb 1876 age 33y in Calais (adv).

v. SAMUEL WILLIAMS, born circa 1838 in St. Stephen, NB (1850 census). Died before 1899 (sister, Sarah's obit). Census: 1850 & 60 in Calais a farmer.

vi. SARAH A. WILLIAMS, born 13 May 1840 (obit) in St. Stephen, NB (1850 census). Died Dec 1899 in Minneapolis, MN (obit in adv copied from Minneapolis Tribune of Dec 4th). Census: 1850 & 60 in Calais. Buried in Lakewood Cemetery Minneapolis. She married 22 Jan 1866 by Rev. S. H. Keeler in Calais (VR) Capt. GEORGE BOYD, Jr. of Ft. Ripley, MN (poss. her sister, Nancy's widower). He was a Captain in the Civil War.

vii. JAMES WILLIAMS, born 9 Feb 1842 in Calais (VR). Died before 1899 (Sarah's obit). Census: 1850 & 60 in Calais.

viii. GEORGE WILLIAMS, born 9 Mar 1843 in Calais (VR). Died after 1899 of Escelator, WI (Sarah's obit, only surviving sibling). Census: 1850 & 60 in Calais.

JOHN & ELLEN WILLIAMS, p. 196

FRANCIS WILLIAMS, age 79, lived in Calais in 1850 in the household of John Williams and family. There was also a Francis Williams, age 27, in the same household. In the Naturalization records at MSA there is a Francis Williams b. 1819 in Granshaw, Ireland. Came from Ireland Mar 1843, arrived Eastport 26 May 1843 and to Calais May 1843. It is possible that the two Francis' are father and brother of the following John Williams. The older Francis was still with John in 1860 at age 90. In the Machias Union are deaths for Francis Williams age 90 on 25 Dec 1860. The Calais Advertiser of 6 Aug 1890 has the death of Francis Williams age 78 in Cambridge, MA on 5 Aug 1890, says he is formerly of Calais and mentions his nephew Edward and brother John who died ca 1878. Francis Williams was Master of St. Croix Lodge, No. 46 in 1851-1853-1858-1860 (lodge:43).

There is an Elizabeth Williams age 62 b. NB d. in Calais in Dec., listed in deaths in 1850 census she may be the wife of above Francis.

JOHN WILLIAMS, born circa 1810, in Graneshaw, Donegal County, Ireland, entered U.S. 1 July 1833 at Eastport, came to Calais 1836 (SJC:8:45). Naturalized 12 Oct 1864 (irmch). Died ca 1874 (brother, Francis' obit). Census: 1840 (2 males, 1 female), 50, 60 & 70 in Calais.

He married before 1840, ELLEN (_____), born circa 1816 in Eastport ME (1850 census). Census: 1850, 60 & 70 in Calais. Children:

i. WILLIAM FRANCIS WILLIAMS, born 11 Jan 1841 (VR). Died 11 Dec 1842 age 1y 11m in Calais (VR:1:235, obit, gaz). Buried in Calais Cemetery.

ii. ELIZABETH 'ELIZA' OSBORN WILLIAMS, born 9 Jul 1843 (twin), died 1 May 1844 age 10m in Calais (VR:1:235, FJ).

iii. EDWARD VERY WILLIAMS, born 9 Jul 1843 (twin) in Calais (VR). Graduate of Calais Academy. He was a shoe-merchant. He was a junior member of the firm William Brothers Boot & Shoe Store, died 26 Nov 1915 age 73 in Chelsea, MA (obit adv) Buried in Calais Cemetery. Census: 1850, 60 & 70 in Calais. He married 24 Sep 1866 by Rev. H. V. Dexter in Calais (VR:3:218) MARY B. McPHAIL, of Baring, who died Mar 1885 in Chelsea, MA, buried in Calais Cemetery (obit adv). Census: 1870 in Calais.

JONATHAN & LUCINDA WILLIAMS, p. 209

JONATHAN WILLIAMS b. bet. 1791-1800 (poss. son of Jonathan Williams & Hannah Porter, beg:127). Baptized 1 May 1836 (congo). He received the rank of P.M. on 16 Aug 1829 in the Militia, 1st Brig. 7th Div (mil). Died in California (congo). Census: 1840 (3 males, 3 females).

He married 21 Nov 1832 in Calais by A. G. Chandler, Esq. (demo) LUCINDA C. DOWNES. Children:

i. HANNAH HAYDEN PORTER WILLIAMS, born 30 Jul 1834 in Calais, died 30 Dec 1835 in Calais (VR:1:237).

ii. SOPHIA MUNROE WILLIAMS, born 10 Oct 1836 in Calais (VR).

iii. GEORGE FREDERICK WILLIAMS, born 25 Aug 1838 in Calais, died 15 Sep 1839 in Calais (VR:1:237, sext). Buried: 16 Sep 1839 in Calais Cemetery.

iv. EDWARD DOWNES WILLIAMS, born 18 Jun 1840 in Calais, died 18 Sep 1841age 15m, in Calais (VR:1:237, sext). Buried: 19 Sep 1841 in Calais Cemetery.
v. EDWARD LEROY WILLIAMS, born 6 Aug 1844 in Calais (VR). Died 27 Oct 1847 age 4y 3m in Calais (VR:1:237, adv, g.s.). Buried in Calais Cemetery.
vi. GEORGE DOWNES WILLIAMS, born 9 Mar 1846 in Calais (VR).

WILLIAM T. & FRANCES WOODBURY, p. 212

WILLIAM T. WOODBURY, born circa 1815 in Wilmot, NS (g.s., 1850 census), born (2) 17 Feb 1819 in NS, entered U.S. May 1833 at Eastport, naturalized 12 Oct 1864 (irmch). He was a brick mason. Died 4 Mar 1879 age 63 in Calais (g.s.). Buried in Calais Cemetery. Census: 1850, 60 & 70 in Calais.

He married 10 June 1838 by John Sargent, Esq. in Calais (cal2:50, gaz), FRANCES D. WINCHELL, born circa 1822 in Grand Manan, NB (g.s., 1850 census). Died 25 Feb 1881 age 59 in Calais (g.s., obit, prbt). Buried in Calais Cemetery. Census: 1850 thru 1880 in Calais. Children:

i. CHARLES REUBEN S. WOODBURY, born (1) 9 Apr 1839 in Calais (VR), born (2): 9 Apr 1838 in Calais (VR:3:246). He served in Civil War in Co C 7th Maine, he was 5'3" with hazel eyes and light hair and was missing in action 4 May 1863 (cwcard). He was a brick mason. Died 3 Apr 1880 in Calais (times, mortality schedule 1880 census). Buried in Calais Cemetery (mil. stone no dates). Census: 1850, 60 & 70 in Calais.
ii. ANNA B. WOODBURY, born 4 Mar 1842 in Calais (VR). Census: 1850, 60 & 70 in Calais. She married (int.) 9 Feb 1872 in Calais (VR: 3) JOHN McLAUGHLIN.
iii. MARY HELEN WOODBURY, born 5 Aug 1843 in Calais (VR). She was a tailoress. Census: 1850, 60 & 70 in Calais. She married after 1870 and before 1881 (_____) CREGAN (her name in mother's estate).
iv. HARRIET MARIA WOODBURY, born (1) 9 Nov 1844 in Calais (VR, 1850 census has Wilmot, NS), born (2) 9 Nov 1845 (VR:3:246). She was a milliner. Census: 1850, 60 & 70 in Calais. She married 7 Nov 1866 by Rev. H. V. Dexter in Calais (VR:3:218) ELISHA B. MURPHY, born ca 1843. He was a lumberman & surveyor. Served in Civil War Co M 1st Heavy Artillery (MSA), he was a clerk 5'6 3/4" with blue eyes and light hair (cwcard). Census: 1870 in Calais (see MURPHY).
v. JEROME W. WOODBURY, born (1) 5 Apr 1845 in Calais (VR), born (2) 5 Apr 1846 in Calais (VR:3:246). Died 4 Jul 1847 age 15m in Calais (VR:3:306, g.s.). Buried in Calais Cemetery.
vi. FRANCES W. WOODBURY, born 10 Aug 1847 in Calais (VR). Died 6 Sep 1848 age 13m in Calais (VR:3:306, g.s. = Sept. 5). Buried in Calais Cemetery.
vii. WILLIAM S. WOODBURY, born 26 Mar 1848 in Calais (VR:3:246). Died 26 June 1889 in Calais age 45 (obit, adv). Buried in Calais Cemetery. Census: 1850 thru 1880 in Calais. He married 7 Nov 1868 by Samuel Lambe, JP in Calais (VR:3:232) ELIZA A. WHEELER of Fredericton, NB, born ca 1848. She was a dressmaker. She divorced him for abuse & non support in Apr 1883 (SJC case #330). Census: 1870 (age 32) in Calais.
viii. GEORGE T. WOODBURY, born 18 Dec 1850 in Calais (VR:3:246). Died 21 Dec 1908 in Chelsea Ma. (obit, adv, name is Geo. P.). Census: 1860 in Calais.
ix. JAMES F. WOODBURY, born 4 Mar 1853 in Calais (VR:3:246). Died (1) 31Dec 1855 in Calais (VR:3:306). Died (2) 30 Dec 1856 in Calais (union, g.s.). Buried in Calais Cemetery.
x. JOSEPH AUSTIN WOODBURY, born 26 Mar 1856 in Calais (VR:3:246, death rec. = 6 May 1855). He was a brick mason, a violinist and also played brass instruments (obit). Died 8 Jan 1918 in Calais (MSA, obit = age 62y 8m 2d, death notice same paper = 64y). Census: 1860 thru 1900 in Calais. He married before 1884 (her death rec., son's death rec.) AMELIA HOVEY. She died 26 Oct 1916 in Fredericton, NB, buried in Calais Cemetery (adv). Census: 1900 in Calais. [Died in Calais 19 Feb 1882 Rose M. Woodbury age 23y wife of Austin Woodbury (SCC), was she his first wife?]
xi. JAMES J. WOODBURY, born 4 Mar 1857 in Calais (VR:3:246). Census: 1860, 70 & 80 in Calais. He married 12 Sep 1879 in Calais (adv) ALICE/OLIVE M. LEGACY born in Frederiction, NB (daughter's death rec.). She died 8 Sept 1887 age 26y in Calais (adv). Buried 6 Sept 1887 in Calais Cemetery (sext).
xii. FANNY ALICE WOODBURY, born 3 Jul 1859 in Calais (VR:3:246). She died after her mother (prbt). Census: 1860 & 70 in Calais. She married 15 Dec 1879 by George Eldridge in Calais (VR:3:328) WILLIAM H. COLE.
xiii. AMY ELLEN WOODBURY, born 8 Jun 1861 in Calais (VR:3:246). Died 15 Apr 1913 age 50y 10m in

Calais (VR, MSA, adv). Census: 1870 thru 1900 in Calais. She married 1 Aug 1882 in Calais by Rev. A. J. Padleford (VR:2:19) ORRIN DAVIDSON, son of GEORGE DAVIDSON and SARAH 'SALLY' SMITH (see DAVIDSON).

xiv. SARAH E. WOODBURY, born 29 Aug 1863 in Calais (VR:3:246). Census: 1870 in Calais.

xv. JOHN WOODBURY, born circa 1867 in Calais. Census: 1870 (age 3) in Calais.

REUBEN & HARRIET WYMAN, p. 193

REUBEN WYMAN. Census: 1840 (3 males, 3 or 4 females) in Calais.

From "Deaths from the Maine Farmer" by David Young, p. 385: 7 May 1842 Reuben Wyman of Calais, died on Monday last, suddenly in a fit, left a wife and little ones at Topsfield, ME.

He married HARRIET(_____). Children:

From marriage records at PNAB: Reuben Wyman of St. George and Harriet Bassett of the same, with consent of parents, were married 3 June 1824, by Rev. Thomson. Witnesses: Francis Lovejoy and Robert Ash, Jr.

i. HANNAH ELIZABETH WYMAN, born 7 Aug 1836 in Calais, died 16 Sep 1837 in Calais (VR:1:233).

ii. HARRIET ANGELINE WYMAN, born 30 Dec 1840 in Calais (VR).

HENRY & OLIVE ZELMA, p. 199

HENRY & OLIVE ZELMA listed in VR of Calais with the birth of one child. Nothing else has been found on this family. He is possibly the son of Augustus and Amelia Zelma and brother of Diannah (Zelma) Ferris (see Ferris).

i. ARALENAH ZELMA, born 27 Aug 1846 in Calais (VR).

REFERENCES

Rev. Seth H. Keeler, a minister in Calais, reported marriages at the end of each year, as required by the state. What he neglected to do was to put the month and day that the event occurred. His listings all read 'marriages I performed from April 18__ to April 18__.

(VR) preceded by a place name = Vital Records of that place.
(AMHI) Augusta Mental Health Institute
(1850 census) The town of birth is written in the listing of names in the county copy of the 1850 census of Calais, at the Machias Probate Office, but not in the federal or state copies on microfilm. This little bit of data was very helpful in locating where many of the families in Calais came from. A place name followed by (1850 census) indicates the data came from this source.

BOOKS

(album) Album, Biographical Records of Soldiers & Citizens in Wisconsin
(amher) Amherst, NH, History of, by Daniel F. Secomb, pub. 1883
(antr) Antrim, NH, History of, by Rev. W. R. Cochrane, 1880
(aroos) History of Aroostook County, compiled by Hon. Edward Wiggin, 1922
(atlas) Illustrated Atlas of Winnebago County, WI, by George A. Randall, 1889
(banhis) Bangor Historical Magazine
(beg) Beginnings or Annals of Calais, Maine, by Rev. I. C. Knowles, 1875
(belf) Belfast, History of, Vol. II, by Joseph Williamson, pub. 1913
(bthl) Bethel, Maine, History of, original pub. 1891 – reprint 1981
(bill) Billerica, History of, by Rev. Henry A. Hazen, 1883.
(biodir) Biographical Directory of American Congress 1774-1971, found at MSA.
(biorev) Biographical Review Vol. XXIX, Somerset, Piscataquis, Hancock, Washington & Aroostook Counties, Maine pub. 1898
(biosk) Biographical Sketches of Maine Senate & House   (vol. IV 1875) (vol. V 1876)
(bowhis) History of Bowdoin College, by Nehemiah Cleaveland, Class of 1813, pub. 1882
(bowcat) Bowdoin College General Catalogue 1794-1950, pub. 1950 (at MSL).
(bowd) Bowdoin Obituaries and/or Alumni file.
(brief) Brief Biographies of Maine Vol. I 1926-1927, edited by Theodore R. Hodgkins.
(brown) Brown University Catalogue 1764-1904, pub. 1905 by University
(CEV) Calais, Eastport & Vicinity – Business Men – by George F. Bacon, 1892
(cal2) Calais, Maine Records, Vol. 2, compiled by Sharon Howland, Picton Press, 2001
(china) China Maine Bicentennial History, by China Historical Society
(cumb) History of Cumberland County Maine
(cutter) Genealogical & Memorial of New England by William Richard Cutter, third series, Vol. I
(cwWI) Civil War Veterans of Winnebago, Co. WI, vol. 2, pub 1994, by David A. Langkau
(dir. 1887) General Directory of Calais, Maine & St. Stephen, NB, 1887
(dir. 1891) General Directory of Calais, Maine & St. Stephen, NB, 1890-1891
(dir. 1901) General Directory of Calais, Maine 1901-1902
(drisko) Machias, Maine, History of, by George W. Drisko, 1904, reprint 1979 and/or
   Index, compiled by Warren H. Hasty, 1992
(durh) Durham, Maine, History by Everett S. Stackpole, reprint 1978, original pub. 1899
(east) Eastport Sentinel, Vital Records, 1818-1900, by Kenneth L. Willey, 1996
(goffs) Goffstown, NH, History of, Volume II, by George P. Hadley, 1920
(gorh) Gorham, Maine, History of, by Hugh D. McLellan, 1903
(harv) Harvard College
(heavy) 1st Maine Heavy Artillery 1862-1865 by Horace H. Shaw & Charles J. House 1903
(indr) Industry, Maine, History of, by William C. Hatch, 1893, reprint 1984
(leed) Leeds, Me, History of the Town of, by J. C. Stinchfield, with additions by David C. Young, pub. 1996 [see also (stanch)]

(lime)	Limerick, ME, Early Families of, by Robert L. Taylor
(litch)	Litchfield, History of, compiled by Oliver B. Clason 1895, reprint 1992
(litt)	Little's Genealogy & Family History of State of Maine, by George Little, Vol III, 1909
(liver)	Livermore, History of by Ira T. Monroe, 1928
(lubec)	Vital Records of Lubec, ME, prior to 1892, compiled by Patricia M. Townsend, 1996.
(mefam)	Maine Families in 1790, Volumes 1-5, Maine Genealogical Society, pub. 1988-1996.
(mrwc)	Marriage Records of Washington County, prior to 1892. Edited by Alice M. Long, 1993.
(massv)	Massachusetts Volunteers in War of 1812 at MSL.
(mss)	Massachusetts Soldiers and Sailors in the Civil War, 1930
(memcen)	Memorial Centennial Anniversary of Machias, 1863
(mop)	Men of Progress, Biographical Sketches & Portraits -- compiled by Richard Herndon, 1897
(newip)	New Ipswich, NH, History, 1735-1914, by Charles H. Chandler, pub. 1914
(NRMS)	No Rich Men's Sons, The Sixth Maine Volunteer Infantry, by James H. Mundy, 1994
(norw)	Norway, Maine, History of, by William B. Lapham 1986
(oxf)	Oxford County, Maine Marriage Returns, prior to 1892 by Rev. D. L. McAllister & L. E. Naas
(paris)	Paris, Maine, History of, by Lapham & Maxim, 1983
(pars)	Parsonsfield, Maine History, 1888- Reprint by Peter E. Randall,
(prf)	Pleasant River Families of Washington County, ME, by Tibbetts & Lamson, 1997
(RMM)	Representative Men of Maine, under direction of Henry Chase, 1893.
(rowley)	Rowley, MA, Early Settlers, by Amos E. Jewett, 1933
(rural)	St. Stephen Rural Cemetery, Tombstone Inscriptions, by NB Gen. Soc., Charlotte Branch
(sanbay)	San Francisco Bay, History, Vol. II by Bailey Millard, 1924 (excerpt sent by Pat Devoe)
(water)	Watertown, MA, Bonds Genealogies of, by Harry Bond, 1860
(weston)	Weston, Maine Memorial Book III, compiled by Marion L. Dunn, edited by Basil E. Kenney
(wey)	Weymouth, MA, Early Families, by George W. Chamberlain, 1984
(wiscnh)	Wisconsin, History of Northern, pub. 1881, on microfilm.

GENEALOGIES

(andrew)	Andrews, Descendants of Lt. John, Vol. I:(5-204), compiled by Elliott M. Andrews, 1961
(balch)	Balch Families in America, by G. B. Balch, MD, 1897
(bang)	Bangs Family in America, by Dean Dudley, pub. 1896
(RBD)	Barnard, Robert of Andover, MA and His Descendants, by Robert M. Barnard, 1899
(bill)	History of Billerica, by Rev. Henry A. Hazen, 1883, found at BPL
(bish)	Bishop Family 'Tangled Roots,' of Horton, Nova Scotia, pub. By Bishop Family Association.
(board)	Boardman Family, a manuscript in St. Andrews Archives
(boy)	Boyden, Thomas, and his Descendants, by Wallace C. Merrill & Amos J. Boyden, 1901
(brack)	Brackett Genealogy, by Herbert Brackett, 1907
(bradb)	Bradbury Memorial, John of Ipswich, MA, by William B. Lapham, 1890
(bradf)	Bradford, Descendants of William, 1951
(chand)	Chandler Family, collected by George Chandler of Worcester, Mass, 1883.
(christie)	Christie, Jessie, Descendants by Donald Melvin Christie 1991 at SSPL
(chute)	Chute Family in America by William E. Chute, 1894
(clinch)	Clinch Genealogy by Blair Meating, Orleans, Ont.1995 at SSPL
(cope)	Copeland Family, by Warren Turner Copeland, 1937
(drum)	Descendants of Alexander Drummond, by Josiah Hayden Drummond, printed 1942
(dem)	Deming Genealogy, Descendants of John, by Judson K. Deming, 1904
(dick)	Dickerman Ancestry, by Edward D. Dickerman and George S. Dickerman, pub. 1897
(dcf)	Drisko-Crocker-Foster by Frances Sterling Drisko, Heritage Books, Inc., 2001
(doe)	The Descendants of Nicholas Doe, by Elmer E. Doe, 1918
(dow)	Book of Dow, compiled by Robert Percy Dow, 1929
(eaton)	Eaton's of Nova Scotia, compiled by Rev. Arthur W. Eaton, 1885
(emery)	Emery, Descendants of John, Sen.
(esta)	Estabrook Family of St. John River, NB by Florence Estabrook 1935

(farns)	Farnsworth Memorial II, by R. Glen Nye, 1974, found at MSL
(felt)	Felt Genealogy, by John E. Morris, 1893, at Cambridge, Mass. Public Library.
(flint)	Flint, Descendants of Thomas, by John Flint and John H. Stone, pub. In 1860.
(fuller)	Fuller, Genealogy, Vol. 3, Descendants of Matthew Fuller, 1914
(fur)	Furlong Genealogy, by Penland Holmes, printed 1990, found at MSL
(gard)	Gardner Family Descendants of Thomas thru Ebenezer, of Machias, ME
(gate)	Gates Family
(hap)	Hapgood Family, Descendants of Shadrach, 1656-1898 by Warren Hapgood, 1908
(haml)	Hamlin Family, Bangor Historical Magazine, Vol. II p. 193
(harm)	Harmon Genealogy, by Artemas C. Harmon, Washington, DC 1920
(hamm)	Hammond Families in America, by Frederick S. Hammond Vol. II, pub. 1904
(heal)	Heal - Heald Genealogy, by Isabel Maresh
(hoyt)	Hoyt, Haight, and Hight Families by David W. Hoyt, pub 1871
(hunt)	Huntley, Descendants of John, of Lyme, CT by Ivy Huntley Horne, 1953
(jord)	The Jordan Memorial, by Tristram Frost Jordan, New England History Press, Somersworth, 1982
(keeler)	Keeler Family by Wesley B. Keeler 1985, at NEHGS, Boston.
(kidd)	Kidder Family Genealogy, by Morgan H. Stafford, pub. Rutland, Vt. no date.
(kimb)	Kimball Family, Vol. II, by Leonard A. Morrison, & Stephen P. Sharples, Boston, 1897.
(ladd)	Ladd Family, by Warren Ladd, New Bedford, Ma, 1890
(leigh)	Leigh/Lee, descendants of John, by William Lee, 1888
(lime)	Limerick Families by Robert Taylor, pub. 1984
(love)	Lovejoy Genealogy 1460-1930, by Clarence E. Lovejoy, 1930
(low)	Lowells of America 1639-1899, by Delmar R. Lowell, 1899
(mck)	McKusick Family, by Charles E. McKusick, 1988, at NEHGS
(mhl)	Moore, Hitchings, & Livingstone, Loyalist Families, by John E. Moore, 1898
(pea)	Peabody Genealogy by William S. Peabody, Boston 1867
(jpike)	Pike, John, Family by A. R. Pike 1995
(port)	Porter, Genealogy of descendants of Richard Porter by Joseph W. Porter, pub 1878
(pott)	Potter Families & their descendants in America by Charles E. Potter 1888
(pres)	Prescott Memorial, Part I by William Prescott, MD, Boston 1870
(pressp)	Prescott – Biography of Harriet Prescott Spofford, by Elizabeth K. Halbeisen, 1935.
(rick)	Ricker, Genealogy of the Ricker Family, by Percy L. Ricker & Elwin R. Holland, Heritage Books, 1996
(sawofne)	Sawyer Families of New England, by Eleanor G. Sawyer, pub. 1995.
(shed)	Shedd, Genealogy of Daniel Shedd at BPL.
(sherdir)	Sherman Directory
(shergen)	Descendants of William Sherman, by Mary Lovering Holman, 1936.
(shop)	Shoppee Family manuscript, found at Cherryfield, Me. Library
(spald)	Spalding Memorial by Charles W. Spalding 1897.
(spragf)	<u>Sprague Families in America</u> 1840-41, Supplement by W. V. Sprague, at CFL
(stack)	Stackpole Family, Genealogy, by Everett S. Stackpole, no date
(stan)	Stanhope Family, manuscript at CFL
(stick)	The Stickney Family, by Matthew A. Stickney, 1869 at Boston Pub. Lib. p 177-178-279
(stinch)	Stinchfield - Stanchfield Family, by Roger A. Stinchfield, 1963 see also (leed)
	[History of the Town of Leeds, by J. C. Stinchfield, with additions by David C. Young, pub. 1996, p. 23, 126, and Stinchfield - Stanchfield Genealogy, p. 148],
(swett)	Swett Genealogy, Desc. of John Swett of Newbury, MA, by Everett S. Stackpole (no date)
(tapp)	Tappan-Toppan Genealogy of Newton, MA, by Daniel L. Tappan, 1915.
(tink)	Tinker, Descendants of John Wescot Tinker, by Frederick J. Libbie, Boston, 1900
(titcom)	Descendants of William Titcomb, of Newbury, MA 1635, by Gilbert M. Titcomb
(topp)	Toppans, by Joshua Coffin, 1862
(tow)	Towers, unpublished manuscript of Towers Family, found at St. Andrews, NB Archives
(varrell)	Varrell - Verrill, Descendants of Samuel, by Harold F. Round, Pub. 1968
(vose)	Vose, Robert and his Descendants, by Ellen F. Vose, printed, 1932.
(wad)	Wadsworth Family in America, pub. 1985, in BPL

(wads) Wadsworth Family in America, by Horace A. Wadsworth, pub 1883
(waite) Waite Family of Malden, MA, by Deloraine P. Corey, 1913
(wake) Wakefield Memorial compiled by Homer Wakefield, M. D., printed 1897, Bloomington, IL
(wnact) Weidknecht, Whitenack(neck/knect) Families, by Everett Whiteneck, Concord, NH, no date, manuscript found at CFL.
(went) Wentworth Genealogy by John Wentworth 1878
(whidd) Whidden, Descendants of Rendol & Sarah, Manuscript no date, found at CFL.
(wtny) Desc. of John Whitney, by Frederick C. Pierce, 1895.
(whit) Desc. of Thomas Whittier & Ruth Green of Salsibury & Haverhill, MA, by Charles D. Whittier, 1937
(wight) The Wights by William Ward Wight, Swain & Tate – printers, Milwaukee, 1890

LIBRARIES

(banglib) Bangor Public Library, Bangor, ME
(boslib) Boston Public Library, Boston, MA
(CFL) Calais Free Library, Calais, ME
(CCA) Charlotte County Archives, St. Andrews, NB
(folg) Folger Library at University of Maine, Orono, ME
(LDS) Family History Library, Later Day Saints, Waterville, ME and Salt Lake City, UT.
(HIL) Harriet Irving Library, University of NB, Fredericton, NB
(MSL) Maine State Library at Augusta ME
(MSA) Maine State Archives at Augusta ME
(MHS) Maine Historical Society in Portland, ME.
(NAW) National Archives at Waltham, Mass.
(NADC) National Archives at Washington, DC
(NEHGS) New England Historical & Genealogical Society, Boston, MA
(oshlib) Oshkosh, Wisconsin Public Library
(PANB) Provincial Archives of New Brunswick, in Fredericton, NB
(SSPL) St. Stephen Public Library, St. Stephen, NB

NEWSPAPERS

(adv) *Calais Advertiser*, Calais, ME   on microfilm at (CFL) and (folg)
(argus) *Daily Eastern Argus*, Portland, ME on microfilm at (MSL)
(bay) *Bay Pilot,* St. Andrews, NB, on microfilm at (HIL)
(call) *Call*, San Francisco, CA, from Pat DeVore
(demo) *Eastern Democrat,* Calais, ME vital records transcribed by Jeffrey Brown, 1990, unpublished.
(eastar) *Eastern Star,* Eastport, ME (County Court House, at Machias).
(FJ) *Frontier Journal*, Calais, ME   on microfilm at (PANB)
(gaz) *Gazette & Advertiser,* Calais, ME vital records 1836-1844, transcribed by Michael McGarry, of St. Stephen, NB, unpublished.
(ithaca) Ithaca Journal-News, Ithaca, NY.
(KJ) *Kennebec Journal,* Augusta, ME on microfilm at (MSL)
(light) *Northern Lights,* Eastport, ME, original papers at Court House, Machias, ME
(north) *Oshkosh Northwestern* , Oshkosh, Wisconsin, at Oshkosh Public Library
(otime) Oshkosh Wisconsin *Weekly Times* at Oshkosh Public Library.
(ppress) *Portland Press Herald,* Portland, ME on microfilm at (MSL)
(pst) Portland Sunday Telegram, Portland, ME on microfilm at (BPL)
(SAS) *St. Andrews Standard,* St. Andrews, NB on microfilm at (PANB)
(SCC) *St. Croix Courier,* St. Stephen, NB on microfilm at (PANB)
(trib) *Calais Tribune*, a political paper, a few copies found in Pike Papers at Folger Library, Orono.
(times) *Times*, Calais, ME, on microfilm at (PANB)
(union) *Machias Union,* Machias, Maine, transcribed records at (MSL) and (banglib), original papers at Court House, Machias, ME.

MISC. RECORDS

(as)	As I Remember It, by Robert L. Wilson, 1977
(achs)	Alexander Crawford Historical Society Newsletter, Alexander, ME
(angch)	Anglican Church Records of St.
(bail)	Baileyville Maine, Early History, by Albert W. Bailey 1972, manuscript found at CFL.
(bible)	Family Bible of Jonathan Dow, received third handed info should be verified.
(bibj)	Family Bible of Isaac Jones, copy from Nichols Jones 3rd
(brownu)	Brown University History Catalogue 1761-1904
(calef)	Robert Calef of Boston & Roxbury, compiled by William W. Lunt, Hingham, MA, 1928
(cath)	Catholic Church records, found in CFL
(CCMR)	Charlotte County Marriage Records in New Brunswick, at PANB
(cityd)	City Directory of South Portland, Me.
(clip)	Clipping from the Minneapolis Journal of Dec. 22, 1907, pub. in Calais Advertiser of 1 Jan 1908.
(congo)	Congregational Church of Calais, ME records found at MHS, and/or First Congregational Church Catalogue of Members printed 1877
(CCP)	Court of Common Pleas, Washington County, at MSA
(cwcard)	Civil War Records at MSA, Adj. General cards, grave records and locations
(colby)	Colby College Alumni Records or Colby College Catalogue
(DEA)	Downeast Ancestry, periodical published from June 1977 to Jan 1993
(DC)	District Court of Washington County, at MSA
(ERE)	Eastport, Early Records, manuscript copied from original by Beulah H. Morse, 1947
(enlist)	Enlistment papers at MSA (Civil War)
(hay)	Haycock Family manuscript found at St. Stephen Public Library, unpaged.
(harv)	Harvard College Catalogue
(hope)	Mt. Hope Cemetery records, Bangor, Maine
(irmch)	Immigration Records at Machias Court House
(irmsa)	Immigration Records found in court records at MSA
(jojc)	Journal of John Chandler at Folger Library, U of M, Folio Em 353,1 CY A3
(kmc)	Kirk McColl Church Records, St. Stephen, NB on film at SSPL
(lodge)	History of St. Croix Lodge No. 46, F. & A. M. by H. E. Lamb 1934, found at CFL
(lord)	Lord, Rev. Isaac, Jr. Baptism, Marriage & Funeral Records, unpublished manuscript, at BPL
(MOCA)	Maine Old Cemeteries Association, records at MSA
(mil)	Maine Militia, Company Rolls records for 1828,29,31,32 found at CFL
(mayf)	Mayflower Quarterly, Nov 1989, p. 304-305.
(milb)	Milburn Connection Newsletter, vol. 1:3:5-6, edited by Beverly Murphy of Arizona, sent by Ruth E. Dow of Nobleboro
(milit)	Maine Militia 1820-1850 Roll # 1 & 2 at MSA
(milnat)	Military Records at National Archives, Washington, DC
(pensrec)	Pension record of James L. Eye, from National Archives, Washington, D.C.
(pkjdt)	Pike, James S. - papers transcribed by James D. Thomas of Calais 1967-69
(pkbib)	Pike family bible, info from Justine Gengras.
(prinvr)	Princeton Maine Vital Records at Princeton, not available at MSA
(prbt)	Probate Records of Washington County, Maine at Machias, ME
(presSA)	Presbyterian Church, St. Andrews, NB, records at PANB
(saint)	St. Anne's Episcopal Church records, Calais, ME
(sfh)	Scholl Funeral Home, Records, Calais, ME
(sext)	Sexton's Records of Calais Cemetery, found at (CFL) or Sexton's Journal published in Downeast Ancestry
(cityd)	South Portland City Directories.
(speak)	Speakers of the Maine House of Representatives from 1820 by James H. Mundy.
(sprag)	Sprague Family, unpublished manuscript, p 203, found in (SSPL)

(SJC) Supreme Judicial Court records of Washington County at MSA
(VR) Vital Records of towns in Maine found at MSA
(VSNB) Vital Statistics from New Brunswick Newspapers, transcribed by Daniel F. Johnson, B.B.A., C.G.
(wwcf) West Washington County Families by Dorothy P. Phelan, unpublished manuscript at (BPL)
(wldr) Wilder Papers, found in Machias
(winn) Winnebago County, WI marriage records on microfilm at LDS Salt Lake City, UT
(wmr) Wisconsin marriage records, found at LDS Salt Lake City, UT
(wdr) Wisconsin death index prior to 1907, micro fiche at LDS

FAMILIY REFERENCES

Descendants of Calais families who have shared their research for this book.

(arnie) Arnold Krause of Saskatoon, Sask, Canada (Thompson, and other families)
(bouch) Boucher, Judy of Fort Meyers, Fl (Bradford family)
(brownj) Brown, Jeffrey, MSA, (Holmes & Smyth Families)
(bruce) Bruce Towers of Prospect CT (Towers Family)
(casey) Casey, Joan, of Waltham, MA (Good family)
(conn) Linda J. Conn, (Clark & Rogers families)
(daveh) David Hodsdon, of Lanham, MD (Hodsdon family)
(devo) Pat Devore,, Bolton, MA (Heal family)
(dowr) Ruth E. Dow of Nobleboro, ME (Dow family)
(diana) Diane Parker, of Cape Elizabeth, Me (Hudson family)
(dows) Susan Dow Countryman, of Yuba City, CA (Sprague Family)
(dlund) Undocumented research of David Lund of England, while serving in the British Embassy in Washington, D.C., sent by Ruth E. Dow of Nobleboro, Me.
(dyerf) Frank Dyer, info on Jones Dyer family, on internet.
(fini) Barbara Crosby Finizia, of Palm Beach Gardens, FL (Gallagher & Crosby family)
(fish) Peggy Fish,, of Dover, NH (Noah Smith family)
(fisher) Carol Smith Fisher, of Brewer, Me (Ferris & Smith families)
(folley) Michelle Folley, of Brewster, MA (Clark, Cheney, Spooner & other families)
(fran) Francis McHugh, of St. John, NB (Spinney family)
(geng) Justine Gengras of Alton, NH (Porter & Greenlaw families)
(gengbr) Bible record provided by Justine Gengras
(howell) Karen Howell of Woburn, MA (Spinney, Lamb, Holt + other families)
(howland) Sharon Howland, of Waltham, MA (Pineo, Pike, + other families)
(jones 3rd) Isaac 'Nick' Jones 3rd of Tampa, FL (Isaac N. Jones family).
(lesko) Chuck Lesko, (Estabrooks, Murphy & Smith families)
(mart) Lois Martin, of Wells, ME (Barry family)
(mason) J. S. Mason, of Seattle, WA (Callighan family)
(mead) Grace Meader, of Calais (Sprague family)
(morin) William Morin of Penn. (McMunn family)
(morris) Tracey Stanchfield Morris on internet (Stanchfield and Wadsworth families)
(pearl) Pearls in America, Edited by Richard H. Pearl, privately published, Las Vagas, NV 1996
(phill) Phillips, Judy of Woburn, MA (Spinney family)
(ps) Paul Sherman of Litchfield, ME (Eye-Brown family)
(rayt) Ray Thomas of Wiscassett, ME (McMunn family)
(rey) Reynolds, Beatrice of Sidney (Hastings family)
(rilla) Rilla Whiteneck (Whiteknact family)
(tina) Tina Vickery of Augusta, Me (Vickery family)
(SRW) Sarah R. Wentworth on internet (Hill family)

1800 Census Calais, Washington County, Maine

Names of heads of families	Free White Males					Free White Females					
	Under 10	10 and under 16	16 and under 26	26 and under 45	of 45 and up	Under 10	10 and under 16	16 and under 26	26 and under 45	of 45 and up	
Bohanan, John		1	2	1	1			2	1		
Conyers, Robert					1						
Dyer, Stephen	4			1		1		1			
Dyer, Jones	2			1		1		1	2	1	
Dyer, Jones, Jun.			1								
Dyer, Widow	2					2	1		1		
Foster, Moses	1			1		1			1		
Gilmore, H. Arthur	4			1		2			1		
Hill, Thomas	1		1					1			
Hill, Daniel		1	1		1					1	
Knight, Jonathan		1	2		1	1	1			1	
Knight, Paul	4	2		2		3	1		1		
Knight, Henry	1			1	1	1			1		
Lane, James	2	1	1	1		1		1			
Noble, John	4	1		1		1	1		1		
Pettygrove, Thomas			1		1			1			
Pettygrove, Thomas, Jun.				1			1				
Pettygrove, Francis				1		2		1			
Stickney, Timothy				1				2			
Sprague, James	1	2	2			2	1	1			
Totals	26	9	11	12	7	18	6	11	9	3	112

1810 Census Calais Washington County Maine

Names of heads of families	Free White Males					Free White Females				
	Under 10	10 and under 16	16 and under 26	26 and under 45	of 45 and up	Under 10	10 and under 16	16 and under 26	26 and under 45	ages 45 and up
Bohanan, Daniel	3			1			1		1	
Bohanan, John	1		1	1	1	2		1		1
Bohanan, John, Jr.	2			1		2			1	
Brewer, Stephen				1		1	1		1	
Campbell, Anna	1					2			1	
Clark, David				1	1	1	2		1	
Crocket, William				1		3		1		
Downes, Shubiel	2		6	3		2	1	1	2	
Dyer, Jones			1		1			1		1
Dyer, Stephen	2	3	1	1		1	1		1	
Dyer, Jones, Jun.	1			1		2	1	2		
Dunn, Samuel	1			1		2			1	
Elliot, Simon	5	2	2	1				1	1	
Foss, Nathan	3			4					1	
Frazier, Oliver	3			1		1	2		1	
Fox, Warren	1	1	1	1		1	1	1	1	1
Frost, Ephraim		1		2					1	
Grover, Stephen					1	1			1	
Griggs, William	1			2				1	1	
Goodwin, John W.	3			1		2			1	
Helms (Holms?), William	2		1			1		1		
Hill, Thomas	5	1		1					1	
Hill, Daniel					1		1			1
Knight, George	1		2	7		1	1	1		
Knight, Jonathan			2	4	1					1
Knight, Westbrook	1			1		1		1		
Knight, Paul	4	2			1	4	2	3	1	
Knight, Henry	1			1		4			1	
Keen, Jarius	4		1	4		1		2		1

Lane, William			1			2				
Lane, Widow			3					1		1
Lane, Clement	3		2	1				1		
McKeen, James	1	1		1		2	1		1	
Marshall, John	2			1		1		1		1
Noble, John	1	2	1	1			2		1	
Nevens, Jonathan			1				1	1		
Pike, William	2		4	5		1		2		
Pettygrove, Thomas			2	1	1			1		
Pettygrove, Thomas, Jr.	3		2		1	2			1	
Pettygrove, Francis	1			2		4		1	1	
Prescott, Joseph	1			1		1	1			
Potter, Zebulon	1				2				1	
Rhoads, Dan'l	1		4	1		2		2		
Russell, Eli			3	3				1		
Robbins, Solomon			3					1		
Sands, Ephraim	2		3	1		1		1		
Sharp, William	1		1	4		1		1	1	
Sprague, James	4		1	1					1	
Spring, Ziba G.	1		1					2		
Sherman, William	2			1		3			1	
Willet, George	1			1		1		1		
Wait, Joseph	3		1	1					1	
Totals	77	*	*	68	11	56	19	35	28	8
* missing on film										

* These two columns have erasures and cross outs, hard to determine exact numbers.

1820

#	Names of heads of families	Free white males						Free white females					Foreign not naturalized
		Under 10	10 under 16	Between 16 & 18	16 under 26	26 under 45	45 & up	Under 10	10 and under 16	16 and under 26	26 and under 45	Ages 45 & up	Foreign not naturalized
1	Sawyer, Abner				1	1		3			2		1
2	Bartlett, Enoch	2				2		1		1			1
3	Choate, Nehemiah	1				1				1			
4	Aldridge, Ezra	3				1				1			
5	Burges, Nathaniel	1				1		2			1		
6	Christopher, George				1			4			1		
7	Brooks, John	5	1				1	1	1		1		
8	Hamilton, Samuel				1	2		1		1	2		
9	Nash, Amaziah	1			1			1	1	1			
10	Crosby, Thomas					1							
11	Martin, Samuel				1								
12	Griggs, William	1	1			1		2		1	1		
13	Lane, Clement		3		1	1		4			1		
14	Lamb, James	1		1	2		1	3	2	2	1		
15	Morril, Ai				1								
16	Foss, Catharine		1	1	1	1		1			1		
17	Redding, Ebenezer	3				1		1	1				
18	Knight, Jonathan		1		1	1			1				1
19	Rice, Jonas						1		1				
20	Dyer, Jones, Jr	2	1			1	1	3	2	2	1		
21	Frost, Jeremiah	2	1			1		2			1		
22	Whitney, Joseph				5	2				1			1
23	Jellison, Theodore					1		1		1	1	1	
24	Bulford, Ira	1			5	4		3		1	1		5
25	Pike, Hannah	3	1			1		1		2	1		
26	Brewer, Sophia								1		2		
27	Hodgman, Thomas					1		3	1	1			2
28	McMillan, (Huey?)				1					1			2
29	Pike, Robert	2			2	1		2		2			1
30	Darling, Samuel	1	2	1	2	1		1		1	1		1
31	Cram, David						1						
32	Watson, Susan				1			2	2	3		1	
33	Pettygrove, Thomas	2	1	2	2		1	2	2		1		
34	O'Brien, Joseph		2			1		2	1	1	1		4
35	Keen, Jarius	4	2	1	2	1			1	1	1		1
36	Rhodes, Daniel	3				1		1	3		1	1	
37	Payne, Thomas	3				1		1			1		
38	Knight, Westbrook	2	1		1	1		1	1		1		1
39	Dyer, Samuel					1		2		1			

40	Dyer, James				1								
41	Foss, William	1	1				1	1				1	
42	Dyer, Jones				1		1					1	
43	Dyer, Stephen	2	3		3	1	1		1		1		1
44	Farnham, Rufus	1			3	2		1		1			1
45	Chase, George W.	1			1	1		1		1	1		
46	Knight, Henry	4					2		1	1	1		
47	Knight, Paul		1	1	4		1		7			1	
48	Hill, Thomas	4	1	2	3		1			1	1		
49	Bohanan, John	4	1	1	1		1	1	1		1		
50	Lane, Daniel				2			2		1		1	
51	Lane, William					1	1	4	2		1		
52	Coleman, Joseph				2		1						
53	Evans, Jonathan	3			1	1		1			1		
54	Scott, Samuel	2				1		3		1	1		
55	Grover, Stephen						1	1		1		1	
56	Lane, John	1			1	1		1					
57	Whitney, Stephen					1							
58	Elliot, Elizabeth		3	1	2			2				1	
59	Pettygrove, Francis		2		1		1	1	3	1			
60	Bassett, David	1		1	1	1	1	3	2	1	1		7
61	Collins, William	3	1		1	1		1	2		1		
62	Kimball, (blank)				1								
63	Gordon, (blank)				1								
64	Corbett, (blank)				1								

1830 Census of Calais, Washington Co. Maine — page 1

#	Names of heads of families	Free White Males										Free White Females										
		Under 5 years	Of 5 and under 10	Of 10 and under 15	Of 15 and under 20	Of 20 and under 30	Of 30 and under 40	Of 40 and under 50	Of 50 and under 60	Of 60 and under 70	Of 70 and under 80	Under 5 years	Of 5 and under 10	Of 10 and under 15	Of 15 and under 20	Of 20 and under 30	Of 30 and under 40	Of 40 and under 50	Of 50 and under 60	Of 60 and under 70	Of 70 and under 80	Of 80 and under 90
1	PIKE, Robert	1	1	2								1	1				1					
2	CHOATE, Nehemiah		2				1					1	1				1					
3	ELLIS, Levi	1				2						1				2						
4	KELLEY, Michael	2					1					1			1	1	1					
5	SHERMAN, William					1										1						
6	BURNS, Thomas					1								1			1					
7	BUTLER, John	2	1	1			1										1					
8	BASTON, Gideon	1					1					2	1			1						
9	EATON, Josiah	1		1			1							1	1		1					
10	TODD, Alexander					1						1				1						
11	KELSEY, Elias		1	1		2	3						2				2					
12	QUIMBY, Daniel	1				1	1					1				2						
13	HAMLIN, Isaac		1			6	1		1						1			1				
14	RINES, Moses						1															
15	HAMILTON, Lemuel			1		1	8		1				1					1				
16	NOYES, Levi	1		1		8	1						1		1	1						
17	BROOKS, John		1	1	2	3			1						1	1						
18	HAYWARD, Foster	1				1								1		1						
19	LIBBY, Delan	1				3										1						
20	AITSON, M.G.			1		2		1						1				1				
21	TOURTELLET, Rueben	1				1	1										1					
22	LOWELL, Reuben	2	1			1	1						1			1	1					
23	REDING, Ebenezer		1	2	1	9	2	1							3		1					
24	HOIT, John P.	1				3						1	2			1						
25	HOW, Isaac		2	1		3	1					1	1	1		1						

1830 Census of Calais, Washington Co. Maine — page 2

#	Name				12	1	1			2	1	
26	BOIES, James	2	2				1		2	1		
27	BOARDMAN, William	2	2	2						1	1	
28	SMITH, William B.	1	2	1	3	1	1		1		1	
29	SMITH, Steward			1	3	1		1			1	
30	EASTES, Amaziah	1			1			1				
31	EASTES, Joseph				2	2	1	1		1	1	
32	BRAGG, James	1				1		1		1		
33	COUSINS, Samuel			1	4	1			1	1		
34	KILBY, William	2			2	2		2		2		
35	LANE, Isaac		1		4	1		2	1	1		
36	ATTWOOD, William B.	1				1		1		1		
37	HUNNEWELL, Alec	1				1		1		1		
38	GATES, Salmon	1		1	4	2	1		1	2		1
39	TUTTLE, Ebenezer	1			2				1	1		
40	RUMRY, Robert E.	2			4					1	1	
41	MORDRIDGE, John				2	1				1		
42	EMERSON, Seth				2	1				1		
43	JOHNSON, Elisha			1	3	1				2		
44	GETCHELL, Josiah				1	2	1			1	1	
45	BLANCHARD, Silas		2		2	1			1	1		
46	SPRING, Ephraim	1			2	1	1	1		1	1	
47	STAPLES, Peter			1	1	1		2	1	2		
48	TURNER, Mrs.					1		1				
49	TOURTELLOT, Mrs.			1							1	
50	STARKEY, David	1		1			1		2	1	1	
51	ALBEE, Mary	1								1	1	
52	MOORE, James	1			1				1	1		
53	JONES, Calvin	1	2		5	1			1			
54	DURIN, Daniel			1	2	1		1	1	1		
55	DOW, Jonathan	1			5					1		
56	WARD, Ethan A.				4				1	1	1	
57	TODD, Abigail			1	8	1			2	1		1
58	SHIRLEY, Moses	2			1	1	1			1		
59	SHIRLEY, Davies				2			1				

1830 Census of Calais, Washington Co. Maine   page 3

60	TURNER, Seth																					
61	ESTABROOKS, David	2		2						2	1											
62	BRADBURY, Simeon		1	1		3	2			1				3	1	1	1					
63	HALL, John			3	3	6	4	1	1							2	1					
64	HICKS, Shepard	1				7				1				1			1					
65	LOVERING, Joseph				1	2								1			1					
66	NEVERS, Nathan					7	1									1						
67	MUNSON, Adanijah	1	1					1		1				2	1		1		1			
68	STICKNEY, John						1							1		1	1				1	
69	TAYLOR, Levi					6	1			1				1		2						
70	WALDRON, John D.			1	1	1		1		1				1	1	1			1	1		
71	COGGINS, Samuel						1	1							1	1			1			
72	KNIGHT, James	2				2	2							1			1					
73	HILL, Ansel					4								1	1	1						
74	WHITNEY, Paul			1	2		1	1						1	2		1		1			
75	GATES, Samuel	1				1									1		1					
76	HANSCOME, Jeremiah		2			1	1							2								
77	RAIRDON, Samuel															1	1					
78	JOHNSON, Samuel			1		3	1							1	1	1	1					
79	TRACEY, Christopher					4	1									1						
80	STARER, Amos	1				2											1					
81	CALLAGHAN, Samuel	2		2		1	1							1	1	1	1					
82	PRATT, Elias	1				1								1	1							
83	MOULTON, John	2				4	1								2	1	1					
84	OLMSTEAD, Ethel			1		1				1						2						
85	SMITH, Abraham	1	3			1	1							1	1		1					
86	VARREL, Peter	1												1			1					
87	GREENLAW, Solomon	2		1				1						1	1	2				1		
88	BATES, Mercy				3	1									1							1
89	WINSHEL, Reuben	2	3					1							2		1		1			
90	LUNT, Joseph	1	1	3				1		2					1							
91	TOWERS, John	2		1	2	10									2		1					
92	FROST, Nathaniel	1				3								1	1		1					
93	McKENNY, Daniel	1	2	1			1							2			1					

1830 Census of Calais, Washington Co. Maine

page 4

#	Name	Values (left to right)
94	SCOTT, Ralph	1 … 1
95	BATES, Adna	8 … 2 … 2
96	DESHON, John P.	2 … 1 … 1 … 1
97	TOWNSEND, Seth	2 … 1 … 1
98	KIMBALL, Jacob	1, 1 … 1 … 1 … 1
99	BARKER, Samuel F.	1 … 1, 1 … 1 … 1 … 1
100	DEMING, William	1 … 1 … 1 … 2
101	POND, Asa A.	1 … 1 … 1 … 2 … 1 … 1
102	PARKER, Jesse	1 … 1 … 2 … 1 … 1
103	HASTINGS, Mathew	1 … 1 … 1 … 1 … 1
104	DANFORD, Mrs.	… 1 … 1
105	ROBINSON, Albert	1 … 1 … 1 … 2 … 1
106	PENEL, Louis	2 … 1 … 1
107	ARNOLD, Benj	1 … 1 … 2 … 1 … 1 … 1 … 2 … 1
108	STEWART, James	3 … 1 … 1 … 1
109	BREWER Thomas	1 … 1 … 1 … 1 … 2 … 1 … 2 … 1
110	BASFORD, David [Basset?]	3 … 1 … 2 … 1
111	JONES, John Y.	7 … 2 … 2
112	TRACEY, Andrew	1 … 2 … 1 … 1 … 1 … 1
113	VANCE, James P.	2 … 1 … 3 … 1 … 1 … 2 … 2
114	WHITNEY, Joseph	1 … 5 … 2 … 2 … 2
115	CHENEY, Nancy	1 … 1 … 8 … 1 … 2 … 1
116	SMITH, Samuel	1 … 1
117	WADSWORTH, Abner	7 … 1 … 2 … 2 … 1 … 2
118	JENKINS, Samuel	2 … 8 … 1 … 1 … 1 … 1 … 1
119	LORD, Jacob	1 … 1 … 1 … 1
120	SHAW, Noel D.	3 … 1 … 1 … 1 … 1 … 1
121	WHEATON, David	1 … 1 … 1 … 1
122	KING, Benjamin	2 … 1 … 1 … 1 … 1
123	JONES, Theodore	1 … 2 … 2 … 1 … 2 … 1 … 1
124	GOODWIN, William	1 … 3 … 1 … 1 … 1
125	CARLTON, Elisa	… 2
126	BASFORD, Asher	1 … 1
127	WILLIAMS, James	1 … 2 … 1 … 1 … 1

1830 Census of Calais, Washington Co. Maine — page 5

#	Name	C1	C2	C3	C4	C5	C6	C7	C8	C9	C10	C11	C12	C13	C14	C15	C16	C17	C18
128	PEARL, Levi				4	2					1	1							
129	SPRING, William				2	1						1	1						
130	ROCKWOOD, Lorenzo	1			5					2	2	1							
131	BARNARD, Abel					1				1	1	1							
132	BARNARD, John					1			1		1	1							
133	SAWYER, Abner	1			2	1	1				2	1	1						
134	PIKE, Hannah		2		4	3						1	2	1					
135	JILLISON, Theodore		1		2	1					2		1				1		
136	STEARNS, Elijah		2	2	8		2				1	2	1						
137	TYLER, William H.	1			1							1							
138	LINCOLN, James M.	1		1	6	2	1		1					3					
139	ALEXANDER, Mathew	1				1		1				1							
140	DELESDERNIER, William		1			2						2							
141	DYER, Jones			3	2	1		1		3	2	2	1						
142	HUME, John	1		1	3	5			1		1								
143	SCOTT, Enos				1				1	1		2							
144	WHIPPLE, D. S. S.	2	1		1	1			1	1		3							
145	DOWNES, George	1			1	1			1	1	1	2							
146	CHURCH, Aaron	1				1			1		1								
147	RICE, Jonas			1	4	1	1				1	1	1						
148	KELLEY, Samuel	1		1	3	4				2		2	1						
149	LAWRENCE, William		1		2			1		3	1	1							
150	WILSON, Lewis					2				1		1	1			1			
151	DILLING, Edward [Dillon?]							1		1		1		1					
152	TRUNDY, William	1			1	1				2		1							
153	BROWN, Michael	1			1	1				1		1							
154	RANDAL, Benjamin	2	1			1	1			1		1							
155	KELLEY, Jeremiah	2				1	1			1		1	1						
156	WATSON, James	1				1				1		1	1						
157	DALY, James					1				1		1							
158	DARLING, Samuel							1			1		1		1				
159	PERKINS, John				2					2									
160	ROGERS, Aaron				2	1	1				2	2							
161	BUTLER, Edward	1			1					1		1		1					

1830 Census of Calais, Washington Co. Maine — page 6

#	Name	M<5	M5-10	M10-15	M15-20	M20-30	M30-40	M40-50	M50-60	M60-70	M70-80	M80-90	M90-100	M100+	F<5	F5-10	F10-15	F15-20	F20-30	F30-40	F40-50	F50-60	F60-70	F70-80	F80-90	F90-100	F100+
162	PIKE, William														3	1		1	1								
163	KEEN, Jarius, Jr.	1				1									2				1								
164	WHITE, Samuel						1												1								
165	HINCKLEY, Andrew	1			4				1							1		1	1								
166	WATSON, Eben	1					1										1		1							1	
167	PETTYGROVE, Thomas	1	1		1		2								1				2	1							
168	KEEN, Jarius	1	2	2	3	1			1	1						1				2		1					
169	PETTYGROVE, John	1			1										2				1								
170	ELLWOOD, Daniel	1	1		1														1	1							
171	RHOADS, Daniel			2		1			1							1	1		2								
172	TOPLIFF, Samuel				2								1			1			1		1						
173	PAINE, Thomas	1	3		1		1								1				1								
174	BOHANAN, Daniel 2nd	1	1	1		1									1				1	1							
175	BOHANAN, Daniel			1		1													2							1	
176	KNIGHT, Westbrook	1	2	2	1		1								1				1	1							
177	DYER, Samuel	1	1		1		1								1			2		1							
178	DYER, Nathan	1	1					1										1									
179	DYER, James	2					1								1												
180	FOX, Warren				2			1											1	1						1	
181	SMITH, William	1					1								2				1	1							
182	JACKSON, Nathaniel	1			1										1				1								
183	WATSON, John	1					1								1				1					1			
184	KNIGHT, Henry		1		1	2			1										1	1							
185	KNIGHT, Paul		1	1	3	1													1	1			1				
186	HILL, Thomas	1	2	2	2		1									1									1		
187	LANE, Daniel				1		1	1							2	2	2	1								1	
188	LANE, Joseph						1								1		1			1							
189	LANE, William		1				1									2	3	1				1					
190	FARNHAM, Rufus	1	3		1		1								2	1		1	1								
191	SCOTT, Samuel	1	1		1		1								1	1	2	1									
192	DYER, Stephen			1	2		1																	1	1		
193	LANE, Thomas	1				1									3		1		1								
194	MERRIFIELD, Isaiah	1			1										1	1			1								
195	GLIDDEN, Joseph W.			1	2				1									2	1		1						

1830 Census of Calais, Washington Co. Maine — page 7

#	Name																				
						6									3						
196	BOWLER, Joel																				
197	NASH, Amasiah	1	1	1		5	1				1	2	1	2		1					
198	BOHANAN, John			1					1				1					1			
199	GROVER, Stephen	1			1		1				1									1		
200	LANE, John	1	1	1	1			1			1	2		1	1	1					
201	SMITH, John	1				1									1						
202	ELLIOT, Elizabeth					4	1								2			1			
203	PETTYGROVE, Francis	1		1		1	2			1	2	1		1	3	1					
204	McPHERSON, E. M.			1		2	1				1	1				1					
205	NOBLE, Nicholas					1					2				2						
206	SMITH, George	1					1								1					1		
207	NOBLE, John					2	1	1			1	1			1						
208	KIDDER, Joseph E. [C]			1		2	1														
209	DAVIDSON, Daniel		1	1			1				1		1	1	1	1					
210	SPRAGUE, Jonathan	1										1	1		1				1		
211	LOMBARD, Luther		1	1	1	1	1			1											
212	BARBER, Elias	1	1	1			1				1	2		2	1	1					
213	LAMBERT, Edward	2	2	2		1					1	1		1	1						
214	FARNHAM, Silas	2				1					1				1						
215	LAMBERT, MATHIES	1	1	1	2	1	1				2		1	1		1					
216	COLLINS, William	1	1	2	1	1		1			1				1						
217	DRESSER, David	2	1	1	1		1				1				1						
218	McPHAIL, Duncan	2	1	1		1	1						1			1					
219	LANE, Melatiah	1				1															
220	LANE, Clement, Jr.	1				1								1							
221	LANE, Clement	1	1			2			1		1		2					1			
222	YOUNG, Jacob Y.	1		1		1								1							
223	GARDNER, Nathaniel						1							1	1						
224	NEVENS, John				1	1	1	1			1	1		1		1					
225	SINCLAIR, Zenah					8															
226	MILLER, Andrew					2									1						
	TOTALS	145	88	77	75	399	145	48	25	5	143	89	67	97	163	68	31	12	6	1	1

GRAND Total 1007 male / 679 female

1840 Census of Calais, Washington Co. Maine

page 1

#	Names of heads of families	Free White Males										Free White Females										
		Under 5 years	5 and under 10	10 and under 15	15 and under 20	20 and under 30	30 and under 40	40 and under 50	50 and under 60	60 and under 70	70 and under 80	Under 5 years	5 and under 10	10 and under 15	15 and under 20	20 and under 30	30 and under 40	40 and under 50	50 and under 60	60 and under 70	70 and under 80	80 and under 90
1	CHASE, George	1					1			1		1			1	1						
2	WHITTIER, Joseph		1	1	3			1					1		1	1		1				
3	BUTLER, Edward			1	1	1		1						1			1	1				
4	FOLSOM, Benjamin				2		2					1	1	1				1				
5	O'BRIEN, Joseph				2				1			1	1		1					1		
6	FURLONG, Samuel	1	1			1	1	1				2					1					
7	BURK, Francis			1										1					1			
8	LOWELL, Sarah		1	2		1							1	1	1			1				
9	HAMILTON, Horace					1									1							
10	TURTLE, Ebenezer	1				1		1					1				1					
11	LAFLIN, Salem	1		1	1	1	1					1			1	1						
12	PLUMMER, Josiah	1				1										2						
13	BARRET, Michael	1	1		2	1	1	1					1			1						
14	KELLEY, Michael			1	1		1						1	1				1				
15	ESTERBROOKS, David	1	2	1	2	1	1					1			1			1				
16	DOW, Jonathan	1	1	1			1	1					1		1		1					
17	BOARDMAN, William			1	2									1				1				
18	DUREN, William	1			4	1									2	1						
19	AVERY, Peter	1		1		1										2						
20	HASTINGS, Mathew		2	1			1						1	1								
21	STICKNEY, John					1		1						1	1		1				1	
22	TYLER, Lendal	1			2		1					1		1	1							
23	STICKNEY, Robert					1	1								1							
24	TODD, William	2			1							1	1		1	1						
25	HACKETT, Moses	3					1					1	1		1	1						

1840 Census of Calais, Washington Co. Maine — page 2

#	Name	C1	C2	C3	C4	C5	C6	C7	C8	C9	C10	C11	C12	C13	C14
26	GATES, Ephraim C.														
27	GILMORE, George W.	3		1					1	1	1				1
28	HAYCOCK, Jones C.	1			1				1	1	1				
29	BROOKS, Alfred	1	1	4	1				2		2	1	1		
30	KELSEY, Elias					1				1		1		1	
31	ALBEE, Mary												1		
32	STILLSON, Elizabeth				1									1	
33	ABBOTT, Levi	1		2	2		1		3	1		1	1		
34	COGGINS, Samuel	1		1		1	1		3	2	1	1	1		
35	McNEAR, Thomas				1	1						1			
36	TUTTLE, Moses				1	1				2					
37	STARKEY, David			1				1	1	1		1		1	
38	RAIRDON, Samuel H.	1				1			2		1		1		
39	BURGES, Zadock T.				1	1				2			1		
40	DOUGLAS, Calista					1									
41	HAYCOCK, Samuel W.	1		1	1				2	1		1			
42	CHOAT, Daniel			1							1		1		
43	BARSTOW, Gideon	1				1			2	2	2			1	
44	SMITH, Thomas	1			1				1	1		1			
45	HOLMES, John C.				1				1			1			
46	WALDRON, Sumner T.	1				1			1	1	1		1		
47	MANSON, Robie	2				1			1	1			1		
48	SMITH, Stewart	1	1		1	1			2		1		1		
49	ESTES, Joseph							1	1		1				
50	McLAUGHLIN, Joseph							1						2	1
51	MERSER, Alexie	1	2	1						1	1		1		1
52	WHITMORE, Daniel	2	1			1				1	1		1		
53	VERREL, James									1	1				
54	KELLEY, William	2	1		1	1			2	2		2		1	
55	PICKENS, Leonard		1		1	1				1	1		1		
56	KIMBALL, James G.	1			1				1		1				
57	GATES, Salmon			1	1		1			1	1	1	1	1	
58	WHITNEY, Paul			1	3		1					2	1	1	
59	FOSS, Edmund					1			2	1					

1840 Census of Calais, Washington Co. Maine — page 3

#	Name	C1	C2	C3	C4	C5	C6	C7	C8	C9	C10	C11	C12
60	HAMILTON, Rosannah			2	2	1				1			
61	BALKAM, James	1		1							1	1	
62	LINSCOTT, David			1			2				1		
63	TWITCHELL, Tinker				1		1				1		
64	HALL, John				1								1
65	JAMES, Sarah						1			1	1		
66	YORK, David	1	2	2	2					2			
67	PEABODY, Charles C.	1		1	1				1		1		
68	SPRING, Ephraim	1		2	1	1		1					1
69	GOODWIN, John H.	1		1			1				1		
70	GRAHAM, James	1	2		1		1	1		1	1		
71	BACON, Elizabeth	1	1				1	1			1		
72	WHITMORE, Joseph			1			2				1		
73	WHITNEY, Levi		2	2		1	1	1		1		1	
74	PINEO, Stephen			4		1					2		
75	BLANCHARD, Stiles	2	1	1	1		1	1			1		
76	HOW, Charles F.	1	1	1	1		1	1		1	1		
77	FAIRFIELD, James M.			1							1		
78	TOZIER, Asa E.	1		1			1	1			1		
79	HEWS, Thomas	1		1				1			1		
80	HUTCHINS, John			1			1				1		
81	HODSDON, Samuel		1	1	2	1	1				1	1	
82	EMERSON, Seth		1	2	1	1		1			1	1	
83	LANE, Isaac			1	1	1				1	1		1
84	BUTLER, John	1	1	1	1					1	1		
85	ATWOOD, William B.		1		1		1	2		1	1	1	
86	FULLER, Thomas J. D.	2			1			1		1	1		
87	CLARK, Amos				1		2	1					
88	BARTLETT, John	1			1		1	1		2		1	
89	HOGAN, Daniel	2			1		1	2				1	
90	SHIRLEY, Moses	1	1	2	1			2				1	
91	GOOLD, William A.		1	1		1	2				1		
92	PARAMETER, James			2		2				2			
93	SMITH, William	2	2	1	2			1		1	1		1

1840 Census of Calais, Washington Co. Maine — page 4

#	Name	C1	C2	C3	C4	C5	C6	C7	C8	C9	C10	C11	C12	C13	C14	C15	C16	C17
94	ELLSWORTH, Reuben	1									1	1	1	1				
95	LOVEJOY, John L.		1				1	3			1	1	1	1		1		
96	FARRIS, John	1						1			1	2		1				
97	DOW, Oliver	2	1					1			2	1		1				
98	McPHERSON, Henry		1						1									
99	BEEDY, James	1						1			1			1				
100	WADSWORTH, Abner					1	1	4		1	1	1	2		1			
101	LORD, Isaac								1		1	1	1	1				
102	HALL, John									1								
103	HALL, James G.		1					1	1		1			2				
104	GRIFFIN, Leonard		1					3	1			1	2		1			
105	MARTIN, James			1				2			1			1				
106	HALL, Denny			1					2			1	1	1				
107	MERRICK, David C.							1			1	2		1				
108	BAYLEY, Thomas							1				1	1					
109	DYKEMAN, James	1						3	1			1		1				
110	SCOTT, Ephraim	1		1		4		1			1	1		1				
111	BOHANAN, Ananiah							1			1	1	2		1			
112	LOVEJOY, Parker		2				1				1				2	1		
113	MOONEY, Newbegin H.	2							1			3			1			
114	NEVERS, Nathan	1	1					1			1	1			1			
115	MOORE, Albert	2							1		2							
116	REDDING, Rebecca, widow					1		4	1					1	1	1		
117	JOURDAN, Charles		1			1	1	2			1	1	1	1	1		1	
118	BROCKWAY, Charles	1				1		1			2	2			2			
119	MURPHY, Sawyer	1				1								1				
120	BROWN, Ebenezer			1	2			2		1	2	2	1		1			
121	SPOONER, Paul	1	1	1				1			1	1						
122	ELSEMORE, Moses									1		1	2		1			
123	DESHON, John P.	1		1							1			1				
124	BRADFORD, John	1									1							
125	THOMPSON, James					1		17					2	1	2	1		1
126	BAYLEY, Thomas H.	1											1	1				
127	POLLEYS, Elizabeth									1		1	2	1				

1840 Census of Calais, Washington Co. Maine   page 5

#	Name	Values (left → right across columns)
128	DOUGAN, William	2; 1, 1, 1
129	GOODWIN, William	1; 1; 1, 3, 2, 2
130	VEAZEY, Joshua	2, 1; 1; 1, 1, 1, 1
131	LEACH, Seth	1, 1; 1; 1, 1, 1
132	PIKE, Newell	1; 1; 1, 1, 1, 1
133	MEGUIRE, Thomas	1; 1, 3, 1
134	GILCHRIST, Robert	1; 1; 1, 2, 2, 2, 1
135	SMITH, Noah, Junr.	1, 3; 1, 2; 1, 2, 1
136	JENKINS, Samuel	2, 2; 1; 1, 1, 1, 1
137	COOPER, James S.	1; 1; 1, 1, 1, 1
138	COLLINS, Bradbury	1, 1; 1; 1, 1, 1
139	COPELAND, Charles	1, 1; 1; 1, 1, 2
140	TODD, Alexander	2; 1; 1, 1, 1, 1
141	VICKERY, Lebbeus	1; 1; 1, 1, 1, 1
142	ELLIS, William	1, 2; 2, 1; 1, 1, 1, 1
143	TOWNSEND, Manley B.	2; 1; 1, 1, 1
144	GRANGER, Joseph	2; 1; 1, 2, 2
145	McLELLAN, George	1; 1; 1, 1, 1, 1
146	FLINT, Benjamin M.	1; 1; 1, 2, 2, 1
147	FLINT, Isaac	1, 2; 1; 2, 3
148	TINKHAM, Spencer	3, 1; 1, 2; 1, 1
149	WHIDDEN, Randol	2, 1; 1; 2, 1, 1
150	REED, Albert	1, 1; 1; 1, 1
151	THOMAS, Israel	1, 1; 1; 1, 1, 1
152	OLMSTEAD, Ethert	1; 1
153	BONNEY, Horatio N.	1; 2, 2; 3, 2, 1, 1
154	BRIDGES, Otis L.	1; 2, 1; 2, 2, 1, 1
155	WILSON, Lewis	1; 1, 1; 2, 1, 2
156	GOODNOW, Calvin R.	1, 2; 2, 1; 1, 1, 2
157	NOBLE, James	1, 1; 1; 1; 1, 1, 1
158	BAKER, Benjamin	1, 1; 1, 2; 1, 1
159	ELLSWORTH, Mark	1, 1; 1; 1, 1, 1
160	ROBINSON, John	1; 1; 1, 1, 2
161	AMES, John	1; 1; 2, 1; 1, 1, 1

1840 Census of Calais, Washington Co. Maine

page 6

#	Name	1	2	3	4	5	6	7	8	9	10	11	12	13	14
162	JENKINS, Samuel	1		2	1				1		1	1	2		1
163	LAWRENCE, William		2	1				1	1	2	1	1			1
164	BOLLE, John					1		1	1						
165	WOODCOCK, Dexter H.	2	1	1		1			1			1	1	1	
166	GALLAGHER, Samuel				1	1				1		1	1		
167	NICHOLS, John	2				1			1			1		1	
168	SCOTT, William H.		1	1							1				
169	VERY, Horace	1			1				1		1		1	1	
170	PEARL, Levi	2	2		1		1						1	1	
171	SMITH, John	2	2	2			1		2	1	1		1	1	
172	HAMMOND, John	2	1			1			1	1	1		1		
173	ARCHESON, John					1			2			1	1	1	
174	HUTCHINS, Mary		1												1
175	MOORE, Hiram	1				1			1			1			
176	GIBSON, James					1									
177	BASSET, David	1	1			1							1	1	
178	WYMAN, Reuben		2			1				1		1			
179	FRENCH, Benjamin					1							1		
180	LORD, Jacob					1	1					1			1
181	STEARNS, Elijah			2			1								1
182	FOSTER, Gilbert	1	1		1				1	1				1	
183	BARKER, Sumner			1									1	1	
184	JOHNSON, Thomas Junr.			1	1								1		
185	TINKER, Ferdinand	1	1		1	1			1	2	1		2	2	
186	WHIPPLE, Shelsmith S.		1	1				1					2		
187	McHENRY, William							1			1	1			1
188	ARNOLD, Mary widow	1							1		1	1	1		1
189	BRADFORD, Perez	1		1		2		1	1	2	1	1		1	
190	EYE, Philip E.	1			1				2	1			1		
191	BARNARD, A. Webster	2		1	1								2		
192	SARGEANT, John	2	2	1	1	1		1		1		2		1	
193	DARLING, Samuel						1								
194	HUME, David					1			2				2		1
195	WILLIAMS, John				1								1		

1840 Census of Calais, Washington Co. Maine — page 7

#	Name	1	2	3	4	5	6	7	8	9	10	11	12	13	14	15	16	17	18	19	20
196	SMITH, George S.				1							2				1	1				
197	SMITH, Thomas D.	1										1					1				
198	BARNARD, G. S.				1	1								1		1	2				
199	HEYWOOD, Zimri B.	2	3		1	1										1	2	1			
200	DEMING, William		1				1					2	1				1				
201	POND, Asa A.			1	2		1							1		1				1	
202	TWEED, Harrison H.									1								1			
203	PRESCOTT, Joseph N.						1			1		1					3			1	
204	BLAKE, Sylvanus L.	2	1		1		1							1		1	1				
205	VICKERY, Matthias	1			2		1									1	1				
206	BURNHAM, Nicholas R.				1												1				
207	RODGERS, Thomas			1				1						2			1	1			
208	JOHNSON, Samuel	1									1			1			1				
209	KIMBALL, Jacob	1										3		1			1				
210	BROWN, Ira W.								1												
211	HAYMAN, Robert	1	1		1			1				1		2		1	1			1	
212	PORTER, Eber									1		1		1		1	1				
213	BATES, Charles	2		3													1				
214	TOWERS, John	1	2	1	2		1			1			2	2			*				
215	SPENCER, Robert T.			1	2							1	2				1				
216	JONES, Lemuel H.	1		1					1					1		1	1			1	
217	COCHRAN, John	1		1	1							1		1		1	1				
218	DIFFIN, Robert	1		2	2		1					1	2					1			
219	KINSMAN, Freeman E.	1			1							2	1				2				
220	SCOTT, Jesse	1	2		3			2					1					1			
221	CALAGHAN, Samuel	1		3	2						1		1			1				1	
222	CALAGHAN, William	2			1																
223	TOWERS, Jesse	1														1					
224	BELEMORE, James	2				1										1					
225	MURPHY, James	1	1		1		1			1		1	1	2			1			1	
226	COY, Solomon		1			2											1	1			
227	JONES, Arthur	1	1		1	2						2		1			2				
228	WILLIAM, Thomas D.								1											1	
229	BRADFORD, James			1	1									1							1

1840 Census of Calais, Washington Co. Maine — page 8

#	Name	C1	C2	C3	C4	C5	C6	C7	C8	C9	C10	C11	C12	C13	C14	C15	C16
230	SPENCER, David D.	1										2	3			1	1
231	BREWER, Thomas A.		1	1			1					2		1			1
232	AVERY, Edward D.				1					1				2			
233	LEE, Joseph A.							*	2					2			
234	HUME, John	1	1	2	1		3			1	1	1	1	1	1		
235	SAWYER, Thomas		1				1			1			2				
236	AMES, John			2				1				1		1	1		
237	TYLER, William H.		1	1			1			1	1	1		1			
238	HEAL, Seth	1	1				1			1			1				1
239	BARNARD, Dwight B.	1		1	1		1			1			2	2			
240	CURTIS, Jeremiah	1			3					1	2			1			
241	MORONG, Frederick	2			1					1					1		
242	CHANEY, Nancy		1		1							1	1	1			
243	GREEN, Elijah						1							2			
244	BARNARD, Edward A.			1	1					1			1		1		
245	SAWYER, Samuel D.			1	1		1			1		1		1	1		
246	ROBBINS, James	1					1			1							
247	RYDER, Lawrence	2	1				1				1				1		
248	WASHBURN, J. C.		1	2	1				1		1		2		1		
249	GARLAND, Dennis			2		1					1						
250	COOPER, Columbus	2	1	1	6		1				1		2	2			
251	WADE, Benjamin F.	3	1								1		1	1	2		
252	SWAN, Francis			3	2		1										
253	WEYMOUTH, Alexander H.	1	1				1			1	1	1	1	1		1	
254	DYER, Edward S.		1		1		1			2	1	1	1	1			
255	GLOVER, Phineas H.						1			1	1			1			
256	PORTER, Charles C. Jr.		1		1					1		1		2			
257	CHASE, Sarah	1	2								1		3	1	2	1	
258	THURLOW, Samuel G.	2	2		3								1	1			
259	WHITE, Luther C.					1				1			1		1		
260	CARMAN, Thomas H.		1		1		3			1	1		1		1		
261	BIXBY, Mary, widow												1	2	1		
262	GARDNER, Nathaniel		2		2					2	5	6		1			1
263	PIKE, Hannah, widow				3		1					1	2	1			

1840 Census of Calais, Washington Co. Maine

264	LOWELL, Levi L.	1			1	1												1			
265	SAWYER, Abner			1	1			1								1	1	1	2		
266	THOMAS, Israel L.	1	1			2										1	1				
267	GUEST, Edward W.	1	1	1	1			1								1			1		
268	HOYT, Justus		2	1				1	1							1			1		
269	RODGERS, Hugh		1	2	1			1					3				1				
270	BRADFORD, Joseph	1				1														1	
271	RENDELL, Benjamin	2	2	2	1			1							1		1	1			
272	HUTTON, Michael		2			1							2				1				
273	WATSON, Mrs. Sally			1																	
274	LAWRENCE, Dudley				1								1		1		1		1		
275	POOL, Witham					1	1											1			
276	LAWRENCE, William D.				2								1			1	1				
277	HUME, Josiah	1				1											1	3			
278	BRADBURY, Bion	1			2								1	1				1			
279	HAPGOOD, Charles	1			1	1															
280	KNIGHT, Joel			1	5			3										2		1	
281	EMERSON, Stephen							1	1												
282	HUSTON, George	1			2	3		2					1				1				
283	EYE, Leonard	1			1	1							1				1				
284	FLEWELLING, Enos	1						1							1			1			
285	SCOTT, Levi		2		2	2		1								1	1	1	1		
286	CALLAGHAN, James					5				1						1			1		
287	GOOLD, David	1														1					
288	LUDDY, John				1	2										1			1		
289	McCALLAM, Margaret			1	2							1									
290	McQUININE, William					1											1	2		1	1
291	McMAHAN, Patrick					1												1			
292	McGOWAN, Michael	2				1							1					1			
293	RYAN, Daniel	1			1											1					
294	LYNCH, Bartholomew	1			1								1			1		1		1	
295	OTIS, John		1		2	2		1					2			1		1			
296	KEEN, Jarius Junr.	1				1							2			1			1		
297	WHITE, Daniel	1	1		1			1					1							1	

page 9

1840 Census of Calais, Washington Co. Maine

page 10

298	TRACY, Andrew	1						1		1	1			
299	BATES, Stephen	1	2					1	1		1			
300	GODFREY, George	1						1			1			
301	EASTMAN, John	1	1		1			1	1	1				
302	PILSBURY, Albert	1	1		1						1			
303	DILLON, Margaret								1	1			1	
304	JOHNSON, Miss Edith									1				
305	DANFORTH, Mary, widow							1		1			1	
306	TRACY, Christopher		2	1		1				2		1		
307	JELLISON, Theodore		1			1				2				
308	BASFORD, Asher B.	1	1		1			1						
309	WHITE, Daniel S.	1	1			1		1	1		1			
310	McCATHERINE, Andrew	1	1			1	1	1	2	1	1		1	1
311	RHOADS, Daniel	1		1	3			2	1	2	1			
312	MILLIKIN, Samuel		1	2				1	2	1	1	1		
313	KELLEY, Samuel	1	1	1		1		1	1	1		1		
314	CHASE, Sarah		1	2	2									
315	FLINT, Isaac								1	3				
316	PORTER, Charles C.			2			1	1	1	2	1		1	
317	HOLMES, Job	1			1	1		3		2				
318	GALVIN, Thomas P.	1	1		1			1	1	3	1			1
319	PURRINGTON, Isaac	1	1		1			1	2	1	1	1		
320	WADSWORTH, George	1	1		1	1			2	3		1		
321	DOWNES, George	1	2		1	1			2	1				
322	ROBINSON, Thomas					1	1	1		1				
323	PIKE, William	1	1		1	1			2	2	1	1		
324	MORRISON, Alexander		1		1			1					1	
325	WEBBER, Luther				1			1	2	1				
326	MORRISON, Samuel		1		1	3		1	1	2		1		
327	McGAGHREN, Patrick	1			4	1		1	1	1				
328	ROBBINS, James		1		2		1	2	1					
329	BARKER, Samuel F.	1	1		1		1	1	1		1	1		
330	HARN??, William		1			1	1	1	2	1	1			
331	BEAN, Seth P.	1			1			1	1	2		1		

1840 Census of Calais, Washington Co. Maine

#	Name	C1	C2	C3	C4	C5	C6	C7	C8	C9	C10	C11	C12	C13	C14	C15	C16	C17	C18
332	SMITH, Uriah	1														1	1		1
333	FROST, George		1	1							1		1			1			
334	BUZZELL, Benjamin			1								3		2	1				
335	SPRAGUE, Charles		1	1							1	3	2			1			
336	MOORE, Albert	1			1							2			1				
337	LYON, Porter		2		1	1								1	1	1			
338	FROST, John		1			1										1			
339	DUNCAN, William	1	2	1		1							1		1	1			
340	DUNKHAM, William			1	1									1	1	1			
341	WILLIAMS, Jonathan	1		1		1					1	1			1				
342	JONES, John Y.	2				1						2	2	1					
343	KEEN, William	1	1	2								1				2			
344	HINKLEY, Andrew	1	1			1				1			1	2		1			
345	VANCE, James P.	2	1	1		1									1	1		1	
346	WATSON, Ebenezer						1						1	1	1				
347	MOULTON, John	1	1	1		1						1	1	1					
348	PETTYGROVE, Thomas			2	1			1							1	1			1
349	TRIMBLE, Richard	1	1		1							2				1			
350	LEAHAN, Dennis	1			1						1		1						
351	KEEN, Jarius			2	3				1				1						
352	WHITE, Samuel	1			2	2			1							2			
353	ELLWOOD, Mary widow		1	1	1							1	1	1	1				
354	McALLISTER, John				1							1	1						
355	PAINE, Thomas			3	1			1			1	1	1						
356	BOHANAN, Daniel Jr.	1		1	3							2	1	1	1				
357	BOHANAN, Daniel			1					1										1
358	BONAHAN, Shubiel	1			1						2	2			1				
359	KNIGHT, Levi				2									1		1			
360	DYER, Samuel	1	1	1				1			2	2	1	1	1				
361	DYER, James	1	2		1						1	1	1		1				
362	HAROLD, John	1		2								1		2					
363	KNIGHT, Sophia, widow			1	3	1				1		1	1	1		1		1	
364	HUNTLEY, Gideon	1			1					1		1							
365	KNIGHT, James		1	2	2		1								1				

page 11

1840 Census of Calais, Washington Co. Maine — page 12

#	Name	C1	C2	C3	C4	C5	C6	C7	C8	C9	C10	C11	C12	C13	C14	C15	C16	C17	C18	C19
366	KNIGHT, Jerome																			
367	KNIGHT, Ellis	2	2							2	2	1			2	1				
368	HILL, Thomas			1	3		1	1				1	1	1	1					1
369	GARDNER, John	2	2		1	1				1										
370	MUNROE, George A.	2			1	1							1			1				
371	LANE, Mary, widow		1		1								2							
372	SCOTT, Atkins	1	1		1					1			1							
373	SCOTT, Samuel	1	2	1			1				1	1				1				
374	NASH, Amaziah	2	2	2	3		1				2	1	2	2	1	1				
375	GEPHERD, George	1	1			1					2		2	1						
376	NASH, Joshua Y.		1	2			1			1	1	2		1						
377	BOHANAN, John							1												
378	WATSON, John	1	2	1		1						1				1				
379	DYER, David W.				1	1						1	1							
380	HILL, Abner	1	1			1							1							
381	BONNEY, Horatio N.									1	2	3	1		1					
382	NEVENS, Jonathan		2		3	1				1		1	1				1			
383	JAMES, Benjamin		1	1				1		2	1									
384	LAMB, Samuel	2	1	1	1	1						1	1							
385	GLIDDEN, John		1		1					2										
386	GLIDDEN, Joseph	2		1		1				1			1							
387	HILL, Thomas S.	1		1		1				2	1	1	1		1					
388	ROWE, Charles			1		1				1			1							
389	GLIDDEN, Joseph								1	1										
390	LANE, Thomas		2	1	1		1			1	1	3	1			1				
391	SMITH, George	2	2				1			1	1				1					
392	KILBURN, John								1											
393	BELYTHER, Benjamin		1	1	3	1				2	1	1	1							
394	ELLIOT, Ethan A.					1	1			1	1	1			1					
395	ELLIOT, Elizabeth, widow					1	1						2	1	1				1	
396	ELLIOT, Samuel	2		1		1			1				1	1	1					
397	PETTYGROVE, Francis	1	1								2	2	1		1	1				
398	LANE, Joseph	1	2			1	1				1	1	1		1					
399	MASON, Hugh		1			1		1		1	1	1	1		1					

1840 Census of Calais, Washington Co. Maine

#	Name	Males (by age group)		Females (by age group)
400	CORSON, Jesse	1, 1		1, 1, 1
401	PETTYGROVE, John	2, 1, 1		2, 1, 1, 1
402	MILLER, John	1, 1		1
403	NOBLE, Nicholas	1, 2, 1		1, 2, 1
404	NOBLE, John	1, 1, 1, 1		1, 1, 1
405	NOBLE, Isaac	1		1, 1
406	McPHERSON, Europe	1		1, 1, 1
407	CHICK, Ebenezer	1, 1		2, 1, 1, 1
408	LEEMAN, John E.	1, 2, 1		1, 1, 1
409	CAMPBELL, Archibald	1, 1, 1		1, 1, 1
410	LOCKHEAD, John	1, 2, 1, 1		1, 1, 1
411	COLEMAN, Thomas	1, 2		1, 1
412	GARDNER, William	1, 2, 2, 1		1, 1, 1
413	LAMBERT, Luther	1, 1		1
414	BARBER, Elias	1, 1, 2, 1, 1		1, 1, 1, 1
415	FORD, William H.	1, 2, 1, 1		1, 1
416	BROWN, James	2, 1, 1		1, 1, 1
417	CARLOW, James	1, 1, 1, 1		1, 2, 1
418	CARLOW, Margaret	1		1
419	GARDNER, Samuel	1, 1, 1, 1		1, 1, 2
420	MINGO, George	1, 3, 1, 1		1, 1
421	McPHAIL, Duncan	1, 2, 2, 1, 1		1, 1
422	COOK, James	1, 1, 2, 1, 1		1, 2, 1, 1
423	COOK, James W.	1, 1, 1, 1		1, 1, 1
424	COOK, John	1, 1, 1, 1		1, 1
425	CARLOW, Richard	1, 1, 1, 1		1, 2, 1, 1
426	NODDIN, Michael	1, 2, 1, 1		1, 1
427	LANE, Silas	1		1, 1
428	NODDIN, Andrew	1, 1, 1		1, 2, 1, 1, 1
429	CHASE, Alexis	1, 1, 1		1, 2, 1
430	MINGO, David	2, 1, 1, 1		1
431	YOUNG, Jacob T.	1, 1, 1, 1		1, 1, 2
432	CARLOW, Gideon C.	1, 1		1, 1
433	LANE, Meltiah	1, 2, 1		1, 1

1840 Census of Calais, Washington Co. Maine   page 14

434	KELLEY, Levi	1	1			1											1			
435	LANE, Clement	3		2	1	1									3	1	1			
436	CAULKINS, William	1	1		3						1						1			
437	SHATTOCK, Benjamin	2	1		1						1					1			1	
438	DRESSER, David		1	2	1			1			1				1	1			1	
439	WADSWORTH, Calvin		1	1					1									1		
440	SHERMAN, Harris							1							1		1			

BURIED NAME INDEX

This index covers the genealogy section only. The census portion of the book was not indexed.

----, Agnes 52 Alice 65 Alvina 121 Amelia Grace 44 Amy 141 Ann 10 72 106 134 Anna 130 Bathiah 131 Bathsheba R 68 Caroline M 32 Catherine 11 85 105 109 128 Charlotte 34 Clarissa 107 Cynthia 133 Dorcas 141 Eliza 24 145 Eliza Ann 30 62 Eliza F 55 Eliza M G 136 Elizabeth 35 45 Elizabeth L 59 Elizabeth S 56 Ella F 37 Ellen 24 47 56 140 184 Emma C 70 Emma S 158 Euphemia 115 138 Evelina C 29 Fannie 158 Frances 82 130 158 Georgia 152 Hannah 5 111 133 179 Harriet 49 186 Hopestill 143 Huldah 168 Isabel 73 Isabella 6 Jane 14 19 167 Jennie 159 Joanna 117 Kate 65 85 Lucretia 22 Lydia 26 Margaret 4 11 39 54 137 Margaret A 104 Margaret C 149 Maria 65 76 Maria Louisa 181 Martha 131 138 175 Martha A 122 Mary 3 23 43-44 54 65 73 109 136 Mary A 50 Mary Ann 35 107 Mary E 152 167 Mary L 81 Mary S 140 Melina A 176 Nancy 60 170 183 Orelia 91 Rebecca 15 125 Ruxby 136 Sarah 31 53 Sarah J 24 Sophia 16 Sophornia 134 Susan 106 Temperance 169 Violetta 182

ABBOTT, Jacob 74 Maletia 37 Mary Jane 74 Sarah A 74
ABELL, Aristine H 100
ADAMS, Martha Burnham 8 S W 8
AHEARN, Austis 35 Katherine 35 Thomas 35
ALBEE, Ada Maria 138 Almira 8 Ann Marple 97 153 Arthur D 138 Hannah 97 James Dellaway 97 Sarah 138 William 97
ALDRICH, Ann Mariah 143 Cynthia 57 Ezra 143 Moses 57
ALLEN, F B 130 Fannie 153 172 Lois 50 Lydia 177 N Glover 176 Ruth 115
ALLEY, Jerome 146 Rev 133
ALLINE, Jane 56 121
AMES, Ann 103 John 66 Susan Louise 66
ANDERSON, A W C 148 159 Alexander F 15 Cassie 15 Catherine E 15 Charles Beauchamp 28 Isabella 166 John 166 Maggie 147 Maria Lowell 28
ANDREWS, Almira 8 Anna C 129 Anna M 8 Isreal J 129 John D 8 Lydia 47
APT, Frederick Bradbury 147 Jessie Maud 146
ARLEY, Lucy 73
ARMSTRONG, Eliza 147 James John 82 Salome A 82
ARNOLD, Benjamin 62 Mary 62 Sarah Elizabeth 62
ASH, John 47 Robert Jr 186 Sophia 47
ASPENWALL, Joseph C 174
ATKINS, Abigail 75 Mary 90
ATWOOD, Jane 37
AVERY, Nancy 20 Peter 20
BABB, Benjamin 151 Benjamin Jr 151 Lydia 151 Perley 151
BABSON, Sarah 153
BACON, Abbie L 164 Betsey 141 Elizabeth 141
BAILEY, Abigail 142-143 Caroline Pike 42 Charlotte 138 Charlotte A 138 Elizabeth 83 Josiah 138 Lydia 144 Lyman C 42 Martha 143 Sarah 17
BAKER, Anne 37 Emma 26 Harrison 47 Henrietta 45 Samuel F 37 Sophronia Abigail 47
BALCH, Emily 3 Horatio Gates 3 Rhoda 3

BALK, A 133 148
BANGS, 170 Joshua 41 Laurina 170 Lorana 170 Lydia 41 Mary 41
BARBER, Mary Ann 170-171 Mercy 163-164 William 163-164
BARBOUR, Catherine 119 Eliza 164
BARCLAY, Andrew 147 Carolyn B 147 Eliza 147 Frank H 147 Hannah 91
BARKER, Catherine 119
BARNARD, Edward Augustus 126 Frances L 38 George Sullivan 38 Harriet Larkin 126 Mary Ann 126 Sarah Elizabeth 38
BARNES, Daniel Webster 93 Ethelbert 93 Julia 65 Lucinda Brackett 93 Zilphia 93
BARR, Irena J 121
BARRETT, Rev Mr 12 162
BARRITT, Nancy 85
BARROWS, Allen 26 149 177
BARRY, Catharine 113
BARTLETT, Annie B Jamison 106 Hananh 101
BARTON, Emeline 3
BASSETT, Harriet 186 Maria 135 Thomas 21
BASSFORD, Anna Eliza 101 Asher 101 Asher Benjamin Jr 101 Lucy Jane 101
BATES, Ambrose 126 Edwin 138 Elizabeth H 126 Henry 14 Mary 14 Mary Ann 15 Mercy 126
BEAL, Bathula 92 Joseph 93 Seth 105
BEALE, Merritt C 120
BEAN, Annie Y 27 Emma Jane 26 George William 27 Stephen 27
BECKFORD, Henry 15 Mary 15 Mary Ann 15
BECKWITH, Eunice E 163
BEEDY, Sarah Ann 6
BELL, Jane M 153 Philip Y 153 Sarah 10
BELMORE, Annie 80 James 3 81 James M 80 Mary Helen 66 80
BENNETT, Charles W 51 Lillian K 105 Rev Mr 169
BENTON, Albert E 167 Sarah J 167
BERNARD, Herbert 51
BERRY, Georgianna 183 Sarah 74 Stephen B 183 Stephen O 15
BIRCHALL, Emma A 35 Minnie 35
BIXBY, Maria 13
BLACK, Jane 114 Sarah 69
BLACKWELL, Hannah 179
BLACKWOOD, Corilla N 98
BLAISDELL, Matilda J 69
BLAKE, Cordelia 39 George 181 Hannah 118 Harriet Emeline 181 Joseph 118 Lydia 117-118
BLANEY, Anna Jane 32 Annie Jane 32 James Edgar 32 Josephine 32 William H 32
BLISH, Sarah 153 158
BLUNT, Clarissa 57
BOARDMAN, Caroline M 64 Esther W 17 William 17
BOHANAN, Frances 53

BOHANNAN, Daniel 156 Martha 156 Mary Ann 156 Sheppard 156
BOICE, Fanny 156 Nancy R 156
BOIES, Fanny 156 Nancy R 156
BOIS, Mary Ann 124
BOVARD, Annie 112 Georgianna H 113 Joseph 113 William 113
BOWEN, Susan 7
BOWLES, Mary K 123 S J 123
BOYD, Almira 79 Edward 79 Eliza 154 George 183 George Jr 183-184 Hannah Miller 129 James 39 Jane 154 John 154 Sarah A 184
BOYDEN, Hannah 4 63 Hannah H 160 Jacob 160 Jane 160 Joseph A 160 Philip 160 Stephen 160 Stephen Arnold 160
BRACKETT, Abigail 120 161 169 Bathula 92 Caroline 120 Emma Adelaide 169 George M C 169 Harriet 90 James 120 James C 134 James Jr 92 John 5 41 90 108 Luther 161 169 Lydia 34 92 Mary Ann 24 41 108 Nancy 5 41 90 108 Permelia 134
BRACY, Bethiah 136
BRADBURY, Annie Eliza 27 Bion 27 85 94 Elizabeth 175 Emily 157 Jeremiah 27 157 Mary Langdon 27 157 Thomas 175
BRADFORD, Amanada 89 Benjamin 113 Deborah 15 71 Eliza 113 Mary S 118 Patrice 158 Perez 118 Perez Jr 71 Salome 71
BRADLEY, Christopher C 93 Cornelia S 93 Elizabeth P 140 Henry E 55 Margaret 93
BRAGG, Roxanna 28
BRALEY, Olive 28
BREEN, Barbary 122 James 122 Mary 134
BRENNAN, Mary 112
BREWER, John 140
BRIDGES, Anna Livingstone 126 Bathsheba 151 Isabella M 160 John 126 Mary 59 Sarah Jane 126 Thomas 151
BRIGGS, Harriet 7
BRITON, Mary Emma 175
BROCKWAY, Adeline Boardman 18 James W 18
BROOKS, 168 Alfred 108 Hannah C 78 Harriet 108 Howard 108 Howard Albertus 108 Lucy B 78 Mary 108 Mary B 84 William 174
BROWKER, Lucy L 110
BROWN, Abigail 119 Alexander 125 Ann 12 Annie Trafton 125 David 53 Fanny Stuart 53 Frances 53 Lucy A 33 Margaret 52 143 Mary C 16 Mary J 179 Mills 169 Nathaniel 171 Rebecca 169 Sarah 125 162 W L 29 Willard 53
BROWNELL, John V 50
BROWNING, Charles L 104
BRUNEL, Martha 70
BRUNELL, Elizabeth W 21
BRUNYERBROECK, Alphonce 109 Harriet Furbush 109
BRYNES, Elizabeth 83 Frances Rebekah 83 William Bradshaw 83 William M 83
BUCHANAN, President 58
BUCK, Lydia Cushing 62
BUCKSTAFF, John 138 John Sr 103 Lucy 138 Ruth Julia 138
BUGBEE, Caroline 88 Caroline A 88
BULLOCK, Charles 149 Eleanor 149 Ellen 149 Mary Ellen 149
BULMER, Margaret 171
BURBANK, Ruth 174
BURDICK, 114 Amelia 120 Elizabeth A 120 Helen Augusta 114 William 120
BURGESS, I J 18 30 70 138 164 J J 45 Rebecca 182

BURGOYNE, 95
BURK, Hannah 94
BURNHAM, John B 143 Louisa Emma 143 Lydia 93 125
BURNS, Bridget 30 Elizabeth 30 George B 111 Hugh 30 Liberty 30 Margaret 128 Sarah A 9
BURRAGE, Abigail 95
BURRELL, Esther 28 Esther Robinson 28 Samuel 28
BURRILL, Mary E 54
BURT, Rev 60
BUTLER, Catherine 77 John 82 Nathaniel 150
BYRON, Catherine Hall 59 Joseph Jr 60 Kate 59
CAHILL, Margaret 133
CALDERWOOD, Edith 102 Mary 102 Samuel 102
CALDWALLDER, Addie 76 John 76
CALDWELL, Abigail 142-143 Charity 143 Harriet 142 J 55 103 Margaret E 147 William 142-143
CALDWOOD, J 13
CALIFF, Mary Ann 45
CALLAGHAN, Lydia Elthea 104 Phebe Abigail 47 Samuel Jr 47
CALLERY, Elizabeth 170
CALLIGAN, Hollis 26 Mary M 26 Rachel 26
CAMERON, Janet 100 Mary 35
CAMPBELL, James 25 Mary 56 Mary L 147 Rachel 16 Sarah Jane 25 Susanna 66 Thomas 66 William H 16
CAMPHOR, Mary Ann 36 180
CANAVAN, Margaret 35
CAPRON, 172 Susan Drew 172
CAREW, Barbara 166 John 166 Lavinia B 166
CAREY, Hattie N 9 Michael 73
CARLE, Abigail 90 Almira 20 90 101 175 Elmira 20 90 101 175 Peter 90
CARLTON, Ann S 116
CARMICHEL, Almeida 16 Daniel 16
CARMODY, Catherine 66 Margaret 111
CARNEY, Mary A 176
CARPENTER, Alfred 23 Benjamin 23 Joanna 23 Joseph 23 Mary 23 108
CARR, 101 Helen Elizabeth 101 Sarah Jane 29
CARRUTHERS, William 8-10 15 36-37 60 63 180
CARVER, Charlotte 96 Fanny 83 Joseph Henry 73 Lucy 73 Mary 8 Priscilla 83 Priscilla F 73 Rufus 83
CARY, Maggie J 13 Michael 73 Theodore 13
CASEY, Nellie 54
CASS, Alice 90
CASWELL, Amos 79 Charlotte E 79
CATES, Cordelia 152
CAVERT, James 32 Mary 32 Susanna 32
CHAMBERLAIN, Anna 152
CHAMBERS, Rebecca 165
CHANDLER, A G 69 184 Anson Gonzalo 122 Catherine 164 Elizabeth Ann 122
CHAPIN, George E 14
CHARLTON, Rebecca 67
CHASE, 7 Ann 48 Charlotte 124 Clara Ann 144 Daniel Kimball 100 George M 27 James M 124 Janet 100 Lucy 47 Minerva 100 Sophia Ann 124
CHENEY, Amasa 28 48 161 Eliza Jane 48 Mary Ann 150 Mary Ann Nichols 28 Nancy Campbell 28 48 161 William 48
CHILD, Hannah 42 157 James 157
CHRISTIE, Charles J 47 James C 47 Jane M 47 John Mcdiarmid 47 Margaret J 47 Mary 47 Mary C 47 Mr 47 Nancy Cassa 179

CHRISTOPER, Mary 131
CHRISTOPHER, Caroline 131 Elizabeth 27 122 Elizabeth Ann 81 George 81 122 Lydai 122 Lydia 131
CHURCH, Asa 61 Carlos D 67 Eleanor 67 Hester A 116 Lucy 61 89 122 175 Rachel 61 Rev Mr 56
CLAPP, Abbie W 67 Almeda M 160
CLARK, Alice Dodge 150 Amos 48 150 161 Caroline N 39 Elizabeth T 111 Eunice 145 Josephine 39 Mary 48 145 Mary Ann 150 161 Rev Mr 164 Sally 74 Sarah 74 Temperance 74 144 150 William 74 145
CLARKE, Joanna 122
CLAXTON, Lydia 96
CLEAVES, Adelaide 43 Emily C 46 James 46
CLENDENING, Andrew 159 Eliza 159 Mary 159
CLENDINON, James 125
CLINCH, Bessie 92 Betsey 92 Conrad 92 Letitia 177 Peter 177 Sarah 177 Sarah Marie 129
COCHRAN, Hannah 122 Joseph W 6 Mary Hannah 25 Sarah Adaline 6 William 25
CODMAN, Annie 157 Randolph A L 157
COFFIN, Betsey 140 Mary Ann 98 Samuel H 98
COFFRIN, Eliza 39
COFFRON, John 165
COGGINS, Clarinda 33 Rebecca 33 Samuel 33
COLBERT, James 32 Mary 32 Susanna 32
COLBY, Dr 39 Mehitable 168
COLE, Benjamin 133 Cynthia 133 Fanny Alice 184 George 178 George E 178 Jerusha 89 Laura Smith 178 Lucy 133 Olivia 178 Patience 175 Phoebe 95 William H 184
COLINS, Hiram P 7
COLLEY, Ruth K 50
COLLINS, 148 Anne Young 28 Bradbury 28 Charity G 28 Charles B 28 Etta M 148 Harriet 7 Joseph E 7 Mercy 50
COLSON, Anna C 32 Annie 15 80 Josiah 32 Mary 32
COLWELL, Jane 172
CONDELL, John 21 Mary 21
CONLY, Lydia Frances 48
CONNELLY, Catherine 158
CONNOR, Edwin Popejon 119 Mary Asenath 119 Mary J 41
CONNORS, Hugh 148 Jane 148 Nancy 148 Patrick 148 Sarah A 148
CONREY, John 166 Julia A 166 Sarah 166
CONTON, Rev Father 35
CONY, Ellen Vesta 75 Joseph S 75 Nellie 75
COOK, Edith 178 Eliza 51-52 Elizabeth A 51 Ella F 37 George L 37 George Warren 52 James Warren 51-52 Mary E 52
COOKSON, Margaret 145
COOPER, Columbus 78 Deliverance 78 Hannah 22 71 Rebecca S 78 William 78
COPELAND, Henry C 86 Henry Clay 100 Julia E 86 Julia Elvira 86 100 Mary Townsend 86 Sarah 100 Thomas Jefferson 86 100
COPP, Timothy 182
CORDWELL, Eunice 169 Tryphosa 169 William 169
COREY, Mary 18
CORLISS, Charles 170 Millie Marie 170 Phebe 170
CORMIER, 33 Harriet Melinda 33
CORNING, Mary R 149
CORSON, Nancy 168
CORWELL, Emma G 125
COTHRAN, Mary 42 86 99
COTTELL, Hampden C 33
COURTNEY, Maggie E 54

COVERT, Susanna 32
COX, Anna 174 Catherine 101 Charles 74 Emerline 148 Evelyn 148 Sarah Priscilla 74
COY, Jane 93 Sarah Jane 93 Solomon 93
COYENS, W J 76
COYLE, Catherine 117 Henry 117 Kate 117 Katherine 117
CRAFTS, Emeline M 88 Lizzie 84
CRAIG, Mary Ellen 34 Mary Jane 137 Nancy A 92 Rebecca Louise 52
CRANGLE, 86 James 23 John 112 Mary Caroline 23
CRAWFORD, William C 163
CREAMER, Jennie 37 Mary E 172 Regina 37
CREGAN, 184 Mary Helen 184
CRESSEY, Amelia B 108 Joseph R 108 Mary Etta 108
CROCKER, Clementina E 162 Sally 74 Sarah 74
CROCKETT, Elizabeth 182
CROSBY, Adelaide E 60 Charles William 60 Sarah Stone 60
CROSS, Joseph 176 Sarah Dean 176
CROWELL, Garrison 125 Nancy W 125
CROWLEY, Cornelius 62 Henora Agnes 62 Nancy 62 Nora Agnes 62
CULVER, Esther 36 180
CUMMINGS, Priscilla 83
CUNNINGHAM, F O 15 Rachel 126 Samuel 126 Susan 126
CURRAN, George A 43
CURRY, Charles H 146
CURTIS, Susan 126
CUSHING, Hannah 157 Ruth 98
CUTTER, Ann Graffam 69 Christina 69 Simon 69
DAILEY, Ansel 131 Laura 131 Mary 131
DAMON, Isaiah 59 Joshua C 108 Mary 59 Minerva Abigail 59 Moses L 59 Ruth Augusta 108
DANBURY, Bathsheba 109 Clarissa 109 John 109
DANFORD, Betsey 86 Betsey L 42 Emeline 86 Emeline Mowbray 99 Mary 42 86 99 Paul 42 86 99
DAVENPORT, William 155
DAVIDSON, Amy Ellen 185 Annie Dorcas 105 Daniel 180 Frances Lavinia 117 George 105 180 186 Maria 180 Marie 180 Mary Ann 180 Orrin 186 Sally 186 Sarah 105 186
DAVIS, A A 108 Agnes 27 Deborah 22 71 Deborah Ellen 23 Florence 27 Hirma T 89 Mary 21 Mercy E 89 Susanna 28 William 27
DEARBORN, Frederick 94 Hannah 94
DEFOREST, Elizabeth 104
DELESDERNIER, Anna Maria 58 Harriet 126
DELUE, Charlotte Downes 162 Elizabeth 154 169 Jacob 169 Tobias 162
DEMICK, John 21 Phebe Sawyer 21
DEMING, Anne D 7 Charles 7 Charles Leonard 10 Mary Elizabeth 173 Mehitable 7 Rebecca 39 Sarah Elizabeth 10 Sarah M 10 173 William 7 10 173 William Jr 173
DENHAM, 124
DENSMORE, Cordelia 6
DESBOW, Rev 162
DEWHURST, Frederick 131
DEWOLF, Nancy 38-39
DEWOLFE, Adelaide Mary 171 Benjamin R 171 Mary Louisa 75
DEXTER, Esther 28 H V 6 21 50 92 95 115 132-134 146 148-149 163-165 169 171 179-180 184 Henry Vaughan 18 Mary Ednah 18 R V 171 Rev 37
DEYOUNG, George A 180 Lucy Ora 180
DICKERMAN, Elvira Adaline 50 Lois 50 Wyatt 50 Wyatt Jr 50

DICKEY, Caroline 19 Susan Y 163 Thomas 163
DILLON, Edward 20 John 114 Margaret 20 Sarah A 114 Sarah Ann 19
DINGLEY, Emma Frances 72
DINSMORE, Amy 6 Lovinia A 37 Samuel 6 Sarah G 87
DITMARS, Catherine 82
DIX, Sarah Jane Maria 51
DOAK, Margaret 46 63 177
DOBSON, Sarah 30
DODGE, Delilah 66
DOE, Mary 115 Simon 115
DOHERTY, Margaret Jane 94 Robert 94
DOKE, Margaret 46 63 177
DOLE, Irene 126 Sarah 155
DOLITTLE, Jennie Elizabeth 58
DONOHUE, Mary 106
DONWORTH, Patrick E 63
DOOR, Julia A 91
DORWIN, 144 Julia Elmy 144
DOUGHTY, Benjamin 103 David 103 Lucy H 103 Martha 103
DOW, Abigail 58 Catherine 66 Jeremiah 58 Jonathan 58 Mary Ann 20 108 Mary Helen 66 Oliver 20 108 Orion S 66 Rebeckah 58
DOWD, Eva 40 Lewis 40
DOWNES, Betsey 86 Clarissa 123 George 39 63 123 132 George Edward 124 Lucinda C 184 Lydia 162 Martha Prescott 124 Shubiel 162 Temperance 162
DOWNS, Jude 115 Judith 114-115
DOYLE, Joseph 57
DRUMMOND, Rev 47
DUDLEY, Thomas 57
DUKE, Margaret 46
DUNCAN, Letitia 58 Martha J 138 Robert 138
DUNCKLEE, Phebe 181
DUNN, Betsey 16 67 90-91
DURELL, George 53 George W 65
DUREN, Mary Califf 45 William 45 66
DURGAN, Ella Josephine 12 Frank 12
DURGIN, Charlotte C 159 Elizabeth 159 Walter 159
DURRELL, G W 142 George W 179
DUTCH, Abigail Todd 181 John 102 John Califf 44 87 155 161 181 Margaret 44 87 102 155 161 181 Margaret Elizabeth 102 Maria Haycock 87 Mary Califf 44 Peggy 44 87 155 161 181 Susan Eliza 155
DUTTON, Rhoda 3
DYCKMAN, Lina 28
DYER, Abigal 134 Betty 134 Christina 69 Edward S 19 George Washington 86 Hannah 36 Helen Elizabeth 142 Henry 134 James 143 James Sr 143 Jones Jr 86 126 134 142 Jones Sr 36 Kate 86 Lydia 86 126 134 142 Margaret 40 63 177 Maria 134 Maria Nancy 177 Martha 143 Mary 36 Mary Elizabeth Shaw 86 Mary Jane 63 78 Samuel 63 143 177 Sophia B 9 126
DYKE, Rev 35
EARL, Charlotte 124
EASTMAN, Hannah 25
EATON, Albion H 178 Anna 39 Anna Louisa 18 Annie Mccullough 178 Betsey 13 Charles H 178 Clement 38-39 Clement Belcher 38 Dan 171 David 39 171 Elisha 39 171 Eliziabeth M 13 H F 18 Henry Franklin 18 Herbert 86 Htomas 171 James 39 171 John 39 171 Jonas 18 Jonathan 39 171 Josiah 40 108 115 143 171 Margaret 171 Mary 18

EATON (cont.)
   Mary Ann 171 Nancy 38-39 Rebecca 39 Rebecca Leonard 38 Rev 14 46 Sarah 178 Thomas 39 William 38-39
EDDY, E B 146 149 164 177 E R 130
EDERSON, Clara Augusta 147 William H 147
EDES, Esther 37
EDGE, Maria 120 Phillip E 120
EDGERLEY, Ida May 120
EDGETT, Joseph 150
EDWARDS, Aaron 28 Elisha 28 Jane 68 Lydia 28 Lydia A 28 Mary Jane 68 Susanna 28
ELDRIDGE, G N 70 George 184
ELLICOTT, Elizabeth 123 Mary 123 Thomas 123
ELLIOT, Bessie Louise 32 Frank 32 Katherine 32 Margaret Ann 149
ELLIS, Deborah 140
ELLSMORE, Bethiah L 85 Lucy 64 85 Lucy Ann 64 Martha 85 Moses 64 85 Phebe Abigail 25
ELLSWORTH, Elizabeth 68 Lydia 103 Mark 173 Oliver 103 Reuben 68
ELSEMORE, Lucy 25
ELSMORE, Moses 25
ELWELL, Maria Ann 78
EMERSON, Electra 9 Elizabeth 100 Mary W 100 Seth 100
EMERY, John 175 Patience 175 Sally 175 Sarah Jane 173 Sarah W 175
EMMA, Hall 57
ESTABROOK, Charles T 88 Mary 89 Sarah Caroline 88
ESTABROOKS, Amanda R 23 David 84 Judith 84 Lilly 24 Nancy J 80 84
ESTEY, Angeline 147 Charles 147 Mary 48 Mary A 147
EVANS, Isabella 57
EVERETT, Flora Etta 39 Francis A 39
EYE, Nancy 107
FAIRBANK, Elizabeth 8
FAIRFIELD, Abigail 20 120
FALEN, James 79 Sarah A 79
FALES, Martha 43
FANJOY, Margaret 25 Rebecca 24
FARLING, James 54
FARNSWORTH, 111 Abi 93 110-111 Abi Sarah 110 Annie 111 Annie L 93 E 156 Jonas 93 110 Lydia Anna 93 Mary 93 111 Mary Gardner 111 Solon 111 Solon Parker 93
FARRAR, George 70 Judith 99 Mary Ball 70 Rebecca 70
FARRISH, John 156 Sophia A 156
FAUGHT, Elijah 70 Ellen 70 Olive 70
FELLOWS, Polly 76
FELT, Mary F 83 Peter 83 Polly 83
FENNEMORE, Isaac 179 Susan 179
FERGERSON, Mary Ann 91
FERRIS, Abigail B 179 Daniel 179 Daniel Jr 113 Diannah 179 186 Emma Sarah 113 Hannah 179 John 179 Martha Zilme 179
FICKETT, Eunice 74
FIELD, Bessie M 14 Giles 121 John 14
FINCH, Clara L 108
FINKLE, Matilda P 167 William 167
FINNEY, Martha 174
FISHER, Ebenezer 151
FITCH, Elizabeth 76
FITZPATRICK, Grace Ennis 105 Jeremiah E 105
FITZSIMMONS, Jane 30
FLEMING, Mary Jane 163 Nellie 167

FLETCHER, Judith 49 84 Maria 49 Polly 83
FLOOD, John 173 Priscilla 173 Priscilla W 173
FLY, Polly 132
FORBES, Marietta 150
FORD, Frederick 121 Marcia 121
FOSTER, Anna A 121 Cyrus Woodin 178 E L 35 175 Edgar L 8 173 Ellen C 66 Gilbert 66 121 Gilbert Henry 124 Hannah Emma 66 Harriet N Miranda 178 Helen Augusta 124 John Wooden Jr 47 Lucy 25 47 Maria L 153 Maria Louisa 124 Mary E 54 Mary Jane 129 Mehitable 47 Mercy 124 Robert 121 Ruth 30 Sally 178 William 66 William Brewer 66
FOWLER, Clara A 129 Ed 175 Hannah 129 John 129
FOX, Kate 143 Katherine 143
FRASEUR, Amy 164 Jannet P 164 Jennie 164 William 164
FRAZER, Jannet P 164 Jennie 164
FRAZIER, Mary 121
FREEBORN, Harriet E 93 William A 93
FREEMAN, C M 141 144
FREIDAY, J A 80
FRISBIE, Hudson Townsend 103 Mary E 103 Timothy 103
FROST, Elizabeth 87 Jane 5 Jeremiah Sr 5 Katherine 32 Oliver R 87 Victoria A 87
FULLER, Catherine 77 Elizabeth 37 Mehitable 7 37 Moses 37 Richard O 77 Thomas J D 85 94
FURGASON, Margaret 59
FURGERSON, Jane 147
FURLONG, Melissa P 74
GAGE, Elizabeth G 107 Isabella 57 107 Jennie Mae L 57 Kennedy 57 107
GALLEGHER, Eva Hannah 138 Patrick 138 Rose Hannah 138
GALLOP, Betsey 181 Chester 181 Sally 181
GAMMON, Mary H 169 Newell 169 Polly 169
GARDNER, Aaron L Raymond 177 Aaron Leeman Raymond 131 Abbie Wilder 131 177 Abi 93 110 Ann Eliza 131 Daniel Morgan 15 22 David 79 Deborah 15 22 Ebenezer 131 George Reynolds 131 177 Harriet Louise 177 Jacob D 22 Jane 155 Julia A 15 Mary 80 Merton David 15 Rachel 79 Sarah 22 131 Zeriah 79
GARLAND, Ann 132
GARNET, Cassie Felica 147 James C 147 Mary 147
GARNETT, Ellsworth Brigham 52 Rebecca Louise 52
GARVEY, 134 Elizabeth 134
GATES, Church E 9 Emeline G 89 Ephraim 10 Ephraim Church 122 Lucy 10 89 122 175 Lucy Caroline 175 Salmon 89 122 175 Vashti R 10 122
GERRISH, Emily Manning 157 Ethel 29 Ethel H 29 Frederick Henry 157 Hiram 29 Oliver 157 Sarah 157
GERRY, Elbridge Joseph 82 Mary 82 Seth 82 Sophia Teresa 82
GETCHELL, Mary Emeline 168 Mehitable M 12
GIBSON, Edward 133 Elizabeth 76 Emma W 133 James 76 Mariam R 76 May 142 May Merrill 178 Susan C 76
GILBERT, Dianthia 108 Hattie 108 William 108
GILE, Mary 86
GILLIS, George 138 George Jr 52 George Sr 52 James 118 Julia Helena 138 Mina 170 Minerva E 170 Robert 170
GILLMOR, Arthur Hill 69 Mary 69 Rebecca Ann 69
GILMORE, Betsey 81 Lillah Elizabeth 175 Mary Emma 175 Robert Joseph 175 Warren 53
GISON, Alfred C 178
GLEASON, Margaret 100
GLIDDEN, Rebeckah 58 Rebekah 40
GOLDEN, Jane L 146

GOLDING, Alice Elizabeth 121 Jane L 146 Lucy A 146 Peter 146 Samuel W 121
GOOD, Catherine 54
GOODNOW, Calvin 4 Calvin Rice 4 Salome 4 Sarah Elizabeth 4
GOODWIN, Augusta Jane 78 John H 46 78 Mary Jane 46 78
GORDON, David 84-85 Mary 85 Mary B 84
GORY, Auathusia 51
GOSS, Jane 83
GOULDRICH, Margaret M 62
GRACIER, Caroline Elizabeth 71 Francis Joseph 71 Francis Joseph Jr 71 Sabra Atherton 71
GRANGER, Anna Caroline 88 Emma Marcelia 38 George Frederick 38 Harriet 38 88 Joseph 10 13 38 88 William Augustus 88
GRANT, Donald 118 Elizabeth Anna 18 Fannie 14 Mahala 118 Margaret M 170 Mehali Ann 118
GRAVES, Joanna 156 Samuel G 156
GRAY, Ellen 148 George 148 Mary 148 Mary Emma 17 Robert J 17
GREEN, Elijah 18 Elijah D 142 Emma Sophia 142 Hannah 18 Hannah C 142 Mary H 123
GREENE, Amy W 179
GREENLAW, Charles Henry 150 Eliza Ann 145 Elizabeth 146 Flora 150 Gilbert H 146 Hannah 105 Jane E 74 Joan 179 Joanna 179 Josie 146 Josphine V 146 Laura Fidella 150 Margaret 145 Margaret Jones 145 Martha 150 Mary 88 Mercy 13 126 Otis 179 Samuel 145 Seth Henry 150 Solomon 145
GREENLOW, Hannah 141
GREENWOOD, Ann Eliza 180 Randolph 180
GREGORY, A 7 D H 120 Elizabeth 167
GRIFFIN, Margaret E 106
GRIMMER, Amy 164 Hattie 96 163-164 Lydia 163 Martha 96 163-164 Mary Ann 66 Thomas 163
GROSVENOR, Charlotte Otis 123 Clarissa 123 Lemuel Putnam 123
GROUT, Dolly 67 Jonathan 67
HAFLIN, Hiram L 169
HALE, Laura 83
HALKSHAW, Sarah 57
HALL, Abner H 46 Amanda J 46 Amelia 124 Ann E 50 Frances Maria 87 Frank 15 Hannah Emma 57 Harriet Elizabeth 46 Jacob B 87 James S 47 James Sullivan 57 152 John 124 Marcia 41 Maria 86 Mary E 57 152
HALLIDAY, Elizabeth 108 Hannah 132 John N 108 Mary E 108
HAM, Henrietta 141 145 Jane 141 145 Martha Almena 145 Rufus 141 145 Rufus Jr 145
HAMBLIN, Lucy W 45
HAMILTON, Abigail 90 Asa 29 Catharine 90 174 Horace 100 Margaret 3 Minerva 100 Sarah 29 Sarah Maria 29
HAMLIN, Anna 75 Cyrus 12 75 Eleazer 75 Lydia 75 Olive 70 Vesta 75
HANCOCK, Thomas 106
HANDY, Letitia 177
HANSCOM, Nathaniel 33 Phoebe 33 Ruth 33
HANSON, Elijah 182 Elizabeth 182 Eunice 151 Jane B 182 Levi F 151 Levi T 151
HARMON, 16 Eleanor 91 Elizabeth M 48 Hannah 102 Lydia 48 102 Nathaniel 48 102
HARRINGTON, Hannah 36

HARRIS, E B 159 E N 33 110 Edward N 28 170 Emma J 148 Isaiah 148 Mary Jane 148 Samuel 82
HART, Mary 85
HARVELL, Cosomy 116
HARVEY, Malinda C 158
HASACK, Sabra Atherton 71
HASKELL, C 155 Sarah 48
HASLEM, Mary 159
HASTINGS, Ann 165 Betsey 144 Hasty 165 Mary 165 Mathew 151 Mr 118
HATCH, Elizabeth 33 Mary 41 Melinda 18
HATCHEN, Amelia B 108
HATT, Sarah C 36
HAVERSTOCK, Almira 164 Elmira 164 Myra 164 Willis N 164
HAY, Mrs 121
HAYCOCK, Hannah 95 Hannah W 86
HAYDEN, Aaron 18 64 Caroline M 64 Charles A 158 Charles Henry 18 64 Eliza S 121 Elizabeth Faxton 71 Fannie E 95 Hannah 18 Hannah C 142 Hannah Claflin 64 Ruth Richards 18 64
HAYMAN, Deborah Elizabeth 21 William H 21
HAYWARD, Allen 126 Eben Smith 126 Mary 32 Mary Amanda 126 Thankful 126
HELMERSHAWSEN, E H 183 Matilda 183
HENDERSON, Daniel 70 Mae 70 Mary Dow 70
HENNIGAN, James G 112
HENRY, Martha C 70 Mary O 70 William 70
HERALD, Widow 90
HERON, C B 155
HERSEY, Caleb 104 Darius Deforest 104 Elizabeth 104 Ezra L 98 Freeman 55 Mary Ann 55 Mary E 104 Sarah A 104 Sarah Persis 98
HEWSON, Charles Wentworth Upham 67 Mary Elizabeth 67
HEYWARD, Hannah 22 Salome 22 William Brewer 22 Zimri 90 Zimri Brewer 22
HEYWOOD, Emily Ardra 17 Theodore A 17
HIBBARD, Lyman 67 Rebecca 67
HIGGINS, Anna 117 Annie 117 Catherine 117 Fannie Billings 59 Margaret 59 Mary Angeline 151 Michael 136 Patrick C 117 Phenneas 68 91 Phineas 156 Simeon 59 Thomas 117
HILL, David 118 Elizabeth 87-88 Hannah 124 Horatio N 100 Japhet 124 Joel 17 Lavinia 87 Mary 9 118 154 Mary H 154 Mary Jamison 17 Mary Jane 17 Naomi 94 Phebe Whitney 100 Priscilla 18 124 159 Rebecca 129 Samuel 129 154 Sarah 68 118 Sarah Waite 134 Socrates 118 Stephen 88 Thomas 129 William T 134
HILTZ, Harriet 114 Harriet Emeline 181 Henry A 181
HINCKLY, Josephine Elizabeth 71
HINDMAN, Mattie F 10
HINDS, Addie M 91
HINES, Richard 82 Salome 82 Sarah 82
HITCHINGS, Almira 97 138 Anna Livingstone 126 Elmira 138 Jane 138 Rev Mr 100 William 138
HLEMER, C D 13
HOBBS, Mary 154
HODGE, Susan 155
HODGEMAN, Mary Josephine 74 Samuel 74
HODGKINS, Sally 149
HODGMAN, Jane E 74
HOLBERT, C M 13 Laura Mehitable 13
HOLBROOK, Laura Mehitable 13 Mrs 13
HOLLIDAY, Archibald 132

HOLMAN, Sarah 19
HOLMES, Charles 150 Charles M 59 Deborah 33 Dr 42 Emily 150 Emma 150 Gilbert A 150 Henrietta 150 James 59 James Francis 144 James Jr 144 150 Job 42 Malissa P 59 Melissa Peaslee 59 Temperance 59 144 150
HOLT, Hannah 146
HOLWAY, Martha 162
HONIGAN, Mary 107
HOOKER, Martha 11
HOOPER, Mary 118
HOPKINS, Hannah 118
HOPPER, J E 87
HORNE, James B 8 Martha Burnham 8
HORTON, Minerva 42 Thomas 42
HOVEY, Amelia 184
HOWARD, Mary Emma 175
HOWE, Abner R 151 Eliza 151 Julie E 151 Juliette 151
HUBBARD, Gov 27 Joseph 59 Louisa Amanda 59
HUCKINGS, James 49
HUCKINS, James 78
HUGHES, Elizabeth Ann 182
HUME, Augusta Jane 63 David W 79 Josiah 63 Josiah Lysander 63 Mary Ann 79 Rebecca S 63 Sabria 79
HUMPHREY, Jane 138
HUNT, Abbie Frances 67 Abbie W 67 Clarence M 72 Harriet Granger 72 Reuben S 67
HUNTER, Isabella 107
HUNTLEY, Alice 133 Almira 78 89 Elsie 133 Gideon G 78 89 Helen M 89 Lorenzo 149-150 Mary 133 Sabra 78 Sabria 78 Sarah 138 William Henry 133 William Lane 78 Zeriah 79
HUNTRESS, Kate 86 Leonard 86
HURLEY, Alice 133 Eleanor 149 Ellen 148-149 Elsie 133
HUSKINS, James 137
HUSON, Louisa 84 Samuel 84 Thomas Albert 84 Victoria Elizabeth 84
HUSSEY, A W 129 Sarah Whidden 129
HUTCHINGS, Benjamin 80 Margaret 80
HUTCHINS, George W 66 George Washington 15 Jessie 66 Joseph 15 115 136 Mary Ann 15 136 Mary Helen 15 66 Vesta H 115
HUTCHINSON, Mary 158
HUTTON, James 173 John 173
HYDE, Rebecca 83
INCHES, Charlotte 117 James 117 Jane E 117
INNESS, Arthur F 85 George 41 Harrison Henry 41 John Alexander 41 Lizzie 41 Lucy B 85 Marcia 41 Martha 85 Mary Elizabeth 41 Sarah Jane 41
IRVIN, Anna 80 Catherine 73 John 73 Martha Ann 73
IRVING, James 55 Lizzie 148
JACK, Margaret Jane 120
JACKSON, Abigail P 104 Elizabeth 36 Jones 36 Keziah 36 Mary 36 Mary E 104 Rev Mr 42 S B 104 Sarah 114 William 36
JAKIN, Nellie 145
JAMES, Eliza 182 Elizabeth 146 Jeremiah 182 Mary Louisa 158 William F 158
JAMESON, Henrietta 46
JAMISON, M 129
JAQUES, Parker 160
JEWELL, Clarrassa 74 Harriet B 74 John 74
JOHNSON, 7 Archie 147 Carrie 26 Edith Anna 176 Emily Louisa 7 Eva 40 George A 149 Judith 20 Maggie 147 Mariam 31 Mary A 20 Mary Ann 20 Mary E 20 147

JOHNSON (cont.)
    Moses S 20 Nancy 5 20 41 90 108 Nellie 149 Rev Mr 164 Sarah 130 Thomas 20 William F 27

JONES, Almeda M 28 160 Calvin 25 73 Catherine Winthrop 56 Elizabeth 122 Ellen C 66 Ellen Cobb 56 Esther W 73 Frances 25 73 Harriet Call 101 Jennie 47 Joanna 23 John Y 28 160 Josephine 32 Katherine Winthrop 38 56 Lemuel H 64 Myra 28 160 Rachel 125 133 Ruth Richards 18 64 Sarah Brinley 38 Sarah D 160 Theodore 38 56 William O 101

JORDAN, Anna 151 Asa 151 Clarissa 57 David 120 Elizabeth 58 Hannah 151 Harriet 120 Henry Cobb 57 Maggie 151 Mary Ann 168 Mary Ellen 57 Olive 157 Samuel 57 Tristram 157

JOY, Andrew Jackson 174 Daniel 174 Ellen 135 Hannah 174 Helen 135 Margaret 135 Martha 174 Robert 135

JUDKINS, Dorcas 179 William S 179

JUSTASON, Katherine 150

KATYING, Mary 72

KEELER, Ev 141 H 62 Rev 63 160 S H 3-4 6 12 16 18 39 41-43 61 77 89 96 98-99 103 141 165 167 176 182-184 Seth H 25

KEEN, Alby Sr 50 80 Capt 46 Nancy J 49 80 Victoria Elizabeth 80

KEENE, Alby Sr 50 Bethiah L 47 Martha 47 Nancy J 49 William 47

KEITH, Abby Hooper 63 Eugene 63 Sarah 178

KELLER, S H 57

KELLEY, 89 Ann 73 Cordelia 153 Cordlia 97 Eliza 154 George 12 Maria 12 Maria Haycock 45 Samuel 87 William 97 153 William Lovejoy 45

KELLY, Mary Plummer 153 Samuel Jr 173

KENDALL, Annie 8-9

KENNEDY, Charlotte Grosvenor 99 Frank A 99

KERR, John 94 Phebe Ann 94 Sarah 94

KETTLE, T Q 101

KIDD, Ann Maria 56

KIDDER, Helen M 79 Jonathan 79 138 Joseph Calvin Sr 79 Mary 79 Mary J 89

KILBURN, Lurena 7

KILDEA, John T 80

KILLMAN, Jane Callahan 89

KIMBALL, David 86 Emeline G 61 Gorham G 71 Huldah 126 Jacob 4 James 61 James G 86 James Gorham 61 Julia 4 Mary 69

KING, 148 Ann G 132 Carrie M 45 Charles 61 89 Charles Willard 89 Edgar 112 Elizabeth 169 Elizabeth Ann Chandler 132 Emeline Danford 86 G G 87 George Gilman 86 George W 112 Gilman 42 Gilman D 86 95 Hannah 95 Hannah W 86 Harriet Emeline 89 Henrietta 45 Henry 183 Henry Harrison 183 Hezekiah 89 Jerusha 89 John Quincy 112 Judson P 112 Julia Norris 98 Lillian A 148 Lyman Leighton 112 Maryetta 112 Minerva 42 Phoebe Sawyer 95 Quincy A 112 Rebecca 183 Rebecca Eliza 183 Samuel T 132 Samuel Tyler 132 Sarah 112 Silvia 112 Susan H 86 Sylvester Munroe 112 Willard Bancroft 95 169 William 69 William Trott 45 William Wallace 98

KINNEY, 35 Caroline 35

KIRK, Isabella 16

KISSAM, Emily 77

KITCHEN, Mary A 147

KNEELAND, Amanda Judith 26 Carrie 26 Ephraim 26

KNIGHT, Abigail E 77 Amelia 78 Benjamin 158 Carolyn A 158 Elizabeth 120 Ephraim 134 Frances 118 Hannah 49 78 124 Jerome H 78 John H 78 Jonathan 49 84 Joshua 87 Lucy 84

KNIGHT (cont.)
    Lydia 86 126 134 142 Malinda 78 Maria Ann 78 Mary 69 158 Mary W 49 100 Melinda 78 Milton E 118 Nancy 118 Paul 49 78 Sarah 87 Thomas Jefferson 120

KNOWLES, Elizabeth S 152 Reuben B 152

KNOWLTON, I C 59 101 171 Isaac C 50 John 15

KUMMELL, Anna Kendall 9 Julius M 9

LABORTIER, Ann Amelia 7

LADD, Almy Wicks 98 Caleb 95 Charles Carroll 95 Emma Gerturde 98 Harriet 138 Joseph W 98 Joseph Warren 95 Joseph Warren Jr 98 Mary Ellen 95

LAFLIN, Almeda S 169 Helen 169 Hiram 169

LAMB, Albert 175 Almira 20 101 103 175 Ann 141 Betsey 16 67 103 Eleanor 16 67 Elmira 20 101 175 Harriet 20 James 16 67 103 Lydia W 122 Mary Briggs 16 Nathaniel 16 20 67 101 103 175 Oramendal 122 Peter Carle 101 Robert 16 67 103 Robert James 122 Sarah Anna 174 Sarah Griggs 101 Seth Turner 20 William 141

LAMBE, Caroline G 132 Carrie 132 Mary 132 Samuel 132 167 184

LAMSON, Mercy 172

LANE, Almira 78-79 89 Clement Jr 52 Elias S 52 Elias Stuart 52 Elizabeth Sarah 52 Lydia A 96 Lydia M 14 Margaret Pendleton 52 Mary 78-79 Mary Ann 78-79 William 78-79

LANGFORD, Elizabeth 76

LANGLANDS, Louisa 22 Robert 22

LANNIGAN, Bridget 134

LARNER, Ann Jane 26 Isaac 26 Jane 26

LATHROP, T S 138

LAUGHTON, Edward S 55 Edwin 55

LAWLER, Mary 85

LAWRENCE, Annie 111 Christina 51 Clara A 51 Gustavus A 34 Lydia 34 Mel 51 Millard D 51 Millard O 51 Samuel A 51 Sarah Jane 34 William 34

LEACH, Lois Starr 31 Louis Starr 31 Tryphosa 169

LEADBETTER, Hannah 153

LEARY, Ellen 11 John J 11

LEAVES, Maria 46

LEDLARD, Jane Wilcox 176 Jennie 176 Perry M 176

LEE, Dorothy 69 Nellie 69

LEEMAN, Carrie M 37 Henry 37 Louisa 179 Maletia 37 Rebecca 174

LEGACY, Alice M 184 Olive M 184

LEIGHTON, Abigail 150 Althea A 166 David 150 Harrison B 135 Louisa 182 Permelia 134 Phoebe 135

LESLIE, Margaret 80

LESUER, Anna Maria 164 Benjamin Lewis 164

LIBBY, Charles E 8 Ellen 8 Joanna 41 Nellie 8

LINCOLN, President 141 Ruth 155 Zelphan 40

LINDSAY, Mary 6 153 Polly 153

LINDSEY, Hannah 153 William 153

LINSCOTT, David 138 Eva Jane 138 Jane 138

LITTLE, Edna 17 Elizabeth 161 Harriet J 161 Robert 161 Sarah 157

LITTLEFIELD, Dianthia 108

LIVERMORE, Anna 75 Elijah 75 Hannah 75 Mary 66

LOGAN, Maria 65 William 65

LOMBARD, Hannah 118

LONG, C C 138 Sally 5

LORD, Lucretia Maria 98 Maria 98-99 Martha 103 Mary L 18 Rufus 98

LORING, Betsey 166 Elizabeth 166 Elmira Swett 114 Janette 5 John 166 Lucius 5 Mahala 166 Peter 83 Peter Jr 114 Rachel 83 125 133 Zacheus 166
LOUDEN, John 166 Lydia 166 Sarah 165 William 166
LOVEJOY, Ann Marple 153 Attai 87 Capt 69 Cordelia 87 Francis 186 Hannah Amy 152 Hannah Emma 152 James Albee 153 John Lorin 153 Lucretia Maria 97 Rev Mr 15 Ruby 97 Thomas Odiorne 97 W W 168 William 87
LOVELL, Deliverance 78 Deliverence 31
LOW, Elizabeth 89 Sabra 78
LOWE, Mary 68 148
LOWELL, Elizabeth 49 Elwell 17-18 Emeline 86 Emily 18 John 18 L L 31 Melinda 18 Reuben Braddock 49 Reuben N 49 Sally 49 Sarah 49
LULL, Fanny 34 Laura A 34 Levi 34 Sophia F 93
LUND, Olive 181
LUNT, Benjamin 20 Esther 20 Jane 20
LYONS, Fanny 108
MABEE, Helen 169
MACK, Annette G 69 Luther J 69 Matilda J 69 Nettie 69
MACLEAN, Alexander 103
MAGNUS, Michaeles 50
MAHER, Alice 11
MAHONEY, Jane 96
MAKER, Alice 70 Alice C 70 James 70
MAKOE, Alice 70 Alice C 70 James 70
MALLOW, Peter 53
MAMBURG, Thedbolia 153
MANN, Mary Catherine 41
MANNING, Nola 177 Penolia Almasetta 177 Richard 157 Sarah Porter 157
MANSELL, Lucy 128
MANSFIELD, Mary Ann 15 80 136
MANSON, Hannah 91 Robert 91 Sarah Griggs 91
MARKS, Abraham H 4 David H 4 Hannah H 4 Lucinda B 4 Nehemiah 4
MARPLE, Hannah 97
MARSH, Hannah 69
MARSHALL, Adelaide A 13 Anna Eliza 13 Annie 148 Bradford 13 Ellen 13 Emma Sarah 113 Fannie A 13 Jessina 13 John M 148 Robert 13 Tressa L 148
MARSHRALL, Margaret 180
MARTIN, Eben 68 Elizabeth 77 Hannah 68 Jacob 77 James 68 John 77 Mrs Frank 113 Sarah Ann 68
MASON, Hannah E 181 Jane 160 John 182 Lydia 182
MATHEWS, M D 16
MAURICE, Caroline 79
MAXELL, Emily Judson 41 Joanna 41 Sarah H 41 Thomas Jefferson 41
MAXFIELD, Martha 106
MAXWELL, Eliza E 163 Emily Judson 41 Sarah H 41
MAYHER, Margaret 93
MAYVILLE, Elizabeth Jane 161 James Theodore 161
MCADAM, Eliza A 135 Jane A 135 John 135
MCALLISTER, Abner 152 Byron 63 Eliza 173 George C 44 John Patterson 45 Keziah Hill 152 Lydia 48 68 102 Margaret Elizabeth 45 Minnie M 63 Rachel 63 William L 10 63 90
MCBEAN, Donald A 156 Fanny 156 Isaac S 183 Nancy 183 Nancy R 156 Serena A 156
MCBRIDE, Jane 165 Nellie A 85
MCCANN, Ann 85 Annie 156 Lorinda 156 Malinda 156 Rodney 156

MCCARTHY, Catharine 77
MCCARTNEY, Margaret J 76
MCCARTY, David 92
MCCATHERINE, Andrew S 160 164 Jane Smith Pineo 160 Mary Amanda 164
MCCELLAN, Isabella 166 Nancy 50
MCCLANAHAN, Ella 41 Sarah Luella 41
MCCLASKEY, James 154
MCCLUSKEE, Jane 148
MCCLUSKEY, James 155 Mary 155
MCCOLLY, Rev 89
MCCONNEGHY, Margaret 114
MCCONNELL, Margaret 35 Mary E 35 Patrick 35
MCCULLUM, Peter 112
MCCULLY, Charles 105 Rev 95
MCCURDY, Agnes 23 Alexander 183 Almira Deborah 50 Ellen 183 Lizzie 183 Lucy 138 Lydia A 112
MCDONALD, Angus 49 Anna E 85 Deborah 6 26 Deborah M 172 Emma Sarah 113 Frank 85 Jane 180 Lucy Harmond 6 Lydia Elthea 26 Mahala 147 174 Maria 46 Mary Ann 49 Randal 26 William 6 26 172
MCDOUGHALD, 172 Arzelia 172
MCEACHERN, Andrew S 164 Charles 160 164 Mary 160 164 Mary Amanda 164
MCELROY, Hannah 107-108 Matthew 108
MCFARLAND, Catherine 34 Laura 102 Sarah 114
MCFARLANE, James 57 Lucy Ann 57
MCGARRITY, Catherine 117
MCGERRY, Annie Dorcas 37 Noah Smith 37
MCGIBBON, Ann 113 Mary A 113 Richard 113
MCGLINCHEY, Ann 113
MCGOULDRICK, Margaret M 62
MCGREGOR, Mary Caroline 8 William H 8
MCKAY, Lucretia 110 Susanna 167 Thomas 58
MCKELLAR, W S 15 96 156
MCKELLER, W S 76 William S 60
MCKENNEY, Eleanor 52 Ellen 52
MCKENZIE, George 96 James 23 Leoniece B 40 Perley 151 Sophia 96
MCKINNON, Lydia 86
MCKUSICK, Adelaide A 13 Levi E 13 Marshall Noah 13
MCKUSKICK, Lucy J 13
MCLAUFLIN, Mira M 89
MCLAUGHLIN, Agnes 27 Amelia 89 Anna B 184 Annie 156 Charles 125 J 89 John 184 Laughlin 89 Marinda 89 Mary 92 106 Mildred 89 Rebecca 169
MCLEAN, Victoria E 124
MCLELLAN, Ann 80 Margaret 80 Martin 80 Mary 50 Nancy 50 80 William 50
MCMAHAN, James 153 James B 153 Rose Emma 153 Thedbolia 153
MCMULLEN, Hugh 61 Mary 61
MCNAMARA, Eliza 159 Emma 159 Thomas 159
MCNEAR, Harriet 24 Mary Ann 20 24 41 Thomas 20 24 41
MCNEIL, Jane G 159
MCNEILL, Margaret 83
MCNELLY, Adalaide Eliza 159 Hannah 159 Joseph 159 Matthew 159
MCNUTT, Daniel 167 Elizabeth 167 Henrietta 167 John 167 Nellie 167
MCPHAIL, Abiah 141 Anna Augusta 97 Ferdinand 97 Hannah 141 John 97 Martha 97 Mary 147 Mary B 184
MCQUADE, Ellen 183

MCQUAY, Jane 107
MCROY, N Sophia 34
MCVAY, Bridget 134 John 134 Mary Ellen 134 Susanna 167
MCWHINNEY, Margaret 171 Thomas 171
MEIGGS, Martha 100
MELVILLE, Mary Sophia 132
MERRIAM, Rev 111
MERRICK, Elizabeth 49
MERRILL, Laura F 10
MERRIMAN, Caroline A 158 Carrie 158 John F 158
MESERVE, Betsey 128-129 Mehitable 47
MILBURN, Jeremiah 40 Sarah 40
MILLAR, Cora Estella 48 George 48 Mary 48
MILLBURN, Elizabeth 40
MILLBURY, Amy 6
MILLER, Joseph 171 Laura L 171 Mary 123 Phebe 170 Sarah 41
MILLIGAN, Isabella 6 16 Margaret E 16 Samuel 6 16
MILLS, Alexander Barry 147 Eliza 159 Frances Maria 126 James 147 Louise Parks 147 Lucy 147 Mary L 147
MINGO, Daniel 30 Frances 30 Michael 30 Sarah 30
MITCHELL, Almeda M 28 Almira Y 167 B M 17 46 124 Corilla N 98 Edward C 79 Eliza S 167 Ira F 98 Jane 154 Jerome 98 John 36 Julia 65 Lucretia Maria 98 Mehitable W 36 Nancy C 91 Ruth 98 Susan Anna 65 Thomas 65
MONDIE, Elizabeth 105 Lizzie 105
MONNEY, Jane 138
MONROE, Abigail 27
MOONEY, Jane 96
MOORE, Agnes 75 Ashal 78 Edward 75 Frank H 82 John Warren 75 Mary Louisa 75 Tristrram 75 William 75
MORELAND, Mary Elizabeth 120
MOREY, 93
MORGAN, Elizabeth 98 Erecta Louise 98 George Nelson 98 Martha 169 Sarah 22 W 6
MORICY, Bridget 72 Mary 72 Timothy 72
MORRILL, Anson P 141
MORRIS, Annie 148 Sarah 112
MORRISCY, Bridget 72
MORRISON, Alexander A 31 Barbara Jane 34 Barbara M 31 George 31 Helen D 144 J H 104 Jane 33 93 John 34 Lydia Ann 77 Margaret 31 Mary 47 Mary E 31 N Sophia 34
MORSE, Hannah 152 Hannah S 66 98 152 William 152
MORSS, Jane 83 Jennie Florence 83 William 83
MOSELEY, Edward A 126 Katherine Montague 126
MOSHER, Charles P 115 Daniel 55 Priscilla 55 173 Susan E 115
MOSS, Julia 120
MOWATT, Henry 147 Margaret 147 Martha 147
MURCHIE, Annie 66 James 66 Jane A 135 Mary Ann 66
MURPHY, Catherine 13 Clara Martha 106 Elisha B 184 Harriet Maria 184 Kate 13 Martha 106 Mary Ann Jane 163 Nancy 118 Samuel 106
MURRAY, Annie 148 E W 21 44 57 76 88 125 Edward W 125 Edwin 68 Edwin R 44
MUSTARD, Annie 147 Jane 147 Robert 147
MYRICK, Elizabeth 49 Melville W 132
NASH, Cynthia 57 Lydia 99
NASON, Betsey 166 Elizabeth 166
NELSON, Cynthia 57 Frank 57 Henrietta Brewer 57 Samuel 57 Thomas 57
NEVENS, Jonathan 96 Lydia A 96 Matilda M 96

NEVERS, Mary 80 Nathan 80 Sophia Eveline 151 Thomas Owen 151 Vesta H 80
NEW, Jane 21 Joseph 21 Mary Ellen 21
NEWELL, Elizabeth 37
NEWHALL, Esther 8-10
NEWNHAM, Elizabeth 117
NEWTON, Abigail 95 Charles Harrison 95 Elizabeth Sparhawk 95 Horace 95 Mr 95 Rachel 61
NICHOLS, Abbie A 145 Abigail 20 45 161 173 Mehitables S 145 Nabby 45 161 173 Rebecca 144 Walter B 145
NICHOLSON, 121
NICKELS, Alexander 162 Martha 162 Mary Ann 162
NICKERSON, Eliza 51-52
NOBLE, Eliza Jane 96 Hannah 140 Jemima 140 151 Joanna 105 John 96 140 151 Mary C 156 Nicholas 156 Priscilla 151-152 Sarah 156 Susan 96
NORDSTROM, Mary O 155
NORRIS, Hannah 112 Jeremiah 112 Rebecca 112 114
NORTON, Fred D 15 Julia A 15 Lydia 121 Nellie 15
NOWELL, W G 122
NOYES, Annie Y 27
NUTT, Harriet Downes 162 James 162 Noel Byron 162 Sarah 162
NUTTING, Georgianna 183
O'BRIEN, Mary A 82 Thomas A 82
O'CONNOR, George 116
O'HARA, Ellen 92 John 92 Mary 92 Sis 92 Thomas 92 Thomas J 92
OLIVER, Bessie L 32 Bessie Louise 32 Catherine 32 Frank 32
OSBORN, David C 117 Elizabeth A 88 Ellen Elizabeth 117 Lizzie 117
OSGOOD, B F 59 Joseph 75 Malissa P 59 Melissa Peaslee 59
OUDESLUYS, Mrs H T 64
OUTHOUSE, Millie 56
OWENS, Edward 33 Josephine L C 33
PADELFORD, Rev 37
PADLEFORD, A J 44 170 186 Rev 132 177 180
PAINE, Mary Sophia 22 Nancy 22 Oliver 22 Thomas 22 Thomas Oliver 22
PALMER, Sarah P 168 Susan 96
PARK, Jonathan Green 69 Linda Ann 69 Mary Lucinda 69 Sarah 69
PARKMAN, John A 130 Mary 130 Mary Augusta 130
PARKS, Lucy A 146
PARSONS, Sarah Stone 60
PATTEN, Emma Sawin 79 John 134 Love M 134 Olivia P 30 Permelia 134 Ruth 30 William 30
PATTERSON, Fanny 96 Hannah 166 Julia Elizabeth W 170 Lavinia S 166 Mr 170 Robert 166 Sarah 166
PATTON, Charity G 28
PAYSON, Edward 176 Nancy 95
PEABODY, Charles 160 Charles P 160 Cordelia 98 Cordelia Evelyn 160 Julia Ann 182 Mary 182 Mary Ann Boies 160 Thomas 182
PEARL, Caroline Brackett 20 Levi 20
PENINGTON, Ada W 33 Thomas 33
PERKINS, Arthur 130 Esther 20 Hannah Maria 130
PERLEY, Caroline A 88 Charles 88 Mary 119
PETTIS, Mary 17
PETTYGROVE, Mrs Frank 118 Sarah E 184
PHELPS, Hannah Rebecca 59 James A 59
PHILBREICK, H A 46
PHILBRICK, Rev 156

PHILBROOK, H A 78 88 152 Rev 173
PHILLIPS, Salome 4 62
PHINNEY, John 55 Mary 55 Mehitable 5
PHIPPS, Cozomy N 151 Eliza 151 Malissa P 59 Melissa P 74 Melissa Peaslee 59 Rufus 74 Rufus D 59 Thomas 151 William 151
PICKARD, Fred V 180 Hepsibah 95 Hepsie 95
PICKENS, Leonard 61 91 Lydia W 91 Vashti 61 91 Vashti R 10 Vashti Randall 61
PICKETT, Valentine 95
PIKE, Abba C 9 Abby 9 Alvin 126 Ann M 77 Anna 118 Elizabeth 27 Elizabeth Ann 27 Elizabeth Ellen 62 Ellen 62 Ethel 164 F A 154 Frances Campbell 42 173 Frances Campbell Todd 56 Frances Elizabeth 173 Frank 126 Frederick Augustus 64 Helen Augusta 56 Maria Louisa 57 Martha Prescott 42 Mary 8-9 Mary Caroline 131 Mary Hayden 64 Mary W 8 Nancy Jane 126 Nellie 62 Oliva Maria B 126 Samuel Dean 8-9 Samuel G 62 William 163-164 William C Sr 27 William Cornelius Jr 42 56 173 William Franklin 126
PINE, James 88 Mary 88
PINEA, Mary Augusta 124
PINEO, David 18 159 David Jr 18 George 124 Hannah Hill 120 159 Marcey 98 Mary Ann 18 Priscilla 18 Stephen S 19
PITTS, Lydia 30
PLAISTED, Ida 150 Marietta 150 William P 150 William Porter 150
PLATT, Medora Caroline 75
POMROY, Sarah 156
POOL, Lydia 93 Nancy Ann B 93 Rachel 83 133 Solomon 83 93 William 93
POOLE, Enos 150 Katherine 150 Mary Ellen 150
POOR, Anna 45 155 Jonathan 155 Sarah 155
PORTER, C W 72 Charles Curtis 9 George Thatcher 9 Harriet Larkin 9 R D 97 Rev 29 Sophia B 9
POTTER, 44 Abigail 87 Martha Mary 44 Mattie 44 Solomon Jr 155 Susan 155 Susan H 155
POWELL, Evan 150
POWERS, Austis 35
PRATT, Abby 29 Abigial 29 George 29 Gideon 75
PREBLE, George B 88 Harriet E 88
PRESCOTT, Albion P 156 E 156 Emily Sophia Green 87 Emma A 156 Emma Sophia Green 87 Jesse 87 John 87 Joseph A 152 Sarah 87 Sarah G 87
PRICE, Cyrena 149 Rebecca 70 Serena 74 149
PRINCE, Sarah Kimball 22
PROCTOR, Georgia 35
PULLEN, Anne E 120 John 120 Permadia 120
PURDY, Jemima 116 140 151
PURINGTON, Isaac Jr 38 Isaac Sr 38 Mary R 38 Sarah Jane 38
PURPLE, Henry K 132 Sarah Caroline 132
PURRINGTON, Theresa Ann 174
PUSHOR, Sarah J 26
PUTNAM, Joshua 179
QUINCY, Horatio G 17 Mary 17
RACKLIFF, B R 126
RAIRDEN, Anne M 148
RAND, Caroline E 76
RANDALL, Vashti 61 91 122
RAWSON, Jerusha 75
REARDON, Anne M 148
REAVES, Abzina 68

REDDING, Anne M 148 Ebenezer 20 Esther 20 Mary Emeline 168 Mary R 168 Otis 168
REDING, Esther 20
REED, Abigail Torrey 50 Eleaza 177 Isaac 141 Joseph 50 135 Martha 135 Mary 182 Mercy 50 Sarah 135 177
REGAN, Mary Ann 5
REYNOLDS, Abbie Wilder 131 177 Bela R 131 Benjamin 52 Jerusha 52 Lucy S 52
RHOADES, Caroline Ellen 104 Daniel 104 Mary 104
RICH, Albion K P 44 Matilda Jane 44
RICHARDS, Hattie Adelica 102 Mary 82 145
RICHARDSON, Arthur St Clair 128 Edith Josephine 128 Hannah 152 Mary 151
RICKER, Ann 132 Anna Garland 132 Charlotte 23 Edward 11 Gershom 132 Humphrey 11 Katherine 11 Martha 11 169 Miss 132
RIOX, Sarah 111
RIPLEY, Adelia 26
ROBBINS, 124 Ann 177 James 35 James H 35 James Henry 123 Laura H 35 Mary 35 Mary Augusta 124 Mary Caroline 123
ROBERT, Bennett 166
ROBERTS, Alma 125 Bennett 83 James Arthur 125 Jemima 20 Jeremiah 125 Mary 98 Minerva Minnie 125
ROBERTSON, James 39 Sarah Ann 39
ROBINSON, Abigail 141 Ardra 16 Chase 182 Eliza 182 Elizabeth 138 Jabez 100 Margaret A 64 Martha 100 Priscilla 182 Rachel 26 Sarah 43 W H 32
ROGERS, Almira E 114 Emeline Gerry 114 Emma 114 Izetta 29 Lydia 83 Ruth 5 Sarah 125 Sarah Jane 29 148 Stephen Edward 29 Thomas 148 William 83 114
ROLFE, Clara H 144 Clorlinda 133 Curlinda 133 Frank 144 Margaret 133 Stephen 133
ROLLINS, Mary 164 Polly 164
ROMAIS, Jane 128 John S 128 Louise R 128
ROMINGEN, Davis 122 Hannah 122
ROSS, 27 Mary 95 134
ROSTER, Jane 121
ROUNDS, C B 9
RUGGLES, Gilbert 20 Mary 20 Mary Ann 20
RUMERY, John 5 Mary Ann 5 Mehitable 5 Robert E 167
RUMNEY, John 5 Mary Ann 5 Mehitable 5
RUNNELLS, Lucinda P 163
RUSSELL, Maggie 180 Margaret 180 Margaret A 180 Solomon 180
RUTHERFORD, A 148 Annie 148 David 148 Etta M 148 William John 148
SALE, Clement 106 Clement S 125 Laura 106 Laura Ann 125
SALLEE, Virginia Almira 119
SAMPSON, Hepsibeth 152 Nancy 108
SANDERSON, Caroline Elizabeth 144
SARGENT, Catherine Winthrop 56 James 12 John 184 Katherine Winthrop 38 56
SAUNDERS, Martha 81
SAVAGE, Andrew 40 Margaret 3 Mary E 40
SAWTELL, Harvey C 94 Martha L 93 Mattie 93
SAWYER, Abner 95 183 Addie 45 Augustus Eben 154 Charles 104 Ebenezer 45 Ennis D 45 Enos 45 Helen 80 James David 104 Lucy W 45 Lydia E 104 Mary 95 Mary Adelaide 45 Mary Ann 80 Mary L 95 Nathaniel 154 Phoebe 95 Sarah 12 80 104 Sarah Archibald 154 Sophia H 154 Stillman Osgood 80 Warren 80
SCAMMON, Reav C 118

SCHOOLS, Elizabeth 140
SCOTT, Anna Maria 40 Daniel 150 Elizabeth 150 Esther 179
    Esther S 92 Fanny 115 Hester 179 Jane P 72 Jane T 72 John
    115 Mary Alice 150 Mary Louise 161 Priscilla B 160
    Rebecca 72 Susan F 115
SCRIPPS, Mildred 89
SCRIPTURE, Mary Elizabeth 171
SCULLIN, Aannie M 147 Ellen 147 William 147
SEARS, John A 60 Martha 60
SEDERQUIST, Amanda Jane 84 Henry 84
SEDGLEY, Amelia 124 Stephen 124
SEWALL, C D 131 Carrie G 131
SEWELL, Rev Mr 90
SHAEFFER, Elizabeth 58
SHARMAN, Clara Estelle 115 Ruth 115 William 115 William
    Allen 115
SHATTUCK, Benjamin 68 143 Elizabeth 75
SHAW, Alvira 160 Annie C 157 Mary 102
SHEA, Dennis 107 Hannah 107 Mary 107
SHEAD, Daniel 173 James 173 Nancy 173 Nancy Folsom 173
    Oliver 173 Zachariah 173
SHEAN, Aannie M 147
SHEED, Nancy Folsom 173
SHEEHAN, Ellen 13 101 Margaret 101 Richard 101
SHELBY, Evan Wiley 119 Susan Isabel 119 Virginia Almira
    119
SHEPARDSON, Frank L 178 Sarah 178
SHEPERD, Hannah 122 James 122
SHEPPARD, David 9 Mary 9 Mary Ann 9 126
SHERMAN, Ann Eliza 6 William 6
SHERWOOD, Cynthia 48 Gilbert 48 Martha D 48
SHIRLEY, George Washington 145 Lydia F 145
SHOPPEE, Betsey 128-129 Emma Phebe 128 Henry C 128
    James Rupert 128-129 Joseph W 129 Matilda Ann 128
SHORT, Mary 17
SILVERSTONE, M 51 Maria Jane 50 Maria L 51 Micheles 50
    Michelis 51 Ophella 51
SIMEZ, Rebecca 104
SIMMONS, Betsey 170 James 50
SIMONTON, Betty 134
SIMPSON, Rachel 103 Sarah A 122
SINCLAIR, Benjamin 46 Margaret 31 Martha Ann 46
SITE, Elizabeth 36
SKILLINGS, Alice Bradbury 99 David Nelson Jr 99
SKOFIELD, Almira J 160
SMALL, Alexander Nicholas 97 Almira 97 Eva Jane 97
    Margaret 107 Robert 107 William Melvin 97
SMITH, 33 Ann 14 Anna Towers 172 Bathsheba 179 Benjamin
    53 Catherine 32 Channing 178 Charles Hart 64 Charlotte
    142 D F 21 94 96 148 Edith K 178 Eliphalet 100 Eliza Jane
    Trafton 175 Elvina Elizabeth 111 Emma Sophia 64 Frank G
    36 Gideon 14 Hannah 105-106 Hannah Draper 64 177
    Hannah Hill 159 Harriet N 36 Helen M 21 Horation Nelson
    175 Isaiah 49 James 114 James E 145 James G 125 Jane 100
    114 172 Joseph 100 Lucinda Barret 33 Martha 100 Mary 4
    Mary Ann 49 Mary Jane 114 Mary Kelly 53 Mary Kilby 53
    Mary O 70 Mila Frances 177 Mrs W W 172 Nathan 159
    Noah Jr 64 177 Randall 109 Sally 36 49 100 186 Sarah 36
    40 49 100 186 Sarah E 137 Thankful 126 Viola Albina 14
    W R 111 W W 105 William H 14 William S 172 William
    Walker 172
SMTIH, Henrietta 145

SMYTH, Charity 74 Clara Jane Greenleaf 95 Frederick K 95
    James 156 Mary Emeline 74 Stewart 74
SMYTHE, Clara Jane Greenleaf 95 Frederick K 95
SNOW, Alvira 160 Mary 118
SOMERS, Hannah 129
SOMES, Eva 66
SOTHM, Daniel S 130
SPARHAWK, Ebenzer 94 Naomi 94 Priscilla 94
SPARROW, Ann S 54
SPENCE, Jane 141 Rufus Jr 141
SPENCER, Almy Wicks 98 Caroline Foster 178 Carrie 178
    Hezekiah Albert 178 Rae M 179
SPINNEY, Emily R 174 Emma Jane 68 John 174 Jonathan 76
    Louisa Ann 79 Mary 68 76 Nathaniel 68 132 Sarah C 76
    Sarah J 132 Stephen 68
SPOFFORD, Amos 126 Frances Maria 126 Harriet Elizabeth
    126 Irene 126 Richard S 126 Richard Smith Jr 126
SPOONER, Alice Dodge 29 Emily 74 Emma S 74 Henrietta 74
    Paul 74 Sanders Gill 29 Serena 74
SPRAGUE, 114 Amanda 74 Bathesheba 115 Charles 115
    Elizabeth 155 Eunice 74 Harriet 114 Howard 36 164 Joseph
    74 Mary 16 168 Mary Ellen 114 Sophia Everline 115
    Thomas 16
SPRING, Ephraim 45 66 88 98 156 Hannah 88 Hannah Amy 98
    Hannah Emma 98 Hannah S 66 98 Long 5 Lucius 5 Lucius
    Stillman 88 Mary E 57 66 Mary Plummer 88
STACKPOLE, Caroline 43 Carrie 43 Charles 43 Cornelius 151
    James 43 James H 151 John 43 Mary 151 Mary Eliza
    Damon 151 Philip 43 Samuel O 43 Sarah 43
STAFFORD, Jane Emeline 145 Zach 145
STAMP, Anna L 149 Hannah L 149
STANHOPE, Jonathan 96 Joseph 96 Mary Ella 132 Peter 96
    Sally 96 Samuel 96 Sarah E 96
STAPLES, Ann 147 Annie 163 Mary Ann 164
STARBOARD, Ebenezer 10 Frances L 10 38 Sarah 10
STARR, Sally 181
STEARNS, Julia Washburn 158 Mary Sophia Gleason 169
    William Henry Clark 169
STEELE, Donald 35 Esther 35 Joseph 35 Mary 35
STEEN, Alexander 167 Jane 167
STEPHENS, Martha Louisa 151
STEPHENSON, Fanny 113 James 113
STETSON, Mary 82
STEVENS, Asenath 119 Lucy 68 172 Martha Louisa 151
    Rachel 172 Susan H 86
STEVENSON, Charles 104 Simez 104
STEWART, Caroline 79 Charles 79 Lucy Jane 12 S J 62 Sarah
    A 79
STICKNEY, Anna 45 Benjamin 45 John 176-177 Robert Clark
    45 Sarah 177 Susan Eliza 45
STILES, 73 Adelia A 170 Della 170 John 170 Margaret M 170
STILLMAN, George 79
STINCHFIELD, Alfreda Hillman 172 Fannie 172 Oliver Otis
    172 Roger 172
STOCKMAN, Hannah 12
STOCKWELL, Rebecca S 63 78
STONE, Hepzibah 60
STORER, Mary Langdon 27 157 Olive 157 Seth 157
STOWELL, Alice Amanda 168 Charles W 178 Florence Maria
    178 Florrie 178
STRATTON, Cordelia 152 George 152 Joseph 152 Keziah H
    152 Keziah Hill 152
STREETER, Mrs 67

STRICKLAND, Mary E 62 Nellie A 62 Philo 62
STROUT, Adelaide Colwell 144 Emma L 91 George D 82 145 George H 144 Lydia 144 Solomon O 144 Solomon Obadiah Jr 144
STUART, Hannah Eliza 146 Lucy Jane 12 Mary 160 164 Robert Thompson 146
STUDLEY, Martha 20
STYLES, Lovina J 170
SULLIVAN, Deborah 112 Hannah 94 Jane 112 Joanna 123 John 112-113
SWAN, Charles Edward 42 51 Francis 42 Hannah 42 Hulda 168 Mary Danford 42 Mehitable 168 Minerva 42 Nathaniel 168
SWEET, Ann 58 Frances Mary 70
SWEETSER, Mary 141 Paul 141
SWETT, Augusta L 90 Daniel 83 125 133 Lydia 83 Lydia G 133 Rachel 83 125 133 Sullivan Clark 70
SWIM, Maria 12 135 Sarah 12 80 135
SYPHER, Sarah 82
TAPPAN, Edna 17 Esther Wigglesworth 17 Stephen 17
TARBOX, Elizabeth 171 George R 95 George Rogers 171 Mary Elizabeth 171
TAYLOR, Lucy H 85 O H 26-27 William B 85
THAYER, Solomon 174
THEOBALD, Isabella A 95 Nancy 95 Philip 95 Philip Ernst Jr 95 Philip Jr 95
THOMAS, Annie 180
THOMPSON, A D 87 Ann 147 Berranga 56 D 87 Duncan 87 Eliza J 149 Fanny 115 James 59 163 Joseph 147 Lydia 163 Lydia R 87 Margaret 59 Mary 59 Mrs 54 Nellie M 147 Rebecca 56 Sam 173 Samuel G 31 William 56 147
THOMSON, Rev 4 186 Samuel 12
THURSTON, Charles Edgar 45 Charlotte C 45
TIBBETTS, Charles 33
TILTON, E W 48 Mrs 48 Nancy Maria 48
TINKER, Ferdinand 120 Hannah 18 124 Hannah Hill 120 Mary Ann Boies 120 Sarah 28
TITCOM, Elizabeth Dordin 58
TITCOMB, Anna Maria 58 John 58 Pearson 58 Penuel 58 Samuel 58 William 58
TOAL, Agnes V 6 Horatio N 6 Martha 6
TODD, 120 160 Abigail 20 45 169 173 Adaline 17 Alexander 20 Ann Elizabeth 88 Anna 17 David 48 Edwin B 10 F H 10 Fannie Paine 10 Frances Campbell 42 124 173 Freeman Hale 17 Hannah 55 155 Hannah Townsley 38 86 173 Hannah W 13 James 48 124 Jeremiah 48 John 48 John C 20 John Camel 45 John Campbell 45 173 John N 20 John Worthy 13 Margaret 44-46 87 155 181 Maria 13 Mary Ann Boies 160 Mary Jamison 17 Mercy 124 Nabby 45 173 Nancy Campbell 28 48 Peggy 44-46 87 155 181 Ruth 155 Sally 155 Samuel 155 Sarah 48 William 17 20 William Jr 88
TOOLE, James 21 Mary Jane 21
TOPPAN, Stephen 17
TOPPING, Martha 43 Nancy Ann 43 Robert 43
TOURTELLOTT, Lucy 128 Reuben 128
TOURTELOTT, Betsey 128 Elizabeth 128
TOWERS, Anna Maria 96 Hattie 96 164 Jennett H 104 Jennette H 172 John 96 164 Martha 96 164 Mercy 164
TOWLE, Hannah 112 Jane 77 Joseph 77
TOWNS, Pheobe 159
TOWNSEND, A S 7 91 101 Augustus L 163 Julia Elvira 86 100 M B 21 Manley B 20 Mercy 163 Nellie 15
TRACEY, Margaret 61 Mary 61 Thomas S 61
TRACY, Cordelia 150 Jane 150 William 150

TRAFTON, Angeline V 164 Angie 164 Eliza 164 Theodore 164
TRAINER, Attia Cordelia 87 William 87
TRASK, Helen S 157
TRAVELLAR, F D 106 Mrs 106
TRAYNOR, A C 87 George W 87
TREFETHER, 11 Eleanora 11 Nora 11
TRICKEY, Ellen 62
TRIPP, Zilphia 93
TROAT, Mary 76
TROKE, Mary 76
TROTE, Mary 148
TROTT, Barbara 166 Mary 148
TRUE, Mary 67
TRYNOR, Attia Cordelia 87 William W 87
TUCKER, Amanda J 109 Amanda Jane 109 Edith 36 Warren A 109
TUFTS, Elizabeth 146 Margaret 146
TUPPER, Allen 142 Ellen Sweetser 142
TURNBULL, John 31
TURNER, Eleanor 88 George W 136 Martha Ellen 136 Sally 178
TWITCHELL, Ada A 183 Elizabeth 182
TYLER, Harriet 138 Jennie Cutter 70 Jenny 69-70 John S L 138 Joseph 70 Salome Bastow 153 Temperance 41 William H 135 138 153
ULSTER, Col 7
UPTON, Sally 54
VARNEY, Eliza Morton 179 Isaac H 179
VARNUM, Eben C 150 Sarah Jane 150
VAUGHAN, Ellen 98
VEAZIE, Elizabeth 95 154 Joshua 154 Lizzie 95 Mary Sophia Gleason 154
VERY, E D 18
VIOLETTE, Maggie 171
VOSE, Edward Howard 62 Eliza Maria 62 Lydia Cushing 62 Myra 28 160 Peter Thacher 62
WADE, Harriet Hall 63 John 63
WADSWORTH, Aaron 68 Aaron Jr 68 Abner 104 Ann Maria Judson 86 Augusta Hale 43 Deborah 26 Deborah M 104 Jennett H 104 Lewis L 43 Lewis Lumber Jr 86 Lewis Lumber Sr 86 Lucy 68 Lucy G 68 Maria 86 Marie H 43
WAGG, Andrew F 115 Charles Herbert 115 Louisa Griffin 115 Sophronia 115
WAIT, 4
WAITE, Benjamin F 161-162 Benjamin Franklin 38 55 Charles 124 Frances Elizabeth 124 Frederick Townsley 55 Hannah 55 Hannah Townsley 86 161 Hannah Townsley Todd 38 Helen Maria 86 Mary Elizabeth 38 Priscilla 55
WAKEFIELD, Ann W 31 Cyrus 147 Emily R 147 Mahala 147
WALDRON, 168 Catharine 90 Sarah Ann 90 Sumner 87 Sumner T 23 90
WALKER, Amelia 89 Frederick P 141 Lucy 141 Maggie 96 Marcellus 96-97 Margaret 96 Margaret E 96 Sophronia 115
WARD, Alpheus H 60 Caroline 174 Elijah 106 Eliza Ann 116 Emeline 106 John 181 John C 116 Lydia 106 Mary Elizabeth 60
WARDWELL, S D 85
WARE, Augustus Lyman 130 Inez Alberti 130 Josiah H 130
WARNER, Elizabeth 98 W W 48
WARR, Mary Ann 170-171
WARREN, Caroline B 71 Mary 144
WASBURN, Flora Ella 183

WASHBURN, Annie Laurie 96 Charles Francis 96 Emily B 158 Frances Caroline 12 George 158 173 George W 12 J C 164 J P 125 147 Japheth C 142 158 174 Japheth Coombs 130 153 Jepheth Coombs 158 Julia Caroline 153 173 Sarah 153 158 Sarah Jane 173 Sophia 96 William G 183

WATSON, R S 154 Sophia H 154

WATT, Christina 51

WATTS, Elsie 70

WAY, Lydia 163

WAYE, Edgar 140 Leonice Howard 140

WEBB, 108 Jonathan 8 Mary 8-9 Nancy 78

WEBSTER, Almira 164 Elmira 164 Myra 164 William 164

WELLS, Margaret 104 Rev Mr 22

WENTWORTH, 61 Abial 73 Giles Merrill 61 Henry Newell 73 James 73 Lucy Caroline 61 Maggie 73 Margaret Hill 73 Mary Ann 73 Nola 171 S 74 Vernon 171

WEST, Charles C 16 Eliza Turner 16

WESTON, Jonathan 45 Mary 119

WEYMOUTH, Mary 115

WHARFF, Maria Nancy 47 Thomas E 47

WHEATON, 129 Abigail 141 Hannah Draper 64 141 177 J 178 James 141

WHEELER, Benjamin 165 Eliza A 184 Hannah E 166 Mary Ann 165 Peter 166

WHIDDEN, Charles 30 Charles Randol 142 Laura S 30 Mila 30 Mila Frances 142 Vashti Harriet 42

WHITAKER, Samuel H 128 Susan Caroline 128

WHITCHER, Mary 27

WHITE, Alice Rosalind 146 Bathsheba 53 Charlotte A 136 Daniel 53 Emma 136 Jerusha 172 John 84 John W T 136 Martha Zilma 53 Nancy Jane 84 Nathaniel 53

WHITEHALL, William 9

WHITEKNACT, Esther 36 John 36 Maria 36 Marie 36 William F 36

WHITELAW, W H 104

WHITMAN, Frances Louise 19 Jason 54 Nathaniel 19 Sarah 19

WHITNEY, 26 Abigail Todd 45 Addie M 91 Amanda J 46 Amy Ellen 177 Catherine 119 Cordealia Evelyn 160 Cordelia Evelyn 119 Daniel 168 Ehpraim 45 George C 178 George Clarkson 177 Hannah 49 78 James 46 James B 91 Joel 49 119 John 26 177 Julia A 91 Lydia 177 Martha 91 Mary 119 132 168 Mary Ann Tyler 119 Pathenia F 26 Paul 119 Phebe Whitney 100 Sallie 168 Sarah A 168 Sarah J 26

WHITTEN, C R 72

WHITTIER, Alice 90 Artemus 90 Artemus N 90 Louise Victoria 103 Mary 27 Sarah A 90

WHITTIKER, David 116 Helen A 116

WHITWELL, William 17 William A 9 155 163

WIGGIN, Kate Douglas 142 177

WILCOX, Benjamin 37 Bethiah Emmeline Atwood 176 Jane 37 Sarah M 10 37 173

WILDER, Bathsheba 151 Rebecca 88

WILDES, Lulu Belle 131

WILKINS, Clara 89 Clarissa 89 Mary 79 88

WILLAMS, James Eveleth 14

WILLIAMS, Betsey 14 Margaret 147 Mary 133 Polly Eveleth 14 Sabra Atherton 71 Thomas D 36 146

WILLIAMSON, Jane 15

WILLIS, Henry A 95

WILSON, Emma Elzora 51 Georgianna 183 Jane 26 John 77 Joseph 183 Mary 51 Mary Caroline 66 Nathaniel I 66 Sarah Cottnam 77 William 51

WINCHELL, Frances D 37 184

WIND, Lydia 30

WING, David 30 Elizabeth 30 Otis 121

WINSTON, Nancy 62

WINTER, Mary 153

WINTHROP, John 57

WISEGARVER, Eleanor 119

WOFFENDALE, Charlotte 117

WOLFF, F R 48

WOLFINGER, Leslie 13

WOODBURY, Amy Ellen 37 Frances D 37 Harriet 113 Samuel 106 William T 37

WOODCOCK, Elsie Watts 70 Harriet 70 John L 70 John T 70 Nancy Jane 126

WOODMAN, Ann 48 85 Clara A 48 Elizabeth 141 Jane 60 John 48 85 Nancy Jane 126 Rodney P 60 Zoa Ann 85

WOODS, Abba E 9 Abbie 9 Abby 9 Francis 138 Frank 138 Georgianna 138 Joseph G 9 Mr 9 W 138

WOODWARD, Daniel 153 Mary 153 Nellie F 153

WOODWORTH, Marcey 98 Ruby 97 William 106 William Jr 98

WORTHLY, Anna 17

WRENTON, Jennie C 44

WRIGHT, Amanda 21 Charlotte 142 Charlotte Eaton 142 David 142 Hannah 181 Myrtle R 181 P V 181

WYATT, Benjamin D 83 Mary Richards 83

WYLIE, Sarah 135

WYMAN, Sabrina K 130

YATES, Martha 169 Mary H 169 Polly 169 Twilliam 169

YORK, Mary 80 Sarah 67

YOUNG, Cyrus 9 Electra 9 Ellen Augusta 9 Emma 60 Margaret Pendleton 52 Margret 60 Maria 60 Nancy 173 Nellie 9 Phebe 146 Susan B 27 William Harrison 60

ZELMA, Amelia 53 Augustus 53 Diannah 53 179